THE COOKBOOK THAT WAS WRITTEN FOR *YOU!*

What we eat, how we prepare it and even who prepares it—all have changed dramatically since 1950 when the first edition of the bestselling *Betty Crocker's Cookbook* appeared. Consequently, when we planned this sixth edition, we did more than revise. We created a book specifically for today's needs.

We monitored your new food tastes and discovered that what was once exotic is now mainstream. We investigated emerging trends, and looked for new twists to add to the basics. Most importantly, we were guided by your letters and telephone calls.

Responsive to change and true to tradition, this new and revised *Betty Crocker's Cookbook* contains all that you have asked for, and offers one more advantage—the dependability you have come to expect from recipes developed and tested in the Betty Crocker Kitchens.

—*The Betty Crocker Editors, from the Foreword*

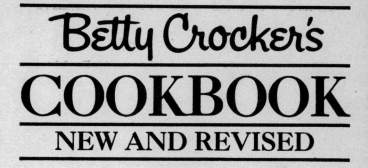

Betty Crocker's
COOKBOOK
NEW AND REVISED

BANTAM BOOKS
TORONTO · NEW YORK · LONDON · SYDNEY · AUCKLAND

BETTY CROCKER'S COOKBOOK

*A Bantam Book / published by arrangement with
Western Publishing Company, Inc.*

PRINTING HISTORY
Golden Press First Edition, August 1986

Betty Crocker is a registered trademark of General Mills, Inc.

Bantam edition / December 1987

*Bantam Books are published by Bantam Books, Inc. Its trademark, consisting
of the words "Bantam Books" and the portrayal of a rooster, is Registered
in U.S. Patent and Trademark Office and in other countries. Marca Registrada.
Bantam Books, Inc., 666 Fifth Avenue, New York, New York 10103.*

PRINTED IN THE UNITED STATES OF AMERICA

O   0 9 8 7 6 5 4 3

THE HERITAGE OF BETTY CROCKER'S COOKBOOK

For most of this century, the name, signature and portrait of Betty Crocker have been symbols of quality recipes and have won the confidence of millions.

Betty Crocker's cookbook and recipe heritage can be traced back to the 1890s—with the purchase and distribution of *Miss Parloa's New Cook Book* by the Washburn Crosby Company, forerunner of General Mills. However, it was not until 1921 that "Betty Crocker" first appeared as the signature on letters replying to thousands of questions about cooking and baking.

In 1936, the Betty Crocker name, by then famous, was given a face when the first official portrait of Betty Crocker was commissioned. In the years that followed, there were five other "sittings." In 1986, the seventh and most recent portrait in the series was introduced. As the previous ones reflected changing times, the current Betty Crocker portrait reflects the 1980s.

In 1950, cooking and baking information was in such great demand that the need for a wide-ranging basic cookbook seemed clear. Simply called *Betty Crocker's Picture Cookbook*, the volume collected under one cover the recipes, advice and expertise accumulated over the years. It was an instant success—the nonfiction best-seller for that year!

Betty Crocker's Picture Cookbook was revised twice before it was replaced in 1969 by *Betty Crocker's Cookbook*. This was later updated and a new edition was published in 1978.

Now new and again revised, this is the sixth edition of *the* all-time best-selling cookbook.

With its straightforward, easy-to-understand language and tested recipes, *Betty Crocker's Cookbook* has introduced millions to the heritage of American cooking. In recognition of this outstanding contribution, *Betty Crocker's Cookbook* received the distinction of becoming the sixth book to be placed in the R.T. French Cookbook Hall of Fame.

Like its predecessors, this edition mirrors an American lifestyle and stands ready to serve a new generation.

CONTENTS

APPETIZERS / BEVERAGES   1

BREADS / GRAINS / PASTA   39

CAKES / PIES   101

COOKIES / CANDY   163

DESSERTS   217

EGGS / CHEESE / LEGUMES   277

FISH / SHELLFISH   315

BEEF / VEAL   351

PORK / LAMB   **401**

POULTRY   **439**

SALADS   **479**

SOUPS / SANDWICHES / SAUCES   **555**

VEGETABLES   **609**

SPECIAL HELPS / NUTRITION CHARTS   **677**

INDEX   **765**

FOREWORD

What we eat, how we prepare it and even *who* prepares it—all have changed dramatically since 1950 when the first edition of the best-selling *Betty Crocker's Cookbook* appeared. Consequently, when we planned and developed this sixth edition of *Betty Crocker's Cookbook*, we did more than revise. We created a book specifically for today's needs. And to assure success, we relied on one indispensable ingredient—you.

We monitored your new food tastes and discovered that what was once exotic is now mainstream. We investigated emerging trends, and looked for new twists to add to the basics. Most importantly, we were guided by your letters and telephone calls. The trained staff of our Consumer Relations Department communicates with nearly 10,000 of you each month.

Your growing awareness of the need for good nutrition became evident—you choose poultry and fish over red meat, eat more fresh fruits and vegetables, and use less fat in cooking. So, with the assistance of our Nutrition Department, we have provided a calorie count with each recipe plus special chapter-by-chapter charts with computer-calculated nutrients.

We found all members of the family sharing the responsibility for food preparation. Therefore our recipes are clearly written, with easy-to-follow directions. How-to illustrations, information charts, special tips—all help even the beginner to feel comfortable and confident in the kitchen.

Since time saving and ease of preparation are so important to you, there are do-ahead tips and microwave variations. Many main dish recipes are flagged "*Easy . . .*" and most main dish recipes feature menu suggestions to help take the guess-work out of go-togethers.

The Special Helps chapter is actually a mini-encyclopedia

of cooking basics and tips, food preparation terms, microwave principles, food storage guidelines and more.

Responsive to change and true to tradition, this new and revised *Betty Crocker's Cookbook* contains all that you have asked for, and offers one more advantage—the dependability you have come to expect from recipes developed and tested in the Betty Crocker Kitchens.

The Betty Crocker Editors

APPETIZERS
BEVERAGES

APPETIZERS

MELON AND PROSCIUTTO

Cut 1 cantaloupe, casaba, honeydew or Spanish melon (about 3 pounds) lengthwise into halves; scoop out seeds and fibers. Cut each half lengthwise into 6 wedges; remove rind. Cut crosswise slits 1½ inches apart in each melon wedge.

Cut ¼ pound thinly sliced prosciutto (Italian ham) into 1-inch strips. Place several strips prosciutto over each wedge; push prosciutto into slits.   **12 servings; 35 calories per serving.**

Melon and Prosciutto Bites: Cut melon into bite-size pieces. Wrap each piece in strips of prosciutto; secure with wooden picks.

SHRIMP COCKTAIL

Prepare Cocktail Sauce (page 603). To serve as individual appetizers, mix 36 shrimp with sauce. For a party snack, fill large bowl with crushed ice and place a dish of sauce in center; arrange shrimp on ice. Serve with wooden picks for dipping shrimp into sauce.   **6 servings; 80 calories per serving.**

OYSTERS ROCKEFELLER

	Rock salt
12	medium oysters in shells
2	tablespoons finely chopped onion
2	tablespoons snipped parsley
2	tablespoons finely chopped celery
¼	cup margarine or butter
½	cup chopped fresh or frozen spinach, partially thawed and drained
⅓	cup dry bread crumbs
¼	teaspoon salt
7	drops red pepper sauce
	Dash of ground anise

Fill three pie plates, 9 × 1¼ inches, ½ inch deep with rock salt; sprinkle with water. Scrub oysters in shells under running cold water. Break off thin end of shell with hammer. Force a table knife or shucking knife between halves of the shell at broken end; pull apart. Cut oyster at muscle to separate from shell. Remove any bits of shell. Place oyster on deep half of shell; discard other half. Arrange filled shells on rock salt base.

Heat oven to 450°. Cook and stir onion, parsley and celery in margarine until onion is tender. Mix in remaining ingredients. Spoon about 1 tablespoon spinach mixture onto oyster in each shell. Bake 10 minutes. **2 servings; 355 calories per serving.**

Oysters Parmesan: Omit spinach mixture. Spoon 1 teaspoon dairy sour cream onto oyster in each shell. Mix ½ cup grated Parmesan cheese, ¼ cup cracker crumbs, ¼ cup margarine or butter, melted, and ½ teaspoon dry mustard. Spoon about 2 teaspoons cheese mixture onto each oyster.

CAVIAR CLASSIC

Mound crushed ice in large glass bowl; place dish of chilled black, golden or red caviar in center of ice. (Or leave caviar in original container.) If desired, sprinkle caviar with sieved hard-cooked eggs, finely chopped onion or snipped chives. Serve with lemon wedges and crisp toast triangles or thinly sliced black bread. **Allow 1 tablespoon caviar per serving;** 140 calories per serving.

STUFFED MUSHROOMS

1	**pound medium mushrooms**
1	**small onion, chopped (about ¼ cup)**
½	**small green pepper, chopped (about ¼ cup)**
3	**tablespoons margarine or butter**
1½	**cups soft bread crumbs**
½	**teaspoon salt**
½	**teaspoon dried thyme leaves**
¼	**teaspoon ground turmeric**
¼	**teaspoon pepper**
1	**tablespoon margarine or butter**

Cut stems from mushrooms; finely chop enough stems to measure ⅓ cup. Cook and stir chopped mushroom stems, onion and green pepper in 3 tablespoons margarine until tender, about 5 minutes; remove from heat. Stir in bread crumbs, salt, thyme, turmeric and pepper.

Heat 1 tablespoon margarine in shallow baking dish until melted. Fill mushroom caps with stuffing mixture; place mushrooms, filled sides up, in baking dish. Bake uncovered in 350° oven 15 minutes.

Set oven control to broil and/or 550°. Broil mushrooms with tops 3 to 4 inches from heat 2 minutes. Serve hot. **About 3 dozen appetizers;** 35 calories per appetizer.

MARINATED MUSHROOMS

1 pound mushrooms
¼ cup lemon juice
½ cup olive or vegetable oil
¼ cup snipped parsley
¾ teaspoon salt
¼ teaspoon freshly ground pepper
2 green onions (with tops), thinly sliced
1 clove garlic, finely chopped
   Paprika
   Parsley sprigs

Cut mushrooms into ⅛-inch slices. Mix mushrooms and lemon juice in 1½-quart bowl. Stir in oil, ¼ cup parsley, the salt, pepper, onions and garlic; toss. Cover and refrigerate, stirring occasionally, at least 3 hours.

Just before serving, remove with slotted spoon. Sprinkle with paprika; garnish with parsley. **10 servings; 40 calories** per serving.

DILLED VEGETABLES

½ medium head cauliflower (about 1 pound)
½ pound green beans
1 small red onion, sliced and separated into rings
½ cup bottled Italian dressing
1 teaspoon dried dill weed
½ teaspoon red pepper flakes

Prepare cauliflower as directed on page 634; separate into flowerets. Prepare green beans as directed on page 617; leave beans whole. Heat 1 inch salted water (½ teaspoon salt to 1 cup water) to boiling. Add cauliflowerets and beans. Cover and heat to boiling; reduce heat. Boil until crisp-tender, 6 to 8 minutes; drain.

Place cauliflowerets, beans and onion rings in shallow glass dish. Shake remaining ingredients in tightly covered container; pour over vegetables. Cover and refrigerate, stirring once, at least 4 hours. Drain before serving. **8 servings; 40** calories per serving.

OLIVES AND ONIONS

1   jar (5 ounces) pimiento-stuffed olives, drained
1   can (6 ounces) small pitted ripe olives, drained
1   jar (7 ounces) cocktail onions, drained
½   cup olive or vegetable oil
¼   cup red wine vinegar
1   teaspoon dried oregano leaves
¼   teaspoon crushed red pepper
2   cloves garlic, finely chopped

Place olives and onions in 1½-quart bowl. Shake remaining ingredients in tightly covered container. Pour over olives and onions. Refrigerate, stirring occasionally, at least 2 hours. Drain before serving. Serve with wooden picks. **15 servings;** 40 calories per serving.

STUFFED CELERY STICKS

7   medium stalks celery
½   cup shredded Swiss cheese (2 ounces)
½   cup finely chopped fully cooked smoked ham
⅓   cup mayonnaise or salad dressing
½   teaspoon prepared mustard

Cut celery into 3-inch pieces (make sure celery is completely dry). Mix remaining ingredients; spread about 1 tablespoon in each piece of celery. Cover and refrigerate 1 hour. **About 14 appetizers;** 65 calories per appetizer.

CHEESY BAGEL BITES

3   bagels, split and toasted
1   tablespoon prepared mustard
⅓   cup mayonnaise or salad dressing
¼   cup grated Parmesan cheese
¼   teaspoon garlic powder
2   green onions (with tops), chopped

Spread bagels with mustard. Mix remaining ingredients; spread to edges of bagels.

Set oven control to broil and/or 550°. Broil bagels with tops about 5 inches from heat until topping is bubbly, about 1 minute. Cut each bagel into 6 pieces. **36 appetizers; 30 calories per appetizer.**

CHILI-CHEESE BALLS

2 cups shredded Cheddar cheese (8 ounces)
1 cup all-purpose flour
½ cup margarine or butter, softened
½ teaspoon salt
1 can (4 ounces) chopped green chilies, well drained

Heat oven to 375°. Mix all ingredients. Shape into ¾-inch balls. Place about 2 inches apart on greased cookie sheet. Bake until set, 15 to 18 minutes. Serve immediately. **About 6 dozen appetizers;** 30 calories per appetizer.

Do-ahead Tip: Shape appetizers and freeze. To serve, bake about 18 minutes.

CHEESE BOARD

An inviting cheese board should include cheeses in a variety of textures and flavors. Plan on 2 ounces of cheese per person. An assortment of crudités (vegetables), thinly sliced breads and crackers should accompany the cheeses; select from suggestions listed below. Plan on about 1 cup vegetable pieces and 8 pieces of bread or crackers per person.

Cheese	Texture	Flavor
Brie	soft	mild to pungent
Camembert	soft	mild to pungent
Gruyère	firm	mild, nutty
Montrachet	soft	mild
Port du Salut	semisoft	mild to robust
Triple Creams:	soft	mild
Brillat-Savarin		
L'Explorateur		
Saint-André		
Cheddar	firm	mild to very sharp

Cheese	Texture	Flavor
Cheshire	firm and crumbly	sharp, salty
Muenster	semisoft	mild to sharp
Blue	firm	tangy, sharp, robust
Roquefort	semisoft	strong, robust, salty
Stilton	semisoft	mellow, piquant

Crudités		
asparagus spears	green onions	turnip spears
broccoli flowerets	mushrooms	white radishes
cauliflowerets	sugar peas	zucchini slices
cherry tomatoes		

Bread	Crackers	
French baguette	rice crackers	stone-ground
pumpernickel	rye crackers	wheat crackers
Swedish limpa	soda crackers	whole wheat flatbread
rye	with unsalted tops	

BROILED POTATO SKINS

- **4 large baking potatoes**
- **2 tablespoons margarine or butter, softened**
- **½ teaspoon salt**
- **1 cup finely shredded Monterey Jack cheese with jalapeño peppers (4 ounces)**
- **4 slices bacon, crisply cooked and crumbled**

Prick potatoes with fork to allow steam to escape. Bake potatoes in 425° oven until tender, about 1 hour; cool slightly.

Cut each potato lengthwise into halves; scoop out insides, leaving a ⅜-inch shell. Spread inside of shells with margarine; sprinkle with salt. Cut each into 6 pieces; sprinkle with cheese and bacon.

Set oven control to broil and/or 550°. Broil potato pieces with tops about 5 inches from heat until cheese is melted, about 2 minutes.   **48 appetizers; 30 calories per appetizer.**

COCKTAIL MEATBALLS

1   pound ground beef
½   cup dry bread crumbs
⅓   cup finely chopped onion
¼   cup milk
1   tablespoon snipped parsley
1   teaspoon salt
½   teaspoon Worcestershire sauce
⅛   teaspoon pepper
1   egg
¼   cup shortening
1   bottle (12 ounces) chili sauce
1   jar (10 ounces) grape jelly

Mix ground beef, bread crumbs, onion, milk, parsley, salt, Worcestershire sauce, pepper and egg; shape into 1-inch balls.

Cook meatballs in shortening in 12-inch skillet until brown. Remove meatballs from skillet; drain fat. Heat chili sauce and jelly in skillet, stirring constantly, until jelly is melted. Add meatballs; stir until coated. Simmer uncovered 30 minutes. Serve hot.   **5 dozen appetizers; 50 calories per appetizer.**

Cocktail Sausages: Substitute 3 cans (5 ounces each) Vienna sausages, cut crosswise into halves, for the meatballs. Decrease simmering time to 20 minutes.

SAUERKRAUT BALLS

1 pound ground pork
1 medium onion, finely chopped
½ pound ground fully cooked smoked ham
1 cup all-purpose flour
½ teaspoon dry mustard
4 drops red pepper sauce
½ cup milk
¼ cup snipped parsley
1 can (16 ounces) sauerkraut, rinsed, well drained and chopped
⅓ cup margarine or butter
2 eggs
¼ cup cold water
¾ cup dry bread crumbs
Mustard Sauce (below)

Cook and stir ground pork and onion in 10-inch skillet over medium heat until pork is done; drain. Stir in ham, flour, mustard and pepper sauce thoroughly. Stir in milk. Cook over medium heat, stirring constantly, until hot, about 5 minutes; remove from heat. Stir in parsley and sauerkraut; cool.

Heat margarine in jelly roll pan, 15½ × 10½ × 1 inch, in 400° oven until melted. Mix eggs and water. Shape pork mixture into 1-inch balls; dip in egg mixture. Coat evenly with bread crumbs. Place in margarine in pan. Bake uncovered 15 minutes; turn. Bake until hot and golden brown, about 15 minutes longer. Serve with Mustard Sauce. **About 5 dozen appetizers**; 70 calories per appetizer.

Mustard Sauce

¼ cup dairy sour cream
¼ cup mayonnaise or salad dressing
1 tablespoon dry mustard
¼ teaspoon sugar

Mix all ingredients until smooth.

BARBECUED RIBS

2 - pound rack pork back ribs, cut lengthwise across bones
    into halves
½ cup catsup
2 tablespoons packed brown sugar
1 tablespoon lemon juice
1 teaspoon salt
½ teaspoon garlic powder
¼ teaspoon ground ginger
3 tablespoons dry mustard
3 tablespoons cold water

Trim excess fat and remove membranes from pork. Mix catsup, brown sugar, lemon juice, salt, garlic powder and ginger; pour over pork, turning to coat both sides. Cover and refrigerate at least 2 hours.

Remove pork; reserve marinade. Place pork on rack in aluminum foil-lined broiler pan. Bake uncovered in 400° oven, brushing occasionally with reserved marinade, 30 minutes. Turn pork; bake, brushing occasionally with marinade, until done, about 30 minutes longer.

Cut between each rib to separate. Mix mustard and water until smooth; let stand 5 minutes. Serve with ribs. **25 appetizers;** 70 calories per appetizer.

PIZZA BITES

2 tablespoons margarine or butter, softened
⅛ teaspoon instant minced garlic
3 English muffins, split and toasted
24 slices pepperoni, each about 1½ inches in diameter
12 cherry tomatoes, cut into halves
1 cup shredded mozzarella cheese (4 ounces)
½ teaspoon dried oregano leaves

Mix margarine and garlic; spread on muffin halves. Cut each muffin half into 4 wedges; do not separate. Place 1 slice pepperoni and 1 tomato half on each muffin wedge. Place in broiler pan. Mix cheese and oregano; sprinkle over muffin wedges.

Set oven control to broil and/or 550°. Broil muffin wedges

with tops about 5 inches from heat until cheese is melted, about 2 minutes. Cut to separate into wedges.   **6 servings;** 65 calories per serving.

RUMAKI

6   **chicken livers**
4   **water chestnuts**
    Teriyaki Sauce (below)
6   **slices bacon**
    Brown sugar

Cut chicken livers into halves; cut each water chestnut into 3 pieces. Pour Teriyaki Sauce on livers and water chestnuts in bowl. Refrigerate at least 4 hours; drain.

Cut bacon slices into halves. Wrap a piece of bacon around a piece of liver and water chestnut; secure with wooden pick. Roll in brown sugar.

Set oven control to broil and/or 550°. Broil rumaki with tops 3 to 4 inches from heat, turning occasionally, until bacon is crisp, about 10 minutes.   **12 appetizers;** 50 calories per appetizer.

Teriyaki Sauce

¼   **cup vegetable oil**
¼   **cup soy sauce**
2   **tablespoons catsup**
1   **tablespoon vinegar**
¼   **teaspoon pepper**
2   **cloves garlic, crushed**

Mix all ingredients.

SHRIMP-BACON BITES

1   **cup cleaned cooked shrimp (about 16)**
½   **clove garlic, slivered**
½   **cup chili sauce**
8   **to 10 slices bacon**

Mix shrimp and garlic; pour chili sauce over mixture. Cover and refrigerate, stirring occasionally, several hours.

Cut bacon slices into halves. Cook bacon until limp; drain. Wrap each shrimp in bacon piece; secure with wooden pick.

Set oven control to broil and/or 550°. Broil with tops 2 to 3 inches from heat until bacon is crisp. **About 16 appetizers;** 30 calories per appetizer.

SAUSAGE-CHEESE CHIPS

  8   ounces fully cooked kielbasa
 36   tortilla chips
1½   cups shredded mozzarella cheese
  1   can (4 ounces) chopped green chilies, drained

Coarsely chop kielbasa; reserve. Arrange chips on greased 12-inch pizza pan. Sprinkle kielbasa and cheese evenly over each chip; top with chilies. Bake uncovered in 375° oven until cheese is melted, 3 to 5 minutes. **6 servings;** 40 calories per serving.

PARTY SANDWICHES

Cheese Sandwiches: Cut each sandwich bread slice into 4 squares. Spread each with 1 teaspoon whipped cream cheese (plain, chive or pimiento). Sprinkle with chopped nuts or garnish each with a nut. 30 calories per appetizer.

Cucumber Sandwiches: Cut each sandwich bread slice into 3 circles. Spread each with ¼ teaspoon margarine or butter, softened, or 1 teaspoon whipped cream cheese. Place a thin cucumber slice between each 2 bread circles. 60 calories per appetizer.

Cucumber-Shrimp Sandwiches: Cut each sandwich bread slice into 3 circles. Spread each with 1 teaspoon whipped cream cheese. Top each with a thin cucumber slice, small amount of cream cheese and cooked small shrimp. 15 calories per appetizer.

Ham Sandwiches: Cut each sandwich bread slice into 2 diamond shapes. Spread each with ¼ teaspoon margarine or butter, softened. Mix deviled ham spread with small amount mayonnaise or salad dressing; spread over diamonds. Garnish with sliced pimiento-stuffed olives. 60 calories per appetizer.

Do-ahead Tip: Place sandwiches on a cardboard tray; cover with plastic wrap. Overwrap with aluminum foil and freeze up to 2 months. (Do not freeze cucumber slices; add them just before serving.) Forty-five minutes before serving, remove foil and let sandwiches stand at room temperature.

NOTE: For an attractive assortment, use a variety of breads; trim crusts and cut sandwiches into different shapes.

HAM PHYLLO ROLLS

2	cups bean sprouts, chopped (about 4 ounces)
1	cup chopped fully cooked smoked ham
1	small onion, chopped (about ¼ cup)
1	tablespoon margarine or butter
2	cups bite-size pieces spinach
½	cup chopped water chestnuts
1	tablespoon finely chopped gingerroot
2	teaspoons cornstarch
2	teaspoons soy sauce
5	frozen phyllo leaves, thawed
1	tablespoon margarine or butter, melted
2	tablespoons dry mustard
1	tablespoon plus 1½ teaspoons cold water

Rinse bean sprouts under running cold water; drain. Cook and stir ham, onion and 1 tablespoon margarine in 10-inch skillet until onion is tender. Stir in bean sprouts, spinach, water chestnuts and gingerroot; cook and stir 2 minutes. Stir in cornstarch and soy sauce.

Cut stack of phyllo leaves lengthwise into halves. Cut each half crosswise into thirds to make 30 squares, about 5½ × 5½ inches. Cover squares with waxed paper, then with damp towel to prevent them from drying out.

Heat oven to 350°. For each roll, use 2 phyllo squares. Place about 2 tablespoons ham mixture slightly below center of square. Fold corner of square closest to filling over filling, tucking point under filling. Fold in and overlap the 2 opposite corners. Roll up; place seam side down on greased cookie sheet. Repeat with remaining phyllo squares. Brush rolls with 1 tablespoon margarine. Bake until golden brown, about 25 minutes. Mix mustard and water until smooth; let stand 5 minutes. Serve with rolls. **15 appetizers;** 75 calories per appetizer.

Do-ahead Tip: Before baking, place rolls on greased cookie sheet. Cover tightly with plastic wrap. Refrigerate up to 24 hours. Brush rolls with margarine. Bake in 350° oven until golden brown, about 25 minutes.

DEVILED EGGS

6	hard-cooked eggs
3	tablespoons mayonnaise, salad dressing or half-and-half
½	teaspoon dry mustard
¼	teaspoon salt
¼	teaspoon pepper

Cut peeled eggs lengthwise into halves. Slip out yolks; mash with fork. Mix in mayonnaise, mustard, salt and pepper. Fill whites with egg yolk mixture, heaping it lightly. Arrange eggs on large serving plate. Cover and refrigerate up to 24 hours. **6 servings; 140 calories per serving.**

Catsup Deviled Eggs: Substitute ¼ cup plus 1 tablespoon catsup for the mayonnaise; decrease salt to ⅛ teaspoon.

Deviled Eggs with Olives: Omit mustard; decrease salt to ⅛ teaspoon. Mix ¼ cup finely chopped ripe olives and ⅛ teaspoon curry powder into egg yolk mixture.

Party Deviled Eggs: Garnish each deviled egg half with cooked shrimp, rolled anchovy fillet or sliced pimiento-stuffed olive.

Zesty Deviled Eggs: Decrease salt to ⅛ teaspoon. Mix ½ cup finely shredded process American cheese (2 ounces) and 2 tablespoons snipped parsley or 1 teaspoon prepared horseradish into egg yolk mixture.

PICKLED EGGS

6	hard-cooked eggs
1	cup cider vinegar
1	cup beet liquid
⅓	cup granulated sugar or packed brown sugar
½	teaspoon salt
1	small onion, chopped (about ¼ cup)
4	whole cloves
	Shredded greens

Place peeled eggs in bowl or jar. Mix vinegar, beet liquid, sugar, salt, onion and cloves; pour over eggs. Cover and refrigerate at least 2 days. Slice eggs; serve on greens.   **6 servings; 145 calories per serving.**

ORIENTAL-STYLE NUTS

2   packages (3¼ ounces each) blanched whole almonds
1   can (7 ounces) dry roasted cashew nuts
1   teaspoon soy sauce
1   teaspoon water
2   tablespoons margarine or butter
1   teaspoon five-spice powder
⅛   teaspoon garlic powder

Place nuts in jelly roll pan, 15½ × 10½ × 1 inch. Mix soy sauce and water; drizzle over nuts, tossing to distribute evenly. Dot with margarine.

Bake uncovered in 350° oven 10 minutes. Mix five-spice powder and garlic powder; sprinkle over nuts. Bake uncovered, stirring occasionally, until golden brown, 8 to 10 minutes longer.   **10 servings; 255 calories per serving.**

POPCORN

Pour ½ cup popcorn and ¼ cup vegetable oil into Dutch oven; tilt pan to distribute popcorn. Cover and cook over medium-high heat until 1 kernel pops; remove from heat. Let stand 1 minute. Return to heat; cook, shaking pan occasionally, until popcorn stops popping.   **About 12 cups popcorn; 90 calories per cup.**

PARMESAN-CURRY POPCORN

½   cup margarine or butter, melted
⅓   cup grated Parmesan cheese
½   teaspoon salt
¼   teaspoon curry powder
12   cups Popcorn (above)

Mix margarine, cheese, salt and curry powder. Pour over Popcorn; toss. **12 cups popcorn; 170 calories per cup.**

MEXI-DIP

½ **pound ground beef**
½ **teaspoon dry mustard**
¼ **to ½ teaspoon chili powder**
1 **small onion, finely chopped**
½ **medium green pepper, finely chopped (about ¼ cup)**
1 **can (16 ounces) mashed refried beans**
1 **can (8 ounces) tomato sauce**
1 **package (1¼ ounces) taco seasoning mix**
  Sour Cream Topping (below)
  Finely shredded lettuce
  Shredded Cheddar cheese

Cook and stir ground beef in 10-inch skillet until brown; drain. Stir in mustard, chili powder, onion, green pepper, beans, tomato sauce and seasoning mix. Heat to boiling, stirring constantly. Spread in ungreased pie plate, 9 × 1¼ inches.

Spread Sour Cream Topping over ground beef mixture. Sprinkle with lettuce and cheese. Serve with corn chips if desired. **About 3½ cups dip; 30 calories per tablespoon.**

Sour Cream Topping
Mix 1 cup dairy sour cream, 2 tablespoons shredded Cheddar cheese and ¼ teaspoon chili powder.

ZIPPY CHILI DIP

½ **pound ground beef**
1 **can (15 ounces) pinto beans, drained and mashed**
1 **jar (12 ounces) salsa**
1 **tablespoon chili powder**
¼ **cup chopped green pepper**

Cook and stir ground beef in 10-inch skillet until brown; drain. Stir in beans, salsa and chili powder. Heat to boiling, stirring constantly; sprinkle with green pepper. Serve warm and, if desired, with tortilla chips, sliced jicama sticks and celery sticks. **About 3 cups dip; 60 calories per tablespoon.**

SPINACH DIP

2   packages (10 ounces each) frozen chopped spinach, thawed and drained
1   can (8 ounces) water chestnuts, drained and finely chopped
1   cup dairy sour cream
1   cup plain yogurt
1   cup finely chopped green onions (with tops)
1   teaspoon salt
½   teaspoon dried tarragon leaves, crushed
½   teaspoon dry mustard
¼   teaspoon pepper
1   clove garlic, crushed

Mix all ingredients. Cover and refrigerate 1 hour. Serve with rye or rice crackers or raw vegetables if desired. **About 4½ cups dip; 10 calories per tablespoon.**

GUACAMOLE

2   ripe avocados, peeled and cut up
1   medium onion, finely chopped (about ½ cup)
1   or 2 green chili peppers, finely chopped
1   tablespoon lemon juice
1   teaspoon salt
½   teaspoon coarsely ground pepper
½   teaspoon ascorbic acid mixture
1   medium tomato, finely chopped (about ¾ cup)
    Corn chips

Beat avocados, onion, chili peppers, lemon juice, salt, pepper and ascorbic acid mixture until creamy. Stir in tomato. Cover and refrigerate at least 1 hour. Serve with corn chips. **About 2 cups dip; 25 calories per tablespoon.**

Bacon Guacamole: Stir in 2 slices bacon, crisply cooked and crumbled.

Creamy Guacamole: Stir ¼ cup mayonnaise or salad dressing and ½ teaspoon garlic salt into avocado mixture before adding tomatoes.

FRUIT-CHEESE KABOBS WITH GINGER DIP

Ginger Dip (below)
30 seedless green grapes
30 pineapple chunks, each about ¾ inch wide (¼ pineapple), or 1 can (8¼ ounces) sliced pineapple in syrup, drained and each slice cut into eighths
26 mandarin orange segments or 1 can (11 ounces) mandarin orange segments, drained
15 strawberries, each cut into halves
24 cheese cubes, each about ¾ inch thick (about 8 ounces caraway, colby, Cheddar, Monterey Jack or cream cheese)

Prepare Ginger Dip. Alternate 3 pieces of any combination of fruit and cheese on plastic or wooden picks. Serve with Ginger Dip. **About 40 appetizers; 65 calories per appetizer.**

Ginger Dip
1 package (8 ounces) cream cheese, softened
1 cup plain yogurt
¼ cup honey
2 teaspoons crushed gingerroot
1 can (8 ounces) crushed pineapple in juice, drained

Beat cream cheese, yogurt, honey and gingerroot until creamy. Fold in pineapple. Cover; refrigerate 1 hour. **About 3 cups dip; 30 calories per tablespoon.**

BUTTERMILK DIP

1 cup dairy sour cream
⅓ cup instant dry buttermilk
½ teaspoon dried dill weed
¼ teaspoon salt
1 clove garlic, crushed

Mix all ingredients. Cover and refrigerate 1 hour. **About 1 cup dip; 40 calories per tablespoon.**

KIELBASA IN FONDUE

1   pound fully cooked kielbasa, cut into ½-inch slices
2   cups beer
2   cups shredded sharp natural Cheddar cheese (8 ounces)
2   cups shredded natural Swiss cheese (8 ounces)
2   tablespoons all-purpose flour
½   teaspoon dry mustard
¼   teaspoon pepper
1   clove garlic, cut into halves
⅛   teaspoon red pepper sauce

Heat kielbasa and ½ cup beer to boiling; reduce heat. Simmer uncovered 10 minutes; drain.

Toss cheeses, flour, mustard and pepper until cheese is coated. Rub bottom and side of 2-quart heavy saucepan or skillet with cut clove of garlic; add remaining beer. Heat over low heat until bubbles rise to surface. Add cheese mixture, about 1 cup at a time and stirring after each addition, until cheese is melted and mixture is smooth. Stir in pepper sauce.

Remove to ceramic fondue dish; keep warm over low heat. Spear kielbasa with long-handled forks; dip and swirl in fondue with stirring motion. If fondue becomes too thick, stir in additional heated beer.   **8 servings; 410 calories per serving.**

CHEESE BALL

2   packages (8 ounces each) cream cheese
¾   cup crumbled blue cheese (4 ounces)
1   cup shredded sharp Cheddar cheese (4 ounces)
1   small onion, finely chopped
1   tablespoon Worcestershire sauce
     Finely snipped parsley

Place cheeses in 1½-quart bowl; let stand at room temperature until softened. Beat in onion and Worcestershire sauce on low speed. Beat on medium speed, scraping bowl frequently, until fluffy. Cover and refrigerate at least 8 hours.

Shape mixture into 1 large ball. Roll in parsley; place on serving plate. Cover and refrigerate until firm, about 2 hours.   **About 12 servings; 205 calories per serving.**

RICOTTA CHEESE SPREAD

1   carton (15 ounces) ricotta cheese
4   radishes, chopped
2   green onions (with tops), chopped
1   clove garlic, finely chopped
2   tablespoons chopped green pepper
2   tablespoons lemon juice
2   tablespoons dairy sour cream
½   teaspoon salt
⅛   teaspoon ground red pepper
    Raw vegetables or assorted crackers

Mix all ingredients except raw vegetables. Cover and refrigerate 1 hour. Serve with vegetables. **2½ cups spread; 45** calories per tablespoon.

MUSHROOM SPREAD

8   ounces mushrooms, coarsely chopped (about 2 cups)
2   tablespoons chopped onion
1   tablespoon margarine or butter
1   package (3 ounces) cream cheese, softened
¼   teaspoon salt
¼   teaspoon dried basil leaves
2   sprigs parsley
18   round butter-flavored crackers

Cook and stir mushrooms and onion in margarine in 10-inch skillet over medium heat until all liquid is absorbed, about 10 minutes.

Place mushroom mixture, cream cheese, salt and basil in blender container. Cover and blend on high speed, stopping blender occasionally to scrape sides, until smooth, about 2 minutes. Add parsley. Cover and blend on high speed just until parsley is chopped, about 30 seconds longer. Pour into serving dish. Cover and refrigerate until firm, about 3 hours.

Garnish with mushroom slices and parsley sprigs if desired. Serve with crackers. **9 servings (2 teaspoons per cracker); 85** calories per serving.

ITALIAN SAUSAGE TERRINE

1	pound bulk mild Italian sausage
1	pound chicken livers
1	medium onion, chopped (about ½ cup)
¼	cup all-purpose flour
¼	cup brandy
1	teaspoon salt
¼	teaspoon ground allspice
¼	teaspoon ground nutmeg
¼	teaspoon ground cloves
¼	teaspoon pepper
2	cloves garlic, chopped
3	eggs
½	pound bacon (about 10 slices)

Cook and stir sausage until brown; drain and reserve. Place remaining ingredients except bacon in blender container. Cover and blend on high speed until smooth, about 45 seconds; stir into sausage.

Line loaf pan, 9×5×3 inches, with heavy-duty aluminum foil, leaving about 3 inches overhanging sides. Place bacon slices crosswise across bottom and up sides of pan, letting slices overhang edges of pan. Pour sausage mixture into pan; fold bacon over top. Place loaf pan in shallow pan; pour very hot water (1 inch) into shallow pan. Bake uncovered in 350° oven 1½ hours.

Remove loaf pan from hot water; fold foil over top. Place weight on terrine. (An unopened 46-ounce juice can makes a good weight.) Press down firmly 2 minutes. Leave weight on terrine; refrigerate until firm, about 6 hours.

To remove terrine, loosen foil from sides of pan and, grasping ends of foil, lift out; remove foil. Cut terrine into ¼-inch slices. Serve with thinly sliced bread if desired. **30 servings; 105 calories per serving.**

BAKED CHEESE SPREAD

1 package (4½ ounces) Camembert cheese
1 package (8 ounces) cream cheese, softened
¼ cup milk
½ teaspoon salt
½ teaspoon dried marjoram leaves
2 eggs
2 green onions (with tops), sliced
Paprika
32 thin slices French bread

Remove rind from Camembert cheese and let cheese stand until room temperature.

Mix cheeses and remaining ingredients except paprika and bread on low speed until smooth. Pour into greased 1-quart casserole; sprinkle with paprika. Bake uncovered in 350° oven until knife inserted 1 inch from edge comes out clean, 30 to 35 minutes. Serve with French bread. **32 servings**; 85 calories per serving.

CHEVRE PATE

4 ounces chèvre cheese
2 tablespoons margarine or butter, softened
2 tablespoons milk
¼ teaspoon paprika
Dash of ground red pepper
¼ cup chopped pecans
2 tablespoons chopped ripe olives
24 toasted rye crackers

Remove rind from cheese and let stand until room temperature.

Place cheese, margarine, milk, paprika and red pepper in blender container. Cover and blend on high speed, stopping blender occasionally to scrape sides, until smooth, about 1 minute. Stir in pecans and olives. Cover and refrigerate until firm, about 2 hours.

Garnish with pecan halves and chopped ripe olives if desired. Serve with crackers. **1 cup pâté** (2 teaspoons pâté per cracker per serving); 60 calories per serving.

SALSA CHEESE BAKE

2 cloves garlic, finely chopped
1 tablespoon vegetable oil
1 jar (12 ounces) salsa
1 can (4 ounces) chopped green chilies, drained
2 tablespoons raisins
¼ teaspoon ground cinnamon
⅛ teaspoon ground cloves
Dash of ground cumin
½ pound bulk Italian sausage
16 ounces Monterey Jack cheese, cut into ¼-inch slices
¼ cup sliced pimiento-stuffed olives
1 package (12 ounces) round tortilla chips

Cook and stir garlic in oil in 1-quart saucepan until garlic is brown, about 1 minute. Stir in salsa, chilies, raisins, cinnamon, cloves and cumin. Heat to boiling, stirring occasionally; reduce heat. Simmer uncovered, stirring occasionally, until mixture is slightly thickened, about 3 minutes. Cook and stir sausage in 10-inch skillet until brown; drain. Stir in 1 cup of the salsa mixture.

Place half of the cheese slices in single layer in ungreased 1-quart shallow casserole or pie plate, 9 × 1¼ inches. Spoon sausage mixture over cheese slices in casserole; top with remaining cheese slices.

Bake uncovered in 400° oven until cheese is melted, 8 to 10 minutes. Heat remaining salsa mixture and the olives until hot; pour over cheese. Serve with tortilla chips. **15 servings**; 295 calories per serving.

MOCK CAVIAR

2 cans (4¼ ounces each) chopped ripe olives, drained
2 tablespoons olive or vegetable oil
1 teaspoon dried tarragon leaves
2 teaspoons lemon juice
¼ teaspoon red pepper sauce
1 small onion, finely chopped
1 hard-cooked egg yolk, sieved
1 tablespoon snipped parsley
36 melba toast rounds

Mix olives, oil, tarragon, lemon juice and pepper sauce. Cover and refrigerate 2 hours.

Spread in pie plate, 8 × 1¼ inches. Top with onion, egg yolk and parsley. Serve with melba toast rounds; garnish with lemon wedges if desired. **12 servings; 90 calories per serving.**

SHRIMP-CHEESE STRATA

    1   **package (8 ounces) cream cheese, softened**
    ¼   **cup dairy sour cream**
    1   **tablespoon lemon juice**
    1   **to 2 teaspoons curry powder**
    ¼   **teaspoon salt**
    1   **can (4¼ ounces) tiny shrimp, rinsed and drained**
    1   **hard-cooked egg, chopped**
    3   **tablespoons finely chopped green onions (with tops)**
        Flatbread

Mix cream cheese, sour cream, lemon juice, curry powder and salt. Spread about ¼ inch thick on 8-inch plate. Top with shrimp and egg; sprinkle with green onions. Serve with flatbread. **3 cups spread; 25 calories per tablespoon.**

YOGURT-SHRIMP SPREAD

    1   **package (8 ounces) cream cheese, softened**
    1   **carton (6 ounces) plain yogurt**
    1   **tablespoon snipped chives**
    1   **teaspoon prepared horseradish**
    ¼   **teaspoon salt**
    1   **can (4½ ounces) small shrimp, rinsed and drained**

Mix all ingredients except shrimp thoroughly. Coarsely chop shrimp; stir into cheese mixture. Cover and refrigerate 2 hours. Serve with bran snack toast if desired. **2 cups spread; 50 calories per tablespoon.**

SALMON MOUSSE

1   can (15½ ounces) salmon, drained and flaked
1   medium stalk celery, chopped (about ½ cup)
¼   cup chopped green onions (with tops)
1½ cups half-and-half
2   tablespoons lemon juice
1   teaspoon instant chicken bouillon
¾   teaspoon dried dill weed
¼   teaspoon salt
2   envelopes unflavored gelatin
½   cup cold water
    Thin slices baguette, lightly toasted

Place salmon, celery, onions, 1 cup of the half-and-half, the lemon juice, bouillon (dry), dill weed and salt in blender container. Cover and blend on high speed until smooth, about 2 minutes.

Sprinkle gelatin on cold water in 1-quart saucepan to soften; stir in remaining half-and-half. Heat over low heat, stirring constantly, until gelatin is dissolved; cool. Mix gelatin mixture and salmon mixture. Pour into lightly oiled 4-cup mold. Refrigerate until firm, about 2 hours. Unmold on serving plate. Serve mousse with baguette slices. **4 cups mousse; 20 calories per tablespoon.**

CAJUN CRABMEAT MOLD

2   packages (8 ounces each) cream cheese, softened
2   tablespoons dairy sour cream
½   teaspoon salt
½   teaspoon paprika
½   teaspoon ground red pepper
¼   teaspoon garlic powder
¼   teaspoon ground thyme
1   cup cooked crabmeat
¼   cup finely chopped green pepper
    Rye crackers

Beat all ingredients except crabmeat, green pepper and crackers in 2½-quart bowl on medium speed until well blended, about 1 minute. Stir in crabmeat and green pepper. Line a deep 1½-pint bowl with plastic wrap; press mixture in bowl. Cover and refrigerate until firm, about 3 hours.

Unmold on serving plate; remove plastic wrap. Garnish with chili peppers if desired. Serve with crackers. **3 cups spread** (2 teaspoons spread per cracker per serving); 60 calories per serving.

BEVERAGES

WASSAIL

1   gallon apple cider
⅔   cup sugar
2   teaspoons whole cloves
2   teaspoons whole allspice
2   three-inch sticks cinnamon
2   oranges, studded with cloves

Heat all ingredients except oranges; reduce heat. Cover and simmer 20 minutes. Strain punch and pour into punch bowl. Float oranges in bowl.   **32 servings** (about ½ cup each); 85 calories per serving.

HOT CRANBERRY PUNCH

½   cup packed brown sugar
7   cups water
1   teaspoon pumpkin pie spice
2   cans (16 ounces) jellied cranberry sauce
¼   cup lemon juice
1   can (12 ounces) frozen orange juice concentrate, thawed

Mix brown sugar, 1 cup of the water and the pumpkin pie spice in Dutch oven. Heat to boiling over high heat, stirring constantly. Boil and stir until sugar is dissolved; remove from heat. Stir in cranberry sauce until well blended. Stir in remaining water, the lemon juice and orange juice concentrate. Heat to boiling; reduce heat. Simmer uncovered 5 minutes.   **24 servings** (about ½ cup each); 100 calories per serving.

HOT ORANGE CIDER

1   can (12 ounces) frozen orange juice concentrate
1½   quarts apple cider
1   orange, cut into 12 slices

Prepare orange juice as directed on can. Heat orange juice
and apple cider just to boiling over low heat. Pour about 1
cup orange juice mixture into each mug. Stir in 2 teaspoons
rum if desired; top with orange slice. Garnish with stick
cinnamon if desired. **12 servings; 135 calories per serving.**

SPARKLING CRANBERRY PUNCH

2   quarts cranberry juice cocktail, chilled
1   can (6 ounces) frozen pink lemonade concentrate,
      thawed
1   bottle (32 ounces) sparkling water, chilled

Mix cranberry juice cocktail and lemonade concentrate in
punch bowl. Just before serving, stir in sparkling water. **25
servings (about ½ cup each); 65 calories per serving.**

SANGRIA PUNCH

⅔   cup lemon juice
⅓   cup orange juice
¼   cup sugar
1   bottle (25½ ounces) dry red wine

Strain juices; add sugar, stirring until dissolved. Mix juice
mixture and wine; add ice. Garnish each serving with twists
of lemon peel if desired. **8 servings (about ½ cup each); 115
calories per serving.**

TOMATO-BEER COOLER

Mix 1½ cups tomato juice, chilled, and 2 cans (12 ounces each)
beer, chilled. Pour into chilled glasses. Serve immediately
with green onions for stirrers and, if desired, with red pepper
sauce, salt and pepper. **6 servings (about ¾ cup each); 75
calories per serving.**

LEMONADE

Mix 3 cups water, 1 cup lemon juice (about 4 lemons) and ½ cup sugar. Serve over ice. **5 servings** (about ¾ cup each); 95 calories per serving.

Limeade: Substitute lime juice (about 10 limes) for the lemons and increase sugar to ¾ cup.

Minted Lemonade: Bruise mint leaves in glasses before pouring Lemonade. Garnish with mint leaves.

Pink Lemonade: Add 2 or 3 drops red food color and, if desired, 2 tablespoons grenadine syrup.

PINK COLADA

2 cans (12 ounces each) frozen limeade concentrate, thawed
1 can (15½ ounces) coconut cream
½ cup grenadine syrup
2 bottles (28 ounces each) sparkling water, chilled

Mix limeade concentrate, coconut cream and grenadine syrup; add sparkling water. Serve over ice and garnish with lime slice and maraschino cherry if desired. **24 servings** (about ½ cup each); 120 calories per serving.

STRAWBERRY SPRITZER

3 cups strawberries, cut into halves*
¼ cup orange-flavored liqueur
1 bottle (25½ ounces) dry white wine, chilled
1 bottle (32 ounces) mineral water or sparkling water, chilled

Place strawberries and orange-flavored liqueur in blender container. Cover and blend on high speed until smooth, about 30 seconds.

*1 package (16 ounces) frozen unsweetened strawberries, partially thawed, can be substituted for the 3 cups strawberries. Garnish each serving with mint leaves if desired.

Pour about 3 tablespoons strawberry mixture over ice in each of 8 glasses; stir in about ⅓ cup wine and ½ cup mineral water. Garnish side of glass with whole strawberry if desired.   **8 servings; 120 calories per serving.**

APRICOT APERITIF

  1   **tablespoon sugar**
      Dash of angostura bitters
  4   **cans (5½ ounces each) apricot nectar, chilled**
  1   **bottle (25½ ounces) dry white wine, chilled**
  1   **bottle (32 ounces) mineral water or sparkling water, chilled**
 10   **thin slices or wedges lime**
      Ground nutmeg

Mix sugar and bitters in 3-quart pitcher. Stir in apricot nectar, wine and mineral water. Pour over ice in each of 10 eight-ounce glasses. Garnish each with lime slice sprinkled with nutmeg.   **10 servings; 110 calories per serving.**

BRANDY CREAM

Place 1 pint vanilla ice cream in 1½-quart bowl; cut ice cream into fourths. Let stand until slightly softened, about 10 minutes. Add 2 to 4 tablespoons brandy; beat on low speed 30 seconds. Cover and freeze until thick, 3 to 5 hours.

Just before serving, stir gently and pour into chilled glasses. Sprinkle with shaved chocolate if desired.   **4 servings** (about ½ cup each); 150 calories per serving.

Fruit Brandy Cream: Substitute apricot-, peach- or cherry-flavored brandy for the brandy.

CHOCOLATE MILK SHAKES

Place ¾ cup milk and ¼ cup chocolate-flavored syrup in blender container. Cover and blend on high speed 2 seconds. Add 3 scoops vanilla ice cream. Cover and blend on low speed until smooth, about 5 seconds longer.   **2 servings** (about 1 cup each); 295 calories per serving.

Cherry Milk Shakes: Substitute cherry ice-cream topping for the chocolate-flavored syrup.

Chocolate Malts: Add 1 tablespoon natural instant malted milk (dry) with the syrup.

Pineapple Milk Shakes: Substitute pineapple ice-cream topping for the chocolate-flavored syrup.

HOT COCOA

⅓   **cup sugar**
⅓   **cup cocoa**
¼   **teaspoon salt**
1½ **cups water**
4½ **cups milk**

Mix sugar, cocoa and salt in 2-quart saucepan. Add water. Heat to boiling, stirring constantly. Boil and stir 2 minutes. Stir in milk; heat just until hot (do not boil). Stir in ¼ teaspoon vanilla if desired.

Beat with hand beater until foamy or stir until smooth. Serve immediately.   **9 servings** (about ⅔ cup each); 115 calories per serving.

HOT CHOCOLATE

2   **ounces unsweetened chocolate**
1   **cup water**
¼   **cup sugar**
    Dash of salt
3   **cups milk**

Heat chocolate and water in 1½-quart saucepan, stirring constantly, until chocolate is melted and mixture is smooth. Stir in sugar and salt. Heat to boiling; reduce heat. Simmer uncovered, stirring constantly, 4 minutes.

Stir in milk; heat just until hot (do not boil). Beat with hand beater until foamy. Serve immediately.   **6 servings** (about ⅔ cup each); 165 calories per serving.

MEXICAN HOT CHOCOLATE

1½   ounces unsweetened chocolate
¼   cup sugar
¾   cup water
1   tablespoon plus 2 teaspoons instant coffee (dry)
½   teaspoon ground cinnamon
¼   teaspoon ground nutmeg
     Dash of salt
2   cups milk

Heat all ingredients except milk in 1½-quart saucepan over low heat, stirring constantly, until chocolate is melted and mixture is smooth. Heat to boiling; reduce heat. Simmer uncovered, stirring constantly, 4 minutes. Stir in milk; heat just until hot (do not boil).

Beat with hand beater until foamy. Top with whipped cream if desired. Serve immediately.   **5 servings** (about ⅔ cup each); 155 calories per serving.

ABOUT COFFEE

■ Start with a thoroughly clean coffee maker. Wash after each use with hot, soapy water and rinse well with hot water; never scour with an abrasive pad. When cleaning an automatic coffee maker, follow the manufacturer's directions.

■ Always use fresh coffee and freshly drawn cold water. Never use hot water, especially in automatic coffee makers; it changes percolating time.

■ Serve steaming-hot coffee as soon as possible after brewing. If coffee must stand any length of time, remove grounds and hold coffee at serving temperature over very low heat.

■ Keep ground coffee tightly covered.

PREPARATION METHODS
Automatic: Follow manufacturer's directions for selecting grind of coffee (special ones are available), measuring and brewing the coffee and holding the coffee at serving temperature.

Drip: Measure cold water and heat to boiling. Preheat coffeepot by rinsing with very hot water. Measure drip-grind coffee into filter paper in cone or into filter section of coffeepot, depending on the type of drip pot used. Pour measured fresh boiling water into upper container; cover. When dripping is completed, remove upper container and filter section.

COFFEE CHART

Strength of Brew	For each serving* Ground Coffee	Water
Weak	1 level tablespoon	¾ cup
Medium	2 level tablespoons	¾ cup
Strong	3 level tablespoons	¾ cup

*Best general recommendation.

CAFE AU LAIT

Prepare coffee as directed at left, using ¾ cup ground coffee and 3 cups water. Heat 3 cups milk. Pour equal amounts of hot coffee and hot milk simultaneously from separate pots into each cup. **8 servings** (about ¾ cup each); 60 calories per serving.

IRISH COFFEE

1   cup chilled whipping cream
¼   cup powdered sugar
1   teaspoon vanilla
¾   cup ground coffee
3   cups water
½   cup Irish whiskey or brandy
4   to 8 teaspoons granulated sugar

Beat whipping cream, powdered sugar and vanilla in chilled 1½-quart bowl until stiff; refrigerate.

Prepare coffee as directed at left, using ¾ cup coffee and 3 cups water.

Heat 4 mugs or Irish coffee glasses by rinsing with boiling water; drain. Place 2 tablespoons whiskey and 1 to 2 teaspoons granulated sugar in each mug; stir. Pour hot coffee into each mug. Top with whipped cream; serve immediately.   **4 servings** (about ¾ cup each); 280 calories per serving.

LARGE-QUANTITY COFFEE

Measure regular-grind coffee into a clean cloth sack; fill only half full to allow for expansion of coffee and free circulation of water. (Soak and rinse sack thoroughly before using.) Tie sack, allowing sufficient length of cord for fastening to handle of kettle.

Heat measured amount of cold water to full rolling boil; reduce heat. Tie sack to handle; submerge in water. Keep kettle over low heat. Brew, pushing sack up and down frequently for proper extraction, 6 to 8 minutes. When coffee is done, remove sack, permitting all extract to drain into kettle.

QUANTITY COFFEE CHART

People	Servings (⅔ cup each)	Ground Coffee	Water
12	23	2 cups	4 quarts
25	46	4 cups	8 quarts

Note: For 25 people, based on half the people using cream and sugar, you will need 1½ cups cream (1 tablespoon per cup) and ½ cup or 25 cubes sugar (1 teaspoon per cup).

ABOUT TEA

The tea you buy is a delicate blend of some 20 to 30 varieties. Quality varies according to the soil, climate and altitude in which it is grown and the age and size of the leaves when they are picked.

Broadly classified, there are three types: black, oolong and green.

Black tea derives its color from a special processing treatment in which the leaves are allowed to oxidize. This turns the leaves black and produces a rich brew.

Oolong tea is semioxidized. Its leaves are brown and green. It brews light in color.

Green tea is not oxidized, thus the leaves remain green. The brew is pale green in color.

PREPARATION METHOD

Whether you use loose tea or tea bags, the preparation method is the same:

■ Start with a spotlessly clean teapot made of glass, china or earthenware. Add rapidly boiling water; allow to stand a few minutes, then pour out.

■ Heat cold water to a full rolling boil.

■ Add tea or bags to the warm pot, allowing 1 teaspoon of loose tea or 1 tea bag for each cup of tea desired. Pour boiling water over tea (¾ cup for each cup of tea); let stand 3 to 5 minutes to bring out the full flavor. Stir the tea once to ensure uniform strength.

■ Do not judge the strength of tea by its color; you must taste it.

■ Strain the tea or remove tea bags. Serve with sugar and milk or lemon if desired.

Prepare instant tea, a concentrate, according to the directions on the jar.

SPICED TEA

½	cup unsweetened lemon-flavored instant iced tea (dry)
¼	cup sugar
¼	cup orange-flavored instant breakfast drink (dry)
¼	teaspoon ground cinnamon
¼	teaspoon ground cloves
⅛	teaspoon ground ginger
12	cups boiling water

Mix all ingredients except boiling water; store in tightly covered container at room temperature up to 1 week.

Pour boiling water over tea mixture; stir until dissolved. Garnish with lemon or orange slices if desired. **16 servings** (about ¾ cup each); 35 calories per serving.

NOTE: For individual serving, mix 1 tablespoon dry tea mixture and 1 cup boiling water until mixture is dissolved.

ICED TEA

Prepare tea as directed on page 37 except—double the amount of tea. Strain tea over ice in pitcher or into ice-filled glasses.

NOTE: Tea that has been steeped too long or refrigerated will become cloudy. Pour a small amount of boiling water into tea to make clear again.

DO-AHEAD ICED TEA

Use 2 teaspoons loose tea or 2 tea bags for each cup of cold water. Place tea in glass container; add water. Cover and refrigerate at least 24 hours. Serve over crushed ice.

BREADS
GRAINS
PASTA

QUICK BREADS

ABOUT QUICK BREADS

As their name suggests, quick breads are just that—fast and very easy to make. Quick breads range from pancakes to tender, flaky biscuits to moist, rich nut breads.

Quick-acting baking powder rather than slower-acting yeast is the leavening agent for quick breads. It consists of an acid, such as cream of tartar, and an alkali, such as baking soda, which react with one another in the presence of moisture to form a gas. In batter or dough this gas forms tiny bubbles that expand quickly, creating the structure of the quick bread. To be sure it is always fresh, purchase only a small quantity of baking powder at a time.

BAKING TIPS
■ Use shiny pans and cookie sheets, which reflect heat, for golden, delicate and tender crusts on muffins, coffee cakes and nut breads.

■ Grease only the bottoms of muffin cups; muffins will then be nicely shaped and have no rim around the top edge.

■ Grease only the bottoms of loaf pans for fruit or nut breads. The ungreased sides provide a surface for the batter to cling to while rising during baking, which helps form a gently rounded top.

■ Cool nut breads completely before slicing to prevent crumbling. Cut with a sharp, thin-bladed knife, using a light sawing motion.

41

BAKING POWDER BISCUITS

½ cup shortening
2 cups all-purpose flour*
1 tablespoon sugar
3 teaspoons baking powder
1 teaspoon salt
¾ cup milk

Heat oven to 450°. Cut shortening into flour, sugar, baking powder and salt with pastry blender until mixture resembles fine crumbs. Stir in milk until dough leaves side of bowl (dough will be soft and sticky).

Turn dough onto lightly floured surface. Knead lightly 10 times. Roll or pat ½ inch thick. Cut with floured 2½-inch round cutter. Place on ungreased cookie sheet about 1 inch apart for crusty sides, touching' for soft sides. Bake until golden brown, 10 to 12 minutes. Immediately remove from cookie sheet. **1 dozen biscuits; 155 calories per biscuit.**

Blue Cheese Biscuits: Add 3 tablespoons crumbled blue cheese and ½ teaspoon Italian seasoning with the flour.

Buttermilk Biscuits: Decrease baking powder to 2 teaspoons and add ¼ teaspoon baking soda with the salt. Substitute buttermilk for the milk. (If buttermilk is thick, it may be necessary to add slightly more than ¾ cup.)

Cornmeal Biscuits: Substitute ½ cup cornmeal for ½ cup of the flour. Sprinkle cornmeal over biscuits before baking.

Drop Biscuits: Increase milk to 1 cup. Drop dough by spoonfuls onto greased cookie sheet.

Herb Biscuits: Add ¾ teaspoon dried dill weed or rosemary leaves, crushed, with the salt.

*If using self-rising flour, omit baking powder and salt.

SCONES

⅓ cup margarine or butter
1¾ cups all-purpose flour*
3 tablespoons sugar
2½ teaspoons baking powder
½ teaspoon salt
1 egg, beaten
½ cup currants or raisins
4 to 6 tablespoons half-and-half
1 egg, beaten

Heat oven to 400°. Cut margarine into flour, sugar, baking powder and salt with pastry blender until mixture resembles fine crumbs. Stir in 1 egg, the currants and just enough half-and-half so dough leaves side of bowl.

Turn dough onto lightly floured surface. Knead lightly 10 times. Roll or pat ½ inch thick. Cut with floured 2-inch round cutter, or cut into diamond shapes with sharp knife. Place on ungreased cookie sheet; brush dough with 1 egg. Bake until golden brown, 10 to 12 minutes. Immediately remove from cookie sheet; cool. Split scones. Spread with margarine and serve with strawberry preserves if desired. **15 scones;** 115 calories per scone.

DUMPLINGS

3 tablespoons shortening
1½ cups all-purpose flour**
2 teaspoons baking powder
¾ teaspoon salt
¾ cup milk

Cut shortening into flour, baking powder and salt with pastry blender until mixture resembles fine crumbs. Stir in milk. Drop dough by spoonfuls onto hot meat or vegetables in boiling stew (do not drop directly into liquid). Cook uncovered 10 minutes. Cover and cook 10 minutes longer. **10 dumplings;** 105 calories per dumpling.

*If using self-rising flour, omit baking powder and salt.
**If using self-rising flour, omit baking powder and salt.

Cheese Dumplings: Add ¼ cup shredded sharp cheese (1 ounce) with the flour.

Herb Dumplings: Add ½ teaspoon herbs (such as dried sage leaves, celery seed or dried thyme leaves) with the flour.

Parsley Dumplings: Add 3 tablespoons snipped parsley or chives with the flour.

FRENCH TOAST

½	cup all-purpose flour*
2	cups milk
1	tablespoon plus 1½ teaspoons sugar
¼	teaspoon salt
6	eggs
18	slices French bread, each 1 inch thick
1	tablespoon margarine or butter

Beat flour, milk, sugar, salt and eggs with hand beater until smooth. Soak bread in egg mixture until saturated.

Heat margarine in skillet until melted. Cook bread until golden brown, about 12 minutes on each side.   **18 slices; 155** calories per slice.

WAFFLES

2	eggs
2	cups all-purpose flour**
½	cup margarine or butter, melted, or vegetable oil
1¾	cups milk
1	tablespoon sugar
4	teaspoons baking powder
½	teaspoon salt

Heat waffle iron. Beat eggs with hand beater until fluffy; beat in remaining ingredients just until smooth. Pour batter from cup or pitcher onto center of hot waffle iron. Bake until steaming stops, about 5 minutes. Remove waffle carefully.

Three 10-inch waffles; 715 calories per waffle.

*If using self-rising flour, omit salt.
**If using self-rising flour, omit baking powder and salt.

Blueberry Waffles: Sprinkle 2 to 4 tablespoons fresh or frozen blueberries (thawed and well drained) over batter immediately after pouring it onto the iron.

Cheese and Bacon Waffles: Stir in 1 cup shredded sharp cheese (4 ounces). Arrange 4 short slices bacon, crisply cooked, on batter immediately after pouring it onto the iron.

Whole Wheat Waffles: Substitute whole wheat flour for the all-purpose flour and packed brown sugar for the granulated sugar. If desired, sprinkle 2 tablespoons wheat germ or sesame seed over batter immediately after pouring it onto the iron.

PANCAKES

1   **egg**
1   **cup all-purpose flour***
¾   **cup milk**
1   **tablespoon sugar**
2   **tablespoons shortening, melted, or vegetable oil**
3   **teaspoons baking powder**
½   **teaspoon salt**

Beat egg with hand beater until fluffy; beat in remaining ingredients just until smooth. For thinner pancakes, stir in additional ¼ cup milk. Grease heated griddle if necessary. (To test griddle, sprinkle with few drops water. If bubbles skitter around, heat is just right.)

For each pancake, pour about 3 tablespoons batter from tip of large spoon or from pitcher onto hot griddle. Cook pancakes until puffed and dry around edges. Turn and cook other sides until golden brown. **Nine 4-inch pancakes; 100 calories per pancake.**

Blueberry Pancakes: Stir in ½ cup fresh or frozen blueberries (thawed and well drained).

Buckwheat Pancakes: Substitute ½ cup buckwheat flour and ½ cup whole wheat flour for the all-purpose flour. Use 1 cup milk. If desired, sprinkle 1 teaspoon whole bran or wheat germ over each pancake just before turning. **10 pancakes.**

Buttermilk Pancakes: Substitute 1 cup buttermilk for the

*If using self-rising flour, omit baking powder and salt.

milk. Decrease baking powder to 1 teaspoon and beat in ½ teaspoon baking soda.   **10 pancakes.**

Ham Pancakes: Omit sugar. Stir in ⅓ to ½ cup ground or cut-up fully cooked smoked ham.

Whole Wheat Pancakes: Substitute whole wheat flour for the all-purpose flour and packed brown sugar for the granulated sugar.

BLUEBERRY MUFFINS

¾	cup milk
½	cup vegetable oil
1	egg
2	cups all-purpose* or whole wheat flour
⅓	cup sugar
3	teaspoons baking powder
1	teaspoon salt
1	cup fresh or drained canned blueberries or ¾ cup frozen blueberries, thawed and well drained

Heat oven to 400°. Grease bottoms only of 12 medium muffin cups, 2½ × 1¼ inches, or line with paper baking cups. Beat milk, oil and egg. Stir in flour, sugar, baking powder and salt, all at once, just until flour is moistened (batter will be lumpy). Fold in blueberries. Divide batter among muffin cups. Sprinkle with sugar if desired. Bake until golden brown, 18 to 20 minutes. Immediately remove from pan.   **1 dozen muffins; 195 calories per muffin.**

Apple Muffins: Omit blueberries. Stir in 1 medium apple, pared and chopped, with the milk and ½ teaspoon ground cinnamon with the salt. Sprinkle batter in pan with brown sugar if desired.

Cranberry-Orange Muffins: Omit blueberries. Stir in 1 cup cranberry halves and 1 tablespoon grated orange peel with the milk. Sprinkle batter in pan with sugar.

Date-Nut Muffins: Omit blueberries. Stir in ½ cup cut-up dates and ⅓ cup chopped nuts with the milk.

French Puffs: Omit blueberries. Immediately roll hot muffins in about ½ cup margarine or butter, melted, then in mixture of ½ cup sugar and 1 teaspoon ground cinnamon.

*If using self-rising flour, omit baking powder and salt.

Oatmeal-Raisin Muffins: Omit blueberries. Stir in 1 cup raisins with the milk. Decrease flour to 1 cup; stir in 1 cup quick-cooking oats, ½ teaspoon ground nutmeg and ¼ teaspoon ground cinnamon with the flour.

BRAN-RAISIN MUFFINS

1½	cups shreds of wheat bran cereal
½	cup raisins
½	cup boiling water
1	egg
1	cup buttermilk
¼	cup vegetable oil
1¼	cups all-purpose flour*
⅔	cup sugar
1¼	teaspoons baking soda
¼	teaspoon salt
¼	teaspoon ground nutmeg

Heat oven to 400°. Grease bottoms only of 12 medium muffin cups, 2½ × 1¼ inches, or line with paper baking cups. Mix cereal, raisins and water; let stand 2 minutes. Beat egg in 2½-quart bowl; stir in buttermilk, oil and cereal mixture. Stir in remaining ingredients, all at once, just until flour is moistened (batter will be lumpy). Fill muffin cups about ¾ full. Bake until golden brown, about 20 minutes. Immediately remove from pan. **About 1 dozen muffins; 190 calories per muffin.**

*If using self-rising flour, omit baking soda and salt.

RAISIN-SPICE COFFEE CAKE

2   cups all-purpose flour*
1   cup sugar
⅓   cup margarine or butter, softened
1   cup milk
3   teaspoons baking powder
1   teaspoon salt
1   teaspoon ground cinnamon
¼   teaspoon ground allspice
¼   teaspoon ground nutmeg
1   egg
½   cup raisins
    Streusel (below)

Heat oven to 350°. Grease square pan, 9 × 9 × 2 inches. Beat all ingredients except raisins and Streusel on low speed 30 seconds. Beat on medium speed, scraping bowl occasionally, 2 minutes. Stir in raisins.

Spread half of the batter in pan; sprinkle with half of the Streusel. Top with remaining batter; sprinkle with remaining Streusel. Bake until wooden pick inserted in center comes out clean, 40 to 45 minutes.   **1 coffee cake (9 servings); 460** calories per serving.

Streusel

⅓   cup firm margarine or butter
½   cup all-purpose flour
⅓   cup packed brown sugar or granulated sugar
1   teaspoon ground cinnamon
½   cup chopped nuts

Cut margarine into flour, brown sugar and cinnamon until crumbly; stir in nuts.

Streusel Coffee Cake: Omit cinnamon, allspice, nutmeg and raisins in batter.

*If using self-rising flour, omit baking powder and salt.

SOUR CREAM COFFEE CAKE

Apple-Nut Filling, Almond Filling or Brown Sugar
Filling (below and page 50)
1½ cups sugar
¾ cup margarine or butter, softened
1½ teaspoons vanilla
3 eggs
3 cups all-purpose* or whole wheat flour
1½ teaspoons baking powder
1½ teaspoons baking soda
¾ teaspoon salt
1½ cups dairy sour cream
Glaze (page 50)

Heat oven to 325°. Grease tube pan, 10 × 4 inches, or 12-cup
bundt cake pan. Prepare one of the fillings; reserve. Beat
sugar, margarine, vanilla and eggs in 2½-quart bowl on medium speed, scraping bowl occasionally, 2 minutes. Beat in
flour, baking powder, baking soda and salt alternately with
sour cream on low speed.

Spread ⅓ of the batter (about 2 cups) in pan; sprinkle with ⅓ of
the filling. Repeat 2 times. Bake until wooden pick inserted
near center comes out clean, about 1 hour; cool 20 minutes.
Remove from pan; drizzle with Glaze. **1 coffee cake** (16
servings); 355 calories per serving.

Apple-Nut Filling

1½ cups chopped apples
⅓ cup packed brown sugar
1 tablespoon all-purpose flour
2 tablespoons margarine or butter
¼ teaspoon ground nutmeg
⅛ teaspoon salt
½ cup finely chopped nuts

Cook all ingredients except nuts over medium heat, stirring
constantly, until apples are tender, 3 to 4 minutes; stir in
nuts.

*If using self-rising flour, omit baking powder, baking soda and salt.

Almond Filling
Heat 1 package (3½ ounces) almond paste, cut up, ½ cup powdered sugar and ¼ cup margarine or butter over medium heat, stirring constantly until smooth. Stir in ½ cup sliced almonds.

Brown Sugar Filling
Mix ½ cup packed brown sugar, ½ cup finely chopped nuts and 1½ teaspoons ground cinnamon.

Glaze
Mix ½ cup powdered sugar, ¼ teaspoon vanilla and 1 to 2 teaspoons milk until smooth.

CAKE DOUGHNUTS

	Vegetable oil
3⅓	cups all-purpose flour*
1	cup sugar
¾	cup milk
2	tablespoons shortening
3	teaspoons baking powder
½	teaspoon salt
½	teaspoon ground cinnamon
¼	teaspoon ground nutmeg
2	eggs

Heat oil (2 to 3 inches) in deep fryer or Dutch oven to 375°. Beat 1½ cups of the flour and the remaining ingredients in 1½-quart bowl on low speed, scraping bowl constantly, 30 seconds. Beat on medium speed, scraping bowl occasionally, 2 minutes. Stir in remaining flour.

Turn the dough onto generously floured cloth-covered board; roll around lightly to coat with flour. Gently roll ⅜ inch thick. Cut with floured doughnut cutter. Slide doughnuts into hot oil with wide spatula. Turn doughnuts as they rise to surface. Fry until golden brown, 1 to 1½ minutes on each side. Remove carefully from oil (do not prick surfaces); drain. Serve plain or shake one at a time in a bag with powdered sugar. **2 dozen doughnuts**; 150 calories per doughnut.

*If using self-rising flour, omit baking powder and salt.

Buttermilk Doughnuts: Do not use self-rising flour. Substitute buttermilk for the milk. Decrease baking powder to 2 teaspoons and beat in 1 teaspoon baking soda.

NOTE: Hot fat cools somewhat when foods are dropped into it. While foods are frying, temperature of fat should be 370 to 380°. If fat is too hot, foods brown before they are cooked through; if too cool, foods become grease-soaked. A deep-fat thermometer is a good investment; checking it helps maintain a constant temperature. Do not use a candy thermometer for deep-fat frying as it does not register high enough.

FRITTERS AND DEEP-FRIED FOODS

FRITTER BATTER
    1   cup all-purpose flour*
    ½   cup milk
    1   teaspoon baking powder
    1   teaspoon salt**
    1   teaspoon vegetable oil
    2   eggs

THIN BATTER
    1   cup all-purpose flour*
    1   cup milk
    ¼   cup vegetable oil
    1   teaspoon baking powder
    ½   teaspoon salt**
    1   egg

Prepare food to be fried. Thaw frozen foods completely before frying. Dry food completely before dipping into batter. Use Fritter Batter with chopped or shredded foods; use Thin Batter when you want to retain shape of food.

Heat vegetable oil (2 to 3 inches) in deep fryer or Dutch oven to 375°. Beat batter ingredients with hand beater until smooth.

Fritters (chopped cooked shrimp or fully cooked smoked ham; cubed luncheon meat; corn; chopped apple or banana; pineapple cubes): Stir about 1 cup food into Fritter Batter;

*If using self-rising flour, omit baking powder and salt.
**If adding salted foods to the batter, omit salt.

drop by level tablespoonsful into hot oil. Fry until completely cooked, about 5 minutes; drain.

Deep-fried Foods (whole shrimp, scallops, oysters, fish fillets, partially cooked chicken pieces, cutlets; eggplant slices, cauliflowerets, onion rings, zucchini slices; pineapple slices, banana quarters, apple slices, apricot halves): Coat food with flour; dip food into Thin Batter with tongs or fork, allowing excess batter to drop into bowl. Fry in hot oil until golden brown; drain.

IRISH SODA BREAD

    3   tablespoons margarine or butter, softened
  2½   cups all-purpose flour*
    2   tablespoons sugar
    1   teaspoon baking soda
    1   teaspoon baking powder
   ½   teaspoon salt
   ⅓   cup raisins, if desired
   ¾   cup buttermilk

Heat oven to 375°. Cut margarine into flour, sugar, baking soda, baking powder and salt with pastry blender until mixture resembles fine crumbs. Stir in raisins and just enough buttermilk so dough leaves side of bowl.

Turn dough onto lightly floured surface. Knead until smooth, 1 to 2 minutes. Shape into round loaf, about 6½ inches in diameter. Place on greased cookie sheet. Cut an X about ½ inch deep through loaf with floured knife. Bake until golden brown, 35 to 45 minutes. Brush with margarine or butter, softened, if desired.   **1 loaf** (12 servings); 125 calories per serving.

POPOVERS

    2   eggs
    1   cup all-purpose flour*
    1   cup milk
   ½   teaspoon salt

*Do not use self-rising flour in this recipe.

Heat oven to 450°. Generously grease six 6-ounce custard cups. Beat eggs slightly; beat in flour, milk and salt just until smooth (do not overbeat).

Fill custard cups about ½ full. Bake 20 minutes. Decrease oven temperature to 350°; bake 20 minutes longer. Immediately remove from cups; serve hot. **6 popovers; 140 calories per popover.**

GRUYERE PUFF RING

1	cup milk
¼	cup margarine or butter
1	cup all-purpose flour*
4	eggs
¾	cup shredded Gruyère or Swiss cheese (3 ounces)
¼	cup grated Parmesan cheese

Heat oven to 400°. Heat milk and margarine to rolling boil in 2-quart saucepan. Stir in flour. Stir vigorously over low heat until mixture forms a ball, about 1 minute; remove from heat. Beat in the eggs, all at once; continue beating until smooth and thickened. Beat in ½ cup of the Gruyère cheese and the Parmesan cheese.

Drop ¾ of the dough by tablespoonfuls into 8 mounds to form a circle on greased cookie sheet. (Each mound of dough should just touch the next one.) Drop a teaspoonful of remaining dough onto center of each mound. Sprinkle with remaining Gruyère cheese. Bake on center oven rack until ring is puffed and golden, 30 to 35 minutes. **1 ring (8 servings); 205 calories per serving.**

*Self-rising flour can be used in this recipe.

CORN BREAD

1½ cups cornmeal
½ cup all-purpose flour*
¼ cup shortening or bacon fat
1½ cups buttermilk
2 teaspoons baking powder
1 teaspoon sugar
1 teaspoon salt
½ teaspoon baking soda
2 eggs

Heat oven to 450°. Mix all ingredients; beat vigorously 30 seconds. Pour into greased round pan, 9 × 1½ inches, or square pan, 8 × 8 × 2 inches. Bake until golden brown, 25 to 30 minutes. Serve warm. **12 servings; 145 calories per serving.**

Chili Corn Bread: Stir in 1 can (4 ounces) chopped green chilies, well drained, and ½ teaspoon chili powder.

Corn Muffins: Fill 14 greased medium muffin cups, 2½ × 1¼ inches, about ⅞ full. Bake about 20 minutes.

Corn Sticks: Fill 18 greased corn stick pans about ⅞ full. Bake 12 to 15 minutes.

Onion-Cheese Corn Bread: Stir in ½ cup shredded process sharp American cheese (2 ounces) and 3 medium green onions, chopped (about ¼ cup).

Skillet Corn Bread: Pour batter into greased 10-inch ovenproof skillet. Bake about 20 minutes.

*If using self-rising flour, decrease baking powder to 1 teaspoon and omit salt.

SPOON BREAD

1½ cups boiling water
1 cup cornmeal
1 tablespoon margarine or butter, softened
3 eggs, separated
1 cup buttermilk
1 teaspoon salt
1 teaspoon sugar
1 teaspoon baking powder
¼ teaspoon baking soda
   Margarine or butter

Heat oven to 375°. Stir boiling water into cornmeal; continue stirring until mixture is lukewarm. Stir in 1 tablespoon margarine and the egg yolks until blended. Stir in buttermilk, salt, sugar, baking powder and baking soda. Beat egg whites just until soft peaks form; fold into batter. Pour into greased 2-quart casserole. Bake until knife inserted near center comes out clean, 45 to 50 minutes. Serve bread with margarine. 8 servings; 155 calories per serving.

ZUCCHINI BREAD

2⅔ cups sugar
⅔ cup shortening
3 cups shredded zucchini (about 2 medium)
⅔ cup water
4 eggs
3⅓ cups all-purpose flour*
2 teaspoons baking soda
1½ teaspoons salt
1 teaspoon ground cinnamon
1 teaspoon ground cloves
2 teaspoons vanilla
½ teaspoon baking powder
⅔ cup coarsely chopped nuts
⅔ cup raisins

*If using self-rising flour, omit baking soda, salt and baking powder.

Heat oven to 350°. Grease bottoms only of 2 loaf pans, 9×5×3 inches, or 3 loaf pans, 8½×4½×2½ inches. Mix sugar and shortening in 2½-quart bowl. Stir in zucchini, water and eggs. Mix in flour, baking soda, salt, cinnamon, cloves, vanilla and baking powder; stir in nuts and raisins. Pour into pans. Bake until wooden pick inserted in center comes out clean, 60 to 70 minutes; cool 5 minutes. Loosen sides of loaves from pans; remove from pans. Cool completely before slicing. **2 or 3 loaves (24 slices each); 125 calories per slice.**

Do-ahead Tip: Wrap and refrigerate no longer than 10 days.

Pumpkin Bread: Substitute 1 can (16 ounces) pumpkin for the zucchini. Omit vanilla. Increase baking time to about 1 hour 10 minutes.

CRANBERRY-ORANGE BREAD

2	cups all-purpose flour*
¾	cup sugar
1½	teaspoons baking powder
¾	teaspoon salt
½	teaspoon baking soda
¼	cup margarine or butter, softened
1	tablespoon grated orange peel
¾	cup orange juice
1	egg
1	cup fresh or frozen cranberries, chopped
½	cup chopped nuts

Heat oven to 350°. Grease bottom only of loaf pan, 8½×4½×2½ or 9×5×3 inches. Mix flour, sugar, baking powder, salt and baking soda; stir in margarine until mixture is crumbly. Stir in orange peel, orange juice and egg just until moistened; stir in cranberries and nuts. Spread in pan. Bake until wooden pick inserted in the center comes out clean, 8-inch loaf 1¼ hours, 9-inch loaf 55 to 65 minutes; cool 5 minutes. Loosen sides of loaf from pan; remove from pan. Cool completely before slicing. **1 loaf (24 slices); 105 calories per slice.**

*If using self-rising flour, omit baking powder and salt. Decrease baking soda to ¼ teaspoon.

BANANA BREAD

1	cup sugar
⅓	cup margarine or butter, softened
2	eggs
1½	cups mashed ripe bananas (3 to 4 medium)
⅓	cup water
1⅔	cups all-purpose flour*
1	teaspoon baking soda
½	teaspoon salt
¼	teaspoon baking powder
½	cup chopped nuts

Heat oven to 350°. Grease bottom only of loaf pan, 8½ × 4½ × 2½ or 9 × 5 × 3 inches. Mix sugar and margarine in 2½-quart bowl. Stir in eggs until blended. Add bananas and water; beat 30 seconds. Stir in remaining ingredients except nuts just until moistened; stir in nuts. Pour into pan. Bake until wooden pick inserted in center comes out clean, 8-inch loaf 1¼ hours, 9-inch loaf 55 to 60 minutes; cool 5 minutes. Loosen sides of loaf from pan; remove from pan. Cool completely before slicing. **1 loaf** (24 slices); 120 calories per slice.

Do-ahead Tip: Wrap and refrigerate no longer than 1 week.

*Do not use self-rising flour in this recipe.

YEAST BREADS

ABOUT YEAST BREADS

INGREDIENTS

Flour: All-purpose flour is the most widely used flour. It contains a special protein called gluten, the structure builder of bread. When mixed with liquid and kneaded or beaten, the gluten stretches and gives elasticity to the dough by trapping bubbles of gas formed by the yeast.

Some flours, such as rye and whole wheat, lack sufficient gluten and usually are used in combination with all-purpose flour. Self-rising flour, which already contains leavening and salt, is not often recommended for yeast breads. However, all recipes were tested with self-rising flour; adjustments are indicated when necessary.

Yeast: Yeast is a live plant that gives off a gas that makes dough rise. It is very sensitive—too much heat will kill it, but cold will stunt its growth. Yeast is available in several forms: regular active dry yeast, quick-acting active dry yeast and compressed yeast. All of our recipes have been tested with dry yeast. Most of the recipes follow the traditional method of dissolving the yeast in warm water (105 to 115°). However, some recipes yield better results by mixing the yeast with the flour, then beating in very warm water (120 to 130°).

Liquids: Water or milk are the most commonly used liquids. Water gives bread a crisper crust; milk, a velvety texture and added nutrients.

Sweeteners: Sugar, honey or molasses provide "food" for the yeast, enhance flavor and help brown the crust.

Salt: A flavor agent that is needed to control the growth of the yeast and prevent overrising, which can cause the bread to collapse.

Fat: Added to contribute to tenderness and flavor.

Eggs: For flavor, richness and color, eggs are sometimes added.

YEAST DOUGHS

There are basically two kinds of yeast doughs—kneaded and batter. Both doughs need to rise before shaping and baking. To let dough rise, cover and keep in a warm, draft-free place. If necessary, place covered bowl of dough on wire rack over a bowl of warm water.

Kneaded dough: Kneading develops the gluten and results in bread with an even texture and a smooth, nicely rounded top.

- After first addition of flour has been beaten in, dough will be very soft and will fall in "sheets" off rubber spatula.

- The second addition of flour makes the dough stiff enough to knead. Mix in only enough flour so dough leaves side of the bowl.

- To knead, fold dough toward you. With heels of hands, push dough away with short rocking motions. Give dough a quarter turn; repeat.

- When dough is properly kneaded, it will feel elastic and the top will be smooth with some blisters appearing on the surface.

- Dough should rise until double. Test by pressing fingertips ½ inch into dough. If impression remains, dough has risen enough.

- Punch down center of dough with your fist. Fold dough over and form into a ball. This releases large air bubbles to produce a finer texture.

- If dough is not sufficiently kneaded, the bread will be coarse, heavy, crumbly and dry.

Batter dough: Batter breads are really shortcut no-knead yeast breads. Because less flour is used, the dough is stickier; instead of being kneaded, it is beaten with a mixer with the first addition of flour. The batter is generally not shaped but spread in the pan. The bread has a coarser texture and pebbled surface.

REFRIGERATING YEAST DOUGH

Yeast dough made with water (except plain bread dough) can be refrigerated up to 5 days. However, if milk and at least ¼ cup sugar are used, refrigerate no longer than 3 days. After mixing dough, grease top well. Cover with moistureproof wrap, then a damp cloth. Keep cloth damp during storage. When ready to bake, shape dough; let rise until double, 1½ to 2 hours. Bake as directed.

BAKING TIPS

■ Use loaf pans of anodized aluminum, darkened metal or glass for bread with well-browned crusts.

■ Shiny cookie sheets or muffin cups produce sweet rolls with tender, golden brown crusts.

■ Stagger loaf pans on a lower shelf of the oven so they do not touch sides of the oven or each other.

■ The top of each pan should be level with, or slightly above, the middle of the oven.

■ If baking round loaves on a cookie sheet, place the sheet on the center rack.

■ Doneness is determined by tapping the crust. The loaf will have a hollow sound when done.

■ Remove loaves from pans immediately and place on wire racks away from draft to cool.

■ For a shiny, soft crust, brush just-baked loaf with margarine, butter or shortening.

STORING

Bread and rolls can be stored in airtight containers in a cool, dry place for 5 to 7 days. Refrigerate only in hot, humid weather. Breads can be stored, tightly wrapped in moistureproof or vaporproof material, labeled and dated, in the freezer for 2 to 3 months. To thaw, let stand wrapped at room temperature for 2 to 3 hours.

RAISED DOUGHNUTS

2	packages regular or quick-acting active dry yeast
¼	cup warm water (105 to 115°)
1½	cups lukewarm milk (scalded then cooled)
½	cup sugar
1	teaspoon salt
2	eggs
⅓	cup shortening
5	cups all-purpose flour*
	Vegetable oil
	Granulated sugar, or Creamy Glaze or Chocolate Glaze (page 62)

Dissolve yeast in warm water in 2½-quart bowl. Add milk, ½ cup sugar, the salt, eggs, shortening and 2 cups of the flour. Beat on low speed, scraping bowl constantly, 30 seconds. Beat on medium speed, scraping bowl occasionally, 2 minutes. Stir in remaining flour until smooth. Cover and let rise in warm place until double, 50 to 60 minutes. (Dough is ready if indentation remains when touched.)

Turn dough onto generously floured surface; roll around lightly to coat with flour. Gently roll dough ½ inch thick with floured rolling pin. Cut with floured doughnut cutter. Cover and let rise until double, 30 to 40 minutes.

Heat vegetable oil (2 to 3 inches) in deep fryer or Dutch oven to 350°. Slide doughnuts into hot oil with wide spatula. Turn doughnuts as they rise to surface. Fry until golden brown, about 1 minute on each side. Remove carefully from oil (do not prick surfaces); drain. Serve sugared or spread with Creamy or Chocolate Glaze while warm. **About 1½ dozen doughnuts;** 230 calories per doughnut.

*If using self-rising flour, omit salt.

Creamy Glaze

- ⅓ cup margarine or butter
- 2 cups powdered sugar
- 1½ teaspoons vanilla
- 4 to 6 tablespoons hot water

Heat margarine until melted; remove from heat. Stir in powdered sugar and vanilla until smooth. Stir in water, 1 tablespoon at a time, until of desired consistency.

Chocolate Glaze

- ⅓ cup margarine or butter
- 4 squares (1 ounce each) semisweet chocolate
- 2 cups powdered sugar
- 1½ teaspoons vanilla
- 4 to 6 tablespoons hot water

Heat margarine and chocolate over low heat until chocolate is melted; remove from heat. Stir in powdered sugar and vanilla until smooth. Stir in water, 1 tablespoon at a time, until of desired consistency.

ENGLISH MUFFINS

- 1 package regular or quick-acting active dry yeast
- 1 cup warm water (105 to 115°)
- 3 cups all-purpose* or whole wheat flour
- ¼ cup shortening
- 2 tablespoons honey
- 1 teaspoon salt
  Cornmeal

Dissolve yeast in warm water in 2½-quart bowl. Stir in flour, shortening, honey and salt until water is absorbed and dough cleans side of bowl. Turn dough onto floured surface. Knead lightly just until easy to handle, 5 to 10 times. Roll ¼ inch thick, adding flour to surface, if necessary, to prevent sticking. Cut into 3½-inch circles.

Sprinkle ungreased cookie sheet with cornmeal. Place cir-

*If using self-rising flour, omit salt.

cles about 1 inch apart on cookie sheet; sprinkle with corn-meal. Cover and let rise in warm place until light and airy, about 1 hour. (Dough is ready if indentation remains when touched; dough does not double.)

Heat ungreased electric griddle or skillet to 375°. Cook circles until deep golden brown, about 7 minutes on each side; cool. To serve, split with fork; toast and spread with margarine or butter and marmalade if desired. **12 muffins;** 155 calories per muffin.

ANGEL BISCUITS

1	package regular or quick-acting active dry yeast
2	tablespoons warm water (105 to 115°)
1	cup shortening
5	cups all-purpose flour*
¼	cup sugar
3	teaspoons baking powder
2	teaspoons salt
1	teaspoon baking soda
2	cups buttermilk

Dissolve yeast in warm water. Cut shortening into flour, sugar, baking powder, salt and baking soda with pastry blender in 4-quart bowl until mixture resembles fine crumbs. Stir in buttermilk and yeast mixture until dough leaves side of bowl (dough will be soft and sticky).

Turn dough onto generously floured surface. Gently roll in flour to coat; shape into ball. Knead lightly 25 to 30 times, sprinkling with flour if dough is too sticky. Roll or pat ½ inch thick. Cut with 2½-inch round cutter. Place about 1 inch apart on ungreased cookie sheet. Cover and let rise in warm place until double, 1 to 1½ hours.

Heat oven to 400°. Bake until golden brown, 12 to 14 minutes. Immediately remove from cookie sheet. **2½ dozen biscuits;** 140 calories per biscuit.

Do-ahead Tip: Place dough in lightly greased bowl, cover with plastic wrap and refrigerate no longer than 3 days.

*If using self-rising flour, omit baking powder and salt.

SOFT BREADSTICKS

1	package regular or quick-acting active dry yeast
1⅓	cups warm water (105 to 115°)
3	to 3½ cups all-purpose flour*
3	tablespoons vegetable oil
1	tablespoon honey
1	teaspoon salt
1	egg white, slightly beaten
	Coarse salt or sesame seed

Dissolve yeast in warm water in 2½-quart bowl. Stir in 1 cup of the flour, the oil, honey and 1 teaspoon salt. Beat until smooth. Stir in enough remaining flour, scraping dough from side of bowl, until soft dough forms. Cover and let rise in warm place until double, about 45 minutes.

Heat oven to 400°. Stir down dough by beating about 25 strokes. Turn dough onto generously floured surface; roll around lightly to coat with flour. Divide into 24 equal parts. Roll and shape each part dough into a rope, about 9 inches long, sprinkling with flour if dough is too sticky. Place on greased cookie sheet. Brush with egg white; sprinkle with coarse salt. Bake until crust is deep golden brown and crisp, about 15 minutes. Immediately remove from cookie sheet. Store loosely covered. **2 dozen breadsticks;** 70 calories per breadstick.

Whole Wheat Soft Breadsticks: Substitute whole wheat flour for the all-purpose flour. Or substitute 1 cup whole wheat flour for 1 cup of the all-purpose flour; stir into yeast mixture.

*If using self-rising flour, omit salt.

EGG BAGELS

1   package regular or quick-acting active dry yeast
1   cup warm water (105 to 115°)
4   cups all-purpose* or unbleached flour
2   tablespoons sugar
2   tablespoons vegetable oil
1½ teaspoons salt
2   eggs
2   quarts water
2   tablespoons sugar
1   egg yolk
1   tablespoon water

Dissolve yeast in warm water in 2½-quart bowl. Stir in 1¼ cups of the flour, 2 tablespoons sugar, the oil, salt and eggs. Beat until smooth. Stir in remaining flour.

Turn dough onto lightly floured surface; knead until smooth and elastic, about 5 minutes. Place in greased 2½-quart bowl; turn greased side up. Cover and let rise in warm place until double, about 45 minutes. (Dough is ready if indentation remains when touched.)

Punch down dough; divide into 16 equal parts. Roll each part into rope, about 6 inches long; moisten ends with water and pinch to form a bagel. Or shape each part into smooth ball; punch hole in center and pull gently to enlarge hole and make uniform shape. Let rise 20 minutes.

Heat oven to 375°. Heat 2 quarts water and 2 tablespoons sugar to boiling in Dutch oven; reduce heat. Add 4 bagels. Simmer uncovered, turning once, 4 minutes; drain on towel. Repeat with remaining bagels, four at a time. Beat egg yolk and 1 tablespoon water slightly; brush over bagels. Bake on greased cookie sheet until golden brown, 30 to 35 minutes; cool.   **16 bagels; 145 calories per bagel.**

*Do not use self-rising flour in this recipe.

TRADITIONAL WHITE BREAD

6	to 7 cups all-purpose* or unbleached flour
3	tablespoons sugar
1	tablespoon salt
2	tablespoons shortening
2	packages regular or quick-acting active dry yeast
2¼	cups very warm water (120 to 130°)

Mix 3½ cups of the flour, the sugar, salt, shortening and yeast in 4-quart bowl; add warm water. Beat on low speed, scraping bowl frequently, 1 minute. Beat on medium speed, scraping bowl frequently, 1 minute. Stir in enough remaining flour, 1 cup at a time, to make dough easy to handle.

Turn dough onto lightly floured surface; knead until smooth and elastic, about 10 minutes. Place in greased 2½-quart bowl; turn greased side up. Cover and let rise in warm place until double, 40 to 60 minutes. (Dough is ready if indentation remains when touched.)

Punch down dough; divide into halves. Let rest 5 minutes. Flatten each half with hands or rolling pin into rectangle, 18 ×9 inches, on lightly floured surface. (If dough shrinks, gently stretch into rectangle.) Fold 9-inch sides crosswise into thirds, overlapping sides. Roll up tightly toward you, beginning at open end. Pinch edge of dough into roll to seal well. Press each end with side of hand to seal; fold ends under loaf. Place loaves, seam sides down, in 2 greased loaf pans, 9×5×3 or 8½×4½×2½ inches. Brush loaves lightly with margarine if desired. Let rise until double, 35 to 50 minutes.

Heat oven to 425°. Place loaves on low rack so that tops of pans are in center of oven. Bake until deep golden brown and loaves sound hollow when tapped, 25 to 30 minutes. Remove from pans. Brush loaves with margarine if desired; cool on wire rack.   **2 loaves** (24 slices each); 65 calories per slice.

Cinnamon-Raisin Bread: Stir in 1 cup raisins with the second addition of flour. Mix ¼ cup sugar and 2 teaspoons ground cinnamon. After flattening dough into rectangles, sprinkle each with 1 tablespoon water and half of the sugar mixture.

*If using self-rising flour, omit salt.

BRIOCHE

  1   **package regular or quick-acting active dry yeast**
 ½   **cup warm water (105 to 115°)**
  2   **tablespoons sugar**
 ½   **teaspoon salt**
  5   **eggs**
  1   **egg white**
 ¾   **cup butter, softened**
3½   **cups all-purpose flour***
  1   **egg yolk**
  1   **tablespoon water**

Dissolve yeast in warm water in 4-quart bowl. Add sugar, salt, 5 eggs, the egg white, butter and 2 cups of the flour. Beat on low speed, scraping bowl constantly, 30 seconds. Beat on medium speed, scraping bowl occasionally, 10 minutes. Stir in remaining flour until smooth. Scrape dough from side of bowl. Cover with plastic wrap and let rise in warm place until double, about 1 hour.

Stir down dough by beating about 25 strokes. Cover bowl tightly with plastic wrap and refrigerate at least 8 hours.

Grease two 4-cup brioche pans or two 1½-quart ovenproof bowls. Stir down dough. (Dough will be very soft and slightly sticky.) Divide dough into halves; refrigerate one half. Shape ¼ of the remaining dough into a cone shape with lightly floured hands. Shape remaining ¾ dough into flattened round, about 3½ inches in diameter.

Place flattened round in pan, patting to fit. Make indentation, about 2 inches in diameter and 1½ inches deep, in center of dough; place cone-shaped dough, pointed side down, in indentation. Repeat with refrigerated dough. Cover and let rise in warm place until double, about 1½ hours.

Heat oven to 375°. Beat egg yolk and 1 tablespoon water slightly; brush over top of dough. (Do not allow egg yolk mixture to accumulate around edges of pans.) Bake until golden brown, 35 to 40 minutes. Immediately remove from pans. **2 loaves** (12 slices each); 150 calories per slice.

Individual Brioches: Grease 24 brioche pans or medium muffin cups, 2½ × 1¼ inches. After stirring down chilled

*Do not use self-rising flour in this recipe.

dough, divide into halves; refrigerate one half. Shape remaining half dough into roll, about 7½ inches long. Cut into 15 slices, each about ½ inch thick.

Working quickly with floured hands (dough will be very soft and slightly sticky), shape 12 of the slices into balls; place in muffin cups. Flatten and make a deep indentation in center of each ball with thumb. Cut each of the remaining 3 slices into 4 equal parts; shape each part into ball. Place 1 ball in each indentation. Repeat with refrigerated dough. Cover and let rise in warm place until double, about 40 minutes.

Heat oven to 375°. Beat egg yolk and 1 tablespoon water slightly; brush over top of dough. (Do not allow egg yolk mixture to accumulate around edges of pans.) Bake until golden brown, 15 to 20 minutes. Immediately remove from pans. **2 dozen individual brioches.**

FRENCH BREAD

1	package regular or quick-acting active dry yeast
1¼	cups warm water (105 to 115°)
1	tablespoon sugar
2	teaspoons salt
3	to 3½ cups all-purpose flour*
1	tablespoon cornmeal
	Cold water
1	egg white
2	tablespoons cold water

Dissolve yeast in warm water in 2½-quart bowl. Stir in sugar, salt and 2 cups of the flour. Beat until smooth. Stir in enough remaining flour to make dough easy to handle (dough will be soft).

Turn dough onto lightly floured surface; knead until smooth and elastic, about 5 minutes. Place in greased 2½-quart bowl; turn greased side up. Cover and let rise at room temperature (about 70°) until slightly more than double, 1½ to 2 hours. (Longer rising gives typical French bread texture.)

Punch down dough; cover and let rest 15 minutes. Grease cookie sheet; sprinkle with cornmeal. Divide dough into halves. Roll each half into rectangle, 15 × 10 inches. Roll up tightly, beginning at 15-inch side. Pinch edge of dough into roll to

*Do not use self-rising flour in this recipe.

seal well. Roll gently back and forth to taper ends. Place both loaves lengthwise on cookie sheet. Make ¼-inch deep slashes across loaves at 2-inch intervals or make 1 lengthwise slash on each loaf. Brush loaves with cold water. Let rise uncovered until slightly more than double, about 1½ hours.

Heat oven to 375°. Pour 1 cup hot water into rectangular pan, 13×9×2 inches; place pan on lowest oven rack. Brush loaves with cold water. Bake 20 minutes. Remove pan of water from oven. Mix egg white and 2 tablespoons cold water; brush over loaves. Bake until loaves are golden brown and sound hollow when tapped, about 30 minutes longer. **2 loaves** (12 slices each); 55 calories per slice.

GARLIC BREAD

Cut 1 loaf (1 pound) French bread into 1-inch slices. Mix ½ cup margarine or butter, softened, and 1 clove garlic, finely chopped; spread over slices. Reassemble loaf; wrap in heavy-duty aluminum foil and seal securely. Heat in 400° oven until hot, 15 to 20 minutes. **1 loaf** (24 slices); 90 calories per slice.

Herb-Cheese Bread: Substitute 2 tablespoons grated Parmesan cheese, 2 teaspoons snipped parsley, ½ teaspoon dried oregano leaves and ⅛ teaspoon garlic salt for the garlic.

Onion Bread: Substitute 2 tablespoons finely chopped onion or snipped chives for the garlic.

DARK PUMPERNICKEL

3	packages regular or quick-acting active dry yeast
1¾	cups warm water (105 to 115°)
½	cup dark molasses
1	tablespoon salt
2	tablespoons vegetable oil
2	teaspoons fennel or caraway seed
2½	cups medium rye flour
1	cup shreds of wheat bran cereal
¼	cup cocoa
2	to 2½ cups all-purpose flour*
	Cornmeal
	Margarine or butter, softened

*If using self-rising flour, decrease salt to 1 teaspoon.

Dissolve yeast in warm water in 4-quart bowl. Stir in molasses, salt, oil, fennel seed, rye flour, cereal and cocoa. Beat until smooth. Stir in enough all-purpose flour for easy handling. Turn onto lightly floured surface. Cover; let rest 10 to 15 minutes. Knead until smooth, about 5 minutes. Place in greased 2½-quart bowl;. turn greased side up. Cover; let rise in warm place until double, about 1 hour. (Dough is ready if indentation remains when touched.)

Grease cookie sheet; sprinkle with cornmeal. Punch down dough; divide into halves. Shape each half into a round, slightly flat loaf. Place loaves in opposite corners of cookie sheet; brush tops lightly with margarine. Let rise until double, 40 to 50 minutes.

Heat oven to 375°. Bake until loaves sound hollow when tapped, 30 to 35 minutes; cool on rack. **2 loaves** (24 slices each); 65 calories per slice.

HONEY-WHOLE WHEAT BREAD

3	cups stone-ground whole wheat or graham flour
⅓	cup honey
¼	cup shortening
1	tablespoon salt
2	packages regular or quick-acting active dry yeast
2¼	cups very warm water (120 to 130°)
3	to 4 cups all-purpose* or unbleached flour

Mix whole wheat flour, honey, shortening, salt and yeast in 4-quart bowl; add warm water. Beat on low speed, scraping bowl frequently, 1 minute. Beat on medium speed, scraping bowl frequently, 1 minute. Stir in enough all-purpose flour, 1 cup at a time, to make dough easy to handle.

Turn dough onto lightly floured surface; knead until smooth and elastic, about 10 minutes. Place in greased 2½-quart bowl; turn greased side up. Cover and let rise in warm place until double, 40 to 60 minutes. (Dough is ready if indentation remains when touched.)

Punch down dough; divide into halves. Let rest 5 minutes. Flatten each half with hands or rolling pin into rectangle,

*If using self-rising flour, decrease salt to 1 teaspoon.

18 × 9 inches, on lightly floured surface. (If dough shrinks, gently stretch into rectangle.) Fold 9-inch sides crosswise into thirds, overlapping sides. Roll up tightly toward you, beginning at open end. Pinch edge of dough into roll to seal well. Press each end with side of hand to seal; fold ends under loaf. Place loaves, seam sides down, in 2 greased loaf pans, 9 × 5 × 3 or 8½ × 4½ × 2½ inches. Brush loaves lightly with margarine and sprinkle with whole wheat flour or crushed rolled oats if desired. Let rise until double, 35 to 50 minutes.

Heat oven to 375°. Place loaves on low rack so that tops of pans are in center of oven. Bake until loaves are deep golden brown and sound hollow when tapped, 40 to 45 minutes. Remove from pans; cool on wire rack. **2 loaves** (24 slices each); 70 calories per slice.

BRAN-OATMEAL BREAD

5   to 5½ cups all-purpose flour*
1   cup shreds of wheat bran cereal
1   cup quick-cooking oats
½   cup molasses
1   tablespoon salt
3   tablespoons shortening
2   packages regular or quick-acting active dry yeast
2   cups very warm water (120 to 130°)
1   egg white, slightly beaten
1   tablespoon cold water
    Quick-cooking oats

Mix 2 cups of the flour, the cereal, 1 cup oats, the molasses, salt, shortening and yeast in 4-quart bowl; add the warm water. Beat on low speed, scraping bowl frequently, 1 minute. Beat on medium speed, scraping bowl frequently, 1 minute. Stir in enough remaining flour, 1 cup at a time, to make dough easy to handle.

Turn dough onto lightly floured surface; knead until smooth and elastic, about 10 minutes. Place in greased 2½-quart bowl; turn greased side up. Cover and let rise in warm place until double, about 1 hour 15 minutes. (Dough is ready if indentation remains when touched.)

*If using self-rising flour, omit salt.

Punch down dough; divide into halves. Let rest 5 minutes. Flatten each half with hands or rolling pin into rectangle, 18 × 9 inches, on lightly floured surface. (If dough shrinks, gently stretch into rectangle.) Fold 9-inch sides crosswise into thirds, overlapping sides. Roll up tightly toward you, beginning at open end. Pinch edge of dough into roll to seal well. Press each end with side of hand to seal; fold ends under loaf. Place loaves, seam sides down, in 2 greased loaf pans, 8½ × 4½ × 2½ inches. Cover and let rise in warm place until double, about 1 hour.

Heat oven to 375°. Mix egg white and 1 tablespoon water; brush over loaves. Sprinkle with oats. Bake until loaves are deep golden brown and sound hollow when tapped, 35 to 40 minutes. Remove from pans; cool on wire rack.   **2 loaves** (20 slices each); 85 calories per slice.

CHEESE CASSEROLE BREAD

1	package regular or quick-acting active dry yeast
½	cup warm water (105 to 115°)
½	cup lukewarm milk (scalded then cooled)
⅔	cup margarine or butter, softened
2	eggs
1	teaspoon salt
3	cups all-purpose flour*
1	cup shredded Swiss or Cheddar cheese (4 ounces)
½	teaspoon pepper
	Margarine or butter, softened

Dissolve yeast in warm water in 2½-quart bowl. Add milk, ⅔ cup margarine, the eggs, salt and 1 cup of the flour. Beat on low speed, scraping bowl constantly, 30 seconds. Beat on medium speed, scraping bowl occasionally, 2 minutes. Stir in remaining flour, the cheese and pepper. Scrape batter from side of bowl. Cover and let rise in warm place until double, about 40 minutes. (Batter is ready if indentation remains when touched with floured finger.)

Stir down batter by beating about 25 strokes. Spread evenly in greased 2-quart casserole. Cover and let rise until double, about 45 minutes.

*If using self-rising flour, omit salt.

Heat oven to 375°. Place loaf on low rack so that top of casserole is in center of oven. Casserole should not touch sides of oven. Bake until loaf is brown and sounds hollow when tapped, 40 to 45 minutes. Loosen side of bread from casserole; immediately remove from casserole. Brush top of bread with margarine; cool on wire rack. **1 loaf** (24 slices); 130 calories per slice.

Onion-Dill Casserole Bread: Omit cheese and pepper. Stir in 1 small onion, finely chopped (about ¼ cup), and 1 tablespoon dried dill weed with the second addition of flour. Brush top of loaf with margarine and sprinkle with sesame seed or poppy seed before baking.

HARD ROLLS

5 to 5¾ cups all-purpose flour*
1 tablespoon sugar
1 tablespoon salt
2 tablespoons margarine or butter, softened
1 package regular or quick-acting active dry yeast
2 cups very warm water (120 to 130°)
1 egg white
2 tablespoons cold water

Mix 3 cups of the flour, the sugar, salt, margarine and yeast in 2½-quart bowl; add warm water. Beat on low speed, scraping bowl frequently, 1 minute. Beat on medium speed, scraping bowl frequently, 1 minute. Stir in enough remaining flour, 1 cup at a time, to make dough easy to handle.

Turn dough onto lightly floured surface; knead until smooth and elastic, about 10 minutes. Place in greased 2½-quart bowl; turn greased side up. Cover with plastic wrap and let rise at room temperature (about 70°) until double, about 1½ hours. (Dough is ready if indentation remains when touched.)

Punch down dough; cover and let rest 15 minutes. Divide dough into 18 equal parts. Shape each part into ball; roll back and forth under palm of hand to form 3-inch oblong shape.

*If using self-rising flour, omit salt.

Place on each of 2 greased cookie sheets. Cover loosely with plastic wrap and let rise until double, about 1 hour.

Mix egg white and 2 tablespoons cold water; brush over rolls. Make slash about ½ inch deep and about 2 inches long on top of each roll.

Heat oven to 375°. Place both cookie sheets in oven; bake 15 minutes. Alternate cookie sheets; bake until golden brown, 15 to 20 minutes longer. Remove rolls from cookie sheets; cool on wire racks.   **18 rolls; 140 calories per roll.**

Do-ahead Tip: After baking, rolls can be covered and stored at room temperature. Heat oven to 350°. Place rolls directly on oven rack. Bake uncovered until rolls are warm, about 10 minutes.

TRADITIONAL ROLL DOUGH

3½   to 3¾ cups all-purpose* or unbleached flour
¼   cup sugar
¼   cup shortening or margarine or butter, softened
1   teaspoon salt
1   package regular or quick-acting active dry yeast
½   cup very warm water (120 to 130°)
½   cup very warm milk (scalded then cooled to 120 to 130°)
1   egg
       Margarine or butter, softened

Mix 2 cups of the flour, the sugar, shortening, salt and yeast in 2½-quart bowl. Add water, milk and egg. Beat on low speed, scraping bowl frequently, 1 minute. Beat on medium speed, scraping bowl frequently, 1 minute. Stir in enough remaining flour to make dough easy to handle.

Turn dough onto lightly floured surface; knead until smooth and elastic, about 5 minutes. Place in greased 2½-quart bowl; turn greased side up. Cover and let rise in warm place until double, about 1 hour. (Dough is ready if indentation remains when touched.)

Punch down dough; cut or roll as directed for any Dinner Rolls recipe (right). Brush with margarine. Cover and let rise until double, about 30 minutes.

*If using self-rising flour, omit salt.

Heat oven to 400°. Bake until golden brown, 12 to 18 minutes.

Whole Wheat Traditional Roll Dough: Substitute 1½ to 1¾ cups whole wheat flour for the second addition of all-purpose flour.

DINNER ROLLS

Cloverleaf Rolls: Cut half of Traditional Roll Dough into 36 pieces; shape into balls. Place 3 balls in each of 12 greased medium muffin cups, 2½ × 1¼ inches. Continue as directed above.   **1 dozen rolls; 100 calories per roll.**

Crescent Rolls: Roll half of Traditional Roll Dough into 12-inch circle on floured surface. Spread with margarine or butter, softened. Cut into 16 wedges. Roll up, beginning at rounded edge. Place rolls, with points underneath, on greased cookie sheet; curve slightly. Continue as directed left.   **16 rolls; 85 calories per roll.**

Fan Tans: Roll half of Traditional Roll Dough into a rectangle, 13 × 9 inches, on floured surface. Spread with margarine or butter, softened. Cut crosswise into 6 strips, each about 1½ inches wide. Stack strips evenly; cut into 12 pieces, each about 1 inch wide. Place cut side down in 12 greased medium muffin cups, 2½ × 1¼ inches. Continue as directed at left.   **1 dozen rolls; 110 calories per roll.**

Pan Rolls: Cut half of Traditional Roll Dough into 24 pieces; shape pieces into balls. Place close together in greased round pan, 9 × 1½ inches. Continue as directed at left.   **2 dozen rolls; 50 calories per roll.**

Parker House Rolls: Roll half of Traditional Roll Dough into rectangle, 12 × 9 inches, on generously floured surface. Cut with floured 3-inch round cutter. Brush each circle with margarine or butter, softened. Make crease across each circle; fold so top half slightly overlaps bottom half. Press edges together. Place close together in greased square pan, 9 × 9 × 2 inches. Continue as directed at left.   **1 dozen rolls; 120 calories per roll.**

Square Rolls: Roll Traditional Roll Dough into rectangle, 13 × 9 inches, on floured surface. Place in greased rectangular pan, 13 × 9 × 2 inches. Cut dough with sharp knife ¼ inch deep to make 15 rolls. Continue as directed at left.   **15 rolls; 160 calories per roll.**

SWEET ROLL DOUGH

1	package regular or quick-acting active dry yeast
½	cup warm water (105 to 115°)
½	cup lukewarm milk (scalded then cooled)
⅓	cup sugar
⅓	cup shortening or margarine or butter, softened
1	teaspoon salt
1	egg
3½	to 4 cups all-purpose flour*

Dissolve yeast in warm water in 2½-quart bowl. Stir in milk, sugar, shortening, salt, egg and 2 cups of the flour. Beat until smooth. Stir in enough remaining flour to make dough easy to handle. Turn onto lightly floured surface; knead until smooth and elastic, about 5 minutes. Place in greased 2½-quart bowl; turn greased side up. Cover; let rise in warm place until double, about 1½ hours. (Dough is ready if indentation remains when touched.) Punch down dough. Use for Orange Rolls (below) and Cinnamon Rolls (page 77).

Do-ahead Tip: After kneading, cover dough and refrigerate in greased bowl no longer than 3 days.

ORANGE ROLLS

1½	cups powdered sugar
3	tablespoons margarine or butter, softened
1	tablespoon grated orange peel
2	tablespoons orange juice
½	Sweet Roll Dough (above)

Beat all ingredients except dough until smooth and creamy. Flatten dough with hands or rolling pin into rectangle, 12 × 7 inches, on lightly floured surface; spread with half of the orange mixture. Roll up tightly, beginning at 12-inch side. Pinch edge of dough into roll to seal well. Stretch roll to make even. Cut into twelve 1-inch slices. Place slightly apart in greased round pan, 8 × 1½ inches. Let rise until double, about 40 minutes.

*If using self-rising flour, omit salt.

Heat oven to 375°. Bake until golden brown, 20 to 25 minutes. Frost with remaining orange mixture while warm.   **1 dozen rolls; 195 calories per roll.**

NOTE: To cut even slices, place a piece of dental floss or heavy thread under roll. Bring ends of floss up and crisscross at top of roll. Pull strings in opposite directions.

CINNAMON ROLLS

½ **Sweet Roll Dough (page 76)**
2 **tablespoons margarine or butter, softened**
¼ **cup sugar**
2 **teaspoons ground cinnamon**
   Glaze (below)

Flatten dough with hands or rolling pin into rectangle, 15 × 9 inches, on lightly floured surface; spread with margarine. Mix sugar and cinnamon; sprinkle over rectangle. Roll up tightly, beginning at 15-inch side. Pinch edge of dough into roll to seal well. Stretch roll to make even. Cut into nine 1½-inch slices. Place slightly apart in greased square pan, 9 × 9 × 2 inches, or in greased medium muffin cups, 2½ × 1¼ inches. Let rise until double, about 40 minutes.

Heat oven to 375°. Bake until golden brown, 25 to 30 minutes. Spread rolls with Glaze while warm.   **9 rolls; 240 calories per roll.**

Glaze
Mix 1 cup powdered sugar, 1 tablespoon milk and ½ teaspoon vanilla until smooth and of desired consistency.

Butterscotch-Pecan Rolls: Before flattening the dough into rectangle, heat ¼ cup margarine or butter until melted; stir in ½ cup packed brown sugar, ½ cup pecan halves and 2 tablespoons corn syrup. Spread in pan. Roll dough, slice, let rise and bake as directed. Immediately invert pan on heatproof serving plate. Let pan remain 1 minute.

HONEY TWIST COFFEE CAKE

1	package regular or quick-acting active dry yeast
¼	cup warm water (105 to 115°)
2½	to 3 cups all-purpose flour*
1	cup plain yogurt
2	tablespoons granulated sugar
2	tablespoons margarine or butter, softened
1	teaspoon salt
1	egg
⅓	cup packed brown sugar
¼	cup margarine or butter, melted
¼	cup honey
	Honey-Nut Filling (below)

Dissolve yeast in warm water in 2½-quart bowl. Add 1½ cups of the flour, the yogurt, granulated sugar, 2 tablespoons margarine, the salt and egg. Beat on low speed until moistened. Beat on medium speed, scraping bowl occasionally, 3 minutes. Stir in enough remaining flour to make dough easy to handle.

Turn dough onto lightly floured surface; knead until smooth and elastic, about 5 minutes. Place in greased 2½-quart bowl; turn greased side up. Cover and let rise in warm place until double, about 1 hour. (Dough is ready if indentation remains when touched.)

Mix the brown sugar, ¼ cup margarine and the honey in ungreased rectangular pan, 13 × 9 × 2 inches; spread evenly in pan. Punch down dough; roll into rectangle, 24 × 9 inches. Spread Honey-Nut Filling crosswise over half of rectangle; fold dough crosswise over filling. Cut rectangle crosswise into six 2-inch strips. Twist each strip loosely; place crosswise in pan. Cover and let rise until double, about 1 hour.

Heat oven to 375°. Bake until golden brown, 20 to 25 minutes. Immediately invert pan on heatproof serving plate. Let pan remain 1 minute. **1 coffee cake** (18 servings); 200 calories per serving.

Honey-Nut Filling
Mix ⅓ cup margarine or butter, softened, ¼ cup finely chopped nuts and ¼ cup honey.

*If using self-rising flour, omit salt.

DANISH PASTRY DOUGH

1½ sticks cold butter*
1 package regular or quick-acting active dry yeast
¼ cup warm water (105 to 115°)
¼ cup lukewarm milk (scalded then cooled)
2 tablespoons sugar
½ teaspoon salt
1 egg
2⅓ cups cake flour or all-purpose** or unbleached flour

Cut whole stick butter crosswise into halves. Place 3 half-sticks butter, side by side, on piece of waxed paper. Cover with second piece waxed paper. Flatten butter into 6-inch square solid sheet with rolling pin. Refrigerate until firm, at least 1½ hours. (Butter must be very cold to prevent sticking when rolling dough.)

Dissolve yeast in warm water in 4-quart bowl. Stir in milk, sugar, salt, egg and 1⅓ cups of the flour. Beat until smooth. Stir in enough remaining flour to make dough easy to handle.

Turn dough onto lightly floured surface; knead until smooth and elastic, about 5 minutes. Place in lightly greased 4-quart bowl; cover with damp cloth. Refrigerate 1½ hours.

Roll dough into 12-inch circle on lightly floured cloth-covered board with floured cloth-covered rolling pin. Place square of butter on center of dough. Fold top and bottom edges of dough to center, covering butter. Fold right and left edges of dough to center; press to seal securely. (Dough should form a square envelope around butter.)

Roll dough into rectangle, 20 × 6 inches. (Dough will be stiff at first.) Fold crosswise into thirds to make 3 layers. (Remove excess flour from dough with pastry brush while folding.) Press edges of rectangle to secure dough and seal seam.

(Work rapidly so that butter does not soften. Generously flour cloth as needed to prevent dough from sticking. If butter breaks through dough onto cloth, generously flour area and continue rolling.)

Turn dough ¼ turn. Roll into rectangle, 20 × 6 inches. Fold

*We do not recommend margarine for this recipe.
**If using self-rising flour, omit salt.

rectangle crosswise into thirds, keeping sides and ends straight (uneven rolling results in less flakiness).

Turn dough ¼ turn; repeat rolling step a third time. Fold rectangle crosswise into thirds; place on tray. Cover with plastic wrap and refrigerate until well chilled, 1½ to 2 hours.

Cut rectangle into halves. Use for Danish Strip (below), Jam Pastries (page 81) or Danish Twists (page 81).

Do-ahead Tip: Dough can be refrigerated no longer than 8 hours before rolling with butter; cover with plastic wrap to prevent drying. Punch down dough; continue as directed.

DANISH STRIP

½ **Danish Pastry Dough (page 79)**
½ **cup Apricot Filling (below) or ⅓ cup apricot preserves**
   Powdered sugar or Powdered Sugar Frosting (below)

Roll dough into rectangle, 15×6 inches, on lightly floured cloth-covered board. Spread Apricot Filling to within ½ inch of edges. Moisten edges of dough. Fold dough lengthwise into thirds; press seam and edges to seal securely. Place seam side down on ungreased cookie sheet. Make diagonal cuts ¼ inch deep at 2-inch intervals with sharp knife. Cover and let rise in warm place until double, about 30 minutes.

Heat oven to 400°. Bake until deep golden brown, about 25 minutes; cool slightly on wire rack. Sprinkle with powdered sugar or drizzle with Powdered Sugar Frosting. **1 strip** (12 servings); 155 calories per serving.

Apricot Filling
Simmer 1 cup dried apricots in just enough water to cover until tender, about 30 minutes; drain and cut up. Mix apricots, ⅓ cup sugar and ¼ teaspoon ground allspice. **About 1 cup filling.**

Powdered Sugar Frosting
Mix 1 cup powdered sugar, 1 tablespoon water or milk and ½ teaspoon vanilla until smooth. If necessary, stir in additional water, ½ teaspoon at a time, until of spreading consistency.

JAM PASTRIES

½   **Danish Pastry Dough (page 79)**
¾   **cup apricot, cherry or raspberry preserves or Apricot Filling (page 80)**
     Water or 1 egg, beaten

Roll dough into 12-inch square on lightly floured cloth-covered board. Cut dough into nine 4-inch squares. Place squares about ½ inch apart on ungreased cookie sheet. Place about 1 tablespoon preserves on center of each square. Bring 2 opposite corners to center; press firmly to seal. Cover pastries and let rise in warm place until double, about 30 minutes. Brush lightly with water.

Heat oven to 400°. Bake until deep golden brown, about 20 minutes. Drizzle with Powdered Sugar Frosting (page 80) if desired.   **9 pastries; 195 calories per pastry.**

DANISH TWISTS

½   **Danish Pastry Dough (page 79)**
¼   **to ½ cup jam, jelly, preserves or Apricot Filling (page 80)**

Roll dough into rectangle, 12×7 inches, on lightly floured cloth-covered board. Cut into twelve 1-inch strips. Shape into snails or figure 8s. For each snail, hold one end of strip on ungreased cookie sheet; wind strip around to form snail shape. Tuck free end under roll. For each figure 8, hold one end of strip in each hand and twist in opposite directions, stretching strip slightly. Bring ends together; shape into figure 8 on ungreased cookie sheet. Cover and let rise in warm place until double, about 30 minutes.

Heat oven to 400°. Make a depression in center of snail or each loop of figure 8s. Fill with 1 teaspoon jam. Bake until golden brown, about 15 minutes.   **12 twists; 120 calories per twist.**

DANISH KRINGLE

½ cup firm margarine or butter
2 cups all-purpose flour*
1 tablespoon sugar
½ teaspoon salt
1 package regular or quick-acting active dry yeast
¼ cup warm water (105 to 115°)
½ cup lukewarm milk (scalded then cooled)
1 egg
   Almond Filling or Pecan Filling (below and right)
   Glaze (right)
¼ cup chopped nuts

Cut margarine into flour, sugar and salt in 2½-quart bowl until mixture resembles fine crumbs. Dissolve yeast in warm water. Stir yeast mixture, milk and egg into flour mixture; beat until smooth (dough will be very soft). Cover and refrigerate at least 2 hours but no longer than 24 hours.

Prepare filling. Divide dough into halves; return one half to refrigerator. Roll remaining half into rectangle, 15 × 6 inches, on floured cloth-covered board with floured cloth-covered rolling pin. Sprinkle half of the filling lengthwise down center of rectangle in 2-inch strip. Fold sides of dough over filling, overlapping 1½ inches. Pinch edges firmly to seal.

Shape rectangle into oval or horseshoe shape; pinch ends together for the former. Carefully place seam side down on greased cookie sheet. Repeat with remaining dough and filling. Cover and let rise in warm place 30 minutes.

Heat oven to 375°. Bake 10 minutes; alternate cookie sheets. Bake until golden brown, 10 to 15 minutes longer. Spread with Glaze; sprinkle with nuts. **2 coffee cakes** (12 servings per coffee cake); 230 calories per serving.

Almond Filling
Mix 1 can (8 ounces) almond paste (1 cup), ½ cup packed brown sugar and ½ cup margarine or butter, softened, until smooth.

*If using self-rising flour, omit salt.

Pecan Filling
Mix 1½ cups chopped pecans, 1 cup packed brown sugar and ½ cup margarine or butter, softened.

Glaze
Mix 1 cup powdered sugar, 1 tablespoon water and ½ teaspoon vanilla until smooth. If necessary, stir in additional water, ½ teaspoon at a time, until of desired consistency.

GRAINS

ABOUT GRAINS

Regular white rice has been milled to remove the hull, germ and most of the bran. It is available both long and short grain, the long grain being a better all-purpose rice. One cup uncooked = 3 cups cooked.

Parboiled (converted) rice contains the vitamins found in brown rice but is polished like white rice. One cup uncooked = 3½ cups cooked.

Precooked (instant) rice is commercially cooked, rinsed and dried before packaging. It is therefore quick and very easy to prepare. One cup uncooked = 2 cups cooked.

Brown rice is unpolished with only the outer hull removed. It has a slightly firm texture and a nutlike flavor. One cup uncooked = 4 cups cooked.

Wild rice is the seed of grass that grows in marshes. It is dark greenish-brown in color and has a distinctive, nutlike flavor. Expensive, it is sometimes combined with white or brown rice. One cup uncooked = 3 cups cooked.

Barley, one of the first grains ever cultivated, is commercially hulled to shorten the cooking time that softens the outer chaff. Pearled barley is the most common variety.

Cornmeal is ground yellow or white corn kernels. *Grits* is meal that has been coarsely ground from hulled kernels of corn.

Bulgur and *cracked wheat* are made from whole wheat kernels. Wheat kernels are parboiled, dried and partially debranned, then cracked into coarse fragments to make bulgur. Cracked wheat is from kernels that are cleaned, then cracked or cut into fine fragments.

Kasha is the kernel inside the buckwheat seed. It is roasted for a nutlike flavor, then coarsely ground.

REGULAR RICE

Heat 1 cup rice, 2 cups water and 1 teaspoon salt, if desired, to boiling, stirring once or twice; reduce heat. Cover and simmer 14 minutes. (Do not lift cover or stir.) Remove from heat. Fluff rice lightly with fork; cover and let steam 5 to 10 minutes. **3 cups rice; 215 calories per cup.**

Lemon Rice: Stir 2 tablespoons margarine or butter, melted, and 2 teaspoons lemon juice into cooked rice.

Mushroom Rice: Heat 1 can (3 or 4 ounces) sliced mushrooms or mushroom stems and pieces, drained, in 2 tablespoons margarine or butter; stir into cooked rice.

Onion Rice: Cook 2 tablespoons finely chopped onion in 2 tablespoons margarine or butter until tender; stir into cooked rice.

Parsley Rice: Stir 2 tablespoons snipped parsley into cooked rice.

BROWN RICE

Heat 1 cup brown rice, 2¾ cups water and 1 teaspoon salt, if desired, to boiling, stirring once or twice; reduce heat. Cover and simmer until tender, 45 to 50 minutes; remove from heat. **4 cups brown rice; 180 calories per cup.**

WILD RICE

Wash 1 cup wild rice by placing in wire strainer; run cold water through it, lifting rice with fingers to clean thoroughly. Heat rice, 2½ cups water and 1 teaspoon salt, if desired, to boiling, stirring once or twice; reduce heat. Cover; simmer until tender, 40 to 50 minutes. After cooking rice 30 minutes, check to see that rice is not sticking to pan. Add ¼ cup water if necessary. **3 cups wild rice; 225 calories per cup.**

OVEN-STEAMED RICE

Heat oven to 350°. Mix 2 cups boiling water, 1 cup uncooked regular rice and 1 teaspoon salt in ungreased 1-quart casserole or rectangular baking dish, $12 \times 7\frac{1}{2} \times 2$ inches. Cover and bake until liquid is absorbed, 25 to 30 minutes.   **3 cups rice; 215 calories per cup.**

RICE WITH ARTICHOKES

1½   cups uncooked instant rice
¼   teaspoon salt
3   green onions (with tops), chopped
1   can (16 ounces) stewed tomatoes
1   can (14 ounces) artichoke hearts, undrained

Mix all ingredients in 10-inch skillet. Heat to boiling, stirring frequently; reduce heat. Cover and simmer until rice is tender, about 10 minutes.   **5 servings; 150 calories per serving.**

LEMON PILAF

1   small onion, chopped (about ¼ cup)
1   small clove garlic, finely chopped
¼   cup margarine or butter
1   cup uncooked regular rice
2   cups water
2   teaspoons instant chicken bouillon (dry)
2   teaspoons finely shredded lemon peel
½   teaspoon salt
¼   teaspoon dry mustard
⅛   teaspoon red pepper sauce
2   medium stalks celery, sliced
2   tablespoons snipped parsley

Cook and stir onion and garlic in margarine in 3-quart saucepan until onion is tender. Stir in remaining ingredients except parsley. Heat to boiling, stirring once or twice; reduce heat. Cover and simmer 14 minutes. (Do not lift cover or stir.) Remove from heat. Stir in parsley lightly with fork; cover and let steam 5 to 10 minutes.   **7 servings** (about ½ cup each); 165 calories per serving.

CURRIED RICE

1   tablespoon finely chopped onion
2   tablespoons margarine or butter
½   to 1 teaspoon curry powder
¼   teaspoon salt
¼   teaspoon pepper
3   cups hot cooked regular or brown rice (page 85)
¼   cup toasted slivered almonds
¼   cup chopped pimiento-stuffed olives or ripe olives

Cook and stir onion in margarine until tender. Stir in curry powder, salt and pepper. Stir in hot rice. Sprinkle with almonds and olives.   **4 servings; 280 calories per serving.**

SAVORY MIXED RICE

¾   cup uncooked brown rice
¼   cup uncooked wild rice
1   medium stalk celery, chopped (about ½ cup)
1   medium onion, chopped (about ½ cup)
3   tablespoons margarine or butter
3   cups chicken broth (page 557)
½   teaspoon salt
¼   teaspoon ground sage
1   can (4 ounces) mushroom stems and pieces, drained
½   cup plain yogurt
2   tablespoons snipped parsley

Cook and stir brown rice, wild rice, celery and onion in margarine in 2-quart saucepan over medium heat until onion is tender, about 6 minutes. Stir in broth, salt, sage and mushrooms. Heat to boiling; reduce heat. Cover and simmer until rice is tender, about 1 hour. Stir in yogurt and parsley.   **5 servings** (about ¾ cup each); 250 calories per serving.

WILD RICE AND MUSHROOMS

1	cup uncooked wild rice
4	ounces mushrooms, sliced (about 1½ cups)
2	green onions (with tops), thinly sliced
2	tablespoons margarine or butter
2¼	cups water
¼	cup dry white wine
1	teaspoon salt
¼	teaspoon pepper
1	cup shredded Monterey Jack cheese (4 ounces)

Cook and stir wild rice, mushrooms and onions in margarine in 10-inch skillet over medium heat until onions are tender, about 5 minutes. Stir in water, wine, salt and pepper. Heat to boiling, stirring occasionally; reduce heat. Cover and simmer until rice is tender, 40 to 50 minutes; drain if necessary. Stir in cheese. **7 servings** (about ½ cup each); 195 calories per serving.

BARLEY WITH MUSHROOMS

8	ounces mushrooms, sliced (about 3 cups)
1	large onion, chopped (about 1 cup)
2	tablespoons margarine or butter
1	cup uncooked barley
3¼	cups boiling water
2	teaspoons instant chicken bouillon (dry)
½	teaspoon salt
	Dash of pepper

Cook and stir mushrooms and onion in margarine 5 minutes. Place in ungreased 1½-quart casserole. Stir in remaining ingredients. Cover and bake in 375° oven, stirring once, until barley is tender, about 1¼ hours. **6 servings;** 180 calories per serving.

CHEESY GRITS

    2   cups milk
    2   cups water
    1   teaspoon salt
    ¼   teaspoon pepper
    1   cup white hominy quick grits
  1½   cups shredded Cheddar cheese (6 ounces)
    ¼   cup sliced green onions (with tops)
    2   eggs, slightly beaten
    1   tablespoon margarine or butter
    ¼   teaspoon paprika

Heat milk, water, salt and pepper to boiling in 2-quart saucepan. Gradually add grits, stirring constantly; reduce heat. Simmer uncovered, stirring frequently, until thick, about 5 minutes. Stir in cheese and onions. Stir 1 cup of the hot mixture into eggs; stir into remaining hot mixture in saucepan. Pour into greased 1½-quart casserole. Dot with margarine; sprinkle with paprika. Bake uncovered in 350° oven until set, 35 to 40 minutes. Let stand 10 minutes. **8 servings; 230** calories per serving.

CORNMEAL MUSH

    ¾   cup cornmeal
    ¾   cup cold water
  2½   cups boiling water
    ¾   teaspoon salt
    2   tablespoons margarine or butter
        Flour

Mix cornmeal and cold water in 2-quart saucepan. Stir in boiling water and salt. Cook, stirring constantly, until mixture thickens and boils; reduce heat. Cover; simmer 10 minutes. Spread in greased loaf pan, 9×5×3 or 8½×4½×2½ inches. Cover and refrigerate until firm, at least 12 hours but no longer than 2 weeks.

Invert pan to unmold; cut loaf into ½-inch slices. Heat margarine in 10-inch skillet until melted. Coat slices with flour; cook in margarine over low heat until brown on both sides. Serve hot with syrup if desired. **4 servings; 155 calories per serving.**

BULGUR PILAF

1   cup uncooked bulgur (cracked wheat)
1   medium onion, chopped (about ½ cup)
1   medium stalk celery, sliced (about ½ cup)
2   tablespoons margarine or butter
1   can (10½ ounces) condensed beef broth
1   can (4 ounces) mushroom stems and pieces, drained
⅔   cup water
½   teaspoon salt
⅛   teaspoon pepper
¼   cup sliced almonds

Cook bulgur, onion and celery in margarine in 2-quart sauce-pan over medium heat, stirring frequently, until onion is tender and bulgur is brown, about 5 minutes. Stir in remaining ingredients except almonds. Heat to boiling; reduce heat. Cover and simmer until liquid is absorbed, 15 to 17 minutes. Stir in almonds.   **8 servings** (about ½ cup each); 145 calories per serving.

PASTA

COOKED MACARONI, SPAGHETTI AND NOODLES

Traditional Method: Add 1 tablespoon salt, if desired, to 3 quarts rapidly boiling water. Gradually add 7 to 8 ounces macaroni, spaghetti or noodles to water so that water continues to boil. (If spaghetti strands are left whole, place one end in water; as they soften, gradually coil them until submerged.)

Boil uncovered, stirring occasionally, just until tender* (7 to 10 minutes or as directed on package). Test by cutting several strands with fork. Drain immediately in colander or sieve. If macaroni product is to be used in a salad, rinse under running cold water. **4 servings.**

Easy Method: Drop 7 to 8 ounces macaroni, spaghetti or noodles into 6 cups rapidly boiling water; add 4 teaspoons salt if desired. Heat to rapid boiling. Cook, stirring constantly, 3 minutes.* Cover tightly; remove from heat. Let stand 10 minutes; drain. If macaroni product is to be used in a salad, rinse under running cold water. **4 servings.**

NOTE: Toss cooked and drained macaroni, spaghetti or noodles with 3 tablespoons margarine or butter; this will keep pieces separated.

*For thicker macaroni products, such as lasagne, kluski noodles, etc., follow manufacturer's directions.

PASTA YIELDS

| | Cooked | |
Uncooked Pasta	Cups	Servings
Macaroni		
6 to 7 ounces or 2 cups	4	4 to 6
Spaghetti		
7 to 8 ounces	4	4 to 6
Noodles		
8 ounces or 4 to 5 cups	4 to 5	4 to 6

EGG NOODLES

2   cups all-purpose* or whole wheat flour
3   egg yolks
1   egg
2   teaspoons salt
¼   to ½ cup water

Make a well in center of flour. Add egg yolks, egg and salt; mix thoroughly. Mix in water, 1 tablespoon at a time, until dough is stiff but easy to roll. Divide dough into 4 equal parts. Roll one part at a time into paper-thin rectangle on generously floured cloth-covered board (keep remaining dough covered). Loosely fold rectangle lengthwise into thirds; cut crosswise into ⅛-inch strips for narrow noodles, ¼-inch strips for wide noodles. Unfold strips and place on towel until stiff and dry, about 2 hours.

Break strips into smaller pieces. Cook in 3 quarts boiling salted water (1 tablespoon salt) until tender, 5 to 7 minutes; drain. (To cook half of the noodles, use 2 quarts water and 2 teaspoons salt.) **7 servings** (about ¾ cup each); 115 calories per serving.

Cornmeal Noodles: Substitute ½ cup cornmeal for ½ cup of the flour.

*If using self-rising flour, omit salt.

SPAETZLE

2	eggs, beaten
¼	cup milk or water
1	cup all-purpose flour*
½	teaspoon salt
	Dash of pepper
2	quarts water
1	teaspoon salt
2	tablespoons margarine or butter, melted

Mix eggs, milk, flour, ½ teaspoon salt and the pepper (batter will be thick). Heat water and 1 teaspoon salt to boiling in Dutch oven. Press batter through colander (preferably one with large holes), a few tablespoons at a time, into boiling water. Stir once or twice to prevent sticking. Cook until spaetzle rise to surface and are tender, about 5 minutes; drain. Pour margarine over spaetzle. **6 servings; 140 calories per serving.**

GREEN FETTUCCINE

8	ounces spinach**
2	eggs
1	tablespoon olive or vegetable oil
1	teaspoon salt
2	cups all-purpose flour†
4½	quarts water
1	tablespoon salt
1	tablespoon olive or vegetable oil

*Do not use self-rising flour in this recipe.
**1 package (10 ounces) frozen spinach can be substituted for the fresh spinach. Cook as directed on package; drain.
†If using self-rising flour, omit the 1 teaspoon salt.

Wash spinach, drain. Cover and cook over medium heat with just the water that clings to the leaves, 3 to 10 minutes. Rinse spinach under running cold water; drain. Place spinach, eggs, 1 tablespoon oil and 1 teaspoon salt in blender container. Cover and blend on medium speed until smooth, about 20 seconds.

Make a well in center of flour. Add spinach mixture; mix thoroughly. (If dough is too dry, mix in a few drops water; if dough is too sticky, mix in small amount flour.) Gather dough into ball. Knead on lightly floured cloth-covered board until smooth and elastic, about 5 minutes. Let stand 10 minutes.

Divide dough into 4 equal parts. Roll one part at a time into paper-thin rectangle on generously floured cloth-covered board with cloth-covered rolling pin (keep remaining dough covered). Loosely fold rectangle lengthwise into thirds; cut crosswise into ¼-inch strips. Unfold strips and place on towel until dry, at least 30 minutes.

Heat water to boiling; stir in 1 tablespoon salt, 1 tablespoon oil and the noodles. Cook until almost tender, 3 to 5 minutes; drain. **8 servings** (about ¾ cup each); 100 calories per serving.

FOUR-CHEESE FETTUCCINE

¼ cup margarine or butter
½ cup half-and-half
½ cup shredded Gruyère cheese (2 ounces)
¼ cup grated Parmesan cheese
½ teaspoon salt
⅛ teaspoon freshly ground pepper
1 clove garlic, finely chopped
8 ounces uncooked fettuccine or Green Fettuccine (page 93)
2 tablespoons olive oil
½ cup crumbled Gorgonzola cheese
½ cup shredded mozzarella cheese (2 ounces)
1 tablespoon snipped parsley

Heat margarine and half-and-half in 2-quart saucepan over low heat until margarine is melted. Stir in Gruyère cheese, Parmesan cheese, salt, pepper and garlic. Cook, stirring occasionally, 5 minutes.

Cook fettuccine as directed on package except—add oil to boiling water; drain. Add hot fettuccine to sauce; add Gorgonzola cheese and mozzarella cheese. Toss with 2 forks; sprinkle with parsley.   **4 servings; 540 calories per serving.**

NOODLES ROMANOFF

    8   ounces uncooked wide egg noodles
    2   cups dairy sour cream
    ¼   cup grated Parmesan cheese
    1   tablespoon snipped chives
    1   teaspoon salt
    ⅛   teaspoon pepper
    1   large clove garlic, crushed
    2   tablespoons margarine or butter
    ¼   cup grated Parmesan cheese

Cook noodles as directed on page 91. Mix sour cream, ¼ cup cheese, the chives, salt, pepper and garlic. Stir margarine into hot noodles; stir in sour cream mixture. Arrange on warm platter; sprinkle with ¼ cup cheese.   **8 servings; 325 calories per serving.**

VERMICELLI AND SPINACH

    8   ounces uncooked vermicelli
    6   slices red onion (¼ inch thick), separated into rings
    2   cloves garlic, crushed
    2   tablespoons olive or vegetable oil
   12   ounces spinach, cut crosswise into ½-inch strips (about
         12 cups)
    2   tablespoons lemon juice
    1   teaspoon dried tarragon leaves
    ¼   teaspoon salt
         Freshly ground pepper
    ¼   cup crumbled Gorgonzola or blue cheese

Cook vermicelli as directed on package; drain. Cook and stir onion and garlic in oil in 12-inch skillet over medium heat until onion is almost tender, about 5 minutes. Stir in spinach, lemon juice, tarragon, salt and pepper. Cook and stir until spinach is slightly limp, about 2 minutes. Toss with hot vermicelli; sprinkle with cheese. **8 servings** (about 1 cup each); 165 calories per serving.

SPAGHETTI WITH MUSHROOMS

7	ounces uncooked spaghetti
5	ounces mushrooms, sliced (2 cups)
2	tablespoons margarine or butter
2	tablespoons all-purpose flour
2	tablespoons lemon juice
½	teaspoon salt
¼	teaspoon pepper
2	cups milk
3	tablespoons snipped parsley

Cook spaghetti as directed on page 91. Cook and stir mushrooms in margarine in 3-quart saucepan over medium heat until tender. Stir in flour, lemon juice, salt and pepper. Cook over low heat, stirring constantly, until mixture is smooth and bubbly; remove from heat.

Gradually stir in milk. Heat to boiling, stirring constantly. Boil and stir 1 minute. Stir in hot spaghetti and parsley. Cover and let stand 10 minutes. **6 servings;** 280 calories per serving.

SPAGHETTI AND ANCHOVIES

  1   medium onion, chopped (about ½ cup)
  1   clove garlic, chopped
  2   tablespoons olive or vegetable oil
  1   can (8 ounces) tomato sauce
  1   can (1¾ ounces) anchovies, drained and chopped
  ¼   cup snipped parsley
  ½   teaspoon dried oregano leaves
  ¼   teaspoon salt
  ⅛   teaspoon pepper
  ¼   cup dry bread crumbs
  1   tablespoon olive oil, margarine or butter
  8   ounces uncooked spaghetti

Cook and stir onion and garlic in 2 tablespoons oil until onion is tender. Stir in tomato sauce, anchovies, parsley, oregano, salt and pepper. Heat to boiling; reduce heat. Cover and simmer 15 minutes. Cook and stir bread crumbs in 1 tablespoon oil until golden brown. Cook spaghetti as directed on page 91; drain. Toss hot spaghetti with sauce; sprinkle with bread crumbs. **6 servings; 245 calories per serving.**

PEPPER MOSTACCIOLI

  1   green pepper, cut into ¼-inch strips
  1   onion, sliced and separated into rings
  1   clove garlic, crushed
  2   tablespoons olive or vegetable oil
1½   cups uncooked mostaccioli
  1   medium tomato, coarsely chopped
  1   tablespoon snipped basil leaves or 1 teaspoon dried basil leaves
  ¼   teaspoon salt
     Freshly ground pepper
  2   tablespoons grated Romano cheese

Cook and stir green pepper, onion and garlic in oil over medium heat until pepper is tender, about 10 minutes. Cook mostaccioli as directed on package; drain. Stir tomato, basil, salt and pepper into green pepper mixture; heat until hot. Toss with hot mostaccioli; sprinkle with grated cheese.   **4 servings** (about ¾ cup each); 170 calories per serving.

RIGATONI AND TOMATOES

  3   medium tomatoes, chopped (about 3 cups)
  3   tablespoons olive or vegetable oil
  2   tablespoons snipped basil leaves or 2 teaspoons dried
         basil leaves
  2   tablespoons capers
  1   tablespoon lemon juice
  1   teaspoon sugar
  ½   teaspoon salt
  ⅛   teaspoon crushed red pepper
  1   clove garlic, finely chopped
  3   cups uncooked rigatoni
  ¼   cup grated Parmesan or Romano cheese

Mix all ingredients except rigatoni and cheese. Cover and refrigerate at least 2 hours but no longer than 24 hours.

Prepare rigatoni as directed on package; drain. Immediately toss with tomato mixture. Serve immediately, or cover and refrigerate until chilled. Sprinkle with cheese.   **6 servings** (about ¾ cup each); 290 calories per serving.

MEXICAN-STYLE MACARONI

  3   cups uncooked macaroni shells (about 12 ounces)
  1   can (4 ounces) chopped green chilies, drained
  1   jar (2 ounces) diced pimientos, drained
  1   cup half-and-half
  ½   cup shredded Cheddar cheese (2 ounces)
  ½   cup sliced ripe olives
  ½   teaspoon salt

Cook macaroni as directed on page 91. Stir in remaining ingredients. Cook over low heat, stirring occasionally, until cheese is melted and sauce is hot, about 5 minutes. **6 servings** (about 1 cup each); 315 calories per serving.

CAKES
PIES

CAKES

ABOUT CAKE BAKING

PAN POINTERS
■ Always use pans of the size called for in the recipe. To check width of the pan, measure across the top from inside edge to inside edge. A cake baked in too large a pan will be pale, flat and shrunken; baked in too small or too shallow a pan, it will bulge and lose its shape.

■ Shiny metal pans are preferred for baking cakes because they reflect heat away from the cake and produce a tender, light brown crust.

■ Cake pans should not be filled more than half full. If you are using an odd-shaped pan (heart, star, bell), measure the capacity by filling with water, then measure the water and use half that amount of batter. Any remaining batter can be used for cupcakes.

■ For shortening-type cakes, place pans in the middle of the oven. Layer pans should not touch and there should be at least 1 inch of space between pan and side of oven.

■ Cool layer pan on wire rack about 5 minutes. Place towel-covered rack on top of layer. Invert as a unit; remove pan. Place original rack on bottom of layer; turn over both racks as a unit. Allow layer to cool completely on rack.

PREPARING PANS
■ For shortening-type cakes, grease bottoms and sides of pans generously with shortening. (Do not use margarine, butter or oil.) Dust each greased pan with flour, shaking pan until bottom and sides are well coated. Shake out excess

flour. When using pans with a nonstick coating, follow the manufacturer's directions.

■ For angel food and chiffon cakes, do not grease and flour the pans. The batter must cling to the side and tube of the pan to rise properly.

■ For fruitcakes, line pans with aluminum foil, then grease. Leave short "ears" so you can easily lift out the baked cake. If you intend to store the cake, extend foil well over sides of pan. When cake has cooled, bring foil up and over the top and seal.

MIXING CAKES
■ The cake recipes in this cookbook have been tested with both standard and portable mixers. Standard mixers are usually more powerful than portables. Also, the power of a portable mixer could be affected by age or condition, so you may need to increase the mixer speed to medium for the initial step of blending ingredients.

■ The one-bowl method was developed using the electric mixer, but you can also mix by hand. Stir the ingredients to moisten and blend them, then beat 150 strokes for each minute of beating time (3 minutes equals 450 strokes). You'll need practice before this seems easy, and while you're practicing, cake volume may suffer.

CAKE YIELDS
■ Our cake and frosting recipes include calories per serving based on the estimated yield from the *first* pan size mentioned in the recipe.

CAKE YIELDS

Size and Kind	Servings
8- or 9-inch layer cake	10 to 16
8- or 9-inch square cake	9
13 × 9 × 2-inch rectangular cake	12 to 15
10 × 4-inch tube cake	12 to 15
12-cup bundt cake	12 to 15

CUTTING CAKES
■ Use a sharp, long, thin knife to cut shortening-type cakes, a long serrated knife for angel food and chiffon cakes. If the frosting sticks, dip the knife in hot water and wipe with a damp towel after cutting each slice.

STORING CAKES
■ Cool unfrosted cakes thoroughly before storing. If covered while warm, they will become sticky.

■ Keep cake with a creamy-type frosting under a cake safe (or large inverted bowl). Or cover cake loosely with aluminum foil, plastic wrap or waxed paper.

■ Serve cake with a fluffy-type frosting the day it's made. If you must store the cake, use a cake safe or inverted bowl, but slip a knife under the edge so the container is not airtight.

■ Cakes with whipped cream toppings, cream fillings or frostings made with cream cheese should be refrigerated.

SHORTENING-TYPE CAKES

All shortening-type cakes are alike in that they contain the same basic ingredients: shortening, margarine or butter; flour; eggs; a liquid; and a leavening agent such as baking powder or soda. Only the flavors differ.

■ If margarine is specified in the recipe, use only the stick-type, not the whipped.

■ Do not substitute oil for shortening, margarine or butter, even when those ingredients are to be melted.

■ To determine if a shortening-type cake has baked long enough, insert a wooden pick into the center of the cake. If it comes out clean, the cake is done.

■ Cool shortening-type layer cakes in their pans on wire racks about 5 minutes. Remove layers from pans; cool completely on racks.

COCOA PECAN TORTE

⅔ cup margarine or butter
1½ cups pecans, ground
1 cup granulated sugar
¾ cup cocoa
1 teaspoon almond flavoring
   Dash of salt
3 eggs, slightly beaten
½ cup chilled whipping cream
1 tablespoon powdered sugar
12 whole pecans

Heat oven to 375°. Grease round pan, 8 × 1½ inches. Heat margarine in 2-quart saucepan over low heat until melted; remove from heat. Stir in ground pecans, granulated sugar, cocoa, almond flavoring, salt and eggs. Pour into pan.

Bake until wooden pick inserted in center comes out clean, 25 to 28 minutes; cool 10 minutes. Loosen side from pan; remove from pan. Cool cake completely.

Beat whipping cream and powdered sugar in chilled 1½-quart bowl until stiff; spread over top of cake. Arrange whole pecans around edge of cake. **12 servings; 355 calories per serving.**

CHOCOLATE MOUSSE CAKE

1 cup granulated sugar
2 cups margarine or butter
1 cup water
1 teaspoon instant coffee, if desired
16 squares (1 ounce each) semisweet chocolate, cut into pieces
8 eggs, slightly beaten
½ cup chilled whipping cream
1 tablespoon powdered sugar

Heat oven to 350°. Grease springform pan, 9 × 3 inches. Heat granulated sugar, margarine, water, coffee (dry) and chocolate in 3-quart saucepan over low heat, stirring constantly, until chocolate is melted and mixture is smooth; remove from heat. Stir in eggs. Pour into pan.

Bake until wooden pick inserted in center comes out clean, 45 to 50 minutes. Cool completely. Remove side of pan. Cover cake with plastic wrap and refrigerate until chilled, at least 4 hours.

Remove plastic wrap. Beat cream and powdered sugar in chilled 1½-quart bowl until stiff. Garnish top of cake with whipped cream and, if desired, whole almonds. Refrigerate any remaining cake. **16 servings;** 480 calories per serving.

NOTE: Batter is very thin. If side and bottom of pan do not fit tightly, line pan with foil.

SOUR CREAM CHOCOLATE CAKE

2	cups all-purpose flour*
2	cups sugar
¾	cup dairy sour cream
¼	cup shortening
1	cup water
1¼	teaspoons baking soda
1	teaspoon salt
1	teaspoon vanilla
½	teaspoon baking powder
2	eggs
4	squares (1 ounce each) unsweetened chocolate, melted and cooled

Heat oven to 350°. Grease and flour rectangular pan, 13 × 9 × 2 inches, 2 round pans, 9 × 1½ inches, or 3 round pans, 8 × 1½ inches. Beat all ingredients on low speed, scraping bowl constantly, 30 seconds. Beat on high speed, scraping bowl occasionally, 3 minutes. Pour into pan(s).

Bake until wooden pick inserted in center comes out clean, rectangle 40 to 45 minutes, rounds 30 to 35 minutes; cool. Frost with Chocolate Sour Cream Frosting (page 131) if desired. **15 servings;** 270 calories per serving.

*If using self-rising flour, decrease baking soda to ¼ teaspoon; omit salt and baking powder.

COCOA FUDGE CAKE

1⅔ cups all-purpose flour* or 2 cups cake flour
1½ cups sugar
⅔ cup cocoa
½ cup shortening
1½ cups buttermilk
1½ teaspoons baking soda
1 teaspoon salt
1 teaspoon vanilla
2 eggs

Heat oven to 350°. Grease and flour rectangular pan, 13 × 9 × 2 inches, 2 round pans, 8 or 9 × 1½ inches, or 12-cup bundt cake pan. Beat all ingredients on low speed, scraping bowl constantly, 30 seconds. Beat on high speed, scraping bowl occasionally, 3 minutes. Pour into pan(s).

Bake until wooden pick inserted in center comes out clean, rectangle 35 to 40 minutes, rounds 30 to 35 minutes, bundt cake 40 to 45 minutes; cool. Frost with Satiny Beige Frosting (page 129) or Creamy Cocoa Frosting (page 132) if desired. **15 servings**; 220 calories per serving.

Cocoa Fudge Cupcakes: Line 30 medium muffin cups, 2½ × 1¼ inches, with paper baking cups. Pour batter into cups, filling each ½ full. Bake 20 minutes. **30 cupcakes.**

Cocoa Spice Cake: Add 2 teaspoons ground cinnamon and ½ teaspoon ground nutmeg with the salt.

Red Devils Food Cake: Substitute ½ cup packed brown sugar for ½ cup of the granulated sugar and 2 squares (1 ounce each) unsweetened chocolate, melted and cooled, for the cocoa.

Triple Fudge Cake: Stir 1 cup miniature semi-sweet chocolate chips into batter. Bake in rectangular pan, 13 × 9 × 2 inches, or 12-cup bundt cake pan. Spread with Chocolate Chip Glaze (page 132).

*If using self-rising flour, decrease baking soda to ¾ teaspoon and omit salt.

GERMAN CHOCOLATE CAKE

½	cup boiling water
1	bar (4 ounces) sweet cooking chocolate
2	cups sugar
1	cup margarine or butter, softened
4	egg yolks
1	teaspoon vanilla
2½	cups cake flour
1	teaspoon baking soda
1	teaspoon salt
1	cup buttermilk
4	egg whites, stiffly beaten
	Coconut-Pecan Frosting (below)

Heat oven to 350°. Grease 2 square pans, 8×8×2 or 9×9×2 inches, or 3 round pans, 8 or 9×1½ inches. Line bottoms of pans with waxed paper. Pour boiling water on chocolate, stirring until chocolate is melted; cool.

Mix sugar and margarine in 2½-quart bowl until light and fluffy. Beat in egg·yolks, one at a time. Beat in chocolate and vanilla on low speed. Mix in flour, baking soda and salt alternately with buttermilk, beating after each addition until batter is smooth. Fold in egg whites. Divide batter among pans.

Bake until wooden pick inserted in center comes out clean, 8-inch squares 45 to 50 minutes, 9-inch squares 40 to 45 minutes, 8-inch rounds 35 to 40 minutes, 9-inch rounds 30 to 35 minutes; cool. Fill layers and frost top of cake with Coconut-Pecan Frosting.   **16 servings; 545 calories per serving.**

Coconut-Pecan Frosting

1	cup sugar
½	cup margarine or butter
1	cup evaporated milk
1	teaspoon vanilla
3	egg yolks
1⅓	cups flaked coconut
1	cup chopped pecans

Mix sugar, margarine, milk, vanilla and egg yolks in saucepan. Cook over medium heat, stirring occasionally, until thick, about 12 minutes. Stir in coconut and pecans. Beat until of spreading consistency.

NOTE: This is the grass roots recipe that swept the country to become a classic.

DOUBLE CHOCOLATE CAKE

1⅔   cups all-purpose flour*
1   cup packed brown sugar or granulated sugar
¼   cup cocoa
1   teaspoon baking soda
½   teaspoon salt
1   cup water
⅓   cup vegetable oil
1   teaspoon vinegar
½   teaspoon vanilla
½   cup semisweet chocolate chips

Heat oven to 350°. Mix flour, brown sugar, cocoa, baking soda and salt with fork in ungreased square pan, 8 × 8 × 2 inches. Mix in remaining ingredients except chocolate chips. Sprinkle chocolate chips over batter.

Bake until wooden pick inserted in center comes out clean, 35 to 40 minutes. Sprinkle with powdered sugar if desired.   **9 servings;** 305 calories per serving.

NOTE: Cake can be mixed in a bowl if desired.

Chocolate-Cherry Cake: Omit water and chocolate chips. Stir ⅓ cup chopped almonds into flour mixture. Mix ¾ cup water and ¼ cup maraschino cherry syrup. Stir in syrup mixture and ¼ cup chopped maraschino cherries with the remaining ingredients.

Chocolate-Spice Cake: Stir 1½ teaspoons ground allspice into flour mixture.

Chocolate-Walnut Cake: Omit cocoa and vanilla if desired. Substitute ⅓ cup miniature chocolate chips and ⅓ cup chopped walnuts for the ½ cup chocolate chips; sprinkle over batter.

*Do not use self-rising flour in this recipe.

Maple-Nut Cake: Omit cocoa, vanilla and chocolate chips. Stir ½ cup chopped nuts into flour mixture. Stir in ½ teaspoon maple extract with the remaining ingredients.

Oatmeal-Molasses Cake: Omit cocoa, vanilla and chocolate chips. Stir ¾ cup quick-cooking oats, ½ cup raisins and 1 teaspoon ground allspice into flour mixture. Stir in 2 tablespoons dark molasses with the remaining ingredients.

Pumpkin Cake: Omit cocoa, vanilla and chocolate chips. Stir 1 teaspoon ground allspice into flour mixture. Decrease water to ½ cup. Stir in ½ cup canned pumpkin pie mix with the remaining ingredients.

SILVER WHITE CAKE

2¼   **cups all-purpose flour***
1⅔   **cups sugar**
 ⅔   **cup shortening**
1¼   **cups milk**
3½   **teaspoons baking powder**
 1   **teaspoon salt**
 1   **teaspoon vanilla**
 5   **egg whites**

Heat oven to 350°. Grease and flour rectangular pan, 13 × 9 × 2 inches, or 2 round pans, 8 or 9 × 1½ inches. Beat all ingredients except egg whites on low speed, scraping bowl constantly, 30 seconds. Beat on high speed, scraping bowl occasionally, 2 minutes. Beat in egg whites on high speed, scraping bowl occasionally, 2 minutes. Pour into pan(s).

Bake until wooden pick inserted in center comes out clean or until cake springs back when touched lightly in center, rectangle 40 to 45 minutes, rounds 30 to 35 minutes. Frost with Cherry-Nut Frosting (page 129) if desired. **15 servings; 240 calories per serving.**

Almond White Cake: Substitute 1 teaspoon almond extract for the vanilla.

Cherry-Nut Cake: Fold ½ cup chopped nuts and ⅓ cup chopped maraschino cherries, well drained, into batter.

Chocolate Chip White Cake: Fold ½ cup miniature or

***Do not use self-rising flour in this recipe.**

finely chopped semisweet chocolate chips into batter. Frost cake with Chocolate Frosting (page 131) if desired.

Hazelnut Cake: Add 1 cup ground hazelnuts with the sugar.

Lemon-filled White Cake: Spread rectangular cake or fill layers with Lemon Filling (page 113) and frost with White Mountain Frosting (page 128). Sprinkle cake with about 1 cup flaked or shredded coconut if desired.

Silver White Cupcakes: Line 30 medium muffin cups, 2½ × 1¼ inches, with paper baking cups. Fill cups about ½ full. Bake 20 to 25 minutes. **30 cupcakes.**

Silver White Sheet Cake: Grease and flour jelly roll pan, 15½ × 10½ × 1 inch. Pour batter into pan. Bake 40 to 45 minutes.

YELLOW CAKE

2	cups all-purpose flour*
1½	cups sugar
½	cup shortening (half margarine or butter, softened, if desired)
1	cup milk
3½	teaspoons baking powder
1	teaspoon salt
1	teaspoon vanilla
3	eggs

Heat oven to 350°. Grease and flour rectangular pan, 13 × 9 × 2 inches, or 2 round pans, 8 or 9 × 1½ inches. Beat all ingredients on low speed, scraping bowl constantly, 30 seconds. Beat on high speed, scraping bowl frequently, 3 minutes. Pour into pan(s).

Bake until wooden pick inserted in center comes out clean, rectangle 40 to 45 minutes, rounds 30 to 35 minutes; cool. Frost with Chocolate Frosting (page 131) if desired. **15 servings;** 220 calories per serving.

Eggnog Cake: Substitute rum flavoring for the vanilla. Beat in 1 teaspoon ground nutmeg and ¼ teaspoon ground ginger.

Lemon-filled Yellow Cake: Spread rectangular cake or fill layers with Lemon Filling (page 113); frost with White Mountain Frosting (page 128).

*If using self-rising flour, omit baking powder and salt.

Lemon Filling

- ¾ cup sugar
- 3 tablespoons cornstarch
- ¼ teaspoon salt
- ⅔ cup water
- 1 tablespoon margarine or butter
- 1 teaspoon grated lemon peel
- ¼ cup lemon juice
- 2 drops yellow food color, if desired

Mix sugar, cornstarch and salt in 1½-quart saucepan. Gradually stir in water. Cook over medium heat, stirring constantly, until mixture thickens and boils. Boil and stir 1 minute; remove from heat. Stir in margarine and lemon peel until margarine is melted. Gradually stir in lemon juice and food color. Press plastic wrap onto filling. Refrigerate until set, at least 2 hours.

Maraschino Cherry Cake: Fold ½ cup finely chopped maraschino cherries, well drained, into batter.

Marble Cake: Pour half of the batter into another bowl. Mix 2 squares (1 ounce each) unsweetened chocolate, melted and cooled, 1 tablespoon sugar, 2 tablespoons warm water and ¼ teaspoon baking soda; stir into one batter. Spoon light and dark batters alternately into pan. Cut through batter several times for marbled effect.

Peanut Cake: Fold ½ cup finely chopped peanuts into batter.

Yellow Cupcakes: Line 36 medium muffin cups, 2½ × 1¼ inches, with paper baking cups. Fill each cup about ½ full. Bake 20 minutes. **36 cupcakes.**

POUND CAKE

- 2¾ cups sugar
- 1¼ cups margarine or butter, softened
- 1 teaspoon vanilla
- 5 eggs
- 3 cups all-purpose flour*
- 1 teaspoon baking powder
- ¼ teaspoon salt
- 1 cup evaporated milk

*Do not use self-rising flour in this recipe.

Heat oven to 350°. Grease and flour 12-cup bundt cake pan or tube pan, 10 × 4 inches. Beat sugar, margarine, vanilla and eggs on low speed, scraping bowl constantly, 30 seconds. Beat on high speed, scraping bowl occasionally, 5 minutes. Beat in flour, baking powder and salt alternately with milk on low speed. Pour into pan.

Bake until wooden pick inserted in center comes out clean, 70 to 80 minutes. Cool 20 minutes; remove from pan. **16 servings**; 385 calories per serving.

Almond Pound Cake: Substitute 1 teaspoon almond extract for the vanilla.

Lemon Pound Cake: Substitute 1 teaspoon lemon extract for the vanilla and fold 2 to 3 teaspoons grated lemon peel into batter.

Orange-Coconut Pound Cake: Fold 1 can (3½ ounces) flaked coconut (1⅓ cups) and 2 to 3 tablespoons shredded orange peel into batter.

PINEAPPLE UPSIDE-DOWN CAKE

2	tablespoons margarine or butter
¼	cup packed brown sugar
1	can (8¼ ounces) sliced pineapple in syrup, drained
1½	cups buttermilk baking mix
½	cup sugar
½	cup milk or water
2	tablespoons shortening
1	teaspoon vanilla
1	egg

Heat oven to 350°. Heat margarine in round pan, 9 × 1½ inches, in oven until melted. Sprinkle with brown sugar. Place 1 pineapple slice in center of pan. Cut remaining slices into halves; arrange halves, cut sides out, around pineapple in center of pan. Place 7 maraschino cherries in center or curves of pineapple slices if desired; arrange 6 pecan halves around center slice if desired.

Beat remaining ingredients on low speed, scraping bowl constantly, 30 seconds. Beat on medium speed, scraping occasionally, 4 minutes. Pour over fruit in pan.

Bake until wooden pick inserted in center comes out clean,

35 to 40 minutes. Immediately invert pan on heatproof serving plate. Let pan remain a few minutes. Serve warm and, if desired, with Sweetened Whipped Cream (page 274). **8 servings**; 255 calories per serving.

Apricot-Prune Upside-down Cake: Substitute 1 can (8¾ ounces) apricot halves (9 halves), drained, and 12 pitted cooked prunes for the pineapple.

Spiced Apple Upside-down Cake: Substitute 1 jar (14 ounces) spiced apple rings, drained, for the pineapple. Cut apple rings into halves; arrange in parallel rows over brown sugar.

FRUIT-TOPPED CAKE

1½	cups buttermilk baking mix
½	cup sugar
½	cup milk or water
2	tablespoons shortening
1	teaspoon vanilla
1	egg
¾	cup apricot preserves
1	tablespoon lemon juice
	Whipped Cream Cheese Topping (page 116)
2	kiwifruit, sliced
½	pint strawberries, cut into halves

Heat oven to 350°. Grease and flour round pan, 9 × 1½ inches. Beat baking mix, sugar, milk, shortening, vanilla and egg on low speed, scraping the bowl constantly, 30 seconds. Beat on medium speed, scraping bowl occasionally, 4 minutes. Pour into pan. Bake until wooden pick inserted in center comes out clean, 30 to 35 minutes. Immediately remove from pan; cool.

Heat apricot preserves and lemon juice to boiling, stirring occasionally. Strain enough of the preserve mixture to measure 2 tablespoons syrup for glaze; reserve. Cool preserve mixture.

Split cake horizontally to make 2 layers. (To split, mark side of cake with wooden picks and cut with long, thin knife.) Spread bottom cake layer with half of the preserve mixture; spread with ¾ cup of the Whipped Cream Cheese Topping. Top with second layer; spread with remaining preserve mixture. Arrange fruit on top. Brush fruit with reserved apricot syrup. Frost side of cake with remaining topping. Serve immediately or refrigerate no longer than 8 hours.   **8 servings;** 425 calories per serving.

NOTE: Any combination of fruit can be used.

Whipped Cream Cheese Topping
Beat 1 package (3 ounces) cream cheese, softened, in chilled 1½-quart bowl until smooth. Add ¼ cup powdered sugar, ¾ cup chilled whipping cream and ½ teaspoon vanilla. Beat on high speed, scraping bowl occasionally, until stiff peaks form.

Apricot Rum Cake: Omit kiwifruit, strawberries and glaze. Before spreading top of cake with remaining preserve mixture, prick cake with skewer or fork. Heat 1 tablespoon sugar, 2 tablespoons water and 1 tablespoon rum or brandy to boiling. Spoon evenly over top of cake. Continue as directed.

DATE-CHOCOLATE CHIP CAKE

1¼	cups boiling water
1	cup cut-up dates
1	teaspoon baking soda
1¾	cups all-purpose flour*
½	cup granulated sugar
½	cup packed brown sugar
⅔	cup vegetable oil
1	teaspoon baking soda
1	teaspoon vanilla
½	teaspoon salt
2	eggs
	Chocolate Chip Topping (page 117)

Pour boiling water on dates in 2½-quart bowl; stir in 1 teaspoon baking soda. Cool to lukewarm.

Heat oven to 350°. Stir remaining ingredients except Chocolate Chip Topping into date mixture. Pour into ungreased square pan, 9 × 9 × 2 inches. Sprinkle with Chocolate Chip Topping. Bake until wooden pick inserted in center comes out clean, 50 to 55 minutes.   **9 servings;** 500 calories per serving.

*If using self-rising flour, omit second teaspoon of baking soda and the salt.

Chocolate Chip Topping

½	**cup semisweet chocolate chips**
¼	**cup packed brown sugar**
¼	**cup all-purpose flour**
2	**tablespoons margarine or butter, softened**

Mix all ingredients.

APPLESAUCE CAKE

2½	**cups all-purpose* or cake flour**
2	**cups sugar**
1	**cup raisins**
½	**cup chopped walnuts**
½	**cup shortening**
1½	**cups applesauce**
½	**cup water**
1½	**teaspoons baking soda**
1½	**teaspoons salt**
¾	**teaspoon ground cinnamon**
½	**teaspoon ground cloves**
½	**teaspoon ground allspice**
¼	**teaspoon baking powder**
2	**eggs**

Heat oven to 350° Grease and flour rectangular pan, 13 × 9 × 2 inches, or 2 round pans, 8 or 9 × 1½ inches. Beat all ingredients on low speed, scraping bowl constantly, 30 seconds. Beat on high speed, scraping bowl occasionally, 3 minutes. Pour into pan(s).

Bake until wooden pick inserted in center comes out clean, rectangle 60 to 65 minutes, rounds 50 to 55 minutes; cool. Frost with Caramel Frosting (page 130) if desired.   **15 servings; 315 calories per serving.**

Small Applesauce Cake: Grease and flour square pan, 9 × 9 × 2 inches. Cut all ingredients in half. Pour batter into pan. Bake 50 to 55 minutes.   **9 servings.**

*Do not use self-rising flour in this recipe.

APPLE CAKE

1½	cups sugar
1	cup vegetable oil
3	eggs
2	cups all-purpose flour*
1½	teaspoons ground cinnamon
1	teaspoon baking soda
1	teaspoon vanilla
½	teaspoon salt
¼	teaspoon ground nutmeg
3	cups chopped tart apples (about 3 medium)
1	cup coarsely chopped nuts

Heat oven to 350°. Grease and flour rectangular pan, 13 × 9 × 2 inches. Mix sugar, oil and eggs until blended; beat 1 minute. Stir in remaining ingredients except apples and nuts; beat 1 minute. Stir in apples and nuts. Pour into pan.

Bake until wooden pick inserted in center comes out clean, 35 to 45 minutes. Frost with Caramel Frosting (page 130) if desired. **15 servings; 350 calories per serving.**

Carrot Cake: Substitute 3 cups shredded carrots for the apples. Frost with Cream Cheese Frosting (page 130) if desired.

BANANA-NUT CAKE

2⅓	cups all-purpose flour**
1⅔	cups sugar
1¼	cups mashed bananas (about 3 medium)
⅔	cup finely chopped nuts
⅔	cup shortening
⅔	cup buttermilk
3	eggs
1¼	teaspoons baking powder
1¼	teaspoons baking soda
1	teaspoon salt

*If using self-rising flour, omit baking soda and salt.
**If using self-rising flour, omit baking powder, baking soda and salt.

Heat oven to 350°. Grease and flour rectangular pan, 13 × 9 × 2 inches, 2 round pans, 9 × 1½ inches, or 3 round pans, 8 × 1½ inches. Beat all ingredients on low speed, scraping bowl constantly, 30 seconds. Beat on high speed, scraping bowl occasionally, 3 minutes. Pour into pan(s).

Bake until wooden pick inserted in center comes out clean, rectangle 45 to 50 minutes, rounds 35 to 40 minutes; cool. Frost with Creamy Vanilla Frosting (page 129) if desired. **15 servings;** 310 calories per serving.

PINEAPPLE-APRICOT CAKE

1	can (8 ounces) crushed pineapple in juice
½	cup cut-up dried apricots
½	cup raisins
2	cups all-purpose flour*
1	cup granulated sugar
½	cup packed brown sugar
½	cup vegetable oil
1¼	teaspoons baking soda
1	teaspoon salt
1	teaspoon ground cinnamon
1	teaspoon vanilla
¼	teaspoon ground nutmeg
3	eggs
	Nut Topping (page 120)

Drain pineapple, reserving juice; add enough water to juice to measure 1 cup. Heat juice mixture to boiling; pour over apricots and raisins in 2½-quart bowl. Let stand 1 hour.

Heat oven to 350°. Grease and flour rectangular pan, 13 × 9 × 2 inches. Add pineapple and remaining ingredients except Nut Topping to apricot mixture. Beat on low speed, scraping bowl constantly, 1 minute. Beat on medium speed, scraping bowl occasionally, 2 minutes. Pour into pan. Sprinkle with Nut Topping.

Bake until wooden pick inserted in center comes out clean, 45 to 50 minutes. Serve slightly warm with Sweetened Whipped Cream (page 274) if desired. **15 servings;** 325 calories per serving.

*If using self-rising flour, decrease baking soda to ½ teaspoon and omit salt.

Nut Topping

Mix ½ cup packed brown sugar and 2 tablespoons margarine or butter, softened, until crumbly; stir in ½ cup chopped nuts.

Prune-Walnut Cake: Grease and flour rectangular pan, 13 × 9 × 2 inches, 9- or 12-cup bundt cake pan or tube pan, 10 × 4 inches. Omit pineapple and Nut Topping. Substitute 1 cup cut-up dried prunes for the apricots and raisins. Pour 1 cup boiling water over prunes; let stand 1 hour. Add 1 cup chopped walnuts with the flour. Bake bundt cake or tube pan 50 to 55 minutes. Frost with Creamy Lemon Frosting (page 129) if desired.

WILLIAMSBURG ORANGE CAKE

2½	cups all-purpose flour* or 2¾ cups cake flour
1½	cups sugar
1	cup golden raisins, cut up
½	cup chopped nuts
½	cup margarine or butter, softened
¼	cup shortening
1½	cups buttermilk
1	tablespoon grated orange peel
1½	teaspoons baking soda
¾	teaspoon salt
1½	teaspoons vanilla
3	eggs

Heat oven to 350°. Grease and flour rectangular pan, 13 × 9 × 2 inches, 2 round pans, 9 × 1½ inches, 3 round pans, 8 × 1½ inches, or 12-cup bundt cake pan. Beat all ingredients on low speed, scraping bowl constantly, 30 seconds. Beat on high speed, scraping bowl occasionally, 3 minutes. Pour into pan(s).

Bake until wooden pick inserted in center comes out clean, rectangle 45 to 50 minutes, rounds 30 to 35 minutes, bundt cake 55 to 60 minutes; cool. Frost with Creamy Orange Frosting (page 129) if desired. **15 servings; 320 calories per serving.**

*Do not use self-rising flour in this recipe.

SOUR CREAM SPICE CAKE

  2   cups all-purpose flour*
1½   cups packed brown sugar
  1   cup raisins, cut up
  1   cup dairy sour cream
  ½   cup chopped walnuts
  ¼   cup margarine or butter, softened
  ¼   cup shortening
  ½   cup water
  2   teaspoons ground cinnamon
1¼   teaspoons baking soda
  1   teaspoon baking powder
  ¾   teaspoon ground cloves
  ½   teaspoon salt
  ½   teaspoon ground nutmeg
  2   eggs

Heat oven to 350°. Grease and flour rectangular pan, 13 × 9 × 2 inches, or 2 round pans, 8 or 9 × 1½ inches. Beat all ingredients on low speed, scraping bowl constantly, 30 seconds. Beat on high speed, scraping bowl occasionally, 3 minutes. Pour into pan(s).

Bake until wooden pick inserted in center comes out clean, rectangle 40 to 45 minutes, rounds 30 to 35 minutes; cool. Frost with Browned Butter Frosting (page 129) if desired. **15 servings; 305 calories per serving.**

*If using self-rising flour, decrease baking soda to ¾ teaspoon and omit baking powder and salt.

ZUCCHINI SPICE CAKE

2 cups all-purpose flour*
2 cups finely chopped zucchini (about 3 medium)
1¼ cups sugar
1 cup chopped nuts
½ cup vegetable oil
⅓ cup water
1¼ teaspoons baking soda
1 teaspoon salt
1 teaspoon ground cinnamon
1 teaspoon ground cloves
1 teaspoon ground nutmeg
1 teaspoon vanilla
3 eggs

Heat oven to 350°. Grease and flour rectangular pan, 13 × 9 × 2 inches. Beat all ingredients on low speed, scraping bowl constantly, until blended, about 1 minute. Beat on medium speed, scraping bowl occasionally, 2 minutes. Pour into pan.

Bake until wooden pick inserted in center comes out clean, 45 to 50 minutes. Frost with Cream Cheese Frosting (page 130) if desired. **15 servings; 265 calories per serving.**

Rhubarb Cake: Substitute ½ package (16-ounce size) frozen cut rhubarb (2 cups), rinsed, drained and chopped, or 1¾ cups finely chopped fresh rhubarb for the zucchini. Frost with Caramel Frosting (page 130) if desired.

*If using self-rising flour, decrease baking soda to ½ teaspoon and omit salt.

JEWELED FRUITCAKE

9   ounces Brazil nuts (about 1½ cups)
8   ounces dried apricots (about 2 cups)
8   ounces pitted dates (about 1½ cups)
5   ounces red and green candied pineapple, cut up (about 1 cup)
1   cup red and green maraschino cherries
¾   cup all-purpose flour*
¾   cup sugar
½   teaspoon baking powder
½   teaspoon salt
1½   teaspoons vanilla
3   eggs

Heat oven to 300°. Line loaf pan, 9×5×3 or 8½×4½×2½ inches, with aluminum foil; grease. Mix all ingredients. Spread in pan.

Bake until wooden pick inserted in center comes out clean, about 1¾ hours. If necessary, cover with aluminum foil during last 30 minutes of baking to prevent excessive browning. Remove from pan; cool. Wrap in plastic wrap; store in refrigerator. **32 servings; 155 calories per serving.**

FOAM-TYPE CAKES

Angel food, sponge and chiffon cakes depend on meringue for lightness, but they differ slightly.

Angel food cakes have no added leavening, shortening or egg yolks. They contain a high proportion of beaten egg whites to flour. *Sponge cakes* use both the whites and yolks of eggs. Sometimes additional leavening is called for, but never shortening. Sponge cakes are used for rolled cakes. *Chiffon cakes* combine the qualities of both foam- and shortening-type cakes, for they use yolks, leavening and shortening.

*If using self-rising flour, omit baking powder and salt.

HINTS FOR SUCCESS

■ Beat egg whites until stiff, straight peaks form. Be sure the bowl and beaters are dry and free from even a speck of grease or egg yolk.

■ To fold in ingredients, cut down through center of egg whites, along bottom and up side; rotate bowl ¼ turn. Repeat.

■ Use a knife to break down large air pockets and to seal batter against side of pan and tube.

■ Bake cakes in tube pans on bottom rack.

■ Don't open oven door before minimum baking time is up.

■ Cakes baked in tube pans are done when cracks in top feel dry and no imprint remains when touched.

■ Foam-type cakes baked in rectangular, layer or jelly roll pans are done when a wooden pick inserted in center comes out clean.

■ Cool cake upside down in tube pan. Put tube on heatproof funnel or bottle so cake does not touch counter.

■ To loosen and remove cooled cake from tube pan, slide metal spatula or table knife up and down between cake and pan. Next, invert pan and hit one side against counter. The cake will slip out.

ANGEL FOOD CAKE

1½   cups powdered sugar
 1   cup cake flour
1½   cups egg whites (about 12)
1½   teaspoons cream of tartar
 1   cup granulated sugar
1½   teaspoons vanilla
 ½   teaspoon almond extract
 ¼   teaspoon salt

Heat oven to 375°. Mix powdered sugar and flour. Beat egg whites and cream of tartar in 3-quart bowl on medium speed until foamy. Beat in granulated sugar on high speed, 2 tablespoons at a time, adding vanilla, almond extract and salt with the last addition of sugar; continue beating until stiff and glossy. Do not underbeat.

Sprinkle sugar-flour mixture, ¼ cup at a time, over meringue, folding in just until sugar-flour mixture disappears. Spread batter in ungreased tube pan, 10×4 inches. Cut gently through batter with metal spatula.

Bake until cracks feel dry and top springs back when touched lightly, 30 to 35 minutes. Invert pan on heatproof funnel; let hang until cake is cold. Remove from pan. Spread top of cake with Vanilla Glaze (page 132) if desired.   **16 servings; 130** calories per serving.

Chocolate Angel Food Cake: Substitute ¼ cup cocoa for ¼ cup of the flour. Omit almond extract.

Coconut Angel Food Cake: Fold in 1 cup shredded coconut, ½ cup at a time, after folding in sugar-flour mixture.

JELLY ROLL

3   eggs
1   cup granulated sugar
⅓   cup water
1   teaspoon vanilla
¾   cup all-purpose flour* or 1 cup cake flour
1   teaspoon baking powder
¼   teaspoon salt
     About ⅔ cup jelly or jam
     Powdered sugar

Heat oven to 375°. Line jelly roll pan, 15½×10½×1 inch, with aluminum foil or waxed paper; grease generously. Beat eggs in 1½-quart bowl on high speed until very thick and lemon colored, about 5 minutes. Pour eggs into 2½-quart bowl. Gradually beat in granulated sugar. Beat in water and vanilla on low speed. Gradually add flour, baking powder and salt, beating just until batter is smooth. Pour into pan.

Bake until wooden pick inserted in center comes out clean,

*If using self-rising flour, omit baking powder and salt.

12 to 15 minutes. Immediately loosen cake from edges of pan; invert on towel generously sprinkled with powdered sugar. Carefully remove foil. Trim off stiff edges of cake if necessary. While hot, carefully roll cake and towel from narrow end. Cool on wire rack at least 30 minutes. Unroll cake; remove towel. Beat jelly slightly with fork to soften; spread over cake. Roll up cake; sprinkle with powdered sugar. **10 servings; 205 calories per serving.**

Chocolate Ice-cream Roll: Beat in ¼ cup cocoa with the flour. Omit jelly. Spread 1 to 1½ pints of your favorite-flavored ice cream, slightly softened, over cake. Roll up; wrap in plastic wrap. Freeze until firm, at least 4 hours. Serve with Fudge Sauce (page 272) if desired.

Lemon Cake Roll: Substitute Lemon Filling (page 113) for the jelly. Serve with Sweetened Whipped Cream (page 274) if desired.

LEMON CHIFFON CAKE

2	cups all-purpose flour* or 2¼ cups cake flour
1½	cups sugar
3	teaspoons baking powder
1	teaspoon salt
¾	cup cold water
½	cup vegetable oil
2	teaspoons vanilla
2	teaspoons grated lemon peel
7	egg yolks (with all-purpose flour) or 5 egg yolks (with cake flour)
1	cup egg whites (about 8)
½	teaspoon cream of tartar

Heat oven to 325°. Mix flour, sugar, baking powder and salt. Beat in water, oil, vanilla, lemon peel and egg yolks until smooth. Beat egg whites and cream of tartar in 3-quart bowl until stiff peaks form. Gradually pour egg yolk mixture over beaten egg whites, folding with rubber spatula just until blended. Pour into ungreased tube pan, 10 × 4 inches.

Bake until top springs back when touched lightly, about 1¼ hours. Invert pan on heatproof funnel; let hang until cake is

*If using self-rising flour, omit baking powder and salt.

cold. Remove from pan. Frost with Creamy Lemon Frosting (page 129) if desired.   **16 servings;** 220 calories per serving.

Orange Chiffon Cake: Omit vanilla; substitute 2 tablespoons grated orange peel for the lemon peel. Spread top of cake with Orange Glaze (page 132) if desired.

FROSTINGS

FROSTING AND GLAZING CAKES

■ Brush away loose crumbs. Place a cool cake layer, rounded side down, on a plate. Spread ⅓ cup creamy-type or ½ cup fluffy-type frosting to within ½ inch of edge. Top with second layer, rounded side up.

■ Spread a very thin layer of frosting around side of cake to seal in any remaining crumbs. Frost side of cake, making a rim about ¼ inch high around top. Spread remaining frosting on top, just to rim.

■ To glaze a chiffon, angel food or bundt cake, pour or spoon a small amount of glaze on top of cake. Spread glaze, allowing some to drizzle down side. Repeat until all glaze is used.

WHITE MOUNTAIN FROSTING

½   cup sugar
¼   cup light corn syrup
2   tablespoons water
2   egg whites
1   teaspoon vanilla

Mix sugar, corn syrup and water in 1-quart saucepan. Cover and heat to rolling boil over medium heat. Uncover and boil rapidly to 242° on candy thermometer (or until small amount of mixture dropped into very cold water forms a firm ball that holds its shape until pressed).

As mixture boils, beat egg whites in 1½-quart bowl just until stiff peaks form. Pour hot syrup very slowly in thin stream into egg whites, beating constantly on medium speed. Add vanilla; beat on high speed until stiff peaks form. Frosts a 13×9-inch cake or fills and frosts two 8- or 9-inch cake layers.   **15 servings; 45 calories per serving.**

128

NOTE: To get an accurate temperature reading on the thermometer, it may be necessary to tilt the saucepan slightly. It takes 4 to 8 minutes for the syrup to reach 242°. Preparing this type of frosting on a humid day may require a longer beating time.

Cherry-Nut Frosting: Stir in ¼ cup cut-up candied cherries, ¼ cup chopped nuts and, if desired, 6 to 8 drops red food color.

Chocolate Revel Frosting: Stir in ½ cup semisweet chocolate chips or 1 square (1 ounce) unsweetened chocolate, coarsely grated.

Cocoa Frosting: Sift ¼ cup cocoa over frosting and fold in until blended.

Coffee Frosting: Beat 1 teaspoon powdered instant coffee into Satiny Beige Frosting (below).

Peppermint Frosting: Stir in ⅓ cup coarsely crushed peppermint candy or ½ teaspoon peppermint extract.

Satiny Beige Frosting: Substitute packed brown sugar for the granulated sugar and decrease vanilla to ½ teaspoon.

CREAMY VANILLA FROSTING

3   cups powdered sugar
⅓   cup margarine or butter, softened
1½   teaspoons vanilla
     About 2 tablespoons milk

Mix powdered sugar and margarine. Stir in vanilla and milk; beat until smooth and of spreading consistency. Frosts a 13 × 9-inch cake or fills and frosts two 8- or 9-inch cake layers.   **15 servings; 140 calories per serving.**

NOTE: To fill and frost three 8-inch layers, use 4½ cups powdered sugar, ½ cup margarine or butter, softened, 2 teaspoons vanilla and about 3 tablespoons milk.

Browned Butter Frosting: Heat margarine over medium heat until delicate brown; cool.

Creamy Cherry Frosting: Stir in 2 tablespoons drained chopped maraschino cherries and 2 drops red food color.

Creamy Lemon Frosting: Omit vanilla and substitute lemon juice for the milk. Stir in ½ teaspoon grated lemon peel.

Creamy Orange Frosting: Omit vanilla and substitute orange juice for the milk. Stir in 2 teaspoons grated orange peel.

Maple-Nut Frosting: Substitute ½ cup maple-flavored syrup for the vanilla and milk. Stir in ¼ cup finely chopped nuts.

Peanut Butter Frosting: Substitute peanut butter for the margarine and increase milk to about ⅓ cup.

Pineapple Frosting: Omit vanilla and milk. Stir in ⅓ cup well-drained crushed pineapple.

CREAM CHEESE FROSTING

    1   package (8 ounces) cream cheese, softened
    1   tablespoon milk
    1   teaspoon vanilla
    4   cups powdered sugar

Beat cream cheese, milk and vanilla in 2½-quart bowl on low speed until smooth. Gradually beat in powdered sugar, 1 cup at a time, until smooth and of spreading consistency. Frosts a 13 × 9-inch cake or fills and frosts two 8- or 9-inch cake layers. Refrigerate any remaining frosted cake. **15 servings; 190** calories per serving.

CARAMEL FROSTING

    ½   cup margarine or butter
    1   cup packed brown sugar
    ¼   cup milk
    2   cups powdered sugar

Heat margarine in 2-quart saucepan until melted. Stir in brown sugar. Heat to boiling, stirring constantly. Boil and stir over low heat 2 minutes; stir in milk. Heat to boiling; remove from heat. Cool to lukewarm. Gradually stir in powdered sugar. Place pan of frosting in bowl of cold water; beat until smooth and of spreading consistency. If frosting becomes too stiff, stir in additional milk, 1 teaspoon at a time. Frosts a 13 × 9-inch cake or fills and frosts two 8- or 9-inch cake layers. **15 servings;** 185 calories per serving.

FUDGE FROSTING

½   **cup granulated sugar**
2   **tablespoons cocoa**
¼   **cup milk**
2   **tablespoons margarine or butter**
1   **tablespoon light corn syrup**
    Dash of salt
½   **to ¾ cup powdered sugar**
½   **teaspoon vanilla**

Mix granulated sugar and cocoa in 1-quart saucepan. Stir in milk, margarine, corn syrup and salt; heat to boiling, stirring frequently. Boil, stirring occasionally, 3 minutes; cool. Beat in powdered sugar and vanilla. Frosts one 8- or 9-inch cake layer.   **8 servings;** 125 calories per serving.

CHOCOLATE
SOUR CREAM FROSTING

⅓   **cup margarine or butter, softened**
3   **squares (1 ounce each) unsweetened chocolate, melted**
    and cooled
3   **cups powdered sugar**
½   **cup dairy sour cream**
2   **teaspoons vanilla**

Mix margarine and chocolate; stir in powdered sugar. Stir in sour cream and vanilla; beat until smooth and of spreading consistency. Frosts a 13×9-inch cake or fills and frosts two 8- or 9-inch cake layers.   **15 servings;** 190 calories per serving.

CHOCOLATE FROSTING

⅓   **cup margarine or butter, softened**
2   **squares (1 ounce each) unsweetened chocolate, melted**
    and cooled
2   **cups powdered sugar**
1½   **teaspoons vanilla**
    About 2 tablespoons milk

Mix margarine and chocolate. Stir in powdered sugar. Beat in vanilla and milk until smooth and of spreading consistency. Frosts a 13×9-inch cake or fills and frosts two 8- or 9-inch cake layers. **15 servings; 130 calories per serving.**

NOTE: To fill and frost three 8-inch layers, use ½ cup margarine or butter, softened, 3 squares (1 ounce each) unsweetened chocolate, melted and cooled, 3 cups powdered sugar, 2 teaspoons vanilla and about 3 tablespoons milk.

Creamy Cocoa Frosting: Substitute ⅓ cup cocoa for the chocolate.

Mocha Frosting: Stir in 1½ teaspoons powdered instant coffee with the powdered sugar.

VANILLA GLAZE

⅓   cup margarine or butter
2   cups powdered sugar
1½   teaspoons vanilla
2   to 4 tablespoons hot water

Heat margarine until melted. Stir in powdered sugar and vanilla. Stir in water, 1 tablespoon at a time, until smooth and of desired consistency. Glazes a 12-cup bundt cake or 10-inch chiffon or angel food cake. **16 servings; 100 calories per serving.**

Butter-Rum Glaze: Substitute 2 tablespoons light rum or 1½ teaspoons rum flavoring for the vanilla; stir in hot water, 1 teaspoon at a time, until smooth and of desired consistency.

Lemon Glaze: Add ½ teaspoon grated lemon peel to melted margarine and substitute lemon juice for the vanilla and water.

Orange Glaze: Add ½ teaspoon grated orange peel to melted margarine and substitute orange juice for the vanilla and water.

CHOCOLATE CHIP GLAZE

½   cup semisweet chocolate chips
2   tablespoons margarine or butter
2   tablespoons corn syrup
1   to 2 teaspoons hot water

Heat chocolate chips, margarine and corn syrup over low heat, stirring constantly, until chocolate is melted; cool slightly. Stir in water, 1 teaspoon at a time, until of desired consistency. Glazes a 12-cup bundt cake or 10-inch angel food or chiffon cake. **16 servings; 50 calories per serving.**

ALMOND TOPPING

Beat 1 cup chilled whipping cream in chilled 1½-quart bowl until stiff; fold in 2 tablespoons almond-flavored liqueur. Serve on slices of angel food or pound cake or squares of chocolate or white cake. **2 cups topping; 115 calories per ¼ cup.**

Crème de Cacao Topping: Substitute 2 tablespoons crème de cacao for the almond-flavored liqueur.

Crème de Menthe Topping: Substitute 1 to 2 tablespoons crème de menthe for the almond-flavored liqueur.

Orange Topping: Substitute 1 to 2 tablespoons orange-flavored liqueur for the almond-flavored liqueur.

COCOA FLUFF

    1   cup powdered sugar
    ½   cup cocoa
    2   cups chilled whipping cream

Beat all ingredients in chilled 2½-quart bowl until stiff. Serve on squares of cake or frost a 10-inch angel food or chiffon cake. **4 cups topping; 150 calories per ¼ cup.**

Caramel Fluff: Substitute ¾ cup packed brown sugar for the powdered sugar and add 1 teaspoon vanilla.

Mocha Fluff: Decrease cocoa to ¼ cup and add 1 teaspoon instant coffee (dry).

Peppermint Fluff: Omit cocoa. Add 1 teaspoon peppermint extract and 6 to 8 drops red food color before beating.

PIES & PASTRY

ABOUT PASTRY FOR PIES

■ To make a perfect pie, use the right bakeware. Choose heat-resistant glass pie plates or dull-finish (anodized) aluminum pans. Never use shiny pans—pie will have a soggy bottom crust.

■ To cut in shortening evenly, a pastry blender is a great help. If you don't have one, use two knives; with the blades almost touching each other, move them back and forth in opposite directions in a parallel cutting motion.

■ If you use self-rising flour, you must omit the salt. Pastry made with self-rising flour will have a slightly different character—mealy and tender rather than flaky and tender.

■ To prevent an unbaked pie shell from puffing up as it bakes, prick pastry thoroughly after it has been placed in the pie plate.

■ Anchor a pastry cloth around a board and use a cloth cover for your rolling pin to keep the dough from sticking. Rub flour into both; this will prevent sticking, yet the flour won't be absorbed by the dough.

■ For a handsome top crust, brush it with milk before baking. You can also moisten it with water, then sprinkle with sugar. Or brush the crust lightly with a beaten egg or an egg yolk mixed with a little water.

NOTE: When recipes are given for both 9- and 10-inch-size pies, the calories and other nutritional information provided are for the 9-inch.

STANDARD PASTRY

ONE-CRUST PIE:
8- OR 9-INCH
- ⅓ cup plus 1 tablespoon shortening or ⅓ cup lard
- 1 cup all-purpose flour*
- ½ teaspoon salt
- 2 to 3 tablespoons cold water

10-INCH
- ½ cup shortening or ¼ cup plus 3 tablespoons lard
- 1⅓ cups all-purpose flour*
- ½ teaspoon salt
- 3 to 4 tablespoons cold water

TWO-CRUST PIE:
8- or 9-INCH
- ⅔ cup plus 2 tablespoons shortening or ⅔ cup lard
- 2 cups all-purpose flour*
- 1 teaspoon salt
- 4 to 5 tablespoons cold water

10-INCH
- 1 cup shortening or ¾ cup plus 2 tablespoons lard
- 2⅔ cups all-purpose flour*
- 1 teaspoon salt
- 7 to 8 tablespoons cold water

Cut shortening into flour and salt until particles are size of small peas. Sprinkle in water, 1 tablespoon at a time, tossing with fork until all flour is moistened and pastry almost cleans side of bowl (1 to 2 teaspoons water can be added if necessary).

Gather pastry into a ball; shape into flattened round on lightly floured cloth-covered board. (For Two-Crust Pie, divide pastry into halves and shape into 2 rounds.)

Roll pastry 2 inches larger than inverted pie plate with floured cloth-covered rolling pin.

Fold pastry into fourths; unfold and ease into plate, pressing firmly against bottom and side.

*If using self-rising flour, omit salt. Pie crusts made with self-rising flour differ in flavor and texture from those made with all-purpose flour.

For One-Crust Pie: Trim overhanging edge of pastry 1 inch from rim of plate. Fold and roll pastry under, even with plate; flute. Fill and bake as directed in recipe.

For Baked Pie Shell: Heat oven to 475°. Prick bottom and side thoroughly with fork. Bake until light brown, 8 to 10 minutes; cool.

For Two-Crust Pie: Turn desired filling into pastry-lined pie plate. Trim overhanging edge of pastry ½ inch from rim of plate. Roll other round of pastry. Fold into fourths; cut slits so steam can escape.

Place over filling and unfold. Trim overhanging edge of pastry 1 inch from rim of plate. Fold and roll top edge under lower edge, pressing on rim to seal; flute.

Fluted Pastry Edges: Cover edge with 2- to 3-inch strip of aluminum foil to prevent excessive browning; remove foil during last 15 minutes of baking. Bake as directed in recipe.

PASTRY BASICS

■ Roll pastry from center to outside edge in all directions, giving it a quarter turn occasionally. For an even thickness, lift the rolling pin as it approaches the edge.

■ When rolling out pastry, keep circular by occasionally pushing edge in gently with sides of hands. To prevent it from sticking to cloth, lift pastry occasionally.

■ Fold pastry into quarters; place in pie plate with point in center. Unfold and gently ease into plate, being careful not to stretch pastry. Trim as directed above.

■ For two-crust pie, let top pastry overhang 1 inch beyond edge of pie plate. Fold and roll overhanging pastry under edge of bottom pastry, pressing to seal.

■ While pinching the top and bottom edges together, form a stand-up rim on the edge of the pie plate—this seals the pastry and also makes fluting easier.

FLUTING PASTRY EDGES

■ *Fork edge:* Flatten pastry evenly on rim of pie plate. Press firmly around edge with tines of fork. Dip fork into flour occasionally to prevent any sticking.

■ *Rope edge:* Place side of thumb on pastry edge at an angle. Pinch pastry edge by pressing the knuckle of your index finger down into pastry toward thumb.

■ *Pinch edge:* Place index finger on inside of pastry edge and knuckles (or thumb and index finger) on outside. Pinch pastry into V shape; pinch again to sharpen.

LATTICE TOP

Prepare pastry as directed for Two-Crust Pie (page 135) except—leave 1-inch overhang on lower crust. Roll circle for top crust; cut into strips about ½ inch wide. (Use pastry wheel if desired.) Place 5 to 7 strips (depending on size of pie) across fruit filling. Weave a cross-strip through center by first folding back every other strip going the other way. Continue weaving lattice, folding back alternate strips each time cross-strip is added. (To save time, do not weave strips; lay second half of strips across first. Trim ends.)

Fold trimmed edge of lower crust over ends of strips. Build up a high pastry edge to help prevent juices from bubbling over. Seal and flute (see above).

BAKED TART SHELLS

Prepare pastry as directed for 8- or 9-inch One-Crust Pie (page 135) except—roll into 13-inch circle about ⅛ inch thick.

Cut circle into eight 4½-inch circles; fit circles over backs of medium muffin cups or 6-ounce custard cups, making pleats so pastry will fit closely. (If using individual pie pans or tart pans, cut pastry circles 1 inch larger than inverted pans; fit into pans.) Prick thoroughly with fork to prevent puffing.

Heat oven to 475°. Place on ungreased cookie sheet. Bake until light brown, 8 to 10 minutes. Cool before removing from pans. Fill each shell with ⅓ to ½ cup of favorite filling. **8 tart shells.**

CRUMB CRUSTS FOR 9-INCH PIES

Name	Crumbs	Margarine or Butter	Sugar	Temperature and Time
Graham Cracker	1½ cups (about 20 squares)	⅓ cup, melted	3 tablespoons	350° 10 minutes
Cookie*	1½ cups	¼ cup, melted		350° 10 minutes
Granola	2 cups crushed granola	¼ cup, melted	2 tablespoons	350° 6–8 minutes
Nut	1½ cups ground nuts	2 tablespoons, softened	3 tablespoons	400° 6–8 minutes

*Vanilla or chocolate wafers or gingersnaps.

Heat oven. Mix crumbs, margarine and sugar. Reserve 3 tablespoons mixture for topping if desired. Press remaining mixture firmly against bottom and side of pie plate, 9 × 1¼ inches. Bake as directed above; cool.

APPLE PIE

9-INCH
   Pastry for 9-inch Two-Crust Pie (page 135)
- ¾   cup sugar
- ¼   cup all-purpose flour*
- ½   teaspoon ground nutmeg
- ½   teaspoon ground cinnamon
     Dash of salt
- 6   cups thinly sliced pared tart apples (about 6 medium)
- 2   tablespoons margarine or butter

10-INCH
   Pastry for 10-inch Two-Crust Pie (page 135)
- 1   cup sugar
- ⅓   cup all-purpose flour*
- 1   teaspoon ground nutmeg
- 1   teaspoon ground cinnamon
     Dash of salt
- 8   cups thinly sliced pared tart apples (about 7 medium)
- 3   tablespoons margarine or butter

*If using self-rising flour, omit salt.

Heat oven to 425°. Prepare pastry. Mix sugar, flour, nutmeg, cinnamon and salt. Stir in apples. Turn into pastry-lined pie plate. Dot with margarine. Cover with top crust that has slits cut in it; seal and flute. Cover edge with 3-inch strip of aluminum foil to prevent excessive browning; remove foil during last 15 minutes of baking. Bake until crust is brown and juice begins to bubble through slits in crust, 40 to 50 minutes.   **6 servings per 9-inch pie;** 600 calories per serving.

Dutch Apple Pie: Prepare 9-inch pie as directed except— make extra large slits in top crust; 5 minutes before end of baking, pour ½ cup whipping cream through slits in top crust. Best served warm.

Easy Apple Pie: Prepare 9-inch pie as directed except— substitute 2 cans (20 ounces each) sliced apples, drained, for the 6 cups apples.

French Apple Pie: Prepare pastry for 9-inch One-Crust Pie (page 135); omit margarine and top apple filling with Crumb Topping: Mix 1 cup all-purpose flour, ½ cup firm margarine or butter and ½ cup packed brown sugar until crumbly. Cover topping with aluminum foil during last 10 minutes of baking. Bake 50 minutes. Best served warm.

APPLE DEEP-DISH PIE

      Pastry for 9-inch One-Crust Pie (page 135)
1½   **cups sugar**
 ½   **cup all-purpose flour***
 1   **teaspoon ground nutmeg**
 1   **teaspoon ground cinnamon**
 ¼   **teaspoon salt**
12   **cups thinly sliced pared tart apples (about 11 medium)**
 2   **tablespoons margarine or butter**

Heat oven to 425°. Prepare pastry as directed except—roll into 10-inch square. Fold pastry into halves; cut slits near center so steam can escape. Mix sugar, flour, nutmeg, cinnamon and salt. Stir in apples. Turn into ungreased square pan, 9×9×2 inches. Dot with margarine. Cover with crust; fold edges under just inside edges of pan. Bake until juice begins to bubble through slits in crust, about 1 hour. Serve slightly warm.   **12 servings;** 305 calories per serving.

*If using self-rising flour, omit salt.

APPLE-SOUR CREAM PIE

      Pastry for 9-inch One-Crust Pie (page 135)
 ¾   cup sugar
 2   tablespoons all-purpose flour
 ⅛   teaspoon salt
 1   cup dairy sour cream
 1   tablespoon vanilla
 ¼   teaspoon ground cinnamon
 1   egg
 2   cups chopped pared tart apples (about 2 medium)
      Brown Sugar Topping (below)

Heat oven to 375°. Prepare pastry. Mix sugar, flour and salt.
Beat in sour cream, vanilla, cinnamon and egg with fork until
smooth. Stir in apples. Pour into pastry-lined pie plate. Bake
until center is set, about 45 minutes.

   Sprinkle Brown Sugar Topping over pie; bake until golden
brown, about 15 minutes.   **8 servings;** 390 calories per serving.

Brown Sugar Topping

 ⅓   cup all-purpose flour
 ⅓   cup packed brown sugar
 2   tablespoons firm margarine or butter
 ¼   teaspoon ground cinnamon
 ⅛   teaspoon ground cloves

Mix all ingredients until crumbly.

APPLE-CINNAMON TART

 ¾   cup red cinnamon candies
 2   tablespoons water
 2   tablespoons light corn syrup
 5   cups thinly sliced pared tart apples (about 5 medium)
 2   tablespoons sugar
 1   tablespoon margarine or butter
      Pastry for 9-inch One-Crust Pie (page 135)

Heat candies, water and corn syrup to boiling; reduce heat.
Simmer uncovered until candies are almost dissolved, about
5 minutes. Pour into ungreased round pan, 9 × 1½ inches; cool.

Heat oven to 425°. Layer half of the apples, overlapping slices, on candy mixture; sprinkle with 1 tablespoon sugar. Layer with remaining apples; sprinkle with remaining sugar. Dot with margarine.

Prepare pastry as directed except—roll into 10-inch circle on lightly floured cloth-covered surface. Fold pastry into halves; carefully place over apples, with fold in center of pan. Unfold; trim edge of pastry to fit pan. Bake until crust is light golden brown, 40 to 45 minutes; cool 1 hour. Invert on serving plate. Serve with Sweetened Whipped Cream (page 274) or ice cream if desired. **8 servings; 275 calories per serving.**

APPLE SQUARES

Pastry (page 142)
1 **cup granulated sugar**
⅓ **cup all-purpose flour**
1 **teaspoon ground nutmeg**
1 **teaspoon ground cinnamon**
Dash of salt
8 **cups thinly sliced pared tart apples (about 7 medium)**
3 **tablespoons margarine or butter**
¾ **cup powdered sugar**
About 1 tablespoon milk

Heat oven to 425°. Prepare Pastry. Gather into a ball; divide into halves. Shape each half into flattened round on lightly floured cloth-covered board. Roll 1 round into rectangle, 18 × 13 inches, with floured cloth-covered rolling pin. Fold pastry into fourths; unfold and ease into ungreased jelly roll pan, 15½ × 10½ × 1 inch.

Roll other round pastry into rectangle, 17 × 12 inches. Fold into fourths; cut slits so steam can escape. Mix granulated sugar, flour, nutmeg, cinnamon and salt. Stir in apples. Turn into pastry-lined pan. Dot with margarine. Cover with crust with slits; seal and flute (page 137).

Bake until crust is golden brown and juice begins to bubble through slits in crust, 35 to 40 minutes; cool slightly. Mix powdered sugar and milk until smooth and of desired consistency; drizzle over crust. Cut into about 3-inch squares. Serve dessert warm with ice cream if desired. **15 squares; 400 calories per square.**

Pastry

1⅓ cups shortening
3½ cups all-purpose flour*
1 teaspoon salt
8 to 9 tablespoons cold water

Cut shortening into flour and salt until particles are size of small peas. Sprinkle in water, 1 tablespoon at a time, tossing with fork until all flour is moistened and pastry almost cleans side of bowl (1 to 2 teaspoons water can be added if necessary).

APPLE DUMPLINGS

Pastry for 8- or 9-inch Two-Crust Pie (page 135)
6 baking apples (each about 3 inches in diameter), cored
3 tablespoons raisins
3 tablespoons chopped nuts
2 cups packed brown sugar
1 cup water

Heat oven to 425°. Prepare pastry as directed except—roll ⅔ of the pastry into 14-inch square; cut into 4 squares. Roll remaining pastry into rectangle, 14 × 7 inches; cut into 2 squares. Place apple on each square.

Mix raisins and nuts; fill each apple. Moisten corners of pastry squares; bring 2 opposite corners up over apple and pinch. Repeat with remaining corners; pinch edges of pastry to seal. Place dumplings in ungreased rectangular baking dish, 12 × 7½ × 2 inches.

Heat brown sugar and water to boiling; carefully pour around dumplings. Bake, spooning syrup over dumplings 2 or 3 times, until crust is golden and apples are tender, about 40 minutes. Serve warm or cool with cream or Sweetened Whipped Cream (page 274) if desired. **6 dumplings; 800 calories per dumpling.**

*If using self-rising flour, omit salt.

BLUEBERRY PIE

Pastry for 9-inch Two-Crust Pie (page 135)
½ cup sugar
⅓ cup all-purpose flour
½ teaspoon ground cinnamon, if desired
4 cups fresh blueberries
1 tablespoon lemon juice
2 tablespoons margarine or butter

Heat oven to 425°. Prepare pastry. Mix sugar, flour and cinnamon. Stir in blueberries. Turn into pastry-lined pie plate; sprinkle with lemon juice. Dot with margarine. Cover with top crust that has slits cut in it; seal and flute. Cover edge with 2- to 3-inch strip of aluminum foil to prevent excessive browning; remove foil during last 15 minutes of baking.

Bake until crust is brown and juice begins to bubble through slits in crust, 35 to 45 minutes.   **6 servings; 550 calories per serving.**

Blackberry, Boysenberry, Loganberry or Raspberry Pie: Substitute 4 cups fresh berries for the blueberries. Increase sugar to 1 cup and omit the lemon juice.

Easy Blueberry Pie: Substitute drained canned blueberries or unsweetened frozen blueberries, partially thawed, for the fresh blueberries.

Plum Pie: Substitute 4 cups purple plum slices for the blueberries and add the cinnamon.

BLUEBERRY GRENADINE PIE

Pastry for 9-inch One-Crust Pie (page 135)
2 cups fresh blueberries
½ cup sugar
1 tablespoon plus 2 teaspoons cornstarch
¼ teaspoon salt
¼ teaspoon ground cinnamon
¾ cup water
¼ cup grenadine syrup
2 teaspoons lemon juice
½ cup chilled whipping cream
1 tablespoon sugar

Prepare pastry as directed except—stir in ¼ cup cornmeal with the flour. Continue as directed for Baked Pie Shell (page 136). Place blueberries in pie shell. Mix ½ cup sugar, the cornstarch, salt and cinnamon in saucepan. Stir in water. Heat to boiling, stirring constantly. Boil and stir 1 minute. Stir in grenadine syrup and lemon juice. Pour over blueberries. Refrigerate until chilled.

Beat whipping cream and 1 tablespoon sugar in chilled 1½-quart bowl until stiff. Cut pie into wedges; top with whipped cream. **6 servings; 420 calories per serving.**

CHERRY PIE

9-INCH
Pastry for 9-inch Two-Crust Pie (page 135)
1⅓ cups sugar
⅓ cup all-purpose flour
2 cans (16 ounces each) pitted red tart cherries, drained
¼ teaspoon almond extract
2 tablespoons margarine or butter

10-INCH
Pastry for 10-inch Two-Crust Pie (page 135)
1⅔ cups sugar
½ cup all-purpose flour
3 cans (16 ounces each) pitted red tart cherries, drained
1 teaspoon almond extract
3 tablespoons margarine or butter

Heat oven to 425°. Prepare pastry. Mix sugar and flour. Stir in cherries. Turn into pastry-lined pie plate; sprinkle with almond extract. Dot with margarine. Cover with top crust that has slits cut in it; seal and flute. Cover edge with 2- to 3-inch strip of aluminum foil to prevent excessive browning; remove foil during last 15 minutes of baking.

Bake until crust is brown and juice begins to bubble through slits in crust, 35 to 45 minutes. **6 servings per 9-inch pie; 690 calories per serving.**

Fresh Cherry Pie: Prepare 9-inch pie as directed except—substitute 4 cups fresh red tart cherries, pitted, for the canned cherries.

Frozen Cherry Pie: Prepare 9-inch pie as directed except—

substitute 4 cups frozen pitted red tart cherries, thawed and drained, for the canned cherries; decrease sugar to ½ cup.

CHERRY PHYLLO PIE

10	frozen phyllo leaves, thawed
½	cup margarine or butter, melted
1	cup sugar
3	tablespoons cornstarch
1	teaspoon lemon juice
3	drops red food color, if desired
2	cans (16 ounces each) pitted red tart cherries, drained

Heat oven to 350°. Cut stack of phyllo leaves into 12-inch squares; discard remaining phyllo strips. Cover squares with damp towel to prevent them from drying out. Carefully separate 1 square; brush with margarine. Place in ungreased pie plate, 9 × 1¼ inches, allowing corners of phyllo to hang over edge of pie plate. Repeat with 4 squares.

Mix sugar and cornstarch. Stir in lemon juice, food color and cherries. Spread in phyllo-lined pie plate. Fold overhanging corners phyllo over filling. Spread each remaining phyllo square with margarine; arrange on filling to make top crust, allowing corners to hang over edge of plate. Fold overhanging corners of phyllo under, between bottom layers and rim of plate. Cut through top layers of phyllo with scissors to make 8 sections. Bake until crust is golden brown and juice begins to bubble through cuts in phyllo, 45 to 50 minutes. **8 servings;** 320 calories per serving.

GLAZED CHERRY TARTS

	Baked Tart Shells (page 137)
2	pounds unstemmed dark sweet cherries
1	cup currant jelly
2	packages (3 ounces each) cream cheese, softened
¼	cup whipped cream

Bake eight 4-inch tart shells; cool. Drop cherries into 3 cups boiling water; reduce heat. Simmer uncovered 3 minutes; drain and cool. Remove pits. Heat jelly over low heat until melted; reserve. Mix cream cheese and whipped cream. Spread 2 tablespoons cheese mixture in bottom of each tart shell. Divide cherries evenly among tart shells. Pour 2 tablespoons jelly over each tart. **8 tarts; 440 calories per tart.**

CHERRY CREAM PIE

	8- or 9-inch Baked Pie Shell (pages 135 and 136)
1	package (about 3½ ounces) vanilla instant pudding and pie filling
½	package (2.8-ounce size) whipped topping mix (1 envelope)
1½	cups milk
½	teaspoon almond extract
1	can (21 ounces) cherry pie filling, drained (reserve syrup)

Bake pie shell. Beat pudding and pie filling (dry), whipped topping mix (dry), milk and almond extract in 2½-quart bowl on low speed until blended. Beat on high speed until soft peaks form, about 3 minutes. Fold in cherries. Pour into pie shell. Refrigerate until firm, at least 2 hours. Top each serving with ½ cup reserved syrup. **8 servings; 360 calories per serving.**

FRUIT SALAD PIE

	Pastry for 9-inch Two-Crust Pie (page 135)
1	medium banana
1	package (10 ounces) frozen strawberries, thawed and drained (reserve syrup)
1	can (20 ounces) pineapple chunks in syrup, drained (reserve syrup)
1	tablespoon lemon juice
½	cup sugar
¼	cup quick-cooking tapioca
¼	teaspoon salt
2	tablespoons margarine or butter
	Sour Cream Topping (page 147)

Heat oven to 425°. Prepare pastry. Slice banana into 2½-quart bowl; add strawberries, pineapple chunks, lemon juice and ¼ cup of the reserved pineapple syrup. Mix sugar, tapioca and salt; stir into fruit mixture. Turn into pastry-lined pie plate. Dot with margarine. Cover with top crust that has slits cut in it; seal and flute. Cover edge with 2- to 3-inch strip of aluminum foil to prevent excessive browning; remove foil during last 15 minutes of baking.

Bake until crust is brown, 40 to 50 minutes; cool. Serve with Sour Cream Topping. **8 servings; 520 calories per serving.**

Sour Cream Topping
Mix 1 cup dairy sour cream and 2 tablespoons reserved strawberry syrup.

PEACH PIE

9-INCH
    Pastry for 9-inch Two-Crust Pie (page 135)
  1 **cup sugar**
  ¼ **cup all-purpose flour**
  ¼ **teaspoon ground cinnamon**
  5 **cups sliced fresh peaches (about 5 medium)**
  1 **teaspoon lemon juice**
  2 **tablespoons margarine or butter**

10-INCH
    Pastry for 10-inch Two-Crust Pie (page 135)
 1¼ **cups sugar**
  ⅓ **cup all-purpose flour**
  ¼ **teaspoon ground cinnamon**
  6 **cups sliced fresh peaches (about 6 medium)**
  1 **teaspoon lemon juice**
  3 **tablespoons margarine or butter**

Heat oven to 425°. Prepare pastry. Mix sugar, flour and cinnamon. Stir in peaches and lemon juice. Turn into pastry-lined pie plate. Dot with margarine. Cover with top crust that has slits cut in it; seal and flute. Cover edge with 2- to 3-inch strip of aluminum foil to prevent excessive browning; remove foil during last 15 minutes of baking.

Bake until crust is brown and juice begins to bubble through slits in crust, 35 to 45 minutes. Serve with ice cream and Raspberry-Currant Sauce (page 274) if desired. **6 servings per 9-inch pie; 595 calories per serving.**

Apricot Pie: Prepare 9-inch pie as directed except—substitute 5 cups apricot halves for the peaches.

Easy Peach Pie: Prepare 9-inch pie as directed except—substitute 2 cans (29 ounces each) sliced peaches, drained, or 5 cups frozen sliced peaches, partially thawed and drained, for the fresh peaches; decrease sugar to ½ cup.

Peach-Apricot Pie: Substitute ¼ cup apricot jam or preserves and ¾ cup packed brown sugar for the granulated sugar; stir jam into peaches and lemon juice before stirring into flour mixture.

PEACH MELBA TARTS

    Baked Tart Shells (page 137)
1   **package (10 ounces) frozen raspberries, thawed**
    Melba Sauce (below)
1½ **cups sliced fresh peaches**
    Vanilla ice cream

Bake tart shells. Drain raspberries, reserving syrup. Prepare Melba Sauce. Mix raspberries and peaches. Divide mixture among tarts; top each tart with ice cream and Melba Sauce. **8 tarts; 340 calories per tart.**

Melba Sauce
Mix ½ cup reserved raspberry syrup, ¼ cup currant jelly and 2 teaspoons cornstarch in 1-quart saucepan. Cook over medium heat, stirring constantly, until mixture thickens and boils. Boil and stir 1 minute; cool.

PEACH-PECAN TART

    Clear Orange Glaze (page 149)
    Butter Crust (page 149)
2   **packages (3 ounces each) cream cheese, softened**
4   **cups sliced fresh peaches (4 medium)**
½   **cup chopped pecans**

Prepare Clear Orange Glaze. Bake Butter Crust. Beat cream cheese until smooth; spread over crust. Arrange peaches on crust; sprinkle with pecans. Pour Clear Orange Glaze over top. Refrigerate until set, about 2 hours. **8 servings; 530 calories per serving.**

Clear Orange Glaze

  1   **cup sugar**
  3   **tablespoons cornstarch**
  ¼   **teaspoon salt**
  1   **cup orange juice**
  ½   **cup water**

Mix sugar, cornstarch and salt in 1-quart saucepan. Gradually stir in orange juice and water. Heat to boiling over medium heat, stirring constantly. Boil and stir 1 minute; cool.

Butter Crust

Heat oven to 400°. Mix 1⅓ cups all-purpose flour, ⅔ cup margarine or butter, softened, and ⅓ cup packed brown sugar with fork until crumbly. Press firmly and evenly against bottom of ungreased 12-inch pizza pan. Bake until light brown, 10 to 15 minutes; cool.

PEAR TART

    Pastry for 8- or 9-inch One-Crust Pie (page 135)
  ½   **cup currant jelly, melted**
  3   **cups thinly sliced pared pears (about 3 medium)**
  1   **to 2 tablespoons packed brown sugar**
    Dairy sour cream or Sweetened Whipped Cream (page 274)

Heat oven to 425°. Prepare pastry as directed except—roll into rectangle, 12 × 10 inches. Trim edges to make even. Place rectangle on ungreased cookie sheet. Brush ½-inch edge around rectangle with water. Fold moistened edges onto rectangle; press lightly with floured fork. Brush half of the currant jelly on rectangle up to folded edges. Arrange pears in rows, overlapping slices, on jelly-covered pastry; sprinkle with brown sugar.

    Bake until pastry is golden brown, 20 to 25 minutes. Brush

remaining currant jelly on pears and pastry edges. Cut into 6 squares. Serve warm or cool topped with sour cream. **6 servings;** 365 calories per serving.

RAISIN-SOUR CREAM PIE

	9-inch Baked Pie Shell (pages 135 and 136)
1	tablespoon plus 1½ teaspoons cornstarch
1	cup plus 2 tablespoons sugar
¾	teaspoon ground nutmeg
¼	teaspoon salt
1½	cups dairy sour cream
1½	cups raisins
1	tablespoon lemon juice
3	egg yolks
	Brown Sugar Meringue (page 155)

Bake pie shell. Heat oven to 400°. Mix cornstarch, sugar, nutmeg and salt in 2-quart saucepan. Stir in sour cream. Stir in raisins, lemon juice and egg yolks. Cook over medium heat, stirring constantly, until mixture thickens and boils. Boil and stir 1 minute. Pour into pie shell.

Prepare meringue; spoon onto hot pie filling. Spread over filling, carefully sealing meringue to edge of crust to prevent shrinking or weeping.

Bake until delicate brown, about 10 minutes. Refrigerate any remaining pie immediately. **8 servings;** 515 calories per serving.

RHUBARB PIE

	Pastry for 9-inch Two-Crust Pie (page 135)
1⅓	to 1⅔ cups sugar
⅓	cup all-purpose flour
½	teaspoon grated orange peel, if desired
4	cups cut-up rhubarb (½-inch pieces)
2	tablespoons margarine or butter

Heat oven to 425°. Prepare pastry. Mix sugar, flour and orange peel. Turn half of the rhubarb into pastry-lined pie plate; sprinkle with half of the sugar mixture. Repeat with remaining rhubarb and sugar mixture. Dot with margarine.

Cover with top crust that has slits cut in it; seal and flute. Sprinkle with sugar if desired. Cover edge with 2- to 3-inch strip of aluminum foil to prevent excessive browning; remove foil during last 15 minutes of baking.

Bake until crust is brown and juice begins to bubble through slits in crust, 40 to 50 minutes. **6 servings; 610 calories per serving.**

Frozen Rhubarb Pie: Decrease sugar to ⅔ cup and substitute 1 package (20 ounces) frozen rhubarb, partially thawed, for the 4 cups cut-up rhubarb.

Rhubarb-Blueberry Pie: Substitute fresh or frozen (thawed) blueberries for half of the rhubarb and use the lesser amount of sugar.

Rhubarb-Strawberry Pie: Substitute sliced strawberries for half of the rhubarb and use the lesser amount of sugar.

FRENCH STRAWBERRY TART

1¼	cups buttermilk baking mix
¼	cup sugar
1	tablespoon grated orange peel
¼	cup margarine or butter, softened
1	pint fresh strawberries, cut into halves
½	cup orange juice
¼	cup water
2	tablespoons sugar
1	tablespoon cornstarch
½	cup chilled whipping cream
2	tablespoons sugar

Heat oven to 400°. Mix baking mix, ¼ cup sugar and the orange peel. Cut in margarine until mixture resembles coarse cornmeal. Press mixture in bottom of ungreased round pan, 9 × 1½ inches. Bake until light brown, 10 to 12 minutes; cool about 30 minutes.

Invert crust on serving plate. Arrange strawberries on crust. Mix orange juice, water, 2 tablespoons sugar and the cornstarch in saucepan. Heat to boiling, stirring constantly. Boil and stir 1 minute; cool completely. Pour orange glaze on strawberries. Refrigerate 1 hour.

Beat whipping cream and 2 tablespoons sugar in chilled 1½-quart bowl until stiff. Garnish tart with whipped cream. 8 servings; 250 calories per serving.

STRAWBERRY GLACE PIE

```
    9-inch Baked Pie Shell (pages 135 and 136)
 6  cups strawberries (about 1½ quarts)
 1  cup sugar
 3  tablespoons cornstarch
½   cup water
 1  package (3 ounces) cream cheese, softened
```

Bake pie shell. Mash enough strawberries to measure 1 cup. Mix sugar and cornstarch in 2-quart saucepan. Gradually stir in water and mashed strawberries. Cook over medium heat, stirring constantly, until mixture thickens and boils. Boil and stir 1 minute; cool.

Beat cream cheese until smooth; spread on bottom of pie shell. Fill shell with remaining strawberries; pour cooked strawberry mixture over top. Refrigerate until set, at least 3 hours. 8 servings; 320 calories per serving.

Peach Glacé Pie: Substitute 5 cups sliced peaches (about 5 medium) for the strawberries. To prevent discoloration, dip peaches in an ascorbic acid mixture as directed on package.

Raspberry Glacé Pie: Substitute 6 cups raspberries for the strawberries.

COCONUT CREAM PIE

```
    9-inch Baked Pie Shell (pages 135 and 136)
⅔   cup sugar
¼   cup cornstarch
½   teaspoon salt
 3  cups milk
 4  egg yolks, slightly beaten
 2  tablespoons margarine or butter, softened
 2  teaspoons vanilla
 1  cup flaked coconut
 1  cup Sweetened Whipped Cream (page 274)
```

Bake pie shell. Mix sugar, cornstarch and salt in saucepan. Gradually stir in milk. Cook over medium heat, stirring constantly, until mixture thickens and boils. Boil and stir 1 minute. Stir at least half of the hot mixture gradually into egg yolks. Stir into hot mixture in saucepan. Boil and stir 1 minute; remove from heat. Stir in margarine, vanilla and ¾ cup of the coconut. Pour into pie shell; press plastic wrap onto filling. Refrigerate at least 2 hours but no longer than 48 hours.

Remove plastic wrap; top pie with whipped cream and remaining coconut. Refrigerate any remaining pie immediately. **8 servings; 485 calories per serving.**

Banana Cream Pie: Increase vanilla to 1 tablespoon plus 1 teaspoon; omit coconut. Press plastic wrap onto filling in saucepan; refrigerate until room temperature. Slice 2 large bananas into pie shell; pour filling over bananas. Refrigerate until serving time. Top pie with whipped cream and garnish with banana slices.

Chocolate Cream Pie: Increase sugar to 1½ cups and cornstarch to ⅓ cup; omit margarine and coconut. Stir in 2 squares (1 ounce each) unsweetened chocolate, cut up, after stirring in milk. Top pie with whipped cream.

CLASSIC FRENCH SILK PIE

9-inch Baked Pie Shell (pages 135 and 136)
1   cup granulated sugar
¾   cup butter,* softened
1½   teaspoons vanilla
¼   teaspoon cream of tartar
3   squares (1 ounce each) unsweetened chocolate, melted
       and cooled
3   eggs
1   cup chilled whipping cream
2   tablespoons powdered sugar

*We do not recommend margarine for this recipe.

Bake pie shell; cool. Beat granulated sugar and butter in 1½-quart bowl until light and fluffy. Stir in vanilla, cream of tartar and chocolate. Beat in eggs until light and fluffy, about 3 minutes. Pour into pie shell. Refrigerate until set, 3 to 4 hours. Or cover with plastic wrap and freeze at least 8 hours.

If pie is frozen, remove from freezer 15 minutes before serving. Beat whipping cream and powdered sugar in chilled 1½-quart bowl until stiff. Top pie with whipped cream and, if desired, chopped nuts or Chocolate Curls (page 681). Refrigerate any remaining pie immediately.   **8 servings;** 580 calories per serving.

Mocha French Silk Pie: Stir in 1½ teaspoons instant coffee (dry) with the chocolate.

CHOCOLATE-BANANA PIE

> Graham Cracker Crust (page 138)
> 1   cup dairy sour cream
> 1   cup milk
> 1   package (about 4 ounces) chocolate instant pudding and
>   pie filling
> 3   medium bananas

Bake pie crust. Beat sour cream and milk with hand beater until smooth. Mix in pudding and pie filling (dry) until smooth and slightly thickened. Slice bananas into pie crust; pour sour cream mixture over bananas. Refrigerate until set, at least 1 hour.   **8 servings;** 360 calories per serving.

ABOUT MERINGUE PIES

Here's how to make high, light-as-air, golden brown meringue toppings for pies:

■ Separate eggs very carefully while cold. Make sure no yolk gets into whites—even a speck of yolk or any grease prevents whites from beating up. For greatest volume, let whites stand at room temperature 30 minutes before beating.

■ Beat in sugar gradually. Continue beating until mixture stands in stiff peaks when beaters are lifted. (Meringue should feel smooth, not gritty, when rubbed between your forefinger and thumb.)

■ Spread meringue over *hot* filling, right up to the crust all the way around. Sealing the meringue against the crust prevents shrinking.

■ Cool baked meringue gradually, away from drafts.

All these precautions will help prevent "weeping" (moisture that collects between meringue and filling).

MERINGUE FOR 9-INCH PIE

    3   egg whites
    ¼   teaspoon cream of tartar
    6   tablespoons sugar
    ½   teaspoon vanilla

Beat egg whites and cream of tartar in 2½-quart bowl until foamy. Beat in sugar, 1 tablespoon at a time; continue beating until stiff and glossy. Do not underbeat. Beat in vanilla.

Brown Sugar Meringue: Substitute packed brown sugar for the granulated sugar.

MERINGUE PIE SHELL

Heat oven to 275°. Generously butter pie plate, 9 × 1¼ inches. Beat 2 egg whites and ¼ teaspoon cream of tartar in 1½-quart bowl until foamy. Beat in ½ cup sugar, 1 tablespoon at a time; continue beating until stiff and glossy. Do not underbeat. Spoon into pie plate, pressing meringue against bottom and side.

Bake 45 minutes; turn off oven. Leave meringue in oven with door closed 45 minutes; remove from oven. Finish cooling away from draft.

LEMON MERINGUE PIE

9-inch Baked Pie Shell (pages 135 and 136)
1½ cups sugar
⅓ cup plus 1 tablespoon cornstarch
1½ cups water
3 egg yolks, slightly beaten
3 tablespoons margarine or butter
2 teaspoons grated lemon peel
½ cup lemon juice
2 drops yellow food color, if desired
Meringue for 9-inch Pie (page 155)

Bake pie shell. Heat oven to 400°. Mix sugar and cornstarch in 1½-quart saucepan. Gradually stir in water. Cook over medium heat, stirring constantly, until mixture thickens and boils. Boil and stir 1 minute. Gradually stir at least half of the hot mixture into egg yolks. Stir into hot mixture in saucepan. Boil and stir 1 minute; remove from heat. Stir in margarine, lemon peel, lemon juice and food color. Pour into pie shell.

Prepare meringue; spoon onto hot pie filling. Spread over filling, carefully sealing meringue to edge of crust to prevent shrinking or weeping.

Bake until delicate brown, 8 to 12 minutes. Cool pie away from draft. Refrigerate any remaining pie immediately. 8 servings; 410 calories per serving.

PUMPKIN PIE

9-INCH
Pastry for 9-inch One-Crust Pie (page 135)
2 eggs
¾ cup sugar
1 can (16 ounces) pumpkin
1 can (12 ounces) evaporated milk
1 teaspoon ground cinnamon
½ teaspoon salt
½ teaspoon ground ginger
¼ teaspoon ground cloves

10-INCH
      Pastry for 10-inch One-Crust Pie (page 135)
  3   eggs
  1   cup sugar
2¾ cups canned pumpkin
2¼ cups evaporated milk
1½ teaspoons ground cinnamon
 ¾ teaspoon salt
 ¾ teaspoon ground ginger
 ½ teaspoon ground cloves

Heat oven to 425°. Prepare pastry. Beat eggs slightly with hand beater; beat in remaining ingredients. Place pastry-lined pie plate on oven rack; pour in filling. Bake 15 minutes.

Reduce oven temperature to 350°. Bake until knife inserted in center comes out clean, 9-inch pie 45 minutes longer, 10-inch pie 55 minutes longer. Refrigerate until chilled, at least 4 hours. Serve with Sweetened Whipped Cream (page 274) if desired. Refrigerate any remaining pie immediately.   **8 servings per 9-inch pie; 310 calories per serving.**

Praline Pumpkin Pie: Prepare 9-inch Pumpkin Pie as directed except—decrease second bake time to 35 minutes. Mix ⅓ cup packed brown sugar, ⅓ cup chopped pecans and 1 tablespoon margarine or butter, softened; sprinkle over pie. Bake until knife inserted in center comes out clean, about 10 minutes longer.

Sweet Potato Pie: Substitute mashed cooked sweet potatoes (page 667) for the pumpkin.

PECAN PIE

      Pastry for 9-inch One-Crust Pie (page 135)
⅔ cup sugar
⅓ cup margarine or butter, melted
1 cup corn syrup
½ teaspoon salt
3 eggs
1 cup pecan halves or broken pecans

Heat oven to 375°. Prepare pastry. Beat sugar, margarine, corn syrup, salt and eggs with hand beater. Stir in pecans. Pour into pastry-lined pie plate.

Bake until set, 40 to 50 minutes. Refrigerate until chilled, at least 2 hours. Refrigerate any remaining pie immediately. **8 servings; 520 calories per serving.**

Do-ahead Tip: After baking, refrigerate pie 2 hours. Freeze uncovered at least 3 hours. Wrap and return to freezer. Store no longer than 1 month. Unwrap pie and thaw in refrigerator 20 minutes.

Brandy-Pecan Pie: Decrease corn syrup to ¾ cup and beat in ¼ cup brandy.

Chocolate-Pecan Pie: Melt 2 squares (1 ounce each) unsweetened chocolate with the margarine.

Peanut-Chocolate Chip Pie: Substitute 1 cup salted peanuts for the pecans. After baking, sprinkle with ½ cup semisweet chocolate chips. Let stand 30 minutes before refrigerating.

CHOCOLATE BROWNIE PIE

	Pastry for 9-inch One-Crust Pie (page 135)
2	tablespoons margarine or butter
2	squares (1 ounce each) unsweetened chocolate
½	cup sugar
¾	cup dark corn syrup
3	eggs
1	cup pecan halves

Heat oven to 375°. Prepare pastry. Heat margarine and chocolate over low heat until melted; cool. Beat chocolate mixture, sugar, corn syrup and eggs with hand beater. Stir in pecans. Pour into pastry-lined pie plate.

Bake just until set, 40 to 50 minutes. Refrigerate until chilled, at least 2 hours. Serve with Sweetened Whipped Cream (page 274) if desired. Refrigerate any remaining pie immediately. **8 servings; 475 calories per serving.**

CUSTARD PIE

Pastry for 9-inch One-Crust Pie (page 135)
4 eggs
⅔ cup sugar
2⅔ cups milk
1 teaspoon vanilla
½ teaspoon salt
¼ teaspoon ground nutmeg

Heat oven to 450°. Prepare pastry. Beat eggs slightly with hand beater; beat in remaining ingredients. Place pastry-lined pie plate on oven rack; pour in filling. Bake 20 minutes.

Reduce oven temperature to 350°. Bake until knife inserted halfway between center and edge comes out clean, 15 to 20 minutes longer. Refrigerate any remaining pie immediately. **8 servings; 295 calories per serving.**

LEMON COCONUT PIE

Pastry for 8-inch One-Crust Pie (page 135)
1½ cups sugar
½ cup shredded coconut
¼ cup margarine or butter, melted
1 tablespoon grated lemon peel
¼ cup lemon juice
¼ cup milk
2 tablespoons all-purpose flour
¼ teaspoon salt
4 eggs
1 cup Sweetened Whipped Cream (page 274)

Heat oven to 375°. Prepare pastry. Beat remaining ingredients except Sweetened Whipped Cream until smooth. Pour into pastry-lined pie plate. Bake until filling is golden brown and set, 40 to 50 minutes. Refrigerate until cool, at least 2 hours. Serve with whipped cream. Refrigerate any remaining pie immediately. **6 servings; 660 calories per serving.**

LEMON CHIFFON PIE

9-inch Baked Pie Shell (pages 135 and 136)
4 egg yolks, slightly beaten
½ cup sugar
⅔ cup water
⅓ cup lemon juice
1 envelope unflavored gelatin
1 tablespoon grated lemon peel
4 egg whites
½ teaspoon cream of tartar
½ cup sugar

Bake pie shell. Mix egg yolks, ½ cup sugar, the water, lemon juice and gelatin in saucepan. Heat just to boiling over medium heat, stirring constantly; remove from heat. Stir in lemon peel. Place pan in bowl of ice and water or refrigerate, stirring occasionally, until mixture mounds when dropped from a spoon.

Beat egg whites and cream of tartar until foamy. Beat in ½ cup sugar, 1 tablespoon at a time; continue beating until stiff and glossy. Do not underbeat. Fold in lemon mixture; mound into pie shell. Refrigerate until set, at least 3 hours. Serve with Sweetened Whipped Cream (page 274) if desired. Refrigerate any remaining pie immediately. **8 servings;** 275 calories per serving.

Lime Chiffon Pie: Substitute lime juice and grated lime peel for the lemon juice and lemon peel.

Orange Chiffon Pie: Substitute 1 cup orange juice for the water and lemon juice and grated orange peel for the lemon peel.

CHOCOLATE ANGEL PIE

Meringue Pie Shell (page 155)
1 bar (4 ounces) sweet cooking chocolate
3 tablespoons hot water
1 teaspoon vanilla
1 cup chilled whipping cream

Bake pie shell. Heat chocolate and hot water over low heat, stirring constantly, until chocolate is melted. Cool to room temperature. Stir in vanilla.

Beat whipping cream in chilled 1½-quart bowl until stiff. Fold in chocolate mixture; spoon into pie shell. Refrigerate at least 12 hours. Garnish with fresh fruit, whipped cream, chopped nuts or grated chocolate if desired. **8 servings; 240 calories per serving.**

COFFEE CORDIAL PIE

Chocolate Cookie Crust or Graham Cracker Crust (page 138)

½	cup water
1	tablespoon instant coffee
32	large jet-puffed marshmallows
¼	cup coffee liqueur
3	tablespoons Irish whiskey
1½	cups chilled whipping cream

Bake pie crust. Heat water, instant coffee (dry) and marshmallows over low heat, stirring constantly, just until marshmallows are melted. Refrigerate, stirring occasionally, until mixture mounds slightly when dropped from a spoon, about 20 minutes. (If mixture becomes too thick, place pan in bowl of warm water; stir mixture until of proper consistency.) Gradually stir in liqueur and whiskey.

Beat whipping cream in chilled 2½-quart bowl until stiff. Fold marshmallow mixture into whipped cream. Pour into crust; sprinkle with grated semisweet chocolate if desired. Refrigerate until set, at least 4 hours. **8 servings; 410 calories per serving.**

Alexander Pie: Substitute ½ cup milk for the water and instant coffee, dark crème de cacao for the coffee liqueur and brandy for the whiskey.

Cherry Cordial Pie: Substitute ½ cup milk for the water and instant coffee and ½ cup kirsch for the coffee liqueur and whiskey. Fold few drops red food color into marshmallow-whipped cream mixture if desired.

Grasshopper Pie: Substitute ½ cup milk for the water and instant coffee, crème de menthe for the coffee liqueur and white crème de cacao for the whiskey. Fold few drops green food color into marshmallow-whipped cream mixture if desired.

FROZEN LEMON PIE

Graham Cracker Crust (page 138)
3 eggs, separated
½ teaspoon cream of tartar
½ cup sugar
1 cup chilled whipping cream
2 teaspoons grated lemon peel
¼ cup lemon juice

Prepare pie crust, reserving 3 tablespoons crumbs. Bake pie crust. Beat egg whites and cream of tartar in 2½-quart bowl until foamy. Beat in sugar, 1 tablespoon at a time; continue beating until stiff and glossy. Beat egg yolks until thick and lemon colored; fold into meringue.

Beat whipping cream in chilled bowl until stiff. Fold whipped cream, lemon peel and juice into egg mixture. Pour into crust; sprinkle with reserved crumbs. Freeze until firm, about 6 hours. Remove from freezer 15 minutes before serving. **8 servings**; 370 calories per serving.

FROZEN PUMPKIN PIE

Gingersnap Crust (page 138)
1 cup canned pumpkin
¼ cup packed brown sugar
1 teaspoon aromatic bitters
½ teaspoon salt
½ teaspoon ground ginger
¼ teaspoon ground nutmeg
¼ teaspoon ground cinnamon
1 container (4½ ounces) frozen whipped topping, thawed
1 pint butter pecan ice cream, softened
2 tablespoons chopped pecans

Bake crust. Mix pumpkin, brown sugar, bitters, salt, ginger, nutmeg and cinnamon. Fold in whipped topping. Spread ice cream in crust. Swirl pumpkin over ice cream. Freeze uncovered at least 3 hours. Remove from freezer 15 minutes before serving. Sprinkle with pecans. **8 servings**; 295 calories per serving.

COOKIES
CANDY

COOKIES

ABOUT COOKIE MAKING

BAKING BASICS
Cookie sheets: Use a shiny cookie sheet at least 2 inches narrower and shorter than the oven. The sheet may be open on one to three sides. If a sheet with a nonstick coating is used, watch carefully—cookies may brown quickly. Grease the cookie sheet only if specified in the recipe. Always place dough on a cool cookie sheet; dough spreads on a hot one.

The "test" cookie: Bake one cookie. If it spreads more than desired, add 1 to 2 tablespoons flour to the dough. If it's too dry, add 1 to 2 tablespoons milk.

Baking: To assure uniform baking, make each cookie the same size and thickness. Bake one sheet of cookies at a time on the center rack. Check at the end of the minimum baking time—just one minute can make a difference. Unless the recipe states otherwise, remove cookies immediately from the sheet with a wide spatula and place on a wire rack to cool.

Storing: Store crisp, thin cookies in a container with a loose-fitting cover. If they soften, recrisp by placing in a 300° oven for 3 to 5 minutes. Store soft cookies in a tightly covered container. A piece of bread or apple in the container will help keep them soft.

DROP COOKIES
■ Use two teaspoons (not measuring spoons) to drop dough on cookie sheet.

■ If edges are dark and crusty, cookies were overbaked or cookie sheet was too large for oven. If center of cookie is doughy, it was underbaked.

■ Excess spreading may be caused by dough being too warm, cookie sheet too hot or oven temperature incorrect. Chilling dough before dropping onto sheet will help prevent this.

BAR COOKIES
■ Use the size pan specified in the recipe. Cookies made in a larger pan will be dry and overbaked; in a smaller pan, underbaked.

■ Cut into bars, squares or triangles when cool unless recipe specifies cutting while warm.

MOLDED COOKIES
■ Rich, soft dough must be chilled before shaping. Work with small amounts, keeping remaining dough refrigerated. If dough is still too soft, mix in 1 to 2 tablespoons flour.

■ If dough is too dry and crumbly, work in 1 to 2 tablespoons milk, water or softened margarine.

■ Roll dough between palms of hands. For even browning, be sure the surface of the dough is smooth. If the recipe recommends flattening the cookies, use the bottom of a glass dipped in flour, or press down with a fork.

■ Take time and care to mold fancy shapes (crescents, candy canes, wreaths, bells) so that cookies are uniform in shape and size.

REFRIGERATOR COOKIES
■ Shape dough firmly into a long, smooth roll of the diameter specified in the recipe.

■ Wrap rolled dough in waxed paper, plastic wrap or aluminum foil, twisting ends.

■ Chill rolled dough until firm enough to slice easily. Use a thin, sharp knife to slice dough.

ROLLED COOKIES
■ To prevent dough from sticking, rub flour into cloth-covered rolling pin and pastry cloth.

■ Roll only part of the chilled dough at a time and keep the remainder refrigerated.

- To ensure even baking, roll dough evenly to maintain uniform thickness.

- Dip cookie cutter into flour; shake off excess.

PRESSED COOKIES
- Use room-temperature margarine, butter or shortening.

- Test dough for consistency before adding all the flour. Put a small amount of dough in cookie press; squeeze out. Dough should be soft and pliable, but not crumbly.

- Chill dough only if specified in the recipe.

- If dough seems too stiff, add 1 egg yolk; if too soft, add 1 to 2 tablespoons flour.

- Be sure cookie sheet is cool. Hold press so that it rests on cookie sheet (unless using star or bar plate).

- Raise press from cookie sheet after enough dough has been released to form a cookie.

CHOCOLATE CHIP COOKIES

    1   cup margarine or butter, softened
    ¾   cup granulated sugar
    ¾   cup packed brown sugar
    1   egg
    2¼ cups all-purpose flour*
    1   teaspoon baking soda
    ½   teaspoon salt
    1   cup coarsely chopped nuts
    1   package (12 ounces) semisweet chocolate chips

Heat oven to 375°. Mix margarine, sugars and egg. Stir in flour, baking soda and salt (dough will be stiff). Stir in nuts and chocolate chips. Drop dough by rounded teaspoonfuls about 2 inches apart onto ungreased cookie sheet. Bake until light brown, 8 to 10 minutes. (Centers will be soft.) Cool slightly; remove from cookie sheet.   **About 6 dozen cookies;** 90 calories per cookie.

*If using self-rising flour, omit baking soda and salt.

Chocolate Chip Bars: Press dough in ungreased rectangular pan, 13 × 9 × 2 inches. Bake until golden brown, about 25 minutes; cool. Cut into bars, about 3 × 1½ inches. **24 bars.**

Crisp Chocolate Chip Cookies: Decrease flour to 2 cups. **About 5 dozen cookies.**

Jumbo Chocolate Chip Cookies: Drop dough by ¼ cupfuls about 3 inches apart onto ungreased cookie sheet. Bake until edges are set, 12 to 15 minutes. Cool completely; remove from cookie sheet. **About 1½ dozen cookies.**

CANDY COOKIES

½ cup granulated sugar
½ cup packed brown sugar
⅓ cup margarine or butter, softened
⅓ cup shortening
1 teaspoon vanilla
1 egg
1½ cups all-purpose flour*
½ teaspoon baking soda
½ teaspoon salt
1 package (8 ounces) candy-coated chocolate candies

Heat oven to 375°. Mix sugars, margarine, shortening, vanilla and egg. Stir in remaining ingredients. Drop dough by heaping teaspoonfuls about 2 inches apart onto ungreased cookie sheet. Bake until light brown, 8 to 10 minutes. (Centers will be soft.) Cool slightly; remove from cookie sheet. **About 3 dozen cookies;** 105 calories per cookie.

Almond Brickle Cookies: Substitute 1 package (6 ounces) almond brickle chips for the candy-coated chocolate candies.

Candy Bars: Press dough in ungreased rectangular pan, 13 × 9 × 2 inches. Bake until golden brown, about 20 minutes; cool. Cut into bars, about 3 × 1½ inches. **24 bars.**

*If using self-rising flour, omit baking soda and salt.

OATMEAL COOKIES

½ cup granulated sugar
½ cup packed brown sugar
¼ cup margarine or butter, softened
¼ cup shortening
½ teaspoon baking soda
½ teaspoon ground cinnamon
½ teaspoon vanilla
¼ teaspoon baking powder
¼ teaspoon salt
1 egg
1½ cups quick-cooking oats
1 cup all-purpose flour*
1 cup raisins or chopped nuts, if desired

Heat oven to 375°. Mix all ingredients except oats, flour and raisins. Stir in oats, flour and raisins. Drop dough by rounded teaspoonfuls about 2 inches apart onto ungreased cookie sheet. Bake until light brown, about 10 minutes. Immediately remove from cookie sheet. **About 2 dozen cookies; 110 calories per cookie.**

Oatmeal Crispies: Omit cinnamon and raisins.

Oatmeal Squares: Press dough in ungreased square pan, 8×8×2 inches. Bake until light brown, about 25 minutes. Cut into about 2-inch squares while warm. **16 squares.**

*If using self-rising flour, omit baking soda, baking powder and salt.

CHOCOLATE-MINT COOKIES

 1   cup sugar
 ½   cup margarine or butter, softened
 1   teaspoon vanilla
 1   egg
 2   squares (1 ounce each) unsweetened chocolate, melted
     and cooled
 1   cup all-purpose flour*
 ½   teaspoon salt
     Peppermint Frosting (below)
 ¼   cup margarine or butter
 2   tablespoons corn syrup
 1   package (6 ounces) semisweet chocolate chips

Heat oven to 375°. Mix sugar, ½ cup margarine, the vanilla, egg and unsweetened chocolate. Stir in flour and salt. Drop dough by rounded teaspoonfuls about 2 inches apart onto ungreased cookie sheet. Flatten each cookie with greased bottom of glass dipped in sugar. Bake until set, about 8 minutes. Cool slightly; remove from cookie sheet. Cool cookies completely.

Spread Peppermint Frosting over each cookie to within ¼ inch of edge. Heat ¼ cup margarine, the corn syrup and chocolate chips over low heat, stirring constantly, until margarine and chocolate are melted. Drizzle mixture over each cookie.   **About 3 dozen cookies; 155 calories per cookie.**

Peppermint Frosting

2½   cups powdered sugar
 ¼   cup margarine or butter, softened
 3   tablespoons milk
 ½   teaspoon peppermint extract

Mix all ingredients until smooth and of spreading consistency.

*If using self-rising flour, omit salt.

CHOCOLATE DROP COOKIES

    1   cup sugar
    ½   cup margarine or butter, softened
    ⅓   cup buttermilk or water
    1   teaspoon vanilla
    1   egg
    2   squares (1 ounce each) unsweetened chocolate, melted
         and cooled
    1¾   cups all-purpose flour*
    1   cup chopped nuts, if desired
    ½   teaspoon baking soda
    ½   teaspoon salt
         Chocolate Frosting (below)

Heat oven to 400°. Mix sugar, margarine, buttermilk, vanilla, egg and chocolate. Stir in flour, nuts, baking soda and salt.

Drop dough by rounded teaspoonsful about 2 inches apart onto ungreased cookie sheet. Bake until almost no indentation remains when touched, 8 to 10 minutes. Immediately remove from cookie sheet; cool. Frost with Chocolate Frosting.   **About 4½ dozen cookies**; 95 calories per cookie.

Chocolate Frosting

    2   squares (1 ounce each) unsweetened chocolate
    2   tablespoons margarine or butter
    3   tablespoons water
         About 2 cups powdered sugar

Heat chocolate and margarine over low heat until melted; remove from heat. Stir in water and powdered sugar until smooth and of spreading consistency.

Chocolate-Cherry Drop Cookies: Omit nuts. Stir in 2 cups cut-up candied or maraschino cherries.

Cocoa Drop Cookies: Increase margarine to ⅔ cup; omit chocolate and stir in ½ cup cocoa.

Double Chocolate Drops: Stir in 1 package (6 ounces) semisweet chocolate chips.

*If using self-rising flour, omit baking soda and salt.

ZUCCHINI COOKIES

½ cup granulated sugar
½ cup packed brown sugar
½ cup margarine or butter, softened
2 eggs
2½ cups all-purpose flour*
1½ cups shredded zucchini (about 1 medium)
½ cup chopped nuts
1 teaspoon grated lemon peel
1 tablespoon lemon juice
2 teaspoons baking powder
1 teaspoon ground nutmeg
¼ teaspoon salt
Lemon Frosting (below)

Heat oven to 375°. Mix sugars, margarine and eggs. Stir in remaining ingredients except Lemon Frosting. Drop dough by rounded teaspoonfuls about 2 inches apart onto ungreased cookie sheet. Bake until almost no indentation remains when touched, 8 to 10 minutes; cool. Frost with Lemon Frosting. **About 5 dozen cookies; 85 calories per cookie.**

Lemon Frosting

3 cups powdered sugar
¼ cup margarine or butter, softened
1 teaspoon grated lemon peel
1 tablespoon lemon juice
1 tablespoon water

Mix powdered sugar, margarine and lemon peel. Beat in lemon juice and water. If necessary, stir in additional water, 1 teaspoon at a time, until of spreading consistency.

Carrot Cookies: Substitute shredded carrots for the zucchini.

*If using self-rising flour, omit baking powder and salt.

CREAM CHEESE COOKIES

½ cup margarine or butter, softened
2 packages (3 ounces each) cream cheese, softened
2¾ cups all-purpose flour*
1½ cups packed brown sugar
1 cup chopped pecans
2 tablespoons milk
1 teaspoon salt
1 teaspoon vanilla
½ teaspoon baking soda
2 eggs

Heat oven to 375°. Mix margarine and cream cheese. Stir in remaining ingredients. Drop dough by rounded teaspoonfuls about 1 inch apart onto ungreased cookie sheet. Bake until almost no indentation remains when touched, 8 to 10 minutes. Immediately remove from cookie sheet; cool. Frost with Caramel Frosting (page 130) if desired. **About 6 dozen cookies;** 70 calories per cookie.

Applesauce Cookies: Omit cream cheese and milk. Stir in ¾ cup applesauce, 1 teaspoon ground cinnamon and ¼ teaspoon ground cloves.

Cherry-Cream Cheese Cookies: Substitute ½ cup chopped maraschino cherries for half of the pecans. Top each cookie with pecan or maraschino cherry half before baking if desired.

COCONUT MACAROONS

3 egg whites
¼ teaspoon cream of tartar
⅛ teaspoon salt
¾ cup sugar
¼ teaspoon almond extract
3 drops red or green food color
2 cups flaked coconut
12 candied cherries, each cut into fourths

*If using self-rising flour, omit salt and baking soda.

Beat egg whites, cream of tartar and salt in 1½-quart bowl until foamy. Beat in sugar, 1 tablespoon at a time; continue beating until stiff and glossy. Do not underbeat. Pour into 2½-quart bowl. Fold in almond extract, food color and coconut.

Heat oven to 300°. Drop mixture by teaspoonfuls about 1 inch apart onto aluminum foil-covered cookie sheet. Place a cherry piece on each cookie. Bake just until edges are light brown, 20 to 25 minutes. Cool 10 minutes; remove from foil.   **3½ to 4 dozen cookies;** 45 calories per cookie.

Do-ahead Tip: Store cookies in airtight container no longer than 2 weeks or freeze no longer than 1 month.

Mint Macaroons: Substitute ¼ teaspoon peppermint extract for the almond extract. After beating, fold in 1 package (6 ounces) semisweet chocolate chips, reserving 3½ to 4 dozen chocolate chips. Substitute reserved chips for the cherry pieces.

COCONUT-MACADAMIA COOKIES

1	cup margarine or butter, softened
1	cup packed brown sugar
½	cup granulated sugar
1	egg
2¼	cups all-purpose flour*
1	teaspoon baking soda
1	cup flaked coconut
1	jar (3½ ounces) macadamia nuts, coarsely chopped

Heat oven to 375°. Mix margarine, sugars and egg. Stir in flour and baking soda (dough will be stiff). Stir in coconut and nuts. Drop dough by heaping teaspoonfuls about 2 inches apart onto ungreased cookie sheet. Bake until light brown, 8 to 10 minutes. (Centers will be soft.) Cool slightly; remove from cookie sheet.   **About 4½ dozen cookies;** 85 calories per cookie.

Coconut-Macadamia Bars: Press dough in ungreased rectangular pan, 13×9×2 inches. Bake until golden brown, about 25 minutes; cool. Cut into bars, about 3×1½ inches.   **24 bars.**

*If using self-rising flour, omit baking soda.

DELUXE BROWNIES

⅔ cup margarine or butter
5 squares (1 ounce each) unsweetened chocolate, cut into
     pieces
1¾ cups sugar
2 teaspoons vanilla
3 eggs
1 cup all-purpose flour*
1 cup chopped nuts

Heat oven to 350°. Heat margarine and chocolate over low heat, stirring constantly, until melted; cool slightly. Beat sugar, vanilla and eggs on high speed 5 minutes. Beat in chocolate mixture on low speed. Beat in flour just until blended. Stir in nuts. Spread in greased square pan, 9 × 9 × 2 inches.

Bake just until brownies begin to pull away from sides of pan, 40 to 45 minutes; cool. Cut into about 2-inch squares.   **16 brownies**; 300 calories per brownie.

COCOA BROWNIES

1 cup sugar
½ cup margarine or butter, softened
1 teaspoon vanilla
2 eggs
⅔ cup all-purpose flour**
½ cup cocoa
½ cup chopped walnuts
½ teaspoon baking powder
½ teaspoon salt

Heat oven to 350°. Mix sugar, margarine, vanilla and eggs. Stir in remaining ingredients. Spread in greased square pan, 8 × 8 × 2 inches.

*Do not use self-rising flour in this recipe.
**If using self-rising flour, omit baking powder and salt.

Bake until wooden pick inserted in center comes out clean, 25 to 30 minutes; cool. Frost with Fudge Frosting (page 131) if desired. Cut into about 2-inch squares. **16 brownies; 160 calories per brownie.**

GRASSHOPPER BARS

	Cocoa Brownies (page 175)
3	cups powdered sugar
⅓	cup margarine or butter, softened
2	tablespoons green crème de menthe
2	tablespoons white crème de cacao
1½	squares (1½ ounces) unsweetened chocolate

Prepare Cocoa Brownies as directed; cool. Mix remaining ingredients except chocolate; spread over brownies. Refrigerate 15 minutes.

Heat chocolate over low heat until melted; spread evenly over powdered sugar mixture. Refrigerate at least 3 hours. Cut into bars, about 1½ × 1 inch. **36 bars; 140 calories per bar.**

Brandy Alexander Bars: Substitute 2 tablespoons brandy for the crème de menthe.

Mint Bars: Substitute ¼ cup milk for the crème de menthe and crème de cacao. Stir in ½ teaspoon peppermint, spearmint or wintergreen extract and 6 drops green food color.

ALMOND BROWNIES

⅔	cup shortening
4	squares (1 ounce each) unsweetened chocolate
2	cups sugar
1¼	cups all-purpose flour*
1	cup chopped almonds
1	cup chopped almond paste
1	teaspoon baking powder
1	teaspoon salt
4	eggs

*If using self-rising flour, omit baking powder and salt.

Heat oven to 350°. Heat shortening and chocolate in 3-quart saucepan over low heat until melted; remove from heat. Stir in remaining ingredients. Spread in greased rectangular pan, 13 × 9 × 2 inches.

Bake until brownies begin to pull away from sides of pan, about 30 minutes. Do not overbake. Cool slightly. Cut into bars, about 2 × 1½ inches. **36 brownies;** 195 calories per brownie.

BUTTERSCOTCH BROWNIES

¼	cup shortening
1	cup packed brown sugar
1	teaspoon vanilla
1	egg
¾	cup all-purpose flour*
½	cup chopped nuts
1	teaspoon baking powder
½	teaspoon salt

Heat oven to 350°. Heat shortening in 1½-quart saucepan over low heat until melted; remove from heat. Mix in brown sugar, vanilla and egg. Stir in remaining ingredients. Spread in greased square pan, 8 × 8 × 2 inches. Bake 25 minutes. Cut into about 2-inch squares while warm. **16 brownies;** 135 calories per brownie.

Brazil Nut Bars: Substitute ¾ cup finely chopped Brazil nuts for the nuts.

Coconut-Butterscotch Brownies: Decrease vanilla to ½ teaspoon. Substitute flaked coconut for the nuts.

Date-Butterscotch Brownies: Decrease vanilla to ½ teaspoon; stir in ½ cup snipped dates with the remaining ingredients.

EASY PRALINE BARS

24	graham cracker squares
½	cup packed brown sugar
½	cup margarine or butter
½	teaspoon vanilla
½	cup chopped pecans

*If using self-rising flour, omit baking powder and salt.

Heat oven to 350°. Arrange crackers in single layer in ungreased jelly roll pan, 15½ × 10½ × 1 inch. Heat brown sugar and margarine to boiling. Boil and stir 1 minute; remove from heat. Stir in vanilla. Pour over crackers; spread evenly. Sprinkle with pecans. Bake until bubbly, 8 to 10 minutes; cool slightly. Cut into bars, about 2¼ × 1¼ inches. **48 bars; 50 calories per bar.**

TOFFEE BARS

  1   **cup packed brown sugar**
  1   **cup margarine or butter, softened**
  1   **teaspoon vanilla**
  1   **egg yolk**
  2   **cups all-purpose flour***
  ¼   **teaspoon salt**
  1   **bar (4 ounces) milk chocolate candy**
  ½   **cup chopped nuts**

Heat oven to 350°. Mix brown sugar, margarine, vanilla and egg yolk. Stir in flour and salt. Press in greased rectangular pan, 13 × 9 × 2 inches.

Bake until very light brown, 25 to 30 minutes (crust will be soft). Immediately place separated pieces of chocolate candy on crust. Let stand until soft; spread evenly. Sprinkle with nuts. Cut into bars, about 2 × 1½ inches, while warm. **32 bars; 140 calories per bar.**

*If using self-rising flour, omit salt.

CASHEW TRIANGLES

½ cup margarine or butter, softened
¼ cup granulated sugar
¼ cup packed brown sugar
½ teaspoon vanilla
1 egg, separated
1 cup all-purpose flour*
⅛ teaspoon salt
1 teaspoon water
1 cup chopped salted cashew nuts, macadamia nuts or
    toasted almonds
1 square (1 ounce) unsweetened chocolate, melted

Heat oven to 350°. Mix margarine, sugars, vanilla and egg yolk. Stir in flour and salt. Press dough in ungreased rectangular pan, 13×9×2 inches, with floured hands. Beat egg white and water; brush over dough. Sprinkle with cashew nuts; press lightly. Bake until light brown, about 25 minutes; cool 10 minutes. Cut into about 3-inch squares; cut each square diagonally into halves. Immediately remove from pan; cool completely.

Drizzle with chocolate. Let stand until chocolate is set, about 2 hours.   **24 triangles; 115 calories per triangle.**

HAZELNUT BARS

¼ cup powdered sugar
¼ cup margarine or butter, softened
1 egg yolk
½ cup all-purpose flour**
½ cup currant or raspberry jelly, softened
    Hazelnut Topping (page 180)

Heat oven to 350°. Mix powdered sugar, margarine and egg yolk. Mix in flour. Press in bottom of ungreased square pan, 8×8×2 or 9×9×2 inches.

*If using self-rising flour, omit salt.
**Do not use self-rising flour in this recipe.

Bake 10 minutes. Spread with jelly, then with Hazelnut Topping. Bake until topping is golden brown, about 20 minutes longer; cool slightly. Cut into bars, about 2 × 1 inch. (If topping sticks to knife, occasionally dip knife into hot water.) **32 bars; 60 calories per bar.**

Hazelnut Topping
- 1   egg white
- ¼   teaspoon ground cinnamon
- ¼   cup sugar
- ½   cup finely chopped hazelnuts

Beat egg white until foamy; add cinnamon. Beat in sugar, 1 tablespoon at a time; continue beating until stiff and glossy. Fold in hazelnuts.

PEANUT BUTTER SQUARES

- ½   cup granulated sugar
- ½   cup packed brown sugar
- ½   cup margarine or butter, softened
- ⅓   cup crunchy peanut butter
- 1   egg
- 1   cup all-purpose flour*
- 1   cup regular oats
- ½   teaspoon baking soda
- ¼   teaspoon salt
     Peanut Butter Frosting (page 181)
- 3   tablespoons cocoa
- 1   tablespoon milk

Heat oven to 350°. Mix sugars, margarine, peanut butter and egg. Stir in flour, oats, baking soda and salt. Spread in greased rectangular pan, 13 × 9 × 2 inches. Bake until golden brown, 17 to 22 minutes; cool.

Prepare Peanut Butter Frosting; reserve ⅓ cup. Stir cocoa and milk into remaining frosting until smooth. If necessary, stir in additional milk until of spreading consistency. Frost with cocoa frosting. Drop Peanut Butter Frosting by teaspoonfuls onto cocoa frosting; swirl for marbled effect. Cut into about 1½-inch squares. **48 squares; 85 calories per square.**

*If using self-rising flour, omit baking soda and salt.

Peanut Butter Frosting
Mix 1½ cups powdered sugar, ¼ cup crunchy peanut butter
and 2 tablespoons milk. Stir in additional milk, ½ teaspoon at
a time, until of spreading consistency.

LEMON SQUARES

1	cup all-purpose flour*
½	cup margarine or butter, softened
¼	cup powdered sugar
2	eggs
1	cup granulated sugar
2	teaspoons grated lemon peel, if desired
2	tablespoons lemon juice
½	teaspoon baking powder
¼	teaspoon salt

Heat oven to 350°. Mix flour, margarine and powdered sugar.
Press in ungreased square pan, 8×8×2 or 9×9×2 inches,
building up ½-inch edges. Bake 20 minutes. Beat remaining
ingredients until light and fluffy, about 3 minutes. Pour over
hot crust. Bake until no indentation remains when touched
lightly in center, about 25 minutes; cool. Cut into about
1½-inch squares. **25 squares; 95 calories per square.**

   Lemon-Coconut Squares: Stir ½ cup flaked coconut into
egg mixture.

CARAMEL-OAT BARS

2	cups quick-cooking or regular oats
½	cup packed brown sugar
½	cup margarine or butter, melted
¼	cup dark corn syrup
1	teaspoon vanilla
½	teaspoon salt
1	package (6 ounces) semisweet chocolate chips

Heat oven to 400°. Mix all ingredients except chocolate chips.
Spread in greased square pan, 9×9×2 inches.

*If using self-rising flour, omit baking powder and salt.

Bake until bubbly, about 8 minutes. Immediately sprinkle with chocolate chips. Let stand until soft; spread evenly. Sprinkle with chopped nuts if desired. Refrigerate at least 1 hour. Cut into bars, about 2 × 1 inch. Store in refrigerator. **36 bars**; 85 calories per bar.

CARAMEL-APPLE BARS

1	cup packed brown sugar
½	cup margarine or butter, softened
¼	cup shortening
1¾	cups all-purpose flour*
1½	cups quick-cooking oats
1	teaspoon salt
½	teaspoon baking soda
4½	cups coarsely chopped pared tart apples (about 3 medium)
3	tablespoons all-purpose flour
1	package (14 ounces) caramel candies

Heat oven to 400°. Mix brown sugar, margarine and shortening. Stir in 1¾ cups flour, the oats, salt and baking soda. Remove 2 cups of the mixture; reserve. Press remaining mixture in ungreased rectangular pan, 13 × 9 × 2 inches.

Toss apples and 3 tablespoons flour; spread over mixture in pan. Heat candies over low heat, stirring occasionally, until melted; pour evenly over apples. Top with reserved oat mixture; press lightly.

Bake until golden brown and apples are tender, 25 to 30 minutes. Cut into bars, about 2 × 1½ inches, while warm. Refrigerate any remaining bars. **36 bars**; 135 calories per bar.

Date Bars: Heat 1 pound dates, cut up (about 3 cups), 1½ cups water and ¼ cup sugar over low heat, stirring constantly, until thickened, about 10 minutes; cool. Substitute date mixture for the apples, 3 tablespoons flour and the caramel candies.

Mincemeat Bars: Mix 1 jar (28 ounces) prepared mincemeat and ½ cup chopped walnuts or almonds. Substitute mincemeat mixture for the apples, 3 tablespoons flour and the caramel candies.

*If using self-rising flour, omit salt and baking soda.

FUDGY OATMEAL BARS

- 2 cups packed brown sugar
- 1 cup margarine or butter, softened
- 1 teaspoon vanilla
- 2 eggs
- 2½ cups all-purpose flour*
- 1 teaspoon baking soda
- ½ teaspoon salt
- 3 cups quick-cooking or regular oats
- 2 tablespoons margarine or butter
- 1 can (14 ounces) sweetened condensed milk
- 1 package (12 ounces) semisweet chocolate chips
- 1 cup chopped nuts
- 1 teaspoon vanilla
- ½ teaspoon salt

Heat oven to 350°. Mix brown sugar, 1 cup margarine, 1 teaspoon vanilla and the eggs. Stir in flour, baking soda and ½ teaspoon salt; stir in oats. Reserve ⅓ of the oat mixture. Press remaining oat mixture in greased jelly roll pan, 15½ × 10½ × 1 inch.

Heat 2 tablespoons margarine, the milk and chocolate chips over low heat, stirring constantly, until chocolate is melted; remove from heat. Stir in nuts, 1 teaspoon vanilla and ½ teaspoon salt. Spread over oat mixture in pan. Drop reserved oat mixture by rounded teaspoonfuls onto chocolate mixture.

Bake until golden brown, 25 to 30 minutes. Cut into bars, about 2 × 1 inch, while warm. **70 bars; 135 calories per bar.**

*If using self-rising flour, omit baking soda and ½ teaspoon salt.

PEANUT BUTTER COOKIES

½	cup granulated sugar
½	cup packed brown sugar
½	cup peanut butter
¼	cup shortening
¼	cup margarine or butter, softened
1	egg
1¼	cups all-purpose flour*
¾	teaspoon baking soda
½	teaspoon baking powder
¼	teaspoon salt

Mix sugars, peanut butter, shortening, margarine and egg. Stir in remaining ingredients. Cover and refrigerate at least 3 hours.

Heat oven to 375°. Shape dough into 1¼-inch balls. Place about 3 inches apart on ungreased cookie sheet. Flatten in crisscross pattern with fork dipped in flour. Bake until light brown, 9 to 10 minutes. Cool 2 minutes; remove from cookie sheet. **About 3 dozen cookies; 85 calories per cookie.**

Peanut Butter and Jelly Cookies: Shape dough into 1-inch balls. Roll balls in ½ cup finely chopped peanuts. Place about 3 inches apart on lightly greased cookie sheet; press thumb in center of each. Bake until set but not hard, 10 to 12 minutes. Spoon small amount jelly or jam into thumbprint. **About 3½ dozen cookies.**

Peanut Butter Fingers: Refrigerate dough 1 hour. Place dough in cookie press with star plate; shape into 2½-inch fingers on ungreased cookie sheet. Bake 8 to 10 minutes. When cool, dip one end of each cookie into melted plain milk chocolate bars, then into ¾ cup finely chopped salted peanuts. **About 8 dozen cookies.**

*If using self-rising flour, omit baking soda, baking powder and salt.

CHOCOLATE CRINKLES

- 2 cups granulated sugar
- ½ cup vegetable oil
- 2 teaspoons vanilla
- 4 squares (1 ounce each) unsweetened chocolate, melted and cooled
- 4 eggs
- 2 cups all-purpose flour*
- 2 teaspoons baking powder
- ½ teaspoon salt
- 1 cup powdered sugar

Mix granulated sugar, oil, vanilla and chocolate. Mix in eggs, one at a time. Stir in flour, baking powder and salt. Cover and refrigerate at least 3 hours.

Heat oven to 350°. Drop dough by teaspoonfuls into powdered sugar; roll around to coat. Shape into balls. Place about 2 inches apart on greased cookie sheet. Bake until almost no indentation remains when touched, 10 to 12 minutes.   **About 6 dozen cookies**; 70 calories per cookie.

GINGERSNAPS

- 1 cup packed brown sugar
- ¾ cup shortening
- ¼ cup molasses
- 1 egg
- 2¼ cups all-purpose flour**
- 2 teaspoons baking soda
- 1 teaspoon ground cinnamon
- 1 teaspoon ground ginger
- ½ teaspoon ground cloves
- ¼ teaspoon salt
  Granulated sugar

Mix brown sugar, shortening, molasses and egg. Stir in flour, baking soda, cinnamon, ginger, cloves and salt. Cover and refrigerate at least 1 hour.

*If using self-rising flour, omit baking powder and salt.
**If using self-rising flour, decrease baking soda to 1 teaspoon and omit salt.

Heat oven to 375°. Shape dough by rounded teaspoonfuls into balls. Dip tops in granulated sugar. Place balls, sugared sides up, about 3 inches apart on lightly greased cookie sheet. Bake cookies just until set, 10 to 12 minutes. Immediately remove from cookie sheet.   **About 4 dozen cookies; 85 calories per cookie.**

PRETZEL COOKIES

>   1   **cup sugar**
>   1   **cup margarine or butter, softened**
> ½   **cup milk**
>   1   **teaspoon vanilla**
>   1   **teaspoon almond extract**
>   1   **egg**
> 3½ **cups all-purpose flour***
>   1   **teaspoon baking powder**
> ¼   **teaspoon salt**
>   **Colored sugar**

Mix 1 cup sugar, the margarine, milk, vanilla, almond extract and egg. Stir in flour, baking powder and salt. Cover and refrigerate at least 4 hours.

Heat oven to 375°. Divide dough into 4 equal parts. Divide one part into 12 equal pieces (keep remaining dough refrigerated). Sprinkle about 1 teaspoon colored sugar on board. Roll each piece of dough on sugared board into pencil-like strip, about 10 inches long. Twist into pretzel shape on ungreased cookie sheet. Repeat with remaining dough. Bake until delicate golden brown, 10 to 12 minutes.   **About 4 dozen cookies; 90 calories per cookie.**

*If using self-rising flour, omit baking powder and salt.

HIDDEN MINT COOKIES

½   cup granulated sugar
¼   cup packed brown sugar
¼   cup margarine or butter, softened
¼   cup shortening
½   teaspoon vanilla
1   egg
1⅔ cups all-purpose flour*
½   teaspoon baking soda
¼   teaspoon salt
    About 48 round or square pastel or
      chocolate wafer mints
    Pastel Glaze (below)

Heat oven to 400°. Mix sugars, margarine, shortening, vanilla and egg. Stir in flour, baking soda and salt. Shape 1 level tablespoonful dough around each mint. Place about 2 inches apart on ungreased cookie sheet. Bake until golden brown, 9 to 10 minutes. Immediately remove from cookie sheet; cool. Dip tops of cookies in Pastel Glaze. **About 4 dozen cookies; 155 calories per cookie.**

Pastel Glaze
Mix 1½ cups powdered sugar, 2 tablespoons milk and 1½ teaspoons vanilla until smooth and of desired consistency. Tint glaze with food color.

COLORFUL COOKIES

1   package (3 ounces) fruit-flavored gelatin
1   cup powdered sugar
1   cup margarine or butter, softened
2¼ cups all-purpose flour**
¼   teaspoon salt
    Colorful Glaze (page 188)

*If using self-rising flour, omit baking soda and salt.
**Do not use self-rising flour in this recipe.

Heat oven to 350°. Reserve 1 tablespoon gelatin (dry) for the glaze. Mix remaining gelatin, the powdered sugar and margarine. Stir in flour and salt. Shape dough into 1-inch balls. Place about 2 inches apart on ungreased cookie sheet. Bake until set but not brown, 8 to 10 minutes. Cool slightly; remove from cookie sheet. Cool completely.

Prepare Colorful Glaze. Dip tops of cookies into glaze. Decorate with coconut, nuts, cherries, colored sugar, small candies or chocolate shot if desired. **About 4½ dozen cookies; 80 calories per cookie.**

Colorful Glaze
Mix reserved 1 tablespoon gelatin and 3 tablespoons hot water. Let stand 5 minutes. Stir in 2 cups powdered sugar and 1 teaspoon vanilla until smooth and of desired consistency.

ACORN COOKIES

```
1    cup sugar
1    cup margarine or butter, softened
½    cup milk
1    teaspoon vanilla
1    teaspoon almond extract
1    egg
3½   cups all-purpose flour*
1    teaspoon baking powder
¼    teaspoon salt
1    package (12 ounces) semisweet chocolate chips
2    cups finely chopped nuts
```

Mix sugar, margarine, milk, vanilla, almond extract and egg. Stir in flour, baking powder and salt. Cover and refrigerate at least 4 hours.

Heat oven to 375°. For each cookie, shape 1 tablespoon dough into 2-inch oval. Taper one end by pinching dough. Place about 1 inch apart on ungreased cookie sheet. Bake until set and very light brown, 9 to 12 minutes. Immediately remove from cookie sheet; cool.

Heat chocolate chips until melted. Dip about ⅓ of the wide, rounded end of each cookie into chocolate, then dip into nuts. **About 9 dozen cookies; 70 calories per cookie.**

*If using self-rising flour, omit baking powder and salt.

Chocolate-Nut Logs: For each cookie, shape 1 teaspoon dough into 2½-inch rope. Bake as directed. Dip ends of cookies into chocolate; dip into nuts. **About 8 dozen cookies.**

Peppermint Candy Canes: Substitute 1 teaspoon peppermint extract for the almond extract. Divide dough into halves. Add ½ teaspoon red food color to 1 half. For each candy cane, shape 1 teaspoon dough from each half into 4-inch rope by rolling back and forth on floured surface. Place 1 red and 1 white rope side by side; press together lightly and twist. Place on ungreased cookie sheet; curve top of cookie down to form handle of cane. Bake as directed. Mix 2 tablespoons finely crushed peppermint candy and 2 tablespoons sugar. Immediately sprinkle over baked cookies. **About 4½ dozen cookies.**

RUSSIAN TEACAKES

1   cup margarine or butter, softened
½   cup powdered sugar
1   teaspoon vanilla
2¼   cups all-purpose flour*
¾   cup finely chopped nuts
¼   teaspoon salt
         Powdered sugar

Heat oven to 400°. Mix margarine, ½ cup powdered sugar and the vanilla. Stir in flour, nuts and salt until dough holds together; shape into 1-inch balls. Place about 1 inch apart on ungreased cookie sheet. Bake until set but not brown, 10 to 12 minutes.

Roll in powdered sugar while warm; cool. Roll in powdered sugar again. **About 4 dozen cookies;** 80 calories per cookie.

Surprise Candy Teacakes: Decrease nuts to ½ cup. Cut 12 vanilla caramel candies into 4 pieces each or cut 1 bar (4 ounces) sweet cooking chocolate into ½-inch squares. Mold portions of dough around pieces of caramels or chocolate to form 1-inch balls.

*Do not use self-rising flour in this recipe.

THUMBPRINT COOKIES

¼   cup packed brown sugar
¼   cup shortening
¼   cup margarine or butter, softened
½   teaspoon vanilla
1   egg, separated
1   cup all-purpose flour*
¼   teaspoon salt
¾   cup finely chopped nuts
    Jelly

Heat oven to 350°. Mix brown sugar, shortening, margarine, vanilla and egg yolk. Stir in flour and salt until dough holds together; shape into 1-inch balls.

Beat egg white slightly. Dip each ball into egg white; roll in nuts. Place about 1 inch apart on ungreased cookie sheet; press thumb deeply in center of each. Bake until light brown, about 10 minutes. Immediately remove from cookie sheet; cool. Fill thumbprints with jelly.   **About 3 dozen cookies; 70** calories per cookie.

CHOCOLATE-NUT SLICES

1   cup granulated sugar
1   cup packed brown sugar
⅔   cup shortening
⅔   cup margarine or butter, softened
2   teaspoons vanilla
2   eggs
3¼ cups all-purpose flour**
1   cup finely chopped nuts
½   cup cocoa
1   teaspoon baking soda
1   teaspoon salt

*If using self-rising flour, omit salt.
**If using self-rising flour, omit baking soda and salt.

Mix sugars, shortening, margarine, vanilla and eggs. Stir in remaining ingredients. Divide dough into halves. Shape each half into roll, about 2 inches in diameter and about 8 inches long. Wrap in plastic wrap and refrigerate at least 8 hours but no longer than 1 month, or freeze no longer than 3 months.

Heat oven to 375°. Cut rolls into ¼-inch slices. Place 2 inches apart on ungreased cookie sheet. Bake until set, about 8 minutes. Immediately remove from cookie sheet. **About 5½ dozen cookies**; 100 calories per cookie.

Butterscotch Slices: Omit cocoa.

Oatmeal-Coconut Slices: Decrease flour to 2¾ cups. Stir in 1 cup flaked coconut and 1 cup quick-cooking oats with the flour.

Toasted Coconut Slices: Stir in 1 cup toasted coconut with the flour. Roll dough in additional toasted coconut before wrapping in plastic wrap if desired.

NOTE: For crisper cookies, cut rolls into ⅛-inch slices. Bake until set, about 6 minutes.

SPUMONI COOKIES

1	cup margarine or butter, softened
½	cup sugar
1	teaspoon vanilla
1	egg
2¼	cups all-purpose flour*
½	teaspoon salt
¼	cup chopped pistachio nuts or toasted almonds
6	drops green food color
1	square (1 ounce) unsweetened chocolate, melted and cooled
2	tablespoons finely chopped maraschino cherries, drained

Mix margarine, sugar, vanilla and egg. Stir in flour and salt. Divide dough into 3 equal parts. Mix pistachio nuts and food color into 1 part. Mix chocolate into 1 part; mix cherries into remaining part. Line bottom and ends of loaf pan, 9×5×3 inches, with aluminum foil, allowing ends of foil to extend 5 inches over each end of pan. Press nut dough evenly in bottom of pan. Press chocolate dough on nut dough; press

*Do not use self-rising flour in this recipe.

cherry dough on chocolate dough. Cover dough with extended ends of foil. Refrigerate at least 2 hours but no longer than 6 weeks.

Heat oven to 375°. Remove foil and dough from pan; remove foil. Cut dough crosswise into ¼-inch slices; cut each slice crosswise into halves. Place about 1 inch apart on ungreased cookie sheet. Bake cookies until set, about 10 minutes. Immediately remove from cookie sheet. **About 6½ dozen cookies**; 45 calories per cookie.

Neapolitan Cookies: Substitute walnuts for the pistachio nuts. Omit green food color.

LEMON COOKIE SANDWICHES

½ cup sugar
½ cup margarine or butter, softened
1 tablespoon water
1 teaspoon vanilla
2 eggs, separated
1½ cups all-purpose flour*
½ teaspoon salt
¼ teaspoon baking soda
⅔ cup finely chopped nuts
Lemon Filling (page 193)

Mix sugar, margarine, water, vanilla and egg yolks. Stir in flour, salt and baking soda. Divide dough into halves. Shape each half into roll, about 1½ inches in diameter and about 7 inches long. Wrap and refrigerate at least 4 hours.

Heat oven to 400°. Cut rolls into ⅛-inch slices. Place about 1 inch apart on ungreased cookie sheet. Beat egg whites slightly; stir in nuts. Spoon ½ teaspoon nut mixture onto each of half of the slices. Bake until edges begin to brown, about 6 minutes. Immediately remove from cookie sheet; cool. Put nut-topped and plain cookies together in pairs with Lemon Filling, placing the nut-topped cookies on top. **About 4 dozen cookies**; 65 calories per cookie.

*If using self-rising flour, omit salt and baking soda.

Lemon Filling
Beat 1 cup powdered sugar, 2 teaspoons margarine or butter,
softened, 1 teaspoon grated lemon peel and 1 tablespoon plus
1½ teaspoons lemon juice.

SOUR CREAM COOKIES

1	cup sugar
¼	cup shortening
¼	cup margarine or butter, softened
1	teaspoon vanilla
1	egg
2⅔	cups all-purpose flour*
½	cup dairy sour cream
1	teaspoon baking powder
½	teaspoon baking soda
½	teaspoon salt
¼	teaspoon ground nutmeg

Heat oven to 425°. Mix sugar, shortening, margarine, vanilla
and egg. Stir in remaining ingredients. Divide dough into 3
equal parts. Roll each part ¼ inch thick on lightly floured
cloth-covered board. Cut with 2-inch cookie cutter; sprinkle
with sugar. Place on ungreased cookie sheet. Bake until no
indentation remains when touched, 6 to 8 minutes. **4 to 5
dozen cookies**; 65 calories per cookie.

SUGAR COOKIES

1½	cups powdered sugar
1	cup margarine or butter, softened
1	teaspoon vanilla
½	teaspoon almond extract
1	egg
2½	cups all-purpose flour**
1	teaspoon baking soda
1	teaspoon cream of tartar
	Granulated sugar

*If using self-rising flour, omit baking powder, baking soda and salt.
**If using self-rising flour, omit baking soda and cream of tartar.

Mix powdered sugar, margarine, vanilla, almond extract and egg. Stir in remaining ingredients except granulated sugar. Cover and refrigerate at least 3 hours.

Heat oven to 375°. Divide dough into halves. Roll each half 3/16 inch thick on lightly floured cloth-covered board. Cut into desired shapes with 2- to 2½-inch cookie cutters; sprinkle with granulated sugar. Place on lightly greased cookie sheet. Bake until edges are light brown, 7 to 8 minutes. **About 5 dozen cookies**; 65 calories per cookie.

Decorated Sugar Cookies: Omit granulated sugar. Frost and decorate cooled cookies with Creamy Vanilla Frosting (page 129) tinted with food color if desired. Decorate with colored sugar, small candies, candied fruit or nuts if desired.

Filled Sugar Cookies: Cook 2 cups raisins, cut-up dates or figs, ¾ cup sugar, ½ cup chopped nuts, and ¾ cup water, stirring constantly, until mixture thickens; cool completely. Roll dough ⅛ inch thick. Cut into 48 circles with 2½-inch doughnut cutter that has center removed. Cut out centers of 24 of the circles with center of doughnut cutter. Place uncut circles on lightly greased cookie sheet. Top with raisin mixture, spreading almost to edges. Top with remaining circles. Press edges together with floured fork. Sprinkle tops with sugar. Bake until light brown, 8 to 10 minutes. **2 dozen cookies.**

Paintbrush Cookies: Omit granulated sugar. Cut no more than 12 cookies at a time to keep them from drying out. Mix 1 egg yolk and ¼ teaspoon water. Divide mixture among several custard cups. Tint each with different food color to make bright colors. (If paint thickens while standing, stir in few drops water.) Paint designs on cookies with small paintbrushes. Bake as directed.

HONEY-SPICE COOKIES

½	cup honey
½	cup molasses
¾	cup packed brown sugar
1	teaspoon grated lemon peel
1	tablespoon lemon juice
1	egg
2¾	cups all-purpose flour*
⅓	cup cut-up citron
⅓	cup chopped nuts
1	teaspoon ground allspice
1	teaspoon ground cinnamon
1	teaspoon ground cloves
1	teaspoon ground nutmeg
½	teaspoon baking soda
	Cookie Glaze (below)

Heat honey and molasses to boiling in 1½-quart saucepan; remove from heat. Cool completely. Mix in brown sugar, lemon peel, lemon juice and egg. Stir in remaining ingredients except Cookie Glaze. Cover and refrigerate at least 8 hours.

Heat oven to 400°. Roll about ¼ of the dough at a time ¼ inch thick on lightly floured cloth-covered board (keep remaining dough refrigerated). Cut into rectangles, 2½ × 1½ inches, or cut with heart-shaped cookie cutter. Place about 1 inch apart on greased cookie sheet. Bake until no indentation remains when touched, 10 to 12 minutes. Brush with glaze; garnish with candied cherries if desired. Immediately remove from cookie sheet. **About 5 dozen cookies; 70 calories per cookie.**

Cookie Glaze
Mix 1 cup powdered sugar, 1 tablespoon warm water and 1 teaspoon light corn syrup until smooth. If necessary, stir in additional warm water, 1 teaspoon at a time, until glaze is of desired consistency.

*Do not use self-rising flour in this recipe.

ITALIAN SWEETS

2½	cups all-purpose flour*
1	cup granulated sugar
¼	cup margarine or butter, softened
½	cup whipping cream
2	teaspoons baking powder
1	teaspoon almond extract
½	teaspoon salt
1	egg, separated
1¾	cups powdered sugar
½	teaspoon almond extract
½	cup chopped almonds
¼	cup cut-up red candied cherries
¼	cup cut-up green candied cherries

Mix flour, granulated sugar, margarine, whipping cream, baking powder, 1 teaspoon almond extract, the salt and egg yolk. Work well with hands to blend. Cover and refrigerate at least 1 hour.

Heat oven to 375°. Divide dough into halves. Roll each half into rectangle, 8 × 6 inches, on generously floured cloth-covered board. Square off rounded corners. Place on greased cookie sheet. Beat egg white until foamy; gradually beat in powdered sugar and ½ teaspoon almond extract. Continue beating until stiff and glossy. Spread meringue over dough; arrange almonds and cherries on top. Cut into strips, about 2 × 1 inch. Bake until edges are light brown, about 10 minutes. Cut into strips again. **About 4 dozen cookies**; 90 calories per cookie.

SCOTCH SHORTBREAD

Heat oven to 350°. Mix ¾ cup margarine or butter, softened, and ¼ cup sugar. Stir in 2 cups all-purpose flour.** (If dough is crumbly, stir in 1 to 2 tablespoons margarine or butter, softened.)

Roll dough about ½ inch thick on lightly floured cloth-

---

*If using self-rising flour, omit baking powder and salt.
**Do not use self-rising flour in this recipe.

covered board. Cut into small shapes (leaves, ovals, squares, triangles, etc.). Place about ½ inch apart on ungreased cookie sheet. Bake until set, about 20 minutes. Immediately remove from cookie sheet. **About 2 dozen 1½ × 1-inch cookies; 95** calories per cookie.

NUT ROLL-UPS

⅓ cup margarine or butter, softened
1 package (3 ounces) cream cheese, softened
¾ cup all-purpose flour*
36 pecan or walnut halves, candied cherry halves or choc-olate, butterscotch-flavored or peanut butter-flavored chips
  Powdered sugar

Mix margarine and cream cheese. Stir in flour until soft dough forms. Cover and refrigerate until firm, at least 8 hours.

Heat oven to 375°. Roll dough into rectangle, 12 × 9 inches, on cloth-covered board generously sprinkled with powdered sugar. Cut dough into rectangles, each 3 × 1 inch. Place 1 pecan half on one end of each rectangle; roll up, beginning at 1-inch end. Pinch end and sides to seal. Place cookies, end seam sides down, on ungreased cookie sheet. Bake until golden brown, 15 to 17 minutes; cool. Sprinkle with pow-dered sugar. **3 dozen cookies;** 45 calories per cookie.

*Self-rising flour can be used in this recipe.

JUMBO MOLASSES COOKIES

1	cup sugar
½	cup shortening
1	cup dark molasses
½	cup water
4	cups all-purpose flour*
1½	teaspoons salt
1	teaspoon baking soda
1½	teaspoons ground ginger
½	teaspoon ground cloves
½	teaspoon ground nutmeg
¼	teaspoon ground allspice
	Sugar

Mix 1 cup sugar and the shortening. Stir in remaining ingredients except sugar. Cover and refrigerate at least 3 hours.

Heat oven to 375°. Roll dough ¼ inch thick on generously floured cloth-covered board. Cut into 3-inch circles; sprinkle with sugar. Place about 1½ inches apart on well-greased cookie sheet. Bake until almost no indentation remains when touched, 10 to 12 minutes. Cool 2 minutes; remove from cookie sheet. **About 3 dozen cookies; 115 calories per cookie.**

GINGERBREAD PEOPLE

1	cup packed brown sugar
⅓	cup shortening
1½	cups dark molasses
⅔	cup cold water
7	cups all-purpose flour**
2	teaspoons baking soda
2	teaspoons ground ginger
1	teaspoon salt
1	teaspoon ground allspice
1	teaspoon ground cloves
1	teaspoon ground cinnamon

Mix brown sugar, shortening, molasses and water. Stir in remaining ingredients. Cover and refrigerate at least 2 hours.

*If using self-rising flour, omit salt and baking soda.
**If using self-rising flour, omit baking soda and salt.

Heat oven to 350°. Roll dough ¼ inch thick on floured board. Cut with floured gingerbread cutter or other favorite shaped cutter. Place about 2 inches apart on lightly greased cookie sheet. Bake until no indentation remains when touched, 10 to 12 minutes; cool. Decorate with colored frosting and candies if desired. **About 2½ dozen 2½-inch cookies; 180 calories per cookie.**

SPRITZ

1	**cup margarine or butter, softened**
½	**cup sugar**
2¼	**cups all-purpose flour***
1	**teaspoon almond extract or vanilla**
½	**teaspoon salt**
1	**egg**

Heat oven to 400°. Mix margarine and sugar. Stir in remaining ingredients.

Place dough in cookie press; form desired shapes on ungreased cookie sheet. Bake until set but not brown, 6 to 9 minutes. Immediately remove from cookie sheet. **About 5 dozen cookies; 50 calories per cookie.**

Chocolate Spritz: Stir 2 ounces melted unsweetened chocolate (cool) into margarine mixture.

Holiday Decorated Spritz: Before baking, top cookies with currants, raisins, candies, nuts, slices of candied fruits or candied fruit peels arranged in attractive patterns. Or, after baking, decorate with colored sugars, nonpareils, red cinnamon candies and finely chopped nuts. Use drop of corn syrup to hold decorations on baked cookies.

*Do not use self-rising flour in this recipe.

ROSETTES

Vegetable oil
1 egg
1 tablespoon sugar
½ teaspoon salt
½ cup all-purpose flour*
½ cup water or milk
1 tablespoon vegetable oil

Heat oil (2 to 3 inches) to 400°. Beat egg, sugar and salt in 1½-quart deep bowl. Beat in flour, water and 1 tablespoon oil until smooth. Heat rosette iron by placing in hot oil 1 minute. Tap excess oil from iron; dip hot iron into batter just to top edge (don't go over top). Fry until golden brown, about 30 seconds. Immediately remove rosette; invert to cool. (If rosette is not crisp, stir small amount of water or milk into batter.)

Heat iron in hot oil and tap off excess oil before making each rosette. (If iron is not hot enough, batter will not stick.) Sprinkle rosettes with powdered sugar just before serving if desired.   **18 rosettes;** 80 calories per rosette.

*If using self-rising flour, omit salt.

CANDY

ABOUT CANDY MAKING

■ Use the recommended saucepan. A smaller or larger pan could affect cooking time and quality.

■ Don't double the recipe—make another batch. Increasing ingredients changes cooking time.

■ A cool, dry day is best for making candy. Heat, humidity and altitude can affect quality. On a rainy day, cook candy to a temperature a degree or so higher than the recipe indicates.

■ Consult an altitude table to determine boiling point in your area, then adjust if necessary.

■ To help prevent crystallization or grainy candy, sugar must dissolve completely over low heat; stir down any grains from side of saucepan. After candy has boiled, do not stir until it has cooled as recipe indicates. To prevent crystals, don't scrape pan or stir candy during cooling.

■ Use a reliable candy thermometer. To get an accurate reading, be sure it stands upright in cooking mixture and bulb does not rest on bottom of pan. Read it at eye level; watch temperature closely. At 200°, it goes up very quickly.

■ If you don't have a thermometer, use the cold water test. Using a clean spoon, drop small amount of cooking mixture into a cupful of very cold water. Test hardness with fingers (see chart). If candy does not pass test, continue cooking.

CANDY COOKING TESTS

Hardness	Temperature	Cold Water Test
Thread	223 to 234°	Forms 2-inch soft thread
Soft ball	234 to 240°	Forms a ball but does not hold its shape
Firm ball	242 to 248°	Forms a ball that holds its shape until pressed
Hard ball	250 to 268°	Forms a ball that holds its shape but is pliable
Soft crack	270 to 290°	Separates into hard but not brittle threads
Hard crack	300 to 310°	Separates into hard, brittle threads
Caramel	320 to 350°	Do not use cold water test. Mixture coats metal spoon and forms light caramel-colored mass when poured on a plate.

CHOCOLATE FUDGE

- 2 **cups sugar**
- ⅔ **cup milk**
- 2 **tablespoons corn syrup**
- ¼ **teaspoon salt**
- 2 **squares (1 ounce each) unsweetened chocolate or ⅓ cup cocoa**
- 2 **tablespoons margarine or butter**
- 1 **teaspoon vanilla**
- ½ **cup coarsely chopped nuts, if desired**

Butter loaf pan, 9×5×3 inches. Cook sugar, milk, corn syrup, salt and chocolate in 2-quart saucepan over medium heat, stirring constantly, until chocolate is melted and sugar is dissolved. Cook, stirring occasionally, to 234° on candy thermometer (or until small amount of mixture dropped into very cold water forms a soft ball that flattens when removed from water); remove from heat.

Add margarine. Cool mixture to 120° without stirring. (Bottom of pan will be lukewarm.) Add vanilla; beat vigorously and continuously until candy is thick and no longer glossy, 5 to 10 minutes. (Mixture will hold its shape when dropped from spoon.) Quickly stir in nuts. Spread in pan; cool until firm. Cut into 1-inch squares. **32 candies;** 85 calories per candy.

Penuche: Substitute 1 cup packed brown sugar for 1 cup of the granulated sugar and omit chocolate.

EASY FUDGE

1   can (14 ounces) sweetened condensed milk
1   package (12 ounces) semisweet chocolate chips
1   square (1 ounce) unsweetened chocolate, if desired
1½ cups chopped nuts, if desired
1   teaspoon vanilla

Butter square pan, 8×8×2 inches. Heat milk, chocolate chips and unsweetened chocolate over low heat, stirring constantly, until chocolate is melted and mixture is smooth; remove from heat. Stir in nuts and vanilla. Spread in pan. Refrigerate until firm. Cut into 1-inch squares. **64 candies;** 50 calories per candy.

COCOA FUDGE

1   cup granulated sugar
¼ cup cocoa
¼ cup margarine or butter
⅓ cup milk
1   tablespoon light corn syrup
⅓ cup chopped nuts
1   teaspoon vanilla
2   to 2¼ cups powdered sugar

Butter loaf pan, 9×5×3 inches. Mix granulated sugar and cocoa in 2-quart saucepan. Stir in margarine, milk and corn syrup. Heat to boiling over medium heat, stirring frequently. Boil and stir 1 minute; remove from heat. Cool, without stirring, until bottom of pan is lukewarm, about 45 minutes. Stir in nuts and vanilla. Stir in powdered sugar until mixture is very stiff. Press in pan. Refrigerate until firm, about 30 minutes. Cut into 1-inch squares. **32 candies;** 85 calories per candy.

Peanut Butter Fudge: Omit cocoa and margarine. Stir in ½ cup peanut butter with the milk. Substitute salted peanuts for the nuts.

ALMOND BARK FUDGE

12   ounces vanilla-flavored candy coating
⅔   cup sweetened condensed milk
1½   cups coarsely chopped toasted almonds
½   teaspoon almond extract

Butter square pan, 8 × 8 × 2 inches. Separate candy coating into squares if necessary. Heat candy coating and milk over low heat, stirring occasionally, until coating is melted and mixture is smooth, about 5 minutes; remove from heat. Stir in almonds and almond extract. Spread in pan. Garnish with additional almonds or cherries if desired. Refrigerate until firm, about 1½ hours. Cut into about 1-inch squares. **64 candies**; 55 calories per candy.

TRUFFLES

6   squares (1 ounce each) semisweet chocolate, cut up
2   tablespoons margarine or butter
¼   cup whipping cream
1   tablespoon shortening
1   package (6 ounces) semisweet or milk chocolate chips

Heat 6 squares semisweet chocolate in heavy 2-quart saucepan over low heat, stirring constantly, until melted; remove from heat. Stir in margarine; stir in whipping cream. Refrigerate, stirring frequently, *just* until thick enough to hold a shape, 10 to 15 minutes. Drop mixture by teaspoonfuls onto aluminum foil-covered cookie sheet; shape into balls. (If mixture is too sticky, refrigerate until firm enough to shape.) Freeze 30 minutes.

Heat shortening and chocolate chips over low heat, stirring constantly, until chocolate is melted and mixture is smooth; remove from heat. Dip truffles, one at a time, into chocolate; place on aluminum foil-covered cookie sheet. Immediately sprinkle some of the truffles with finely chopped nuts if desired. Refrigerate truffles until coating is set, about 10 minutes. Drizzle some of the truffles with a mixture of ¼ cup powdered sugar and ½ teaspoon milk if desired; refrigerate just until set. Serve at room temperature. Cover and store any remaining truffles in cool, dry place. **15 candies; 155 calories per candy.**

Almond Truffles: Stir 2 tablespoons almond-flavored liqueur into whipping cream.

Apricot Truffles: Soak 3 tablespoons chopped apricots in 1 tablespoon brandy 15 minutes. Stir into whipping cream mixture.

Cashew Truffles: Stir 3 tablespoons chopped cashew nuts into whipping cream mixture.

Cherry Truffles: Stir 2 tablespoons cherry-flavored brandy into whipping cream.

Orange Truffles: Stir 2 tablespoons orange-flavored liqueur into whipping cream.

DIVINITY

2⅔   **cups sugar**
⅔   **cup light corn syrup**
½   **cup water***
2   **egg whites**
1   **teaspoon vanilla**
⅔   **cup broken nuts**

Cook sugar, corn syrup and water in 2-quart saucepan over low heat, stirring constantly, until sugar is dissolved. Cook, without stirring, to 260° on candy thermometer (or until small amount of mixture dropped into very cold water forms a hard ball).

Beat egg whites in 1½-quart bowl until stiff peaks form. Continue beating while pouring hot syrup in a thin stream into egg whites. Add vanilla; beat until mixture holds its shape and becomes slightly dull. (Mixture may become too stiff for mixer.) Fold in nuts.

Drop mixture from buttered spoon onto waxed paper. Let stand at room temperature, turning candy over once, until outside of candy is firm, at least 12 hours. Store in airtight container. **About 4 dozen candies;** 70 calories per candy.

*Use 1 tablespoon less water on humid days.

ALMOND BUTTER CRUNCH

1   cup sugar
1   cup butter
2   tablespoons water
1   tablespoon light corn syrup
¾   cup chopped toasted almonds
½   cup semisweet chocolate chips

Butter square pan, 9 × 9 × 2 inches. Heat sugar, butter, water and corn syrup to boiling in heavy 2-quart saucepan over medium heat, stirring constantly. Cook, stirring constantly, to 290° on candy thermometer, 12 to 15 minutes (mixture will be light brown and thickened); remove from heat.

Stir in almonds. Spread evenly in pan. Sprinkle chocolate chips evenly over hot candy. Cover until chocolate is softened, 1 to 2 minutes; carefully spread over candy. Let stand at room temperature until chocolate is firm, about 3 hours.

Loosen candy from sides of pan; remove from pan. Break candy into pieces with knife. Cover and refrigerate any remaining candy.   **About 6 dozen candies; 50 calories per candy.**

PEANUT BRITTLE

1½   teaspoons baking soda
1   teaspoon water
1   teaspoon vanilla
1½   cups sugar
1   cup water
1   cup light corn syrup
3   tablespoons margarine or butter
1   pound shelled unroasted peanuts

Butter 2 cookie sheets, 15½ × 12 inches; keep warm. Mix baking soda, 1 teaspoon water and the vanilla; reserve. Mix sugar, 1 cup water and the corn syrup in 3-quart saucepan. Cook over medium heat, stirring occasionally, to 240° on candy thermometer (or until small amount of mixture dropped into very cold water forms a soft ball that flattens when removed from water).

Stir in margarine and peanuts. Cook, stirring constantly, to 300° (or until small amount of mixture dropped into very cold water separates into threads that are hard and brittle). Watch carefully so mixture does not burn. Immediately remove from heat; stir in baking soda mixture.

Pour half of the candy mixture onto each cookie sheet and quickly spread about ¼ inch thick; cool. Break into pieces. **About 6 dozen candies;** 70 calories per candy.

CARAMELS

½ cup finely chopped nuts
2 cups sugar
½ cup margarine or butter
2 cups half-and-half
¾ cup light corn syrup

Butter square pan, 8 × 8 × 2 inches. Spread nuts in pan. Heat sugar, margarine, 1 cup of the half-and-half and the corn syrup to boiling in 3-quart saucepan over medium heat, stirring constantly. Stir in remaining half-and-half. Cook over medium heat, stirring frequently, to 245° on candy thermometer (or until small amount of mixture dropped into very cold water forms a firm ball). Immediately spread over nuts in pan; cool. Cut into about 1-inch squares. **64 candies;** 65 calories per candy.

Chocolate Caramels: Heat 2 squares (1 ounce each) unsweetened chocolate with the sugar.

PRALINES

2 cups packed light brown sugar
1 cup granulated sugar
1¼ cups milk
¼ cup light corn syrup
⅛ teaspoon salt
1 teaspoon vanilla
1½ cups pecan halves (5½ ounces)

Heat sugars, milk, corn syrup and salt to boiling in 3-quart saucepan, stirring constantly. Cook, without stirring, to 236° on candy thermometer (or until small amount of mixture dropped into very cold water forms a soft ball that flattens when removed from water). Immediately remove thermometer. Cool, without stirring, until saucepan is cool to touch, about 1½ hours.

Add vanilla and pecans. Beat with spoon until mixture is slightly thickened and just coats pecans but does not lose its gloss, about 1 minute. Drop by spoonfuls onto waxed paper. (Try to divide pecans equally.) Cool until candies are firm and no longer glossy, 12 to 18 hours.

Wrap individually in plastic wrap or waxed paper and store tightly covered at room temperature. **About 1½ dozen candies;** 235 calories per candy.

SPONGE CANDY

---

    1   **cup sugar**
    1   **cup dark corn syrup**
    1   **tablespoon cider vinegar**
    1   **tablespoon baking soda**

Heat sugar, corn syrup and vinegar to boiling in 2-quart saucepan over medium heat, stirring constantly, until sugar is dissolved. Boil, without stirring, to 300° on candy thermometer (or until small amount of mixture dropped into very cold water separates into threads that are hard and brittle); remove from heat. Quickly stir in baking soda thoroughly. Pour mixture into ungreased rectangular pan, 13 × 9 × 2 inches. Do not spread; cool. Break into pieces. **About 3 dozen candies;** 50 calories per candy.

TAFFY

---

    1   **cup sugar**
    1   **tablespoon cornstarch**
    ¾   **cup light corn syrup**
    ⅔   **cup water**
    2   **tablespoons margarine or butter**
    1   **teaspoon salt**
    2   **teaspoons vanilla**
    ¼   **teaspoon food color, if desired**

Butter square pan, $8 \times 8 \times 2$ inches. Mix sugar and cornstarch in 2-quart saucepan. Stir in corn syrup, water, margarine and salt. Heat to boiling over medium heat, stirring constantly. Cook, without stirring, to 256° on candy thermometer (or until small amount of mixture dropped into very cold water forms a hard ball), about 30 minutes; remove from heat. Stir in vanilla and food color. Pour into pan.

When just cool enough to handle, pull taffy with lightly buttered hands until satiny, light in color and stiff. Pull into long strips ½ inch wide. Cut strips into 1½-inch pieces with scissors. Wrap pieces individually in plastic wrap or waxed paper (candy must be wrapped to hold its shape). **About 4 dozen candies;** 35 calories per candy.

Almond Taffy: Stir in 2 teaspoons almond extract with the vanilla.

Peppermint Taffy: Substitute 1 tablespoon peppermint extract for the vanilla. Stir in ¼ teaspoon red food color with the peppermint extract.

EASY TURTLE CANDIES

72	pecan halves (about 4 ounces)
24	caramel candies
1	teaspoon shortening
1	package (6 ounces) semisweet chocolate chips

Heat oven to 300°. Cover cookie sheet with aluminum foil, shiny side up; grease. For each candy, place 3 pecan halves in Y shape on foil. Place 1 caramel candy in center of each pecan Y. Bake just until candy is melted, 9 to 10 minutes.

Heat shortening and chocolate chips over low heat, stirring constantly, just until chocolate is melted. Spread mixture over candies, leaving ends of pecans uncovered. Refrigerate just until chocolate is firm, about 30 minutes. **24 candies;** 100 calories per candy.

CASHEW CLUSTERS

Heat 1 teaspoon shortening and 1 package (6 ounces) semisweet chocolate chips in 2-quart saucepan over low heat, stirring constantly, until chocolate is melted and mixture is smooth; remove from heat. Stir in 3 cups salted cashew nuts, macadamia nuts or peanuts. Drop mixture by teaspoonfuls into mounds onto waxed paper-covered cookie sheet. Refrigerate until firm, about 30 minutes. Cover tightly and refrigerate any remaining candies. **About 3 dozen candies; 100** calories per candy.

Coconut Clusters: Substitute 3 cups flaked coconut for the cashew nuts.

Raisin Clusters: Substitute 3 cups raisins for the cashew nuts.

Raisin-Nut Clusters: Substitute 1½ cups raisins and 1½ cups salted peanuts for the cashew nuts.

PEANUT BUTTER CANDY BARS

1¼   cups creamy peanut butter
½   cup margarine or butter, softened
4   cups honey graham cereal, crushed
2   cups powdered sugar
1   tablespoon shortening
1   package (5.75 ounces) milk chocolate chips
      (about 1 cup)

Mix peanut butter and margarine; stir in cereal. Mix in powdered sugar, ⅓ at a time. Press mixture firmly in ungreased square pan, 9×9×2 inches.

Heat shortening in 1-quart saucepan over low heat until melted. Add chocolate chips. Heat over very low heat, stirring constantly, until chocolate is melted and mixture is smooth. Spread chocolate mixture over cereal mixture. Refrigerate until chilled, about 1 hour. Remove from refrigerator 10 minutes before serving. Cut into bars, about 2¼×1½ inches. Refrigerate any remaining bars. **24 bars; 210 calories per bar.**

Peanut Butter Cups: Press about 2 tablespoons cereal mixture in each of 24 to 30 small foil or paper baking cups. Spread tops with chocolate mixture.

BOURBON BALLS

3 cups finely crushed vanilla wafers (about 75)
2 cups powdered sugar
1 cup finely chopped pecans or walnuts (about 4 ounces)
¼ cup cocoa
½ cup bourbon
¼ cup light corn syrup
　Granulated or powdered sugar

Mix crushed wafers, powdered sugar, pecans and cocoa. Stir in bourbon and corn syrup. Shape mixture into 1-inch balls. Roll in granulated sugar. Cover tightly and refrigerate several days before serving. **About 5 dozen candies; 65 calories per candy.**

　Brandy Balls: Substitute ½ cup brandy for the bourbon.

　Rum Balls: Substitute ½ cup light rum for the bourbon.

MINT WAFERS

3½ to 4 cups powdered sugar
⅔ cup sweetened condensed milk
½ teaspoon peppermint, spearmint or wintergreen extract

Mix 3½ cups powdered sugar, the milk and, if desired, a few drops food color. Knead in extract and enough additional powdered sugar to make a smooth, creamy mixture. Shape mixture into 1-inch balls. Place about 1 inch apart on waxed paper-covered cookie sheet. Flatten each ball with fork to about ¼-inch thickness. Let stand uncovered at room temperature until firm, about 1 hour.

　Turn candies over and let stand until tops are firm, about 1 hour longer. Store tightly covered at room temperature. **About 8 dozen candies; 25 calories per candy.**

　Easy Bonbons: Substitute ¾ teaspoon vanilla or almond extract for the peppermint extract. For each bonbon, mold about 1 measuring teaspoonful mixture around piece of candied or dried fruit or nut to form a ball. Or shape mixture into 1-inch balls; decorate with candied or dried fruit and nuts. **About 5 dozen candies.**

SWEET SNACKS

CANDIED CITRUS PEEL

3	oranges
3	lemons
1½	cups sugar
¾	cup water
½	cup sugar

Cut peel of each orange and lemon into 4 sections with sharp knife. Remove peel carefully with fingers. Scrape white membrane from peel with spoon (back of peel will appear porous when membrane is removed). Cut peel lengthwise into strips about ¼ inch wide. Heat peel and enough water to cover to boiling in 1½-quart saucepan; reduce heat. Simmer uncovered 30 minutes; drain. Repeat simmering process.

Heat 1½ cups sugar and ¾ cup water to boiling in 1½-quart saucepan, stirring constantly, until sugar is dissolved. Stir in peel. Simmer uncovered, stirring occasionally, 45 minutes; drain in strainer. Roll in ½ cup sugar; spread on waxed paper to dry. Store tightly covered at room temperature no longer than 1 week. **12 servings** (about ¼ cup each); 120 calories per serving.

CARAMEL-NUT CORN

12	cups popped popcorn (page 17)
3	cups walnut halves, pecan halves and/or unblanched whole almonds
1	cup packed brown sugar
½	cup margarine or butter
¼	cup light corn syrup
½	teaspoon salt
½	teaspoon baking soda

212

Divide popcorn and nuts between 2 ungreased rectangular pans, 13 × 9 × 2 inches. Cook brown sugar, margarine, corn syrup and salt over medium heat, stirring occasionally, until bubbly around edges. Continue cooking 5 minutes; remove from heat. Stir in baking soda until foamy. Pour over popcorn and nuts, stirring until corn is well coated. Bake uncovered in 200° oven, stirring every 15 minutes, 1 hour. **15 servings** (about 1 cup each); 300 calories per serving.

Caramel Corn: Increase popped popcorn to 15 cups; omit nuts.

POPCORN BALLS

½ cup sugar
¼ cup margarine or butter
½ cup light corn syrup
½ teaspoon salt
 Few drops food color
8 cups popped popcorn (page 17)

Heat all ingredients except popcorn to simmering in Dutch oven over medium-high heat, stirring constantly. Stir in popcorn. Cook, stirring constantly, until popcorn is well coated, about 3 minutes; cool slightly.

Dip hands into cold water; shape mixture into 8 about 2½-inch balls. Place on waxed paper; cool completely. Wrap individually in plastic wrap, or place in plastic bags and tie. **8 popcorn balls;** 205 calories per ball.

Caramel Popcorn Balls: Substitute packed brown sugar for the granulated sugar and dark corn syrup for the light corn syrup; omit food color.

Chocolate Popcorn Balls: Add 2 tablespoons cocoa with the sugar; omit food color.

CHOCOLATE-CARAMEL APPLES

6 wooden skewers or ice-cream sticks
6 medium apples
½ cup chopped nuts
¼ cup semisweet chocolate chips
2 tablespoons water
1 package (14 ounces) caramel candies

Insert skewer in stem end of each apple. Divide nuts into 6 mounds on waxed paper.

Heat chocolate chips, water and candies over low heat, stirring occasionally, until candies are melted and mixture is smooth. Keep mixture over very low heat. Dip each apple into chocolate mixture, spooning mixture over apple until completely coated. (If chocolate mixture hardens while coating apples, heat over low heat.) Place each on mound of nuts; sprinkle loose nuts on top of apple around skewer.   **6 servings;** 415 calories per serving.

Caramel Apples: Omit nuts and chocolate chips. Dip each apple into caramel candy mixture, spooning mixture over apple until about ¾ coated. Place on waxed paper; refrigerate until caramel coating is firm.

MARSHMALLOW BARS

32 **large marshmallows or 3 cups miniature marshmallows**
¼ **cup margarine or butter**
½ **teaspoon vanilla**
5 **cups crispy corn puff, toasted oat, cornflake or whole wheat flake cereal**

Butter square pan, 9 × 9 × 2 inches. Heat marshmallows and margarine in 3-quart saucepan over low heat, stirring constantly, until marshmallows are melted and mixture is smooth; remove from heat. Stir in vanilla. Stir in half of the cereal at a time until evenly coated. Press in pan; cool. Cut into bars, about 2 × 1 inch.   **36 bars; 35 calories per bar.**

Chocolate-Marshmallow Bars: Heat 1 package (6 ounces) semisweet chocolate chips over low heat, stirring frequently, until melted; spread over cereal mixture in pan.

Coconutty-Marshmallow Bars: Substitute ½ cup flaked coconut and ½ cup coarsely chopped nuts for 1 cup of the cereal.

Gumdrop-Marshmallow Bars: Stir in ¼ teaspoon ground cinnamon with the vanilla. Stir in 1 cup small gumdrops, cut into halves, with the cereal.

Peanut Butter-Marshmallow Bars: Stir ½ cup peanut butter into marshmallow-margarine mixture until melted.

S'MORE BARS

⅓ cup light corn syrup
1 tablespoon margarine or butter
1 package (5.75 ounces) milk chocolate chips or 5 bars (1.2 ounces each) milk chocolate, broken into pieces
½ teaspoon vanilla
4 cups honey graham cereal
1½ cups miniature marshmallows

Butter square pan, 9×9×2 inches. Heat corn syrup and margarine to boiling in 3-quart saucepan; remove from heat. Stir in chocolate chips and vanilla until chocolate is melted. Gradually fold in cereal until evenly coated; fold in marshmallows. Press in pan with buttered back of spoon. Let stand at room temperature at least 1 hour. Cut into bars, about 2¼×1½ inches. **24 bars; 80 calories per bar.**

GRANOLA BARK

Separate 1 package (16 ounces) vanilla- or chocolate-flavored candy coating into squares if necessary. Heat in 3-quart saucepan over low heat, stirring occasionally, until melted; remove from heat. Stir in 3 cups granola. Spread on waxed paper-covered cookie sheet. Refrigerate until firm, about 30 minutes. Break into bite-size pieces. Cover; refrigerate remaining candy. **About 80 candies; 45 calories per candy.**

DESSERTS

FRUIT DESSERTS

GLAZED APPLE RINGS

¼   cup margarine or butter
4   apples, cored and cut into ½-inch rings
½   cup dry white wine or apple juice
1   tablespoon lemon juice
¼   teaspoon ground ginger
¼   teaspoon ground cinnamon
½   cup sugar

Heat margarine in 10-inch skillet over medium heat until melted. Fry several apple rings at a time, turning once, until golden brown. (Add more margarine if necessary.)

Return all apple rings to skillet. Mix wine, lemon juice, ginger and cinnamon; pour over apples. Sprinkle with sugar. Cover and cook over medium heat just until apples are tender and glazed, about 5 minutes. Serve warm and, if desired, with Sweetened Whipped Cream (page 274). **4 servings; 290 calories per serving.**

BAKED APPLES

Core baking apples (Rome Beauty, Golden Delicious, Greening) and pare 1-inch strip of skin from around middle of each apple or pare upper half of each to prevent splitting. Place apples upright in ungreased baking dish. Place 1 to 2 tablespoons granulated or packed brown sugar, 1 teaspoon margarine or butter and ⅛ teaspoon ground cinnamon in center of each apple. Pour water (¼ inch deep) into baking dish.

Bake uncovered in 375° oven until tender when pierced with fork, 30 to 40 minutes. (Time will vary with size and variety of apple.) Spoon syrup in dish over apples several times during baking. Serve with cream or Sweetened Whipped Cream (page 274). 185 calories per apple.

Baked Grenadine Apples: Substitute grenadine syrup for the sugar.

Baked Honey Apples: Substitute honey for the sugar.

Baked Mincemeat Apples: Omit sugar, margarine and cinnamon. Fill each apple with 1 to 2 tablespoons prepared mincemeat.

APPLESAUCE

4 medium cooking apples, each cut into fourths
½ cup water
½ cup packed brown sugar or ⅓ to ½ cup granulated sugar
¼ teaspoon ground cinnamon
⅛ teaspoon ground nutmeg

Heat apples and water to boiling over medium heat; reduce heat. Simmer uncovered, stirring occasionally to break up apples, until tender, 5 to 10 minutes. Stir in remaining ingredients. Heat to boiling. Boil and stir 1 minute. **4 servings** (1 cup each); 190 calories per serving.

APPLE CRISP

4 cups sliced tart apples (about 4 medium)
⅔ to ¾ cup packed brown sugar
½ cup all-purpose flour*
½ cup oats
⅓ cup margarine or butter, softened
¾ teaspoon ground cinnamon
¾ teaspoon ground nutmeg

Heat oven to 375°. Arrange apples in greased square pan, 8 × 8 × 2 inches. Mix remaining ingredients; sprinkle over apples.

Bake until topping is golden brown and apples are tender, about 30 minutes. Serve warm and, if desired, with cream or ice cream. **6 servings;** 295 calories per serving.

*Self-rising flour can be used in this recipe.

Apricot Crisp: Substitute 2 cans (17 ounces each) apricot halves, drained, for the apples, and use the lesser amount of brown sugar.

Cherry Crisp: Substitute 1 can (21 ounces) cherry pie filling for the apples, and use the lesser amount of brown sugar.

Peach Crisp: Substitute 1 can (29 ounces) sliced peaches, drained, for the apples, and use the lesser amount of brown sugar.

Pineapple Crisp: Substitute 2 cans (13½ ounces each) pineapple chunks, drained, or 2 cans (20 ounces each) crushed pineapple, drained, for the apples, and use the lesser amount of brown sugar.

APRICOT-BANANA CREAM

- 1 **can (17 ounces) apricot halves, drained**
- 1 **package (3¾ ounces) banana instant pudding and pie filling**
- 1 **cup whipping cream**

Place apricot halves in blender container. Cover and blend on high speed until smooth, about 20 seconds. Add pudding and pie filling (dry) and whipping cream. Cover and blend on high speed, stopping blender frequently to scrape sides, until smooth and thickened, about 30 seconds. Sprinkle with ground nutmeg if desired. **4 servings; 375 calories per serving.**

Peach-Banana Cream: Substitute 1 can (16 ounces) sliced peaches, drained, for the apricot halves.

WHIPPED AVOCADO DESSERT

- 2 **avocados, peeled and cut into pieces**
- ⅓ **cup powdered sugar**
- ¼ **cup whipping cream**
- 3 **tablespoons lime juice**

Place all ingredients in blender container. Cover and blend on high speed until smooth and creamy. **3 servings; 345 calories per serving.**

CARIBBEAN BANANAS

¼ cup margarine or butter
4 medium bananas
⅓ cup packed brown sugar
1 tablespoon lemon juice
½ teaspoon ground allspice
¼ cup light rum

Place margarine in square baking dish, 9 × 9 × 2 inches. Heat in 350° oven until melted; rotate dish to coat bottom. Cut bananas crosswise into halves; cut each half lengthwise into halves. Place cut sides down in baking dish. Mix brown sugar, lemon juice and allspice; drizzle over bananas.

Bake uncovered 15 minutes. Heat rum until warm; ignite and pour over bananas. **4 servings; 300 calories per serving.**

FRESH BLUEBERRY COBBLER

½ cup sugar
1 tablespoon cornstarch
4 cups blueberries
1 teaspoon lemon juice
3 tablespoons shortening
1 cup all-purpose flour*
1 tablespoon sugar
1½ teaspoons baking powder
½ teaspoon salt
½ cup milk

Heat oven to 400°. Mix ½ cup sugar and the cornstarch in 2-quart saucepan. Stir in blueberries and lemon juice. Cook, stirring constantly, until mixture thickens and boils. Boil and stir 1 minute. Pour into ungreased 2-quart casserole; keep blueberry mixture hot in oven.

Cut shortening into flour, 1 tablespoon sugar, the baking powder and salt until mixture resembles fine crumbs. Stir in milk. Drop dough by 6 spoonfuls onto hot blueberry mixture.

*If using self-rising flour, omit baking powder and salt.

Bake until topping is golden brown, 25 to 30 minutes. Serve warm and, if desired, with Cinnamon Whipped Cream (page 275).   **6 servings; 275 calories per serving.**

Fresh Cherry Cobbler: Substitute 4 cups pitted red tart cherries for the blueberries; increase sugar in cherry mixture to 1¼ cups, cornstarch to 3 tablespoons, and add ¼ teaspoon ground cinnamon with the cornstarch. Substitute ¼ teaspoon almond extract for the 1 teaspoon lemon juice.

Fresh Peach Cobbler: Substitute 4 cups sliced peaches (about 6 medium) for the blueberries. Add ¼ teaspoon ground cinnamon with the cornstarch.

Fresh Plum Cobbler: Substitute 4 cups sliced plums (about 14 large) for the blueberries; increase sugar in plum mixture to ¾ cup, cornstarch to 3 tablespoons, and add ½ teaspoon ground cinnamon with the cornstarch.

CHERRIES JUBILEE

        Vanilla ice cream
   ¼   cup rum
   2   cups pitted dark sweet cherries*
   ¾   cup currant jelly
   1   teaspoon grated orange peel
   ¼   cup brandy

Scoop ice cream into serving-size portions onto cookie sheet; freeze. Pour rum over cherries; refrigerate 4 hours.

Just before serving, heat jelly in chafing dish or saucepan over low heat until melted. Stir in cherry mixture and orange peel. Heat to simmering, stirring constantly. Heat brandy in saucepan until warm; ignite and pour over cherries. Serve hot over ice cream in dessert dishes.   **8 to 10 servings; 325 calories per serving.**

*1 can (16½ ounces) pitted dark sweet cherries can be substituted for the 2 cups cherries. Drain cherries, reserving ¼ cup syrup. Mix reserved cherry syrup and the rum; pour over cherries.

CHERRIES AND KIWIFRUIT

1   cup pitted dark sweet cherries
4   kiwifruit, pared and cut into ¼-inch slices
¾   cup coconut cream
¾   teaspoon finely shredded lemon peel

Divide cherries and kiwifruit among 6 dessert dishes. Mix coconut cream and lemon peel; pour over fruit. Garnish with additional pitted dark sweet cherries if desired.   **6 servings; 150 calories per serving.**

FRUIT AMBROSIA

1   banana, sliced
1   cup seedless green grape halves
2   large oranges, pared and sectioned
¾   cup shredded coconut
⅓   cup orange-flavored liqueur or orange juice

Layer banana, grapes and oranges in serving bowl or 6 dessert dishes, sprinkling coconut between layers. Sprinkle top layer with coconut; drizzle with liqueur.   **6 servings; 125 calories per serving.**

FRUIT IN ORANGE CREAM

1   cup chilled whipping cream
3   tablespoons frozen orange juice concentrate, partially thawed
3   tablespoons honey
¼   teaspoon ground ginger
3   medium kiwifruit, pared and cut into ¼-inch slices
1   medium banana, sliced
6   whole strawberries

Beat whipping cream, orange juice concentrate, honey and ginger in chilled 1½-quart bowl until stiff; reserve 2 tablespoons. Divide remaining mixture among 6 dessert dishes. Arrange kiwifruit and banana on top. Cut each strawberry into fourths, cutting almost through to bottom. Fill each with 1 teaspoon cream mixture; place on banana.   **6 servings; 255 calories per serving.**

FRESH FRUIT CUPS

1 cup seedless green grapes
1 cup cantaloupe balls or pineapple cubes
1 cup strawberries
1 can (6 ounces) frozen fruit juice concentrate (pineapple, orange, lemonade or cranberry juice cocktail), partially thawed

Divide fruit among 6 dessert dishes. Just before serving, spoon 1 to 2 tablespoons fruit juice concentrate onto each serving. **6 servings; 90 calories per serving.**

WINTER-FRUIT COMPOTE

1 jar (17 ounces) figs, drained (reserve syrup)
1 jar (16 ounces) prunes, drained (reserve syrup)
1 three-inch stick cinnamon
1 can (29 ounces) peach halves, drained
1 lime, cut into wedges

Heat reserved syrup and the cinnamon stick to boiling in 3-quart saucepan; boil 5 minutes. Stir in figs, prunes and peach halves; heat through. Remove cinnamon stick. Serve fruit warm; garnish with lime wedges. **6 to 8 servings; 250 calories per serving.**

FRUIT-WINE COMPOTE

⅓ cup packed brown sugar
⅓ cup margarine or butter
¼ teaspoon ground nutmeg
1 can (16½ ounces) pitted dark sweet cherries, drained
1 can (16 ounces) pear halves, drained
1 can (11 ounces) mandarin orange segments, drained
1 cup dry white wine
1 tablespoon cornstarch

Heat brown sugar, margarine and nutmeg in 12-inch skillet over low heat, stirring frequently, until sugar and margarine are melted. Pat fruit with towel to dry; gradually add fruit to skillet, turning to coat. Shake ½ cup of the wine and the cornstarch in tightly covered container. Stir into remaining wine; stir into fruit. Heat to boiling; reduce heat. Simmer uncovered, stirring once or twice, until fruit is heated through, about 10 minutes. **6 to 8 servings; 240 calories per serving.**

CREAMY FILLED MANGO

Mix ¼ cup dairy sour cream and 1 tablespoon packed brown sugar. Cut 1 large unpared mango (about 1½ pounds) into fourths, cutting around seed. If necessary, cut thin slice from bottom of each piece to keep it from tipping. Fill cavities with sour cream mixture. Sprinkle with ground nutmeg if desired. **4 servings; 135 calories per serving.**

MELON BALLS IN WINE

    2   cups cantaloupe balls
    3   tablespoons sugar, if desired
    ½   cup dry red wine

Sprinkle cantaloupe with sugar; stir gently. Pour wine over cantaloupe. Cover and refrigerate at least 1 hour. **4 servings; 90 calories per serving.**

Peaches in Wine: Substitute 2 cups peach slices for the cantaloupe balls.

Strawberries in Wine: Substitute 1 pint strawberries, cut into halves, for the cantaloupe balls and ½ cup dry white wine, champagne or ginger ale for the dry red wine.

WATERMELON SUPREME

1 large oblong watermelon
1 cantaloupe
1 honeydew melon
1 pineapple
2 peaches or nectarines
2 cups blueberries
Honey-Wine Sauce or Citrus Sauce (below)

Cut top third lengthwise from watermelon; cover and refrigerate to use as desired. Scoop balls from larger section of watermelon. Remove seeds; cover balls and refrigerate. Scoop remaining pulp from watermelon with large spoon to form shell. (For decorative edge on shell, cut a saw-toothed or scalloped design.) Drain shell. Cut thin slice from bottom of shell to keep it from tipping; refrigerate.

Scoop melon balls from cantaloupe and honeydew melon (about 3 cups each). Remove rind and core from pineapple. Cut fruit into bite-size pieces. Mix with cantaloupe and honeydew melon balls; cover and refrigerate.

Just before serving, slice peaches. Drain melon balls and pineapple pieces. Mix all fruit in large bowl; drizzle with Honey-Wine Sauce. Spoon fruit into watermelon shell and garnish with mint leaves if desired. Serve immediately. **20 servings;** 80 calories per serving.

Honey-Wine Sauce
Mix ½ cup white wine or ginger ale, 3 tablespoons honey and 2 tablespoons lime juice.

Citrus Sauce

⅔ cup sugar
⅓ cup water
2 tablespoons strained orange juice
2 tablespoons strained lemon juice
2 tablespoons strained lime juice

Mix all ingredients until sugar is dissolved.

MINTED MELON

¼   cup sugar
⅓   cup water
1   tablespoon snipped mint leaves
2   tablespoons orange, pineapple or grapefruit juice
2   cups melon balls, pineapple spears, strawberries, apple wedges, pear slices or blueberries
    Mint leaves

Heat sugar and water to boiling, stirring occasionally; reduce heat. Cover; simmer 5 minutes. Sprinkle with snipped mint; refrigerate 1 hour. Strain mint mixture; stir in orange juice. Pour mint sauce over melon. Garnish with mint leaves.   **4 servings; 85 calories per serving.**

CINNAMON ORANGES

Pare and thinly slice 4 large chilled oranges. Arrange each sliced orange on crushed ice in dessert dish. Just before serving, sprinkle each serving with ¼ teaspoon ground cinnamon and 2 tablespoons flaked or shredded coconut.   **4 servings; 110 calories per serving.**

ORANGE DESSERT OMELETS

2   egg whites
⅛   teaspoon cream of tartar
2   tablespoons granulated sugar
2   egg yolks
2   tablespoons water
2   tablespoons all-purpose flour
3   oranges, pared and sectioned
    Powdered sugar

Beat egg whites and cream of tartar in 2½-quart bowl until foamy. Gradually beat in granulated sugar; continue beating until stiff and glossy. Do not overbeat. Beat egg yolks and water until thick and lemon colored, about 5 minutes. Stir in flour; fold into egg whites.

Heat oven to 400°. Grease and flour 2 round pans, 9 × 1½ inches. Divide egg mixture between pans. Bake until puffy and light brown, 8 to 10 minutes; remove from pans. Spoon half of the oranges onto half of each omelet. Fold other half of each omelet over oranges; sprinkle with powdered sugar. Garnish with orange sections if desired.   **6 servings** (⅓ omelet each); 100 calories per serving.

GINGERED PINEAPPLE

1   **pineapple (with green leaves)**
¼   **cup dark rum**
1   **teaspoon ground ginger**
½   **cup flaked or shredded coconut**

Cut pineapple lengthwise into halves through green top; cut each half into halves. Cut core from each quarter and cut along curved edges of fruit with grapefruit knife. Cut fruit crosswise into ¾-inch slices; then cut lengthwise down center of slices, leaving the cut fruit in the shell. Mix rum and ginger; spoon over pineapple. Cover and refrigerate at least 4 hours but no longer than 24 hours.

Bake coconut in ungreased square pan, 8 × 8 × 2 inches, in 350° oven, stirring occasionally, until golden brown, 8 to 10 minutes. Sprinkle coconut over fruit-filled pineapple quarters. Garnish with strawberries and mint leaves if desired.   **4 servings**; 150 calories per serving.

PAPAYA DESSERT

3   **papayas, pared**
½   **cup chilled whipping cream**
2   **tablespoons powdered sugar**
2   **tablespoons orange-flavored liqueur**
½   **lime**
1   **kiwifruit, pared and sliced**

Cut 2 of the papayas lengthwise into slices. Cut remaining papaya into pieces. Place papaya pieces in blender container. Cover and blend on high speed, stopping blender occasionally to scrape sides, until smooth, about 1 minute.

Beat whipping cream and powdered sugar in chilled bowl until thick but not stiff. Fold in pureed papaya and liqueur. Arrange papaya slices on 4 dessert plates; squeeze juice from lime over papaya. Spoon whipped cream mixture onto papaya; top with kiwifruit. **4 servings; 225 calories per serving.**

Cantaloupe Dessert: Substitute 1 small cantaloupe, pared, for the 3 papayas. Cut ¾ of the cantaloupe into slices. Cut remaining cantaloupe into pieces. Place pieces in blender container; continue as directed.

PEACH MELBA

1   cup sugar
2   cups water
4   peaches, peeled and cut into halves*
     Raspberry-Currant Sauce (page 274)
     Vanilla or pistachio ice cream

Heat sugar and water to boiling in 10-inch skillet. Place peaches, cut sides down, in skillet; reduce heat. Cover and simmer until peaches are tender, 10 to 15 minutes.

Place 2 peach halves in each of 4 dessert dishes. Prepare Raspberry-Currant Sauce; pour over peaches. Refrigerate until chilled. Top each serving with 1 scoop ice cream. **4 servings; 435 calories per serving.**

PEACHES FLAMBE

½   cup coarsely chopped pecans
1   quart vanilla ice cream, slightly softened
½   cup water
⅓   cup apricot jam
3   tablespoons packed brown sugar
6   large peaches, peeled and sliced, or 2 cans (16 ounces
     each) sliced peaches, drained
2   teaspoons lemon juice
½   cup light rum

Stir pecans into ice cream; freeze until firm. Scoop ice cream into serving-size portions onto chilled cookie sheet; freeze.

---

*8 canned peach halves can be substituted for the 1 cup sugar, 2 cups water and 4 peaches.

Mix water, jam and brown sugar in 2-quart saucepan or chafing dish. Heat to simmering over low heat. Simmer uncovered until syrupy, about 5 minutes. Stir in peaches; cook over low heat until peaches are almost tender, about 3 minutes. Stir in lemon juice.

Heat rum in saucepan until warm; ignite and pour over peaches. Stir well before serving. Serve hot over ice cream. **6 servings; 420 calories per serving.**

APRICOT-GLAZED PEARS

Mix ⅓ cup orange juice and ⅓ cup apricot jam in ungreased square baking dish, 8 × 8 × 2 inches, or 2-quart casserole. Cut 4 pears into halves; remove cores. Place cut sides down in dish. Cover and bake in 350° oven until pears are tender when pierced with fork, 25 to 30 minutes. Serve warm or chilled. Garnish with Sweetened Whipped Cream (page 274) and ground nutmeg if desired. **4 servings; 175 calories per serving.**

Apricot-glazed Peaches: Substitute 4 peaches, peeled and cut into halves, for the pears.

PEARS HELENE

- 1 **cup sugar**
- 2 **cups water**
- 1 **teaspoon vanilla**
- 3 **medium pears, pared and cut into halves***
  Fudge Sauce (page 272)
  Vanilla ice cream

Heat sugar and water to boiling in 10-inch skillet; reduce heat. Add vanilla. Place pears, cut sides down, in skillet. Cover and simmer until tender, about 15 minutes. Turn pears over; refrigerate pears in syrup until chilled.

Just before serving, prepare Fudge Sauce. Place 1 scoop ice cream in each of 6 dessert dishes; top with pear half and 1 tablespoon warm Fudge Sauce. **6 servings; 240 calories per serving.**

*6 canned pear halves, drained, can be substituted for the sugar, water, vanilla and 3 pears; refrigerate until chilled.

POACHED PLUMS

¾ to 1 cup sugar
2 cups water
2 tablespoons lemon juice
⅛ teaspoon salt
   Dash of ground allspice
2 sticks cinnamon
2 pounds plums (Santa Rosa, Greengage, Damson, Italian
   prune)

Heat all ingredients except plums to boiling in 3-quart saucepan; add plums. Cook uncovered over medium heat just until
plums are tender, about 15 minutes. Refrigerate until chilled.
Serve as breakfast fruit, dessert or meat accompaniment.   8
servings; 140 calories per serving.

RASPBERRIES ROMANOFF

1 pint fresh raspberries or strawberries
2 tablespoons sugar
2 tablespoons orange-flavored liqueur or ½ teaspoon
   grated orange peel
⅓ cup frozen (thawed) whipped topping
½ pint vanilla ice cream, slightly softened

Reserve 5 berries for garnish. Mix remaining berries, the
sugar and liqueur. Cover and refrigerate, stirring occasionally, 2 hours.

Just before serving, quickly mix whipped topping and ice
cream. Fold into berry mixture. Garnish with berries.   5
servings; 115 calories per serving.

RHUBARB WITH MACAROONS

4 cups 1-inch pieces rhubarb
1 cup sugar
2 tablespoons orange juice
2 cups macaroon pieces (about 4 macaroons)
½ cup chilled whipping cream
⅛ teaspoon almond extract
¼ cup toasted sliced almonds

Cook rhubarb, sugar and orange juice over medium heat, stirring frequently, until rhubarb is tender and slightly transparent, about 10 minutes; cool. Alternate the macaroon pieces and rhubarb sauce in each of 6 parfait glasses. Refrigerate until chilled, about 4 hours.

Just before serving, beat whipping cream and almond extract in chilled 1½-pint bowl until stiff. Top each serving with whipped cream and almonds. **6 servings; 300 calories per serving.**

RHUBARB SAUCE

Cut enough rhubarb into 1-inch pieces to measure 4 cups (about 1 pound). Heat ¾ to 1 cup sugar and ½ cup water to boiling in 2-quart saucepan, stirring occasionally. Add rhubarb; reduce heat. Simmer uncovered until rhubarb is tender and slightly transparent, about 10 minutes. Stir in few drops red food color if desired; refrigerate. **5 servings; 130 calories per serving.**

Strawberry-Rhubarb Sauce: Substitute 1 cup fresh strawberries, cut into halves, for 1 cup of the rhubarb. After cooking rhubarb, stir in strawberries; heat just to boiling.

STRAWBERRY SHORTCAKES

1	quart strawberries, sliced
1	cup sugar
⅓	cup shortening
2	cups all-purpose flour*
2	tablespoons sugar
3	teaspoons baking powder
1	teaspoon salt
¾	cup milk
	Margarine or butter, softened
	Sweetened Whipped Cream (page 274)

Mix strawberries and 1 cup sugar; let stand 1 hour.

Heat oven to 450°. Cut shortening into flour, 2 tablespoons sugar, the baking powder and salt until mixture resembles fine crumbs. Stir in milk just until blended. Gently smooth

*If using self-rising flour, omit baking powder and salt.

dough into a ball on lightly floured cloth-covered board. Knead 20 to 25 times. Roll to ½-inch thickness; cut with floured 3-inch cutter. Place about 1 inch apart on ungreased cookie sheet.

Bake until golden brown, 10 to 12 minutes. Split crosswise while hot. Spread with margarine; fill and top with whipped cream and strawberries.   **6 servings;** 575 calories per serving.

Pat-in-the-Pan Shortcake: Do not smooth dough into a ball. Pat in greased round pan, $8 \times 1½$ inches. Bake 15 to 20 minutes.

BAKED & COOKED DESSERTS

HOT FUDGE SUNDAE CAKE

- 1   cup all-purpose flour*
- ¾   cup granulated sugar
- 2   tablespoons cocoa
- 2   teaspoons baking powder
- ¼   teaspoon salt
- ½   cup milk
- 2   tablespoons vegetable oil
- 1   teaspoon vanilla
- 1   cup chopped nuts, if desired
- 1   cup packed brown sugar
- ¼   cup cocoa
- 1¾   cups hottest tap water
-     Ice cream

Heat oven to 350°. Mix flour, granulated sugar, 2 tablespoons cocoa, the baking powder and salt in ungreased square pan, 9×9×2 inches. Mix in milk, oil and vanilla with fork until smooth. Stir in nuts. Spread in pan. Sprinkle with brown sugar and ¼ cup cocoa. Pour hot water over batter.

Bake 40 minutes. Serve warm, topped with ice cream. Spoon sauce from pan onto each serving. **9 servings; 475** calories per serving.

Butterscotch Sundae Cake: Substitute 1 package (6 ounces) butterscotch chips for the nuts. Decrease brown sugar to ½ cup and the ¼ cup cocoa to 2 tablespoons.

Mallow Sundae Cake: Substitute 1 cup miniature marshmallows for the nuts.

*If using self-rising flour, omit baking powder and salt.

Peanutty Sundae Cake: Substitute ½ cup peanut butter and ½ cup chopped peanuts for the nuts.

Raisin Sundae Cake: Substitute 1 cup raisins for the nuts.

LEMON PUDDING CAKE

 2 eggs, separated
⅔ cup milk
 1 teaspoon grated lemon peel
¼ cup lemon juice
 1 cup sugar
¼ cup all-purpose flour*
¼ teaspoon salt

Heat oven to 350°. Beat egg whites until stiff peaks form. Beat egg yolks slightly; beat in milk, lemon peel and lemon juice. Beat in remaining ingredients until smooth; fold into egg whites. Pour into ungreased 1-quart casserole. Place casserole in square pan, 9 × 9 × 2 inches, on oven rack; pour very hot water (1 inch deep) into pan.

Bake until golden brown, 45 to 50 minutes. Remove casserole from water. Serve warm or cool and, if desired, with whipped cream.   **6 servings;** 195 calories per serving.

Lime Pudding Cake: Substitute 1½ teaspoons grated lime peel and ¼ cup lime juice for the lemon peel and lemon juice.

Saucy Pudding Cake: Increase milk to 1 cup.

*If using self-rising flour, omit salt.

PLUM PUDDING CAKE

---

  1   **cup all-purpose flour***
 ¾   **cup granulated sugar**
  2   **teaspoons baking powder**
 ¼   **teaspoon salt**
 ½   **cup milk**
  3   **tablespoons vegetable oil**
  2   **cups sliced fresh red plums (7 to 8 large)**
  1   **cup packed brown sugar**
  1   **teaspoon ground cinnamon**
  1   **cup boiling water**

Heat oven to 350°. Mix flour, granulated sugar, baking powder and salt. Beat in milk and oil until smooth. Pour into ungreased square pan, 8 × 8 × 2 inches. Top with plums. Mix brown sugar and cinnamon; sprinkle over plums. Pour boiling water on plums. Bake until wooden pick inserted in center comes out clean, 60 to 70 minutes. Serve warm and, if desired, with Sweetened Whipped Cream (page 274).   **6 servings; 410 calories per serving.**

RUM-CRACKER TORTE

---

  6   **eggs, separated**
 ½   **cup sugar**
  2   **tablespoons vegetable oil**
  1   **tablespoon rum flavoring**
 ½   **cup sugar**
 ¼   **cup all-purpose flour****
1¼   **teaspoons baking powder**
  1   **teaspoon ground cinnamon**
 ½   **teaspoon ground cloves**
  1   **cup fine graham cracker crumbs (about 12 squares)**
  1   **cup finely chopped nuts**
  1   **square (1 ounce) unsweetened chocolate, grated**
       Rum-flavored Whipped Cream (page 238)

*If using self-rising flour, omit baking powder and salt.
**If using self-rising flour, decrease baking powder to 1 teaspoon.

Heat oven to 350°. Line bottoms of 2 round pans, 8 or 9 × 1½ inches, with aluminum foil. Beat egg whites in 2½-quart bowl until foamy. Beat in ½ cup sugar, 1 tablespoon at a time; continue beating until stiff and glossy.

Beat egg yolks, oil and rum flavoring in 1½-quart bowl on low speed until blended. Add ½ cup sugar, the flour, baking powder, cinnamon and cloves; beat on medium speed 1 minute. Fold egg yolk mixture into egg whites. Fold in cracker crumbs, nuts and chocolate. Pour into pans.

Bake until top springs back when touched lightly, 30 to 35 minutes. Cool 10 minutes. Loosen edge of layers with knife; invert pan and hit sharply on table. (Cake will drop out.) Remove foil; cool cake completely.

Split cake to make 4 layers. Fill layers and frost top of torte with Rum-flavored Whipped Cream. Garnish with Chocolate Curls (page 681) if desired. Refrigerate at least 7 hours. (Torte mellows and becomes moist.) **12 servings; 425 calories per serving.**

Rum-flavored Whipped Cream
Beat 2 cups chilled whipping cream, ½ cup powdered sugar and 2 teaspoons rum flavoring in chilled bowl until stiff.

PLANTATION CAKE

⅔ cup shortening
½ cup packed brown sugar
2 cups all-purpose flour*
¼ teaspoon salt
⅔ cup water
⅔ cup light molasses
¾ teaspoon baking soda
   Lemon Sauce (page 273)
   Cream Cheese Topping (page 239)

Heat oven to 350°. Beat shortening and brown sugar in 1½-quart bowl on high speed, scraping bowl occasionally, 5 minutes. Mix in flour and salt. Press half of the sugar mixture in greased square pan, 8 × 8 × 2 inches.

*Do not use self-rising flour in this recipe.

Mix water, molasses and baking soda; pour half over sugar mixture in pan. Sprinkle with half of the remaining sugar mixture. Pour remaining molasses mixture over top; sprinkle with remaining sugar mixture.

Bake 40 minutes. Serve warm with Lemon Sauce and Cream Cheese Topping.   **9 servings;** 470 calories per serving.

Cream Cheese Topping
Beat 2 packages (3 ounces each) cream cheese, softened, and 2 to 3 tablespoons milk until smooth and creamy.

GINGERBREAD

2⅓   **cups all-purpose flour***
 ⅓   **cup sugar**
 ½   **cup shortening**
 1   **cup molasses**
 ¾   **cup hot water**
 1   **teaspoon baking soda**
 1   **teaspoon ground ginger**
 1   **teaspoon ground cinnamon**
 ¾   **teaspoon salt**
 1   **egg**

Heat oven to 325°. Grease and flour square pan, 9×9×2 inches. Beat all ingredients on low speed, scraping bowl constantly, 30 seconds. Beat on medium speed, scraping bowl occasionally, 3 minutes. Pour into pan.

Bake until wooden pick inserted in center comes out clean, about 50 minutes.   **9 servings;** 330 calories per serving.

*Do not use self-rising flour in this recipe.

BAKED CHOCOLATE SOUFFLE

⅓ cup sugar
⅓ cup cocoa
¼ cup all-purpose flour
1 cup milk
3 egg yolks
2 tablespoons margarine or butter, softened
1 teaspoon vanilla
4 egg whites
¼ teaspoon cream of tartar
⅛ teaspoon salt
3 tablespoons sugar
 Best Sauce (below)

Mix ⅓ cup sugar, the cocoa and flour in saucepan. Gradually stir in milk. Heat to boiling, stirring constantly; remove from heat. Beat egg yolks with fork. Beat in about ⅓ of the cocoa mixture. Gradually stir in remaining cocoa mixture. Stir in margarine and vanilla; cool slightly.

Place oven rack in lowest position. Heat oven to 350°. Butter and sugar 6-cup soufflé dish. Make a 4-inch band of triple-thickness aluminum foil 2 inches longer than circumference of dish. Butter and sugar one side of band. Extend dish by securing band, buttered side in, around outside edge.

Beat egg whites, cream of tartar and salt in 2½-quart bowl until foamy. Beat in 3 tablespoons sugar, 1 tablespoon at a time; continue beating until stiff and glossy. Do not underbeat. Stir about ¼ of the egg whites into chocolate mixture; fold in remaining egg whites. Carefully pour into soufflé dish. Place dish in square pan, 9 × 9 × 2 inches, on oven rack; pour very hot water (1 inch deep) into pan. Bake 1¼ hours. Prepare Best Sauce. Serve soufflé immediately with Best Sauce.   6 servings; 435 calories per serving.

Best Sauce
Beat ½ cup powdered sugar and ½ cup margarine or butter, softened, in saucepan until creamy. Beat ½ cup chilled whipping cream in chilled 1½-pint bowl until stiff. Fold whipped cream into sugar mixture. Heat to boiling, stirring occasionally.

Do-ahead Tip: Before baking, cover and refrigerate soufflé up to 6 hours.

LINDY'S CHEESECAKE

1	cup all-purpose flour
½	cup margarine or butter, softened
¼	cup sugar
1	tablespoon grated lemon peel
1	egg yolk
5	packages (8 ounces each) cream cheese, softened
1¾	cups sugar
3	tablespoons all-purpose flour
1	tablespoon grated orange peel
1	tablespoon grated lemon peel
¼	teaspoon salt
5	eggs
2	egg yolks
¼	cup whipping cream
¾	cup chilled whipping cream
⅓	cup toasted slivered almonds, if desired

Heat oven to 400°. Lightly grease springform pan, 9 × 3 inches; remove bottom. Mix 1 cup flour, the margarine, ¼ cup sugar, 1 tablespoon lemon peel and 1 egg yolk with hands. Press ⅓ of the mixture evenly on bottom of pan; place on cookie sheet. Bake until golden, 8 to 10 minutes; cool.

Assemble bottom and side of pan; secure side. Press remaining mixture all the way up side of pan.

Heat oven to 475°. Beat cream cheese, 1¾ cups sugar, 3 tablespoons flour, the orange peel, 1 tablespoon lemon peel, the salt and 2 of the eggs in large bowl until smooth. Continue beating, adding remaining eggs and 2 egg yolks, 1 at a time. Beat in ¼ cup whipping cream on low speed. Pour into pan. Bake 15 minutes.

Reduce oven temperature to 200°. Bake 1 hour. Turn off oven; leave cheesecake in oven 15 minutes. Cover and refrigerate at least 12 hours but no longer than 48 hours.

Loosen cheesecake from side of pan; remove side of pan. Beat ¾ cup whipping cream in chilled bowl until stiff. Spread whipped cream over top of cheesecake; decorate with almonds. Refrigerate any remaining cheesecake immediately. **20 servings**; 410 calories per serving.

Lindy's Cheesecake Squares: Heat oven to 400°. Increase almonds to ½ cup. Lightly grease rectangular pan, 13 × 9 × 2 inches. Press the crust mixture evenly on bottom of pan. Do not place pan on cookie sheet. Bake 15 minutes.

Heat oven to 475°. Pour cream cheese mixture into pan. Bake 15 minutes. Reduce oven temperature to 200°. Bake until center is set, about 45 minutes. Leave cheesecake in oven 15 minutes. Cover and refrigerate at least 12 hours but no longer than 48 hours.

Continue as directed with whipping cream and almonds. Cut cheesecake into 2½-inch squares.   **20 squares.**

PEANUT CHEESECAKE

¼	cup creamy peanut butter
3	tablespoons sugar
3	tablespoons margarine or butter
1½	cups graham cracker crumbs (about 20 squares)
2	packages (8 ounces each) cream cheese, softened
¾	cup sugar
2	teaspoons vanilla
2	eggs
½	cup finely chopped salted peanuts
½	cup chilled whipping cream
½	teaspoon vanilla
¼	cup finely crushed peanut brittle

Heat oven to 350°. Heat peanut butter, 3 tablespoons sugar and the margarine in 1½-quart saucepan over low heat, stirring frequently, until margarine is melted. Stir in cracker crumbs. Press firmly against bottom and side of ungreased pie plate, 9 × 1¼ inches, or on bottom only of ungreased square pan, 9 × 9 × 2 inches.

Beat cream cheese slightly in 2½-quart bowl. Add ¾ cup sugar, 2 teaspoons vanilla and the eggs; beat on medium speed until smooth, about 2 minutes. Fold in peanuts; pour over crumb mixture.

Bake until firm, about 30 minutes. Cover and refrigerate at least 2 hours but no longer than 48 hours.

Beat whipping cream and ½ teaspoon vanilla in chilled 1½-pint bowl until stiff. Spread over cheesecake; sprinkle with peanut brittle. Refrigerate any remaining cheesecake immediately.   **8 servings; 410 calories per serving.**

CHOCOLATE CHEESECAKE

1¼   cups chocolate wafer or graham cracker crumbs (about 18 wafers or 16 squares)
2   tablespoons sugar
3   tablespoons margarine or butter, melted
2   packages (8 ounces each) plus 1 package (3 ounces) cream cheese, softened
1   cup sugar
¼   cup cocoa
2   teaspoons vanilla
3   eggs
    Coconut-Pecan Topping (below) or Sour Cream Topping (page 244)

Heat oven to 350°. Mix crumbs and 2 tablespoons sugar; mix in margarine thoroughly. Press evenly on bottom of ungreased springform pan, 9 × 3 inches. Bake 10 minutes; cool.

Reduce oven temperature to 300°. Beat cream cheese in 3-quart bowl. Gradually beat in 1 cup sugar and the cocoa until fluffy; add vanilla. Beat in eggs, one at a time. Pour over crumb mixture. Bake until center is firm, about 1 hour. Cover and refrigerate at least 3 hours but no longer than 48 hours.

Prepare Coconut-Pecan Topping; spread over cheesecake. Loosen cheesecake from side of pan; remove side of pan. Refrigerate any remaining cheesecake immediately. **12** servings; 425 calories per serving.

Coconut-Pecan Topping

⅓   cup evaporated milk
2   tablespoons margarine or butter
2   tablespoons packed brown sugar
2   egg yolks or 1 egg
½   cup chopped pecans
½   cup flaked coconut
½   teaspoon vanilla

Cook milk, margarine, brown sugar and egg yolks in 1-quart saucepan over low heat, stirring constantly, until thickened; remove from heat. Stir in remaining ingredients; cool.

Sour Cream Topping
Beat 1 cup dairy sour cream, 2 tablespoons sugar and 2 teaspoons vanilla until blended.

Lemon Cheesecake: Omit cocoa and decrease vanilla to ¼ teaspoon. Stir in 2 teaspoons grated lemon peel with the vanilla. Bake and cool as directed. Spread with Sour Cream Topping.

PUMPKIN CHEESECAKE

1¼	cups gingersnap cookie crumbs (about twenty 2-inch cookies)
¼	cup margarine or butter, melted
3	packages (8 ounces each) cream cheese, softened
1	cup sugar
1	teaspoon ground cinnamon
1	teaspoon ground ginger
½	teaspoon ground cloves
1	can (16 ounces) pumpkin
4	eggs
2	tablespoons sugar
12	walnut halves
¾	cup chilled whipping cream

Heat oven to 350°. Mix cookie crumbs and margarine. Press evenly on bottom of ungreased springform pan, 9 × 3 inches. Bake 10 minutes; cool.

Reduce oven temperature to 300°. Beat cream cheese, 1 cup sugar, the cinnamon, ginger and cloves in 4-quart bowl on medium speed until smooth and fluffy. Add pumpkin. Beat in eggs, one at a time, on low speed. Pour over crumb mixture. Bake until center is firm, about 1¼ hours. Cover and refrigerate at least 3 hours but no longer than 48 hours.

Cook and stir 2 tablespoons sugar and the walnuts over medium heat until sugar is melted and nuts are coated. Immediately spread on dinner plate or aluminum foil; cool. Carefully break nuts apart to separate if necessary. Cover tightly and store at room temperature up to 3 days.

Loosen cheesecake from side of pan; remove side of pan. Beat whipping cream in chilled 1½-quart bowl until stiff. Spread whipped cream over top of cheesecake; arrange walnuts on top. Refrigerate any remaining cheesecake immediately. **12 servings; 465 calories per serving.**

CREAM PUFFS

1   **cup water**
½   **cup margarine or butter**
1   **cup all-purpose flour***
4   **eggs**
    Cream Filling (below) or Sweetened Whipped Cream (page 274)
    Powdered sugar

Heat oven to 400°. Heat water and margarine to rolling boil in 2½-quart saucepan. Stir in flour. Stir vigorously over low heat until mixture forms a ball, about 1 minute; remove from heat. Beat in eggs, all at once; continue beating until smooth. Drop dough by scant ¼ cupfuls about 3 inches apart onto ungreased cookie sheet.

Bake until puffed and golden, 35 to 40 minutes. Cool away from draft. Cut off tops; pull out any filaments of soft dough. Fill puffs with Cream Filling. Replace tops; sprinkle with powdered sugar. Refrigerate until serving time. **12 cream puffs; 430 calories each.**

Cream Filling

⅓   **cup sugar**
2   **tablespoons cornstarch**
⅛   **teaspoon salt**
2   **cups milk**
2   **egg yolks, slightly beaten**
2   **tablespoons margarine or butter, softened**
2   **teaspoons vanilla**

Mix sugar, cornstarch and salt in 2-quart saucepan. Gradually stir in milk. Cook over medium heat, stirring constantly, until mixture thickens and boils. Boil and stir 1 minute. Stir at least half of the hot mixture gradually into egg yolks. Stir into hot mixture in saucepan. Boil and stir 1 minute; remove from heat. Stir in margarine and vanilla; cool.

Chocolate Cream Puffs: Decrease flour to ¾ cup plus 2 tablespoons. Mix 2 tablespoons cocoa and 1 tablespoon granulated sugar with the flour. Omit Cream Filling and powdered

*Self-rising flour can be used in this recipe.

sugar; fill puffs with chocolate or peppermint ice cream and frost with Chocolate Frosting (below).

Eclairs: Drop regular or chocolate dough by scant ¼ cupfuls onto ungreased cookie sheet. Shape each into finger 4½ inches long and 1½ inches wide with spatula. Bake; cool. Fill with Cream Filling (page 245). Frost with Chocolate Frosting (below). Refrigerate until serving time. **12 eclairs.**

Chocolate Frosting

Heat 1 square (1 ounce) unsweetened chocolate and 1 teaspoon margarine or butter over low heat until melted; remove from heat. Stir in 1 cup powdered sugar and about 2 tablespoons hot water. Beat until smooth and of spreading consistency.

CREPES

1½	cups all-purpose flour*
1	tablespoon sugar
½	teaspoon baking powder
½	teaspoon salt
2	cups milk
2	tablespoons margarine or butter, melted
½	teaspoon vanilla
2	eggs

Mix flour, sugar, baking powder and salt in 1½-quart bowl. Stir in remaining ingredients. Beat with hand beater until smooth. Lightly butter 6- to 8-inch skillet; heat over medium heat until bubbly. For each crepe, pour scant ¼ cup of the batter into skillet; *immediately* rotate skillet until thin film covers bottom.

Cook until light brown. Run wide spatula around edge to loosen; turn and cook other side until light brown. Stack crepes, placing waxed paper between each. Keep covered.

If desired, thinly spread applesauce, sweetened strawberries, currant jelly or raspberry jam on warm crepes; roll up. (Be sure to fill crepes so the more attractive side is on the outside.) Sprinkle with powdered sugar if desired. **12 crepes; 115 calories per crepe.**

---

*If using self-rising flour, omit baking powder and salt.

NOTE: Crepes can be frozen up to 3 months. To freeze, cool; keep crepes covered to prevent them from drying out. Make 2 stacks of 6 crepes each, with waxed paper between crepes. Wrap each stack in aluminum foil, label and freeze.

CHERRY BLINTZES

    Crepes (page 246)
1   cup dry cottage cheese
½   cup dairy sour cream
2   tablespoons sugar
1   teaspoon vanilla
½   teaspoon grated lemon peel
¼   cup margarine or butter
1   cup dairy sour cream
1   can (21 ounces) cherry pie filling

Prepare Crepes except—brown only one side. Cool, keeping crepes covered to prevent them from drying out.

Mix cottage cheese, ½ cup sour cream, the sugar, vanilla and lemon peel. Spoon about 1½ tablespoons of the cheese mixture onto browned side of each crepe. Fold sides of crepe up over filling, overlapping edges; roll up.

Heat margarine in 12-inch skillet over medium heat until bubbly. Place blintzes, seam sides down, in skillet. Cook, turning once, until golden brown. Top each with rounded tablespoon sour cream and about 3 tablespoons pie filling.   **6 servings; 555 calories per serving.**

RASPBERRY CREPES

    Crepes (page 246)
1   package (3½ ounces) vanilla instant pudding and pie filling
2   cups half-and-half
½   teaspoon almond extract
2   tablespoons cornstarch
2   packages (10 ounces each) frozen raspberries, thawed
    Sliced almonds

Prepare Crepes. Prepare pudding and pie filling as directed on package for pudding except—substitute half-and-half for the milk and beat in almond extract; refrigerate until chilled.

Place cornstarch in 1½-quart saucepan; gradually stir in raspberries. Cook over medium heat, stirring constantly, until mixture thickens and boils. Boil and stir 1 minute; cool. Spoon generous 2 tablespoons pudding mixture onto each crepe; roll up. Place 2 crepes, seam sides down, on each dessert plate. Top with raspberry mixture and sprinkle with sliced almonds.   **6 servings** (2 crepes each); 540 calories per serving.

BAKED CUSTARD

3	eggs, slightly beaten
⅓	cup sugar
1	teaspoon vanilla
	Dash of salt
2½	cups milk, scalded
	Ground nutmeg

Heat oven to 350°. Mix eggs, sugar, vanilla and salt. Gradually stir in milk. Pour into six 6-ounce custard cups; sprinkle with nutmeg. Place cups in rectangular pan, 13 × 9 × 2 inches, on oven rack. Pour very hot water into pan to within ½ inch of tops of cups.

Bake until knife inserted halfway between center and edge comes out clean, about 45 minutes. Remove cups from water. Serve warm or chilled. Refrigerate any remaining custards immediately.   **6 servings;** 150 calories per serving.

Caramel Custard: Before preparing custard, heat ½ cup sugar in heavy 1-quart saucepan over low heat, stirring constantly, until melted and golden brown. Divide syrup among custard cups; tilt cups to coat bottoms. Allow syrup to harden in cups about 10 minutes. Pour custard mixture over syrup; bake. To unmold, carefully loosen side of custard with tip of knife. Place plate on top of custard cup; invert both the plate and cup. Shake gently; remove cup. Serve warm or, if desired, refrigerate and unmold at serving time. Caramel syrup will run down sides of custard, forming a sauce.

Raspberry Custard: Mix ⅓ cup raspberry preserves and 1 tablespoon orange-flavored liqueur; divide among six 6-ounce

custard cups. Continue as directed except—mix in 1 teaspoon orange-flavored liqueur with the salt; omit nutmeg. Refrigerate and unmold at serving time. Serve with raspberries.

CREME BRULEE

    4   egg yolks
    3   tablespoons granulated sugar
    2   cups whipping cream
    ⅓   cup packed brown sugar
    4   cups cut-up fresh fruit

Beat egg yolks in 1½-quart bowl on high speed until thick
and lemon colored, about 5 minutes. Gradually beat in granulated sugar. Heat whipping cream in 2-quart saucepan over
medium heat just until hot. Stir at least half of the hot cream
gradually into egg yolk mixture; stir into hot cream in saucepan. Cook over low heat, stirring constantly, until mixture
thickens, 5 to 8 minutes (do not boil). Pour custard into
ungreased pie plate, 9 × 1¼ inches. Cover and refrigerate at
least 2 hours but no longer than 24 hours.

Set oven control to broil and/or 550°. Sprinkle brown sugar
over custard. Broil with top about 5 inches from heat until
sugar is melted and forms a glaze, about 3 minutes. Spoon
over fruit. Refrigerate any remaining sauce immediately. **8
servings;** 325 calories per serving.

CHOCOLATE POTS DE CREME

    ⅔   cup semisweet chocolate chips
    1   cup half-and-half
    2   eggs
    3   tablespoons sugar
    2   tablespoons rum, if desired
        Dash of salt

Heat oven to 350°. Heat chocolate chips and half-and-half,
stirring constantly, until chocolate is melted and mixture is
smooth; cool slightly. Beat remaining ingredients; gradually
stir into chocolate mixture. Pour into 4 or 5 ovenproof pot de
crème cups or 4 ungreased 6-ounce custard cups.

Place cups in baking pan on oven rack. Pour boiling water into pan to within ½ inch of tops of cups. Bake 20 minutes; cool slightly. Cover and refrigerate at least 4 hours but no longer than 24 hours. Refrigerate any remaining pudding immediately. **4 or 5 servings; 315 calories per serving.**

VANILLA PUDDING

⅓   **cup sugar**
2   **tablespoons cornstarch**
⅛   **teaspoon salt**
2   **cups milk**
2   **egg yolks, slightly beaten**
2   **tablespoons margarine or butter, softened**
2   **teaspoons vanilla**

Mix sugar, cornstarch and salt in 2-quart saucepan. Gradually stir in milk. Cook over medium heat, stirring constantly, until mixture thickens and boils. Boil and stir 1 minute. Stir at least half of the hot mixture gradually into egg yolks; stir into hot mixture in saucepan. Boil and stir 1 minute; remove from heat. Stir in margarine and vanilla. Pour into dessert dishes; refrigerate. **4 servings; 240 calories per serving.**

Butterscotch Pudding: Substitute ⅔ cup packed brown sugar for the granulated sugar and decrease vanilla to 1 teaspoon.

Chocolate Pudding: Increase sugar to ½ cup and stir ⅓ cup cocoa into sugar mixture. Omit margarine.

ENGLISH TRIFLE

½ cup sugar
3 tablespoons cornstarch
¼ teaspoon salt
3 cups milk
½ cup dry sherry or other dry white wine
3 egg yolks, beaten
3 tablespoons margarine or butter
1 tablespoon vanilla
2 packages (3 ounces each) ladyfingers
½ cup strawberry preserves
1 package (12 ounces) frozen strawberries, thawed
1 cup chilled whipping cream
2 tablespoons sugar
2 tablespoons toasted slivered almonds

Mix ½ cup sugar, the cornstarch and salt in 3-quart saucepan. Gradually stir in milk and sherry. Heat to boiling over medium heat, stirring constantly. Boil and stir 1 minute. Stir at least half of the hot mixture gradually into egg yolks; stir into hot mixture in saucepan. Boil and stir 1 minute; remove from heat. Stir in margarine and vanilla. Cover and refrigerate at least 3 hours.

Cut ladyfingers lengthwise into halves; spread each half with strawberry preserves. Layer ¼ of the ladyfingers, cut sides up, half of the strawberries and half of the pudding in 2-quart serving bowl; repeat. Arrange remaining ladyfingers around edge of bowl in upright position and with cut sides toward center. (It may be necessary to gently ease ladyfingers down into pudding about 1 inch so they remain upright.) Cover and refrigerate.

Beat whipping cream and 2 tablespoons sugar in chilled 1½-quart bowl until stiff; spread over dessert. Sprinkle with almonds.   **8 to 10 servings;** 465 calories per serving.

APPLE PUDDING

¾   cup sugar
⅓   cup all-purpose* or whole wheat flour
1½ teaspoons baking powder
⅛   teaspoon salt
1   teaspoon vanilla
1   egg
1   medium apple, finely chopped
½   cup chopped nuts

Heat oven to 350°. Beat sugar, flour, baking powder, salt, vanilla and egg in 1½-quart bowl on medium speed until smooth, about 1 minute. Stir in apple and nuts. Pour into greased pie plate, 9 × 1¼ inches. Bake until golden brown, about 30 minutes. Cut into wedges. Serve warm. **6 servings; 215 calories per serving.**

BREAD PUDDING

2   cups milk
¼   cup margarine or butter
2   eggs, slightly beaten
½   cup sugar
1   teaspoon ground cinnamon or nutmeg
¼   teaspoon salt
6   cups dry bread cubes (8 slices bread)
½   cup raisins, if desired

Heat oven to 350°. Heat milk and margarine over medium heat until margarine is melted and milk is scalded. Mix eggs, sugar, cinnamon and salt in 4-quart bowl; stir in bread cubes and raisins. Stir in milk mixture; pour into ungreased 1½-quart casserole. Place casserole in pan of very hot water (1 inch deep).

Bake uncovered until knife inserted 1 inch from edge of casserole comes out clean, 40 to 45 minutes. Serve warm and, if desired, with cream. **8 servings; 355 calories per serving.**

*If using self-rising flour, decrease baking powder to 1 teaspoon and omit salt.

RICE PUDDING

⅔ cup uncooked regular rice
1⅓ cups water
2 eggs or 4 egg yolks
½ cup sugar
½ cup raisins
2 cups milk
½ teaspoon vanilla or 1 tablespoon grated orange peel
¼ teaspoon salt
   Ground nutmeg

Heat rice and water to boiling, stirring once or twice; reduce heat. Cover and simmer 14 minutes. (Do not lift cover or stir.) All water should be absorbed.

Heat oven to 325°. Beat eggs in ungreased 1½-quart casserole. Stir in sugar, raisins, milk, vanilla, salt and hot rice; sprinkle with nutmeg. Bake uncovered, stirring occasionally, until knife inserted halfway between center and edge comes out clean, 50 to 60 minutes. Serve warm or cold and, if desired, with cream. Refrigerate any remaining pudding immediately. **6 to 8 servings; 250 calories per serving.**

Rice-Nut Pudding: Butter casserole; sprinkle bottom and side with bread crumbs. Stir in ½ cup chopped nuts with the raisins.

RICE PUDDING MOLD

½ cup sugar
½ cup water
½ teaspoon salt
2 envelopes unflavored gelatin
1½ cups cooked rice (page 85)
2 cups milk
2 teaspoons vanilla
1 cup chilled whipping cream
   Raspberry-Currant Sauce (page 274)

Heat sugar, water, salt and gelatin in 2-quart saucepan, stirring constantly, until gelatin is dissolved, about 1 minute. Stir in rice, milk and vanilla. Place saucepan in bowl of iced water, stirring occasionally, until mixture mounds slightly when dropped from a spoon, about 15 minutes.

Beat whipping cream in chilled 1½-quart bowl until stiff. Fold whipped cream into rice mixture. Pour into ungreased 1½-quart mold. Cover and refrigerate until firm, about 3 hours; unmold. Serve with Raspberry-Currant Sauce. **8 servings;** 280 calories per serving.

NOODLE-RAISIN PUDDING

1	package (8 ounces) wide egg noodles
2	eggs, slightly beaten
1	cup dairy sour cream
1	cup creamed cottage cheese (small curd)
½	cup golden raisins
½	cup sugar
½	teaspoon salt
¼	teaspoon ground cinnamon
⅛	teaspoon ground nutmeg

Cook noodles as directed on package; drain. Mix remaining ingredients; toss with noodles. Pour into greased 2-quart casserole. Bake uncovered in 350° oven until golden brown, 40 to 50 minutes. Refrigerate any remaining pudding immediately. **6 to 8 servings;** 380 calories per serving.

STEAMED CHOCOLATE PUDDING

1	cup sugar
2	tablespoons margarine or butter, softened
1	egg
2	squares (2 ounces) unsweetened chocolate, melted
1¾	cups all-purpose flour*
1	teaspoon salt
¼	teaspoon cream of tartar
¼	teaspoon baking soda
1	cup milk
	Nutmeg Sauce (page 273)

Beat sugar, margarine, egg and chocolate in 1½-quart bowl with hand beater until blended. Mix remaining ingredients except milk and Nutmeg Sauce; stir into chocolate mixture alternately with milk. Pour into greased 4-cup mold. Cover tightly with aluminum foil.

Place mold on rack in Dutch oven or steamer; pour boiling water into Dutch oven halfway up mold. Cover Dutch oven. Keep water boiling over low heat until wooden pick inserted in center of pudding comes out clean, about 2 hours.

Prepare Nutmeg Sauce. Remove mold from Dutch oven and let stand 5 minutes; unmold. Serve hot with Nutmeg Sauce. **8 servings; 505 calories per serving.**

STEAMED MOLASSES PUDDING

Hard Sauce (page 256) or Lemon Sauce (page 273)
1   **egg**
2   **tablespoons shortening**
½   **cup boiling water**
½   **cup molasses**
1⅓   **cups all-purpose flour****
2   **tablespoons sugar**
1   **teaspoon baking soda**
¼   **teaspoon salt**

Prepare Hard Sauce. Beat egg in 1½-quart bowl on high speed until very thick and lemon colored, about 5 minutes. Heat shortening in boiling water until melted. Beat shortening mixture, molasses, flour, sugar, baking soda and salt into egg on low speed. Pour into well-greased 4-cup mold. Cover tightly with aluminum foil.

Place mold on rack in Dutch oven or steamer; pour boiling water into Dutch oven halfway up mold. Cover Dutch oven. Keep water boiling over low heat until wooden pick inserted in center of pudding comes out clean, about 1½ hours.

Remove mold from Dutch oven and let stand 5 minutes; unmold. Serve warm with Hard Sauce. **6 servings; 445 calories per serving.**

*If using self-rising flour, omit salt, cream of tartar and baking soda.
**Do not use self-rising flour in this recipe.

Hard Sauce
Beat ½ cup margarine or butter, softened, on high speed until fluffy and light, about 5 minutes. Gradually beat in 1 cup powdered sugar. Stir in 2 teaspoons vanilla or 1 tablespoon brandy. Refrigerate 1 hour.

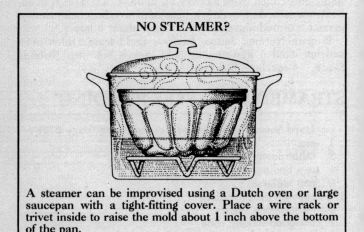

NO STEAMER?

A steamer can be improvised using a Dutch oven or large saucepan with a tight-fitting cover. Place a wire rack or trivet inside to raise the mold about 1 inch above the bottom of the pan.

FUDGY MERINGUE MALLOW

6	egg whites
½	teaspoon cream of tartar
¼	teaspoon salt
1½	cups sugar
⅓	cup cocoa
2	packages (3 ounces each) cream cheese, softened
½	cup sugar
1	teaspoon vanilla
½	teaspoon almond extract
2	cups chilled whipping cream
2	cups miniature marshmallows
	Chocolate-flavored syrup

Heat oven to 275°. Grease rectangular pan, 13 × 9 × 2 inches. Beat egg whites, cream of tartar and salt in 2½-quart bowl until foamy. Beat in 1½ cups sugar, 1 tablespoon at a time; beat until stiff and glossy. Do not underbeat. Beat in cocoa on low speed just until mixed. Spread in pan. Bake 1 hour. Turn off oven; leave meringue in oven with door closed at least 12 hours.

Mix cream cheese, ½ cup sugar, the vanilla and almond extract. Beat whipping cream in chilled 2½-quart bowl until stiff. Fold cream cheese mixture and marshmallows into whipped cream. Spread over meringue; refrigerate at least 12 hours.

Cut into serving pieces; serve with chocolate-flavored syrup. Garnish each serving with a whole strawberry if desired.   **10 servings;** 510 calories per serving.

LEMON SCHAUM TORTE

> **Meringue Shell (page 258)**
> ¾   **cup sugar**
> 3   **tablespoons cornstarch**
> ¼   **teaspoon salt**
> ¾   **cup water**
> 3   **egg yolks, slightly beaten**
> 1   **tablespoon margarine or butter**
> 1   **teaspoon grated lemon peel**
> ⅓   **cup lemon juice**
> 1   **cup chilled whipping cream**

Bake Meringue Shell. Mix sugar, cornstarch and salt in 2-quart saucepan. Gradually stir in water. Cook over medium heat, stirring constantly, until mixture thickens and boils. Boil and stir 1 minute. Stir at least half the thickened hot mixture gradually into egg yolks; stir into hot mixture in saucepan. Boil and stir 1 minute; remove from heat.

Stir in margarine, lemon peel and lemon juice. Cool to room temperature. Spoon into shell. Refrigerate at least 12 hours.

Beat whipping cream in chilled 1½-quart bowl until stiff; spread over filling. Refrigerate any remaining dessert immediately.   **8 to 10 servings;** 305 calories per serving.

Lime Schaum Torte: Substitute grated lime peel and lime juice for the lemon peel and lemon juice. Stir in 1 or 2 drops green food color.

PAVLOVA

3   egg whites
¼   teaspoon cream of tartar
¾   cup sugar
½   teaspoon vanilla
1   cup chilled whipping cream
2   tablespoons sugar
3   kiwifruit, pared and sliced*

Heat oven to 225°. Line bottom of round pan, 8 or 9 × 1½ inches, with brown paper. Beat egg whites and cream of tartar until foamy. Beat in ¾ cup sugar, 1 tablespoon at a time, and the vanilla; continue beating until stiff and glossy. Do not underbeat. Spread in pan. Bake 1½ hours. Turn off oven; leave meringue in oven with door closed 1 hour. Finish cooling meringue at room temperature.

Loosen edge of layer with knife; hit pan sharply on table to remove meringue. Invert on plate. (Meringue will be crumbly on bottom and around edge.) Remove paper. Beat whipping cream and 2 tablespoons sugar in chilled 1½-quart bowl until stiff. Frost side and top of meringue with whipped cream, building up edge slightly. Arrange kiwifruit on top. Cut into wedges.   **8 servings; 220 calories per serving.**

MERINGUE SHELL

Heat oven to 275°. Cover cookie sheet with heavy brown paper. Beat 3 egg whites and ¼ teaspoon cream of tartar in 1½-quart bowl until foamy. Beat in ¾ cup sugar, 1 tablespoon at a time; continue beating until stiff and glossy. Do not underbeat. Shape meringue on brown paper into 9-inch circle with back of spoon, building up side.

Bake 1½ hours. Turn off oven; leave meringue in oven

*1½ to 2 cups fresh strawberries, cut into halves, raspberries, blueberries or combination of these can be substituted for the kiwifruit.

with door closed 1 hour. Finish cooling meringue at room temperature. **8 servings; 75 calories per serving.**

Cinnamon Meringue: Mix ½ teaspoon ground cinnamon with the sugar before beating into egg whites. Fill baked meringue with vanilla ice cream and top with sliced peaches or oranges.

Coffee-Peach Meringue: Mix 1 teaspoon powdered instant coffee with the sugar. Beat ½ cup chilled whipping cream, 1 tablespoon sugar and ¼ teaspoon ground ginger in chilled 1½-pint bowl until stiff. Fill meringue with whipped cream mixture and sliced peaches.

Crème de Menthe Meringue: Fold 1 square (1 ounce) unsweetened chocolate, coarsely grated, into meringue after beating. Fill baked meringue with French vanilla ice cream and top with green crème de menthe.

Heart Meringue: Fold several drops red food color into meringue. Shape into heart shape, building up side. Fill baked meringue with strawberry ice cream and top with sliced strawberries.

Ice Cream Meringue: Fill baked meringue with ice cream and top with fresh berries, cut-up fruit or Fudge Sauce (page 272) or Butterscotch Sauce (page 271).

Individual Meringues: Drop meringue by ⅓ cupfuls onto brown paper. Shape into circles, building up sides. Bake 1 hour. Turn off oven; leave meringues in oven with door closed 1½ hours. Finish cooling meringues at room temperature. **8 to 10 shells.**

REFRIGERATED & FROZEN DESSERTS

LEMON SOUFFLE

¾ **cup sugar**
1 **cup water**
¾ **cup lemon juice (3 to 4 lemons)**
¼ **teaspoon salt**
2 **envelopes unflavored gelatin**
4 **eggs, separated**
2 **teaspoons grated lemon peel**
¾ **cup sugar**
2 **cups chilled whipping cream**

Make a 4-inch band of triple-thickness aluminum foil 2 inches longer than circumference of 6-cup soufflé dish. Extend dish by securing band around outside edge. (A 2-quart round casserole can be used instead of soufflé dish and foil band.)

Mix ¾ cup sugar, the water, lemon juice, salt and gelatin in saucepan. Beat egg yolks slightly; stir into gelatin mixture. Heat just to boiling over medium heat, stirring constantly; remove from heat. Stir in lemon peel. Place pan in bowl of ice and water, or refrigerate, stirring occasionally, just until mixture mounds slightly when dropped from a spoon, 20 to 30 minutes. If mixture becomes too thick, place pan in bowl of hot water; stir constantly until mixture is of proper consistency.

Beat egg whites in 2½-quart bowl until foamy. Beat in ¾ cup sugar, 1 tablespoon at a time; continue beating until stiff and glossy. Do not underbeat. Fold gelatin mixture into egg whites.

Beat whipping cream in chilled 2½-quart bowl until stiff. Fold whipped cream into egg white mixture. Carefully turn into soufflé dish. Refrigerate until set, about 8 hours.

Just before serving, carefully remove foil band. Refrigerate any remaining soufflé immediately. **12 servings;** 275 calories per serving.

ORANGE BAVARIAN

1   **cup boiling water**
1   **package (3 ounces) orange-flavored gelatin**
½   **cup sugar**
1   **tablespoon grated orange peel**
1   **cup orange juice**
1   **cup chilled whipping cream**

Pour boiling water on gelatin in 1½-pint bowl; stir until gelatin is dissolved. Stir in sugar, orange peel and juice. Refrigerate, stirring occasionally, until mixture mounds slightly when dropped from a spoon.

Beat whipping cream in chilled 1½-quart bowl until stiff. Beat gelatin mixture until foamy; fold in whipped cream. Pour into 4-cup mold or 6 to 8 dessert dishes or molds. Refrigerate until firm, about 4 hours; unmold. **6 to 8 servings;** 275 calories per serving.

WATERMELON MOUSSE

2   **cups 1-inch pieces watermelon, seeded**
2   **tablespoons grenadine**
½   **teaspoon grated lemon peel**
1   **envelope unflavored gelatin**
1   **egg white**
⅛   **teaspoon cream of tartar**
⅛   **teaspoon salt**
¼   **cup sugar**
½   **cup chilled whipping cream**

Place watermelon, grenadine and lemon peel in blender container. Cover and blend on high speed until smooth. Pour into saucepan; sprinkle with gelatin. Heat over low heat, stirring constantly, until gelatin is dissolved; remove from heat. Place in bowl of ice and water, or refrigerate, stirring occasionally, until mixture mounds slightly when dropped from a spoon.

Beat egg white, cream of tartar and salt in 1½-quart bowl until foamy. Beat in sugar, 1 tablespoon at a time; continue beating until stiff and glossy. Fold in watermelon mixture.

Beat whipping cream in chilled 1½-pint bowl until stiff. Fold whipped cream into meringue mixture. Spoon into dessert dishes. Refrigerate at least 2 hours.

Garnish with small, thin watermelon wedges if desired. Refrigerate any remaining desserts immediately.   **6 servings;** 150 calories per serving.

CHOCOLATE MOUSSE

- 4   squares (1 ounce each) semisweet chocolate, cut into pieces
- 3   eggs, separated
- 1   teaspoon vanilla
- ¾   teaspoon cream of tartar
- ½   cup sugar
- 1   cup chilled whipping cream

Heat chocolate in heavy 2-quart saucepan over low heat, stirring occasionally, until melted; remove from heat. Beat egg yolks slightly; stir yolks and vanilla into chocolate. Beat egg whites and cream of tartar in 2½-quart bowl until foamy. Beat in sugar, 1 tablespoon at a time; continue beating until stiff and glossy. Stir about ¼ of the meringue into chocolate mixture. Fold into remaining meringue.

Beat whipping cream in chilled 1½-quart bowl until stiff. Fold into chocolate meringue. Spoon into dessert dishes. Refrigerate at least 2 hours but no longer than 48 hours.

Top each serving with Sweetened Whipped Cream (page 274) and grated chocolate if desired. Refrigerate any remaining desserts immediately.   **8 servings** (about ½ cup each); 265 calories per serving.

Brandy Chocolate Mousse: Fold in 2 tablespoons brandy with the whipped cream.

ORANGE MOUSSE

 6   ounces (6 squares) vanilla-flavored candy coating
 3   egg whites
 ¾   teaspoon cream of tartar
 ¼   cup sugar
 1   teaspoon vanilla
 1   cup chilled whipping cream
 2   tablespoons orange-flavored liqueur
 1   teaspoon grated orange peel

Heat candy coating in heavy saucepan over low heat, stirring constantly, until melted; remove from heat.

Beat egg whites and cream of tartar in 2½-quart bowl until foamy. Beat in sugar, 1 tablespoon at a time, and vanilla; continue beating until stiff and glossy. Fold in candy coating until blended.

Beat whipping cream in chilled 1½-quart bowl until stiff. Fold whipped cream, orange-flavored liqueur and orange peel into egg white mixture. Spoon into dessert dishes. Refrigerate at least 2 hours. Sprinkle with grated semisweet chocolate if desired. Refrigerate any remaining desserts immediately.   **8 servings; 255 calories per serving.**

GRAHAM CRACKER TORTE

 2   cups chilled whipping cream
 ½   cup chocolate-flavored syrup
33   graham crackers (each 2½ inches square)

Beat whipping cream and syrup in chilled 2½-quart bowl until stiff. Spread small amount of cream mixture on each of 3 crackers. Arrange crackers, frosted sides down and with edges touching to form a rectangle, on serving plate; spread with about ¼ cup cream mixture. Layer with 3 crackers. Repeat layers 9 times. Gently press torte together. Carefully turn torte on its side with spatula so crackers are vertical. Frost sides and top with remaining cream mixture. Refrigerate at least 6 hours (torte will mellow and become moist). Drizzle top with 1 tablespoon chocolate-flavored syrup if desired.   **10 servings; 390 calories per serving.**

CHERRY LAYER DESSERT

30 graham cracker squares
1 cup dairy sour cream or plain yogurt
2 cups milk
1 package (about 6 ounces) vanilla instant pudding
    and pie filling
1 can (21 ounces) cherry pie filling

Arrange half of the crackers in ungreased rectangular pan, 13 × 9 × 2 inches. Beat sour cream and milk with hand beater until smooth. Beat in pudding and pie filling (dry) until smooth and slightly thickened, about 2 minutes. Spread half of the pudding mixture over crackers in pan. Top with remaining crackers; spread with remaining pudding mixture. Top with cherry pie filling. Cover and refrigerate at least 3 hours. Cut into squares. **12 servings; 245 calories per serving.**

CRANBERRY ICE

1 pound cranberries
2 cups water
2 cups sugar
¼ cup lemon juice
1 teaspoon grated orange peel
2 cups cold water

Cook cranberries in 2 cups water until skins are broken, about 10 minutes. Rub cranberries through sieve to make smooth pulp. Stir in sugar, lemon juice and orange peel. Stir in 2 cups cold water. Pour into square baking dish, 8 × 8 × 2 inches. Freeze, stirring several times to keep mixture smooth, until firm. Let stand at room temperature 10 minutes before serving. **8 servings; 225 calories per serving.**

FROZEN LEMON CREAM

2 cups chilled whipping cream
1¼ cups sugar
2 tablespoons grated lemon peel
⅓ cup lemon juice (about 1½ lemons)
1 or 2 drops yellow food color

Beat all ingredients in chilled 2½-quart bowl until stiff. Pour into square pan, 8×8×2 inches. Freeze until firm, about 2 hours. **4 servings** (about 1 cup each); 330 calories per serving.

SHERBET-BERRY PARFAITS

1	tablespoon sugar
2	teaspoons cornstarch
1	teaspoon grated orange peel
2	tablespoons orange juice
1	package (10 ounces) frozen raspberries, partially thawed
1	quart orange sherbet

Mix sugar and cornstarch in 2-quart saucepan. Stir in orange peel, orange juice and raspberries. Cook over medium heat, stirring constantly, until mixture thickens and boils. Boil and stir 1 minute. Refrigerate until chilled.

Layer orange sherbet and raspberry sauce in each of 6 parfait glasses. Freeze until firm. Remove from freezer to soften slightly before serving. Top with Sweetened Whipped Cream (page 274) if desired. **6 servings**; 250 calories per serving.

CHERRY FREEZE

1	envelope unflavored gelatin
¼	cup cold water
3	cartons (6 ounces each) cherry yogurt (about 2 cups)
½	package (16-ounce size) frozen cherries (1½ cups), partially thawed
¼	cup sugar

Sprinkle gelatin on cold water in 1-quart saucepan to soften; heat over low heat, stirring constantly, until gelatin is dissolved. Place yogurt, cherries and sugar in blender container. Cover and blend on high speed until smooth, 10 to 15 seconds. Add gelatin mixture. Cover and blend 5 seconds. Pour into rectangular baking dish, 13×9×2 inches. Freeze until partially frozen, about 1 hour.

Beat cherry mixture in chilled 2½-quart bowl on low speed until smooth and airy but not completely thawed, about 30 seconds. Do not overbeat (mixture will contain some ice crystals). Return cherry mixture to dish. Cover and freeze until consistency of sherbet, 1 to 2 hours. (If frozen longer than 2 hours, remove from freezer 15 minutes before serving.)   **4 servings** (about 1 cup each); 220 calories per serving.

FROZEN CHOCOLATE CREAM

	Orange Fudge Sauce (page 272)
14	ladyfingers
2	tablespoons orange-flavored liqueur
1	tablespoon water
3	cups chilled whipping cream
¼	cup orange-flavored liqueur

Prepare Orange Fudge Sauce. Remove 1 cup of the sauce; cool. Cover and refrigerate remaining sauce. Cut ladyfingers lengthwise into halves. Place ladyfingers, cut sides toward center, on bottom and upright around side of springform pan, 7 × 3 inches. Mix 2 tablespoons of liqueur and the water; brush on ladyfingers. Beat whipping cream in chilled 2½-quart bowl until stiff. Mix the 1 cup Orange Fudge Sauce and ¼ cup liqueur; fold into whipped cream. Spoon into pan; smooth top. Freeze until firm, about 8 hours.

Place in refrigerator at least 1 hour but no longer than 2 hours before serving. Heat refrigerated Orange Fudge Sauce, stirring occasionally, just until warm. Loosen dessert from side of pan; remove side of pan. Cut Frozen Chocolate Cream into wedges; serve with Orange Fudge Sauce.   **18 servings;** 360 calories per serving.

NOTE: A springform pan, 9 × 3 inches, can be used. Increase ladyfingers to 17, the 2 tablespoons liqueur to ⅓ cup and water to 3 tablespoons; dip cut surface of each ladyfinger half into liqueur mixture. Continue as directed.

CHOCOLATE FRANGO

2	cups chilled whipping cream
¼	cup almond-flavored liqueur
1	can (5.5 ounces) chocolate-flavored syrup

Beat whipping cream in chilled 1½-quart bowl until stiff. Fold liqueur and syrup into whipped cream. Pour into ungreased square pan, 9×9×2 inches. Cover and freeze at least 4 hours but no longer than 48 hours.   **8 servings** (about ½ cup each); 280 calories per serving.

ANGEL TOFFEE DESSERT

    6   **bars (1¹⁄₁₆ ounces each) chocolate-covered toffee candy**
    2   **cups chilled whipping cream**
    ¼   **cup sugar**
    1   **baked 10-inch Angel Food Cake (page 124)**

Refrigerate candy bars until chilled. Crush or finely chop candy bars; reserve ⅓ cup. Beat whipping cream and sugar in chilled 2½-quart bowl until stiff; fold in remaining crushed candy.

Tear cake into about 1-inch pieces. Fold cake pieces into whipped cream mixture. Press lightly in ungreased rectangular pan, 13×9×2 inches; sprinkle with reserved crushed candy. Freeze until firm, at least 1½ hours.   **About 15 servings;** 315 calories per serving.

CHOCOLATE BAKED ALASKA

    1   **half-gallon brick chocolate chip ice cream**
        Double Chocolate Cake (page 110)
    4   **egg whites**
    ½   **teaspoon cream of tartar**
    ⅔   **cup packed brown sugar**

Cut ice cream lengthwise into halves; place one half on plate; freeze. Return remaining ice cream to freezer for another use. Prepare cake as directed except—mix in bowl and grease and flour pan. Bake as directed; cool. Cover cookie sheet with aluminum foil. Place cake on cookie sheet; place ice cream on cake 1 inch from one side. Trim other side of cake around ice cream, leaving a 1-inch edge. Freeze cake and ice cream.

Heat oven to 500°. Beat egg whites and cream of tartar until foamy. Beat in brown sugar, 1 tablespoon at a time;

continue beating until stiff and glossy. Working quickly, completely cover cake and ice cream with meringue, sealing it to foil on cookie sheet. (If desired, dessert can be frozen up to 24 hours at this point.)

Bake on lowest oven rack until meringue is light brown, 3 to 5 minutes. Trim foil to edge of meringue; transfer cake to serving plate. Cut into 6 slices; cut each slice into halves. Serve immediately.   **12 servings;** 260 calories per serving.

VANILLA ICE CREAM

      3   **egg yolks, beaten**
    ½   **cup sugar**
      1   **cup milk**
    ¼   **teaspoon salt**
      2   **cups chilled whipping cream**
      1   **tablespoon vanilla**

Mix egg yolks, sugar, milk and salt in 2-quart saucepan. Cook over medium heat, stirring constantly, just until bubbles appear around edge. Refrigerate in chilled bowl until room temperature, 2 to 3 hours.

Stir whipping cream and vanilla into milk mixture. Pour into freezer can; put dasher in place. Cover and adjust crank. Place can in freezer tub. Fill freezer tub ⅓ full of ice; add remaining ice alternately with layers of rock salt (6 parts ice to 1 part rock salt). Turn crank until it turns with difficulty. Drain water from freezer tub. Remove lid; take out dasher. Pack mixture down; replace lid. Repack in ice and rock salt. Let stand several hours to ripen.   **1 quart ice cream** (eight ½-cup servings); 300 calories per serving.

Chocolate Ice Cream: Increase sugar to 1 cup. Beat 2 squares (1 ounce each) unsweetened chocolate, melted, into milk mixture before cooking. Decrease vanilla to 1 teaspoon.

Chocolate Sandwich Cookie Ice Cream: After removing the dasher from frozen ice cream, stir in 1 cup coarsely broken chocolate sandwich cookies.

Fresh Peach Ice Cream: Decrease vanilla to 1 teaspoon. Mash 4 to 5 peaches to yield 2 cups. Stir ½ cup sugar into peaches; stir into milk mixture after adding vanilla.

Fresh Strawberry Ice Cream: Decrease vanilla to 1 teaspoon. Mash 1 pint strawberries with ½ cup sugar; stir into milk mixture after adding vanilla. Stir in few drops red food color if desired.

Frozen Strawberry Ice Cream: Decrease vanilla to 1 teaspoon. Stir 1 package (16 ounces) frozen strawberry halves, thawed, into milk mixture after adding vanilla. Stir in few drops red food color if desired.

Nut Brittle Ice Cream: Stir 1 cup crushed almond, pecan or peanut brittle into milk mixture after adding vanilla.

Peppermint Ice Cream: Decrease vanilla to 1 teaspoon. Stir ½ cup crushed peppermint candy sticks into milk mixture after adding vanilla. Stir in few drops green or red food color.

Vanilla Bean Ice Cream: Omit vanilla. Add one 3-inch piece of vanilla bean to milk mixture before cooking. Before cooling, remove bean and split lengthwise into halves. Scrape the seeds into cooked mixture with tip of small knife; discard bean.

ICE-CREAM BOMBE

2 pints chocolate ice cream
1 pint French vanilla ice cream
1 pint coffee ice cream, slightly softened

Cut chocolate ice cream into 1-inch slices. Line bottom and side of chilled 1½- to 2-quart metal mold or bowl with slices; press firmly with spoon to form even layer. Freeze until firm, at least 1 hour. Repeat with French vanilla ice cream. Freeze until firm, at least 1 hour. Press coffee ice cream in center of mold. Cover and freeze until firm, about 24 hours.

Invert mold on chilled serving plate. Dip a cloth into hot water; wring out cloth and place over top of mold for just a few minutes. Lift off mold. Return ice cream to freezer until ready to serve. Remove from freezer 10 to 15 minutes before serving. Garnish as desired with Sweetened Whipped Cream (page 274), maraschino cherries, preserved kumquats or mint leaves. **8 to 10 servings;** 270 calories per serving.

NOTE: Your favorite ice-cream combinations can be substituted.

COCONUT SNOWBALLS

Spread 2 cups flaked coconut in shallow pan or on plate. Line 12 medium muffin cups, $2\frac{1}{2} \times 1\frac{1}{4}$ inches, with paper or foil baking cups. Scoop 1 half-gallon any flavor ice cream into 12 balls; roll each in coconut, using 2 forks for rolling. Place balls in muffin cups. Freeze until firm. Cover and freeze up to 2 weeks.   **12 servings; 240 calories per serving.**

Tinted Coconut Snowballs: Shake coconut and 4 drops red or green food color in tightly covered container until coconut is evenly tinted.

DESSERT SAUCES

BUTTERSCOTCH SAUCE

⅔ cup sugar
⅓ cup margarine or butter
⅓ cup buttermilk
2 teaspoons light corn syrup
¼ teaspoon baking soda
1 tablespoon rum or 1 teaspoon rum flavoring, if desired

Heat all ingredients except rum to boiling over medium heat, stirring constantly. Boil, stirring frequently, 5 minutes; remove from heat. Stir in rum; cool completely. ¾ cup sauce; 95 calories per tablespoon.

CARAMEL SAUCE

2 egg yolks, beaten
½ cup packed brown sugar
½ cup granulated sugar
¼ cup margarine or butter
½ cup water
1 teaspoon vanilla

Heat all ingredients to boiling over medium heat, stirring constantly. Boil and stir 1 minute. Serve warm or cold. Store any remaining sauce in tightly covered container in refrigerator up to 4 weeks. **About 1⅓ cups sauce; 65 calories per** tablespoon.

CRUNCHY CHOCOLATE SAUCE

¼ cup margarine or butter
1 cup chopped walnuts or pecans
½ teaspoon vanilla
1 package (6 ounces) milk chocolate or
   semisweet chocolate chips

Heat margarine in heavy skillet until melted. Cook walnuts in margarine over low heat, stirring constantly, until margarine is light brown; remove from heat. Stir in vanilla and chocolate chips until chocolate is melted. Serve warm. **1¼ cups sauce; 110 calories per tablespoon.**

FUDGE SAUCE

1 can (12 ounces) evaporated milk
1 package (12 ounces) semisweet chocolate chips
1 cup sugar
1 tablespoon margarine or butter
1 teaspoon vanilla

Heat milk, chocolate chips and sugar to boiling over medium heat, stirring constantly; remove from heat. Stir in margarine and vanilla. Serve either warm or cold. Store any remaining sauce in tightly covered container in refrigerator up to 4 weeks. **About 3 cups sauce; 55 calories per tablespoon.**

Orange Fudge Sauce: Substitute 2 teaspoons orange-flavored liqueur for the 1 teaspoon vanilla.

MARSHMALLOW SAUCE

⅔ cup sugar
¼ cup water
3 tablespoons light corn syrup
2 cups miniature marshmallows*
¾ teaspoon vanilla
   Dash of salt

*20 large marshmallows, cut into fourths, can be substituted for the miniature marshmallows.

Heat sugar, water and corn syrup to boiling; reduce heat. Simmer uncovered, stirring occasionally, 4 minutes; remove from heat. Stir in remaining ingredients until marshmallows are melted and mixture is smooth. Refrigerate any remaining sauce in tightly covered container up to 1 week. To reheat, pour into saucepan and heat over low heat, stirring constantly, until sauce is warm.   **1½ cups sauce; 40 calories per tablespoon.**

NUTMEG SAUCE

1   **cup sugar**
½   **cup margarine or butter**
½   **cup half-and-half**
½   **teaspoon ground nutmeg**

Cook all ingredients in heavy 1-quart saucepan over low heat 5 minutes, stirring occasionally. (Watch carefully; mixture burns easily.) Serve warm or cool.   **About 1 cup sauce; 110 calories per tablespoon.**

LEMON SAUCE

½   **cup sugar**
2   **tablespoons cornstarch**
1   **cup water**
2   **tablespoons margarine or butter**
1   **tablespoon grated lemon peel**
1   **tablespoon lemon juice**

Mix sugar and cornstarch in saucepan. Gradually stir in water. Cook over medium heat, stirring constantly, until mixture thickens and boils. Boil and stir 1 minute; remove from heat. Stir in remaining ingredients. Serve warm or cool. **About 1 cup sauce; 40 calories per tablespoon.**

ORANGE SAUCE

    1   cup sugar
    2   tablespoons cornstarch
    1   tablespoon all-purpose flour
    ¼   teaspoon salt
    1¼   cups orange juice
    ½   cup water
    ¼   cup lemon juice
    1   tablespoon margarine or butter
    1   teaspoon grated orange peel
    1   teaspoon grated lemon peel

Mix sugar, cornstarch, flour and salt in saucepan. Stir in
orange juice, water and lemon juice. Heat to boiling over low
heat, stirring constantly. Boil and stir 3 minutes; remove
from heat. Mix in remaining ingredients. Serve warm. **2
cups sauce**; 35 calories per tablespoon.

RASPBERRY-CURRANT SAUCE

    ½   cup currant jelly
    1   package (10 ounces) frozen raspberries, thawed
    1   tablespoon cold water
    1½   teaspoons cornstarch

Heat jelly and raspberries (with syrup) to boiling. Mix water
and cornstarch; stir into raspberries. Heat to boiling, stirring
constantly. Boil and stir 1 minute; cool. Press through sieve
to remove seeds if desired. **About 1⅓ cups sauce**; 35 calories
per tablespoon.

SWEETENED WHIPPED CREAM

For 1 cup whipped cream: Beat ½ cup chilled whipping
cream and 1 tablespoon granulated or powdered sugar in
chilled bowl until stiff. **1 cup whipped cream**; 55 calories
per tablespoon.

    For 1½ cups whipped cream: Use ¾ cup chilled whipping
cream and 2 tablespoons sugar.

    For 2⅓ cups whipped cream: Use 1 cup chilled whipping
cream and 3 tablespoons sugar.

Flavored Whipped Cream: Beat one of the following into 1 cup whipping cream and 3 tablespoons sugar:

☐ ½ teaspoon almond extract
☐ ½ teaspoon ground cinnamon
☐ ½ teaspoon ground ginger
☐ 1 teaspoon grated lemon or orange peel
☐ ¼ teaspoon maple flavoring
☐ ½ teaspoon ground nutmeg
☐ ½ teaspoon peppermint extract
☐ ½ teaspoon rum flavoring
☐ 1 teaspoon vanilla

EGGS
CHEESE
LEGUMES

EGGS

ABOUT EGGS

BUYING EGGS

Eggs are marketed according to size, grade and color. Standards for grade and size of eggs are established by the U.S. Department of Agriculture.

Size: Eggs are most often available as extra large, large and medium. Our recipes were tested with large eggs.

Grade: The quality of both the egg and its shell at the time the egg was packed determines the grade. There is very little difference in quality between Grades AA and A, and there is no difference in nutritive content. Almost no Grade B eggs are sold in the retail market.

Color: Egg shell color—white or brown—and yolk color—pale or deep yellow—vary with the breed and diet of the hen. White eggs are most in demand, but in some parts of the country brown are preferred. Flavor, nutritive value and cooking performance are the same for white and brown eggs.

EGG BASICS

■ Purchase eggs from a refrigerated case and refrigerate immediately upon arriving home.

■ Look for egg shells that are clean and not cracked. If a shell cracks between the market and home, use the egg as soon as possible in a fully cooked dish.

■ Store fresh eggs in their carton to help prevent them from absorbing refrigerator odors.

■ Store eggs with the large ends up to help keep the yolk in the center.

■ To measure 1 cup, you need 4 to 6 whole eggs, 8 to 10 whites or 12 to 14 yolks.

■ Freeze raw egg whites in a plastic ice cube tray; remove to a plastic bag for storage. Thaw frozen egg whites in the refrigerator. When measuring, note that 2 tablespoons thawed liquid egg white are equal to 1 fresh egg white.

■ Hard-cooked egg yolks can be frozen successfully, but hard-cooked egg whites become tough and watery.

SOFT-COOKED EGGS

Cold Water Method: Place eggs in saucepan; add enough cold water to come at least 1 inch above eggs. Heat rapidly to boiling; remove from heat. Cover and let stand until desired doneness, 1 to 3 minutes. Immediately cool eggs in cold water several seconds to prevent further cooking. Cut eggs into halves; scoop eggs from shells.

Boiling Water Method: Place eggs in bowl of warm water to prevent shells from cracking. Fill saucepan with enough water to come at least 1 inch above eggs; heat to boiling. Transfer eggs from warm water to boiling water with spoon; remove from heat. Cover and let stand until desired doneness, 6 to 8 minutes. Immediately cool eggs in cold water several seconds to prevent further cooking. Cut eggs into halves; scoop eggs from shells.

HARD-COOKED EGGS

Cold Water Method: Place eggs in saucepan; add enough cold water to come at least 1 inch above eggs. Heat rapidly to boiling; remove from heat. Cover and let stand 22 to 24 minutes. Immediately cool eggs in cold water to prevent further cooking. Tap egg to crackle shell. Roll egg between hands to loosen shell, then peel. Hold egg under running cold water to help ease off shell.

Boiling Water Method: Place eggs in bowl of warm water to prevent shells from cracking. Fill saucepan with enough water to come at least 1 inch above eggs; heat to boiling. Transfer eggs from warm water to boiling water with spoon; reduce heat to below simmering. Cook uncovered 20 min-

utes. Immediately cool eggs in cold water to prevent further
cooking. Tap egg to crackle shell. Roll egg between hands to
loosen shell, then peel. Hold egg under running cold water
to help ease off shell.

POACHED EGGS

Heat water (1½ to 2 inches) to boiling; reduce to simmering.
Break each egg into custard cup or saucer; holding cup or
saucer close to water's surface, slip 1 egg at a time into water.

Cook until desired doneness, 3 to 5 minutes. Remove eggs
from water with slotted spoon.

FRIED EGGS

Heat margarine, butter or bacon fat in heavy skillet to ⅛-inch
depth just until hot enough to sizzle a drop of water. Break
each egg into custard cup or saucer; carefully slip 1 egg at a
time into skillet. Immediately reduce heat to low.

Cook, spooning margarine onto eggs, until whites are set
and a film forms over yolks (sunny-side up). Or gently turn
eggs over when whites are set and cook until desired doneness.

Poached-Fried Eggs: Heat just enough margarine, butter
or bacon fat to grease skillet. Cook eggs over low heat until
edges turn white. Add ½ teaspoon water for 1 egg, decreasing proportion slightly for each additional egg. Cover and
cook until desired doneness.

SCRAMBLED EGGS

For each serving, stir 2 eggs, 2 tablespoons milk or cream, ¼
teaspoon salt and dash of pepper with fork. Stir thoroughly
for a uniform yellow, or slightly for streaks of white and
yellow.

Heat 1½ teaspoons margarine or butter in skillet over
medium heat just until hot enough to sizzle a drop of water.
Pour egg mixture into skillet.

As mixture begins to set at bottom and side, gently lift
cooked portions with spatula so that thin, uncooked portion
can flow to bottom. Avoid constant stirring. Cook until eggs

are thickened throughout but still moist, 3 to 5 minutes.

Fancy Scrambled Eggs: For each serving, stir in 2 tablespoons of one or more of the following: shredded Cheddar, Monterey Jack or Swiss cheese; chopped mushrooms; snipped chives; snipped parsley; crisply cooked and crumbled bacon;* finely shredded dried beef;* chopped fully cooked smoked ham.*

BAKED (SHIRRED) EGGS

For each serving, carefully break 1 egg into buttered 6-ounce custard cup. Sprinkle with salt and pepper. If desired, top each with 1 tablespoon milk or half-and-half, dot with margarine or butter, softened, or sprinkle with 1 tablespoon shredded Cheddar cheese. Bake eggs uncovered in 325° oven until desired doneness, 15 to 18 minutes. (Whites should be set but yolks soft.)

EGGS ON ENGLISH MUFFINS

2	English muffins, split
2	tablespoons margarine or butter, softened
8	ounces mushrooms, sliced
1	clove garlic, finely chopped
1	tablespoon vegetable oil
2	green onions (with tops), thinly sliced
1	medium tomato, chopped (about 1 cup)
½	teaspoon salt
	Freshly ground pepper
4	Poached Eggs (page 281)
2	tablespoons grated Parmesan cheese

Spread split sides of muffins with margarine. Cook muffins, split sides down, in 10-inch skillet over medium heat until brown; remove muffins from skillet. Cook and stir mushrooms and garlic in oil in same skillet over medium heat until mushrooms are tender, 6 to 8 minutes. Stir in onions, tomato, salt and pepper; keep warm.

Prepare Poached Eggs. Remove eggs from water with slot-

*Omit salt.

ted spoon. Place 1 egg on each muffin half; spoon mushroom mixture over eggs. Sprinkle with cheese. **4 servings; 280 calories per serving.**

Cooked Canadian-style Bacon (page 427) and Creamy Filled Mango (page 226) are nice with this entrée.

EGGS BENEDICT CASSEROLE

2½   cups cut-up fully cooked smoked ham
10   Poached Eggs (page 281)
¼   teaspoon pepper
     Mornay Sauce (below)
1   cup crushed cornflakes (about 2 cups uncrushed)
¼   cup margarine or butter, melted

Sprinkle ham in ungreased rectangular baking dish, 13 × 9 × 2 inches. Prepare Poached Eggs except—cook until egg is just set, about 3 minutes. Remove from water with slotted spoon; place on ham. Repeat with remaining eggs (place eggs in 2 rows on ham). Sprinkle with pepper. Prepare Mornay Sauce; pour over eggs. Toss cornflakes and margarine; sprinkle over sauce in rectangle around each egg. Cover and refrigerate no longer than 24 hours.

Bake uncovered in 350° oven until hot and bubbly, 35 to 40 minutes. Garnish each serving with a piece of ripe olive if desired. **10 servings; 395 calories per serving.**

Serve this casserole at brunch with sliced tomatoes, Fruit Platter (page 538) and Danish Kringle (page 82).

Mornay Sauce
¼   cup margarine or butter
¼   cup all-purpose flour
½   teaspoon salt
⅛   teaspoon ground nutmeg
2½   cups milk
1½   cups shredded Gruyère or Swiss cheese (6 ounces)
½   cup grated Parmesan cheese

Heat margarine in 2-quart saucepan over low heat until melted. Stir in flour, salt and nutmeg. Cook over low heat, stirring constantly, until smooth and bubbly; remove from heat. Stir in milk. Heat to boiling, stirring constantly. Boil and stir 1 minute. Add cheeses; cook and stir until cheese is melted and mixture is smooth.

EGGS ON TORTILLAS

    Vegetable oil
6   corn tortillas (each about 6 inches in diameter)
1   jar (12 ounces) Mexican salsa
6   eggs
1½ cups shredded Monterey Jack cheese (6 ounces)

Heat oil (⅛ inch) in 8-inch skillet over medium heat just until hot. Cook tortillas, one at a time, in hot oil, turning once, until crisp, about 3 minutes; drain. Sprinkle with salt if desired. Keep warm.

Heat salsa to boiling in 10-inch skillet until hot; reduce heat. Break each egg into custard cup or saucer; carefully slip one egg at a time into salsa. Cover and cook until desired doneness, 6 to 8 minutes. Place 1 egg on each tortilla; spoon salsa over egg. Top with cheese; sprinkle with snipped parsley if desired.   **6 servings; 345 calories per serving.**

Nice served with Fruit Platter (page 538) and Lemon Pudding Cake (page 236).

EGGS BENEDICT

    Hollandaise Sauce (page 600)
3   English muffins
    Margarine or butter, softened
6   thin slices fully cooked Canadian-style bacon or
      smoked ham
1   teaspoon margarine or butter
6   Poached Eggs (page 281)

Prepare Hollandaise Sauce; keep warm. Split English muffins; toast. Spread each muffin half with margarine; keep warm. Cook Canadian-style bacon in 1 teaspoon margarine over medium heat until light brown. Prepare Poached Eggs. Place 1 slice bacon on split side of each muffin half; top with poached egg. Spoon warm sauce over eggs. **6 servings; 410 calories per serving.**

Add asparagus spears and fresh fruit for a spring brunch.

FRENCH OMELET

Mix 3 eggs with fork just until whites and yolks are blended. Heat 1 tablespoon margarine or butter in 8-inch skillet or omelet pan over medium-high heat just until margarine begins to brown. As margarine melts, tilt skillet to coat bottom completely.

Quickly pour eggs, all at once, into skillet. Slide skillet back and forth rapidly over heat and, at the same time, stir quickly with fork to spread eggs continuously over bottom of skillet as they thicken. Let stand over heat a few seconds to lightly brown bottom of omelet. (Do not overcook—omelet will continue to cook after folding.)

Tilt skillet; run fork under edge of omelet, then jerk skillet sharply to loosen eggs from bottom of skillet. Fold portion of omelet nearest you just to center. (Allow for portion of omelet to slide up side of skillet.)

Grasp skillet handle; turn omelet onto warm plate, flipping folded portion of omelet over so far side is on bottom. Tuck sides of omelet under if necessary. **1 serving; 365 calories.**

Bacon Omelet: Just before folding omelet, sprinkle with 3 slices bacon, crisply cooked and crumbled.

Cheese Omelet: Just before folding omelet, sprinkle with ¼ cup shredded Cheddar cheese (1 ounce).

Chive Omelet: Just before folding omelet, sprinkle with 1 tablespoon snipped chives.

Green Chili Omelet: Just before folding omelet, place 2 tablespoons canned green chilies on ½ of omelet and sprinkle with ¼ cup shredded Monterey Jack cheese (1 ounce). Serve with Mexican salsa if desired.

Herbed Omelet: Just before folding omelet, sprinkle with dried basil, chervil, thyme or marjoram leaves, 1 tablespoon snipped chives and 1 tablespoon snipped parsley.

Jelly Omelet: Just before folding omelet, dot with 2 table-spoons jelly or preserves.

Western Omelet: Mix in ¼ cup finely chopped fully cooked smoked ham, 2 tablespoons chopped onion and 2 tablespoons chopped green pepper.

PUFFY OMELET

<hr>

    4 eggs, separated
    ¼ cup water
    ¼ teaspoon salt
    ⅛ teaspoon pepper
    1 tablespoon margarine or butter

Heat oven to 325°. Beat egg whites, water and salt on high speed until stiff but not dry. Beat egg yolks and pepper on high speed until very thick and lemon colored, about 3 minutes. Fold into egg whites.

Heat margarine in 10-inch ovenproof skillet over medium heat just until hot enough to sizzle drop of water. As margarine melts, tilt skillet to coat bottom completely. Pour egg mixture into skillet. Level surface gently; reduce heat. Cook over low heat until puffy and light brown on bottom, about 5 minutes. (Lift omelet carefully at edge to judge color.) Bake uncovered in oven until knife inserted in the center comes out clean, 12 to 15 minutes.

Tilt skillet; slip pancake turner or spatula under omelet to loosen. Fold omelet in half, being careful not to break it. Slip onto warm plate. Serve with Avocado or Garlic-Tomato Sauce (below and page 287) if desired.   **2 servings; 230 calories per serving.**

Nice with Brioche (page 67).

Avocado Sauce

    ¾ cup dairy sour cream
    ½ teaspoon salt
    ⅛ teaspoon dried dill weed
    1 large tomato, diced and drained
    1 small avocado, diced

Heat sour cream, salt and dill weed until hot. Gently stir in tomato; heat 1 minute. Carefully stir in avocado.

Garlic-Tomato Sauce

      1   clove garlic, finely chopped
      1   green onion (with top), chopped
      1   teaspoon olive or vegetable oil
      1   medium tomato, chopped (about 1 cup)
    ¼   teaspoon dried basil leaves
    ⅛   teaspoon salt
          Dash of sugar
          Freshly ground pepper

Cook and stir garlic and onion in oil over medium heat until onion is tender, about 1 minute. Stir in remaining ingredients. Heat uncovered, stirring occasionally, until hot, about 3 minutes.

Easy ... OVEN OMELET

      2   cups shredded Cheddar cheese (8 ounces)
      1   can (4 ounces) chopped green chilies, drained
      2   cups shredded Monterey Jack cheese (8 ounces)
   1¼   cups milk
      3   tablespoons all-purpose flour
    ½   teaspoon salt
      3   eggs
      1   can (8 ounces) tomato sauce

Layer Cheddar cheese, chilies and Monterey Jack cheese in greased square baking dish, 8 × 8 × 2 inches. Beat milk, flour, salt and eggs; pour over cheese mixture. Bake uncovered in 350° oven until set in center and top is golden brown, about 40 minutes. Let stand 10 minutes before cutting. Heat tomato sauce until hot; serve with omelet.   **8 servings; 300** calories per serving.

Complete with English Muffins (page 62) and Winter Fruit Salad (page 538).

BROCCOLI OVEN OMELET

9 eggs
1 package (10 ounces) frozen chopped broccoli, thawed and drained
⅓ cup finely chopped onion
¼ cup grated Parmesan cheese
2 tablespoons milk
½ teaspoon salt
½ teaspoon dried basil leaves
¼ teaspoon garlic powder
1 medium tomato, cut into 6 slices
¼ cup grated Parmesan cheese

Beat eggs with hand beater in 2½-quart bowl until light and fluffy. Stir in broccoli, onion, ¼ cup cheese, the milk, salt, basil and garlic powder. Pour into ungreased rectangular baking dish, 11 × 7½ × 2 inches. Arrange tomato slices on top; sprinkle with ¼ cup cheese. Bake uncovered in 325° oven until set, 25 to 30 minutes.   **6 servings; 190 calories per serving.**

Serve with Cranberry-Orange Bread (page 56).

VEGETABLE FRITTATA

1 jar (6 ounces) marinated artichoke hearts
  Olive or vegetable oil
1 medium red pepper, chopped (about 1 cup)
1 medium onion, chopped (about ½ cup)
8 eggs
½ teaspoon salt
⅛ teaspoon pepper
½ cup shredded Swiss cheese (2 ounces)
2 tablespoons shredded Swiss cheese

Drain artichoke hearts, reserving marinade. Add enough oil to marinade to measure ⅓ cup. Cook and stir red pepper and onion in marinade mixture in 10-inch skillet over medium heat until onion is tender, about 5 minutes. Stir in artichoke hearts. Beat eggs, salt and pepper; stir in ½ cup cheese. Pour egg mixture over vegetable mixture. Cover and cook over medium-low heat until eggs are set and light brown on bottom, 8 to 10 minutes.

Set oven control to broil and/or 550°. Broil frittata with top about 5 inches from heat until golden brown, about 2 minutes. Sprinkle with 2 tablespoons cheese; cut into wedges. **6 servings**; 290 calories per serving.

Serve with Soft Breadsticks (page 64).

EGGS IN ROLLS

6	Kaiser rolls or steak buns, each 4 inches in diameter
¼	cup margarine or butter, melted
6	eggs, separated
¼	cup milk
½	teaspoon salt
⅛	teaspoon pepper
1	cup shredded mozzarella cheese (4 ounces)
1	can (4½ ounces) deviled ham
1	tablespoon margarine or butter
¼	teaspoon cream of tartar

Heat oven to 425°. Cut a hole about 2 inches in diameter in top of each roll; scoop out inside, leaving ½-inch wall. Place rolls in ungreased rectangular pan, 13×9×2 inches. Brush insides of rolls with ¼ cup margarine.

Mix egg yolks, 3 of the egg whites, the milk, salt and pepper with fork until of uniform color. Stir in cheese and deviled ham. Heat 1 tablespoon margarine in 10-inch skillet just until hot enough to sizzle a drop of water. Pour egg mixture into skillet. As mixture begins to set at bottom and side, gently lift cooked portions with spatula so that thin, uncooked portions can flow to bottom. Avoid constant stirring. Cook until eggs are thickened throughout but still moist. Spoon eggs into rolls.

Beat 3 egg whites and the cream of tartar on high speed until stiff but not dry. Spoon over cooked egg mixture, carefully sealing to edge of rolls. Bake until topping is golden, about 8 minutes. **6 servings**; 460 calories per serving.

Serve with Fruit-Wine Compote (page 225).

EGG FOO YONG

2 tablespoons vegetable oil
3 eggs
1 cup bean sprouts, drained
½ cup chopped cooked pork
2 tablespoons chopped onion
¾ teaspoon salt
Brown Sauce (below)

Heat oil in 10-inch skillet until hot. Beat eggs until thick and lemon colored, about 5 minutes. Stir in bean sprouts, pork, onion and salt.

Pour ¼ cup egg mixture at a time into skillet. Push cooked egg up over pork with broad spatula to form a patty. Cook until patty is set; turn. Cook over medium heat until other side is brown. Serve with Brown Sauce. **2 servings;** 435 calories per serving.

For an easy meal, serve with Lemon Rice (page 85) and melon wedges.

Brown Sauce

½ cup water
1 teaspoon cornstarch
1 teaspoon sugar
1 teaspoon vinegar
2 tablespoons plus 1½ teaspoons soy sauce

Cook all ingredients, stirring constantly, until mixture thickens and boils. Boil and stir 1 minute.

Do-ahead Tip: Cover and freeze cooked patties no longer than 1 month. Heat frozen patties uncovered in 375° oven until hot, about 15 minutes.

CREAMED EGGS WITH HAM

    3   tablespoons margarine or butter
    3   tablespoons all-purpose flour
    ½   teaspoon dry mustard
    ¼   teaspoon salt
    ⅛   teaspoon pepper
  2¼   cups milk
    1   cup diced fully cooked smoked ham
    4   Hard-cooked Eggs (page 280), each cut into fourths

Heat margarine in 2-quart saucepan over low heat until melted.
Stir in flour, mustard, salt and pepper. Cook over low heat,
stirring constantly, until smooth and bubbly; remove from
heat. Stir in milk. Heat to boiling, stirring constantly. Boil
and stir 1 minute. Gently stir in ham and eggs; heat
through.   **5 servings; 265 calories per serving.**
  Spoon over English Muffins (page 62) or toast and complete with fresh fruit.
  Creamed Eggs: Omit mustard and ham and increase eggs
to 6.
  Creamed Eggs with Seafood: Omit mustard and ham; stir
in 1 can (7¾ ounces) salmon, drained and flaked, or 1 can (6½
ounces) tuna, drained, with the eggs.

EGG-BACON BAKE

    ¼   cup dry bread crumbs
    1   tablespoon margarine or butter, melted
    5   Hard-cooked Eggs (page 280), sliced
    3   slices bacon, cut up
    1   cup dairy sour cream
    3   tablespoons finely chopped onion
    1   tablespoon milk
    ½   teaspoon salt
    ¼   teaspoon paprika
    ⅛   teaspoon pepper
    ½   cup shredded Cheddar cheese (2 ounces)

Toss bread crumbs and margarine; divide among 4 buttered
10-ounce custard cups or casseroles. Layer egg slices over
bread crumbs.

Cook bacon until crisp; drain. Mix bacon, sour cream, onion, milk, salt, paprika and pepper; spoon onto eggs. Top with cheese. Bake uncovered in 350° oven until cheese is melted, 10 to 15 minutes.   **4 servings;** 360 calories per serving.

Herb Biscuits (page 42) and Gingered Pineapple (page 229) are nice additions.

CHEESE SOUFFLE

- ¼   **cup margarine or butter**
- ¼   **cup all-purpose flour**
- ½   **teaspoon salt**
- ¼   **teaspoon dry mustard**
-       **Dash of ground red pepper**
- 1   **cup milk**
- 1   **cup shredded Cheddar cheese (4 ounces)**
- 3   **eggs, separated**
- ¼   **teaspoon cream of tartar**

Heat oven to 350°. Butter 4-cup soufflé dish or 1-quart casserole. Make a 4-inch band of triple-thickness aluminum foil 2 inches longer than circumference of dish; butter 1 side. Secure foil band, buttered side in, around dish.

Heat margarine in 2-quart saucepan over low heat until melted. Stir in flour, salt, mustard and red pepper. Cook over low heat, stirring constantly, until smooth and bubbly; remove from heat. Stir in milk. Heat to boiling, stirring constantly. Boil and stir 1 minute. Stir in cheese until melted; remove from heat.

Beat egg whites and cream of tartar in 2½-quart bowl on high speed until stiff but not dry. Beat egg yolks on high speed until very thick and lemon colored, about 3 minutes; stir into cheese mixture. Stir about ¼ of the egg white mixture into cheese mixture. Fold cheese mixture into remaining egg white mixture.

Carefully pour into soufflé dish. Bake uncovered until knife inserted halfway between center and edge comes out clean, 50 to 60 minutes. Carefully remove foil band and divide soufflé into sections with 2 forks. Serve immediately.   **3 servings;** 465 calories per serving.

Accompany soufflé with Leeks in Tomato Sauce (page 645), dinner rolls and Peaches in Wine (page 226).

CHEESE

ABOUT CHEESE

KINDS OF CHEESE

Natural cheese: The solid portion of the milk known as curds is separated from the liquid portion, or whey, and pressed into various forms to make natural cheeses. The length of time that natural cheese is allowed to ripen determines the flavor—mild, medium or sharp.

Pasteurized process cheese: A blend of one or more varieties of natural cheeses that are heated or pasteurized. The heating stops the ripening, so the cheese has a uniform flavor and texture.

Pasteurized cheese food: Cheese food is made by the same methods as process cheese. However, it has less fat and more moisture.

Pasteurized cheese spread: Cheese spread is made by the same method as cheese food. However, it has a slightly lower fat content and slightly higher moisture content.

Coldpack (club) cheese food: This is a soft, spreadable blend of one or more varieties of cheeses that are mixed without using heat.

Unripened, fresh cheese: Cottage cheese and cream cheese are fresh cheeses. Because they are not cured, they have a bland, mild flavor.

COOKING WITH CHEESE

Keep cooking temperature low and the cooking time short. High heat and overcooking cause cheese to become stringy and tough. When adding cheese to other ingredients, cut it into small pieces so it melts evenly and quickly.

CHEESE BASICS

■ The flavor of cheese is best at room temperature (except cottage cheese or cream cheese). Remove cheese from refrigerator and let stand covered about 1 hour before serving.

■ All cheese should be wrapped and stored in the refrigerator.

■ Unripened, fresh cheeses do not improve with age and should be used soon after purchasing.

■ Four ounces of shredded, crumbled or grated cheese equal 1 cup.

■ Refrigerated cheese is firmer and therefore easier to shred than room-temperature cheese.

VARIETIES OF NATURAL CHEESES

Texture	Flavor	Use
HARD		
Parmesan	piquant, sharp	cooking, salad
Provolone	mild to sharp, smoky	cooking, pasta
Romano	piquant, sharp	cooking, pasta
Swiss	mild, nutty, sweet	appetizer, cooking, sandwich, dessert
FIRM		
Blue	tangy, sharp, robust	appetizer, salad, dessert
Cheddar	mild to very sharp	cooking, with fruit, dessert
Cheshire	sharp, salty	cooking, with fruit
Edam, Gouda	milky, nutty	appetizer, dessert
Fontina	mellow, mild	appetizer, eggs, dessert
Gjetost	caramel, sweet	sandwich, snack
Gorgonzola	piquant, salty	salad, dessert
Gruyère	mild, nutty	cooking, dessert
SEMISOFT		
Bel Paese	creamy, mild	cooking, dessert
Brick	mild to sharp	appetizer, sandwich
Feta	salty, sharp	cooking, salad
Havarti	mild	appetizer, dessert
Monterey Jack	creamy, mild	appetizer, cooking, sandwich
Mozzarella	mild	cooking, pizza

Texture	Flavor	Use
SEMISOFT		
Muenster	mild to sharp	appetizer, sandwich, dessert
Port du Salut	mild to robust	appetizer, sandwich, dessert
Roquefort	salty, sharp	appetizer, salad, dessert
Stilton	piquant, mellow	salad, dessert, snack
SOFT		
Brie	mild to pungent	appetizer, dessert
Camembert	mild to pungent	appetizer, sandwich, dessert
Cottage	mild	cooking, salad
Cream	very mild	cooking, dessert
Liederkranz	pungent	appetizer, dessert
Montrachet (Chèvre)	mild	appetizer, cooking
Neufchâtel	mild	cooking, spread
Ricotta	mild	cooking

IMPOSSIBLE BROCCOLI PIE

   2   **packages (10 ounces each) frozen chopped broccoli**
   3   **cups shredded Cheddar cheese (12 ounces)**
  ⅔   **cup chopped onion**
 1⅓   **cups milk**
   3   **eggs**
  ¾   **cup buttermilk baking mix**
  ¾   **teaspoon salt**
  ¼   **teaspoon pepper**

Heat oven to 400°. Grease pie plate, 10 × 1½ inches. Rinse broccoli under running cold water to thaw; drain thoroughly. Mix broccoli, 2 cups of the cheese and the onion in plate. Beat milk, eggs, baking mix, salt and pepper until smooth, 15 seconds in blender on high or 1 minute with hand beater. Pour into plate. Bake until knife inserted in center comes out clean, 25 to 35 minutes. Top with remaining cheese. Bake just until cheese is melted, 1 to 2 minutes longer. Let stand 5 minutes. Garnish with tomato slices if desired.   **6 servings;** 405 calories per serving.

Nice served with Mixed Fruit Salad (page 537).

Easy . . . CHEESE PIE

1 cup shredded Cheddar cheese (4 ounces)
1 cup shredded mozzarella cheese (4 ounces)
1 cup shredded Monterey Jack cheese (4 ounces)
1 medium onion, chopped (about ½ cup)
2 tablespoons all-purpose flour
4 eggs
1 cup milk
½ teaspoon salt
½ teaspoon dry mustard
½ teaspoon Worcestershire sauce
2 medium tomatoes, sliced

Mix cheeses, onion and flour. Spread in greased pie plate, 10 × 1½ inches, or quiche dish, 9 × 1½ inches. Beat eggs slightly; beat in milk, salt, mustard and Worcestershire sauce. Pour over cheese mixture. Bake uncovered in 350° oven until set, 35 to 40 minutes. Let stand 10 minutes; arrange tomato slices around edge of pie, overlapping slices slightly. **8 servings;** 230 calories per serving.

Serve this with broccoli and Apple-Pear Salad (page 541).

QUICHE LORRAINE

Pastry for 9-inch One-Crust Pie (page 135)
12 slices bacon, crisply cooked and crumbled
1 cup shredded natural Swiss cheese (4 ounces)
⅓ cup finely chopped onion
4 eggs
2 cups whipping cream
¾ teaspoon salt
¼ teaspoon pepper
⅛ teaspoon ground red pepper

Heat oven to 425°. Prepare pastry. Sprinkle bacon, cheese and onion in pastry-lined pie plate. Beat eggs slightly; beat in remaining ingredients. Pour into pie plate. Bake uncovered 15 minutes.

Reduce oven temperature to 300°. Bake until knife inserted in center comes out clean, about 30 minutes longer. Let stand 10 minutes before cutting. **6 servings;** 625 calories per serving.

Serve with Cauliflower Salad (page 520) and Fresh Fruit Cups (page 225).

Do-ahead Tip: After sprinkling pastry with bacon, cheese and onion, cover and refrigerate. Beat remaining ingredients; cover and refrigerate. Store no longer than 24 hours. Stir egg mixture before pouring into pie plate. Continue as directed except—increase second bake time to about 45 minutes.

Chicken Quiche: Substitute 1 cup cut-up cooked chicken for the bacon and ½ teaspoon dried thyme leaves for the red pepper. Increase salt to 1 teaspoon.

Crab Quiche: Substitute 1 cup chopped cooked crabmeat or seafood sticks for the bacon. Pat crabmeat dry. Increase salt to 1 teaspoon.

Mushroom Quiche: Add 1 can (4 ounces) mushroom stems and pieces, drained, and 1 jar (2 ounces) diced pimientos, well drained, with the bacon. Increase salt to 1 teaspoon.

CHEESE PIZZA

	Pizza Dough (page 298)
1	can (8 ounces) tomato sauce
1	small onion, chopped (about ¼ cup)
2	teaspoons dried oregano leaves
½	teaspoon salt
½	teaspoon garlic powder
¼	teaspoon pepper
3	cups shredded mozzarella cheese (12 ounces)
¼	cup grated Parmesan or Romano cheese

Heat oven to 425°. Prepare Pizza Dough. Mix tomato sauce, onion, oregano, salt, garlic powder and pepper. Divide dough into halves. Pat each half into 11-inch circle on greased cookie sheet or 12-inch pizza pan with floured fingers. Spread tomato sauce mixture over circles to within ½ inch of edge; sprinkle with cheeses. Bake on lowest oven rack until cheese is light brown, 15 to 20 minutes. **2 pizzas** (6 slices each); 205 calories per slice.

Pizza Dough

1	package active dry yeast
1	cup warm water (105 to 115°)
2½	cups all-purpose flour*
2	tablespoons vegetable oil
1	teaspoon sugar
1	teaspoon salt

Dissolve yeast in warm water in 2½-quart bowl. Stir in remaining ingredients; beat vigorously 20 strokes. Let rest 5 minutes.

Hamburger Pizza: Cook and stir ½ pound ground beef until light brown; drain. Sprinkle ground beef over pizzas before adding cheeses. Decrease mozzarella cheese to 2 cups.

Italian Sausage Pizza: Cook and stir ½ pound bulk Italian sausage until light brown; drain. Sprinkle sausage, 1 cup sliced mushrooms and ½ cup chopped green pepper over pizzas before adding cheeses. Decrease mozzarella cheese to 2 cups.

Pepperoni Pizza: Arrange 1 package (4 ounces) sliced pepperoni over pizzas before adding cheeses. Decrease mozzarella cheese to 2 cups.

MACARONI AND CHEESE

1	to 1½ cups uncooked elbow macaroni, rigatoni or spinach egg noodles (about 6 ounces)
¼	cup margarine or butter
1	small onion, chopped (about ¼ cup)
½	teaspoon salt
¼	teaspoon pepper
¼	cup all-purpose flour
1¾	cups milk
8	ounces process sharp American or Swiss cheese, process American cheese loaf or process cheese spread loaf, cut into ½-inch cubes

Cook macaroni as directed (page 91). Cook and stir margarine, onion, salt and pepper over medium heat until onion is slightly tender. Stir in flour. Cook over low heat, stirring

*If using self-rising flour, omit salt.

constantly, until mixture is smooth and bubbly; remove from heat. Stir in milk. Heat to boiling, stirring constantly. Boil and stir 1 minute; remove from heat. Stir in cheese until melted.

Place macaroni in ungreased 1½-quart casserole. Stir cheese sauce into macaroni. Bake uncovered in 375° oven 30 minutes. **5 servings; 435 calories per serving.**

Serve with Baked Plum Tomatoes (page 673), Cucumber Salad (page 521) and Sherbet-Berry Parfaits (page 265) for a good weekend meal.

Ham Macaroni and Cheese: Stir 1 cup cut-up fully cooked smoked ham into cheese sauce. **7 servings.**

Olive Macaroni and Cheese: Stir ¼ cup chopped pimiento-stuffed olives into cheese sauce.

Pepper Macaroni and Cheese: Stir ⅓ cup chopped green and/or red peppers or 1 can (4 ounces) green chilies, drained and chopped, into cheese sauce.

Tomato Macaroni and Cheese: Stir ¼ cup sliced ripe olives into macaroni in casserole. Arrange 1 large tomato, cut into 5 slices, around edge of casserole before baking.

Tuna Macaroni and Cheese: Stir 1 can (6½ ounces) tuna, drained, into cheese sauce. **7 servings.**

MANICOTTI

1 package (8 ounces) manicotti shells
1½ cups creamed cottage cheese
¼ cup grated Parmesan cheese
1 tablespoon instant chicken bouillon (dry)
½ teaspoon garlic powder
⅛ teaspoon dried thyme leaves
2 eggs
1 small onion, chopped (about ¼ cup)
1 package (10 ounces) frozen chopped spinach, thawed and drained
1 can (8 ounces) tomato sauce
1 cup shredded mozzarella cheese (4 ounces)

Cook manicotti shells as directed on package; drain. Mix remaining ingredients except tomato sauce and mozzarella cheese. Fill manicotti shells with spinach mixture; arrange in greased rectangular pan, 13 × 9 × 2 inches. Pour tomato sauce over manicotti; sprinkle with mozzarella cheese. Cover and bake in 350° oven until hot and bubbly, about 25 minutes. **5 servings; 360 calories per serving.**

Nice served with Italian-style Beans (page 619) and Pear Salad (page 544).

Easy . . . CHEESE STRATA

⅓	cup margarine or butter, softened
½	teaspoon dry mustard
1	clove garlic, crushed
10	slices white bread (crusts removed)
2	cups shredded sharp Cheddar cheese (8 ounces)
2	tablespoons snipped parsley
2	tablespoons chopped onion
1	teaspoon salt
½	teaspoon Worcestershire sauce
⅛	teaspoon pepper
	Dash of ground red pepper
4	eggs
2½	cups milk

Mix margarine, mustard and garlic. Spread over each slice bread. Cut each slice into thirds. Line bottom and sides of ungreased square baking dish, 8 × 8 × 2 inches, with some of the bread slices, buttered sides down.

Mix cheese, parsley, onion, salt, Worcestershire sauce, pepper and red pepper; spread evenly in dish. Top with remaining bread slices, buttered sides up. Beat eggs; stir in milk. Pour over bread. Cover and refrigerate at least 2 hours.

Bake uncovered in 325° oven until knife inserted in center comes out clean, about 1¼ hours. Let stand 10 minutes before cutting. **6 servings; 475 calories per serving.**

Accompany this dish with refreshing Mandarin Salad (page 512).

CHEESY FRENCH BREAD BAKE

½ loaf (1-pound size) French bread
2 cups shredded Muenster or
      Monterey Jack cheese (8 ounces)
¼ pound prosciutto or fully cooked smoked ham, finely
      chopped (about 1 cup)
4 green onions (with tops), sliced
4 eggs, slightly beaten
1½ cups milk
½ cup dry white wine or water
1 tablespoon Dijon-style mustard
¼ teaspoon red pepper sauce
2 tablespoons grated Parmesan cheese

Cut bread into 16 slices. Arrange 8 slices bread in ungreased rectangular baking dish, 11 × 7½ × 2 inches. Top with Muenster cheese, prosciutto and onions. Arrange remaining bread on top. Beat remaining ingredients except Parmesan cheese; pour over bread. Sprinkle with Parmesan cheese.

Bake uncovered in 325° oven until knife inserted in center comes out clean, 1 to 1¼ hours. Let stand 10 minutes before serving.   **8 servings; 305 calories per serving.**

Serve this with Walnut Tossed Salad (page 511) for lunch.

WELSH RABBIT

¼ cup margarine or butter
¼ cup all-purpose flour
½ teaspoon salt
¼ teaspoon pepper
¼ teaspoon dry mustard
¼ teaspoon Worcestershire sauce
1 cup milk
½ cup beer or medium white wine*
2 cups shredded Cheddar cheese (8 ounces)
4 slices toast

*Beer or wine can be omitted; increase milk to 1½ cups.

Heat margarine in saucepan over low heat until melted. Stir in flour, salt, pepper, mustard and Worcestershire sauce. Cook over low heat, stirring constantly, until smooth and bubbly; remove from heat. Stir in milk. Heat to boiling, stirring constantly. Boil and stir 1 minute. Gradually add beer; stir in cheese. Heat over low heat, stirring constantly, until cheese is melted. Serve over toast. Sprinkle with paprika if desired.   **4 servings; 475 calories per serving.**

Accompany with Stir-fried Asparagus (page 617) and Apple-Cherry Salad (page 530).

CHEESE ENCHILADAS

1	large onion, chopped (about 1 cup)
2	large cloves garlic, crushed
1	tablespoon chili powder
2	tablespoons vegetable oil
1	teaspoon dried oregano leaves
1	teaspoon ground cumin
½	teaspoon salt
⅛	teaspoon pepper
1	can (28 ounces) whole tomatoes, undrained
1½	cups shredded Cheddar cheese (6 ounces)
1½	cups shredded Monterey Jack cheese (6 ounces)
½	cup vegetable oil
1	package (9 ounces) 6- or 7-inch corn tortillas (12 tortillas)
1½	cups shredded lettuce
⅓	cup sliced radishes
¼	cup sliced ripe olives

Cook and stir onion, garlic and chili powder in 2 tablespoons oil in 3-quart saucepan until onion is tender, about 5 minutes. Stir in oregano, cumin, salt, pepper and tomatoes; break up tomatoes. Heat to boiling; reduce heat. Simmer uncovered until thickened, about 30 minutes.

Mix cheeses. Heat ½ cup oil in 8-inch skillet until hot. Dip each tortilla lightly into hot oil to soften; drain. Dip each tortilla into tomato mixture to coat both sides. Spoon about 2 tablespoons cheese on each tortilla; roll tortilla around cheese. Place seam side down in ungreased rectangular baking dish, 13 × 9 × 2 inches. Pour remaining tomato mixture over the enchiladas; sprinkle with remaining cheese. Bake uncovered in 350° oven until cheese is melted and enchiladas are hot, about 20 minutes. Top each serving with lettuce, radishes and olives. Serve with dairy sour cream if desired.   **6 servings; 490 calories per serving.**

CHEESE FONDUE

    2 **cups shredded natural Swiss cheese (8 ounces)***
    2 **cups shredded Gruyère cheese (8 ounces)**
    1 **tablespoon cornstarch**
    1 **clove garlic, cut into halves**
    1 **cup dry white wine**
    1 **tablespoon lemon juice**
    3 **tablespoons kirsch or dry sherry**
    ½ **teaspoon salt**
    ⅛ **teaspoon white pepper**
    1 **loaf (1 pound) French bread, cut into 1-inch cubes**

Toss cheeses and cornstarch. Rub garlic on bottom and side of heavy saucepan or skillet; add wine. Heat over low heat just until bubbles rise to surface (wine should not boil); stir in lemon juice.

Gradually add cheeses, about ½ cup at a time, stirring constantly with wooden spoon over low heat until cheeses are melted. Stir in kirsch, salt and white pepper. Remove to earthenware fondue dish; keep warm over low heat. Spear bread cubes with fondue forks; dip and swirl in fondue with stirring motion. If fondue becomes too thick, stir in ¼ to ½ cup heated wine.   **4 servings; 850 calories per serving.**

   Swiss Cheese Fondue: Omit Gruyère cheese. Increase Swiss cheese to 4 cups.

*Swiss cheese should be aged at least 6 months.

LEGUMES

ABOUT LEGUMES

Legumes are dried beans, peas and lentils from pods containing one row of seeds. Dried beans can be used interchangeably; substitute a similar bean if you can't find the kind called for in the recipe (see chart page 306).

Most legumes need to be softened before cooking. A quick way to soften legumes is to cover them with water. Heat to boiling and boil uncovered 2 minutes. Remove from heat; cover and let stand 1 hour. Continue to cook as directed in recipe.

Lentils do not need to be softened and can be cooked in a shorter time.

To prevent the water from foaming when cooking dried beans, add 1 tablespoon of oil or shortening to the water during the first cooking period.

Dried beans double or triple in volume as they cook, so be sure to choose a sufficiently large casserole or pan.

BOSTON BAKED BEANS

6	cups water
1½	pounds dried navy beans (3 cups)
1	large onion, sliced
¼	pound thinly sliced salt pork (with rind)
¼	cup packed brown sugar
¾	cup molasses
1	teaspoon salt
1	teaspoon dry mustard
⅛	teaspoon pepper

Heat water and beans to boiling in Dutch oven. Boil 2 minutes; remove from heat. Cover and let stand 1 hour. Add enough water to beans to cover if necessary. Heat to boiling; reduce heat. Cover and simmer until tender, 1 to 1½ hours (do not boil or beans will burst).

Drain beans, reserving liquid. Layer beans, onion and salt pork in ungreased 4-quart bean pot, casserole or Dutch oven. Mix brown sugar, molasses, salt, mustard, pepper and bean liquid; pour over beans. Add enough water to almost cover beans. Cover; bake in 350° oven, stirring occasionally, 3 hours. Uncover; bake until beans are of desired consistency, about 30 minutes longer.   **8 servings; 390 calories per serving.**

BAKED BLACK BEANS

  5   **cups water**
 12   **ounces dried black beans (about 1¾ cups)**
  2   **medium onions, chopped**
  2   **cloves garlic, finely chopped**
  1   **tablespoon plus 1 teaspoon instant beef bouillon**
  1   **teaspoon salt**
 ¼   **teaspoon pepper**
 ½   **cup rum or water**
  4   **slices bacon, cut into ¼-inch pieces**
 ¼   **cup snipped parsley**
  4   **cups hot cooked rice (page 85)**

Heat water and beans to boiling in Dutch oven. Boil 2 minutes; remove from heat. Cover and let stand 1 hour.

Stir onions, garlic, bouillon (dry), salt and pepper into beans. Add enough water to beans to cover if necessary. Heat to boiling; reduce heat. Cover and simmer until beans are tender, 1 to 1½ hours (do not boil or beans will burst). Stir in rum and bacon.

Place bean mixture in ungreased 2½- or 3-quart casserole. Cover and bake in 350° oven 1½ hours. Sprinkle with parsley. Serve over rice.   **8 servings; 370 calories per serving.**

Cabbage Salad (page 517) adds color and crunch.

TYPES OF LEGUMES

Type	Color	Size and Shape	Use
Black beans	black	small, oval	baked, soups, stews
Black-eyed peas	white with a black spot	small, oval	casseroles
Garbanzo beans (chick-peas)	brown	small, irregular	dips, casseroles, salads, soups, stews
Great northern beans	white	medium, oval	baked, casseroles, chowder, soups, stews
Kidney beans	red	medium, oval	casseroles, chili, salads, soups
Lentils	brown or green	small, round disk	casseroles, salads, soups
Lima beans	white	large, flat	casseroles, soups
Navy beans	white	small, round	baked, soups
Pinto beans	pink speckled with brown	medium, oval	baked, casseroles, soups
Red beans	red	small, round	casseroles, chili
Soybeans	tan	small, round	casseroles, salads
Split peas	green or yellow	small, round	soups

BAKED PINTO BEANS

4	cups water
1	pound dried pinto beans (about 2½ cups)
½	cup packed brown sugar
¼	cup water
1	tablespoon vinegar
1	teaspoon salt
¼	teaspoon ground cloves
¼	teaspoon pepper
¼	teaspoon celery seed
½	cup strong cold coffee
2	tablespoons brandy
1	medium onion, sliced
4	slices bacon

Heat 4 cups water and the beans to boiling in 3-quart sauce-pan. Boil 2 minutes; remove from heat. Cover and let stand 1 hour.

Add enough water to beans to cover if necessary. Heat to boiling; reduce heat. Cover and simmer until tender, about 1½ hours (do not boil or beans will burst).

Drain beans, reserving liquid. Heat brown sugar, ¼ cup water, the vinegar, salt, cloves, pepper and celery seed to boiling, stirring occasionally. Stir in coffee and brandy.

Place half of the beans in ungreased 2-quart casserole; arrange onion on top. Pour half of the coffee mixture over onion; top with remaining beans. Pour remaining coffee mixture and the bean liquid over beans. Cover and bake in 350° oven 1½ hours. Stir beans. Arrange bacon on top and bake uncovered 30 minutes longer. **6 servings; 285 calories per serving.**

SAVORY BAKED BEANS

4	cups water
1	pound dried lima or great northern beans (about 2 cups)
2	teaspoons salt
2	tablespoons margarine or butter
¾	cup chopped onion
¾	cup chopped green pepper
1	clove garlic, finely chopped
½	cup chopped ripe olives
¼	cup grated Parmesan cheese
2	to 3 teaspoons chili powder
1	teaspoon salt
1	can (6 ounces) tomato paste

Heat water and beans to boiling in Dutch oven. Boil 2 minutes; remove from heat. Cover and let stand 1 hour.

Add enough water to beans to cover if necessary. Add 2 teaspoons salt. Heat to boiling; reduce heat. Cover and simmer until tender, 45 to 60 minutes (do not boil or beans will burst).

Drain beans, reserving liquid. Add enough water to bean liquid, if necessary, to measure 1 cup. Heat margarine in 10-inch skillet until melted. Add onion, green pepper and garlic; cook and stir until onion is tender. Mix in beans, bean liquid and the remaining ingredients. Pour into ungreased 2-quart casserole. Bake uncovered in 375° oven until hot and bubbly, about 30 minutes. **6 servings; 325 calories per serving.**

Add Hard Rolls (page 73) and Orange-Jicama Salad (page 543) for texture.

CHALUPAS

Vegetable oil
6   corn tortillas (each about 6 inches in diameter)
1   can (16 ounces) refried beans
2   teaspoons chili powder
½   teaspoon garlic powder
½   teaspoon dried oregano leaves
1½   cups shredded Monterey Jack or
     Cheddar cheese (6 ounces)
1   medium avocado, sliced
1   medium tomato, cut into wedges
     Mexican salsa

Heat oil (⅛ inch) in 8-inch skillet over medium heat until hot.
Place tortillas, one at a time, in hot oil, bending one side up
about 1 inch with tongs until set, about 15 seconds. Repeat,
bending opposite side to form a shallow "boat." Fry tortilla
until crisp, 1½ to 2 minutes longer; drain.

Mix beans, chili powder, garlic powder and oregano. Spread
about ¼ cup on each tortilla; top with cheese. Place on
ungreased cookie sheet. Set oven control to broil and/or 550°.
Broil chalupas with tops 4 to 6 inches from heat until cheese
is melted, 2 to 3 minutes. Serve with avocado, tomato and
salsa.   **6 servings;** 380 calories per serving.

For dessert, serve Caramel Custard (page 248).

ITALIAN LIMA BEANS

4   cups water
1   pound dried lima beans (about 2 cups)
2   teaspoons salt
½   cup sliced ripe olives
¼   cup grated Parmesan or Romano cheese
1   teaspoon dried basil leaves
1   medium onion, finely chopped (about ½ cup)
1   medium green pepper, chopped (about 1 cup)
1   can (15 ounces) tomato sauce

Heat water, beans and salt to boiling in Dutch oven. Boil 2
minutes; remove from heat. Cover and let stand 1 hour.

Add enough water to beans to cover if necessary. Heat to boiling; reduce heat. Cover and simmer until tender, 1¼ to 1½ hours (do not boil or beans will burst). Add more water during cooking if necessary.

Drain beans. Mix with remaining ingredients in ungreased 2-quart casserole. Bake uncovered in 375° oven until hot and bubbly, about 30 minutes. **6 servings; 285 calories per serving.**

Serve with Cooked Canadian-style Bacon (page 427) and Garlic Bread (page 69).

CHEESY LENTILS

2   cups water
6   ounces dried lentils (about 1 cup)
1   tablespoon instant chicken bouillon
1   medium onion, chopped (about ½ cup)
1   medium green pepper, chopped (about 1 cup)
1   medium tomato, chopped (about 1 cup)
½   cup crumbled Gorgonzola or blue cheese

Heat water and lentils to boiling in 2-quart saucepan; stir in bouillon (dry). Cover and simmer until lentils are tender, about 30 minutes. Add more water during cooking if necessary.

Stir in onion and green pepper; simmer uncovered 5 minutes. Stir in tomato. Sprinkle with cheese. **6 servings; 155 calories per serving.**

Accompany this dish with Creamy Cucumber Salad (page 521).

THREE-BEAN CASSEROLE

1	pound pork sausage
2	medium stalks celery, sliced (about 1 cup)
1	medium onion, chopped (about ½ cup)
1	large clove garlic, crushed
2	cans (21 ounces each) baked beans in tomato sauce
1	can (17 ounces) lima beans, drained
1	can (15 ounces) kidney beans, drained
1	can (8 ounces) tomato sauce
1	tablespoon dry mustard
2	tablespoons honey
1	tablespoon vinegar
1	teaspoon salt
¼	teaspoon red pepper sauce

Cook and stir sausage, celery, onion and garlic until sausage is done, about 10 minutes; drain. Mix sausage mixture and remaining ingredients in ungreased 3-quart casserole. Bake uncovered in 400° oven, stirring once, until hot and bubbly, about 45 minutes. 8 servings; 525 calories per serving.

French Bread (page 68) and crisp carrot sticks provide crunch.

CHILI BEANS WITH DUMPLINGS

6	slices bacon, cut up
1	medium onion, chopped (about ½ cup)
1	medium stalk celery, sliced (about ½ cup)
2	cans (15 ounces each) chili beans
¾	cup buttermilk baking mix
½	cup shredded Cheddar cheese (2 ounces)
⅓	cup cornmeal
⅓	cup milk

Cook bacon in 3-quart saucepan until crisp. Remove bacon with slotted spoon; reserve. Drain fat, reserving 2 tablespoons in saucepan. Cook and stir onion and celery in fat until onion is tender. Stir in beans and bacon. Heat to boiling.

Mix remaining ingredients until soft dough forms; beat vigorously 20 strokes. Drop dough by 4 spoonfuls onto boiling bean mixture; reduce heat. Simmer uncovered 10 minutes; cover and simmer 10 minutes longer.   **4 servings; 490 calories per serving.**

Make an easy supper with Marinated Carrot Salad (page 519) and Poached Plums (page 232).

Easy . . . WESTERN-STYLE BEANS

¾ pound pork sausage
1 medium onion, chopped (about ½ cup)
2 cloves garlic, finely chopped
2 cans (16 ounces each) pinto beans, drained
1 can (8 ounces) whole tomatoes, undrained
1 can (8 ounces) tomato sauce
1 tablespoon sugar
1 tablespoon vinegar
2 teaspoons chili powder
1 teaspoon dry mustard
½ teaspoon salt
¼ teaspoon red pepper sauce, if desired

Cook and stir sausage, onion and garlic until sausage is done, about 10 minutes; drain. Mix sausage mixture and remaining ingredients in ungreased 2-quart casserole; break up tomatoes. Bake uncovered in 375° oven, stirring once, until beans are hot and bubbly, about 45 minutes.   **6 servings; 525 calories per serving.**

Serve with Spoon Bread (page 55) and Coleslaw (page 515).

RED BEANS AND RICE

2 cups water
8 ounces dried kidney beans* (about 1 cup)
2 ounces salt pork (with rind), diced, or 3 slices bacon, cut up
1 medium onion, chopped (about ½ cup)
1 medium green pepper, chopped (about 1 cup)
1 cup uncooked regular rice
1½ teaspoons salt

*1 can (16 ounces) red kidney beans, drained, can be substituted for the cooked dried kidney beans.

Heat water and beans to boiling in 3-quart saucepan. Boil 2 minutes; remove from heat. Cover and let stand 1 hour.

Add enough water to beans to cover if necessary. Heat to boiling; reduce heat. Cover and simmer until tender, 1 to 1½ hours (do not boil or beans will burst).

Drain beans, reserving liquid. Cook salt pork in 10-inch skillet until crisp; add onion and green pepper. Cook and stir until onion is tender. Add enough water to bean liquid, if necessary, to measure 2 cups. Add bean liquid, salt pork, onion, green pepper, rice and salt to beans in 3-quart saucepan. Heat to boiling, stirring once or twice; reduce heat. Cover and simmer 14 minutes. (Do not lift cover or stir.) Remove from heat. Fluff with fork; cover and let steam 5 to 10 minutes. **12 servings; 270 calories per serving.**

Serve with Skillet Corn Bread (page 54) and Cantaloupe Salads (page 542).

Hoppin' John: Substitute 1 cup black-eyed peas for the kidney beans. Omit green pepper.

REFRIED BEAN BAKE

 1   **can (17 ounces) refried beans**
 1   **medium onion, finely chopped (about ½ cup)**
 1   **small green pepper, finely chopped (about ½ cup)**
 4   **eggs**
1½   **cups shredded Cheddar cheese (6 ounces)**
 1   **teaspoon chili powder**
 ⅛   **teaspoon garlic powder**
 1   **jar (12 ounces) Mexican salsa**

Mix beans, onion, green pepper, eggs, ¾ cup of the cheese, the chili powder and garlic powder. Pour into ungreased square pan, 9×9×2 inches; sprinkle with remaining cheese. Bake uncovered in 350° oven until hot and firm, about 30 minutes. Heat salsa, stirring occasionally, until hot; serve with beans. **8 servings; 190 calories per serving.**

Easy . . . SKILLET BEANS

> 3 slices bacon, cut into 1-inch pieces
> 1 medium onion, chopped (about ½ cup)
> ¼ cup chili sauce
> 1 teaspoon prepared mustard
> 2 cans (16 ounces each) pork and beans

Cook and stir bacon and onion in 10-inch skillet until bacon is crisp. Stir in remaining ingredients. Heat to boiling; reduce heat. Simmer uncovered, stirring occasionally, until all liquid is absorbed, 15 to 20 minutes. **4 servings; 410 calories per serving.**

Add warm Chili Corn Bread (page 54) for a quick and easy lunch.

FISH
SHELLFISH

FISH

ABOUT FISH

Across the country, fish is appearing on menus more frequently. There are good reasons for this increase in popularity: in addition to being quick-cooking, fish is an excellent source of protein and other nutrients, and is generally low in fat. All this is suited to today's more healthful lifestyle, with its emphasis on lighter eating. Fish also contributes a vast variety of textures and flavors to any meal.

TIPS FOR SELECTING FRESH FISH
- The eyes should be bright, clear, full, bulging.

- Gills should be reddish-pink.

- Scales should be bright in color, with a sheen.

- The flesh should be firm and elastic, and will spring back when pressed.

- Fresh fish does not have a "fishy" odor.

TIPS FOR SELECTING FROZEN FISH
- Be sure the package is frozen solid and tightly wrapped, with little or no airspace between the fish and the wrapping.

- There should be no discoloration, which might indicate freezer burn.

- There should be little or no odor.

HOW MUCH FISH TO BUY
The amount of fresh or frozen fish you buy will depend upon the form you select. While individual appetites dictate the

size of the serving, here is a general guide to use when purchasing fish.

Whole fish is just as it comes from the water. Allow 1 pound per serving.

Drawn fish is whole but eviscerated (internal organs removed). Allow 1 pound per serving.

Dressed and *pan-dressed fish* are eviscerated and scaled. Head, tail and fins have usually been removed. Smaller fish (less than 1 pound) are called pan-dressed. Allow ½ pound per serving.

Steaks are taken from large dressed fish. They are cross-section slices cut about ¾ inch thick. Allow ⅓ pound per serving.

Fillets are the sides of the fish cut lengthwise away from the backbone. They are practically boneless, with little or no waste. *Butterfly fillets* are double fillets held together by the intact skin along the back. Allow ⅓ pound per serving.

Sticks are uniform cuts from frozen blocks of fish. They are breaded, partially cooked, packaged and frozen. Allow ¼ pound per serving.

FAT AND LEAN FISH

Fish is divided into two classifications: fat and lean (less than 5% fat). It is best to select from within the same classification when substituting one fish for another.

Fat	Lean	
Lake trout	Catfish	Orange roughy
Pompano	Cod	Pike
Salmon	Flounder	Red snapper
Whitefish	Grouper	Sea bass
	Haddock	Sole
	Halibut	Swordfish
	Ocean perch	

METHODS OF COOKING FISH

Fish may be steamed, poached, fried, boiled, broiled, baked or planked (literally cooked on a wooden plank). Broiling, baking or planking are usually best for fat fish, while lean fish remain firm and moist when steamed or poached. Exceptions may be made if lean fish are basted. Both fat and lean fish are suitable for frying.

DONENESS TEST

Fish is already tender. Overcooking makes it dry and tough. To test for doneness, insert a fork at an angle into the thickest part of the fish and twist gently. When done, the fish will flake very easily and the flesh will be opaque. In addition, for food safety reasons, we recommend an internal temperature of 175°.

Easy . . . BAKED FISH

- 1 **pound fish fillets**
- ½ **teaspoon salt**
  Dash of pepper
- 2 **tablespoons margarine or butter, melted**
- 1 **tablespoon lemon juice**
- 1 **teaspoon finely chopped onion**

Heat oven to 400°. If fish fillets are large, cut into 3 serving pieces. Arrange fish in ungreased square baking dish, 8 × 8 × 2 inches; sprinkle with salt and pepper. Mix margarine, lemon juice and onion; drizzle over fish. Bake uncovered until fish flakes very easily with fork and is opaque in center, 25 to 30 minutes. Sprinkle with paprika if desired.   **3 servings; 265 calories per serving.**

Serve with Hashed Browns (page 662), buttered green beans and lettuce wedges with French Dressing (page 548).

CREOLE CATFISH

- 2 **pounds catfish, red snapper, cod or haddock fillets**
- ⅓ **cup chopped green pepper**
- 2 **tablespoons snipped parsley**
- 1 **tablespoon lemon juice**
- ½ **teaspoon salt**
- ½ **teaspoon ground red pepper**
- 1 **medium onion, chopped**
- 1 **clove garlic, crushed**
- 1 **can (28 ounces) whole tomatoes, undrained**
- 3 **cups hot cooked rice (page 85)**

Heat oven to 450°. If fish fillets are large, cut into 6 serving pieces. Place in ungreased rectangular baking dish, $11 \times 7 \times 1\frac{1}{2}$ inches. Mix remaining ingredients except rice; break up tomatoes. Pour over fish.

Bake uncovered, spooning tomato mixture over fish occasionally, until fish flakes very easily with fork, 25 to 30 minutes. Serve over rice. Garnish fish with lemon slices sprinkled with snipped parsley if desired. **6 servings; 265 calories per serving.**

Nice with buttered zucchini, Corn Sticks (page 54), large tossed salad and Lemon Chiffon Pie (page 160).

■ **To Microwave:** Arrange fillets, thickest parts to outside edges, in rectangular microwavable dish, $11 \times 7 \times 1\frac{1}{2}$ inches. Drain tomatoes. Mix tomatoes and remaining ingredients except rice; break up tomatoes. Pour over fish. Cover tightly and microwave on high (100%) 6 minutes; rotate dish ½ turn. Microwave until fish flakes very easily with fork, 4 to 5 minutes longer. Let stand covered 3 minutes.

HALIBUT WITH GRAPEFRUIT SAUCE

3   **halibut steaks, 1 inch thick (about 2 pounds)**
1   **teaspoon salt**
⅛   **teaspoon dried dill weed**
½   **small onion, thinly sliced**
¼   **cup margarine or butter, melted**
2   **tablespoons lemon juice**
    Grapefruit Sauce (page 321)

Heat oven to 450°. Cut each halibut steak into halves. Place in ungreased rectangular baking dish, $11 \times 7 \times 1\frac{1}{2}$ inches. Sprinkle with salt and dill weed; top with onion. Mix margarine and lemon juice; pour over fish.

Bake uncovered until fish flakes easily with fork, 20 to 25 minutes. Prepare Grapefruit Sauce; serve over fish. Garnish with dill weed or parsley if desired. **6 servings; 295 calories per serving.**

Complete this with green peas, Walnut Tossed Salad (page 511), Cornmeal Biscuits (page 42) and Sherbet-Berry Parfaits (page 265).

Grapefruit Sauce

 ½ cup unsweetened pink grapefruit juice
 ⅛ teaspoon salt
   Dash of dried dill weed
 1 tablespoon cold water
 1 teaspoon cornstarch
 1 pink grapefruit, pared and sectioned

Heat grapefruit juice, salt and dill weed to boiling in 1½-quart saucepan. Mix cold water and cornstarch; stir into grapefruit juice. Heat to boiling, stirring constantly. Boil and stir 1 minute. Carefully stir in grapefruit.

VEGETABLE-STUFFED SOLE

 1½ teaspoons salt
  ½ teaspoon dried dill weed
  ¼ teaspoon pepper
  6 sole fillets (about 2 pounds)
 24 carrot strips, each about 3 × ¼ inch (about 2 medium carrots)
 18 green pepper strips, each about 3 × ¼ inch (about 1 medium green pepper)
  ¼ cup dry white wine
  2 tablespoons margarine or butter
  2 tablespoons all-purpose flour
  ½ teaspoon salt
  ⅛ teaspoon pepper
  1 cup milk
  ¼ cup dry white wine

Heat oven to 350°. Mix 1½ teaspoons salt, the dill weed and ¼ teaspoon pepper; sprinkle over sole fillets. Divide carrot and green pepper strips among fillets. Roll up; place seam sides down in ungreased rectangular baking dish, 13 × 9 × 2 inches. Pour ¼ cup wine over fish. Cover with aluminum foil and bake until fish flakes very easily with fork, about 40 minutes.

Heat margarine in 1½-quart saucepan until melted; stir in the flour, ½ teaspoon salt and ⅛ teaspoon pepper. Cook and stir 1 minute; remove from heat. Stir in milk and ¼ cup wine. Heat to boiling, stirring constantly. Boil and stir 1 minute.

Arrange fish on serving platter; pour sauce over fish. Garnish with fresh dill weed if desired. **6 servings; 180 calories per serving.**

■ **To Microwave:** Place carrot strips in rectangular microwavable dish, $11 \times 7 \times 1\frac{1}{2}$ inches; add 1 tablespoon wine. Cover tightly and microwave on high (100%) until crisp-tender, about 4 minutes. Remove with slotted spoon. Prepare sole fillets as directed on page 321; arrange seam sides down around sides of dish. Drizzle with 3 tablespoons wine. Cover tightly and microwave on high (100%) 5 minutes; rotate dish ½ turn. Microwave until fish flakes very easily with fork, 5 to 7 minutes longer. Let stand covered 3 minutes. Remove to warm platter; keep warm.

Microwave margarine in 4-cup microwavable measure uncovered on high (100%) until melted, 15 to 30 seconds; stir in flour, ½ teaspoon salt and ⅛ teaspoon pepper. Gradually stir in milk and ¼ cup wine. Microwave uncovered on high (100%), stirring every minute, until thickened, about 4 minutes.

COD AND VEGETABLE BAKE

2	pounds cod fillets
3	tablespoons lemon juice
1½	teaspoons salt
⅛	teaspoon pepper
½	cup margarine or butter, melted
½	teaspoon salt
½	teaspoon ground sage
½	teaspoon ground thyme
5	slices bread (crusts removed), cut into cubes
2	medium carrots, coarsely shredded
1	large stalk celery, finely chopped
1	medium onion, chopped (about ½ cup)
3	tablespoons dry bread crumbs
2	tablespoons snipped parsley
½	teaspoon paprika

If cod fillets are large, cut into 6 serving pieces. Arrange fish in ungreased rectangular baking dish, $12 \times 7\frac{1}{2} \times 2$ inches, or square baking dish, $8 \times 8 \times 2$ inches. Sprinkle with lemon juice, 1½ teaspoons salt and the pepper.

Mix margarine, ½ teaspoon salt, the sage, thyme, bread cubes, carrots, celery and onion. Spread evenly over fish. Mix bread crumbs, parsley and paprika; sprinkle over vegetables. Cover and bake in 350° oven until fish flakes easily with fork, about 35 minutes.   **6 servings; 425 calories per serving.**

Serve with Apple-Cheese Coleslaw (page 516) and Lemon Coconut Pie (page 159).

BAKED STUFFED FISH

8- **to 10-pound fish (salmon, cod, snapper or lake trout), cleaned**
   Salt and pepper
   Garden Vegetable Stuffing (page 324)
   Vegetable oil
½ **cup margarine or butter, melted**
¼ **cup lemon juice**

Rub cavity of fish with salt and pepper; stuff with Garden Vegetable Stuffing. Close opening with skewers and lace with string. Spoon any remaining stuffing into baking dish; cover and refrigerate. Heat in oven 20 minutes before serving.

Brush fish with oil; place in shallow roasting pan. Mix margarine and lemon juice. Bake fish uncovered in 350° oven, brushing occasionally with margarine mixture, until fish flakes very easily with fork, about 1½ hours.   **10 servings; 330 calories per serving.**

Serve with Pea Pods and Peppers (page 637), Cherry Layered Salad (page 531) and Chocolate Frango (page 266) for dessert.

Garden Vegetable Stuffing

1	large onion, chopped (about 1 cup)
¼	cup margarine or butter
2	cups dry bread cubes
1	cup coarsely shredded carrot
½	cup snipped parsley
2	teaspoons salt
1	tablespoon plus 1½ teaspoons lemon juice
¼	teaspoon dried marjoram leaves
¼	teaspoon pepper
1	egg
3	ounces mushrooms, chopped
1	clove garlic, finely chopped

Cook and stir onion in margarine until tender. Gently stir in remaining ingredients.

Easy . . . FISH IN FOIL

1	package (16 ounces) frozen skinless halibut, cod, sole or perch fillets
¼	cup margarine or butter, melted
1	teaspoon salt
⅛	teaspoon pepper

Heat oven to 450°. Remove frozen fish fillets from package; wrap fish securely in 20 × 12-inch piece of heavy-duty aluminum foil. Bake on ungreased cookie sheet 25 minutes.

Turn back foil; pour margarine over fish. Sprinkle with salt and pepper. Bake uncovered until fish flakes very easily with fork and is opaque in center, about 10 minutes longer. **3 servings; 385 calories per serving.**

Complete this with Skillet Corn (page 639), buttered noodles, a fruited gelatin salad and Jumbo Chocolate Chip Cookies (page 168).

Easy . . . BROILED FISH STEAKS

3	fish steaks, 1 inch thick (about 1 pound)
½	teaspoon salt
	Dash of pepper
2	tablespoons margarine or butter, melted

CARVING A WHOLE FISH

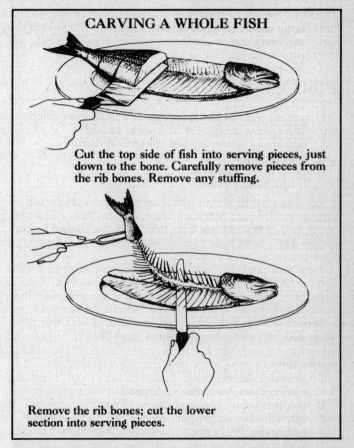

Cut the top side of fish into serving pieces, just down to the bone. Carefully remove pieces from the rib bones. Remove any stuffing.

Remove the rib bones; cut the lower section into serving pieces.

Sprinkle both sides of fish with salt and pepper; brush with half of the margarine. Set oven control to broil and/or 550°. Broil with tops about 4 inches from heat until light brown, about 6 minutes; brush fish with margarine. Turn carefully; brush with margarine. Broil until fish flakes very easily with fork and is opaque in center, 4 to 6 minutes longer. **3 servings;** 265 calories per serving.

Broiled Fish Fillets: Substitute 1 pound fish fillets for the steaks. If fish fillets are large, cut into serving pieces. For fish

fillets less than ¾ inch thick, brush with all of the margarine.
Broil with tops about 4 inches from heat until fish flakes very
easily with fork and is opaque in center, 5 to 6 minutes (do
not turn).

FISH WITH GARLIC SALSA

    2   pounds cod, haddock, halibut or red snapper fillets
    2   tablespoons margarine or butter, melted
    1   tablespoon finely snipped cilantro, if desired
    ½   teaspoon salt
    1   clove garlic, crushed
         Garlic Salsa (below)

If fish fillets are large, cut into 6 serving pieces. Place fish on
rack in broiler pan. Mix margarine, cilantro, salt and garlic.
Brush half of the mixture over fish. Set oven control to broil
and/or 550°. Broil with tops about 4 inches from heat until
light brown, about 6 minutes.

Turn fish carefully; brush with remaining margarine mixture. Broil until fish flakes very easily with fork, 4 to 6
minutes longer. Serve with Garlic Salsa; garnish with lime
wedges if desired.   **6 servings; 245 calories per serving.**

Serve fish with buttered sliced zucchini, Cauliflower Salad
(page 520) and warm French Bread (page 68).

Garlic Salsa

    3   cloves garlic, crushed
    2   medium tomatoes, finely chopped
    1   medium onion, chopped (about ½ cup)
    1   canned jalapeño pepper, seeded and finely chopped
    1   tablespoon finely snipped cilantro, if desired
    1   tablespoon lemon juice
    ½   teaspoon dried oregano leaves
    1½   teaspoons vegetable oil

Heat all ingredients over medium heat, stirring occasionally,
until hot and bubbly, about 5 minutes.

Easy . . . ORANGE ROUGHY WITH TARRAGON

1	pound orange roughy fillets
¼	teaspoon salt
1	tablespoon margarine or butter, melted
½	teaspoon snipped tarragon or
	⅛ teaspoon dried tarragon leaves
	Paprika

Place orange roughy fillets on greased rack in broiler pan; sprinkle with salt. Drizzle with margarine; sprinkle with tarragon. Set oven control to broil and/or 550°. Broil with tops about 4 inches from heat until fish flakes very easily with fork and is opaque in center, 5 to 6 minutes. Sprinkle with paprika.   **3 servings;** 210 calories per serving.

Serve with Bulgur Pilaf (page 90), steamed carrots and lemon sherbet with Raspberry-Currant Sauce (page 274).

MUSTARD-TOPPED FISH

4	small halibut steaks, 1 inch thick (about 1½ pounds)
½	teaspoon salt
⅛	teaspoon pepper
2	tablespoons margarine or butter, melted
2	egg whites
¼	cup grated Parmesan cheese
2	tablespoons Dijon-style mustard
2	tablespoons chopped green onion (with top)

Sprinkle halibut steaks with salt and pepper. Place on rack in broiler pan; brush with half of the margarine. Set oven control to broil and/or 550°. Broil with tops 2 to 3 inches from heat until light brown, about 5 minutes. Turn; brush with remaining margarine. Broil until fish flakes very easily with fork, 5 to 8 minutes longer.

Beat egg whites until stiff but not dry; fold in cheese, mustard and onion. Spread over fish. Broil until topping is golden brown, about 1½ minutes.   **4 servings;** 355 calories per serving.

Nice with Apple-Raisin Stuffing (page 472), Three-Bean Salad (page 515) and Fresh Fruit Cups (page 225).

COLD POACHED SALMON

2 cups water
1 cup dry white wine
1 teaspoon salt
¼ teaspoon dried thyme leaves
¼ teaspoon dried tarragon leaves
5 peppercorns
4 parsley sprigs
1 small onion, sliced
1 stalk celery (with leaves), chopped
1 bay leaf
4 salmon steaks, 1 inch thick (2 pounds)
  Green Sauce (below)

Heat water, wine, salt, thyme, tarragon, peppercorns, parsley, onion, celery and bay leaf to boiling in 12-inch skillet; reduce heat. Cover and simmer 5 minutes. Place salmon steaks in skillet; add water, if necessary, to cover. Heat to boiling; reduce heat. Simmer uncovered until fish flakes easily with fork, 12 to 15 minutes.

Carefully remove fish with slotted spatula; drain on wire rack. Carefully remove skin; cut fish lengthwise into halves. Cover and refrigerate until cold, at least 4 hours. Serve fish with Green Sauce. **4 servings; 495 calories per serving.**

Complete this with green beans, Four-Cheese Fettuccine (page 94), Fruit-Walnut Salad (page 536) and Chocolate Mousse Cake (page 106).

Green Sauce

1 cup parsley sprigs
1½ cups creamed cottage cheese (large curd)
1 tablespoon lemon juice
1 tablespoon milk
½ teaspoon dried basil leaves
½ teaspoon salt
⅛ teaspoon pepper
4 to 6 drops red pepper sauce

Place all ingredients in blender container. Cover; blend on high speed, stopping blender occasionally to scrape sides, until smooth, about 3 minutes.

■ **To Microwave:** Rinse salmon steaks under gently running cold water. Place fish in rectangular microwavable dish, 12 × 7½ × 2 inches. Place salt, thyme, tarragon, peppercorns, parsley, onion, celery and bay leaf on fish. Pour 1 cup water and ½ cup wine over fish. Cover tightly and microwave on high (100%) 3 minutes; rotate dish ½ turn. Microwave until small ends of fish flake easily with fork, 5 to 7 minutes longer. Let stand covered 3 minutes.

Easy . . . PANFRIED FISH

    2 pounds fish fillets, steaks or pan-dressed fish
    1 teaspoon salt
    ⅛ teaspoon pepper
    1 egg
    1 tablespoon water
    1 cup all-purpose flour, cornmeal or
          grated Parmesan cheese
       Shortening (part margarine or butter)

If fish fillets are large, cut into 6 serving pieces. Sprinkle both sides of fish with salt and pepper. Beat egg and water until blended. Dip fish into egg, then coat with flour.

Heat shortening (⅛ inch) in skillet until hot. Fry fish in hot shortening over medium heat, turning fish carefully, until brown on both sides, about 10 minutes. **6 servings; 355** calories per serving.

Easy . . . FISH A LA MEUNIERE

    1 pound fish fillets
    ½ cup all-purpose flour or cornmeal
    ½ teaspoon salt
       Dash of pepper
    ¼ cup milk
    ⅓ cup vegetable oil
    2 tablespoons margarine or butter
    ¼ cup margarine or butter
    1 tablespoon lemon juice
       Snipped parsley

If fish fillets are large, cut into 4 serving pieces. Mix flour, salt and pepper. Dip fish into milk; coat with flour mixture. Heat oil and 2 tablespoons margarine in 10-inch skillet over medium heat until hot. Cook half of the fish in oil mixture, turning once, until fish is golden brown and flakes very easily with fork, 6 to 8 minutes. Remove fish; keep warm. Repeat with remaining fish.

Drain drippings from skillet. Heat ¼ cup margarine in skillet over low heat until light golden brown; remove from heat. Stir in lemon juice. Pour over fish; sprinkle with parsley.   4 servings; 445 calories per serving.

Serve with Barley with Mushrooms (page 88) and strawberries with cream.

Easy . . . OVEN-FRIED FISH

1   **pound fish fillets**
2   **tablespoons cornmeal**
2   **tablespoons dry bread crumbs**
¼   **teaspoon salt**
¼   **teaspoon paprika**
⅛   **teaspoon dried dill weed**
     Dash of pepper
¼   **cup milk**
3   **tablespoons margarine or butter, melted**

Move oven rack to position slightly above middle of oven. Heat oven to 500°. Cut fish fillets into 2 × 1½-inch pieces. Mix cornmeal, bread crumbs, salt, paprika, dill weed and pepper. Dip fish into milk; coat with cornmeal mixture.

Place fish in generously greased rectangular pan, 13 × 9 × 2 inches. Pour margarine over fish. Bake uncovered until fish flakes very easily with fork, about 10 minutes.   3 servings; 350 calories per serving.

Complete this with Potato Salad (page 523), crisp vegetable relishes and Whipped Avocado Dessert (page 221).

DEEP-FRIED FISH

Vegetable oil or shortening
2 pounds fish fillets, steaks or pan-dressed fish
1 cup all-purpose flour
1 teaspoon salt
⅛ teaspoon pepper
2 eggs, slightly beaten
1 cup dry bread crumbs

Heat oil (2 to 3 inches) in deep fryer or Dutch oven to 375° or heat oil (1½ to 2 inches) in skillet until hot. If fish fillets are large, cut into 6 serving pieces. Mix flour, salt and pepper; coat fish with flour mixture. Dip into eggs; coat with bread crumbs. Fry in deep fryer or skillet until golden brown, about 4 minutes. **6 servings; 440 calories per serving.**

Batter-fried Fish: Prepare Thin Batter (page 51). Coat fish with flour mixture, then dip into batter. Fry in deep fryer until golden brown, about 3 minutes, or fry in skillet until golden brown, about 4 minutes.

TUNA SPAGHETTI

1 package (7 ounces) thin spaghetti
2 cloves garlic, finely chopped
¼ cup margarine or butter
¾ cup half-and-half
1 teaspoon dried basil leaves
¼ teaspoon dried oregano leaves
1 can (9¼ ounces) tuna, drained
½ cup sliced pimiento-stuffed olives
¼ cup grated Parmesan cheese

Cook spaghetti as directed on package; drain. Cook garlic in margarine in 2-quart saucepan until garlic is golden brown. Stir in half-and-half, basil and oregano. Heat to boiling. Stir in tuna, olives and cheese. Boil and stir 1 minute. Pour over hot spaghetti. Sprinkle with snipped parsley if desired. **5 servings; 375 calories per serving.**

Easy . . . CURRIED TUNA

¼ cup margarine or butter
2 teaspoons curry powder
2 green onions (with tops), thinly sliced
3 cups cooked regular rice (page 85)
¼ cup hot water
½ teaspoon salt
¼ teaspoon ground ginger
⅛ teaspoon garlic powder
⅛ teaspoon ground red pepper
1 can (12½ ounces) tuna in water, drained
1 hard-cooked egg, chopped
1 tablespoon snipped parsley

Cook and stir margarine, curry powder and onions in 10-inch skillet over medium heat until margarine is melted. Stir in rice, water, salt, ginger, garlic powder, red pepper and tuna. Cook and stir until tuna is hot, about 5 minutes. Sprinkle with egg and parsley. Serve with chutney if desired. **6 servings; 290 calories per serving.**

Nice with Cucumbers and Tomatoes (page 520) and Soft Breadsticks (page 64).

■ **To Microwave:** Place margarine, curry powder and onions in 2-quart microwavable casserole. Cover tightly and microwave on high (100%) until margarine is melted, 1 to 2 minutes. Omit water. Stir rice, salt, ginger, garlic powder, red pepper and tuna into casserole. Cover tightly and microwave until tuna is hot, 3 to 5 minutes.

CREAMY TUNA CASSEROLE

8	ounces uncooked noodles
1	can (12½ ounces) tuna, drained
1	can (4 ounces) sliced mushrooms, drained
1	jar (2 ounces) sliced pimientos, drained
1½	cups dairy sour cream
¾	cup milk
1	teaspoon salt
¼	teaspoon pepper
¼	cup dry bread crumbs
¼	cup grated Parmesan cheese
2	tablespoons margarine or butter, melted
	Snipped parsley

Cook noodles as directed (page 91); drain. Mix noodles, tuna, mushrooms, pimientos, sour cream, milk, salt and pepper in 2-quart casserole. Mix bread crumbs, cheese and margarine; sprinkle over tuna mixture.

Bake uncovered in 350° oven until hot and bubbly, 35 to 40 minutes. Sprinkle with parsley. **6 servings; 430 calories per serving.**

Serve with buttered Italian-style green beans and Herb Biscuits (page 42).

■ **To Microwave:** Decrease milk to ⅔ cup. Mix noodles, tuna, mushrooms, pimientos, sour cream, milk, salt and pepper in 2-quart microwavable casserole. Cover tightly and microwave on medium (50%) 10 minutes; stir. Mix bread crumbs, cheese and margarine; sprinkle over tuna mixture. Microwave uncovered until hot and bubbly, 4 to 7 minutes longer.

SALMON PUFF

½ cup milk
2 tablespoons margarine or butter, melted
4 slices bread, torn into pieces
3 tablespoons lemon juice
2 teaspoons finely chopped onion
1 teaspoon salt
½ teaspoon pepper
2 eggs, separated
1 can (15½ ounces) salmon, drained and flaked
Paprika

Mix milk, margarine and bread; stir in lemon juice, onion, salt, pepper, egg yolks and salmon. Beat egg whites until stiff; fold into salmon mixture. Pour into greased 1½-quart casserole; sprinkle with paprika. Bake uncovered in 350° oven 1 hour. **6 servings; 225 calories per serving.**

Serve with Parmesan Sprouts (page 628) and Mixed Fruit Salad (page 537).

■ **To Microwave:** Use ungreased microwavable casserole. Microwave uncovered on high (100%) until top is dry and set, 5 to 7 minutes.

CRUSTLESS SALMON QUICHE

1 can (15½ ounces) salmon, drained and flaked
1 cup shredded Swiss cheese (4 ounces)
1 medium onion, chopped (about ½ cup)
2 tablespoons all-purpose flour
4 eggs
1 cup milk
¾ teaspoon salt
⅛ teaspoon red pepper sauce

Toss salmon, cheese, onion and flour. Spread in greased pie plate or quiche pan, 9 × 1¼ inches. Beat eggs slightly; beat in remaining ingredients. Pour egg mixture over salmon mixture. Bake uncovered in 350° oven until knife inserted in center comes out clean, 35 to 40 minutes. Let stand 10 minutes before cutting. **6 servings; 280 calories per serving.**

Nice with tossed green salad and Cheese Casserolè Bread (page 72).

Crustless Tuna Quiche: Substitute 2 cans (6½ ounces each) tuna in water, drained, for the salmon.

SALMON LOAF

2	cans (15½ ounces each) salmon, drained and flaked (reserve liquid)
2	eggs
	Milk
3	cups coarse cracker crumbs
2	tablespoons lemon juice
2	teaspoons chopped onion
¼	teaspoon salt
¼	teaspoon pepper

Mix salmon and eggs. Add enough milk to reserved salmon liquid to measure 1½ cups. Stir liquid mixture and remaining ingredients into salmon mixture. Spoon lightly into greased loaf pan, 9 × 5 × 3 inches. Bake uncovered in 350° oven until done, about 45 minutes. Garnish with lemon wedges if desired.   **8 servings; 355 calories per serving.**

Serve with Dill Sauce (page 599), buttered new potatoes and green peas.

Easy . . . SALMON SHORTCAKES

2⅓	cups buttermilk baking mix
½	cup milk
3	tablespoons margarine or butter, melted and cooled slightly
½	cup water
¼	cup sliced ripe olives
1	tablespoon chopped pimiento
1	teaspoon parsley flakes
1	can (10¾ ounces) condensed cream of mushroom soup
1	can (15½ ounces) salmon, drained and flaked

Heat oven to 450°. Mix baking mix, milk and margarine with fork until soft dough forms. Turn dough onto lightly floured cloth-covered board. Knead 8 to 10 times. Roll dough ½ inch thick. Cut into 5 circles with floured 3-inch cutter. Bake on ungreased cookie sheet until golden brown, about 10 minutes.

Heat remaining ingredients except salmon to boiling over medium heat, stirring frequently. Stir in salmon. Split warm shortcakes; serve salmon mixture between halves and over tops. **5 servings; 495 calories per serving.**

Serve with Glazed Carrots (page 633) and Winter Fruit Salad (page 538).

Tuna Shortcakes: Substitute 1 can (12½ ounces) tuna, drained, for the salmon.

SHELLFISH

ABOUT SHELLFISH

Shellfish such as shrimp, crab and lobster have always enjoyed special popularity in great restaurants and with great cooks. Today, these shellfish and others are more readily available almost everywhere, and can be featured in a wide variety of recipes.

HOW TO PURCHASE SHELLFISH
Shellfish are available frozen, canned, smoked, breaded and, in some areas, live. The amount you need to buy varies considerably; consult your recipe or your dealer.

Oysters, scallops and *clams* are partially prepared when purchased shucked in their own liquid. *Raw shrimp* is available either with or without shells. *Crab* and *shrimp* can be purchased fully cooked in the deli or seafood section of many supermarkets. The flesh of partially prepared and prepared shellfish should be firm and spring back when pressed, indicating freshness.

Live *mussels* and *clams* should have tightly closed shells. An open shell will close when tapped if the shellfish is alive. However, if it is not alive, do not use it.

Freshly caught shellfish are often commercially frozen for shipment in prime condition to locations thousands of miles from the sea. Properly frozen packages of seafood are hard, never soft, to the touch and are free of ice crystals and frost. Avoid seafood with a strong, rancid odor or with white or discolored patches, which indicate freezer burn.

SEAFOOD STICKS

Seafood sticks have a distinctive flavor similar to real crab and other shellfish. Composed mainly of Alaska pollock, they are low in fat, cholesterol and calories but high in nutritive value. Moderate price and versatility make seafood sticks a perfect substitute for more expensive shellfish.

COOKING SHELLFISH

Shellfish are usually steamed, boiled, fried, broiled or baked.
  The most important rule is: *Don't overcook.*

COOKED SHRIMP

1½   **pounds fresh or frozen raw shrimp (in shells)**
  4   **cups water**
  2   **tablespoons salt**

Peel shrimp. (If shrimp is frozen, do not thaw; peel under running cold water.) Make a shallow cut lengthwise down back of each shrimp; wash out sand vein.

  Heat water to boiling. Add salt and shrimp. Cover and heat to boiling; reduce heat. Simmer 5 minutes; drain. Remove any remaining particles of sand vein.   **2 cups cleaned cooked shrimp** (¾ pound).

  NOTE: To cook shrimp before peeling, increase salt to ¼ cup. After cooking shrimp, drain and peel. Remove sand vein.

SKEWERED SHRIMP

---

  1   **pound fresh or frozen raw shrimp (18 to 20 in shells)**
  ¾   **cup Italian dressing**
  1   **can (8¼ ounces) pineapple chunks, drained**
 18   **large pitted ripe olives**
 12   **whole mushrooms**
  2   **green peppers, cut into 1½-inch squares**

Peel shrimp. (If shrimp is frozen, do not thaw; peel under running cold water.) Make a shallow cut lengthwise down back of each shrimp; wash out sand vein.

  Pour dressing over shrimp and remaining ingredients in rectangular baking dish, 13 × 9 × 2 inches. Cover and refrigerate, stirring occasionally, at least 4 hours but no longer than 6 hours.

Set oven control to broil and/or 550°. Alternate shrimp, pineapple chunks, mushrooms, green peppers and olives on each of six 15-inch metal skewers, placing an olive on end of each skewer; reserve dressing. Broil kabobs about 4 inches from heat, turning and brushing once with dressing, until shrimp is pink, about 5 minutes. Serve with lemon wedges if desired. **6 servings; 200 calories per serving.**

Serve with Lemon Pilaf (page 86) and Cherry Cordial Pie (page 161).

CHINESE-FRIED SHRIMP

1	pound fresh or frozen raw shrimp (21 to 30 in shells)
	Vegetable oil
½	cup all-purpose flour
¾	teaspoon salt
¼	teaspoon ground ginger
¼	teaspoon pepper
3	egg whites
1½	cups shredded coconut
	Plum Sweet-and-Sour Sauce (page 340)

Peel shrimp, leaving tails intact. (If shrimp is frozen, do not thaw; peel under running cold water.) Make a shallow cut lengthwise down back of each shrimp; wash out sand vein.

Heat oil (2 to 3 inches) in deep fryer or Dutch oven to 325°. Mix flour, salt, ginger and pepper. Beat egg whites just until foamy. Coat shrimp with flour mixture; dip into egg whites. Pat coconut onto shrimp, covering completely. Fry shrimp, turning once, until coconut is golden brown, about 2 minutes; drain. Serve with Plum Sweet-and-Sour Sauce or, if desired, with soy sauce. **4 servings; 535 calories per serving.**

Complete this with rice, Chinese pea pods and Orange Mousse (page 263).

Plum Sweet-and-Sour Sauce

½	cup canned crushed pineapple in syrup
¼	cup sugar
¼	cup water
¼	cup vinegar
¾	teaspoon soy sauce
1½	teaspoons cornstarch
1½	teaspoons cold water
¼	cup plum jam

Heat pineapple (with syrup), sugar, ¼ cup water, the vinegar and soy sauce to boiling in 2-quart saucepan. Mix cornstarch and 1½ teaspoons cold water; stir into pineapple mixture. Heat to boiling, stirring constantly; cool to room temperature. Stir in jam.

Do-ahead Tip: Fry shrimp. Cover; refrigerate no longer than 2 hours. To serve, heat uncovered in 350° oven until hot, about 10 minutes.

STIR-FRIED SHRIMP WITH VEGETABLES

¾	pound fresh or frozen raw shrimp (in shells)
½	teaspoon cornstarch
½	teaspoon soy sauce
¼	teaspoon salt
⅛	teaspoon sesame oil
	Dash of white pepper
8	ounces bok choy (about 4 large stalks)
4	ounces Chinese pea pods
1	tablespoon cornstarch
1	tablespoon cold water
2	tablespoons vegetable oil
1	clove garlic, finely chopped
1	teaspoon finely chopped gingerroot
¼	cup vegetable oil
4	ounces mushrooms, cut into ½-inch slices
2	tablespoons oyster sauce or 1 tablespoon soy sauce
1	teaspoon salt
¼	cup chicken broth (page 557)
2	green onions (with tops), cut into 2-inch pieces

Peel shrimp. (If shrimp is frozen, do not thaw; peel under running cold water.) Make a shallow cut lengthwise down back of each shrimp; wash out sand vein. Cut shrimp lengthwise almost into halves. Toss shrimp, ½ teaspoon cornstarch, ½ teaspoon soy sauce, ¼ teaspoon salt, the sesame oil and white pepper in glass or plastic bowl. Cover and refrigerate 30 minutes.

Separate bok choy leaves from stems. Cut leaves into 2-inch pieces; cut stems diagonally into ¼-inch slices (do not combine leaves and stems). Remove strings from pea pods. Place pea pods in boiling water. Cover and cook 1 minute; drain. Immediately rinse under running cold water; drain. Mix 1 tablespoon cornstarch and the water; reserve.

Heat wok until 1 or 2 drops of water bubble and skitter when sprinkled in wok. Add 2 tablespoons vegetable oil; rotate wok to coat side. Add garlic and gingerroot; stir-fry until garlic is light brown. Add shrimp; stir-fry until shrimp is pink. Remove shrimp from wok.

Add ¼ cup vegetable oil to wok; rotate to coat side. Add bok choy stems and mushrooms; stir-fry 1 minute. Stir in bok choy leaves, oyster sauce and 1 teaspoon salt. Stir in chicken broth; heat to boiling. Stir in cornstarch mixture; cook and stir until thickened, about 10 seconds. Add shrimp and pea pods; cook and stir 30 seconds. Garnish with green onions. **5** servings; 245 calories per serving.

SHRIMP JAMBALAYA

1	large onion, chopped (about 1 cup)
½	medium green pepper, chopped (about ½ cup)
1	clove garlic, finely chopped
3	tablespoons olive or vegetable oil
1	pound fresh or frozen raw shrimp (in shells)
1	cup uncooked regular rice
2	cups chicken broth (page 557)
1	teaspoon salt
⅛	teaspoon pepper
⅛	teaspoon ground thyme
⅛	teaspoon red pepper sauce
1	bay leaf, crumbled
1	can (16 ounces) whole tomatoes, undrained
½	pound cubed fully cooked smoked ham (about 1½ cups)

Cook and stir onion, green pepper, garlic and 2 tablespoons of the oil in Dutch oven over low heat 3 minutes. Add shrimp. Cook, stirring frequently, until shrimp is pink, about 5 minutes. Remove shrimp mixture; reserve.

Cook remaining 1 tablespoon oil and the rice in Dutch oven over medium-high heat, stirring frequently, until rice is light brown, about 10 minutes. Stir in chicken broth, salt, pepper, thyme, pepper sauce, bay leaf and tomatoes. Heat to boiling; reduce heat. Cover and simmer until rice is tender, about 15 minutes. Stir in shrimp mixture and the ham. Cover and cook just until shrimp and ham are hot. **6 servings; 305** calories per serving.

Serve with Orange-Avocado Salad (page 543) and Pecan Pie (page 157).

Easy . . . BROILED GINGER SCALLOPS

- 1 **pound scallops**
- ¼ **cup soy sauce**
- 2 **tablespoons finely chopped gingerroot**
- ¼ **cup lemon juice**
- 2 **tablespoons vegetable oil**
- 1 **tablespoon honey**

If scallops are large, cut into halves. Arrange scallops in single layer in square baking dish, 8 × 8 × 2 inches. Heat soy sauce to boiling. Add gingerroot; reduce heat. Simmer uncovered 5 minutes. Stir in remaining ingredients; pour over scallops. Cover and refrigerate, stirring occasionally, 2 hours.

Set oven control to broil and/or 550°. Remove scallops from marinade with slotted spoon. Arrange in single layer on rack in broiler pan. Broil with tops 3 to 4 inches from heat until opaque in center, about 5 minutes. **3 servings; 155** calories per serving.

Easy . . . SCALLOPS IN CREAM SAUCE

---

1   **pound scallops**
1   **green onion (with top), thinly sliced**
¼   **cup margarine or butter**
¼   **teaspoon salt**
¼   **cup dry white wine**
2   **teaspoons cornstarch**
½   **cup whipping cream**
4   **cups hot cooked spinach noodles or fettuccine**
½   **cup finely shredded Swiss cheese**

If scallops are large, cut into halves. Cook and stir onion in margarine in 10-inch skillet over medium-high heat until tender. Stir in scallops and salt. Cook, stirring frequently, until scallops are white, 3 to 4 minutes.

Mix wine and cornstarch; stir into scallop mixture. Heat to boiling, stirring constantly. Boil and stir 1 minute; reduce heat to medium. Stir in whipping cream. Heat until hot, 1 to 2 minutes. Toss noodles and cheese. Spoon scallop mixture over noodles. Serve with freshly ground pepper if desired.   **6 servings; 355 calories per serving.**

Complete this with Baked Stuffed Tomatoes (page 672), croissants, Mandarin Salad (page 512) and Pavlova (page 258).

STEAMED CLAMS

Wash 6 pounds shell clams ("steamers") thoroughly, discarding any broken-shell or open (dead) clams. Place in steamer* with ½ cup boiling water. Steam until clams open, 5 to 10 minutes. Serve hot in shells with melted margarine or butter and cups of broth.   **6 servings.**

---

*If a steamer is not available, add 1 inch boiling water to Dutch oven with clams; cover tightly.

BOILED HARD-SHELL CRABS

  6   **quarts water**
 ⅓   **cup salt**
 24   **live hard-shell blue crabs**
      Cocktail Sauce (page 603)

Heat water and salt to boiling in Dutch oven. Drop crabs into Dutch oven. Cover and heat to boiling; reduce heat. Simmer 15 minutes; drain. Serve crabs hot or cold with Cocktail Sauce.   **6 servings.**

   NOTE: To remove meat, grasp body of crab. Break off large claws. Pull off top shell. Cut or break off legs. Scrape off the gills; carefully remove organs located in center part of body.

BOILED DUNGENESS CRABS

Have your fish retailer dress 3 live Dungeness crabs for eating. Wash body cavity of each. Heat 8 quarts water and ½ cup salt to boiling in Dutch oven. Drop crabs into Dutch oven. Cover and heat to boiling; reduce heat. Simmer 15 minutes; drain.

   Crack claws and legs. Serve hot with margarine or butter, melted. Or refrigerate crabs until chilled and serve with mayonnaise or salad dressing.   **6 servings.**

COMPANY CRAB CASSEROLE

1	medium onion, chopped (about ½ cup)
1	large clove garlic, finely chopped
2	tablespoons olive or vegetable oil
1	can (16 ounces) whole tomatoes, undrained
1	can (8 ounces) tomato sauce
½	teaspoon dried marjoram leaves
½	teaspoon dried basil leaves
½	teaspoon dried oregano leaves
¼	teaspoon salt
	Dash of red pepper sauce
	Lemon Oven Rice (below)
2	cups cooked crabmeat or ½-inch pieces seafood sticks
½	cup crumbled feta cheese (3 ounces)*

Cook and stir onion and garlic in oil in 3-quart saucepan until onion is tender. Stir in tomatoes, tomato sauce, marjoram, basil, oregano, salt and pepper sauce; break up tomatoes. Heat to boiling; reduce heat. Cover and simmer 45 minutes.

Prepare Lemon Oven Rice. Stir crabmeat and cheese into tomato mixture; spoon over rice. Bake uncovered in 350° oven 20 minutes. Garnish with parsley if desired.   **6 servings; 200 calories per serving.**

Serve with broccoli, warm French Bread (page 68) and Elegant Tossed Salad (page 510).

Lemon Oven Rice

2	cups boiling water
1	cup uncooked regular rice
1	teaspoon salt
2	tablespoons margarine or butter
1	tablespoon lemon juice

Heat oven to 350°. Mix boiling water, rice and salt in ungreased rectangular baking dish, 11 × 7 × 1½ inches. Cover and bake until liquid is absorbed, 25 to 30 minutes. Stir in margarine and lemon juice.

*1 package (3 ounces) cream cheese, cut into cubes, can be substituted for the feta cheese.

BOILED LOBSTER

Heat 3 quarts water and 3 tablespoons salt to boiling in Dutch oven. Plunge 2 live lobsters (about 1 pound each) headfirst into water. Cover and heat to boiling; reduce heat. Simmer 10 minutes; drain. Place each lobster on its back. Cut lengthwise into halves with sharp knife.

Remove the stomach, which is just behind the head, and the intestinal vein, which runs from the stomach to the tip of the tail. Do not discard the green liver and coral roe. Crack the claws. **2 servings.**

BROILED LOBSTER TAILS

> 2 quarts water
> 2 tablespoons salt
> 1 package (24 ounces) frozen South African rock lobster tails
> ⅓ cup margarine or butter, melted
> Lemon Butter Sauce (below)

Heat water and salt to boiling in saucepan. Add lobster tails. Cover and heat to boiling; reduce heat. Simmer 15 minutes; drain.

Cut away thin undershell (covering meat of lobster tails) with kitchen scissors. To prevent tail from curling, insert long metal skewer from meat side through tail to shell side, then back through shell and meat at opposite end. Place tails, meat sides up, on broiler rack. Brush with margarine.

Set oven control to broil and/or 550°. Broil with tops about 3 inches from heat until hot, 2 to 3 minutes. Remove skewers; serve lobster with Lemon Butter Sauce. **3 servings; 570 calories per serving.**

Complete this with baked potatoes, corn on the cob and Deluxe Brownies (page 175).

Lemon Butter Sauce

> ½ cup margarine or butter
> 1 tablespoon lemon juice
> 1 tablespoon snipped parsley
> ¼ teaspoon red pepper sauce

Heat all ingredients over low heat, stirring constantly, until margarine is melted; keep warm.

LOBSTER NEWBURG WITH POPOVERS

Popovers (page 52)
¼ cup margarine or butter
3 tablespoons all-purpose flour
½ teaspoon salt
½ teaspoon dry mustard
¼ teaspoon pepper
2 cups milk
2 cups cut-up cooked lobster
2 tablespoons dry white wine

Prepare Popovers. Heat margarine in 3-quart saucepan over low heat until melted. Stir in flour, salt, mustard and pepper. Cook, stirring constantly, until mixture is smooth and bubbly; remove from heat. Stir in milk. Heat to boiling, stirring constantly. Boil and stir 1 minute. Stir in lobster and wine. Serve over hot split Popovers. **6 servings; 320 calories per serving.**

Complete this meal with buttered asparagus spears, Spinach Tossed Salad (page 506) and Pears Helene (page 231).

Crab Newburg with Popovers: Substitute 2 cups cooked crabmeat or seafood sticks for the lobster.

Easy . . . SCALLOPED OYSTERS

---

1 pint shucked select or large oysters, undrained
½ to ¾ cup half-and-half
3 cups soft bread crumbs
½ cup margarine or butter, melted
2 teaspoons celery seed
1 teaspoon salt
¼ teaspoon pepper

Arrange oysters in greased rectangular baking dish, 12 × 7½ × 2 inches. Pour about ¼ cup of the half-and-half over oysters.

Mix remaining ingredients except half-and-half; sprinkle over oysters. Top with remaining half-and-half (liquid should come about ¾ of the way up on oysters). Sprinkle with paprika if desired. Bake uncovered in 375° oven until hot, 30 to 40 minutes.   **4 servings; 600 calories per serving.**

Nice with Hard Rolls (page 73) and Caesar Salad (page 509).

SEAFOOD LASAGNE

½	cup margarine or butter
2	cloves garlic, crushed
½	cup all-purpose flour
½	teaspoon salt
2	cups milk
2	cups chicken broth (page 557)
2	cups shredded mozzarella cheese (8 ounces)
½	cup sliced green onions (with tops)
1	teaspoon dried basil leaves
¼	teaspoon pepper
8	ounces uncooked lasagne noodles (9 or 10 noodles)
1	cup creamed cottage cheese
1	can (7½ ounces) crabmeat, drained and cartilage removed
1	can (4½ ounces) tiny shrimp, drained
½	cup grated Parmesan cheese

Heat margarine in 3-quart saucepan over low heat until melted; add garlic. Stir in flour and salt. Cook, stirring constantly, until bubbly; remove from heat. Stir in milk and broth. Heat to boiling, stirring constantly. Boil and stir 1 minute. Stir in mozzarella cheese, onions, basil and pepper. Cook over low heat, stirring constantly, until cheese is melted.

Spread ¼ of the cheese sauce (about 1½ cups) in ungreased rectangular baking dish, 13×9×2 inches; top with 3 or 4 uncooked noodles, overlapping if necessary. Spread cottage cheese over noodles in dish. Repeat with ¼ of the cheese sauce and 3 or 4 noodles. Top with crabmeat, shrimp, ¼ of the cheese sauce, the remaining noodles and cheese sauce. Sprinkle with Parmesan cheese. Bake uncovered in 350° oven until noodles are done, 35 to 40 minutes. Let stand 15 minutes before cutting.   **12 servings; 295 calories per serving.**

DEEP-FRIED SHELLFISH

Vegetable oil
½   cup all-purpose flour
1   teaspoon salt
¼   teaspoon pepper
Shellfish (see Timetable)
2   eggs, slightly beaten
1   cup dry bread crumbs

Heat oil (2 to 3 inches) in deep fryer or Dutch oven to 375°.
Mix flour, salt and pepper. Coat shellfish with flour mixture;
dip into beaten eggs, then coat with bread crumbs. Fry until
golden brown (see Timetable).

Batter-fried Shellfish: Prepare Thin Batter (page 51). Coat
shellfish with flour; dip into batter. Fry in deep fryer, turning
once, until golden brown (see Timetable).

Panfried Oysters or Clams: Fry oysters or clams in ⅛ inch
melted margarine or butter over medium heat until golden
brown, about 2 minutes on each side.

TIMETABLE FOR DEEP-FRYING
SHELLFISH

Shellfish	Cooking Time
Deep-fried	
1 pound shrimp	2 to 3 minutes
12 ounces scallops	3 to 4 minutes
1 pint oysters	2 to 3 minutes
1 pint clams	2 to 3 minutes
Batter-fried	
1 pound shrimp	4 to 5 minutes
12 ounces scallops	3 to 4 minutes

BEEF
VEAL

MEAT IDENTIFICATION CHART

Many cuts of meat are named for the bones they contain (rib, arm, leg, for example). The shape of the bone also indicates the tenderness of the cut. Beef, lamb, pork and veal contain bones that are almost identical in appearance. The chart below is a guide to meat cuts and appropriate cooking methods.

Type of Bone	Common Name	Braise	Cook in Liquid	Broil	Panfry	Roast
Arm	**beef** chuck arm steak	■	■			
	beef chuck arm pot roast	■	■			
	lamb shoulder arm chop			■	■	
	lamb shoulder arm roast					■
	pork shoulder arm steak	■			■	
	pork shoulder arm roast					■
	veal shoulder arm steak	■			■	
	veal shoulder arm roast	■				■
Blade center cuts	**beef** chuck blade steak	■	■			
	beef chuck blade pot roast	■	■			
	lamb shoulder blade chop	■		■	■	
	lamb shoulder blade roast					■
	pork shoulder blade steak	■		■	■	
	pork shoulder blade Boston roast	■				■
	veal shoulder blade steak	■			■	
	veal shoulder blade roast	■				■
Rib back bone and rib bone	**beef** rib steak			■	■	
	beef rib roast					■
	lamb rib chop			■	■	
	lamb rib roast					■
	pork rib chop	■		■	■	
	pork rib roast					■
	veal rib chop	■			■	
	veal rib roast					■
Loin back bone (T-shape)	**beef** loin steak (T-bone, porterhouse)			■	■	
	beef loin tenderloin roast or steak			■		■
	lamb loin chop			■	■	
	lamb loin roast					■
	pork loin chop	■		■	■	
	pork loin roast					■
	veal loin chop	■			■	
	veal loin roast	■				■

Type of Bone	Common Name	Braise	Cook in Liquid	Broil	Panfry	Roast
Hip	**beef** sirloin steak			■	■	
pin bone	**beef** loin tenderloin roast or steak			■		■
(near short loin)	**lamb** sirloin chop			■	■	
	lamb leg roast					■
flat bone	**pork** sirloin chop	■		■		
(center cuts)	**pork** sirloin roast					■
	veal sirloin steak	■			■	
	veal leg sirloin roast					■
wedge bone						
(near round)						
Leg	**beef** round steak	■			■	
leg or	**beef** rump roast		■			■
round bone	**lamb** leg steak			■	■	
	lamb leg roast					■
	pork leg (ham) steak	■		■	■	
	pork leg roast (fresh or smoked)					■
	veal leg round steak	■			■	
	veal leg roast					■
Breast	**beef** brisket (fresh or corned)	■	■			
breast and rib	**beef** plate short rib	■	■			
	lamb breast	■	■			■
	lamb breast riblet	■	■			
	pork bacon (side pork)			■	■	
	pork sparerib	■	■			■
	veal breast	■				■
	veal breast riblet	■	■			

BEEF

ABOUT BEEF AND VEAL

As a result of new breeding and feeding techniques, beef is lower in fat, calories and cholesterol than ever before. Veal has fewer calories than beef because it has less fat.

GRADES OF MEAT
The round stamp bearing the abbreviations for "U.S. Inspected and Passed" is your guarantee that the meat is wholesome and met federal standards of cleanliness during processing. The stamp need not be trimmed from the meat because the marking fluid is harmless.

The U.S. Department of Agriculture's grades of meat quality are found in a shield-shaped stamp. In descending order, these grades are USDA Prime, Choice, Good, Standard, Commercial and Utility.

Most meats sold in retail stores are Choice. Prime is usually available only in special restaurants. Grades below Good are ordinarily used by the packers in combination meats and are not sold in retail stores.

Look for flecks of fat within the lean in beef; this is referred to as "marbling." It increases juiciness, flavor and tenderness.

The color of the lean part of beef should be bright red. Vacuum-packed beef and the interior of ground beef have a darker, purplish-red color. The beef should return to a bright red when it is exposed to air. Veal has a light pink color.

Ribs and loins of high-quality beef are usually aged. Aging develops additional tenderness and characteristic flavor.

SERVINGS PER POUND
The number of servings per pound of meat varies according to the cut of meat. The following chart can be used as a guide.

Cut	Allow for one serving
Boneless (ground beef, tenderloin)	¼ pound
Small to Medium Bone-in (rib roasts, pot roasts)	½ pound
Large Bone-in (short ribs, shanks)	¾ pound

CARVING A STANDING RIB ROAST

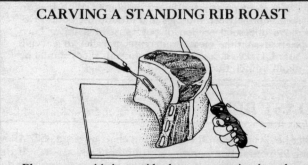

Place roast with large side down on carving board or platter. If necessary, remove wedge-shaped slice from large end so roast will stand firmly. To carve, insert fork below first rib. Slice from outside of roast toward rib side.

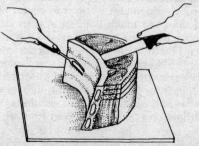

After making several slices, cut along inner side of rib bone with knife. As each slice is released, slide knife under it and lift to plate.

CARVING A BLADE POT ROAST

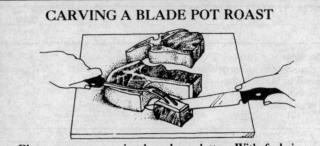

Place roast on carving board or platter. With fork in meat, cut between muscles and around the bones. Remove one solid section of pot roast at a time. Turn section so that meat grain runs parallel to carving board. Carve across the grain of meat; slices should be about ¼ inch thick.

ROAST BEEF

Select beef roast from those listed in chart on page 357. Allow about ½ pound per person (less for boneless roasts). If desired, sprinkle with salt and pepper before, during or after roasting (salt permeates meat only ¼ to ½ inch).

Place beef, fat side up, on rack in shallow roasting pan. The rack keeps the meat out of the drippings. (With a rib roast, the ribs form a natural rack.) It is not necessary to baste.

Insert meat thermometer so tip is in center of thickest part of beef and does not touch bone or rest in fat. Do not add water. Do not cover. Roast in 325° oven. (It is not necessary to preheat oven.) Roast to desired degree of doneness (see Timetable), using the thermometer reading as final guide.

Roasts are easier to carve if allowed to set 15 to 20 minutes after removing from oven. Meat continues to cook after removal from oven; if roast is to set, it should be removed from oven when thermometer registers 5 to 10° lower than desired doneness. To serve au jus, spoon hot beef juices over carved beef. Or serve beef with Oven-browned Potatoes (page 357), Pan Gravy (page 358) or Yorkshire Pudding (page 358).

OVEN-BROWNED POTATOES

About 1½ hours before beef roast (left) is done, prepare and boil 6 medium potatoes as directed on page 657 except— decrease cooking time to 10 minutes. (Make thin crosswise cuts almost through potatoes before cooking if desired.) Place potatoes in beef drippings in pan, turning each potato to coat completely. Or brush potatoes with margarine or butter, melted, and place on rack with beef. Continue cooking, turning potatoes once, until tender and golden brown, about 1¼ hours. Sprinkle with salt and pepper.   **6 servings.**

TIMETABLE FOR ROASTING BEEF
(Oven Temperature 325°F)

Cut	Approximate Weight (Pounds)	Meat Thermometer Reading (°F)	Approximate Cooking Time (Minutes per Pound)
Rib	6 to 8	140° (rare)	23 to 25
		160° (medium)	27 to 30
		170° (well)	32 to 35
Boneless Rib	4 to 6	140° (rare)	26 to 32
		160° (medium)	34 to 38
		170° (well)	40 to 42
Rib Eye (Delmonico)*	4 to 6	140° (rare)	18 to 20
		160° (medium)	20 to 22
		170° (well)	22 to 24
Rolled Rump (high quality)	4 to 6	150 to 170°	25 to 30
Tip (high quality)	3½ to 4	140 to 170°	35 to 40
	6 to 8	140 to 170°	30 to 35
Top Round (high quality)	4 to 6	140 to 170°	25 to 30

			Total Cooking Time
Tenderloin (whole)**	4 to 6	140° (rare)	45 to 60 minutes
Tenderloin (half)**	2 to 3	140° (rare)	45 to 50 minutes

*Roast at 350° **Roast at 425°

PAN GRAVY

    2   tablespoons meat drippings (fat and juices)
    2   tablespoons all-purpose flour
    1   cup liquid (meat juices, broth, water)
        Salt and pepper to taste

Place meat on warm platter; keep warm while preparing gravy. Pour drippings from pan into bowl, leaving brown particles in pan. Return 2 tablespoons drippings to pan. (Measure accurately because too little fat makes gravy lumpy.)

Stir in flour. (Measure accurately so gravy is not greasy.) Cook over low heat, stirring constantly, until mixture is smooth and bubbly; remove from heat. Stir in liquid. Heat to boiling, stirring constantly. Boil and stir 1 minute. Stir in few drops browning sauce if desired. Sprinkle with salt and pepper. **1 cup gravy.**

Creamy Gravy: Substitute milk for half of the liquid. Serve with turkey, chicken, pork chops or veal.

Thin Gravy: Decrease drippings to 1 tablespoon and flour to 1 tablespoon.

YORKSHIRE PUDDING

    1   cup all-purpose flour
    1   cup milk
    ½   teaspoon salt
    2   eggs

Thirty minutes before rib roast or boneless rib roast (page 356) is done, mix all ingredients with hand beater just until smooth. Heat square pan, 9×9×2 inches, in oven. Remove beef from oven; spoon off drippings and add enough melted shortening to drippings, if necessary, to measure ½ cup.

Increase oven temperature to 425°. Return beef to oven. Place hot drippings in heated square pan; pour in pudding batter. Bake 10 minutes. Remove beef; continue baking pudding until deep golden brown, 25 to 30 minutes longer. Cut pudding into squares and serve with beef. **6 servings.**

FRENCH-STYLE BEEF ROAST

3 - pound beef boneless chuck or rolled rump roast
1 teaspoon salt
1 teaspoon dried thyme leaves
6 whole cloves
5 peppercorns
1 bay leaf
1 large clove garlic, cut into fourths
4 cups water
4 medium carrots, cut crosswise into halves or fourths
2 medium onions, cut into fourths
2 medium turnips, cut into fourths
2 medium stalks celery, cut into 1-inch pieces

Place beef roast, salt, thyme, cloves, peppercorns, bay leaf and garlic in Dutch oven; add water. Heat to boiling; reduce heat. Cover and simmer 2½ hours.

Add remaining ingredients. Cover and simmer until beef and vegetables are tender, about 30 minutes. Remove beef and vegetables; cut beef into ¼-inch slices. Strain broth; serve with beef and vegetables. **8 servings; 300 calories per serving.**

Serve with Cherry Layered Salad (page 531) and Baking Powder Biscuits (page 42).

NEW ENGLAND POT ROAST

4 - pound beef arm, blade or cross rib pot roast*
1 tablespoon salt
1 teaspoon pepper
1 jar (5 ounces) prepared horseradish
1 cup water
8 small potatoes, cut into halves
8 medium carrots, cut into fourths
8 small onions
   Pot Roast Gravy (page 360)

*3-pound beef bottom round, rolled rump, tip or chuck eye roast can be substituted; decrease the salt to 2 teaspoons.

Cook beef in Dutch oven over medium heat until brown; reduce heat. Sprinkle with salt and pepper. Spread horseradish over both sides of beef. Add water. Heat to boiling; reduce heat. Cover and simmer on top of range or bake in 325° oven 2½ hours. Add vegetables. Cover and cook until beef and vegetables are tender, about 1 hour longer. Remove to warm platter; keep warm. Prepare Pot Roast Gravy; serve with beef and vegetables.   **8 servings; 355 calories per serving.**

Pot Roast Gravy

Skim excess fat from broth. Add enough water to broth to measure 2 cups. Shake ½ cup cold water and ¼ cup all-purpose flour in tightly covered container; gradually stir into broth. Heat to boiling, stirring constantly. Boil and stir 1 minute.

Barbecue Pot Roast: Decrease salt to 1½ teaspoons and pepper to ½ teaspoon. Omit horseradish and water. Prepare Barbecue Sauce (page 604). After browning beef, pour on Barbecue Sauce. Omit gravy. Skim fat from sauce; spoon sauce over beef and vegetables.

Dilled Pot Roast: Omit horseradish. Sprinkle beef with 1 teaspoon dried dill weed. Prepare gravy as directed except— add enough water to broth to measure 1½ cups. After heating to boiling, reduce heat. Stir in ½ cup dairy sour cream and 1 teaspoon dried dill weed; heat gravy just until hot.

Fruited Pot Roast: Omit horseradish. Substitute 1 cup dry white wine for the water. Substitute 1 cup dried apricots, ½ cup raisins and 1 large onion, sliced, for the vegetables. Remove beef and fruit mixture to warm platter; keep warm. Omit gravy. Skim excess fat from broth. Add enough water to broth to measure 2 cups; heat to boiling. Mix 1 tablespoon cornstarch, 2 tablespoons cold water and ½ teaspoon dry mustard; gradually stir into broth. Heat to boiling, stirring constantly. Boil and stir 1 minute. Serve with beef and fruit mixture.

Herbed Pot Roast: Decrease salt to 1½ teaspoons and pepper to ½ teaspoon. Omit horseradish. After browning beef roast, sprinkle with 1 teaspoon dried marjoram leaves, 1 teaspoon dried thyme leaves, ½ teaspoon dried oregano leaves and 3 cloves garlic, crushed. Substitute 1 can (10½ ounces) condensed beef broth for the 1 cup water.

Easy . . . BEEF BRISKET BARBECUE

4 to 5	pound well-trimmed beef brisket
1½	teaspoons salt
½	cup finely chopped onion
½	cup catsup
¼	cup vinegar
1	tablespoon Worcestershire sauce
1½	teaspoons liquid smoke
¼	teaspoon pepper
1	bay leaf, finely crushed

Rub surface of beef brisket with salt. Place in ungreased rectangular pan, 13×9×2 inches. Mix remaining ingredients; pour over beef. Cover and bake in 325° oven until tender, about 3 hours.

Cut thin diagonal slices across the grain at an angle from 2 or 3 "faces" of beef. Spoon any remaining pan juices over sliced beef if desired. **12 servings; 255 calories per serving.**

For a family picnic, serve with Garden Potato Salad (page 524) and Kidney Bean Salad (page 514).

NOTE: Beef Brisket Barbecue can be grilled. After rubbing surface of beef with salt, place on 20×15-inch piece of heavy-duty aluminum foil. Mix remaining ingredients; pour over beef. Wrap securely in foil. Grill about 5 inches from medium coals, turning once, until tender, about 1½ hours.

CORNED BEEF AND CABBAGE

2	pound well-trimmed corned beef boneless brisket or round
1	small onion, cut into fourths
1	clove garlic, crushed
1	small head green cabbage, cut into 6 wedges

Pour enough cold water on corned beef in Dutch oven just to cover. Add onion and garlic. Heat to boiling; reduce heat. Cover and simmer until beef is tender, about 2 hours.

Remove beef to warm platter; keep warm. Skim fat from broth. Add cabbage. Heat to boiling; reduce heat. Simmer uncovered 15 minutes. **6 servings; 250 calories per serving.**

Serve with slices of warm Dark Pumpernickel (page 69).

New England Boiled Dinner: Decrease simmering time of beef to 1 hour 40 minutes. Skim fat from broth. Add 6 small onions, 6 medium carrots, 3 potatoes, cut into halves, and, if desired, 3 turnips, cut into cubes. Cover and simmer 20 minutes. Remove beef to warm platter; keep warm. Add cabbage. Heat to boiling; reduce heat. Simmer uncovered until vegetables are tender, about 15 minutes.

CARVING A BEEF BRISKET

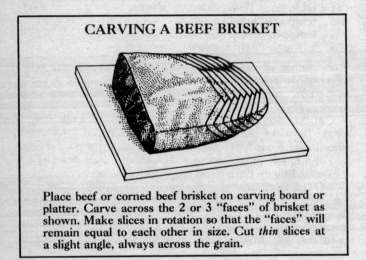

Place beef or corned beef brisket on carving board or platter. Carve across the 2 or 3 "faces" of brisket as shown. Make slices in rotation so that the "faces" will remain equal to each other in size. Cut *thin* slices at a slight angle, always across the grain.

BROILED BEEF STEAKS

For each serving, allow about ½ pound of any steak with a bone; allow about ¼ pound for boneless cuts.

Slash diagonally outer edge of fat on beef steaks at 1-inch intervals to prevent curling (do not cut into lean). Set oven control to broil and/or 550°. Place steaks on rack in broiler pan; place broiler pan so tops of ¾- to 1-inch steaks are 2 to 3 inches from heat, 1- to 2-inch steaks are 3 to 5 inches from heat. Broil until brown. The steaks should be about half done (see Timetable).

Sprinkle brown side with salt and pepper if desired. (Always season after browning because salt tends to draw moisture to the surface, delaying browning.) Turn steaks; broil until brown.

TIMETABLE FOR
BROILING BEEF STEAKS

Cut	Approximate Total Cooking Time (Minutes)	
	Rare (140°F)	Medium (160°F)
Tenderloin		
(filet mignon, 4 to 8 ounces)	10 to 15	15 to 20
T-bone Steak		
1 inch	20	25
1½ inches	30	35
Porterhouse Steak		
1 inch	20	25
1½ inches	30	35
Sirloin Steak		
1 inch	20	25
1½ inches	30	35
Top Loin Steak		
1 inch	15	20
1½ inches	25	30
2 inches	35	45
Rib or Rib Eye Steak		
1 inch	15	20
1½ inches	25	30
2 inches	35	45
Chuck Eye Steak		
(high quality)		
1 inch	24	30
1½ inches	40	45

Easy . . . LONDON BROIL

    1 - pound high-quality beef flank steak
    2   medium onions, thinly sliced
    ¼   teaspoon salt
    1   tablespoon margarine or butter
    2   tablespoons vegetable oil
    1   teaspoon lemon juice
    ½   teaspoon salt
    ¼   teaspoon pepper
    2   cloves garlic, crushed

Cut both sides of beef steak into diamond pattern ⅛ inch deep. Cook and stir onions and ¼ teaspoon salt in margarine until onions are tender; keep warm. Mix remaining ingredients; brush half of the mixture on beef.

Set oven control to broil and/or 550°. Broil beef with top 2 to 3 inches from heat until brown, about 5 minutes. Turn beef; brush with remaining oil mixture and broil 5 minutes longer.

Cut beef across grain at slanted angle into thin slices; serve with onions.   **4 servings; 275 calories per serving.**

Add Caesar Salad (page 509) and Dinner Rolls (page 75). For dessert, offer fresh fruit, cheese and crackers.

BEEF TERIYAKI

    1   pound beef boneless sirloin steak
    ¼   cup soy sauce
    ¼   cup dry sherry or white wine
    1   tablespoon vegetable oil
    2   teaspoons chopped gingerroot or
          ½ teaspoon ground ginger
    1   teaspoon sugar
    1   clove garlic, chopped

Trim fat from beef steak; cut beef into ¾-inch cubes. Place beef in glass or plastic bowl. Mix remaining ingredients; pour over beef. Cover and refrigerate, stirring occasionally, at least 1 hour.

Thread 6 beef cubes on each of 4 skewers; brush with marinade. Set oven control to broil and/or 550°. Broil kabobs

with tops about 4 inches from heat 5 to 6 minutes; turn.
Brush with marinade; broil until done, 5 to 6 minutes longer.
Brush with marinade.   **4 servings; 270 calories per serving.**

Serve with rice, Chinese pea pods and Fruit-Walnut Salad
(page 536).

Easy . . . MUSHROOM MINUTE STEAKS

6   beef cube steaks (about 2 pounds)
2   teaspoons salt
¼   teaspoon lemon pepper
½   cup dry white or red wine
1   medium green pepper, chopped (about 1 cup)
1   small onion, chopped (about ¼ cup)
2   cans (4 ounces each) sliced mushrooms, undrained

Sprinkle beef steaks with salt and lemon pepper. Cook a few
steaks at a time in 10-inch skillet over medium heat, until
brown, 5 to 10 minutes on each side. Return steaks to skillet.
Add wine, green pepper, onion and mushrooms. Heat over
low heat until mushrooms are hot, about 5 minutes.   **6
servings; 265 calories per serving.**

Serve with Potato Planks (page 659) and Tomato-Cheese
Salads (page 525).

Easy . . . BEEF WITH MUSTARD SAUCE

1 -   pound beef tenderloin
2   tablespoons margarine or butter
¼   cup thinly sliced green onions (with tops)
¼   cup dry white wine
½   cup milk
1   tablespoon Dijon-style mustard
½   teaspoon salt
3   slices bread, toasted and buttered

Cut beef tenderloin crosswise into 6 slices. Flatten beef slices to ½-inch thickness. Cook 3 pieces of beef in margarine in 10-inch skillet over medium-high heat, turning once, until medium doneness, about 2 minutes each side. Remove from skillet; keep beef warm. Repeat with remaining beef.

Add green onions and wine to hot skillet. Stir in milk, mustard and salt. Heat to boiling, stirring occasionally. Spoon mustard sauce over beef. Remove crust from toast; cut each slice toast into 4 triangles. Serve beef and mustard sauce with toast triangles. **6 servings; 200 calories per serving.**

Complete this with buttered new potatoes, broccoli spears and Walnut Tossed Salad (page 511).

Easy . . . MUSHROOM STEAK

2	tablespoons all-purpose flour
½	teaspoon salt
⅛	teaspoon pepper
1½-	to 2-pound beef boneless round, tip or chuck steak, about ¾ inch thick
1	tablespoon vegetable oil
1	medium onion, sliced
1	teaspoon salt
1	teaspoon dry mustard
1	teaspoon Worcestershire sauce
⅛	teaspoon red pepper sauce
½	cup water
1	can (4 ounces) mushroom stems and pieces, undrained

Mix flour, salt and pepper. Sprinkle one side of beef steak with half of the flour mixture; pound in. Turn beef and pound in remaining flour mixture. Cut beef into 6 serving pieces.

Heat oil in 10-inch skillet until hot. Cook beef in oil over medium heat, turning once, until brown, about 10 minutes. Add onion. Mix remaining ingredients except water and mushrooms; stir in water and mushrooms. Pour over beef. Heat to boiling; reduce heat. Cover and simmer until beef is tender, about 1 hour. **6 servings; 180 calories per serving.**

Add buttered noodles, Ratatouille Salad (page 517) and warm Dinner Rolls (page 75).

BEEF STEAK PROVENÇALE

2	tablespoons all-purpose flour
½	teaspoon salt
⅛	teaspoon pepper
1½ -	pound beef boneless round steak, about ¾ inch thick
1	tablespoon vegetable oil
1	cup dry red wine
½	cup water
2	cloves garlic, crushed
½	cup pitted ripe olives
6	medium carrots, cut into 1-inch pieces
2	medium onions, cut into fourths
2	tablespoons snipped parsley

Mix flour, salt and pepper. Sprinkle one side of beef steak with half of the flour mixture; pound in. Turn beef and pound in remaining flour mixture. Cut beef into 6-serving pieces.

Heat oil in 10-inch skillet until hot. Cook beef in oil over medium-high heat, turning once, until brown, about 10 minutes. Add wine, water and garlic. Heat to boiling; reduce heat. Cover and simmer 1 hour.

Add olives, carrots and onions. Cover and simmer until beef and carrots are tender, about 40 minutes. Sprinkle with parsley.   **6 servings;** 250 calories per serving.

Serve with buttered noodles and romaine with Classic French Dressing (page 548); complete with Cherry Freeze (page 265).

Beef Stew Provençale: Substitute 1½-pound beef boneless chuck, tip or round roast for the steak. Cut beef into 1-inch cubes. Toss with flour mixture. Cook as directed.

SWISS STEAK

3   tablespoons all-purpose flour
1   teaspoon dry mustard
½   teaspoon salt
1½ - pound beef boneless round, tip or chuck steak,
      about ¾ inch thick
2   tablespoons vegetable oil
1   can (16 ounces) whole tomatoes, undrained
2   cloves garlic, finely chopped
1   cup water
1   large onion, sliced
1   large green pepper, sliced

Mix flour, mustard and salt. Sprinkle one side of beef steak
with half of the flour mixture; pound in. Turn beef and
pound in remaining flour mixture. Cut beef into 6 serving
pieces.

Heat oil in 10-inch skillet until hot. Cook beef in oil over
medium heat, turning once, until brown, about 15 minutes.
Add tomatoes and garlic; break up tomatoes. Heat to boiling;
reduce heat. Cover and simmer until beef is tender, about
1¼ hours. Add water, onion and green pepper. Heat to
boiling; reduce heat. Cover and simmer until vegetables are
tender, 5 to 8 minutes.   **6 servings; 270 calories per serving.**

Nice served with Mashed Potatoes (page 658) and Corn
with Basil (page 638).

Do-ahead Tip: After simmering beef until tender, cover
and refrigerate no longer than 48 hours. About 15 minutes
before serving, add water, onion and green pepper to Swiss
Steak. Heat to boiling; reduce heat. Cover and simmer until
beef is hot and vegetables are tender, 5 to 8 minutes.

FAJITAS

1½ - pound beef boneless sirloin steak,
    about 1½ inches thick
¼ cup vegetable oil
¼ cup red wine vinegar
1 teaspoon sugar
1 teaspoon dried oregano leaves
1 teaspoon chili powder
½ teaspoon garlic powder
½ teaspoon salt
¼ teaspoon pepper
10 large flour tortillas
2 large onions, sliced
2 medium green or red peppers, cut into ¼-inch strips
2 tablespoons vegetable oil
1 jar (8 ounces) picante sauce
1 cup shredded Cheddar or
    Monterey Jack cheese (4 ounces)
    Guacamole (page 19) or 2 containers (6 ounces each)
    frozen guacamole, thawed
¾ cup dairy sour cream

Trim excess fat from beef steak. Prick beef with fork in several places. Mix ¼ cup oil, the vinegar, sugar, oregano, chili powder, garlic powder, salt and pepper in ungreased square baking dish, 8×8×2 inches. Place beef in dish, turning once to coat both sides. Cover and refrigerate, turning beef occasionally, at least 8 hours but no longer than 24 hours.

Wrap tortillas in aluminum foil and heat in 325° oven until warm, about 15 minutes. Remove from oven; keep tortillas wrapped. Remove beef from marinade; reserve marinade. Set oven control to broil and/or 550°. Broil beef with top about 3 inches from heat until brown, about 8 minutes. Turn beef; brush with marinade and broil until medium doneness, 7 to 8 minutes longer. While beef broils, cook and stir onions and green peppers in 2 tablespoons oil until crisp-tender, about 10 minutes. Slice beef diagonally into very thin slices.

For each serving, place some beef, onion mixture, picante sauce, cheese, Guacamole and sour cream in center of tortilla. Fold 1 end up about 1 inch over beef mixture; fold right and left sides over folded end. **5 servings** (2 fajitas per serving); 780 calories per serving.

Start with Sangria Punch (page 30) and end meal with Caramel Custard (page 248).

BEEF STROGANOFF

1½ pounds beef tenderloin or boneless top loin steak, about ½ inch thick
2 tablespoons margarine or butter
1½ cups beef broth (page 561)
2 tablespoons catsup
1 teaspoon salt
1 small clove garlic, finely chopped, or ⅛ teaspoon instant minced garlic
8 ounces mushrooms, sliced
1 medium onion, chopped (about ½ cup)
3 tablespoons all-purpose flour
1 cup dairy sour cream

Cut beef tenderloin across grain into strips, each about 1½ × ½ inch. (For ease in cutting, partially freeze beef.) Cook and stir beef in margarine in 10-inch skillet over low heat until brown. Reserve ⅓ cup of the broth. Stir remaining broth, the catsup, salt and garlic into skillet. Heat to boiling; reduce heat. Cover and simmer until beef is tender, about 10 minutes.

Stir in mushrooms and onion. Cover and simmer until onion is tender, about 5 minutes. Shake reserved broth and the flour in tightly covered container; gradually stir into beef mixture. Heat to boiling, stirring constantly. Boil and stir 1 minute; reduce heat. Stir in sour cream; heat through. Serve over hot cooked noodles or rice if desired. **6 servings;** 320 calories per serving.

Complete this meal with Glazed Carrots (page 633), Avocado-Apple Salad (page 541) and warm, crusty bread.

Economy Beef Stroganoff: Substitute 1½ pounds beef stew meat, cut into ⅛-inch slices, for the beef tenderloin. Increase first simmering time to 1-1½ hours.

STIR-FRIED BEEF

   1 - pound beef flank steak or boneless sirloin steak
   1   tablespoon vegetable oil
   1   teaspoon cornstarch
   1   teaspoon salt
   1   teaspoon sugar
   1   teaspoon soy sauce
 ⅛   teaspoon white pepper
   8   ounces Chinese pea pods
   2   green onions (with tops)
 ¼   cup cold water
   1   tablespoon cornstarch
   1   tablespoon soy sauce
   3   tablespoons vegetable oil
   1   teaspoon finely chopped gingerroot
   1   teaspoon finely chopped garlic
   2   tablespoons vegetable oil
   1   can (8½ ounces) sliced bamboo shoots, drained
   1   jar (4½ ounces) sliced mushrooms, drained
 ½   cup chicken broth

Trim fat from beef steak; cut beef with grain into 2-inch strips. Cut strips across grain into ⅛-inch slices. Toss beef, 1 tablespoon oil, 1 teaspoon cornstarch, the salt, sugar, 1 teaspoon soy sauce and the white pepper in glass or plastic bowl. Cover and refrigerate 30 minutes.

Remove strings from pea pods. Place pea pods in boiling water. Cover and cook 1 minute; drain. Immediately rinse under running cold water; drain. Cut green onions into 2-inch pieces; cut pieces lengthwise into thin strips. Mix water, 1 tablespoon cornstarch and 1 tablespoon soy sauce.

Heat wok or 12-inch skillet until 1 or 2 drops of water bubble and skitter when sprinkled in wok. Add 3 tablespoons oil; rotate wok to coat side. Add beef, gingerroot and garlic; stir-fry until beef is brown, about 3 minutes. Remove beef from wok.

Add 2 tablespoons oil to wok; rotate to coat side. Add bamboo shoots and mushrooms; stir-fry 1 minute. Stir in chicken broth; heat to boiling. Stir in beef; heat to boiling. Stir in cornstarch mixture; cook and stir until thickened, about 30 seconds. Add pea pods; cook and stir 30 seconds. Garnish

with green onions. Serve with hot cooked rice if desired.
5 servings; 345 calories per serving.

■ **Microwave Reheat Directions:** Prepare Stir-fried Beef as
directed except—omit green onions; cover and refrigerate no
longer than 48 hours. Just before serving, prepare green
onions. Place beef mixture on microwavable platter or in
bowl. Cover tightly and microwave on high (100%) 4 minutes;
stir. Cover tightly and microwave until hot, about 4 minutes
longer. Garnish with green onions.

BEEF STEW

1   pound beef boneless chuck, tip or round roast, cut into
     1-inch cubes
1   tablespoon shortening
3   cups hot water
½   teaspoon salt
⅛   teaspoon pepper
2   medium carrots, cut into 1-inch pieces (about 1 cup)
1   large potato, cut into 1½-inch pieces (about 1¼ cups)
1   medium turnip, cut into 1-inch pieces (about 1 cup)
1   medium green pepper, cut into 1-inch pieces (about 1
     cup)
1   medium stalk celery, cut into 1-inch pieces (about ½
     cup)
1   small onion, chopped (about ¼ cup)
½   teaspoon browning sauce, if desired
1½ teaspoons salt
1   beef bouillon cube
1   bay leaf
     Parsley Dumplings (pages 43 and 44)
½   cup cold water
2   tablespoons all-purpose flour

Cook and stir beef in shortening in 12-inch skillet or Dutch
oven until beef is brown, about 15 minutes. Add 3 cups hot
water, ½ teaspoon salt and the pepper. Heat to boiling;
reduce heat. Cover and simmer until beef is almost tender, 2
to 2½ hours.

Stir in carrots, potato, turnip, green pepper, celery, onion,
browning sauce, 1½ teaspoons salt, the bouillon cube and bay

leaf. Cover and simmer until vegetables are tender, about 30 minutes. Remove bay leaf.

Prepare Parsley Dumplings. Shake ½ cup cold water and the flour in tightly covered container; gradually stir into stew. Heat to boiling, stirring constantly. Boil and stir 1 minute; reduce heat.

Drop dumpling dough by 10 to 12 spoonfuls onto hot stew (do not drop directly into liquid). Cook uncovered 10 minutes. Cover and cook 10 minutes longer.   **5 servings; 220** calories per serving.

Do-ahead Tip: After boiling and stirring 1 minute, cover and refrigerate stew no longer than 48 hours. To serve, heat to boiling over medium-high heat. Continue as directed.

Oxtail Stew: Substitute 2 pounds oxtails for the beef. Increase first simmering time to 3½ hours.

BEEF BURGUNDY POPOVERS

Popovers (page 52)
2   **pounds beef boneless round steak, cut into 1-inch cubes**
2   **tablespoons shortening**
2   **tablespoons all-purpose flour**
1   **teaspoon salt**
¼   **teaspoon dried marjoram leaves**
¼   **teaspoon dried thyme leaves**
¼   **teaspoon pepper**
1   **cup dry red wine**
½   **cup beef broth**
1   **large onion, sliced**
8   **ounces mushrooms, sliced**

Bake Popovers. Cook and stir beef in shortening in Dutch oven until beef is brown. Mix flour, salt, marjoram, thyme and pepper. Coat beef with flour mixture. Heat beef and remaining ingredients to boiling in Dutch oven; reduce heat. Cover and simmer until beef is tender, about 1¼ hours. Stir in 2 to 3 teaspoons browning sauce if desired. Cut Popovers lengthwise into halves. Fill each half with beef mixture. Serve immediately.   **6 servings; 420 calories per serving.**

Do-ahead Tip: Wrap Popovers in aluminum foil and freeze. To serve, place frozen Popovers on ungreased cookie sheet and heat in 350° oven, until thawed and warm, about 10 minutes.

SKILLET HASH

2 cups chopped cooked lean beef or corned beef
2 cups chopped cooked potatoes
1 medium onion, chopped
1 tablespoon snipped parsley
½ teaspoon salt
⅛ teaspoon pepper
¼ cup shortening

Mix all ingredients except shortening. Heat shortening in 10-inch skillet over medium heat until melted. Spread beef evenly in skillet. Fry, turning frequently, until brown, 10 to 15 minutes. **4 servings; 340 calories per serving.**

Oven Hash: Omit shortening. Spread beef mixture evenly in greased square baking dish, 8 × 8 × 2 inches. Bake uncovered in 350° oven until hot, about 20 minutes.

Red Flannel Skillet Hash: Use 1½ cups chopped corned beef and 1½ cups chopped cooked potatoes. Mix in 1 can (16 ounces) diced or shoestring beets, drained.

Easy . . . SESAME BEEF

1 pound beef boneless sirloin steak
2 tablespoons sugar
2 tablespoons vegetable oil
2 tablespoons soy sauce
¼ teaspoon pepper
3 green onions (with tops), finely chopped
2 cloves garlic, crushed
1 tablespoon sesame seed
1 tablespoon vegetable oil
3 cups hot cooked rice (page 85)

Trim fat from beef steak; cut beef diagonally across grain into ⅛-inch slices. (For ease in cutting, partially freeze beef, about 1½ hours.) Mix sugar, 2 tablespoons oil, the soy sauce, pepper, onions and garlic in glass or plastic bowl; stir in beef until well coated. Cover and refrigerate 30 minutes.

Drain beef. Cook and stir sesame seed in 10-inch skillet over medium heat until golden brown; remove from skillet. Heat 1 tablespoon oil in same skillet until hot; add beef. Cook and stir beef in oil over medium-high heat until light brown, 3 to 4 minutes. Sprinkle with sesame seed. Serve over rice. **5 servings;** 320 calories per serving.

· Buttered carrots and Cucumber Salad (page 521) are nice accompaniments.

SAVORY BEEF SHORT RIBS

4   **pounds beef short ribs, cut into pieces**
2   **tablespoons vegetable oil**
1   **can (10½ ounces) condensed beef broth**
1   **jar (5 ounces) prepared horseradish**
½   **teaspoon salt**
2   **large onions, sliced**
¼   **cup cold water**
2   **tablespoons all-purpose flour**
½   **cup dairy sour cream**

Cook beef ribs in oil in Dutch oven over medium heat until brown; drain. Stir in broth, horseradish and salt. Heat to boiling; reduce heat. Cover and simmer until beef is tender, about 2 hours.

Remove beef from broth; keep warm. Add onions to broth. Cover and simmer until tender, 5 to 8 minutes. Skim excess fat from broth. Add enough water to broth to measure 2 cups. Shake water and flour in tightly covered container; gradually stir into broth. Heat to boiling, stirring constantly. Boil and stir 1 minute; remove from heat. Stir in sour cream. Serve over beef.   **8 servings;** 725 calories per serving.

Try with buttered noodles and Brussels sprouts.

Do-ahead Tip: After simmering beef, cover and refrigerate beef and broth no longer than 48 hours. About 30 minutes before serving, remove fat from broth. Add onions to beef and broth. Heat to boiling; reduce heat. Simmer uncovered until beef is hot, about 20 minutes. Remove beef from broth; keep warm. Continue as directed.

MUSTARD SHORT RIBS

4   pounds beef short ribs, cut into pieces
⅓   cup prepared mustard
1   tablespoon sugar
2   tablespoons lemon juice
1   teaspoon salt
½   teaspoon pepper
2   cloves garlic, crushed
4   medium onions, sliced

Place beef ribs in shallow glass dish. Mix mustard, sugar, lemon juice, salt, pepper and garlic; spread over beef. Top with onions. Cover and refrigerate, turning beef occasionally, 24 hours.

Remove beef from marinade; reserve onions and marinade. Cook beef in Dutch oven over medium heat until brown; drain. Add onions and pour marinade on beef. Cover and bake in 350° oven until beef is tender, about 2 hours.   **4 servings; 895 calories per serving.**

Add Maple Acorn Squash (page 665) and buttered new potatoes.

HAMBURGER PATTIES

1   pound ground beef
3   tablespoons finely chopped onion, if desired
3   tablespoons water
½   teaspoon salt
¼   teaspoon pepper

Mix all ingredients. Shape mixture into 4 patties, each about 1 inch thick.

Set oven control to broil and/or 550°. Broil with tops about 3 inches from heat until desired doneness (5 to 7 minutes on each side for medium).   **4 servings; 270 calories per serving.**

To Oven-bake: Place patties on rack in shallow pan. Bake in 350° oven until desired doneness (about 35 minutes for medium).

To Panfry: Cook over medium heat, turning frequently, until desired doneness (about 10 minutes for medium).

■ **To Microwave:** Place patties on microwavable rack in microwavable dish. Cover loosely and microwave on high (100%) 3 minutes; rotate dish ½ turn. Microwave until patties are almost done, 3 to 4 minutes longer. Let stand covered 3 minutes.

GIANT BURGER

1½ pounds ground beef
1½ teaspoons salt
 1 tablespoon prepared horseradish
 1 tablespoon prepared mustard
 1 package (3 ounces) cream cheese, softened

Mix ground beef and salt; divide into halves. Pat one half in bottom of ungreased pie plate, 9 × 1¼ inches. Mix remaining ingredients; spread to within 1 inch of edge of beef mixture in pie plate. Shape remaining half into 9-inch circle. Place on cheese mixture; pinch edge together to seal securely.

Bake uncovered in 350° oven until done, 40 minutes for medium, 50 minutes for well done. Remove from plate. Cut into wedges to serve. **6 servings; 320 calories per serving.**

CHEVRE BURGERS

    Bordelaise Sauce (page 601)
 ½ cup crumbled chèvre such as feta, chabis, pyramide or
      log (4 ounces)
 ¼ cup sliced green onions (with tops)
 1 teaspoon dried tarragon leaves
 ½ teaspoon salt
 ½ teaspoon coarsely ground pepper
1½ pounds ground beef

Prepare Bordelaise Sauce. Mix cheese, onions, tarragon, salt and pepper. Shape ground beef into 8 patties, each about 3 inches in diameter. Top 4 of the patties with cheese mixture; top with remaining patties. Pinch edges together to seal securely.

Set oven control to broil and/or 550°. Broil with tops about 3 inches from heat until medium doneness, 5 to 7 minutes on each side. Serve hamburgers with sauce. **4 servings**; 435 calories per serving.

SALISBURY STEAKS

1 **pound ground beef**
⅓ **cup dry bread crumbs**
½ **teaspoon salt**
¼ **teaspoon pepper**
1 **egg**
1 **large onion, sliced**
1 **can (10½ ounces) condensed beef broth**
1 **can (4 ounces) mushroom stems and pieces, drained**
2 **tablespoons cold water**
2 **teaspoons cornstarch**

Mix ground beef, bread crumbs, salt, pepper and egg; shape into 4 oval patties, each about ¾ inch thick. Cook patties in 10-inch skillet over medium heat, turning occasionally, until brown, about 10 minutes; drain. Add onion, broth and mushrooms. Heat to boiling; reduce heat. Cover and simmer until beef is done, about 10 minutes.

Remove patties; keep warm. Heat onion mixture to boiling. Mix water and cornstarch; stir into onion mixture. Boil and stir 1 minute. Serve over patties. **4 servings**; 360 calories per serving.

Serve with Mashed Potatoes (page 658), Skillet Corn (page 639) and Baked Honey Apples (pages 219 and 220) for an inexpensive fall dinner.

Easy . . . MEAT-AND-POTATO PIE

Prepare Meat Loaf (page 379) as directed except—spread beef mixture in ungreased pie plate, 9 × 1¼ inches. Omit catsup and decrease baking time to 40 to 50 minutes; drain. Prepare mashed potato mix as directed on package for 4 servings. Spread hot potatoes evenly over beef mixture; sprinkle with ½ cup shredded Cheddar cheese. Bake until cheese is melted, 2 to 4 minutes. **6 servings**; 475 calories per serving.

Complete with Herbed Green Beans (page 618) and lettuce wedges with Blue Cheese Dressing (page 551).

MEAT LOAF

1½   pounds ground beef
3   slices bread, torn into small pieces*
1   egg
1   cup milk
1   small onion, chopped (about ¼ cup)
1   tablespoon Worcestershire sauce
1   teaspoon salt
½   teaspoon dry mustard
¼   teaspoon pepper
¼   teaspoon rubbed sage
⅛   teaspoon garlic powder
½   cup catsup, chili sauce or barbecue sauce

Mix all ingredients except catsup. Spread mixture in ungreased loaf pan, 8½×4½×2½ or 9×5×3 inches, or shape into loaf in ungreased rectangular pan, 13×9×2 inches. Spoon catsup over top. Bake uncovered in 350° oven until done, 1 to 1¼ hours. Remove from pan.   **6 servings; 370 calories per serving.**

Individual Meat Loaves: Shape meat mixture into 6 small loaves; place in ungreased rectangular pan, 13×9×2 inches. Bake as directed above except—decrease baking time to 45 minutes.

Spanish Meat Loaf: Omit sage. Substitute ⅓ cup tomato sauce and ⅔ cup milk for the milk. Mix in 8 large pimiento-stuffed olives, sliced. Substitute ⅔ cup tomato sauce for the catsup. Bake as directed above.

Stuffed Meat Loaf: Spread half of the meat mixture in ungreased loaf pan, 9×5×3 inches. Toss 2 cups seasoned bread cubes and ½ cup hot water; spread evenly over meat in pan. Top with remaining meat mixture. Spoon catsup on top. Bake as directed above. Let stand 5 minutes before slicing.

Vegetable Meat Loaf: Increase salt to 1½ teaspoons. Mix in 1 small green pepper, chopped, 1 medium carrot, coarsely shredded, and 1 can (4 ounces) mushroom stems and pieces, chopped. Omit catsup. Bake as directed in 9×5×3-inch loaf pan; drain. Arrange 1 tomato, thinly sliced, down center of

*½ cup dry bread crumbs or ¾ cup quick-cooking oats can be substituted for the 3 slices bread.

meat loaf. Top with 3 slices process American cheese, cut diagonally into halves. Bake until cheese is melted, 3 to 5 minutes.

MEATBALLS

1   pound ground beef
½   cup dry bread crumbs
¼   cup milk
¾   teaspoon salt
½   teaspoon Worcestershire sauce
¼   teaspoon pepper
1   small onion, chopped (about ¼ cup)
1   egg

Mix all ingredients; shape into twenty 1½-inch meatballs. Place in ungreased rectangular pan, 13 × 9 × 2 inches. Bake uncovered in 400° oven until done and light brown, 20 to 25 minutes.   **4 servings; 355 calories per serving.**

   To Panfry: Cook over medium heat, turning occasionally, until brown, about 20 minutes.

■ **To Microwave:** Place meatballs in rectangular microwavable dish, 12 × 7½ × 2 inches. Cover loosely; microwave on high (100%) 3 minutes. Rearrange meatballs. Cover loosely and microwave until no longer pink inside, 5 to 7 minutes longer. Let stand covered 3 minutes; drain.

Easy . . . SAUCY MEATBALLS

     Meatballs (above)
⅓   cup milk
⅛   teaspoon ground nutmeg
1   can (10¾ ounces) condensed cream of chicken soup
½   cup dairy sour cream

Prepare Meatballs; drain. Mix milk, nutmeg and soup; add Meatballs. Heat to boiling, stirring occasionally; reduce heat. Cover and simmer 15 minutes. Stir in sour cream; heat through.   **4 servings; 480 calories per serving.**

   Serve with noodles with parsley and Pickled Beets (page 519).

■ **To Microwave:** Cover tightly and microwave Meatballs in square microwavable dish, 8×8×2 inches, on high (100%) until almost done, about 6 minutes; drain. Mix milk, nutmeg, soup and sour cream; stir into Meatballs. Cover tightly and microwave until bubbly, about 5 minutes.

SPAGHETTI AND MEATBALLS

1	large onion, chopped (about 1 cup)
1	clove garlic, crushed
1	teaspoon sugar
1	teaspoon dried oregano leaves
¾	teaspoon salt
¾	teaspoon dried basil leaves
½	teaspoon dried marjoram leaves
1	can (16 ounces) whole tomatoes, undrained
1	can (8 ounces) tomato sauce
	Meatballs (left)
4	cups hot cooked spaghetti (page 91)

Mix all ingredients except Meatballs and spaghetti in 3-quart saucepan; break up tomatoes. Heat to boiling; reduce heat. Cover and simmer, stirring occasionally, 30 minutes.

Prepare Meatballs; drain. Stir Meatballs into tomato mixture. Cover and simmer, stirring occasionally, 30 minutes longer. Serve over spaghetti and, if desired, with grated Parmesan cheese.   **6 servings;** 385 calories per serving.

Nice served with a crisp, tossed green salad and Hard Rolls (page 73).

Spaghetti and Beef Sauce: Omit Meatballs. Cook and stir 1 pound ground beef, the onion and garlic in 10-inch skillet until beef is light brown; drain. Stir in remaining ingredients except spaghetti; break up tomatoes. Heat to boiling; reduce heat. Cover and simmer, stirring occasionally, 1 hour.

Spaghetti and Chicken Sauce: Omit Meatballs. Cover and simmer sauce 1 hour. Stir in 1½ cups cut-up cooked chicken or turkey; heat through.

BEEF IN POTATO SHELLS

3 large baking potatoes
1 tablespoon margarine or butter, melted
1 pound ground beef
1 can (16 ounces) whole tomatoes, undrained
1 envelope (about 1¼ ounces) taco seasoning mix
½ cup shredded Cheddar or
    Monterey Jack cheese (2 ounces)
⅓ cup dairy sour cream
2 green onions (with tops), sliced

Prepare and bake potatoes as directed on pages 657 and 658. Heat oven to 475°. Cut each potato lengthwise into halves. Scoop out potatoes, leaving a ¼-inch shell. (Use potatoes as desired.) Brush outsides and insides of shells with margarine. Place shells, cut sides up, on ungreased cookie sheet. Bake uncovered until edges are brown, 15 to 20 minutes.

Cook and stir ground beef in 10-inch skillet until brown; drain. Stir in tomatoes and seasoning mix; break up tomatoes. Heat to boiling; reduce heat. Simmer uncovered, stirring occasionally, 20 minutes. Spoon beef mixture into shells; sprinkle with cheese. Heat just until cheese is melted. Top each with dollop of sour cream and sprinkle with green onions. 6 servings; 380 calories per serving.

Serve with buttered green peas and Sweet-sour Cabbage Slaw (page 516).

Chicken in Potato Shells: Substitute 2 cups cut-up cooked chicken for the cooked beef.

Do-ahead Tip: Bake potatoes and prepare shells. Cover and refrigerate no longer than 24 hours. Bake shells as directed.

STUFFED CABBAGE ROLLS

12	cabbage leaves
1	pound ground beef
½	cup uncooked instant rice
1	can (15 ounces) tomato sauce
1	teaspoon salt
⅛	teaspoon pepper
⅛	teaspoon garlic salt
1	medium onion, chopped (about ½ cup)
1	can (4 ounces) mushroom stems and pieces, undrained
1	teaspoon sugar
½	teaspoon lemon juice
1	tablespoon cornstarch
1	tablespoon water

Cover cabbage leaves with boiling water. Cover and let stand until leaves are limp, about 10 minutes. Remove leaves; drain.

Mix ground beef, rice, ½ cup of the tomato sauce, the salt, pepper, garlic salt, onion and mushrooms. Place about ⅓ cup beef mixture at stem end of each leaf. Roll leaf around beef mixture, tucking in sides.

Place cabbage rolls, seam sides down, in ungreased square baking dish, 8 × 8 × 2 inches. Mix remaining tomato sauce, the sugar and lemon juice; pour over cabbage rolls. Cover and bake in 350° oven until beef is done, about 45 minutes.

Pour the liquid from cabbage rolls into 1-quart saucepan. Mix cornstarch and water; stir into cabbage liquid. Heat to boiling, stirring constantly. Boil and stir 1 minute. Serve sauce with cabbage rolls.   4 servings; 345 calories per serving.

NOTE: To separate leaves from cabbage head easily, remove core and cover cabbage with cold water. Let stand about 10 minutes; remove leaves.

■ **To Microwave:** Place cabbage leaves and ¼ cup cold water in 3-quart microwavable casserole. Cover tightly and microwave on high (100%) until limp, 4 to 5 minutes. Continue as directed except—use microwavable dish. Mix remaining tomato sauce, the sugar, lemon juice, cornstarch and water; pour over cabbage rolls. Cover with vented plastic wrap and microwave 7 minutes; rotate dish ¼ turn. Microwave until beef is done, 8 to 9 minutes longer. Let stand covered 1 minute. Remove cabbage rolls to platter. Stir sauce in dish; pour over cabbage rolls.

Easy . . . IMPOSSIBLE CHEESEBURGER PIE

    1   pound ground beef
1½ cups chopped onion
    ½   teaspoon salt
    ¼   teaspoon pepper
1½ cups milk
    3   eggs
    ¾   cup buttermilk baking mix
    2   tomatoes, sliced
    1   cup shredded Cheddar or
        process American cheese (4 ounces)

Heat oven to 400°. Grease pie plate, 10 × 1½ inches. Cook and stir ground beef and onion over medium heat until beef is brown; drain. Stir in salt and pepper. Spread in plate. Beat milk, eggs and baking mix until smooth, 15 seconds in blender on high or 1 minute with hand beater. Pour into plate. Bake 25 minutes. Top with tomatoes; sprinkle with cheese. Bake until knife inserted in center comes out clean, 5 to 8 minutes longer. Cool 5 minutes.   **6 servings;** 420 calories per serving.

This makes a lunchtime meal with a crisp, green salad and tall glasses of chocolate milk.

Easy . . . TACO DINNER

1   pound ground beef
1   large onion, chopped (about 1 cup)
1   cup water
1   envelope (about 1¼ ounces) taco seasoning mix
1   package (12 ounces) tortilla chips
½   head lettuce, shredded
2   medium tomatoes, chopped
1   can (2¼ ounces) sliced ripe olives, drained
1   cup shredded Cheddar or
       Monterey Jack cheese (4 ounces)
⅔   cup dairy sour cream

Cook and stir ground beef and onion in 10-inch skillet until beef is light brown; drain. Stir in water and seasoning mix. Heat to boiling; reduce heat. Simmer uncovered, stirring occasionally, 10 minutes. Spoon beef mixture onto chips. Top with remaining ingredients. **6 servings; 635 calories per serving.**

Nice served with Triple-Orange Salad (page 532).

MEXICAN HASH

1   pound ground beef
1   medium onion, chopped (about ½ cup)
1   clove garlic, chopped
2   medium tomatoes, chopped (about 2 cups)
1   medium green pepper, chopped (about 1 cup)
¼   cup raisins
1½   teaspoons salt
⅛   teaspoon ground cinnamon
⅛   teaspoon ground cloves
¼   cup slivered almonds
¼   cup sliced pimiento-stuffed olives
3   cups hot cooked rice (page 85)

Cook and stir ground beef, onion and garlic in 10-inch skillet until beef is light brown; drain. Add tomatoes, green pepper, raisins, salt, cinnamon and cloves. Cover and simmer 10 minutes.

Cook and stir almonds over medium heat until golden, 2 to

3 minutes. Stir almonds and olives into beef mixture. Serve with rice. **4 servings; 565 calories per serving.**

Broiled Zucchini (page 663), avocado slices and warm flour tortillas make this an easy Mexican-style dinner.

TORTILLA CASSEROLE

1 **pound ground beef**
1 **medium onion, chopped (about ½ cup)**
1 **jar (8 ounces) green Mexican salsa**
½ **cup dairy sour cream**
1 **can (10¾ ounces) condensed cream of chicken soup**
1 **jar (2 ounces) sliced pimientos, drained**
6 **corn tortillas, cut into 1-inch strips**
2 **cups shredded Cheddar cheese (8 ounces)**

Cook and stir ground beef and onion until beef is brown; drain. Spread ½ cup of the salsa in bottom of ungreased square baking dish, 8 × 8 × 2 inches. Mix remaining salsa, the sour cream, soup and pimientos. Layer half of the tortilla strips, beef mixture, soup mixture and cheese on salsa; repeat.

Bake uncovered in 350° oven until casserole is hot and bubbly, about 30 minutes. Let stand 10 minutes. Garnish with olives if desired. **6 servings; 490 calories per serving.**

■ **To Microwave:** Crumble ground beef into 2-quart microwavable casserole; add onion. Cover loosely and microwave on high (100%) 3 minutes; break up beef and stir. Cover loosely and microwave until very little pink remains in beef, 2 to 3 minutes longer; drain. Place ½ cup salsa in casserole. Continue as directed except—omit last layer of cheese. Cover tightly and microwave 4 minutes; rotate casserole ½ turn. Microwave until center is hot, 4 to 5 minutes longer. Sprinkle with remaining cheese; cover and let stand 5 minutes.

CHILI CON CARNE

1	pound ground beef
1	large onion, chopped (about 1 cup)
2	cloves garlic, crushed
1	tablespoon chili powder
1	teaspoon salt
1	teaspoon ground cumin
1	teaspoon dried oregano leaves
1	teaspoon cocoa
½	teaspoon red pepper sauce
1	can (16 ounces) whole tomatoes, undrained
1	can (15½ ounces) red kidney beans, undrained

Cook and stir ground beef, onion and garlic in 3-quart saucepan until beef is brown; drain. Stir in remaining ingredients except beans; break up tomatoes. Heat to boiling; reduce heat. Cover and simmer, stirring occasionally, 1 hour.

Stir in beans. Heat to boiling; reduce heat. Simmer uncovered, stirring mixture occasionally, until of desired consistency, about 20 minutes.   **4 servings; 425 calories per serving.**

Warm Corn Bread (page 54) is an appropriate accompaniment.

Cincinnati-style Chili: Prepare Chili con Carne as directed. For each serving, spoon about ¾ cup beef mixture over 1 cup hot cooked spaghetti. Sprinkle each serving with ¼ cup shredded Cheddar cheese and 2 tablespoons chopped onion. Top with dollop of dairy sour cream if desired.   **5 servings.**

Easy Chili con Carne: Increase chili powder to 2 tablespoons; omit cumin, oregano, cocoa and pepper sauce.

LASAGNE ROLL-UPS

6	uncooked lasagne noodles
6	uncooked spinach lasagne noodles
1	pound ground beef
1	large onion, chopped (about 1 cup)
1	jar (15½ ounces) spaghetti sauce
1	can (8 ounces) mushroom stems and pieces, undrained
2	cups ricotta or creamed cottage cheese
1	package (10 ounces) frozen chopped spinach, thawed and well drained
¼	cup grated Parmesan cheese
1	teaspoon salt
¼	teaspoon pepper
2	cloves garlic, crushed

Cook noodles as directed on package; drain. Cover noodles with cold water. Cook and stir beef and onion in 10-inch skillet until beef is brown; drain. Stir in spaghetti sauce and mushrooms; heat to boiling. Pour into ungreased rectangular baking dish, 13 × 9 × 2 inches.

Mix remaining ingredients. Drain noodles. Spread 3 tablespoons of the cheese mixture to edges of 1 noodle. Roll up; cut roll into halves. Repeat with remaining noodles. Place rolls, cut sides down, in beef mixture. Cover and bake in 350° oven until hot and bubbly, about 30 minutes. 8 servings; 445 calories per serving.

HIDDEN BEEF RING

1	pound ground beef
1	medium onion, chopped (about ½ cup)
3	tablespoons catsup
2	tablespoons prepared mustard
1	can (10¾ ounces) condensed chicken gumbo soup
3	cups buttermilk baking mix
⅔	cup milk
2	tablespoons margarine or butter, softened
2	eggs

Cook and stir ground beef and onion in 10-inch skillet until beef is brown; drain. Stir in catsup, mustard and soup. Heat to boiling; reduce heat. Simmer uncovered 5 minutes.

Heat oven to 375°. Generously grease 12-cup bundt cake pan. Mix remaining ingredients; beat vigorously 30 seconds. Spread 2 cups of the batter in bottom and about 2 inches up side and center of pan. Spoon ground beef mixture evenly onto center of batter. Drop remaining batter by teaspoonfuls about ½ inch apart onto ground beef mixture. Bake until light brown and firm, about 25 minutes. Invert on heatproof serving plate.   **8 servings; 405 calories per serving.**

STUFFED PEPPERS

- 6   large green, red or yellow peppers
- 1   pound ground beef
- 2   tablespoons chopped onion
- 1   cup cooked rice (page 85)
- 1   teaspoon salt
- ⅛   teaspoon garlic salt
- 1   can (15 ounces) tomato sauce
- ¾   cup shredded mozzarella cheese (3 ounces)

Cut thin slice from stem end of each pepper. Remove seeds and membranes; rinse peppers. Cook peppers in enough boiling water to cover 5 minutes; drain.

Cook and stir ground beef and onion in 10-inch skillet until beef is light brown; drain. Stir in rice, salt, garlic salt and 1 cup of the tomato sauce; heat through.

Stuff each pepper with beef mixture; stand upright in ungreased square baking dish, 8 × 8 × 2 inches. Pour remaining sauce over peppers. Cover dish and bake in 350° oven 45 minutes. Uncover; bake 15 minutes longer. Sprinkle with cheese.   **6 servings; 290 calories per serving.**

All this one-dish meal needs to be complete is a colorful fruit salad and Garlic Bread (page 69).

Do-ahead Tip: Reserve ⅓ cup of the tomato sauce; pour remaining sauce over stuffed peppers. Cover and bake 30 minutes. Refrigerate peppers and reserved tomato sauce no longer than 24 hours. Pour reserved sauce over peppers. Bake uncovered in 350° oven 35 minutes.

■ **To Microwave:** Prepare peppers as directed (do not cook). Place peppers, cut sides up, in microwavable pie plate, $9 \times 1\frac{1}{4}$ or $10 \times 1\frac{1}{2}$ inches. Cover with vented plastic wrap and microwave on high (100%) until hot, 3 to $3\frac{1}{2}$ minutes. Mix uncooked ground beef, onion, cooked rice, salt, garlic salt and 1 cup of the tomato sauce. Stuff each pepper with about $\frac{1}{2}$ cup beef mixture. Pour remaining sauce over peppers. Cover with vented plastic wrap and microwave 6 minutes; rotate plate $\frac{1}{4}$ turn. Microwave until mixture is done, 6 to 7 minutes longer. Sprinkle with cheese.

VEAL

ROAST VEAL

Select roast from those in chart below. Allow about ⅓ pound per person—less for boneless roasts, more for roasts with a bone. If desired, sprinkle with salt and pepper.

Place veal fat side up on rack in shallow pan. (With a rib roast, the ribs form a natural rack.) It is not necessary to baste. If veal roast has little or no fat, place 2 or 3 slices bacon or salt pork on top of roast.

Insert meat thermometer so tip is in center of thickest part of veal and does not touch bone or rest in fat. Do not add water. Do not cover.

Roast in 325° oven to desired doneness (see Timetable below), using thermometer as final guide. Roasts are easier to carve if allowed to set 15 to 20 minutes after removing from

TIMETABLE FOR ROASTING VEAL
(Oven Temperature 325°F)

Cut	Approximate Weight (Pounds)	Approximate Cooking Time* (Minutes per Pound)
Round or Sirloin	5 to 8	25 to 35
Loin	4 to 6	30 to 35
Rib	3 to 5	35 to 40
Boneless Rump	3 to 5	40 to 45
Boneless Shoulder	4 to 6	40 to 45

*Meat thermometer reading 170°F

oven. Meat continues to cook out of the oven; it should be removed when thermometer registers 5 to 10° lower than desired doneness.

VEAL WITH TUNA SAUCE

2-pound veal boneless shoulder roast
2 tablespoons olive or vegetable oil
½ cup chicken broth (page 557)
½ cup dry white wine
½ teaspoon salt
½ teaspoon dried basil leaves
¼ teaspoon pepper
1 medium onion, chopped (about ½ cup)
2 large cloves garlic, crushed
1 can (6½ ounces) tuna in water, drained
¼ cup olive or vegetable oil
1 tablespoon lemon juice
¼ teaspoon salt
2 tablespoons capers
2 tablespoons snipped parsley

Cook veal roast in 2 tablespoons oil in Dutch oven over medium heat, turning occasionally, until brown. Add chicken broth, wine, ½ teaspoon salt, the basil, pepper, onion and garlic. Heat to boiling; reduce heat. Cover and simmer until veal is tender, about 2 hours. Remove veal from broth; cover and refrigerate until cold, at least 12 hours. Reserve ½ cup broth; cover and refrigerate.

Place tuna, reserved broth, ¼ cup oil, the lemon juice and ¼ teaspoon salt in blender container. Cover and blend on medium speed, stopping blender occasionally to scrape sides, until mixture is smooth and creamy, about 2 minutes. Cut veal into thin slices. Spoon tuna mixture over veal; sprinkle with capers and parsley. Garnish with lemon slices if desired. **10 servings; 250 calories per serving.**

On a warm summer evening, serve this to guests with Ratatouille Salad (page 517), crusty Italian bread and Cocoa Pecan Torte (page 106).

VEAL OSCAR

6   veal cutlets (about 1 pound)
1   egg, slightly beaten
1   tablespoon water
⅔   cup dry bread crumbs
1   teaspoon salt
½   teaspoon pepper
¼   cup all-purpose flour
2   tablespoons margarine or butter
2   tablespoons vegetable oil
1   package (10 ounces) frozen asparagus spears
    Hollandaise Sauce (page 600)

Pound veal cutlets until ¼ inch thick. Mix egg and water. Mix bread crumbs, salt and pepper. Coat veal with flour. Dip veal into egg mixture; coat with bread crumb mixture. Heat 1 tablespoon of the margarine and 1 tablespoon of the oil in 10-inch skillet over medium heat until hot. Cook half of the cutlets in margarine mixture, turning once, until done, about 10 minutes. Remove veal; keep warm. Repeat with remaining margarine, oil and veal.

Cook asparagus as directed on package; drain. Prepare Hollandaise Sauce. Place 3 or 4 asparagus spears on top of each cutlet; spoon sauce over top.   **6 servings; 440 calories per serving.**

Delight your guests with Wild Rice and Mushrooms (page 88), Pear Salad (page 544), croissants and Cherry Phyllo Pie (page 145).

VEAL SAUTE

    2   pounds veal round steak, about ½ inch thick
    ½   cup all-purpose flour
    2   teaspoons salt
    1   teaspoon paprika
    ¼   teaspoon pepper
    ¼   cup vegetable or olive oil
    1   cup dry white wine
    ½   cup water
    8   ounces tiny pearl onions, peeled (1½ cups)
    8   to 10 tiny carrots or 4 medium carrots, cut into strips
    ½   teaspoon dried rosemary or thyme leaves
    ½   teaspoon salt

Cut veal steak into 8 serving pieces. Mix flour, 2 teaspoons salt, the paprika and pepper. Coat veal with flour mixture; pound until ¼ inch thick. Heat oil in 12-inch skillet until hot. Cook veal in oil until brown; drain. Add wine, water, onions, carrots and rosemary. Sprinkle with ½ teaspoon salt. Heat to boiling; reduce heat. Cover and simmer until veal and vegetables are tender, about 45 minutes (Add water if necessary.)

Place veal and vegetables on platter; pour pan juices on top. Sprinkle with snipped parsley if desired.   **8 servings;** 285 calories per serving.

Serve with Bulgur Pilaf (page 90) and a fresh fruit salad; finish with a light, refreshing Lemon Soufflé (page 260).

BRAISED VEAL SHANKS

    4   pounds veal shanks, cut into 2½-inch pieces
    1   teaspoon salt
    ¼   teaspoon pepper
    ¼   cup all-purpose flour
    3   tablespoons vegetable or olive oil
    ⅓   cup dry white wine
    1   can (10½ ounces) condensed beef broth
    1   clove garlic, crushed
    1   bay leaf
    2   tablespoons snipped parsley
    1   teaspoon grated lemon peel
    3   cups hot cooked spaghetti (page 91)

Trim excess fat from veal shanks if necessary. Sprinkle veal with salt and pepper; coat with flour. Cook and turn veal in oil in Dutch oven over medium heat until brown on all sides, about 20 minutes.

Stir in wine, broth, garlic and bay leaf. Heat to boiling; reduce heat. Cover and simmer until veal is tender, 1½ to 2 hours.

Remove veal; skim fat from broth. Return veal to broth. Sprinkle veal mixture with parsley and lemon peel. Heat to boiling; reduce heat. Cover and simmer 5 minutes; remove bay leaf. Serve veal mixture on spaghetti; sprinkle with grated Romano cheese if desired.   **4 servings; 690 calories per serving.**

Buttered green peas and Garlic Tomato Slices (page 524) add color to this meal.

Braised Beef Shanks: Substitute 4 pounds beef shanks, cut into 2½-inch pieces, for the veal.

VARIETY MEATS

LIVER

Beef and pork livers are frequently braised or panfried and are sometimes ground for loaves and patties. (If liver is to be ground, cook slowly in 2 to 3 tablespoons vegetable oil about 5 minutes. This makes grinding much easier.) Baby beef, veal (calf) and lamb livers are usually panfried or broiled. Have liver sliced ½ to ¾ inch thick. Peel or trim any membrane from liver before cooking.

To Braise: Coat sliced beef or pork liver with flour. Heat shortening until melted. Fry liver until brown; sprinkle with salt. Add ¼ cup liquid. Heat to boiling; reduce heat. Cover and simmer until done, 20 to 30 minutes.

To Broil: Dip sliced veal or lamb liver into melted margarine, butter or bacon fat. Set oven control to broil and/or 550°. Broil with tops 3 to 5 inches from heat just long enough to change color and become brown, about 3 minutes on each side.

To Panfry: Coat sliced liver with flour. Heat 2 tablespoons shortening until melted. Fry liver over medium-high heat until brown, 2 to 3 minutes on each side.

LIVER AND ONIONS

Have 1 pound liver sliced ½ to ¾ inch thick. Cook and stir 2 medium onions, thinly sliced, and 3 tablespoons margarine or butter in 10-inch skillet until tender. Remove from skillet; keep warm.

Heat ¼ cup shortening in same skillet until melted. Coat liver slices with flour. Fry liver in shortening over medium heat until brown, 2 to 3 minutes on each side. Sprinkle with salt and pepper. Add the onions during the last minute of cooking to heat through.   **5 servings;** 340 calories per serving.

HEART

Heart is flavorful but one of the less tender variety meats. Braising and cooking in liquid are the preferred methods of cooking.

To Braise: Cook whole heart on all sides in small amount vegetable oil until brown. Add small amount liquid (about ½ cup). Sprinkle with salt and pepper. Heat to boiling; reduce heat. Cover and simmer on top of range or in 300 to 325° oven until tender, 3 to 4 hours for beef heart, 2½ to 3 hours for lamb, pork or veal heart.

To Cook in Liquid: Cover heart with water; add 1 teaspoon salt for each quart water. Heat to boiling; reduce heat. Cover and simmer until tender, 3 to 4 hours for beef heart, 2½ to 3 hours for lamb, pork or veal heart.

KIDNEYS

Because beef kidney is less tender than other kidneys, cook in liquid or braise. Cook lamb, pork and veal kidneys in liquid, braise or broil. Remove membrane and hard parts from kidney before cooking.

To Cook in Liquid: Cover with liquid (usually water). Heat to boiling; reduce heat. Cover and simmer until tender, 1 to 1½ hours for beef kidney, ¾ to 1 hour for lamb, pork or veal kidney.

To Braise: Roll halves or pieces of kidney in flour or crumbs seasoned with salt and pepper. Heat vegetable oil in skillet until hot. Cook kidney in oil until brown. Add small amount liquid. Cover and cook until tender, 1½ to 2 hours for beef kidney, ¾ to 1 hour for lamb kidney, 1 to 1½ hours for pork or veal kidney.

To Broil: Cut lamb kidney lengthwise into halves or leave whole. Cut veal kidney into slices. Brush kidney with margarine or butter, melted, or marinate in French Dressing (page 548). Set oven control to broil and/or 550°. Broil until done, about 5 minutes on each side. Or wrap kidney in slices of bacon and broil, or broil on a skewer.

TONGUE

Purchase tongue fresh, pickled, corned, smoked or canned. Tongue is one of the less tender variety meats and requires long, slow cooking in liquid. Smoked, corned or pickled tongue may require soaking before cooking. Lamb and pork tongues are usually sold ready-to-serve.

To Cook in Liquid: Cover tongue with water. If cooking fresh tongue, add 1 teaspoon salt for each quart water. Heat to boiling; reduce heat. Cover and simmer until tender, 3 to 4 hours for beef tongue, 2 to 3 hours for veal tongue. Drain; plunge into cold water. Peel skin from tongue; cut away roots, bones and cartilage. If serving tongue cold, reserve cooking liquid. After removing skin, roots, bones and cartilage, allow tongue to cool in reserved liquid.

GLAZED BEEF TONGUE

Cook 3- to 3½-pound beef tongue as directed above. Place in ungreased rectangular pan, 13 × 9 × 2 inches. Mix 1 can (8¼ ounces) crushed pineapple, drained, ¼ cup packed brown sugar and 1 teaspoon grated orange peel; spread over tongue. Cover and bake in 350° oven 30 minutes. **6 servings; 545** calories per serving.

BRAINS AND SWEETBREADS

Brains and sweetbreads, soft in consistency and very tender, have a delicate flavor. If not cooked immediately after purchase, precook and refrigerate no longer than 24 hours. Precooking makes them firm; then they can be broiled, fried or braised.

To Precook: Heat 1 quart water, 1 tablespoon lemon juice and 1 teaspoon salt to boiling. Add 1 pound brains or sweetbreads. Heat to boiling; reduce heat. Cover and simmer 20 minutes. Drain; plunge into cold water. Remove membrane with sharp knife.

To Broil (after precooking): Mix ¼ cup margarine or butter, melted, and 1 clove garlic, crushed. Brush half of the margarine mixture over 1 pound brains or sweetbreads. Set oven control to broil and/or 550°. Broil with tops about 3 inches from heat 5 minutes. Turn; brush with remaining ingredients. Broil 5 minutes longer.

To Braise (without precooking): Remove membrane with sharp knife. Coat brains or sweetbreads with flour. Heat shortening until melted. Fry brains in shortening until brown. Cover and cook until done, about 20 minutes.

To Panfry (without precooking): Prepare as directed for braising except—do not cover. Fry, turning occasionally, until done, about 20 minutes.

PORK
LAMB

PORK

ABOUT PORK

The U.S. Department of Agriculture confirms that today's pork is a lean product, containing only about 198 calories per three-ounce serving. Previous nutrition research was conducted when hogs were 50 percent fatter. Pork contains less cholesterol than lamb and veal and about the same amount as beef.

Fresh pork should be cooked to 170°. Hams labeled "cook before eating" should be cooked to an internal temperature of 160°. Hams labeled "fully cooked" can be eaten without further cooking. To serve fully cooked hams hot, heat to an internal temperature of 140°. To be safe, an unlabeled ham should be cooked before eating.

ROAST PORK

Select fresh pork roast from those listed in Timetable. Allow about ⅓ pound per person—less for boneless roasts, more for roasts with a bone. Sprinkle pork with salt and pepper if desired.

Place pork, fat side up, on rack in shallow roasting pan. The rack keeps the meat out of the drippings. (With a rib roast, the ribs form a natural rack.) It is not necessary to baste.

Insert meat thermometer so tip is in center of thickest part of pork and does not touch bone or rest in fat. Do not add water. Do not cover.

Roast in 325° oven. (It is not necessary to preheat oven.) Roast to desired degree of doneness (see Timetable), using thermometer reading as final guide.

Roasts are easier to carve if allowed to set 15 to 20 minutes after removing from oven.

TIMETABLE FOR ROASTING FRESH PORK
(Oven Temperature 325°F)

Cut	Approximate Weight (Pounds)	Meat Thermometer Reading (°F)	Approximate Cooking Time (Minutes per Pound)
Fresh Loin			
Center	3 to 5	170°	30 to 35
Half	5 to 7	170°	35 to 40
Blade or Sirloin	3 to 4	170°	40 to 45
Boneless Top (double)	3 to 5	170°	35 to 45
Boneless Top	2 to 4	170°	30 to 35
Fresh Arm Picnic	5 to 8	170°	30 to 35
Fresh Boston Shoulder			
Boneless Blade Boston	3 to 5	170°	35 to 40
Blade Boston	4 to 6	170°	40 to 45
Fresh Leg (ham)			
Whole (bone-in)	12 to 14	170°	22 to 26
Boneless	10 to 14	170°	24 to 28
Half (bone-in)	5 to 8	170°	35 to 40

			Total Cooking Time
Fresh Tenderloin	½ to 1	170°	¾ to 1 hour
Fresh Spareribs, Back Ribs and Country-style Ribs		Cooked well done	1½ to 2½ hours

PORK ROAST WITH ROSEMARY

    4 - pound pork boneless top loin roast
    ½   teaspoon salt
    ¼   teaspoon pepper
    1   teaspoon dried rosemary leaves, crushed
    2   cloves garlic, crushed
        Pork Wine Gravy (page 405)

Sprinkle pork roast with salt and pepper; rub with rosemary and garlic. Place pork, fat side up, on rack in shallow roasting pan. Insert meat thermometer so tip is in center of thickest part of pork and does not rest in fat. Roast uncovered in 325° oven until thermometer registers 170°, about 2½ hours.

Remove pork and rack from pan; drain drippings from pan, reserving ¼ cup. Prepare Pork Wine Gravy; serve with pork. **12 servings; 305 calories per serving.**

Serve with Mashed Potatoes (page 658) and Glazed Carrots (page 633).

Pork Wine Gravy

Pour reserved pork drippings into 1½-quart saucepan. Stir in ¼ cup all-purpose flour and ½ teaspoon salt. Cook over low heat, stirring constantly, until mixture is smooth and bubbly; remove from heat. Stir in 1¾ cups water and ¼ cup dry white wine. Heat to boiling, stirring constantly. Boil and stir 1 minute.

CARVING A PORK LOIN ROAST

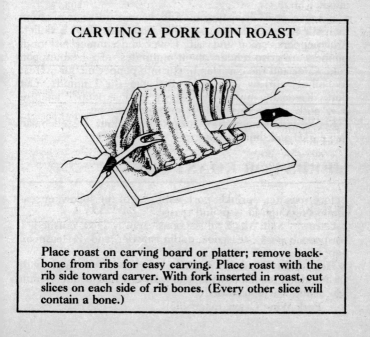

Place roast on carving board or platter; remove backbone from ribs for easy carving. Place roast with the rib side toward carver. With fork inserted in roast, cut slices on each side of rib bones. (Every other slice will contain a bone.)

TENDERLOIN WITH PEPPERS

      1   tablespoon vegetable oil
      1   teaspoon dried thyme leaves
      1   clove garlic, crushed
      1   pork tenderloin (about 1 pound)
    ½   cup water
      1   medium green pepper, cut into ¼-inch strips
      1   medium red pepper, cut into ¼-inch strips
      1   medium onion, thinly sliced and separated into rings
    ½   teaspoon salt
      1   tablespoon cold water
      1   teaspoon cornstarch

Mix oil, thyme and garlic; brush over pork tenderloin. Place on rack in shallow roasting pan. Insert meat thermometer horizontally so tip is in center of thickest part of pork. Roast uncovered in 325° oven until thermometer registers 170°, about 1 hour.

Remove pork; keep warm. Add ½ cup water to roasting pan; stir to loosen brown particles. Pour into 10-inch skillet. Add peppers, onion and salt. Cover and simmer just until peppers are crisp-tender, about 5 minutes. Mix 1 tablespoon cold water and the cornstarch; stir into pepper mixture. Heat to boiling, stirring constantly. Boil and stir 1 minute. Cut pork diagonally into ¼-inch slices. Spoon pepper mixture over pork. **4 servings; 395 calories per serving.**

Serve with Lemon Rice (page 85), Walnut Tossed Salad (page 511) and dinner rolls.

HERBS FOR ROAST PORK

Before roasting, sprinkle pork with one of the following seasonings (enough for 4-pound roast):

Caraway Salt: Mix 2 tablespoons caraway seed, crushed, 1 teaspoon salt, ½ teaspoon garlic powder and ¼ teaspoon pepper.

Herb Salt: Cut 1 clove garlic into halves; rub pork with garlic. Mix 1 teaspoon dried sage leaves, 1 teaspoon marjoram leaves and 1 teaspoon salt.

FRESH HAM WITH STUFFING

4-	pound pork boneless leg (fresh ham)
	Salt
3	cups water
6	medium onions, chopped
1	egg, beaten
2	cups soft bread cubes
1	tablespoon dried sage leaves, crushed
2	tablespoons margarine or butter
1	teaspoon salt
¼	teaspoon pepper

Spread pork leg flat; sprinkle lightly with salt. Heat water to boiling; add onions. Cook 5 minutes; drain. Mix egg, onions and remaining ingredients. Spread half of the mixture on pork; roll up. Fasten with metal skewers.

Place pork, fat side down, on rack in shallow roasting pan. Spoon remaining onion mixture over top of pork. Insert meat thermometer so tip is in center of thickest part of pork and does not rest in stuffing. Roast uncovered in 325° oven until thermometer registers 170°, 3 to 3½ hours. **16 servings;** 660 calories per serving.

Serve with green beans, tomato salad and Lemon Cake Roll (page 126).

BROILED FRESH PORK

Slash diagonally outer edge of fat on pork chops or steaks at 1-inch intervals to prevent curling (do not cut into lean). Set oven control to broil and/or 550°. Place pork on rack in broiler pan; place broiler pan so top of pork is 3 to 5 inches from heat. Broil until light brown. The pork should be about half done (see Timetable).

Sprinkle brown side with salt and pepper if desired. (Always season after browning because salt tends to draw moisture to surface, delaying browning.) Turn pork; broil until brown.

TIMETABLE FOR
BROILING FRESH PORK

Cut	Approximate Total Cooking Time
Chops	
¾ to 1 inch	20 to 25 minutes
Blade Steaks	
½ to ¾ inch	20 to 22 minutes
Ground Pork Patties	
1 inch	20 to 25 minutes

Easy . . . BREADED PORK CHOPS

Prepare Pork Coating Mix (below). Dip 4 pork rib or loin chops, ½ to ¾ inch thick, into ¼ cup milk. Shake each in Pork Coating Mix, coating both sides. Bake on rack in shallow roasting pan in 425° oven until done and brown, 30 to 35 minutes.   **4 servings; 285 calories per serving.**

Complete your meal with Pepper Mostaccioli (page 97). Cheese Cauliflower (page 634) and Applesauce (page 220).

Pork Coating Mix

    2   tablespoons yellow cornmeal
    2   tablespoons whole wheat flour
    1   teaspoon salt
    1   teaspoon ground sage
    ½   teaspoon onion powder
    ½   teaspoon sugar
    ½   teaspoon paprika

Shake all ingredients in plastic or paper bag.

Easy . . . LEMON PORK CHOPS

   4   **pork loin or rib chops, about ¾ inch thick**
       Salt
   4   **thin onion slices**
   4   **thin lemon slices**
   4   **tablespoons packed brown sugar**
   4   **tablespoons catsup**

Sprinkle both sides of pork chops with salt. Place pork chops
in ungreased shallow baking pan or dish. Top each pork chop
with onion slice, lemon slice, 1 tablespoon brown sugar and 1
tablespoon catsup. Cover and bake in 350° oven 30 minutes.
Uncover and bake, spooning sauce onto pork chops occasionally,
until done, about 30 minutes longer.   **4 servings; 425 calories per serving.**

   Nice with Potatoes with Toppers (page 660), buttered broccoli, Waldorf Salad (page 540) and Cherry Freeze (page 265).

PORK WITH PARSNIPS

   4   **pork loin or rib chops, about ½ inch thick**
   3   **medium parsnips, cut crosswise into ½-inch slices**
   1   **medium onion, sliced**
   ½   **cup chicken broth (page 557)**
   1   **teaspoon dry mustard**
   ½   **teaspoon salt**
   ¼   **teaspoon ground allspice**
   ⅛   **teaspoon pepper**
   1   **medium apple, cut into ¼-inch wedges**
   2   **tablespoons snipped parsley**

Cook pork chops in 10-inch skillet over medium heat until
brown on both sides. Place parsnips and onion on pork. Mix
chicken broth, mustard, salt, allspice and pepper; pour over
vegetables. Heat to boiling; reduce heat. Cover and simmer
until pork is done, 35 to 40 minutes. Arrange apple on
vegetables. Cover and cook just until apple is tender, about
3 minutes. Sprinkle with parsley.   **4 servings; 360 calories
per serving.**

   Serve with Wilted Lettuce Salad (page 508), Drop Biscuits
(page 42) and ice cream with Butterscotch Sauce (page 271).

PORK COOKED IN LIQUID

Cook pork in small amount of shortening over medium heat until brown; drain. Pour enough water, bouillon or tomato juice over pork to cover to assure uniform cooking without turning; reduce heat. Cover and simmer until pork is done (see Timetable).

TIMETABLE FOR COOKING
FRESH AND SMOKED PORK IN LIQUID

Cut	Approximate Weight (Pounds)	Approximate Cooking Time (Hours)
Fresh		
Spareribs		2 to 2½
Country-style Ribs		2 to 2½
Hocks		2 to 2½
Smoked Ham		
(cook before eating)		
Whole (country-style)	10 to 16	4½ to 5
Half (country-style)	5 to 8	3 to 4
Smoked Arm Picnic		
(cook before eating)	5 to 8	3½ to 4
Smoked Shoulder		
Roll (butt)	2 to 4	1½ to 2
Smoked Hocks		2 to 2½

BRAISED FRESH PORK

Cook pork over medium heat until brown; drain. Sprinkle with salt, pepper, herbs or spices if desired; reduce heat. Pour small amount of liquid (water or apple, pineapple or vegetable juice) over pork. Cover and simmer until done (see Timetable).

TIMETABLE FOR BRAISING FRESH PORK

Cut	Approximate Cooking Time
Chops	
¾ to 1½ inches	45 to 60 minutes
Blade Steaks	
¾ inch	45 to 60 minutes
Cubes	
1 to 1¼ inches	45 to 60 minutes
Spareribs	1½ hours
Back Ribs	1½ hours
Country-style Ribs	1½ to 2 hours

SWEET AND ZESTY SPARERIBS

4½   pounds fresh pork spareribs, cut into serving pieces
¼   cup vinegar
¼   cup molasses
¼   cup chili sauce
2   tablespoons soy sauce
¼   teaspoon ground ginger
⅛   teaspoon red pepper sauce
1   medium clove garlic, crushed
1   can (8 ounces) crushed pineapple in juice, undrained

Place pork spareribs, meaty sides up, on rack in shallow roasting pan. Roast uncovered in 325° oven 1½ hours.

Mix remaining ingredients; brush over pork. Roast, turning and brushing frequently with pineapple mixture, until pork is done, about 45 minutes longer. (Use about half of the pineapple mixture to brush pork.) Heat remaining pineapple mixture to boiling, stirring occasionally. Serve with pork. **6 servings; 665 calories per serving.**

Easy . . . MUSTARD SPARERIBS

Cut 4½ pounds fresh pork spareribs into serving pieces. Place meaty sides up on rack in shallow roasting pan. Roast uncovered in 325° oven 1 hour.

Brush pork with Mustard Sauce (page 412). Roast, turning and brushing frequently with sauce, until done, about 45 minutes longer. **6 servings; 860 calories per serving.**

Serve with Scalloped Potatoes (page 662), Skillet Cherry Tomatoes (page 671) and Fresh Fruit Cups (page 225).

Mustard Sauce
Mix ½ cup molasses and ⅓ cup Dijon-style mustard; stir in ⅓ cup cider vinegar.

COUNTRY-STYLE RIBS

    3   pounds pork country-style ribs
    ⅔   cup chili sauce
    ½   cup grape jelly
    1   tablespoon dry red wine
    1   teaspoon Dijon-style mustard

Cut pork ribs into serving pieces if necessary. Arrange meaty sides up in ungreased rectangular pan, 13 × 9 × 2 inches. Cover and bake in 325° oven until tender, about 2 hours; drain.

Heat remaining ingredients, stirring occasionally, until jelly is melted; pour over pork. Bake uncovered, spooning sauce over pork occasionally, until pork is hot and glazed, about 30 minutes. Serve sauce over pork.   **6 servings;** 495 calories per serving.

Serve with Herbed Green Beans (page 618) and Bulgur Pilaf (page 90).

PORK PICCATA

    ¾ - pound pork tenderloin, cut into 6 pieces
    1   egg, slightly beaten
    1   tablespoon water
    ½   cup dry bread crumbs
    ½   teaspoon salt
    ¼   teaspoon pepper
    ⅛   teaspoon garlic powder
    ¼   cup all-purpose flour
    2   tablespoons margarine or butter
    2   tablespoons vegetable oil
    2   tablespoons lemon juice
    2   tablespoons dry white wine

Pound pork tenderloin slices until ¼ inch thick. Mix egg and water. Mix bread crumbs, salt, pepper and garlic powder. Coat pork with flour; dip into egg mixture. Coat with crumb mixture. Heat 1 tablespoon margarine and 1 tablespoon oil in 10-inch skillet over medium heat until hot. Cook 3 pieces pork, turning once, until done, about 12 minutes. Remove pork from skillet; keep warm. Repeat with remaining margarine, oil and pork. Remove pork from skillet; stir lemon juice and wine into skillet. Heat to boiling; pour over pork. Sprinkle with snipped parsley and serve with lemon wedges if desired.   **6 servings; 250 calories per serving.**

Accompany with Noodles Romanoff (page 95) and a tossed green salad.

Chicken Piccata: Substitute 3 chicken breast halves (about 1½ pounds) for the pork. Skin, bone and cut each breast half into halves. Cook about 8 minutes.

Veal Piccata: Substitute 1-pound veal round steak, about ½ inch thick and cut into 6 pieces, for the pork. Cook about 8 minutes.

PORK PIES

    1   pound bulk pork sausage
    1   cup cubed fully cooked smoked ham
    ½   teaspoon ground sage
    ⅛   teaspoon pepper
    1   medium green pepper, chopped (about 1 cup)
    1   medium onion, chopped (about ½ cup)
    1   medium stalk celery, thinly sliced (about ½ cup)
    1   can (10¾ ounces) condensed cream of chicken soup
    4   cups thinly sliced apples (about 4 medium)
         Pastry (page 414)

Cook and stir sausage in 10-inch skillet until done, about 10 minutes; drain. Stir in ham, sage, pepper, green pepper, onion, celery and soup. Divide the mixture among 6 ungreased 10-ounce casseroles or custard cups. Place apples on sausage mixture in each casserole.

Prepare Pastry. Gather into ball; divide into 6 equal parts. Roll each part 1 inch larger than casserole. Fold into halves. Place on casserole and unfold. Seal pastry to edge of casserole; cut several slits in top. Bake in 375° oven until crust is

brown, about 30 minutes.   **6 servings; 500 calories per serving.**
Serve with Caesar Salad (page 509) and Pears Helene (page 231).

Pastry

⅓	cup plus 1 tablespoon shortening
1	cup all-purpose flour
¼	cup grated Parmesan cheese
½	teaspoon salt
2	to 3 tablespoons cold water

Cut shortening into flour, cheese and salt until particles are size of small peas. Sprinkle in water, 1 tablespoon at a time, tossing with fork until all flour is moistened and pastry almost cleans side of bowl (1 to 2 teaspoons water can be added if necessary).

SWEET-AND-SOUR PORK

2	pounds pork boneless top loin
	Vegetable oil
½	cup all-purpose flour
¼	cup cornstarch
½	cup cold water
1	teaspoon salt
1	egg
1	can (20 ounces) pineapple chunks in syrup, drained (reserve syrup)
½	cup packed brown sugar
½	cup vinegar
1	teaspoon salt
2	teaspoons soy sauce
2	carrots, cut diagonally into thin slices
1	clove garlic, finely chopped
2	tablespoons cornstarch
2	tablespoons cold water
1	green pepper, cut into ¾-inch pieces
	Hot cooked rice (page 85)

Trim excess fat from pork; cut pork into ¾-inch pieces. Heat oil (1 inch) in deep fryer or Dutch oven to 360°. Beat flour, ¼ cup cornstarch, ½ cup cold water, 1 teaspoon salt and the egg with hand beater until smooth. Stir pork into batter until well coated. Add pork pieces, one at a time, to oil. Fry about 20 pieces at a time, turning 2 or 3 times, until golden brown, about 5 minutes; drain and keep warm.

Add enough water to reserved pineapple syrup to measure 1 cup. Heat syrup mixture, brown sugar, vinegar, 1 teaspoon salt, the soy sauce, carrots and garlic to boiling in Dutch oven; reduce heat. Cover and simmer until carrots are crisp-tender, about 6 minutes. Mix 2 tablespoons cornstarch and 2 tablespoons cold water; stir into sauce. Add pork, pineapple and green pepper. Heat to boiling, stirring constantly. Boil and stir 1 minute. Serve with rice. **8 servings; 605** calories per serving.

Accompany with Corn Sticks (page 54) and Cranberry Ice (page 264).

Do-ahead Tip: After frying pork, cover and refrigerate no longer than 24 hours. Heat uncovered in 400° oven until hot, about 7 minutes.

PORK FRIED RICE

1   cup bean sprouts
2   tablespoons vegetable oil
1   cup sliced mushrooms
3   cups cold cooked regular rice (page 85)
1   cup cut-up cooked pork
2   green onions (with tops), sliced (about 2 tablespoons)
2   eggs, slightly beaten
3   tablespoons soy sauce
    Dash of white pepper

Rinse bean sprouts under running cold water; drain. Heat 1 tablespoon oil in 10-inch skillet until hot; rotate skillet until oil covers bottom. Cook and stir mushrooms in oil over medium heat until coated, about 1 minute. Add bean sprouts, rice, pork and onions; cook and stir over medium heat, breaking up rice, until hot, about 5 minutes.

Push rice mixture to side of skillet; add 1 tablespoon oil to skillet. Add eggs; cook and stir over medium heat until eggs are thickened throughout but still moist. Stir eggs into rice mixture. Stir in soy sauce and white pepper. **4 servings** (about 1 cup each); 425 calories per serving.

Nice served with Easy Fruit Salad (page 537) and lemon sherbet.

Chicken Fried Rice: Substitute 1 cup cut-up cooked chicken for the pork.

PORK CHOW MEIN

1 - pound pork blade or arm steak, cut into thin strips
1 tablespoon vegetable oil
2 cups beef broth (page 561)
2 tablespoons soy sauce
2 medium stalks celery, sliced (about 1 cup)
1 medium onion, chopped (about ½ cup)
1 can (4 ounces) mushroom stems and pieces,
    drained (reserve ¼ cup liquid)
3 tablespoons cornstarch
1 can (16 ounces) Chinese vegetables, drained
1 tablespoon brown gravy sauce (molasses type)
3 cups chow mein noodles

Cook and stir pork steak in oil in 10-inch skillet over medium heat until brown. Stir in broth, soy sauce, celery and onion. Heat to boiling; reduce heat. Cover and simmer 30 minutes.

Shake reserved mushroom liquid and the cornstarch in tightly covered container; gradually stir into pork mixture. Add mushrooms, Chinese vegetables and gravy sauce. Heat to boiling, stirring constantly. Boil and stir 1 minute. Serve over noodles. **5 servings** (about 1 cup each); 385 calories per serving.

For a complete meal, serve with broccoli spears and Almond Brownies (page 176).

PORK HOCKS WITH SAUERKRAUT

4 smoked pork hocks (about 4 pounds)
4 cups water
½ teaspoon dried marjoram leaves
1 onion, sliced
2 cans (16 ounces each) sauerkraut, drained
½ teaspoon celery seed
1 apple, cut into eighths

Heat pork hocks, water, marjoram and onion to boiling in Dutch oven; reduce heat. Cover and simmer 1½ hours.

Drain liquid from Dutch oven, reserving 1 cup. Stir reserved liquid, the sauerkraut and celery seed into pork hocks. Cover and simmer 15 minutes. Add apple; cover and simmer 15 minutes longer.   **4 servings; 415 calories per serving.**

Nice with Cucumber-Relish Mold (page 529), dinner rolls and Apricot-glazed Pears (page 231).

BAKED HAM

Select ham or other cut from those listed in Timetable (page 418). Allow about ⅓ pound per person—less for a boneless roast, more for a roast with a bone.

Place ham, fat side up, on rack in shallow roasting pan. The rack keeps the meat out of the drippings. It is not necessary to baste.

Insert meat thermometer so tip is in center of thickest part of meat and does not touch bone or rest in fat. Do not add water. Do not cover.

Roast in 325° oven. (It is not necessary to preheat oven.) Roast to desired degree of doneness (see Timetable), using thermometer reading as final guide.

Ham is easier to carve if allowed to set 15 to 20 minutes after removing from oven. (See carving illustration, pages 418 and 419.)

GLAZES FOR BAKED HAM

For a glazed ham, remove ham 30 minutes before it is done. Pour drippings from pan. Remove any skin from ham. Score fat surface of ham lightly, cutting uniform diamond shapes. If desired, insert whole clove in each. Pat or brush on your choice of the following glazes (enough for 4-pound ham); continue baking 30 minutes.

Brown Sugar Glaze: Mix 1 cup brown sugar (packed), ½ teaspoon dry mustard and 1 tablespoon vinegar.

Pineapple Glaze: Mix 1 cup brown sugar (packed), 1 tablespoon cornstarch and ¼ teaspoon salt in small saucepan. Stir in 1 can (8½ ounces) crushed pineapple (with syrup), 2 tablespoons lemon juice and 1 tablespoon prepared mustard. Cook over medium heat, stirring constantly, until mixture thickens and boils. Boil and stir 1 minute.

TIMETABLE FOR ROASTING SMOKED PORK
(Oven Temperature 325°F)

Cut	Approximate Weight (Pounds)	Meat Thermometer Reading (°F)	Approximate Cooking Time (Minutes per Pound)
Smoked Loin	3 to 5	160°	25 to 30
Smoked Arm Picnic			
(cook before eating)	5 to 8	170°	30 to 35
(fully cooked)	5 to 8	140°	25 to 30
Smoked Shoulder			
Roll (butt)	2 to 3	170°	35 to 40
Smoked Ham			
(cook before eating)			
Whole	10 to 14	160°	18 to 20
Half	5 to 7	160°	22 to 25
Shank Portion	3 to 4	160°	35 to 40
Rump (butt) Portion	3 to 4	160°	35 to 40
Smoked Ham			
(fully cooked)			
Whole	10 to 15	140°	15 to 18
Half	5 to 7	140°	18 to 24
Canadian-style Bacon			
(fully cooked)	2 to 4	140°	20 to 30

CARVING A WHOLE HAM

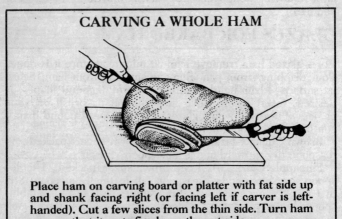

Place ham on carving board or platter with fat side up
and shank facing right (or facing left if carver is left-
handed). Cut a few slices from the thin side. Turn ham
over so that it rests firmly on the cut side.

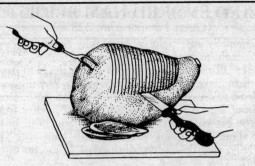

Make slices down to bone. Run knife horizontally along bone to release slices.

CARVING AN ARM PICNIC

Cut off a lengthwise slice from ham. Turn ham over so that it rests firmly on the cut side. Make vertical cuts as shown; turn knife and cut horizontally along bone to remove boneless piece to another surface for slicing. For more servings, cut remaining meat from arm bone and slice.

COOKED SMOKED HAM SLICE

Slash diagonally outer edge of fat of fully cooked smoked ham slice at 1-inch intervals to prevent curling.

To Bake: Place ham slice (about 1 inch thick) in ungreased baking dish. Bake uncovered in 325° oven 30 minutes.

To Broil: Set oven control to broil and/or 550°. Broil ham slice (about 1 inch thick) with top about 3 inches from heat until light brown, about 10 minutes. Turn; broil until light brown, about 6 minutes longer. Brush ham with 3 tablespoons jelly, slightly beaten, during last 2 minutes of broiling if desired.

To Panfry: Rub skillet with small piece of fat cut from ham slice (ham slice should be about ½ inch thick). Cook ham over medium heat until light brown, about 3 minutes. Turn; cook until light brown, about 3 minutes longer.

HAM WITH SPICED FRUITS

2	bananas, each cut into fourths
12	maraschino cherries, cut into halves
1	can (8 ounces) sliced peaches, undrained
1	can (8 ounces) sliced pears, undrained
¼	teaspoon pumpkin pie spice
1½ -	pound fully cooked boneless smoked ham
1	can (23 ounces) sweet potatoes, drained and cut into halves
1	cup packed brown sugar
1	teaspoon dry mustard

Mix bananas, cherries, peaches, pears and pumpkin pie spice. Remove ½ cup syrup from fruit mixture; reserve. Refrigerate fruit mixture.

Place ham in ungreased rectangular baking dish, 12 × 7½ × 2 inches, or square baking dish, 8 × 8 × 2 inches. Arrange sweet potatoes around ham. Mix brown sugar, reserved fruit syrup and the mustard; pour over ham and potatoes. Bake uncovered in 350° oven, spooning sauce onto ham and potatoes occasionally, 30 minutes.

Drain fruit mixture; arrange on top of and around ham. Bake uncovered 15 minutes. **6 servings; 515 calories per serving.**

Accompany with green peas, Confetti Cabbage Mold (page 527) and Baked Custard (page 248).

GINGERED HAM SLICE

1   fully cooked smoked ham slice,
       1 inch thick (about 2 pounds)
1   cup ginger ale
1   teaspoon finely chopped gingerroot or
       ½ teaspoon ground ginger
2   green onions (with tops), chopped
2   teaspoons cornstarch
       Green Onion Tassels (below)

Slash diagonally outer edge of fat of ham at 1-inch intervals; place in rectangular baking dish, $11 \times 7 \times 1\frac{1}{2}$ inches. Mix ginger ale, gingerroot and green onions; pour over ham. Cover and refrigerate, turning ham 2 or 3 times, at least 4 hours.

Drain marinade from ham; reserve marinade. Bake ham uncovered in 325° oven 30 minutes; brush with marinade. Bake until hot, about 15 minutes longer. Mix cornstarch and remaining marinade in saucepan. Heat to boiling, stirring constantly. Boil and stir 1 minute. Garnish ham with Green Onion Tassels; serve with sauce.   **8 servings;** 280 calories per serving.

Green Onion Tassels
Trim root end and green top from green onions, leaving white and some of the green, to about 4 inches. Slit ends 4 or 5 times almost to center. Place in iced water until chilled; drain.

Serve with French Bread (page 68) and Twice-baked Yams (page 669).

Easy . . . HAM AND SCALLOPED POTATOES

Prepare Scalloped Potatoes (page 662) as directed except— arrange 1½ cups cubed or ½ pound sliced fully cooked smoked ham between layers of potatoes.   **6 servings;** 290 calories per serving.

Serve with Saucy Green Beans (page 618), Pineapple Ring Salads (page 544) and coffee ice cream with Crunchy Chocolate Sauce (page 272).

Easy . . . HAM LOAF

1½ pounds ground ham
½ cup dry bread crumbs
¼ cup finely chopped onion
¼ cup finely chopped green pepper
½ cup milk
½ teaspoon dry mustard
¼ teaspoon pepper
2 eggs

Mix all ingredients. Spread in ungreased loaf pan, 9 × 5 × 3 or 8½ × 4½ × 2½ inches. Bake uncovered in 350° oven until done, about 1½ hours. Let stand 5 minutes; remove from pan. 8 servings; 255 calories per serving.

Accompany with Horseradish Sauce (page 602) or Mustard Sauce (page 599).

CHOUCROUTE

4 slices bacon, cut into 1-inch pieces
1 medium onion, chopped (about ½ cup)
1 to 2 tablespoons packed brown sugar
1 can (16 ounces) sauerkraut, drained
2 medium potatoes, cut into fourths
2 tart apples, sliced
6 whole peppercorns
2 whole cloves
1 sprig parsley
1 bay leaf
4 smoked pork loin chops, ½ inch thick
4 frankfurters, slashed diagonally
2 cups chicken broth (page 557)

Cook and stir bacon and onion in Dutch oven or 12-inch skillet until bacon is crisp; drain. Stir in brown sugar and sauerkraut. Add potatoes and apples.

Tie the peppercorns, cloves, parsley and bay leaf in a cheesecloth bag or place in a tea ball; add to sauerkraut mixture. Add pork chops and frankfurters. Pour chicken broth over meat. Heat to boiling; reduce heat. Cover and simmer until meat is done and potatoes are tender, about 30 minutes. Remove cheesecloth bag. Remove sauerkraut, potatoes and apples to large platter with slotted spoon. Arrange meat around edge.   **4 servings;** 725 calories per serving.

Complete meal with Hard Rolls (page 73) and Chocolate Pots de Crème (page 249).

COOKED SAUSAGE (UNCOOKED SMOKED OR FRESH)

To Bake: Arrange sausages in single layer in shallow baking pan. Bake uncovered in 400° oven, turning sausages to brown evenly, until well done, 20 to 30 minutes. Spoon off drippings as they accumulate.

To Panfry: Place pork sausage links or patties in cold skillet. Add 2 to 4 tablespoons water. Heat to boiling; reduce heat. Cover and simmer until done, 5 to 8 minutes (depending on size or thickness). Uncover and cook, turning sausages to brown evenly, until well done.

ITALIAN SAUSAGE LASAGNE

1	pound bulk Italian sausage
1	medium onion, chopped (about ½ cup)
1	clove garlic, crushed
2	tablespoons parsley flakes
1	teaspoon sugar
1	teaspoon dried basil leaves
½	teaspoon salt
1	can (16 ounces) whole tomatoes, undrained
1	can (15 ounces) tomato sauce
12	uncooked lasagne noodles (about 12 ounces)
1	carton (16 ounces) ricotta or creamed cottage cheese (2 cups)
¼	cup grated Parmesan cheese
1	tablespoon parsley flakes
1½	teaspoons dried oregano leaves
2	cups shredded mozzarella cheese (8 ounces)
¼	cup grated Parmesan cheese

Cook and stir sausage, onion and garlic in 10-inch skillet until sausage is brown; drain. Stir in 2 tablespoons parsley, the sugar, basil, salt, tomatoes and tomato sauce; break up tomatoes. Heat to boiling, stirring occasionally; reduce heat. Simmer uncovered until slightly thickened, about 45 minutes.

Cook noodles as directed on package; drain. Mix ricotta cheese, ¼ cup Parmesan cheese, 1 tablespoon parsley and the oregano.

Spread 1 cup of the sauce mixture in ungreased rectangular baking dish, 13 × 9 × 2 inches; top with 4 noodles. Spread 1 cup of the cheese mixture over noodles; spread with 1 cup of the sauce mixture. Sprinkle with ⅔ cup of the mozzarella cheese. Repeat with 4 noodles, the remaining cheese mixture, 1 cup of the sauce mixture, and ⅔ cup of the mozzarella cheese. Top with remaining noodles and sauce mixture; sprinkle with remaining mozzarella and Parmesan cheese. Bake uncovered in 350° oven until hot and bubbly, about 45 minutes. Let stand 15 minutes before cutting. **8 servings; 455 calories per serving.**

NOTE: Uncooked lasagne noodles can be used. Break noodles as necessary to fit dish. Noodles will cook as lasagne bakes.

Accompany lasagne with Elegant Tossed Salad (page 510), Garlic Bread (page 69) and ice cream.

Beef Lasagne: Substitute 1 pound ground beef for the Italian sausage.

COOKED SMOKED SAUSAGES AND FRANKFURTERS

Frankfurters or other cooked smoked sausage links do not require cooking; they need only to be heated. Do not pierce with fork.

To Broil: Brush frankfurters with margarine, butter or shortening. Set oven control to broil and/or 550°. Broil with tops about 3 inches from heat, turning with tongs, until evenly brown.

To Panbroil: Cook frankfurters in 1 to 2 tablespoons shortening, turning with tongs, until brown.

To Simmer: Drop frankfurters into boiling water; reduce heat. Cover and simmer until hot, 5 to 10 minutes (depending on size).

Easy . . . POLISH SAUSAGE IN BEER

Cover and heat ½ to ¾ cup beer or water and 1 pound precooked Polish sausage to boiling; reduce heat. Cover and simmer 10 minutes. (If using uncooked Polish sausage, increase cooking time to 20 minutes.)   **4 servings;** 345 calories per serving.

Nice with Hot German Potato Salad (page 523) and Dark Pumpernickel (page 69).

Bratwurst in Beer: Substitute 1 pound fully cooked bratwurst for the Polish sausage; cook bratwurst in 2 teaspoons margarine or butter until brown before cooking in beer.

CORN DOGS

1 pound frankfurters
  Vegetable oil
1 cup all-purpose flour*
2 tablespoons cornmeal
1½ teaspoons baking powder
½ teaspoon salt
3 tablespoons shortening
¾ cup milk
1 egg, beaten
1 medium onion, grated, if desired

Pat frankfurters dry. Heat oil (2 to 3 inches) in deep fryer or Dutch oven to 365°. Mix the flour, cornmeal, baking powder and salt. Cut in shortening. Stir in remaining ingredients. Dip frankfurters into batter, allowing excess to drip into bowl. Fry, turning once, until brown, about 6 minutes; drain. Insert wooden skewer in end of each frankfurter if desired.   4 servings; 580 calories per serving.

Accompany with carrot and celery sticks, potato chips and ice cream with Crunchy Chocolate Sauce (page 272).

COOKED BACON

To Bake: Place separated slices of bacon on rack in broiler pan. Bake in 400° oven, without turning, until brown, about 10 minutes.

To Broil: Set oven control to broil and/or 550°. Broil separated slices of bacon about 3 inches from heat until brown, about 2 minutes. Turn; broil 1 minute longer.

To Panfry: Place slices of bacon in cold skillet. Cook over low heat, turning bacon to brown evenly on both sides, 8 to 10 minutes.

Bacon Curls: Cut bacon slices into halves. Roll up; secure with wooden picks. Set oven control to broil and/or 550°. Broil with tops 4 to 5 inches from heat 2 minutes. Turn; broil until crisp, about 2 minutes longer.

*If using self-rising flour, omit baking powder and salt.

COOKED CANADIAN-STYLE BACON (FULLY COOKED)

To Bake: Place 2-pound piece fully cooked Canadian-style bacon, fat side up, on rack in shallow baking pan. Insert meat thermometer so tip is in center of bacon. Bake uncovered in 325° oven until thermometer registers 140°, 20 to 30 minutes.

To Broil: Set oven control to broil and/or 550°. Broil ¼-inch slices Canadian-style bacon with tops 2 to 3 inches from heat until brown, about 3 minutes. Turn; broil 3 minutes longer.

To Panfry: Place ⅛-inch slices Canadian-style bacon in cold skillet. Cook over low heat, turning bacon to brown evenly on both sides, 8 to 10 minutes.

BACON-CHEESE PASTRIES

½   package (17¼-ounce size) frozen puff pastry, thawed (1 sheet)

1   package (6 ounces) sliced fully cooked Canadian-style bacon

4   ounces round longhorn colby cheese, cut into six ¼-inch slices

⅓   cup chopped green onions (with tops)

1   tablespoon margarine or butter, melted

Heat oven to 425°. Roll pastry into rectangle, 15 × 10 inches, on lightly floured surface. Cut lengthwise into halves; cut each half crosswise into thirds. Place 2 slices bacon on each square; top each with cheese slice and about 1 tablespoon onion. Bring corners of pastry up over bacon; pinch edges to seal. Place seam sides up on ungreased cookie sheet. Brush pastry with margarine. Bake 15 minutes.

Reduce oven temperature to 325°. Bake until pastry is puffed and deep golden brown, about 10 minutes longer. (Pastry may open slightly during baking.) **6 servings; 315 calories per serving.**

Serve with Cabbage and Sour Cream (page 631) and Elegant Tossed Salad (page 510).

LAMB

ABOUT LAMB

The term *genuine lamb*, as specified by the U.S. Department of Agriculture, refers to meat that comes from sheep that are less than 1 year old. Quality lamb is derived from a young animal and will have fine-textured reddish-pink meat with very little marbling (flecks of fat within the lean). In addition, the meat of quality lamb has a smooth covering of brittle white fat.

SEASONINGS FOR ROAST LAMB

Before roasting, sprinkle lamb with one of the following (enough for a 4-pound roast):

Curried Onion Salt: Mix 2 teaspoons curry powder, 1½ teaspoons instant minced onion, ½ teaspoon salt and ¼ teaspoon pepper.

Dill-Rosemary Salt: Mix 2 teaspoons dried dill weed, 1 teaspoon salt, ½ teaspoon dried rosemary leaves and ¼ teaspoon pepper.

ROAST LAMB

Select lamb roast from those listed in Timetable (page 429). Sprinkle roast with salt and pepper if desired. For a quick seasoning, cut 4 or 5 small slits in lamb with tip of sharp knife and insert slivers of garlic; be sure to remove garlic before serving.

Place lamb, fat side up, on rack in shallow roasting pan. The rack keeps the meat out of the drippings. (With a rib roast, the ribs form a natural rack.) It is not necessary to baste.

Insert meat thermometer so tip is in center of thickest part of lamb and does not touch bone or rest in fat. Do not add water. Do not cover.

Roast in 325° oven. (It is not necessary to preheat oven.) Roast to desired degree of doneness (see Timetable), using thermometer reading as final guide.

Roasts are easier to carve if allowed to set 15 to 20 minutes after removing from oven. Because meat continues to cook after removal from oven, if roast is to set, remove from oven when thermometer registers 5 to 10° lower than desired doneness.

TIMETABLE FOR ROASTING LAMB
(Oven Temperature 325°F)

Cut	Approximate Weight (Pounds)	Meat Thermometer Reading (°F)	Approximate Cooking Time (Minutes per Pound)
Leg	7 to 9	140° (rare)	15 to 20
		160° (medium)	20 to 25
		170° (well)	25 to 30
Leg	5 to 7	140° (rare)	20 to 25
		160° (medium)	25 to 30
		170° (well)	30 to 35
Leg, Boneless	4 to 7	140° (rare)	25 to 30
		160° (medium)	30 to 35
		170° (well)	35 to 40
Leg, Shank Half	3 to 4	140° (rare)	30 to 35
		160° (medium)	40 to 45
		170° (well)	45 to 50
Leg, Sirloin Half	3 to 4	140° (rare)	25 to 30
		160° (medium)	35 to 40
		170° (well)	45 to 50
Shoulder, Boneless	3½ to 5	140° (rare)	30 to 35
		160° (medium)	35 to 40
		170° (well)	40 to 45

CARVING A LEG OF LAMB

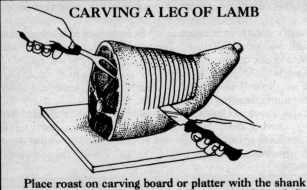

Place roast on carving board or platter with the shank bone to carver's right (or to left if carver is left-handed). Cut a few lengthwise slices from the thin side. Turn the leg over so that it rests firmly on the cut side. Make vertical slices to the leg bone, then cut horizontally along bone to release slices.

STUFFED LAMB SHOULDER

4 -	pound lamb boneless shoulder roast, untied
1	teaspoon salt
½	teaspoon pepper
1	cup grated carrots
1	cup thinly sliced celery
¼	cup thinly sliced green onions (with tops)
2	tablespoons margarine or butter
2	tablespoons snipped mint or 2 teaspoons crushed dried mint leaves
1	tablespoon dry white wine
1	tablespoon lemon juice
1	cup water
1	tablespoon cornstarch
1	tablespoon cold water
¼	teaspoon salt

Sprinkle lamb roast with 1 teaspoon salt and the pepper. Cook and stir carrots, celery and onions in margarine in 10-inch skillet over medium heat until vegetables are crisp-tender, about 5 minutes. Stir in mint, wine and lemon juice. Spread vegetable mixture evenly over lamb. Roll up; tie securely with string.

Place lamb, fat side up, on rack in shallow roasting pan. Insert meat thermometer horizontally so tip is in center of thickest part of lamb and does not rest in stuffing. Roast uncovered in 325° oven to desired degree of doneness, medium (160°) about 2 hours, well done (170°) about 2½ hours.

Remove lamb to warm platter; keep warm. Let stand 10 minutes before slicing. Pour drippings from pan into bowl, leaving brown particles in pan. Reserve 2 tablespoons drippings. Add 1 cup water to pan; stir to loosen brown particles. Pour into 1-quart saucepan; add reserved drippings. Heat to boiling. Mix cornstarch and 1 tablespoon cold water; stir into drippings mixture. Add ¼ teaspoon salt. Heat to boiling, stirring constantly. Boil and stir 1 minute. Remove string from lamb; cut lamb into slices. Serve with the gravy. Garnish with fresh mint or celery leaves if desired. **12 servings;** 385 calories per serving.

Complete your meal with small new potatoes, Citrus Salad (page 532) and Rum-Cracker Torte (page 237).

BROILED LAMB

Choose loin, rib or shoulder lamb chops, allowing 1 or 2 chops for each person. Remove fell (the paperlike covering) if it is on chops. Slash diagonally outer edge of fat on lamb chops at 1-inch intervals to prevent curling (do not cut into lean).

Set oven control to broil and/or 550°. Place chops on rack in broiler pan; place broiler pan so that tops of ¾- to 1-inch chops are 2 to 3 inches from heat, 1- to 2-inch chops are 3 to 5 inches from heat. Broil until brown. The chops should be about half done (see Timetable).

Sprinkle brown side with salt and pepper if desired. (Always season after browning because salt tends to draw moisture to surface, delaying browning.) Turn chops; broil until brown.

TIMETABLE FOR
BROILING LAMB CHOPS AND PATTIES

Thickness	Approximate Total Cooking Time*.
¾ to 1 inch	12 minutes
1½ inches	18 minutes
2 inches	22 minutes

*Time given is for medium doneness; lamb chops are not usually served rare.

SHISH KABOBS

1	pound lamb boneless shoulder
¼	cup lemon juice
2	tablespoons olive or vegetable oil
2	teaspoons salt
½	teaspoon dried oregano leaves
¼	teaspoon pepper
1	green pepper, cut into 1-inch pieces
1	medium onion, cut into eighths
1	cup cubed eggplant

Trim excess fat from lamb shoulder; cut lamb into 1-inch cubes. Place lamb in glass or plastic bowl. Mix lemon juice, oil, salt, oregano and pepper; pour over lamb. Cover and refrigerate, stirring occasionally, at least 6 hours.

Remove lamb; reserve marinade. Thread lamb cubes on four 11-inch metal skewers, leaving a space between each. Set oven control to broil and/or 550°. Broil lamb with tops about 3 inches from heat 5 minutes. Turn; brush with reserved marinade. Broil 5 minutes longer.

Alternate green pepper, onion and eggplant on each of four 11-inch metal skewers, leaving space between each. Place vegetables on rack in broiler pan with lamb. Turn lamb; brush lamb and vegetables with reserved marinade. Broil kabobs, turning and brushing twice with marinade, until brown, 4 to 5 minutes. **4 servings; 360 calories per serving.**

Nice with Curried Rice (page 87), Summer Fruit Salad (page 536) and Pound Cake (page 113) with Lemon Sauce (page 273).

MUSTARD LAMB CHOPS

6   lamb sirloin or shoulder chops, about ¾ inch thick
2   tablespoons Dijon-style mustard
1   teaspoon dried thyme leaves
2   teaspoons vegetable oil
½   teaspoon salt
2   medium carrots, cut into 2 × ½-inch strips
2   medium zucchini, cut into 2 × ½-inch strips
½   small head cauliflower, separated into flowerets
2   tablespoons margarine or butter, melted
½   teaspoon salt
¼   teaspoon pepper

Slash diagonally outer edge of fat on lamb chops at 1-inch intervals to prevent curling (do not cut into lean). Place lamb on rack in broiler pan. Mix mustard, thyme, oil and ½ teaspoon salt; brush half of the mustard mixture evenly over lamb.

Place steamer basket in ½ inch water (the water should not touch bottom of basket). Place carrots, zucchini and cauliflower in basket. Cover tightly and heat to boiling; reduce heat. Steam until tender, 12 to 15 minutes.

Set oven control to broil and/or 550°. Broil lamb with tops about 3 inches from heat until brown, about 6 minutes; turn. Brush lamb with remaining mustard mixture. Broil until medium doneness, 5 to 8 minutes longer. Mix margarine, ½ teaspoon salt and the pepper. Spoon over vegetables; serve with lamb.   **6 servings; 500 calories per serving.**

Accompany with Wild Rice or Brown Rice (page 85), Mixed Fruit Salad (page 537) and Chocolate Frango (page 266).

ITALIAN LAMB SHANKS

1 cup Italian Dressing (page 547)
4 lamb shanks (each about 12 ounces)
½ cup grated Parmesan cheese
¼ cup all-purpose flour
1 tablespoon parsley flakes
½ teaspoon salt
¼ teaspoon onion salt
⅓ cup shortening
   Grated Parmesan cheese

Pour Italian Dressing on lamb shanks in shallow glass dish. Cover and refrigerate, turning lamb occasionally, at least 5 hours.

Remove lamb, reserving marinade. Mix ½ cup cheese, the flour, parsley, salt and onion salt. Coat lamb with cheese mixture, reserving remaining cheese mixture.

Heat shortening in 12-inch skillet or Dutch oven until melted. Cook lamb in hot shortening, turning occasionally, until brown; drain. Sprinkle remaining cheese mixture over lamb in skillet. Add reserved marinade. Heat to boiling; reduce heat. Cover and simmer, turning occasionally, until tender, about 2½ hours. Serve with cheese.   **4 servings; 660** calories per serving.

IRISH STEW

2 pounds lamb boneless neck or shoulder
6 medium potatoes (about 2 pounds)
3 medium onions, sliced
2 teaspoons salt
¼ teaspoon pepper
2 cups water
   Snipped parsley

Trim excess fat from lamb neck; cut lamb into 1-inch cubes. Cut potatoes into ½-inch slices. Layer half each of the lamb, potatoes and onions in Dutch oven; sprinkle with half each of the salt and pepper. Repeat; add water.

Heat to boiling; reduce heat. Cover and simmer until lamb

is tender, 1½ to 2 hours. Skim fat from broth.* Sprinkle stew with snipped parsley.   **6 servings; 330 calories per serving.**

LAMB AND COUSCOUS

1½	pounds lamb boneless shoulder
1	tablespoon olive or vegetable oil
1	cup water
1	teaspoon salt
1	teaspoon ground coriander
¼	teaspoon ground red pepper
¼	teaspoon ground turmeric
4	small carrots, cut into 2-inch pieces
2	cloves garlic, finely chopped
1	medium onion, cut into ¼-inch slices
2	medium green peppers, cut into ½-inch strips
	Couscous (below)

Trim excess fat from lamb shoulder; cut lamb into ¾-inch pieces. Cook and stir lamb in oil in Dutch oven over medium-high heat until brown, about 15 minutes; drain. Add water, salt, coriander, red pepper, turmeric, carrots, garlic and onion. Heat to boiling; reduce heat. Cover and simmer until carrots are almost tender, about 35 minutes. Add green peppers; cover and simmer until green peppers are crisp-tender, about 10 minutes longer.

Prepare Couscous; mound around edge of heated platter. Spoon lamb and vegetables onto center of platter.   **6 servings; 345 calories per serving.**

Complete your meal with pita bread, Spinach Tossed Salad (page 506) and Sherbet-Berry Parfaits (page 265).

Couscous

1	cup water
2	tablespoons margarine or butter
½	teaspoon salt
1	cup couscous (wheat-grain semolina)
½	teaspoon ground ginger
¼	teaspoon ground turmeric
1	medium tomato, chopped

*To remove fat easily, prepare stew the day before, cover and refrigerate. Remove fat before reheating.

Heat water, margarine and salt to boiling in 2-quart sauce-pan. Stir in couscous. Cover and let stand until all water is absorbed, about 3 minutes. Stir in ginger, turmeric and tomato. Heat over low heat, stirring occasionally, until hot, 2 to 3 minutes.

LAMB RAGOUT

2	pounds lamb boneless shoulder
2	tablespoons vegetable oil
3	cups water
3	tablespoons tomato paste
3	teaspoons instant chicken bouillon
1	teaspoon salt
¼	teaspoon pepper
6	small onions
6	small new potatoes
3	medium carrots, cut into 1½-inch pieces
3	small turnips, cut into fourths
1	package (10 ounces) frozen green peas
¼	cup cold water
2	tablespoons all-purpose flour

Trim excess fat from lamb shoulder; cut lamb into 1-inch cubes. Cook and stir lamb in oil in Dutch oven over medium-high heat until brown, about 20 minutes; drain. Add 3 cups water, the tomato paste, bouillon (dry), salt and pepper. Heat to boiling; reduce heat. Cover and simmer until lamb is almost tender, about 45 minutes.

Stir in onions, potatoes, carrots and turnips. Cover and simmer until vegetables are almost tender, about 30 minutes. Stir in peas. Cover and simmer until vegetables are tender, about 10 minutes longer.

Shake ¼ cup water and the flour in tightly covered container; gradually stir into ragout. Heat to boiling, stirring constantly. Boil and stir 1 minute.   **6 servings; 410 calories** per serving.

Beef Ragout: Substitute 2 pounds beef boneless chuck, tip or round for the lamb and beef bouillon for the chicken bouillon. Increase first simmering time to about 1 hour.

LAMB WITH KASHA

1½   pounds lamb boneless shoulder
1   tablespoon olive or vegetable oil
1¼   cups water
2   tablespoons lemon juice
1   teaspoon salt
½   teaspoon dried thyme leaves
½   teaspoon dried oregano leaves
1   medium onion, chopped (about ½ cup)
1   large clove garlic, finely chopped
1   package (10 ounces) frozen cut green beans
½   cup medium kasha

Trim excess fat from lamb shoulder. Cut lamb into ¾-inch pieces. Cook and stir lamb in oil in Dutch oven over medium heat until brown, about 10 minutes. Add water, lemon juice, salt, thyme, oregano, onion and garlic. Heat to boiling; reduce heat. Cover and simmer until lamb is tender, about 1 hour.

Rinse frozen green beans under running cold water to separate; drain. Stir beans and kasha into lamb mixture. Heat to boiling; reduce heat. Cover and simmer until beans are tender and liquid is absorbed, 10 to 12 minutes. **6 servings;** 235 calories per serving.

Serve with Mandarin Salad (page 512) and Fudgy Meringue Mallow (page 256).

POULTRY

POULTRY

ABOUT CHICKEN

When shopping for chicken, a good rule of thumb is to allow about ½ pound per serving. The following types are commonly available.

Broiler-fryer: This all-purpose chicken weighs from 2½ to 3½ pounds. It is very popular because it is so versatile. The best bargain is the whole bird (the bigger the bird, the more meat in proportion to the bone). Cut-up chicken is a convenience and some extra cost per pound should be expected for this service. Some chicken parts sold separately will contain more meat per pound than a whole broiler-fryer.

Roaster: A little older and larger than the broiler-fryer, the roaster weighs 3½ to 6 pounds and has tender meat.

Stewing chicken (hen): This chicken weighs 4½ to 6 pounds and provides a generous amount of meat. It is a mature, less tender bird and is best cooked by simmering or used in stews and soups.

Rock Cornish hen (game hen): This is a small, specially bred bird usually weighing 1 to 1½ pounds. Allow one-half to one small hen per person. The Rock Cornish hen is generally prepared by roasting or broiling.

ROAST CHICKEN, DUCK OR GOOSE

Rub cavity of bird lightly with salt if desired. Do not salt cavity if bird is to be stuffed. Stuff just before roasting—not ahead of time. (See Rice Stuffing and Bread Stuffing, pages 471 and 472). Fill wishbone area with stuffing first. Fasten neck skin to back with skewer. Fold wings across back with tips touching. Fill body cavity lightly. (Do not pack—stuffing will expand while cooking.) Tie or skewer drumsticks to tail.

441

Place breast side up on rack in shallow roasting pan. Brush with shortening, vegetable oil or melted margarine or butter. Do not add water. Do not cover.

Follow Timetable (below). Chicken, duck or goose is done when drumstick meat feels very soft when pressed between fingers.

TIMETABLE FOR ROASTING

Ready-to-Cook Weight	Oven Temperature (°F)	Approximate Total Cooking Time
Broiler-Fryer		
1½ to 2 pounds	400°	¾ to 1 hour
2 to 2½ pounds	400°	1 to 1¼ hours
2½ to 3 pounds	375°	1¼ to 1¾ hours
3 to 4 pounds	375°	1¾ to 2¼ hours
Capon (stuffed)		
5 to 8 pounds	325°	2½ to 3½ hours
Duck		
3½ pounds	350°	2 hours
5½ pounds	350°	3 hours
Goose		
7 to 9 pounds	350°	2½ to 3 hours
9 to 11 pounds	350°	3 to 3½ hours
11 to 13 pounds	350°	3½ to 4 hours

Times given are for unstuffed chickens, ducks or geese; stuffed birds require 15 to 30 minutes longer.

GIBLETS

Cover gizzard, heart and neck with water; sprinkle with ½ teaspoon salt, 2 peppercorns, 2 cloves, a small bay leaf and 2 tablespoons chopped onion. Heat to boiling; reduce heat. Remove bay leaf. Simmer uncovered until gizzard is fork-tender. Liver is very tender; fry, broil or simmer liver in water 5 to 10 minutes.

Use giblet broth in stuffing, gravy and recipes where chicken broth is specified. Cut up cooked giblets and add to gravy or stuffing.

CUTTING UP A CHICKEN

1. Remove wings by cutting into wing joint with a sharp knife, rolling knife to let the blade follow through at curve of the joint.

2. Remove legs by cutting skin between thigh and body; cut through meat between tail and hip joint. Bend leg back until hip joint pops out; cut around bone and through remaining meat and skin.

3. Separate drumsticks from thighs by cutting toward the drumstick at about ⅛ inch from the line of fat that runs crosswise between drumstick and thigh.

4. Cut breast from backbone by holding body, neck end down, and cutting down along each side of the backbone through the rib joints.

5. Placing breast with skin side down, cut just through white cartilage at V of neck to expose end of keel bone (the dark bone at center of breast).

6. Bend back both sides of the breast to pop out keel bone; remove bone. Cut breast into halves with knife or kitchen scissors.

AUTUMN ROAST CHICKEN

2½-   to 3-pound broiler-fryer chicken
½   cup margarine or butter, melted
¼   cup lemon juice
2   tablespoons honey
2   teaspoons dried rosemary leaves, crushed
1   clove garlic, finely chopped
3   pounds winter squash, cut into 1-inch rings or slices
6   medium onions, cut into halves

Prepare chicken as directed in Roast Chicken, Duck or Goose (page 441). Place breast side up on rack in shallow roasting pan. Mix margarine, lemon juice, honey, rosemary and garlic. Arrange squash and onions around chicken. Brush chicken and vegetables with margarine mixture. Roast uncovered in 375° oven, brushing chicken and vegetables several times with remaining margarine mixture, until chicken and vegetables are done, about 1½ hours. **6 servings; 520 calories per serving.**

Spoon Bread (page 55) would lend an unexpected touch to a meal featuring this chicken.

MICROWAVED STUFFED CHICKEN

Prepare and stuff 3½-pound broiler-fryer chicken as directed in Roast Chicken, Duck or Goose (page 441) except—use wooden skewer. Mix ¼ cup margarine or butter, melted, and ½ teaspoon paprika; brush half of the mixture over chicken. Place breast down on microwavable rack in microwavable dish. Cover with waxed paper and microwave on medium-high (70%) 15 minutes. Turn chicken, breast up. Brush with remaining margarine mixture. Cover with waxed paper and microwave until drumstick meat feels very soft when pressed between fingers, 13 to 18 minutes longer. Let stand covered 15 minutes.

FRIED CHICKEN

½   cup all-purpose flour
1   teaspoon salt
1   teaspoon paprika
¼   teaspoon pepper
2½-   to 3-pound broiler-fryer chicken, cut up
     Vegetable oil

Mix flour, salt, paprika and pepper. Coat chicken with flour mixture.

Heat oil (¼ inch) in 12-inch skillet over medium-high heat until hot. Cook chicken in oil until light brown on all sides, about 10 minutes; reduce heat. Cover tightly and simmer, turning once or twice, until thickest pieces are done, about 35 minutes longer. If skillet cannot be covered tightly, add 1 to 2 tablespoons water. Remove cover during last 5 minutes of cooking to crisp chicken.   **6 servings; 305 calories per serving.**

Buttermilk Fried Chicken: Increase flour to 1 cup, salt to 1½ teaspoons and paprika to 2 teaspoons. Dip chicken in 1 cup buttermilk before coating with flour mixture.

Maryland Fried Chicken: Coat chicken with flour mixture. Beat 2 eggs and 2 tablespoons water. Mix 2 cups cracker crumbs, dry bread crumbs or 1 cup cornmeal and ½ teaspoon salt. Dip flour-coated chicken into egg mixture; coat chicken with cracker crumb mixture.

OVEN-FRIED CHICKEN

¼   cup margarine or butter
½   cup all-purpose flour
1   teaspoon salt
1   teaspoon paprika
¼   teaspoon pepper
2½-   to 3-pound broiler-fryer chicken, cut up

Heat margarine in rectangular pan, 13 × 9 × 2 inches, in 425° oven until melted. Mix flour, salt, paprika and pepper. Coat chicken with flour mixture. Place skin sides down in pan. Bake uncovered 30 minutes. Turn chicken; bake until thickest pieces are done, about 30 minutes longer.   **6 servings; 265 calories per serving.**

Crunchy Oven-fried Chicken: Substitute 1 cup cornflake crumbs for the ½ cup flour. Dip chicken in ¼ cup margarine or butter, melted, before coating with crumb mixture.

BATTER-FRIED CHICKEN

2-	to 2½-pound broiler-fryer chicken, cut up
	Vegetable oil
	Thin Fritter Batter (page 51)
½	cup all-purpose flour
1	teaspoon salt
1	teaspoon celery salt
½	teaspoon pepper

Place chicken in Dutch oven with enough water to cover. Heat to boiling; reduce heat. Cover and simmer 20 minutes. Remove chicken from broth; drain and pat dry.

Heat oil (3 to 4 inches) in deep fryer or Dutch oven to 360°. Prepare Thin Fritter Batter.

Mix flour, salt, celery salt and pepper. Coat chicken with flour mixture. Dip chicken into batter, allowing excess batter to drip into bowl.

Fry chicken in hot oil until rich golden brown and done, 5 to 7 minutes; drain.   **6 servings; 515 calories per serving.**

Serve crispy Batter-fried Chicken with Peas and Onions (page 653) and Walnut Tossed Salad (page 511).

GOLDEN NUGGETS

1	whole chicken breast (about 1 pound)
	Vegetable oil
⅓	cup all-purpose flour
¼	teaspoon salt
1½	teaspoons vinegar
¼	teaspoon baking soda
⅓	cup water
	Sweet-and-Sour Sauce or Mustard Sauce (right) or honey

Remove bones and skin from chicken; cut chicken into
1 × ½-inch pieces.

Heat oil (2 to 3 inches) in deep fryer or Dutch oven to
360°. Mix flour and salt. Mix vinegar and baking soda. Stir
vinegar mixture and water into flour mixture; beat until smooth.
Dip chicken into batter, allowing excess batter to drip into
bowl.

Fry chicken in hot oil, 4 or 5 pieces at a time, turning
once, until golden brown and done, about 4 minutes; drain.
Serve with Sweet-and-Sour Sauce.   **4 servings;** 310 calories
per serving.

Surprise your family with these chicken bites, Cheese Cauliflower (page 634) and Cabbage Salad (page 517).

Sweet-and-Sour Sauce
Heat ¼ cup chili sauce and ¼ cup plum or grape jelly over
low heat, stirring constantly, until jelly is melted.

Mustard Sauce
Mix 2 tablespoons dry mustard, 2 to 3 tablespoons water and
1 teaspoon soy sauce.

OVEN-BARBECUED CHICKEN

2½-   to 3-pound broiler-fryer chicken, cut up
  ¾   cup chili sauce
  2   tablespoons honey
  2   tablespoons soy sauce
  1   teaspoon dry mustard
  ½   teaspoon prepared horseradish
  ½   teaspoon red pepper sauce

Place chicken, skin sides up, in ungreased rectangular pan,
13 × 9 × 2 inches. Mix remaining ingredients; pour over chicken.
Cover and bake in 375° oven 30 minutes. Spoon sauce over
chicken; bake uncovered until thickest pieces are done, about
30 minutes longer.   **7 servings;** 175 calories per serving.

Serve with traditional accompaniments—Confetti Slaw (page
516) and Garlic Bread (page 69).

■ **To Microwave:** Arrange chicken, skin sides up, with meatiest parts to outside edges in rectangular microwavable dish, 12 × 7½ × 2 inches. Mix remaining ingredients; pour over chicken. Cover with waxed paper and microwave on high (100%) 10 minutes. Spoon sauce over chicken; rotate dish ½ turn. Cover with waxed paper and microwave until thickest pieces are done, 6 to 10 minutes longer.

STIR-FRIED CHICKEN

2	whole chicken breasts (about 2 pounds)
1	egg white
1	teaspoon cornstarch
1	teaspoon salt
1	teaspoon soy sauce
	Dash of white pepper
4	ounces Chinese pea pods
2	tablespoons cornstarch
2	tablespoons cold water
3	tablespoons vegetable oil
2	cloves garlic, finely chopped
1	teaspoon finely chopped gingerroot
2	tablespoons vegetable oil
1	pound mushrooms, cut into ½-inch slices
½	cup chicken broth
1	tablespoon oyster sauce

Remove bones and skin from chicken; cut chicken into ¼-inch slices. Mix egg white, 1 teaspoon cornstarch, the salt, soy sauce and white pepper in glass or plastic bowl; stir in chicken. Cover and refrigerate 30 minutes.

Remove strings from pea pods. Place pea pods in boiling water. Cover and boil 1 minute; drain. Immediately rinse under running cold water; drain. Mix 2 tablespoons cornstarch and the cold water; reserve.

Heat wok or 12-inch skillet until 1 or 2 drops of water bubble and skitter when sprinkled in wok. Add 3 tablespoons oil; rotate wok to coat side. Add chicken, garlic and gingerroot; stir-fry until chicken is white. Remove chicken from wok.

Add 2 tablespoons oil to wok; rotate to coat side. Add mushrooms; stir-fry 1 minute. Stir in chicken and chicken broth; heat to boiling. Stir in cornstarch mixture; cook and stir until thickened, about 10 seconds. Add pea pods and oyster sauce; cook and stir 30 seconds.   **6 servings; 245 calories per serving.**

Traditionally served with hot cooked white rice (page 85). Serve Fresh Fruit Cups (page 225) for a welcome dessert.

■ **Microwave Reheat Directions:** Prepare Stir-fried Chicken; cover and refrigerate up to 24 hours. Cover tightly and microwave on microwavable platter or in microwavable bowl on high (100%) 4 minutes; stir. Cover tightly and microwave until hot, about 5 minutes longer.

CHICKEN LIVERS WITH BACON

    5   slices bacon
    8   ounces chicken livers, each cut into halves or fourths
    4   ounces mushrooms, sliced (about 1½ cups)*
    1   medium onion, chopped (about ½ cup)
    ½   cup cold water
    1   tablespoon all-purpose flour
    ½   teaspoon instant chicken bouillon
    ¼   teaspoon garlic salt
    ⅛   teaspoon pepper
        Snipped parsley

Cook bacon in 10-inch skillet until crisp; drain. Drain fat, reserving 2 tablespoons in skillet. Cook livers in fat over medium heat, stirring occasionally, until brown, about 4 minutes. Push to side of skillet. Cook and stir mushrooms and onion in skillet until onion is tender, about 5 minutes.

Shake water, flour, bouillon (dry), garlic salt and pepper in tightly covered container; gradually stir into skillet. Heat to boiling, stirring constantly. Boil and stir 1 minute. Reserve a slice of bacon; crumble remaining bacon over liver mixture and stir. Serve over toast triangles or hot cooked noodles if desired; garnish with parsley and reserved bacon slice, crumbled.   **4 servings; 155 calories per serving.**

Try with Dill Wilted Lettuce Salad (page 508) and Squash with Salsa (page 666).

*1 can (4 ounces) mushroom stems and pieces can be substituted for the fresh mushrooms; drain and use mushroom liquid for part of the water.

Chicken Livers with Sour Cream: Increase garlic salt to ½ teaspoon. Stir in ½ cup dairy sour cream with the crumbled bacon; heat just until sauce is hot.

COUNTRY BROILED CHICKEN

2½ - pound broiler-fryer chicken, cut up
½ cup margarine or butter
¼ cup vegetable oil
2 tablespoons lemon juice
2 teaspoons salt
2 teaspoons sugar
½ teaspoon paprika
½ teaspoon ground ginger
1 small onion, finely chopped (about ¼ cup)
1 medium clove garlic, crushed

Place chicken, skin sides down, on rack in broiler pan. Heat remaining ingredients, stirring occasionally, until margarine is melted; brush on chicken.

Set oven control to broil and/or 550°. Place broiler pan so top of chicken is 5 to 7 inches from heat. Brush with margarine mixture every 10 to 15 minutes and turn chicken as it browns; broil until thickest pieces are done, 40 to 50 minutes.   6 servings; 370 calories per serving.

Corn on the cob and Garden Potato Salad (pages 523 and 524) make this entrée a harvest special.

BROILED CHICKEN

Chickens weighing 2½ pounds or less can be broiled. They should be cut into halves, quarters or pieces.

For halves or quarters, turn wing tips onto back side. Set oven control to broil and/or 550°. Brush chicken with melted margarine or butter. Place skin sides down on rack in broiler pan. Place broiler pan so top of chicken is 7 to 9 inches from heat. (If not possible to place broiler pan this far from heat, reduce oven temperature to 450°.)

Broil chicken 30 minutes. Sprinkle brown side with salt and pepper. Turn chicken; brush with melted margarine or butter. Broil until chicken is brown and crisp and thickest pieces are done, 20 to 30 minutes longer.

Broiled Chili-Chicken: Mix 2 tablespoons margarine or butter, melted, 2 tablespoons white wine vinegar, 1½ teaspoons chili powder and ½ teaspoon salt. Brush on chicken. Broil as directed, brushing occasionally with margarine mixture.

Broiled Lemon Chicken: Cut 1 lemon crosswise into halves; rub and squeeze cut sides of lemon over chicken. Mix ½ teaspoon salt, ½ teaspoon paprika and ⅛ teaspoon pepper. Brush chicken with 2 tablespoons margarine or butter, melted; sprinkle with salt mixture. Broil as directed.

POACHED CHICKEN

Cut 2½- to 3-pound broiler-fryer chicken into pieces; remove any excess fat. Place chicken and ¼ cup water in Dutch oven; sprinkle with ½ teaspoon salt. Heat to boiling; reduce heat. Cover and simmer until thickest pieces are done, 45 to 60 minutes. Remove chicken from Dutch oven; cool 10 minutes. Remove chicken from bones and skin. Cover and refrigerate up to 2 days.   **3 to 4 cups cut-up cooked chicken.**

NOTE: Use Poached Chicken in salads, casseroles and other recipes. Use this method when you don't need the broth.

STEWED CHICKEN

4-	to 5-pound stewing chicken, cut up
½	cup chopped celery (with leaves)
1	medium carrot, sliced (about ½ cup)
1	small onion, sliced
1	sprig parsley
2	teaspoons salt
½	teaspoon pepper

Remove any excess fat from chicken. Place chicken, giblets and neck in Dutch oven; add just enough water to cover. Add remaining ingredients. Heat to boiling; reduce heat. Cover and simmer until thickest pieces of chicken are tender, 2½ to 3½ hours. If not serving immediately, refrigerate chicken in broth until cool.

When cool, remove chicken from bones and skin in pieces as large as possible. Skim fat from broth. Cover and refrigerate chicken pieces and broth separately; use within 24 hours. For longer storage, freeze chicken and broth together. **About 5 cups cut-up cooked chicken and 5 to 6 cups broth.**

CHICKEN FRICASSEE

- 1   **cup all-purpose flour**
- 2   **teaspoons salt**
- 2   **teaspoons paprika, if desired**
- ¼   **teaspoon pepper**
- 4 - **pound stewing chicken, cut up**
        Shortening or vegetable oil
- 1   **cup water**
- 3   **tablespoons all-purpose flour**
        Milk
        Chive Dumplings (see Parsley Dumplings, pages 43 and 44)

Mix 1 cup flour, the salt, paprika and pepper. Coat chicken with flour mixture. Heat thin layer of shortening in 12-inch skillet or Dutch oven until hot. Cook chicken in shortening until brown on all sides. Drain fat from skillet; reserve. Add water and, if desired, chopped onion, lemon juice or herbs, such as dried rosemary or thyme leaves, to chicken. Cover and cook over low heat, adding water if necessary, until thickest pieces are tender, 2½ to 3½ hours.

Remove chicken; keep warm. Drain liquid from skillet; reserve. Heat 3 tablespoons reserved fat in skillet. Stir in 3 tablespoons flour. Cook over low heat, stirring constantly, until mixture is smooth and bubbly; remove from heat. Add enough milk to reserved liquid to measure 3 cups; pour into skillet. Heat to boiling, stirring constantly. Boil and stir 1 minute. Return chicken to gravy.

Prepare Chive Dumplings; drop by spoonfuls onto hot chicken. Cook uncovered 10 minutes; cover and cook 20 minutes longer. **8 servings; 460 calories per serving.**

Very good served with Marinated Carrot Salad (page 519) and buttered peas.

NOTE: To fricassee a 2¼- to 3-pound broiler-fryer chicken, cook over low heat about 45 minutes.

CHICKEN IN RED WINE

6	slices bacon
½	cup all-purpose flour
1	teaspoon salt
¼	teaspoon pepper
2½-	to 3-pound broiler-fryer chicken, cut up
1	pound mushrooms (about 4 cups)
8	ounces tiny pearl onions (about 2 cups)
8	baby carrots
2½	cups dry red wine
1½	cups chicken broth (page 557)`
1	teaspoon salt
2	cloves garlic, finely chopped
	Bouquet Garni (below)
	Snipped parsley

Cook bacon in Dutch oven until crisp; drain and crumble. Reserve fat in skillet. Mix flour, 1 teaspoon salt and the pepper. Coat chicken with flour mixture. Cook chicken in hot bacon fat over medium heat until light brown, 15 to 20 minutes; remove chicken. Cook mushrooms, onions and carrots until light brown; drain fat.

Return chicken to Dutch oven; crumble bacon over chicken and vegetables. Stir in wine, chicken broth, 1 teaspoon salt, the garlic and Bouquet Garni. Heat to boiling; reduce heat. Cover and simmer until thickest pieces of chicken are done, 35 to 40 minutes. Skim fat; remove Bouquet Garni. Sprinkle with parsley; serve in soup bowls.   **6 servings; 340 calories per serving.**

This French favorite is traditionally accompanied by parsley potatoes.

Bouquet Garni
Tie 4 sprigs parsley, 2 bay leaves and 1 teaspoon dried thyme leaves in cheesecloth bag or place in tea ball.

CHICKEN WITH VEGETABLES

2½-	to 3-pound broiler-fryer chicken, cut up
1	teaspoon salt
1	teaspoon paprika
2	tablespoons vegetable oil
1	teaspoon dried oregano leaves
1	teaspoon chili powder
½	teaspoon ground cumin
3	medium tomatoes, cut into wedges
2	cloves garlic, finely chopped
1	medium zucchini, cut into ¼-inch slices
1	medium onion, chopped (about ½ cup)
1	can (16½ ounces) whole kernel corn, drained

Remove skin from chicken; sprinkle chicken with salt and paprika. Heat oil in 12-inch skillet or Dutch oven until hot. Cook chicken in oil over medium heat until light brown on all sides, 15 to 20 minutes; reduce heat. Cover and cook 20 minutes. Stir in remaining ingredients. Heat to boiling; reduce heat. Cover and cook until zucchini is crisp-tender and vegetables are heated through, 5 to 10 minutes. Remove vegetables with slotted spoon; serve with chicken.   **7 servings; 230 calories per serving.**

Complete this entrée with Buttermilk Biscuits (page 42).

CHICKEN JAMBALAYA

2½-	to 3-pound broiler-fryer chicken, cut up
2	cups water
1½	teaspoons salt
¼	teaspoon pepper
8	pork sausage links
1	cup uncooked regular rice
½	teaspoon dried thyme leaves
⅛	to ¼ teaspoon ground red pepper
1	medium onion, chopped (about ½ cup)
1	large clove garlic, finely chopped
1	can (16 ounces) stewed tomatoes, undrained
	Snipped parsley

Remove skin from chicken if desired. Place chicken, water, salt and pepper in Dutch oven. Heat to boiling; reduce heat. Cover and simmer 20 minutes. Remove chicken from broth. Skim fat from broth; strain broth.

Cook pork sausage in Dutch oven until brown. Drain fat, reserving 1 tablespoon in Dutch oven. Add chicken; stir in broth and remaining ingredients except parsley. Heat to boiling, stirring once or twice; reduce heat. Cover and simmer until thickest pieces of chicken are done and rice is tender, 30 to 40 minutes. Sprinkle with parsley. **6 servings; 430** calories per serving.

This meal-in-a-dish is complete with Cauliflower Salad (page 520) or Sweet-sour Cabbage Slaw (page 516).

BRUNSWICK STEW

3-	to 3½-pound broiler-fryer chicken, cut up
2	cups water
1½	teaspoons salt
¼	teaspoon pepper
	Dash of ground red pepper
2	cans (16 ounces each) whole tomatoes, undrained
1	can (17 ounces) whole kernel corn, undrained
1	can (16 ounces) lima beans, undrained
1	medium potato, cubed (about 1 cup)
1	medium onion, chopped (about ½ cup)
¼	pound lean salt pork, cut into 1-inch pieces
½	cup cold water
2	tablespoons all-purpose flour

Remove any excess fat from chicken. Heat chicken, giblets, neck, 2 cups water and the salt to boiling in Dutch oven; reduce heat. Cover and simmer until thickest pieces of chicken are tender, about 40 minutes.

Skim fat from broth. Remove chicken from bones if desired; return chicken to broth. Stir in pepper, red pepper, tomatoes, corn, beans, potato, onion and pork. Heat to boiling; reduce heat. Cover and simmer about 45 minutes. Shake ½ cup cold water and the flour in tightly covered container; stir into stew. Heat to boiling, stirring constantly. Boil and stir 1 minute. **8 servings; 370 calories per serving.**

This hearty stew is good with Cornmeal Biscuits (page 42).

CHICKEN PAPRIKA

2	tablespoons vegetable oil
2½-	to 3-pound broiler-fryer chicken, cut up
2	medium onions, chopped
1	clove garlic, chopped
½	cup water
2	tablespoons paprika
1	teaspoon salt
½	teaspoon instant chicken bouillon
¼	teaspoon pepper
1	medium tomato, chopped
1	green pepper, cut into ½-inch strips
1	cup dairy sour cream

Heat oil in 12-inch skillet until hot. Cook chicken in oil over medium heat until brown on all sides, about 15 minutes; remove chicken. Cook and stir onions and garlic in oil until onions are tender; drain fat from skillet. Stir water, paprika, salt, bouillon (dry), pepper and tomato into skillet; loosen brown particles from bottom of skillet. Add chicken. Heat to boiling; reduce heat. Cover and simmer 20 minutes. Add green pepper; cover and cook until thickest pieces of chicken are done, 10 to 15 minutes longer.

Remove chicken; keep warm. Skim fat from skillet. Stir sour cream into liquid in skillet. Heat just until hot. Serve with chicken. **6 servings; 270 calories per serving.**

Dumplings (page 43) are the traditional accompaniment for this dish.

WHEAT-STUFFED DRUMSTICKS

¾   cup uncooked bulgur (cracked wheat)
¾   cup cold water
⅓   cup chopped green onions (with tops)
¼   teaspoon salt
¼   teaspoon ground sage
⅛   teaspoon pepper
8   chicken drumsticks (about 2 pounds)
2   tablespoons margarine or butter
2   tablespoons vegetable oil
½   cup whole wheat or all-purpose flour
1   teaspoon paprika
½   teaspoon salt
¼   teaspoon ground sage
¼   teaspoon pepper

Cover bulgur with cold water. Let stand 1 hour. Mix bulgur, onions, ¼ teaspoon salt, ¼ teaspoon sage and ⅛ teaspoon pepper. Carefully separate skin from meat all around each chicken drumstick, beginning at wide end. Fill opening with wheat mixture. Wipe off excess filling on outside of drumstick. Heat margarine and oil in rectangular pan, 13 × 9 × 2 inches, in 375° oven until margarine is melted. Mix remaining ingredients. Coat drumsticks with flour mixture; place in pan. Bake uncovered 30 minutes. Turn drumsticks; bake until done, about 30 minutes longer.   **4 servings; 505 calories per serving.**

Stir-fried Asparagus (page 617), Waldorf Salad (page 540) and fruit and cookies for dessert complement this chicken dish.

CHICKEN WITH YOGURT

¼ cup sliced almonds
1 tablespoon margarine or butter
8 chicken drumsticks (about 2 pounds)
1 tablespoon margarine or butter
½ teaspoon paprika
¼ teaspoon salt
¼ teaspoon dried dill weed
⅓ cup water
1 teaspoon instant chicken bouillon
1 medium onion, sliced
½ cup plain yogurt
1½ teaspoons cornstarch
¼ cup cold water

Cook and stir almonds in 1 tablespoon margarine in 10-inch skillet over medium heat until almonds are golden brown. Remove with slotted spoon; drain and reserve.

Remove skin from chicken drumsticks. Cook drumsticks in 1 tablespoon margarine over medium heat until brown on all sides; reduce heat. Sprinkle with paprika, salt and dill weed. Mix ⅓ cup water and the bouillon (dry); pour over chicken. Add onion. Cover and simmer until drumsticks are done, about 30 minutes. Remove drumsticks; keep warm. Stir yogurt into liquid in skillet. Mix cornstarch and ¼ cup cold water; gradually stir into yogurt mixture. Heat to boiling, stirring constantly. Boil and stir 1 minute. Pour yogurt sauce over drumsticks; sprinkle with almonds. **4 servings;** 360 calories per serving.

Serve with a fresh fruit garnish and Curried Rice (page 87).

CHICKEN CURRY

⅓ cup margarine or butter
1½ teaspoons curry powder
1 small onion, coarsely chopped
1 clove garlic, chopped
¼ cup all-purpose flour
2 teaspoons sugar
½ teaspoon ground ginger
¼ teaspoon dry mustard
¼ teaspoon pepper
1 medium tomato, chopped
1 medium tart apple, chopped
4 ounces fully cooked smoked ham, chopped
¼ cup shredded coconut
2 cups chicken broth (page 557)
2 pounds chicken or turkey thighs and breasts, skinned, boned and cut into ½-inch slices
4 cups hot cooked rice (page 85)
    Desired Condiments (below)

Cook and stir margarine, curry powder, onion and garlic in 3-quart saucepan until onion is transparent. Stir in flour, sugar, ginger, mustard, pepper, tomato, apple and ham. Cook, stirring occasionally, 5 minutes. Stir in coconut and chicken broth. Heat to boiling; reduce heat. Cover and simmer, stirring occasionally, 1 hour.

Rub mixture through sieve. Return liquid to saucepan; add chicken. Heat to boiling; reduce heat. Cover and simmer until chicken is tender, 25 to 30 minutes. Serve with rice and desired Condiments. **6 servings; 390 calories per serving.**

Condiments
Shredded coconut, chopped peanuts, finely chopped hard-cooked eggs, chutney, finely chopped crystallized ginger, snipped parsley or raisins.

Shrimp Curry: Substitute 1½ pounds fresh or frozen medium shrimp (in shells), cleaned and deveined, for the chicken and Indian hot curry powder for the curry powder. Increase flour to ⅓ cup. Heat sauce to boiling; add shrimp. Heat to boiling; reduce heat. Simmer uncovered, stirring occasionally, just until shrimp is done, about 3 minutes.

OVEN CHICKEN KIEV

¼	cup margarine or butter, softened
1	tablespoon snipped chives or parsley
⅛	teaspoon garlic powder
6	small chicken breast halves (about 3 pounds)
3	cups cornflakes, crushed (about 1½ cups)
2	tablespoons snipped parsley
½	teaspoon paprika
¼	cup buttermilk or milk

Mix margarine, chives and garlic powder; shape into rectangle, 3 × 2 inches. Cover and freeze until firm, about 30 minutes.

Remove bones and skin from chicken breast halves. Flatten each chicken breast half to ¼-inch thickness between plastic wrap or waxed paper. Cut margarine mixture crosswise into 6 pieces. Place 1 piece on center of each chicken breast half. Fold long sides over margarine; fold ends up and secure with wooden pick. Mix cornflakes, parsley and paprika. Dip chicken into buttermilk; coat evenly with cornflake mixture. Place chicken, seam sides down, in greased square pan, 9 × 9 × 2 inches. Bake uncovered in 425° oven until chicken is done, about 35 minutes; remove wooden picks. **6 servings; 265 calories per serving.**

Serve with Wild Rice (page 85), Pea Pods and Peppers (page 637) and Cherries Jubilee (page 223) for a very festive dinner.

■ **Microwave Directions:** Arrange coated chicken breast halves, seam sides down, on a microwavable rack in microwavable dish. Microwave uncovered on high (100%) 4 minutes; rotate dish ½ turn. Microwave uncovered until chicken is done, 4 to 6 minutes longer. Let stand uncovered 5 minutes.

Oven Cordon Bleu: Omit margarine, chives and garlic powder. Divide 1 package (4 ounces) thinly sliced fully cooked ham and ¾ cup shredded Swiss or Gruyère cheese (3 ounces) among flattened chicken breasts.

Easy . . . CHICKEN AND PEPPERS

2   medium green peppers, cut into ¼-inch strips
1   small onion, chopped (about ¼ cup)
1   clove garlic, finely chopped
2   tablespoons vegetable oil
4   small chicken breast halves (about 2 pounds),
        boned, skinned and cut into 1-inch pieces, or
        1 pound turkey tenderloin, cut into 1-inch pieces
1   teaspoon salt
⅛   teaspoon pepper
     Lemon wedges

Cook and stir green peppers, onion and garlic in oil in 10-inch skillet over medium-high heat until peppers are almost tender, about 5 minutes. Add chicken, salt and pepper. Cook and stir until chicken is done, about 8 minutes. Serve with lemon wedges.   **4 servings** (1 cup each); 225 calories per serving.

Four-Cheese Fettuccine (page 94) and Carrot Casserole (page 633) complement this entrée.

Chicken Cilantro: Omit green peppers. Stir 2 tablespoons snipped cilantro into the cooked chicken.

TANDOORI-STYLE CHICKEN

8   chicken breast halves (about 4 pounds),
        skinned and boned
½   teaspoon water
¼   teaspoon dry mustard
1   cup plain yogurt
¼   cup lemon juice
1½   teaspoons salt
1½   teaspoons paprika
½   teaspoon ground cardamom
½   teaspoon each red and yellow food color, if desired
¼   teaspoon ground ginger
¼   teaspoon ground cumin
¼   teaspoon crushed dried red pepper
¼   teaspoon pepper
1   clove garlic, crushed

Place chicken in glass bowl. Mix water and mustard; stir in remaining ingredients. Pour over chicken; turn to coat well. Cover and refrigerate at least 12 hours but no longer than 24 hours. Remove chicken from marinade; place chicken in ungreased baking dish, 13 × 9 × 2 inches. Bake uncovered in 375° oven until done, about 45 minutes. **8 servings;** 130 calories per serving.

Bulgur-Tomato Salad (page 503) and poppadums are traditional accompaniments.

CHICKEN A LA KING

    1   small green pepper, chopped (about ½ cup)
    1   can (4 ounces) mushroom stems and pieces,
            drained (reserve liquid)
    ½   cup margarine or butter
    ½   cup all-purpose flour
    1   teaspoon salt
    ¼   teaspoon pepper
  1½   cups milk
  1¼   cups chicken broth (page 557)
    2   cups cut-up cooked chicken
    1   jar (2 ounces) chopped pimientos, drained
        Corn Bread (page 54), Popovers (page 52)
            or Baking Powder Biscuits (page 42)

Cook and stir green pepper and mushrooms in margarine in 3-quart saucepan over medium heat 5 minutes. Stir in flour, salt and pepper. Cook over low heat, stirring constantly, until bubbly; remove from heat. Stir in milk, broth and reserved mushroom liquid. Heat to boiling, stirring constantly. Boil and stir 1 minute. Stir in chicken and pimientos; heat until hot. Serve over Corn Bread. **6 servings;** 455 calories per serving.

A friendly family entrée to serve with Peas and Onions (page 653).

CHICKEN TOSTADAS

6   six-inch tostada shells
1   can (16 ounces) refried beans
1½   cups cut-up cooked chicken or turkey
1   teaspoon chili powder
½   teaspoon dried oregano leaves
½   teaspoon salt
¼   teaspoon ground cumin
1   can (8 ounces) tomato sauce
1   medium avocado
     Lemon juice
¾   cup shredded Cheddar or Monterey Jack cheese
2   medium tomatoes, sliced
3   cups shredded lettuce
     Dairy sour cream
     Hot taco sauce

Heat tostada shells as directed on package. Heat beans over
medium heat until hot. Heat chicken, chili powder, oregano,
salt, cumin and tomato sauce until hot. Peel and cut avocado
lengthwise into slices; sprinkle with lemon juice.

Spread about ¼ cup of the beans on each tostada shell;
spread with about ¼ cup chicken mixture. Sprinkle 2 tablespoons cheese over each. Arrange tomato and avocado slices
and lettuce on top. Serve with sour cream and taco sauce.   6
tostadas; 320 calories per tostada.

Fruit Ambrosia (page 224) will complete this light meal.

Easy . . . MACARONI CASSEROLE

1½   cups cut-up cooked chicken or turkey
1   cup shredded Cheddar cheese (4 ounces)
1   cup milk
½   teaspoon salt
½   teaspoon curry powder
1   can (10¾ ounces) condensed cream of chicken soup
1   package (7 ounces) elbow macaroni
1   can (4 ounces) mushroom stems and pieces, undrained
1   jar (2 ounces) diced pimientos

Mix all ingredients in ungreased 1½-quart casserole or rectangular baking dish, 10×6×1½ inches. Cover and bake in 350° oven until macaroni is tender, 55 to 60 minutes. **5 servings;** 405 calories per serving.

Carrot-Raisin Salad (page 519) is a familiar accompaniment for this casserole.

■ **Microwave Directions:** Mix all ingredients in 3-quart microwavable casserole. Cover tightly and microwave on high (100%), stirring every 6 minutes, until macaroni is tender, 15 to 18 minutes. Let stand covered 5 minutes.

Easy . . . CHICKEN-PASTA PRIMAVERA

1	cup chopped broccoli
⅓	cup chopped onion
2	cloves garlic, finely chopped
1	carrot, cut into very thin strips
3	tablespoons vegetable oil
2	cups cut-up cooked chicken or turkey
1	teaspoon salt
2	medium tomatoes, chopped
4	cups hot cooked macaroni shells or wheels (page 91)
⅓	cup freshly grated Parmesan cheese
2	tablespoons snipped parsley

Cook and stir broccoli, onion, garlic and carrot in oil in 10-inch skillet over medium heat until broccoli is crisp-tender, about 10 minutes. Stir in chicken, salt and tomatoes; heat just until chicken is hot, about 3 minutes. Spoon chicken mixture over macaroni; sprinkle with cheese and parsley. **6 servings;** 290 calories per serving.

Try this pasta dish with Soft Breadsticks (page 64) and Mushrooms and Cucumbers (page 646).

Easy . . . DINNER CASSEROLE

1   package (10 ounces) frozen peas and carrots
1   can (10¾ ounces) condensed cream of chicken soup
1   can (8 ounces) small whole onions, drained
1   can (4 ounces) mushroom stems and pieces, undrained
2   cups cut-up cooked chicken or turkey
1   cup crushed potato chips

Rinse frozen peas and carrots under running cold water to separate; drain. Mix peas and carrots and remaining ingredients except chips in ungreased 2-quart casserole or square baking dish, 8×8×2 inches. Sprinkle with chips. Bake uncovered in 350° oven until hot and bubbly, 35 to 40 minutes. **6 servings; 185 calories per serving.**

This meal-in-a-dish needs only a crisp salad and hard rolls to be complete.

■ **Microwave Directions:** Mix all ingredients except chips in 2-quart microwavable casserole. Cover tightly; microwave on high (100%) 5 minutes; stir. Cover tightly and microwave until hot, 5 to 7 minutes longer. Sprinkle with chips.

Easy . . . CHICKEN-RICE SUPPER

¼   cup margarine or butter
⅓   cup all-purpose flour
1½   teaspoons salt
⅛   teaspoon pepper
1½   cups milk
1   cup chicken broth (page 557)
2   cups cut-up cooked chicken or turkey
1½   cups cooked white rice or wild rice (page 85)
⅓   cup chopped green pepper
¼   cup slivered almonds
2   tablespoons chopped pimiento
1   can (4 ounces) mushroom stems and pieces, drained

Heat margarine in 2-quart saucepan until melted. Stir in flour, salt and pepper. Cook over low heat, stirring constantly, until bubbly; remove from heat. Stir in milk and broth. Heat to boiling, stirring constantly. Boil and stir 1 minute. Stir in remaining ingredients. Pour into ungreased 2-quart casserole or rectangular baking dish, 10 × 6 × 1½ inches. Bake uncovered in 350° oven until bubbly, 40 to 45 minutes. Garnish with parsley if desired.   **6 servings; 315 calories per serving.**

Mandarin Salad (page 512) is a crisp, colorful accompaniment for this casserole.

■ **Microwave Directions:** Microwave margarine uncovered in 2-cup microwavable measure on high (100%) until melted, about 45 seconds. Stir in flour, salt and pepper. Cover and microwave until hot and bubbly, 45 to 60 seconds. Decrease milk to ½ cup. Stir milk and broth into margarine mixture. Cover and microwave 4 minutes; stir. Cover and microwave 2 minutes longer. Pour into 2-quart microwavable casserole. Stir in remaining ingredients. Cover and microwave on high (100%) until hot and bubbly, about 5 minutes.

TURKEY POT PIE

1	package (10 ounces) frozen peas and carrots
⅓	cup margarine or butter
⅓	cup all-purpose flour
⅓	cup chopped onion
½	teaspoon salt
¼	teaspoon pepper
1¾	cups turkey or chicken broth
⅔	cup milk
2½	to 3 cups cut-up cooked turkey or chicken
	Pastry for 9-inch Two-Crust Pie (page 135)

Rinse frozen peas and carrots under running cold water to separate; drain. Heat margarine in 2-quart saucepan over low heat until melted. Stir in flour, onion, salt and pepper. Cook, stirring constantly, until mixture is bubbly; remove from heat. Stir in broth and milk. Heat to boiling, stirring constantly. Boil and stir 1 minute. Stir in turkey and vegetables.

Prepare pastry. Roll ⅔ of the pastry into 13-inch square; ease into ungreased square pan, 9 × 9 × 2 inches. Pour turkey mixture into pastry-lined pan. Roll remaining pastry into 11-inch square; cut out designs with small cookie cutter. Place square over filling; turn edges under and flute. Bake in 425° oven until golden brown, about 35 minutes.   **6 servings; 645 calories per serving.**

The old-fashioned goodness of this dish would be enhanced by the addition of Apple-Cherry Salad (page 530) and Cranberry Ice (page 264).

Easy . . . IMPOSSIBLE TURKEY PIE

- 2 **cups cut-up cooked turkey or chicken**
- 1 **jar (4½ ounces) sliced mushrooms, drained**
- ½ **cup sliced green onions (with tops)**
- ½ **teaspoon salt**
- 1 **cup shredded natural Swiss cheese (4 ounces)**
- 1½ **cups milk**
- ¾ **cup buttermilk baking mix**
- 3 **eggs**

Heat oven to 400°. Grease pie plate, 10 × 1½ inches. Sprinkle turkey, mushrooms, onions, salt and cheese in pie plate. Beat remaining ingredients until smooth, 15 seconds in blender on high speed or 1 minute with hand beater. Pour into pie plate. Bake until golden brown and knife inserted halfway between center and edge comes out clean, 30 to 35 minutes. Let stand 5 minutes before cutting.   **7 servings; 145 calories per serving.**

Finish this light meal with Mixed Vegetable Salad (page 518) and Poached Plums (page 232).

Impossible Ham Pie: Substitute 2 cups cut-up fully cooked smoked ham for the turkey.

Easy . . . TURKEY DIVAN

¼ cup margarine or butter
¼ cup all-purpose flour
½ teaspoon salt
2 cups chicken broth (page 557)
2 tablespoons dry white wine
⅛ teaspoon ground nutmeg
1½ pounds broccoli, cooked and drained, or 2 packages (10 ounces each) frozen broccoli spears, cooked and drained
5 large slices cooked turkey or
    chicken breast meat (about ¾ pound)
½ cup grated Parmesan cheese

Heat margarine in 2-quart saucepan until melted. Stir in flour and salt. Cook over medium heat, stirring constantly, until bubbly; remove from heat. Stir in broth. Heat to boiling, stirring constantly. Boil and stir 1 minute; remove from heat. Stir in wine and nutmeg.

Place hot broccoli in ungreased rectangular baking dish, 12 × 7½ × 2 inches; top with turkey. Pour sauce over turkey; sprinkle with cheese.

Set oven control to broil and/or 550°. Broil with top 3 to 5 inches from heat until cheese is golden brown, about 2 minutes. **5 servings; 290 calories per serving.**

For a summer supper, serve with Summer Fruit Salad (page 536).

ABOUT TURKEY

Whole ready-to-cook turkeys range in size from 4 to 24 pounds. Quality does not vary between fresh and frozen. Turkey halves, quarters, pieces and breast roasts are available. Boneless rolled turkey roasts, ground raw turkey, fresh turkey tenderloins, breast slices and drumstick steaks are popular convenience items.

ROAST TURKEY

Rub cavity of turkey lightly with salt if desired. Do not salt cavity if turkey is to be stuffed. Stuff just before roasting—not ahead of time. (See Rice Stuffing and Bread Stuffing, pages 471 and 472.) Fill wishbone area with stuffing. Fasten neck skin to back with skewer. Fold wings across back with tips touching. Fill body cavity lightly. (Do not pack—stuffing will expand.) Tuck drumsticks under band of skin at tail or tie or skewer to tail.

Place breast side up on rack in shallow roasting pan. Brush with shortening, vegetable oil or melted margarine or butter. Insert meat thermometer so tip is in thickest part of inside thigh muscle or thickest part of breast meat and does not touch bone. Do not add water. Do not cover. Roast in 325° oven. Follow Timetable (below) for approximate total cooking time. Place a tent of aluminum foil loosely over turkey when it begins to turn golden. When ⅔ done, cut band or remove skewer holding legs.

TIMETABLE FOR ROASTING TURKEY

Ready-to-Cook Weight	Approximate Total Cooking Time	Internal Temperature (°F)
6 to 8 pounds	3 to 3½ hours	185°
8 to 12 pounds	3½ to 4½ hours	185°
12 to 16 pounds	4½ to 5½ hours	185°
16 to 20 pounds	5½ to 6½ hours	185°
20 to 24 pounds	6½ to 7 hours	185°

This timetable is based on chilled or completely thawed stuffed turkeys at a temperature of about 40°. Time will be slightly less for unstuffed turkeys. Differences in the shape and tenderness of individual turkeys can also necessitate increasing or decreasing the cooking time slightly. For best results, use a meat thermometer. For prestuffed turkeys, follow package directions very carefully; do not use Timetable.

There is no substitute for a meat thermometer for determining the doneness of a turkey. Placed in thigh muscle, it should register 185° when turkey is done. If turkey is stuffed, the thermometer point can be inserted in center of stuffing and will register 165° when done. If meat thermometer is not used, test for doneness about 30 minutes before Timetable so indicates. Move drumstick up and down—if done, the joint should give readily or break. Or press drumstick meat between fingers; meat should be very soft.

When turkey is done, remove from oven and let stand about 20 minutes for easiest carving. If desired, prepare Pan Gravy (page 358). As soon as possible after serving, remove every bit of stuffing from turkey. Cool stuffing, turkey meat and any gravy promptly; refrigerate separately. Use gravy or stuffing within 1 or 2 days; heat thoroughly before serving. Serve cooked turkey meat within 2 or 3 days after roasting. (If frozen, it can be kept up to 3 weeks.)

NOTE: When buying turkeys under 12 pounds, allow about ¾ pound per serving. For heavier turkeys (12 pounds and over), allow about ½ pound per serving.

HALVES AND QUARTERS

Prepare half and quarter turkey according to basic directions for whole turkey except—skewer skin to meat along cut edges to prevent shrinking during roasting. Place skin side up on rack in shallow roasting pan. Insert meat thermometer so tip is in thickest part of thigh muscle or breast meat and does not touch bone.

TIMETABLE FOR ROASTING HALVES AND QUARTERS

Ready-to-Cook Weight	Approximate Total Cooking Time	Internal Temperature (°F)
5 to 8 pounds	2½ to 3 hours	185°
8 to 10 pounds	3 to 3½ hours	185°
10 to 12 pounds	3½ to 4 hours	185°

RICE STUFFING

⅔   cup uncooked regular rice
1   medium stalk celery, chopped (about ½ cup)
1   small onion, chopped (about ¼ cup)
2   tablespoons margarine or butter
½   teaspoon salt
⅛   teaspoon pepper
½   cup chopped walnuts
⅓   cup raisins
¼   teaspoon paprika
4   slices bacon, crisply cooked and crumbled

Cook rice as directed on page 85. Cook celery, onion, margarine, salt and pepper in 10-inch skillet until celery is tender; remove from heat. Stir in rice, walnuts, raisins, paprika and bacon.   **4 cups stuffing; 325 calories per ½ cup.**

Fruited Rice Stuffing: Omit raisins. Stir in ⅓ cup cut-up prunes and ⅓ cup cut-up dried apricots.

NOTE: Allow ¾ cup stuffing for each pound of poultry. A 1- to 1¼-pound Rock Cornish hen requires about 1 cup stuffing. Allow ¼ to ⅓ cup stuffing for each rib pork chop and about ½ cup per pound of dressed fish. Stuff poultry, pork or fish just before cooking.

CARVING TURKEY OR CHICKEN

Gently pulling leg away from body, cut through joint between thigh and body. Remove leg. Cut between drumstick and thigh; slice off meat. Make a deep horizontal cut into breast just above wing. Insert fork in top of breast and, starting halfway up breast, carve thin slices down to the cut, working upward. (To carve duckling, cut into quarters or halves with kitchen scissors.)

BREAD STUFFING

1½   cups chopped celery (with leaves)
¾   cup finely chopped onion
¾   cup margarine or butter
9   cups soft bread cubes
1   teaspoon salt
½   teaspoon ground sage
½   teaspoon dried thyme leaves
¼   teaspoon pepper

Cook and stir celery and onion in margarine in Dutch oven until celery is tender; remove from heat. Stir in remaining ingredients. **5 cups stuffing; 410 calories per cup.**

Apple-Raisin Stuffing: Increase salt to 1½ teaspoons. Add 3 cups finely chopped apples and ¾ cup raisins with the remaining ingredients.

Casserole Stuffing: Place stuffing in ungreased 2-quart casserole. Cover and bake in 375° oven until hot and bubbly, about 30 minutes.

Corn Bread Stuffing: Substitute corn bread cubes for the soft bread cubes.

Giblet Stuffing: Simmer heart, gizzard and neck from chicken or turkey in seasoned water until tender, 1 to 2 hours. Add the liver during the last 5 to 15 minutes of cooking. Drain giblets; chop and add with the remaining ingredients.

Mushroom Stuffing: Cook and stir 2 cups sliced mushrooms with the celery and onion.

Oyster Stuffing: Add 2 cans (8 ounces each) oysters, drained and chopped, with the remaining ingredients.

Sausage Stuffing: Omit salt. Add 1 pound bulk pork sausage, crumbled and browned, with the remaining ingredients. Substitute sausage drippings for part of the margarine.

Vegetable Stuffing: Increase celery to 2 cups. Add 2 cups shredded carrots, 1 cup snipped parsley and 1 tablespoon lemon juice with the remaining ingredients.

NOTE: Allow ¾ cup stuffing for each pound of poultry. A 1- to 1¼-pound Rock Cornish hen requires about 1 cup stuffing. Allow ¼ to ⅓ cup stuffing for each rib pork chop and about ½ cup per pound of dressed fish. Stuff poultry, pork or fish just before cooking.

Easy . . . TURKEY WITH PINEAPPLE

4½-	to 5-pound turkey breast
1	pineapple
½	cup dry white wine
2	tablespoons honey
2	tablespoons soy sauce
1	teaspoon finely chopped gingerroot or ½ teaspoon ground ginger
1	large clove garlic, finely chopped
2	teaspoons cornstarch
2	tablespoons cold water

Place turkey breast, skin side up, on rack in shallow roasting pan. Insert meat thermometer so tip is in thickest part of meat and does not touch bone. Roast uncovered in 325° oven 1 hour.

Pare pineapple; cut lengthwise into halves. Remove core; cut each half crosswise into 8 slices.

Mix wine, honey, soy sauce, gingerroot and garlic. Arrange pineapple on rack around turkey. Brush turkey and pineapple with wine mixture. Roast uncovered, brushing turkey and pineapple frequently with wine mixture, until thermometer registers 185°, about 1 hour longer. Remove turkey and pineapple; keep warm.

Pour drippings into measuring cup; skim off any excess fat. Add enough water to drippings to measure 1 cup. Heat drippings to boiling in 1-quart saucepan. Mix cornstarch and cold water; stir into drippings. Boil and stir 1 minute. Serve with turkey.   **16 servings** (about 3 ounces turkey and 1 slice pineapple each); 190 calories per serving.

Flavorful accompaniments are Twice-baked Yams (page 669) and Brussels sprouts.

Easy . . . TURKEY MEATBALLS

1	pound ground raw turkey
¼	cup buttermilk baking mix
¼	cup chopped onion
¼	cup grated Parmesan cheese
¼	teaspoon garlic salt
⅛	teaspoon ground allspice
1	bottle (12 ounces) chili sauce

Heat oven to 400°. Grease bottom of jelly roll pan, 15½ × 10½ × 1 inch. Mix all ingredients except chili sauce. Shape into about twenty 1½-inch balls (for ease in shaping meatballs, wet hands slightly). Bake until brown, 15 to 20 minutes; drain. Heat chili sauce until hot. Serve with meatballs.   **5 servings** (4 meatballs each); 265 calories per serving.

Try with Rigatoni and Tomatoes (page 98), green beans and Pineapple Crisp (pages 220 and 221).

PHEASANT AND GRAVY

1 pheasant, cut into quarters
⅓ cup chopped onion
½ cup apple cider
1 tablespoon plus 1 teaspoon Worcestershire sauce
¾ teaspoon salt
1 clove garlic, finely chopped
1 can (10¾ ounces) condensed cream of chicken soup
1 can (4 ounces) mushroom stems and pieces, drained
   Paprika

Place pheasant in ungreased square baking dish, 9×9×2 inches. Mix remaining ingredients except paprika; pour over pheasant. Generously sprinkle with paprika.

Bake uncovered in 350° oven, spooning sauce onto pheasant occasionally, until done, 1½ to 2 hours. After baking pheasant 1 hour, generously sprinkle again with paprika. **2 servings;** 740 calories per serving.

Parsley Rice (page 85) is a natural accompaniment for pheasant.

Chicken and Brown Gravy: Substitute a 2- to 2½-pound broiler-fryer chicken, cut into quarters, for the pheasant. Bake until done, about 1½ hours. **4 servings.**

CORNISH HENS WITH GLAZED ORANGES

3 Rock Cornish hens (about 1½ pounds each)
2 tablespoons margarine or butter, melted
   Glazed Oranges (page 476)
½ cup orange juice
1 tablespoon honey
½ teaspoon salt
¼ teaspoon dry mustard
⅛ teaspoon paprika

Place hens, breast sides up, on rack in shallow roasting pan; brush with margarine. Roast uncovered in 350° oven 30 minutes.

Prepare Glazed Oranges. Mix remaining ingredients; brush half of the orange juice mixture over hens. Roast uncovered, brushing with remaining orange juice mixture, until hens are done, about 45 minutes longer. Cut each hen along backbone from tail to neck into halves with kitchen scissors. Serve with Glazed Oranges. **6 servings; 325 calories per serving.**

Try Spinach Tossed Salad (page 506), Herbed Green Beans (page 618), Individual Brioches (page 67) and Caramel Custard (page 248) for an elegant meal.

Glazed Oranges

    3   medium oranges
    2   tablespoons margarine or butter
  ¼   cup light corn syrup
    1   tablespoon honey

Cut off ends of oranges; cut each orange into ⅛-inch slices. Heat margarine in 12-inch skillet over medium heat until melted. Stir in corn syrup and honey. Heat to boiling; add oranges and reduce heat. Simmer uncovered, spooning sauce frequently over oranges, until oranges are tender and glazed, about 25 minutes.

STEWED RABBIT

  ⅓   cup all-purpose flour
  ½   teaspoon salt
  ¼   teaspoon pepper
2½-   to 3-pound domestic rabbit or 2 wild rabbits, cut up
    6   slices bacon, cut up
    1   large onion, sliced
    2   medium carrots, cut crosswise into ½-inch slices
    2   medium cloves garlic, crushed
    1   bay leaf
1¼   cups water
  ¾   cup dry red wine
    1   tablespoon packed brown sugar
  ½   teaspoon salt
  ½   teaspoon dried rosemary leaves
  ½   teaspoon paprika
    1   tablespoon cornstarch
    2   tablespoons cold water

Mix flour, ½ teaspoon salt and the pepper. Coat rabbit with flour mixture. Cook bacon in Dutch oven until crisp; drain and crumble. Drain fat, reserving 2 tablespoons in Dutch oven. Cook rabbit in hot fat over medium heat, turning occasionally, until brown. Add onion, carrots, garlic, bacon and bay leaf. Mix 1¼ cups water, the wine, brown sugar, ½ teaspoon salt, the rosemary and paprika; pour over rabbit. Heat to boiling; reduce heat. Cover and simmer until rabbit is tender, 1 to 1½ hours. Remove bay leaf.

Remove rabbit and vegetables; keep warm. Mix cornstarch and 2 tablespoons cold water; stir into liquid in Dutch oven. Heat to boiling, stirring constantly. Boil and stir 1 minute. Pour sauce over rabbit and vegetables.   **6 servings;** 380 calories per serving.

VENISON SAUERBRATEN

3-	to 3½-pound venison chuck roast
2	onions, sliced
2	bay leaves
12	peppercorns
12	juniper berries, if desired
6	whole cloves
1½	cups red wine vinegar
1	cup boiling water
2	teaspoons salt
2	tablespoons shortening
12	gingersnaps, crushed (about ¾ cup)
2	teaspoons sugar

Place venison roast in glass or earthenware bowl or baking dish with onions, bay leaves, peppercorns, berries, cloves, vinegar, boiling water and salt. Cover tightly and refrigerate, turning venison twice a day, at least 3 days. Never pierce when turning.

Remove venison from marinade; reserve marinade. Cook venison in shortening in heavy skillet until brown on all sides. Add the marinade mixture. Heat to boiling; reduce heat. Cover and simmer until venison is tender, 3 to 3½ hours. Remove venison and onions from skillet; keep warm.

Strain and measure liquid in skillet. Add enough water to liquid, if necessary, to measure 2½ cups. Pour liquid into skillet. Cover and simmer 10 minutes. Stir gingersnaps and sugar into liquid. Cover and simmer 3 minutes. Serve venison and onions with gravy.　**10 servings; 235 calories per serving.**

Baked potatoes and Citrus Salad (page 532) are suggested serve-withs.

SALADS

MAIN DISH SALADS

ORIENTAL CHICKEN SALAD

    Ginger Dressing (below)
    Vegetable oil
1   package (3¾ ounces) cellophane noodles (bean threads)*
½   head lettuce, shredded (about 4 cups)
3   cups cut-up cooked chicken or turkey
1   medium carrot, shredded (about ½ cup)
¼   cup sliced green onions (with tops)
1   tablespoon toasted sesame seed

Prepare Ginger Dressing. Heat oil (1 inch) in Dutch oven to 425°. Fry ¼ of the noodles at a time, turning once, until puffed, about 5 seconds; drain.

Pour Ginger Dressing over lettuce, chicken, carrot and onions in 4-quart bowl. Toss with half of the noodles. Spoon salad over remaining noodles; sprinkle with sesame seed. **6 servings; 315 calories per serving.**

Ginger Dressing

⅓   cup vegetable oil
¼   cup white wine vinegar
1   tablespoon sugar
2   teaspoons soy sauce
½   teaspoon salt
½   teaspoon pepper
½   teaspoon ground ginger

*5 cups chow mein noodles can be substituted for the fried cellophane noodles; toss half of the noodles with chicken-dressing mixture; continue as directed.

Shake all ingredients in tightly covered container. Refrigerate at least 2 hours.

Do-ahead Tip: Cellophane noodles can be fried as directed and stored in airtight container at room temperature no longer than 5 days.

MARINATED CHICKEN SALAD

6 small chicken breast halves (about 2 pounds)
2 tablespoons margarine or butter
1 tablespoon vegetable oil
2 tablespoons soy sauce
1 tablespoon toasted sesame seed
1 tablespoon lemon juice
1 clove garlic, crushed
1 small head iceberg lettuce, shredded (about 6 cups)
2 medium tomatoes, chopped (about 2 cups)
2 green onions, sliced
2 cups sliced medium mushrooms
1 package (6 ounces) frozen Chinese pea pods, thawed
   Classic French Dressing (page 548)

Remove skin and bones from chicken. Cook chicken in margarine and oil in 10-inch skillet over medium heat until done, about 6 minutes on each side; cool slightly. Cut into thin slices. Mix soy sauce, sesame seed, lemon juice and garlic; toss with chicken. Cover and refrigerate at least 4 hours.

Mix lettuce and tomatoes; spoon onto serving platter or divide among 6 individual plates. Arrange chicken on top; sprinkle with green onions. Arrange mushroom slices and pea pods around lettuce mixture. Serve with Classic French Dressing. **6 servings; 400 calories per serving.**

CLUB SALADS

10   cups bite-size pieces salad greens
 4   medium tomatoes, sliced
 2   cups ¼-inch strips cooked chicken or
         turkey (about 8 ounces)
 ¾   cup Thousand Island Dressing (page 551) or
         bottled Thousand Island dressing
 4   slices bacon, crisply cooked and crumbled
 4   slices buttered toast, cut into fourths

Divide salad greens among 4 salad plates; top with tomatoes
and chicken. Spoon dressing over top; sprinkle with bacon.
Garnish with toast points.   4 servings; 450 calories per
serving.

CHICKEN SALAD

 ½   cup mayonnaise or salad dressing
 1   tablespoon lemon juice
 ½   teaspoon salt
 ¼   teaspoon pepper
 2   cups cut-up cooked chicken or turkey
 ⅓   cup toasted slivered almonds or chopped nuts
 2   medium stalks celery, sliced (about 1 cup)

Mix mayonnaise, lemon juice, salt and pepper; toss with
chicken, almonds and celery. Cover and refrigerate at least 3
hours. Serve on salad greens garnished with avocado slices or
in cantaloupe halves if desired.   4 servings (¾ cup each); 400
calories per serving.

Chicken-Bacon Salad: Stir 4 slices bacon, crisply cooked
and crumbled, into salad just before serving.

Fruited Chicken Salad: Stir 1 cup seedless grapes or 1 can
(11 ounces) mandarin orange segments, drained, into salad
just before serving.

Seafood Salad: Substitute 2 cups mixed cooked canned or
frozen (thawed) seafood (crabmeat, lobster, shrimp, scallops)
for the chicken.

Tuna Salad: Decrease mayonnaise to ⅓ cup and salt to ¼
teaspoon. Substitute 2 cans (6¼ ounces each) tuna, drained,
for the chicken.

Stuffed Tomatoes: Cut stem ends from 4 chilled medium tomatoes. Place tomatoes cut side down; cut each into sixths to within 1 inch of bottom. Carefully spread out sections. Spoon about ½ cup salad into each tomato.

CHICKEN SALAD CUPS

	Chicken-Almond Salad (below)
1	cup water
½	cup margarine or butter
1	cup all-purpose flour
¼	teaspoon salt
4	eggs

Prepare Chicken-Almond Salad. Heat oven to 400°. Grease 12 medium muffin cups, 2½ × 1¼ inches. Heat water and margarine to rolling boil in 2-quart saucepan; stir in flour and salt. Stir vigorously over low heat until mixture forms a ball, about 30 seconds; remove from heat. Cool 10 minutes. Beat in eggs, all at once; continue beating until smooth. Spread 2 rounded tablespoonfuls dough in bottom and up side of each muffin cup. Bake until puffed and dry in center, about 30 minutes. Immediately remove from pan; cool.

Just before serving, fill each with about ¼ cup chicken salad. **6 servings; 560 calories per serving.**

Chicken-Almond Salad

2	cups cut-up cooked chicken or turkey
1	cup chopped celery
½	cup slivered almonds
½	cup mayonnaise or salad dressing
1	tablespoon lemon juice
1	teaspoon salt
¼	teaspoon pepper
1	jar (2 ounces) sliced pimientos, drained

Mix all ingredients; refrigerate until chilled, at least 1½ hours.

NOTE: Twelve greased 6-ounce custard cups can be substituted for the muffin pan. Increase chicken to 3 cups. Spread dough in bottom and 1 inch up side of each cup. Place cups in jelly roll pan, 15½ × 10½ × 1 inch. Continue as directed.

CURRIED CHICKEN SALAD

- 3 cups cold cooked rice (page 85)
- 2 cups cut-up cooked chicken or turkey
- 1 cup sliced celery
- ½ cup chopped green pepper
- 1 can (13¼ ounces) pineapple chunks in syrup, drained
- 1 cup mayonnaise or salad dressing
- ¾ teaspoon curry powder
- ¼ teaspoon salt
- ¼ teaspoon ground ginger
  Salad greens
- 2 medium tomatoes, cut into wedges
- 6 slices bacon, crisply cooked and crumbled

Mix rice, chicken, celery, green pepper and pineapple. Mix mayonnaise, curry powder, salt and ginger; stir into chicken mixture. Refrigerate until chilled, at least 2 hours.

Just before serving, spoon chicken mixture onto salad greens. Garnish with tomato wedges; sprinkle with bacon. **6 servings; 525 calories per serving.**

TURKEY-VEGETABLE SALADS

- 3 cups cut-up cooked turkey or chicken
- 8 slices bacon, crisply cooked and crumbled
- ½ small head cauliflower, separated into tiny flowerets (about 2 cups)
- ¼ cup sliced radishes
- ⅓ cup plain yogurt
- 2 tablespoons mayonnaise or salad dressing
- 1 green onion (with top), sliced
- ¼ teaspoon dried dill weed
- ⅛ teaspoon salt
  Dash of pepper
  Lettuce cups or leaves
- 1 medium avocado, cut into 12 slices

Mix turkey, bacon, cauliflowerets and radishes. Mix yogurt, mayonnaise, onion, dill weed, salt and pepper; toss with turkey mixture. Spoon into lettuce cups; arrange 2 avocado slices on each salad. **6 servings** (about 1 cup each); 320 calories per serving.

FRUITED TURKEY SALAD

---

    3 cups cut-up cooked turkey or chicken
   ¾ cup seedless grape halves
    2 medium stalks celery, thinly sliced (about 1 cup)
    2 green onions, thinly sliced
    1 can (11 ounces) mandarin orange segments, drained
    1 can (8 ounces) water chestnuts, drained and sliced
    1 carton (6 ounces) lemon, peach or
          orange yogurt (about ⅔ cup)
    2 tablespoons soy sauce

Mix turkey, grapes, celery, onions, orange segments and water chestnuts. Mix yogurt and soy sauce. Pour over turkey mixture; toss. Cover and refrigerate at least 2 hours. **6 servings**; 215 calories per serving.

TURKEY-FRUIT SALAD

       Honey Dressing (page 487)
    3 cups cut-up cooked turkey or chicken
  1½ cups seedless grapes
   ¼ cup sliced green onions (with tops)
   ¼ cup chopped green pepper
    1 can (8 ounces) water chestnuts, drained and chopped
    2 oranges, pared and sectioned
   ¼ head lettuce, torn into bite-size pieces (about 3 cups)
   ¼ cup toasted slivered almonds

Toss Honey Dressing with turkey, grapes, onions, green pepper and water chestnuts. Cover and refrigerate until chilled, at least 2 hours.

Toss turkey mixture with orange sections and lettuce. Spoon onto salad greens if desired; sprinkle with almonds. **6 servings** (about 1½ cups each); 325 calories per serving.

Honey Dressing

¼ cup vegetable oil
2 tablespoons vinegar
1 tablespoon honey
¾ teaspoon salt
Dash of pepper
4 to 6 drops red pepper sauce

Shake all ingredients in tightly covered container.

TURKEY-PASTA SALAD

Spinach Sauce (below)
2 packages (5 ounces each) spiral macaroni
3 cups cut-up cooked turkey or chicken
½ cup sliced ripe olives
1 tablespoon olive or vegetable oil
1 teaspoon vinegar
1 tablespoon pine nuts or slivered almonds

Prepare Spinach Sauce. Cook macaroni as directed on package; drain. Rinse under running cold water; drain. Toss macaroni with ½ cup Spinach Sauce. Toss turkey, olives, oil and vinegar; spoon into center of macaroni mixture. Sprinkle with pine nuts. Serve with remaining Spinach Sauce.   **6 servings** (about 1½ cups each); 410 calories per serving.

Spinach Sauce

4 cups spinach leaves
1 cup parsley sprigs
¼ cup lemon juice
3 large cloves garlic, cut into halves
½ cup grated Parmesan cheese
2 tablespoons olive or vegetable oil
1 teaspoon dried basil leaves
½ teaspoon pepper

Place half each of the spinach, parsley, lemon juice and garlic in blender container. Cover and blend on medium speed, stopping blender frequently to scrape sides, until spinach leaves are finely chopped, about 3 minutes. Repeat with remaining spinach, parsley, lemon juice and garlic. Place all spinach mixture in blender container. Add cheese, oil, basil and pepper. Cover and blend on medium speed, stopping blender frequently to scrape sides, until mixture is smooth, about 2 minutes.

MACARONI-SHRIMP SALAD

1½   cups uncooked elbow or spiral macaroni (about 6 ounces)
1   package (10 ounces) frozen green peas
1   cup shredded Cheddar cheese (4 ounces)
¾   cup mayonnaise or salad dressing
½   cup sliced green onions (with tops)
⅓   cup sweet pickle relish
½   teaspoon salt
1   stalk celery, sliced (about ½ cup)
1   can (4½ ounces) tiny shrimp, rinsed and drained
½   head iceberg lettuce, torn into bite-size pieces (about 3 cups)
6   slices bacon, crisply cooked and crumbled

Cook macaroni as directed on package. Rinse frozen peas under running cold water to separate; drain. Mix macaroni, peas and remaining ingredients except lettuce and bacon. Refrigerate until chilled, at least 4 hours.

Just before serving, toss macaroni mixture with lettuce and bacon. **6 servings; 455 calories per serving.**

Macaroni-Bologna Salad: Omit shrimp. Increase cheese to 2 cups. Substitute 1 cup cut-up bologna (about 4 ounces) for the bacon.

Macaroni-Cheese Salad: Omit shrimp. Increase cheese to 2 cups.

Macaroni-Chicken Salad: Substitute ½ cup cut-up cooked chicken or turkey for the shrimp.

Macaroni-Frank Salad: Omit shrimp. Increase cheese to 2 cups. Substitute 3 frankfurters, sliced, for the bacon.

CURRIED SHRIMP SALAD

 Curry Dressing (below)
8 cups bite-size pieces Bibb lettuce
¼ cup coarsely chopped red onion
1 pound small shrimp, cooked and cleaned
1 can (11 ounces) mandarin orange segments, drained
½ green pepper, thinly sliced

Toss all ingredients. **6 servings; 190 calories per serving.**

Curry Dressing
⅓ cup vegetable oil
1 tablespoon vinegar
1 teaspoon curry powder
1 teaspoon sugar
½ teaspoon salt
1 small clove garlic, crushed

Shake all ingredients in tightly covered container.

SEAFOOD-WILD RICE SALAD

½ cup mayonnaise or salad dressing
1 tablespoon lemon juice
1 teaspoon curry powder
2 cups cold cooked wild rice (page 85)
½ cup frozen green peas, thawed
2 tablespoons chopped pimiento
2 packages (6 ounces each) frozen crabmeat, thawed, drained and cartilage removed
2 cans (4½ ounces each) medium shrimp, rinsed and drained
 Salad greens
 Cherry tomatoes or tomato wedges

Mix mayonnaise, lemon juice and curry powder in 2½-quart bowl. Add wild rice, peas, pimiento, crabmeat and shrimp; toss. Cover and refrigerate at least 1 hour.

 Spoon onto salad greens; garnish with cherry tomatoes. **5 servings; 340 calories per serving.**

 Chicken-Wild Rice Salad: Substitute 3 cups cut-up cooked chicken or turkey for the crabmeat and shrimp.

SEAFOOD-STUFFED SHELLS

15 uncooked jumbo macaroni shells
2   cups creamed cottage cheese (small curd)
¼   cup plus 2 tablespoons milk
1   tablespoon lemon juice
1   teaspoon salt
⅛   teaspoon pepper
½   cup parsley sprigs
½   teaspoon dried basil leaves
2   cloves garlic, crushed
2   medium stalks celery, sliced (about 1 cup)
1   medium zucchini, coarsely shredded
1   medium onion, chopped (about ½ cup)
6   seafood legs, cut into ½-inch pieces
2   cans (4½ ounces each) large shrimp, rinsed and drained
    Salad greens

Prepare macaroni shells as directed on package; refrigerate at least 1 hour.

Place cottage cheese, milk, lemon juice, salt and pepper in blender container. Cover and blend on high speed, stopping blender occasionally to scrape sides, until smooth, about 2 minutes. Remove ½ cup; reserve. Add parsley, basil and garlic to remaining mixture in blender container. Cover and blend on high speed until smooth, about 45 seconds; refrigerate.

Mix celery, zucchini, onion, seafood legs, shrimp and reserved ½ cup cottage cheese mixture. Spoon into macaroni shells. Refrigerate at least 1 hour.

Place stuffed shells on salad greens; serve parsley mixture with shells. (If parsley mixture is too thick, stir in additional milk until of desired consistency.) **5 servings;** 300 calories per serving.

SMOKED FISH SALAD

2   pounds new potatoes (about 16 small)
2   cartons (6 ounces each) lemon yogurt (about 1⅓ cups)
1   jar (2 ounces) diced pimientos, drained
2   teaspoons snipped dill weed or ½ teaspoon dried dill
    weed
1   teaspoon salt
1   teaspoon dry mustard
2 - pound smoked whitefish or salmon
3   medium tomatoes, sliced
1   medium onion, thinly sliced
    Salad greens

Prepare and cook potatoes as directed on page 656; cool. Cut
into ¼-inch slices. Mix yogurt, pimientos, dill weed, salt and
mustard in 4-quart glass bowl. Add potatoes; toss. Cover and
refrigerate at least 3 hours.

Remove head, skin and bones from fish. Divide fish into
serving pieces. Arrange potato mixture, fish, tomatoes and
onion on salad greens. Garnish with fresh dill weed if desired.   **8 servings; 315 calories per serving.**

FISH AND PEPPER SALAD

6   large green or red peppers
1   teaspoon salt
½   lemon, sliced
1½ pounds cod fillets
2   tomatoes, sliced
⅓   cup lemon juice
⅓   cup vegetable or olive oil
2   tablespoons snipped parsley
1¼ teaspoons salt
1   teaspoon dried basil leaves
½   teaspoon dried oregano leaves
¼   teaspoon pepper
2   large cloves garlic, finely chopped
2   green onions (with tops), chopped

Set oven control to broil and/or 550°. Broil green peppers with tops 4 to 5 inches from heat until skin is blistered and brown, about 5 minutes on each side. Wrap in towels; let stand 5 minutes. Remove skins, stems, seeds and membranes from peppers; cut peppers into ¼-inch strips.

Heat 1½ inches water, 1 teaspoon salt and the lemon slices to boiling in 12-inch skillet; reduce heat. Place fish in single layer in skillet. Heat to boiling; reduce heat. Simmer uncovered until fish flakes easily with fork, 4 to 6 minutes. Remove fish with slotted spoon; cool slightly. Separate fish into bite-size pieces.

Place pepper strips on serving platter or divide among 6 individual plates. Arrange tomato slices on peppers. Spoon fish over tomatoes. Shake remaining ingredients in tightly covered container; pour evenly over salad. Cover and refrigerate at least 4 hours. Serve with lemon wedges or slices if desired.   **6 servings; 310 calories per serving.**

TUNA-PASTA TOSS

2	cans (6½ ounces each) tuna in water, drained
2	medium tomatoes, chopped (about 1½ cups)
2	cloves garlic, crushed
1	small onion, thinly sliced and separated into rings
½	cup pitted small ripe olives
2	tablespoons snipped parsley
2	tablespoons olive or vegetable oil
½	teaspoon salt
½	teaspoon dried basil leaves
¼	teaspoon dried oregano leaves
⅛	teaspoon coarsely ground pepper
2	cups uncooked pasta bows

Mix all ingredients except pasta bows. Cover and refrigerate at least 2 hours but not longer than 24 hours.

Cook bows as directed on package; drain. Immediately toss with tuna mixture. Serve salad on lettuce leaves and garnish with anchovies if desired.   **5 servings** (about 1 cup each); 315 calories per serving.

TUNA-MACARONI SALAD

1 cup uncooked elbow or spiral macaroni
1 cup chopped cucumber
¾ cup mayonnaise or salad dressing
1 tablespoon finely chopped onion
1 tablespoon snipped parsley, if desired
½ teaspoon salt
¼ teaspoon pepper
1 can (9¾ ounces) tuna, drained
4 cups bite-size pieces salad greens

Cook macaroni as directed on package; drain. Rinse under running cold water; drain. Mix macaroni and remaining ingredients except salad greens. Cover and refrigerate at least 1 hour. Spoon onto salad greens. Garnish with tomato wedges if desired. 4 servings; 525 calories per serving.

Chicken-Macaroni Salad: Substitute 2 cups cut-up chicken or turkey for the tuna.

Salmon-Macaroni Salad: Substitute 1 can (16 ounces) salmon, drained and flaked, for the tuna.

TUNA-BEAN SALAD

3 cans (15 ounces each) cannellini beans or
    great northern beans, drained
1 jar (2 ounces) diced pimientos, drained
1 large green pepper, chopped (about 1 cup)
1 medium onion, chopped (about ½ cup)
¼ cup snipped parsley
¼ cup olive or vegetable oil
2 tablespoons lemon juice
2 tablespoons capers
½ teaspoon salt
¼ teaspoon red pepper sauce
    Lettuce leaves
1 can (6½ ounces) tuna in water, drained

Mix beans, pimientos, green pepper, onion and parsley. Shake oil, lemon juice, capers, salt and pepper sauce in tightly covered container; toss with bean mixture. Spoon onto lettuce; top with tuna. Serve with lemon wedges if desired. **5 servings** (about 1¼ cups each); 365 calories per serving.

TUNA-CANTALOUPE SALADS

  1 package (6 ounces) frozen Chinese pea pods
  2 cans (6½ ounces each) tuna, drained
  3 cups cooked rice (page 85)
  ⅓ cup mayonnaise or salad dressing
  1 teaspoon instant chicken bouillon
  ¼ teaspoon ground ginger
  3 small cantaloupes
  ⅓ cup cashew nuts or salted peanuts, coarsely chopped

Rinse frozen pea pods under running cold water to separate; drain. Mix pea pods, tuna, rice, mayonnaise, bouillon (dry) and ginger. Cover and refrigerate at least 2 hours.

Cut cantaloupes crosswise into halves; scoop out seeds. (For decorative edge on shells, cut a saw-toothed or scalloped design.) Cut thin slice from bottom of each half to prevent tipping if necessary. Spoon about 1 cup tuna mixture into each half; sprinkle with cashew nuts. **6 servings**; 465 calories per serving.

MEDITERRANEAN SALAD

  4 medium tomatoes, each cut into 3 slices
  1 red onion, thinly sliced
  1 can (14 ounces) artichoke hearts, cut into halves
     Garlic-Basil Dressing (page 495)
 18 thin slices provolone
     or mozzarella cheese (about 8 ounces)
 24 thin slices salami (about 4 ounces)
     Lettuce leaves
 18 pitted ripe olives

Place tomatoes, onion and artichoke hearts in ungreased rectangular baking dish, 11 × 7 × 1½ inches. Pour Garlic-Basil Dressing evenly over vegetables. Cover and refrigerate at least 4 hours.

Remove vegetables from dressing with slotted spoon; reserve dressing. Arrange vegetables, cheese and salami on lettuce. Garnish with olives. Serve with reserved dressing. **6 servings; 500 calories per serving.**

Garlic-Basil Dressing
- ¾ cup vegetable or olive oil
- ¼ cup vinegar
- 1 teaspoon salt
- 1 teaspoon dried basil leaves
- ⅛ teaspoon pepper
- 3 cloves garlic, crushed

Shake all ingredients in tightly covered container.

HAM-PASTA SALAD

Parmesan Dressing (page 496)
- 1 package (10 ounces) frozen chopped broccoli, cooked and drained
- 1 package (10 ounces) pasta bows, cooked and drained
- 1 pound fully cooked smoked ham, cut into julienne strips
- 1 small green pepper, chopped (about ½ cup)
- 2 tablespoons finely chopped onion

Toss all ingredients. Cover and refrigerate at least 6 hours. **6 servings; 505 calories per serving.**

Parmesan Dressing

¼	cup grated Parmesan cheese
¼	cup olive or vegetable oil
2	tablespoons snipped parsley
2	tablespoons lemon juice
2	tablespoons vinegar
1	teaspoon dry mustard
1	teaspoon dried basil leaves
¼	teaspoon dried oregano leaves
¼	teaspoon dried marjoram leaves
⅛	teaspoon pepper
1	medium clove garlic, crushed

Shake all ingredients in tightly covered container.

HAM-SWISS CHEESE SALAD

	Sesame Seed Dressing (below)
8	ounces fully cooked smoked ham, cut into cubes (about 2 cups)
4	ounces Swiss cheese, cut into ¼-inch strips
1½	cups cherry tomatoes, cut into halves
6	green onions (with tops), sliced
1	medium cucumber, thinly sliced
7	cups bite-size pieces salad greens

Mix Sesame Seed Dressing, ham, cheese, tomatoes, onions and cucumber in 4-quart bowl. Add salad greens; toss. **6 servings; 135 calories per serving.**

Sesame Seed Dressing

¼	cup vegetable oil
2	tablespoons wine vinegar
1	tablespoon toasted sesame seed
1	teaspoon salt
1	teaspoon sugar
¼	teaspoon pepper

Shake all ingredients in tightly covered container.

GLAZED HAM SALAD

Parsley Dressing (below)
2   medium stalks celery, sliced
1   medium onion, chopped
1   package (9 ounces) frozen French-style green beans,
        cooked and drained
¼   cup water
2   tablespoons Dijon-style mustard
2   tablespoons corn syrup
¼   teaspoon red pepper sauce
3   cups cut-up fully cooked smoked ham
½   cup broken walnut pieces
1   small head iceberg lettuce, torn into
        bite-size pieces (about 6 cups)
1   tart apple, cut into thin wedges

Toss Parsley Dressing with celery, onion and green beans.
Cover and refrigerate at least 3 hours.

Heat water, mustard, corn syrup and pepper sauce to
boiling in 10-inch skillet, stirring constantly. Boil and stir 1
minute. Stir in ham and walnuts until lightly glazed, about 3
minutes; cool. Arrange ham mixture and vegetables on lettuce. Garnish with apple wedges. **6 servings; 240 calories**
per serving.

Parsley Dressing
¼   cup vegetable oil
2   tablespoons snipped parsley
1   tablespoon lemon juice
2   teaspoons Dijon-style mustard
¼   teaspoon salt
⅛   teaspoon pepper

Shake all ingredients in tightly covered container.
Glazed Smoked Turkey Salad: Substitute 3 cups cut-up
fully cooked smoked turkey for the ham.

CHEF'S SALAD

½ cup ¼-inch strips cooked meat
    (beef, smoked ham or tongue)
½ cup ¼-inch strips cooked chicken or turkey
½ cup ¼-inch strips Swiss cheese
½ cup chopped green onions (with tops)
1 medium head lettuce, torn into bite-size pieces
1 small bunch romaine, torn into bite-size pieces
1 medium stalk celery, sliced (about ½ cup)
½ cup mayonnaise or salad dressing
¼ cup French Dressing (page 548)
    or bottled French dressing
2 hard-cooked eggs, sliced
2 tomatoes, cut into wedges
   Pitted ripe olives

Reserve a few strips of meat, chicken and cheese. Toss remaining meat, chicken and cheese, the onions, lettuce, romaine and celery.

Mix mayonnaise and French Dressing; pour on lettuce mixture and toss. Top with reserved meat, chicken and cheese strips, the eggs, tomatoes and olives. **5 servings; 410 calories per serving.**

BEEF-BULGUR SALAD

½ cup bulgur (cracked wheat)
2 cups bite-size pieces cooked beef
½ cup alfalfa sprouts
½ cup mayonnaise or salad dressing
½ teaspoon salt
¼ teaspoon dried sage leaves
1 medium tomato, chopped and drained (about ¾ cup)
½ medium cucumber, chopped (about ½ cup)
6 medium tomatoes

Cover bulgur with cold water. Let stand until tender, about 1 hour; drain.

Toss bulgur and remaining ingredients except whole tomatoes. Place tomatoes stem sides down; cut each into sixths almost through to bottoms. Spoon about ½ cup beef mixture into each tomato. **6 servings; 335 calories per serving.**

BEEF-EGGPLANT SALAD

     1   medium eggplant (about 1½ pounds)
    ¼   cup olive or vegetable oil
     2   tablespoons lemon juice
     1   teaspoon dried oregano leaves
    ½   teaspoon salt
    ¼   teaspoon pepper
     1   pound cold cooked roast beef, cut into julienne strips
     1   tablespoon snipped parsley
     1   medium tomato, cut into 8 wedges
     8   pitted Greek or large ripe olives

Prepare and cook eggplant, cut into ½-inch strips, as directed
on page 641. Place eggplant in glass or plastic bowl. Mix oil,
lemon juice, oregano, salt and pepper; toss with eggplant.
Cover and refrigerate at least 5 hours.

Arrange beef strips on lettuce leaves if desired; top with
eggplant. Sprinkle with parsley. Garnish with tomato wedges
and olives.   **8 servings** (about ¾ cup each); 295 calories per
serving.

VEGETABLE-BEEF SALAD

     2   pounds beef boneless sirloin steak
     1   bottle (8 ounces) Italian dressing
     1   package (10 ounces) frozen green peas
     2   medium stalks celery, sliced (about 1 cup)
     1   medium green pepper, cut into strips
     1   medium red onion, sliced and separated into rings
     1   small head lettuce, torn into bite-size pieces (about 6 cups)
     6   slices bacon, crisply cooked and crumbled
     2   tomatoes, cut into wedges

Cut beef across grain into ⅛-inch slices. Cook and stir beef in
2 tablespoons of the dressing until beef is brown; drain. Rinse
frozen peas under running cold water to separate; drain. Mix
beef, peas, celery, green pepper, onion and remaining dressing. Cover and refrigerate at least 4 hours.

Toss lettuce with beef mixture; sprinkle with bacon. Garnish with tomatoes.   **8 servings** (1½ cups each); 475 calories
per serving.

TACO SALADS

Tortilla Shells (below)
1   pound ground beef
⅔   cup water
1   tablespoon chili powder
1½   teaspoons salt
¼   teaspoon garlic powder
¼   teaspoon ground red pepper
1   can (15½ ounces) kidney beans, drained
        (reserve empty can)
1   medium head lettuce, torn into bite-size pieces
1   cup shredded Cheddar cheese
⅔   cup sliced ripe olives
2   medium tomatoes, coarsely chopped
1   medium onion, chopped
¾   cup Thousand Island Dressing (page 551)
1   avocado, peeled and thinly sliced
    Dairy sour cream

Prepare Tortilla Shells. Cook and stir ground beef in 10-inch skillet until brown; drain. Stir in water, chili powder, salt, garlic powder, red pepper and kidney beans. Heat to boiling; reduce heat. Simmer uncovered, stirring occasionally, 15 minutes; cool 10 minutes.

Mix lettuce, cheese, olives, tomatoes and onion in 3-quart bowl; toss with Thousand Island Dressing. Pour ground beef mixture on top; toss. Divide among Tortilla Shells; garnish with avocado and sour cream. Serve immediately.   **8 servings** (about 1½ cups salad per shell); 550 calories per serving.

Tortilla Shells
Remove label and both ends of kidney bean can; wash and dry. Heat 1½ inches vegetable oil in 3-quart saucepan to 375°. (Diameter of saucepan should be at least 9 inches.) Place 1 of 8 flour tortillas (10-inch diameter) on top of saucepan; place can on center of tortilla with long-handled tongs. Push tortilla into oil by gently pushing can down. Fry tortilla until slightly set, about 5 seconds; remove can with tongs. Continue frying tortilla, turning tortilla in oil, until tortilla is crisp and golden brown, 1 to 2 minutes longer. Carefully remove tortilla from oil; drain excess oil from inside. Turn tortilla shell upside down; cool. Repeat with remaining tortillas.

PASTA & GRAIN SALADS

DILLED PASTA SALAD

½   cup mayonnaise or salad dressing
¼   cup dairy sour cream
1   tablespoon snipped fresh dill weed or
     ½ teaspoon dried dill weed
½   teaspoon salt
½   teaspoon dry mustard
¼   teaspoon pepper
2   cups uncooked rotini or spiral macaroni,
     cooked and drained
½   cup sliced ripe olives
1   medium zucchini, thinly sliced
1   medium carrot, coarsely shredded
1   small onion, chopped (about ¼ cup)

Mix mayonnaise, sour cream, dill weed, salt, mustard and pepper in 2½-quart bowl. Add remaining ingredients; toss. Cover and refrigerate at least 3 hours. **8 servings** (about ⅔ cup each); 200 calories per serving.

TOMATO-PASTA SALAD

2   medium tomatoes, chopped (about 2 cups)
2   green onions (with tops), chopped
2   cloves garlic, finely chopped
¼   cup snipped parsley
2   tablespoons vegetable or olive oil
½   teaspoon salt
½   teaspoon dried basil leaves
⅛   teaspoon coarsely cracked pepper
1   package (7 ounces) macaroni shells

Mix tomatoes, onions, garlic, parsley, oil, salt, basil and pepper. Prepare macaroni as directed on package; drain. Toss with tomato mixture. Cover and refrigerate at least 2 hours.   **6 servings** (about ¾ cup each); 170 calories per serving.

RICE-SPINACH SALAD

1   package (10 ounces) frozen chopped spinach
3   cups cooked wild rice (page 85)
1½   cups cooked regular rice (page 85)
½   cup toasted slivered almonds
¼   cup sliced green onions (with tops)
4   slices bacon, crisply cooked and crumbled
    Soy Sauce Dressing (below)

Rinse frozen spinach under running cold water to separate; drain thoroughly. Mix spinach and remaining ingredients except dressing. Pour Soy Sauce Dressing over rice mixture; toss. Cover and refrigerate at least 3 hours.   **8 servings** (about ¾ cup each); 265 calories per serving.

Soy Sauce Dressing
½   cup vegetable oil
2   tablespoons vinegar
2   tablespoons soy sauce
1   teaspoon sugar
½   teaspoon salt
¼   teaspoon pepper

Shake all ingredients in tightly covered container.

BULGUR-TOMATO SALAD

1   cup bulgur (cracked wheat)
2   medium tomatoes, chopped (about 2 cups)
1   medium onion, chopped (about ½ cup)
½   cup finely snipped parsley
¼   cup finely chopped green pepper
2   tablespoons finely snipped mint
¼   cup vegetable or olive oil
¼   cup lemon juice
1   teaspoon salt
⅛   teaspoon pepper
     Lettuce leaves

Cover bulgur with cold water. Let stand until tender, about 1 hour; drain.

Mix bulgur, tomatoes, onion, parsley, green pepper and mint. Sprinkle with oil, lemon juice, salt and pepper; stir until evenly coated. Cover and refrigerate at least 2 hours.

Spoon bulgur onto lettuce leaves. Garnish with mint leaves if desired.   **8 servings** (about ½ cup each); 155 calories per serving.

TOSSED SALADS

SALAD GREENS

SELECTING SALAD GREENS

Of the four main groups of lettuce, *crisphead* (notably *iceberg*) is probably the most popular. The other three groups are *butterhead*, including *Boston* and *Bibb*, with its tender, pliable leaves; *romaine* (also called *cos*) with crisp, elongated dark leaves; and *leaf lettuce*, red or green, with tender "leafy" leaves that don't form heads.

The *endive* family includes *curly endive* (sometimes miscalled chicory), a frilly, narrow-leaved bushy plant; *escarole*, a less frilly, broader-leaved variety; and *Belgian* or *French endive*, with narrow, blanched leaves in tight upright clusters. *Radicchio*, another member of the endive family, is rapidly gaining in popularity. Traditionally imported from Italy, its domestic production in California is increasing and it is now available in most well-stocked produce markets. It resembles a small, loose-leaf cabbage, but its leaves are smooth and very tender. There are two varieties: *Rosso* has light red or rose leaves with white veins, and *Castelfranco*, both blander and sweeter, has leaves that are sprinkled with bright colors.

Among the hundreds of green cousins, look for watercress, parsley, arugula (also called rocket), spinach, Swiss chard, fresh beet and mustard tops, collards, Chinese cabbage, even dandelion and nasturtium leaves.

Whatever the green, herb or other salad "sparker," such as red, green or savoy cabbage, be sure it's fresh when purchased. Iceberg lettuce should be firm but resilient, "giving" slightly when squeezed. When buying butterhead and leaf lettuce, look for a bright green color. Choose well-trimmed heads of cabbage that are firm and heavy for their size (early spring cabbage is not as firm as the winter varieties).

STORING SALAD GREENS

Greens should always be placed in a covered container, plastic bag or the crisper section of the refrigerator as soon as possible. However, watercress, parsley and fresh herbs should be refrigerated in large screwtop jars. These, as well as romaine and iceberg lettuce, will keep up to a week. Most other greens will droop within a few days.

Wash greens several hours before using—they need time to crisp. Wash thoroughly in several changes of cold water or under running cold water, then shake off the excess moisture. Toss in a cloth towel, or gently blot dry to remove the remaining moisture; refrigerate. Or use a salad spinner instead of the towel to remove any excess moisture.

If you are going to use iceberg lettuce within a day or so, remove the core before washing. Strike the core end against a flat surface, then twist and lift out core. Hold the head, cored end up, under running cold water to separate and clean leaves. Turn right side up and drain thoroughly. Refrigerate in a plastic bag or bowl with an airtight lid.

SERVING SALAD GREENS

Use a variety of greens for a complementary medley of textures, flavors and colors. And, remember, fresh herbs can perk up even the simplest combinations.

Mix dark greens with light, crisp with tender and straight with curly. Team pale iceberg lettuce with dark green spinach, romaine and curly endive. Red leaf (bronze) lettuce provides both color and delicate flavor. Red cabbage and radicchio add color and texture accents, too.

Combine mild-flavored greens, such as romaine, iceberg lettuce, spinach, Boston lettuce, Bibb lettuce, oakleaf lettuce and radicchio, with greens that have a tangy, pleasant sharpness, such as curly endive, escarole, Belgian endive, sorrel, watercress or dandelion leaves.

Tear—do not cut—salad greens into bite-size pieces. (Exceptions are shredded lettuce, cut wedges of iceberg lettuce and lengthwise quarters or pulled-off leaves of Belgian endive.) Use the small inner whole leaves of butterhead, Boston or Bibb lettuce and romaine in the salad. The larger outer leaves can be torn into bite-size pieces or used whole for lettuce "beds."

Blot up any leftover moisture you find in the crevices; the drier the leaves the better. Pour on the dressing just before serving, using only enough to coat the ingredients lightly, then toss. Or serve the salad with the dressing on the side so that each person can add the desired amount.

SPINACH TOSSED SALAD

	Chutney Dressing (below)
1	pound spinach, torn into bite-size pieces (about 8 cups)
4	ounces mushrooms, sliced (about 1½ cups)
1	cup bean sprouts
1	cup unseasoned croutons
¼	cup crumbled blue cheese
6	red onion slices, separated into rings

Toss all ingredients. Serve with freshly ground pepper if desired. **6 servings** (about 1⅔ cups each); 215 calories per serving.

Chutney Dressing

⅓	cup vegetable oil
¼	cup chutney
2	tablespoons vinegar
½	teaspoon onion salt

Shake all ingredients in tightly covered container.

SPINACH-MUSHROOM SALAD

⅓	cup vegetable oil
¼	cup wine vinegar
¼	teaspoon salt
	Generous dash of freshly ground pepper
1	clove garlic, crushed
1	pound spinach, torn into bite-size pieces (about 8 cups)
8	ounces mushrooms, sliced (about 3 cups)
2	slices bacon, crisply cooked and crumbled
1	hard-cooked egg, chopped

TOSSED SALAD CHART
(for 6 to 8 servings)

Salad Greens	Add Salad Sparkers		Toss with	Garnish with
Choose one or more to total 12 cups	*Choose one or more to total 1½ cups*		*Shake to mix*	*Choose one or two to total ⅓ to ½ cup*
Iceberg lettuce	**Fresh vegetables**	**Cooked vegetables**	**Dressing**	French-fried onions
Boston lettuce	Alfalfa sprouts	Artichoke bottoms or	⅓ cup vegetable or	Croutons
Bibb lettuce	Asparagus, sliced	hearts, plain or	olive oil or	Bacon, crisply fried,
Leaf lettuce	Carrots, sliced	marinated	combination	crumbled
Romaine	Cauliflowerets	Dilled green beans	2 tablespoons cider,	Hard-cooked eggs, sliced
Escarole	Cucumbers, sliced	Green peas, beans or	wine or tarragon	Salted nuts
Spinach	Green peppers, diced	sliced carrots,	vinegar	Blue cheese, crumbled
Watercress	or sliced	marinated	¾ teaspoon salt	Toasted wheat germ
Endive (Belgian	Mushrooms, sliced		⅛ to ¼ teaspoon	Sunflower nuts
or French)	Onions, sliced or diced	**Meat and fish**	pepper	Olives, sliced
Curly endive	Radishes, sliced	Turkey or chicken,	1 small clove garlic,	
	Tomato wedges	ham, tongue, cold	crushed	
	Zucchini, sliced	cuts, cut into ¼-inch		
		strips or cubes		
	Fruit	Shrimp, crabmeat or		
	Apple wedges	lobster, cut up		
	Avocados, sliced			
	Orange sections	**Cheese**		
		Swiss or Cheddar, cut		
		into ¼-inch strips or		
		cubes		

Shake oil, vinegar, salt, pepper and garlic in tightly covered container. Toss with spinach and mushrooms; sprinkle with bacon and egg.   **8 servings** (about 1¼ cups each); 120 calories per serving.

LETTUCE-MUSHROOM SALAD

    2 heads Boston lettuce, torn into
           bite-size pieces (about 8 cups)
    8 ounces mushrooms, sliced (about 3 cups)
       Mustard Dressing (below)
       Freshly ground pepper

Place lettuce in salad bowl; top with mushrooms. Serve with Mustard Dressing and pepper.   **8 servings;** 170 calories per serving.

Mustard Dressing
Place ½ cup plus 2 tablespoons vegetable or olive oil, 2 tablespoons Dijon-style mustard and 2 tablespoons vinegar in blender container. Cover and blend on high speed until mixture begins to thicken, about 15 seconds.

WILTED LETTUCE SALAD

    4 slices bacon, diced
   ¼ cup vinegar
    2 bunches leaf lettuce, coarsely shredded
    5 green onions (with tops), chopped (about ⅓ cup)
    2 teaspoons sugar
   ¼ teaspoon salt
   ⅛ teaspoon pepper

Cook bacon in 12-inch skillet until crisp; add vinegar. Heat through; remove from heat. Add lettuce and onions. Sprinkle with sugar, salt and pepper; toss until lettuce is wilted, 1 to 2 minutes.   **4 servings;** 160 calories per serving.

Dill Wilted Lettuce Salad: Stir ½ teaspoon dried dill weed and ½ teaspoon dry mustard into vinegar.

EASY CAESAR SALAD

3 anchovy fillets
⅓ cup grated Parmesan cheese
⅓ cup bottled Caesar dressing
1 large bunch romaine, torn into
     bite-size pieces (about 10 cups)
1 cup onion-garlic-flavored croutons

Mash anchovies with fork in 3-quart bowl. Stir in cheese and dressing; toss with romaine and croutons. **8 servings;** 130 calories per serving.

CAESAR SALAD

Coddled Egg (page 510)
1 clove garlic, cut into halves
8 anchovy fillets, cut up
⅓ cup olive oil
1 teaspoon Worcestershire sauce
½ teaspoon salt
¼ teaspoon dry mustard
   Freshly ground pepper
1 large or 2 small bunches romaine, torn into bite-size
     pieces (about 10 cups)
1 lemon, cut into halves
1 cup garlic-flavored croutons
⅓ cup grated Parmesan cheese

Prepare Coddled Egg. Rub large wooden salad bowl with cut clove of garlic. Allow a few small pieces of garlic to remain in bowl if desired. Mix anchovies, oil, Worcestershire sauce, salt, mustard and pepper in bowl; toss with romaine until leaves glisten. Break Coddled Egg onto salad. Squeeze lemon over salad; toss. Sprinkle with croutons and cheese; toss. **6 servings;** 195 calories per serving.

Coddled Egg

Place cold egg in warm water. Heat enough water to boiling to cover egg completely. Immerse egg in boiling water with spoon; remove from heat. Cover and let stand 30 seconds. Immediately cool egg in cold water to prevent further cooking; refrigerate.

GREEK SALAD

Lemon Dressing (below)
5 cups bite-size pieces spinach
4 cups bite-size pieces Boston lettuce
½ cup crumbled feta cheese
¼ cup sliced green onions
24 pitted ripe olives
3 tomatoes, cut into wedges
1 cucumber, sliced

Toss all ingredients.   **8 servings; 135 calories per serving.**

Lemon Dressing
¼ cup vegetable oil
2 tablespoons lemon juice
½ teaspoon sugar
1½ teaspoons Dijon-style mustard
¼ teaspoon salt
⅛ teaspoon pepper

Shake ingredients in tightly covered container.

ELEGANT TOSSED SALAD

Cheese-Mustard Dressing (page 511)
4 slices French bread, each ½ inch thick
2 large cloves garlic, cut lengthwise into halves
2 tablespoons olive or vegetable oil
4 ounces watercress (about 4 cups)
4 ounces mushrooms, sliced (about 1½ cups)
1 medium leek, thinly sliced
½ head Boston lettuce, torn into bite-size pieces
½ small bunch romaine, torn into bite-size pieces

Prepare Cheese-Mustard Dressing. Tear bread into ½-inch pieces. Cook and stir garlic in oil in 8-inch skillet over medium heat until garlic is deep golden brown; remove garlic and discard. Add bread to oil. Cook and stir until bread is golden brown and crusty; cool.

Shake Cheese-Mustard Dressing; toss with watercress, mushrooms, leek, lettuce and romaine. Sprinkle with bread. **8 servings** (about 1¼ cups each); 70 calories per serving.

Cheese-Mustard Dressing

  2 tablespoons olive or vegetable oil
  1 tablespoon red wine vinegar
  2 teaspoons grated Parmesan cheese
  2 teaspoons Dijon-style mustard
 ¼ teaspoon salt

Shake all ingredients in tightly covered container. Refrigerate at least 1 hour.

WINTER VEGETABLE TOSS

  6 cups bite-size pieces salad greens
 ¼ cup sliced carrot
 ¼ cup thinly sliced celery
  2 tablespoons coarsely chopped green pepper
  2 small green onions (with tops), thinly sliced
 ¼ cup bottled oil-and-vinegar dressing

Toss all ingredients. **4 servings;** 95 calories per serving.

WALNUT TOSSED SALAD

 ½ cup coarsely chopped walnuts
 ¼ cup vegetable oil
 ½ teaspoon salt
  3 tablespoons tarragon wine vinegar
  1 teaspoon sugar
  4 cups bite-size pieces salad greens
  1 small red onion, thinly sliced

Cook and stir walnuts in oil in 8-inch skillet until toasted, about 4 minutes; remove from heat. Remove walnuts with slotted spoon; drain. Sprinkle with salt. Stir vinegar and sugar into oil in skillet. Pour over salad greens and onion; toss. Sprinkle with walnuts. **6 servings; 165 calories per serving.**

MANDARIN SALAD

¼ cup sliced almonds
1 tablespoon plus 1 teaspoon sugar
   Sweet-Sour Dressing (below)
¼ head lettuce, torn into bite-size pieces
¼ bunch romaine, torn into bite-size pieces
2 medium stalks celery, chopped (about 1 cup)
2 green onions (with tops), thinly sliced (about 2 tablespoons)
1 can (11 ounces) mandarin orange segments, drained

Cook almonds and sugar over low heat, stirring constantly, until sugar is melted and almonds are coated; cool and break apart. Store at room temperature. Prepare Sweet-Sour Dressing.

Place lettuce and romaine in plastic bag; add celery and onions. Pour Sweet-Sour Dressing into bag; add orange segments. Close bag tightly and shake until salad greens and orange segments are evenly coated; add almonds and shake. **6 servings; 155 calories per serving.**

Sweet-Sour Dressing

¼ cup vegetable oil
2 tablespoons sugar
2 tablespoons vinegar
1 tablespoon snipped parsley
½ teaspoon salt
   Dash of pepper
   Dash of red pepper sauce

Shake all ingredients in tightly covered container; refrigerate.

VEGETABLE SALADS

ASPARAGUS SALAD

¾ cup mayonnaise or salad dressing
2 tablespoons bottled French dressing
2 tablespoons pickle relish
1 tablespoon chopped pimiento
1 package (10 ounces) frozen asparagus spears
Salad greens
3 hard-cooked eggs, sliced
4 slices bacon, crisply cooked and crumbled

Mix mayonnaise, dressing, relish and pimiento. Cover and refrigerate at least 2 hours. Cook asparagus as directed on package; drain. Refrigerate until chilled.

Arrange 3 or 4 asparagus spears on salad greens; top with egg slices. Spoon dressing over top; sprinkle with bacon. **6 servings; 240 calories per serving.**

KIDNEY BEAN SALAD

    1   can (20 ounces) white kidney beans, drained
    1   can (15 ounces) red kidney beans, drained
    1   can (15 ounces) garbanzo beans, drained
    3   medium tomatoes, diced (about 1½ cups)
    1   hot pepper, seeded and finely chopped
    1   medium red or sweet white onion,
          chopped (about ¾ cup)
    ½   large green or red pepper, chopped
    5   green onions (with tops), sliced (about ⅓ cup)
    1   cup French Dressing (page 548)
    ½   teaspoon salt
    2   or 3 drops red pepper sauce
        Lettuce leaves

Mix all ingredients except lettuce. Cover and refrigerate, stirring occasionally, at least 3 hours.

Just before serving, remove salad to lettuce-lined bowl with slotted spoon.   **12 servings; 180 calories per serving.**

GARBANZO BEAN SALAD

    4   ounces small mushrooms
    ½   medium green pepper, cut into thin strips
    ½   cup sliced pitted ripe olives
    ¼   cup sliced green onions (with tops)
    1   can (15 ounces) garbanzo beans, drained
        Yogurt Dressing (page 515)
        Lettuce leaves
    2   small tomatoes, cut into wedges

Mix mushrooms, green pepper, olives, onions and beans. Refrigerate until chilled, at least 2 hours.

Just before serving, toss salad with Yogurt Dressing. Serve on lettuce leaves; garnish with tomato wedges.   **4 servings; 300 calories per serving.**

Yogurt Dressing

½   cup plain yogurt
¼   cup mayonnaise or salad dressing
½   teaspoon ground cumin
1½   teaspoons lemon juice
¼   teaspoon garlic salt
⅛   teaspoon ground turmeric

Mix all ingredients.

THREE-BEAN SALAD

1   can (16 ounces) green beans, drained
1   can (16 ounces) wax beans, drained
1   can (15 ounces) kidney beans, drained
4   green onions (with tops), chopped (about ¼ cup)
¼   cup snipped parsley
1   cup Italian Dressing (page 547) or bottled Italian dressing
1   tablespoon sugar
2   cloves garlic, crushed
     Lettuce leaves

Mix beans, onions and parsley. Mix Italian Dressing, sugar
and garlic; pour over salad and toss. Cover and refrigerate,
stirring occasionally, at least 3 hours.

Just before serving, remove salad to lettuce-lined salad
bowl with slotted spoon.   **6 servings;** 150 calories per serving.

COLESLAW

½   cup dairy sour cream or plain yogurt
¼   cup mayonnaise or salad dressing
1   teaspoon sugar
½   teaspoon dry mustard
½   teaspoon seasoned salt
⅛   teaspoon pepper
½   medium head cabbage, finely shredded or
        chopped (about 4 cups)
1   small onion, chopped (about ¼ cup)

Mix sour cream, mayonnaise, sugar, mustard, seasoned salt and pepper; toss with cabbage and onion. Sprinkle with paprika or dried dill weed if desired. **8 servings** (about ½ cup each); 100 calories per serving.

Apple-Cheese Coleslaw: Omit onion; toss 1 tart apple, chopped, and ¼ cup crumbled blue cheese with the cabbage.

Pineapple-Marshmallow Coleslaw: Omit onion; toss 1 can (8 ounces) crushed pineapple, drained, and 1 cup miniature marshmallows with the cabbage.

SWEET-SOUR CABBAGE SLAW

1	egg
¼	cup sugar
¼	cup vinegar
2	tablespoons water
2	tablespoons margarine or butter
1	teaspoon salt
½	teaspoon dry mustard
½	medium head green cabbage, finely shredded or chopped (about 4 cups)
1	small green pepper, chopped (about ½ cup)

Beat egg until thick and lemon colored. Heat sugar, vinegar, water, margarine, salt and mustard to boiling, stirring constantly. Gradually stir at least half of the hot mixture into egg; stir into hot mixture in saucepan. Cook over low heat, stirring constantly, until thickened, about 5 minutes. Pour over cabbage and green pepper; toss. **6 servings** (¾ cup each); 100 calories per serving.

CONFETTI SLAW

1	small head red cabbage, chopped (about 3 cups)
1	medium tomato, chopped (about 1 cup)
⅓	cup sliced pimiento-stuffed olives
1	small onion, chopped (about ¼ cup)
¼	cup crumbled feta cheese
1	tablespoon snipped cilantro, if desired
	Cumin Dressing (page 517)

Mix all ingredients except Cumin Dressing; toss with dressing. **7 servings** (about ½ cup each); 125 calories per serving.

Cumin Dressing
 ¼ cup vegetable oil
 2 tablespoons tarragon or wine vinegar
 ¾ teaspoon salt
 ½ teaspoon ground cumin
    Dash of pepper
 1 small clove garlic, crushed

Shake all ingredients in tightly covered container.

CABBAGE SALAD

 ½ medium head green cabbage, finely
     shredded or chopped (about 4 cups)
 ½ small green pepper, chopped (about ¼ cup)
 ⅓ cup white vinegar
 3 tablespoons vegetable oil
 2 tablespoons sugar
 1 tablespoon chopped pimiento
 1 teaspoon instant minced onion
 1 teaspoon salt
 ½ teaspoon celery seed
 ½ teaspoon dry mustard
 ¼ teaspoon pepper

Mix all ingredients. Cover and refrigerate 3 hours. Just before serving, drain salad. **6 servings**; 40 calories per serving.

RATATOUILLE SALAD

 1 small eggplant (about 1 pound)
 2 medium tomatoes, chopped (about 1½ cups)
 1 medium zucchini, thinly sliced
 1 small onion, sliced and separated into rings
 1 small green pepper, chopped
 ⅓ cup snipped parsley
    Basil Dressing (page 518)

Prepare eggplant as directed on page 641; cut into ½-inch cubes. Cook as directed; cool.

Mix eggplant, tomatoes, zucchini, onion, green pepper and parsley; toss with Basil Dressing. Cover and refrigerate at least 4 hours. Serve on lettuce leaves if desired. **8 servings** (about ½ cup each); 110 calories per serving.

Basil Dressing
- ⅓ **cup olive or vegetable oil**
- 2 **tablespoons lemon juice**
- 1 **teaspoon salt**
- ½ **teaspoon dried basil leaves**
- ½ **teaspoon dry mustard**
- ⅛ **teaspoon pepper**

Shake all ingredients in tightly covered container.

MIXED VEGETABLE SALAD

- 2 **cups cauliflowerets**
- 2 **cups bite-size pieces broccoli flowerets and stems**
- 1 **package (10 ounces) frozen green peas**
- ⅓ **cup mayonnaise or salad dressing**
- ¼ **cup plain yogurt**
- 1 **tablespoon lemon juice**
- 1 **teaspoon salt**
- ¼ **teaspoon pepper**
- 1 **medium carrot, thinly sliced (about ¾ cup)**
- 2 **cups cherry tomatoes, cut into halves**

Heat 1 inch salted water (½ teaspoon salt to 1 cup water) to boiling. Add cauliflowerets and broccoli. Cover and heat to boiling; reduce heat. Cook 5 minutes; drain. Rinse under running cold water; drain. Rinse peas under running cold water to separate; drain.

Mix mayonnaise, yogurt, lemon juice, salt and pepper in 2½-quart bowl. Add cauliflowerets, broccoli, peas and carrot; toss. Cover and refrigerate at least 4 hours. Stir in tomatoes. **8 servings** (about ¾ cup each); 135 calories per serving.

PICKLED BEETS

2   cans (16 ounces each) sliced beets,
       drained (reserve liquid)
2   cups sugar
1   cup vinegar
2   sticks cinnamon

Add enough water to beet liquid to measure 2 cups. Heat
liquid mixture, sugar, vinegar and cinnamon to boiling. Pour
over beets. Cover and refrigerate at least 12 hours.   **8 servings** (about ½ cup each); 110 calories per serving.

MARINATED CARROT SALAD

1½   pounds carrots*
1   bottle (8 ounces) French dressing
2   teaspoons prepared mustard
½   teaspoon Worcestershire sauce
1   small green pepper, chopped (about ½ cup)
1   small onion, thinly sliced

Prepare and cook carrots, cut crosswise into ¼-inch slices, as
directed on page 632.

Mix dressing, mustard and Worcestershire sauce in 2-quart
glass or plastic bowl. Stir in carrots, green pepper and onion
until coated. Cover and refrigerate at least 8 hours.   **8 servings** (about ½ cup each); 240 calories per serving.

CARROT-RAISIN SALAD

2½   cups shredded carrots (about 3 large)
1   medium stalk celery, sliced (about ½ cup)
½   cup raisins
½   cup mayonnaise or salad dressing
1   teaspoon lemon juice

*2 jars (16 ounces each) whole baby carrots, drained, can be substituted
for the 1½ pounds carrots.

Mix all ingredients. Serve on salad greens if desired. **5 servings** (½ cup each); 235 calories per serving.

Carrot-Pineapple Salad: Omit lemon juice. Stir in 1 can (8¼ ounces) crushed pineapple, well drained.

CAULIFLOWER SALAD

1 medium head cauliflower (about 2 pounds), separated into flowerets
2 tablespoons vinegar
2 tablespoons vegetable oil
½ teaspoon salt
  Dash of pepper
  Romaine
  Guacamole (page 19)
2 tablespoons slivered almonds

Heat 1 inch water to boiling. Add cauliflowerets; cover and heat to boiling. Cook 4 minutes; drain. Immediately rinse under running cold water; drain. Mix vinegar and oil in 2½-quart glass or plastic bowl. Add cauliflowerets, salt and pepper; toss. Cover and refrigerate at least 1 hour.

Just before serving, arrange cauliflowerets on romaine. Top with Guacamole; sprinkle with almonds. **6 servings;** 155 calories per serving.

CUCUMBERS AND TOMATOES

2 medium cucumbers
2 green onions (with tops), chopped
1 teaspoon salt
2 tomatoes, chopped
2 tablespoons snipped parsley or cilantro
½ teaspoon ground cumin
⅛ teaspoon pepper
½ clove garlic, finely chopped
1 cup plain yogurt

Cut cucumbers lengthwise into halves. Scoop out seeds; chop cucumbers. Mix cucumbers, green onions and salt. Let stand 10 minutes; add tomatoes. Mix remaining ingredients except yogurt; toss with cucumber mixture. Cover and refrigerate at least 1 hour.

Just before serving, drain salad thoroughly; fold in yogurt. **6 servings;** 50 calories per serving.

CUCUMBER SALAD

- 2 medium cucumbers, thinly sliced
- ⅓ cup cider vinegar
- ⅓ cup water
- 2 tablespoons sugar
- ½ teaspoon salt
- ⅛ teaspoon pepper

Place cucumbers in 1½-quart glass or plastic bowl. Mix remaining ingredients; pour over cucumbers. Cover and refrigerate, stirring occasionally, at least 3 hours.

Drain salad; sprinkle with snipped dill weed or parsley if desired. **6 servings;** 10 calories per serving.

CREAMY CUCUMBER SALAD

- ½ cup plain yogurt or mayonnaise or salad dressing
- ½ teaspoon salt
- ¼ teaspoon dried dill weed
- ⅛ teaspoon pepper
- 2 medium cucumbers, thinly sliced
- 1 small onion, thinly sliced and separated into rings

Mix all ingredients. Cover and refrigerate at least 4 hours. **7 servings** (about ½ cup each); 25 calories per serving.

CUCUMBERS AND SHRIMP

¼ cup vinegar
1 tablespoon sugar
1 teaspoon soy sauce
½ teaspoon salt
1 can (4½ ounces) shrimp, drained
2 medium cucumbers, thinly sliced
Lettuce leaves
1 tablespoon toasted sesame seed

Mix vinegar, sugar, soy sauce and salt in 1½-quart glass or plastic bowl. Add shrimp and cucumbers; toss. Cover and refrigerate at least 1 hour.

Remove salad to 6 lettuce-lined salad plates with slotted spoon; sprinkle with sesame seed. **6 appetizer servings;** 60 calories per serving.

MARINATED PEPPERS

6 large red or green peppers
¼ cup olive or vegetable oil
2 tablespoons snipped parsley
2 tablespoons lemon juice
2 tablespoons lime juice
½ teaspoon salt
¼ teaspoon dried oregano leaves
¼ teaspoon dried basil leaves
⅛ teaspoon dried sage leaves
⅛ teaspoon pepper
2 large cloves garlic, finely chopped

Set oven control to broil and/or 550°. Broil red peppers with tops 4 to 5 inches from heat until skin is blistered and brown, about 5 minutes on each side. Wrap in towels; let stand 5 minutes.

Remove skin, stems, seeds and membranes from peppers; cut peppers into ¼-inch slices. Shake remaining ingredients in tightly covered container; pour over peppers. Cover and refrigerate, stirring occasionally, at least 4 hours. **8 servings** (about ½ cup each); 95 calories per serving.

HOT GERMAN POTATO SALAD

1½ pounds potatoes (about 4 medium), cut into halves
3   slices bacon
1   medium onion, chopped
1   tablespoon all-purpose flour
1   tablespoon sugar
1   teaspoon salt
¼   teaspoon celery seed
    Dash of pepper
½   cup water
¼   cup vinegar

Heat 1 inch salted water (½ teaspoon salt to 1 cup water) to boiling. Add potatoes. Heat to boiling; reduce heat. Cover and cook until tender, 20 to 25 minutes; drain.

Cook bacon in 8-inch skillet until crisp; remove bacon and drain. Cook and stir onion in bacon fat until tender. Stir in flour, sugar, salt, celery seed and pepper. Cook over low heat, stirring constantly, until mixture is bubbly; remove from heat. Stir in water and vinegar. Heat to boiling, stirring constantly. Boil and stir 1 minute; remove from heat. Crumble bacon into hot mixture, then slice in warm potatoes. Cook, stirring gently to coat potato slices, until hot and bubbly. **5 servings; 195 calories per serving.**

POTATO SALAD

2   pounds potatoes (about 6 medium)
1½ cups mayonnaise or salad dressing
1   tablespoon vinegar
1   tablespoon prepared mustard
1   teaspoon salt
¼   teaspoon pepper
2   medium stalks celery, chopped (about 1 cup)
1   medium onion, chopped (about ½ cup)
4   hard-cooked eggs, chopped

Prepare and boil potatoes as directed on pages 657 and 658; cool slightly. Cut into cubes (about 6 cups).

Mix mayonnaise, vinegar, mustard, salt and pepper in 4-quart glass or plastic bowl. Add potatoes, celery and onion; toss.

Stir in eggs. Cover and refrigerate at least 4 hours. **10 servings** (about ¾ cup each); 260 calories per serving.

California-style Potato Salad: Omit eggs. Stir in 1 can (4 ounces) chopped green chilies, drained, with the vegetables. Just before serving, stir in 2 avocados, chopped, and 2 tomatoes, chopped.

Garden Potato Salad: Stir in ½ cup thinly sliced radishes, ½ cup chopped cucumber and ½ cup chopped green pepper. Garnish with tomato wedges.

Scandinavian-style Potato Salad: Stir in 1 jar (8 ounces) pickled herring, drained and chopped, 1 can (8¼ ounces) julienne beets, drained, and 1 teaspoon dried dill weed.

MARINATED WHOLE TOMATOES

6	medium tomatoes, peeled
¾	cup vinegar
½	cup vegetable oil
2	teaspoons sugar
½	teaspoon red pepper sauce
1	small onion, finely chopped (about ¼ cup)
1	clove garlic, crushed

Place tomatoes in square baking dish, 9×9×2 inches. Mix remaining ingredients; spoon over tomatoes. Cover and refrigerate, turning tomatoes occasionally, at least 8 hours. Sprinkle with snipped parsley if desired. **6 servings;** 80 calories per serving.

GARLIC TOMATO SLICES

4	medium tomatoes, cut into ¼-inch slices
¼	cup vegetable or olive oil
2	tablespoons red wine vinegar
⅛	teaspoon salt
3	drops red pepper sauce
2	large cloves garlic, finely chopped

Place tomatoes in glass or plastic dish. Shake remaining ingredients in tightly covered container; pour over tomatoes. Cover and refrigerate at least 3 hours. Serve on lettuce leaves if desired. **8 servings;** 75 calories per serving.

TOMATO-CHEESE SALADS

 3   large tomatoes, each cut into 6 slices
     Bottled Italian dressing
 ¾   cup shredded Cheddar or Swiss cheese (3 ounces)
 2   green onions (with tops), thinly sliced

Arrange 3 tomato slices on each of 6 salad plates. Drizzle with
dressing; sprinkle with cheese and onions. **6 servings;** 100
calories per serving.

BROILED TOMATO SALADS

 2   medium tomatoes, each cut into 6 slices
 ¾   cup Blue Cheese Dressing (page 551)
 ¼   cup sliced green onions (with tops)
 1   firm large head iceberg lettuce, cut into 6 slices
 4   slices bacon, crisply cooked and crumbled

Place 2 tomato slices, overlapping slightly, on ungreased
cookie sheet; repeat with remaining tomato slices. Mix dressing and onions; spoon over tomatoes.

Set oven control to broil and/or 550°. Broil tomatoes with
tops 2 to 3 inches from heat just until dressing bubbles, about
2 minutes. Place 2 tomato slices on each lettuce slice; sprinkle tops with bacon. **6 servings;** 150 calories per serving.

MOLDED SALADS

MAKING MOLDED SALADS

SALAD MOLDS
Molds can be plain or fancy, large, or small and individual.
Gelatin will thicken more quickly and the salad unmold more
easily if the mold is made of a thin metal.

To determine the size of a mold, fill it with water and then
measure the water. And don't try to adjust ingredient amounts
to fit an odd-size mold. It is better to use a smaller mold than
to use one that is too large—the gelatin salad may break as it
is being unmolded if there is too much headspace in the
mold. Pour any extra gelatin into a small container and refrigerate; use it to accent another meal or for a snack.

FLAVORED AND UNFLAVORED GELATIN
Follow package or recipe directions carefully because flavored and unflavored gelatin are dissolved by different methods. Gelatin must be completely dissolved in order for it to
jell. To dissolve unflavored gelatin, first sprinkle it over cold
liquid and allow to stand until softened and translucent. Then
stir in hot liquid to dissolve all the granules completely. In
packaged flavored gelatin, the gelatin is premixed with sugar so
that it does not need to be softened before the hot liquid is added.

ADDING SOLIDS
Before adding solids, the gelatin mixture should be chilled
until thickened to the consistency of unbeaten egg whites. If
the gelatin mixture becomes too thick, soften over hot water
until it reaches the desired consistency. If the gelatin mixture
is not thick enough, the solid pieces may float to the surface
or sink to the bottom.

LAYERING SALADS
Arrange fruits, vegetables or other solids in the bottom of the mold, then carefully add the thickened gelatin. (Drain fruits and vegetables thoroughly to avoid diluting the gelatin.) Or pour a layer of gelatin into the mold and arrange solids in desired pattern. Allow each layer to become firm before proceeding with the next.

UNMOLDING SALADS
Quickly dip mold into warm water that comes just to the rim of the mold. Loosen the edge of the salad with the tip of a knife. Tip the mold slightly to release gelatin from the side of the mold and let air in to break the vacuum. Rotate the tipped mold so that air can loosen gelatin all the way around. Center a plate (preferably chilled) on top of the mold and, holding both tightly, invert plate and mold. Shake gently, then carefully remove mold. Repeat process if necessary.

To unmold without dipping, place the chilled plate on top of the mold and, holding firmly, invert both. Soak a cloth towel in hot water, wring it out thoroughly and press it around the mold and into any crevices. Shake the mold gently and carefully remove. If the salad does not slide out easily, reapply the hot damp towel.

CONFETTI CABBAGE MOLD

1	cup boiling water
1	package (3 ounces) lemon-flavored gelatin
½	cup mayonnaise or salad dressing
½	cup cold water
2	tablespoons vinegar
¼	teaspoon salt
1½	cups finely shredded cabbage
½	cup sliced radishes
½	cup diced celery
¼	cup chopped green pepper
1	tablespoon chopped onion

Pour boiling water on gelatin; stir until gelatin is dissolved. Stir in mayonnaise, cold water, vinegar and salt. Refrigerate until mixture mounds slightly when dropped from a spoon.

Beat until fluffy. Stir in remaining ingredients. Pour into 4-cup mold or 6 individual molds. Refrigerate until firm; unmold. Garnish with salad greens and radishes if desired. **6 servings; 200 calories per serving.**

CARROT-PINEAPPLE SALAD

>　1　**cup boiling water**
>　1　**package (3 ounces) orange-flavored gelatin**
>　½　**cup cold water**
>　⅛　**teaspoon salt**
>　1　**can (8¼ ounces) crushed pineapple in syrup, undrained**
>　1　**cup shredded carrot (about 1 medium)**

Pour boiling water on gelatin; stir until gelatin is dissolved. Stir in cold water, salt and pineapple. Refrigerate until slightly thickened.

Stir in carrot. Pour into 3-cup mold or 6 individual molds. Refrigerate until firm; unmold. Garnish with salad greens if desired. **6 servings; 90 calories per serving.**

Zucchini-Pineapple Salad: Substitute 1 package (3 ounces) lime-flavored gelatin for the orange-flavored gelatin and 1 cup shredded zucchini for the carrot.

CORN-RELISH MOLD

>　1　**cup boiling water**
>　1　**package (3 ounces) lemon-flavored gelatin**
>　⅔　**cup cold water**
>　1　**tablespoon vinegar**
>　¼　**teaspoon salt**
>　1　**medium stalk celery, chopped (about ½ cup)**
>　1　**small green pepper, chopped (about ½ cup)**
>　¼　**cup sliced green onions (with tops)**
>　1　**teaspoon prepared horseradish**
>　1　**can (8 ounces) whole kernel corn, drained**
>　1　**jar (2 ounces) diced pimientos, drained**

Pour boiling water on gelatin; stir until gelatin is dissolved. Stir in cold water, vinegar and salt. Refrigerate until slightly thickened.

Stir in remaining ingredients. Pour into 4-cup mold or 6 individual molds. Refrigerate until firm; unmold. Garnish with salad greens if desired. **6 servings;** 90 calories per serving.

CUCUMBER-RELISH MOLD

1½   cups boiling water
1   package (3 ounces) lime-flavored gelatin
1   cup drained shredded cucumber
1   cup thinly sliced celery
3   tablespoons thinly sliced green onions
½   teaspoon salt

Pour boiling water on gelatin; stir until gelatin is dissolved. Refrigerate until slightly thickened.

Stir in remaining ingredients. Pour into 4-cup mold or 4 individual molds. Refrigerate until firm; unmold. Garnish with salad greens. **4 servings;** 95 calories per serving.

ARTICHOKE SALAD

2   cups boiling water
1   package (6 ounces) lemon-flavored gelatin
¾   cup cold water
¼   cup lemon juice
½   teaspoon salt
⅛   teaspoon red pepper sauce
1   can (14 ounces) artichoke hearts, drained and cut into halves
8   pitted ripe olives, cut into halves
1   jar (2 ounces) sliced pimientos, drained
2   tablespoons mayonnaise or salad dressing
½   cup sliced green onions (with tops)
1   medium stalk celery, sliced (about ½ cup)

Pour boiling water on gelatin; stir until gelatin is dissolved. Stir in cold water, lemon juice, salt and pepper sauce. Remove ½ cup; reserve remaining gelatin mixture. Arrange artichoke hearts, olives and pimientos in 6½-cup ring mold. (Chop and reserve any remaining sliced pimientos.) Pour half of the ½ cup gelatin mixture carefully around vegetables.

Refrigerate until set but not firm, about 20 minutes. Pour remaining ¼ cup gelatin mixture over vegetables. Refrigerate until set but not firm, about 20 minutes. Refrigerate reserved gelatin mixture until slightly thickened.

Beat gelatin mixture and mayonnaise until fluffy. Stir in reserved pimientos, the onions and celery. Pour over vegetables in mold. Refrigerate until firm; unmold. Garnish with salad greens and additional pitted ripe olives if desired.   8 servings; 135 calories per serving.

APPLE-CHERRY SALAD

    1   **cup boiling water**
    1   **package (3 ounces) cherry-flavored gelatin**
    1   **cup cranberry juice**
    1   **tablespoon lemon juice**
    2   **tart apples, chopped (about 2½ cups)**
    ½   **cup thinly sliced celery**
    ⅓   **cup chopped nuts, if desired**

Pour boiling water on gelatin; stir until gelatin is dissolved. Stir in cranberry juice and lemon juice. Refrigerate until slightly thickened.

Stir in remaining ingredients. Pour into 4-cup mold. Refrigerate until firm; unmold. Serve with mayonnaise or salad dressing if desired.   **6 servings; 115 calories per serving.**

MOLDED APRICOT SALAD

    1   **envelope unflavored gelatin**
    1   **cup cold water**
    1   **can (5½ ounces) apricot nectar**
    1   **package (8 ounces) cream cheese, softened**
    1   **can (17 ounces) apricot halves in juice,**
        well drained and chopped
        Salad greens

Sprinkle gelatin on cold water in 1-quart saucepan to soften. Heat over low heat, stirring constantly, until gelatin is dissolved; remove from heat. Stir in apricot nectar.

Beat cream cheese in 2½-quart bowl on medium speed until fluffy. Gradually beat in gelatin mixture on low speed, scraping bowl frequently, until smooth. Refrigerate until slightly thickened.

Stir apricots into cream cheese mixture. Pour into 4-cup mold. Refrigerate until firm; unmold. Garnish with salad greens. **6 servings;** 55 calories per serving.

Molded Nectarine Salad: Substitute 1 nectarine, chopped (about 1¼ cups), for the apricots.

BERRY-WINE SALAD

    1   cup boiling water
    1   package (3 ounces) strawberry-flavored gelatin
    1   package (10 ounces) frozen sliced strawberries,
            partially thawed
    1   cup seedless grapes
    ⅔   cup sweet white wine
    1   carton (6 ounces) strawberry yogurt

Pour boiling water on gelatin; stir until gelatin is dissolved. Stir in strawberries; break apart with fork. Stir in grapes and wine. Pour into 4-cup mold. Refrigerate until firm; unmold. Garnish with salad greens if desired. Serve with yogurt. **6 servings;** 150 calories per serving.

CHERRY LAYERED SALAD

    1   cup boiling water
    1   package (3 ounces) lemon-flavored gelatin
    1   package (3 ounces) cream cheese, softened
    1   teaspoon grated lemon peel
    1   envelope unflavored gelatin
    2   tablespoons lemon juice
    ½   cup boiling water
    ¼   teaspoon ground cinnamon
    1   can (21 ounces) cherry pie filling

Pour 1 cup boiling water on lemon-flavored gelatin in 2½-quart bowl; stir until gelatin is dissolved. Beat in cream cheese and lemon peel on medium speed until smooth. Pour into 5-cup mold. Refrigerate until firm, about 1½ hours.

Sprinkle unflavored gelatin on lemon juice in 1½-quart

bowl to soften; stir in ½ cup boiling water until gelatin is dissolved. Stir in cinnamon and pie filling; pour over cream cheese mixture. Refrigerate until firm; unmold. Garnish with salad greens if desired.   **8 servings; 55 calories per serving.**

CRAN-RASPBERRY MOLD

    2   cups boiling water
    1   package (6 ounces) raspberry-flavored gelatin
    1   can (16 ounces) whole berry cranberry sauce
    1   cup dairy sour cream

Pour boiling water on gelatin; stir until gelatin is dissolved. Stir in cranberry sauce. Refrigerate until slightly thickened.

Beat in sour cream with hand beater. Pour into 5-cup mold. Refrigerate until firm; unmold.   **8 servings; 235 calories per serving.**

CITRUS SALAD

1½   cups boiling water
    1   package (6 ounces) lemon-flavored gelatin
    2   cups ginger ale, chilled
    4   oranges
    2   grapefruit

Pour boiling water on gelatin; stir until gelatin is dissolved. Stir in ginger ale. Refrigerate until slightly thickened.

Pare and section oranges and grapefruit. Cut sections into 1-inch pieces; stir into gelatin mixture. Pour into 8-cup mold. Refrigerate until firm, about 4 hours; unmold. Garnish with additional orange sections and salad greens if desired.   **12 servings; 60 calories per serving.**

TRIPLE-ORANGE SALAD

    2   cups boiling water
    1   package (6 ounces) orange-flavored gelatin
    1   pint orange sherbet or vanilla ice cream
    1   can (11 ounces) mandarin orange segments, drained

Pour boiling water on gelatin; stir until gelatin is dissolved. Stir in sherbet until melted. Refrigerate until slightly thickened.

Stir orange segments into gelatin mixture. Pour into 6-cup mold. Refrigerate until firm; unmold. Garnish with additional orange segments and salad greens if desired.   8 servings; 170 calories per serving.

AMBROSIA SALAD MOLD

1   cup boiling water
1   package (3 ounces) orange-flavored gelatin
1   can (8 ounces) crushed pineapple in juice,
       drained (reserve juice)
½   cup dairy sour cream
2   oranges, pared, sectioned and cut up
½   cup flaked coconut

Pour boiling water on gelatin in 2½-quart bowl; stir until gelatin is dissolved. Add enough cold water to reserved pineapple juice to measure 1 cup; stir into gelatin. Refrigerate until slightly thickened.

Beat gelatin mixture and sour cream until light and fluffy. Stir in pineapple, oranges and coconut. Pour into 5-cup mold. Refrigerate until firm; unmold. Garnish with additional orange sections and salad greens if desired.   8 servings; 135 calories per serving.

SPICED PEACH MOLD

1   can (16 ounces) sliced peaches, drained (reserve syrup)
2   tablespoons vinegar
1½ teaspoons whole cloves
1   four-inch stick cinnamon
1   package (3 ounces) orange-flavored gelatin

Heat reserved syrup, the vinegar, cloves and cinnamon to boiling; reduce heat. Simmer uncovered 10 minutes; remove cloves and cinnamon. Add enough hot water to hot syrup mixture to measure 2 cups. Pour mixture on gelatin; stir until gelatin is dissolved. Refrigerate until slightly thickened.

Stir in peaches; pour into 4-cup mold. Refrigerate until firm; unmold. Garnish with salad greens if desired.   **8 servings;** 85 calories per serving.

Spiced Apricot Mold: Substitute 1 can (17 ounces) apricot halves for the peaches. Cut apricot halves into fourths.

STRAWBERRY-CHEESE SALAD

  1   **cup boiling water**
  1   **package (3 ounces) strawberry-flavored gelatin**
  ½   **cup sweet red wine or cranberry juice cocktail**
  ¼   **cup cold water**
  1   **package (3 ounces) cream cheese, softened**
  ⅓   **cup finely chopped nuts**
  2   **cups strawberry halves**
  1   **tablespoon sugar**

Pour boiling water on gelatin; stir until gelatin is dissolved. Stir in wine and cold water. Refrigerate until slightly thickened.

Shape cream cheese into 18 balls; roll in nuts. Mix strawberries and sugar. Pour ⅓ cup thickened gelatin into 6-cup ring mold. Arrange cheese balls evenly in gelatin in mold. Spoon strawberries over cheese balls. Carefully pour remaining gelatin over strawberries. Refrigerate until firm; unmold.   **6 servings;** 190 calories per serving.

SANGRIA MOLD

  1¼   **cups dry red wine**
  1   **package (3 ounces) lemon-flavored gelatin**
  1   **package (3 ounces) black cherry-flavored gelatin**
  2   **cups ginger ale**
  3   **oranges, pared, sectioned and cut into bite-size pieces**

Heat wine to boiling. Pour over lemon and black cherry gelatin; stir until gelatin is dissolved. Stir in ginger ale. Refrigerate until slightly thickened.

Stir orange pieces into gelatin mixture. Pour into 4-cup mold. Refrigerate until firm; unmold. Garnish with salad greens and additional orange sections if desired. Serve with mayonnaise if desired.   **6 servings;** 210 calories per serving.

FROZEN FRUIT SALAD

- 1 **package (8 ounces) cream cheese, softened**
- 1 **cup dairy sour cream**
- ¼ **cup sugar**
- ¼ **teaspoon salt**
- 1 **can (17 ounces) apricot halves, drained**
- 1 **can (16½ ounces) pitted dark sweet cherries, drained**
- 1 **can (8¼ ounces) crushed pineapple in syrup, drained**
- 1 **cup miniature marshmallows**

Beat cream cheese in 2½-quart bowl until smooth. Beat in sour cream, sugar and salt on low speed. Cut apricot halves into halves. Reserve a few cherries for garnish. Stir apricots, remaining cherries, the pineapple and marshmallows into cheese mixture. Pour into 4½-cup mold or 6 individual molds. Cover and freeze at least 8 hours.

Remove mold(s) from freezer and let stand at room temperature 10 to 15 minutes; unmold. Garnish with reserve cherries. **6 servings; 345 calories per serving.**

FROZEN RASPBERRY SALAD

- ½ **cup boiling water**
- 1 **package (3 ounces) raspberry-flavored gelatin**
- 1 **package (10 ounces) frozen raspberries, thawed**
- 1 **cup dairy sour cream**
- 2 **packages (3 ounces each) cream cheese, softened**
- 1 **can (16 ounces) whole berry cranberry sauce**
- ⅛ **teaspoon salt**
  Salad greens
- 1 **carton (6 ounces) raspberry yogurt**

Pour boiling water on gelatin; stir until gelatin is dissolved. Stir in raspberries (with syrup). Mix sour cream, cream cheese, cranberry sauce and salt; stir into gelatin mixture. (Salad will be slightly lumpy.) Pour into square pan, 8 × 8 × 2 or 9 × 9 × 2 inches. Cover and freeze at least 24 hours but no longer than 2 months.

Remove pan from freezer and let stand at room temperature 10 minutes. Cut into serving pieces. Place on salad greens; serve with yogurt. **9 servings; 300 calories per serving.**

FRUIT SALADS

SUMMER FRUIT SALAD

 Honey-Sour Cream Dressing (below)
½ cup strawberry halves or 1 cup whole raspberries
½ cup seedless grapes, cut into halves
2 medium peaches or nectarines, sliced
2 small bananas, sliced
 Lettuce cups

Prepare Honey-Sour Cream Dressing. Mix strawberries, grapes, peaches and bananas. Spoon fruit mixture into lettuce cups and, if desired, garnish with mint leaves. Serve with Honey-Sour Cream Dressing. **5 servings; 210 calories per serving.**

Honey-Sour Cream Dressing
Mix 1 cup dairy sour cream, 2 tablespoons honey and 2 tablespoons orange or grapefruit juice. Cover and refrigerate 1 hour.

FRUIT-WALNUT SALAD

2 cups melon balls
2 oranges, pared and cut into ¼-inch slices
1 cup seedless grapes, cut into halves
4 cups bite-size pieces salad greens
20 walnut halves
 Yogurt Dressing (page 537) or bottled yogurt dressing.

Arrange fruit on greens; garnish with walnuts. Drizzle with Yogurt Dressing. **4 servings; 200 calories per serving.**

Yogurt Dressing
Mix 1 cup plain yogurt, 1 tablespoon orange juice, 1 tablespoon lemon juice and 1 tablespoon honey.

EASY FRUIT SALAD

1   cup seedless grapes
1   can (11 ounces) mandarin orange segments,
        chilled and drained
1   can (8¼ ounces) pineapple chunks in syrup,
        chilled and drained
1   red apple, sliced
    Salad greens
    Fruit Salad Yogurt Dressing (page 552)

Mix grapes, orange segments, pineapple and apple. Spoon
onto salad greens. Serve with Fruit Salad Yogurt Dressing.   **4 servings; 160 calories per serving.**

MIXED FRUIT SALAD

2   cups blueberries or strawberry halves
2   papayas or 1 small cantaloupe, cut up
2   kiwifruit, sliced
    Honey Dressing (below)

Mix blueberries, papayas and kiwifruit; toss with Honey Dressing. Serve on salad greens and sprinkle with toasted almonds
if desired.   **6 servings; 165 calories per serving.**

Honey Dressing
Shake ½ cup bottled red wine vinegar and oil dressing, 2
tablespoons honey and ½ teaspoon poppy seed in tightly
covered container.

WINTER FRUIT SALAD

2   **medium apples, cut into ¼-inch slices**
    Lime Dressing (below)
2   **oranges, pared and sliced**
1   **grapefruit, pared and sectioned**
2   **cups seedless grapes**
    Salad greens

Dip apple slices in Lime Dressing. Arrange apples, oranges, grapefruit and grapes on salad greens. Serve with Lime Dressing.   **8 servings; 225 calories per serving.**

Lime Dressing
Beat ⅓ cup frozen limeade concentrate, thawed, ⅓ cup honey and ⅓ cup vegetable oil with hand beater until smooth.

FRUIT PLATTER

3   **oranges, pared and cut into slices**
2   **grapefruit, pared and sectioned**
2   **kiwifruit, pared and sliced**
1   **jar (17 ounces) figs, drained**
1   **jar (16 ounces) stewed prunes, drained**
    Lettuce leaves

Arrange fruit on lettuce leaves. Cover and refrigerate up to 3 hours.   **8 servings; 135 calories per serving.**

FRUIT AND CHEESE SALAD

⅓   **cup dairy sour cream**
½   **teaspoon Dijon-style mustard**
1   **cup shredded Cheddar cheese (4 ounces)**
6   **slices bacon, crisply cooked and crumbled**
2   **pears, cut into cubes**
    Lettuce leaves
2   **peaches or nectarines, sliced**

Mix sour cream and mustard; stir in cheese, bacon and pears. Spoon onto lettuce leaves; garnish with peaches.   **5 servings; 205 calories per serving.**

CHOW MEIN FRUIT SALAD

2   medium bananas, sliced
1   can (16 ounces) sliced peaches, drained and cut into
       halves, or 2 fresh peaches, peeled and sliced
1   large red apple, cut into cubes
1   can (8 ounces) crushed pineapple in juice, well drained
       (reserve 2 tablespoons juice)
2   cups chow mein noodles
6   slices bacon, crisply cooked and crumbled
    Sour Cream Dressing (below)

Toss bananas, peaches, apple and pineapple. Top with chow
mein noodles; sprinkle with bacon. Serve with Sour Cream
Dressing.   **6 servings; 245 calories per serving.**

Sour Cream Dressing

½   cup dairy sour cream
2   tablespoons reserved pineapple juice
1   tablespoon honey
½   teaspoon curry powder

Mix all ingredients.

TWENTY-FOUR-HOUR SALAD

    Whipped Cream Dressing (page 540)
1   can (16½ ounces) pitted light or
       dark sweet cherries, drained
2   cans (13¼ ounces each) pineapple chunks in syrup,
       drained (reserve 2 tablespoons syrup)
3   oranges, pared, sectioned and cut up, or 2 cans (11
       ounces each) mandarin orange segments, drained
1   cup miniature marshmallows

Prepare Whipped Cream Dressing. Mix cherries, pineapple,
oranges and marshmallows; toss with Whipped Cream Dressing. Cover and refrigerate at least 12 hours but no longer
than 24 hours.   **8 servings; 250 calories per serving.**

Whipped Cream Dressing

2 eggs, beaten
2 tablespoons sugar
2 tablespoons vinegar or lemon juice
2 tablespoons reserved pineapple syrup
1 tablespoon margarine or butter
Dash of salt
¾ cup chilled whipping cream

Heat all ingredients except whipping cream just to boiling, stirring constantly; cool. Beat whipping cream in chilled 1½-quart bowl until stiff; fold in egg mixture.

FRUIT-PRUNE SALAD

1 can (20 ounces) pineapple chunks in juice, drained (reserve 2 tablespoons juice)
1 cup cut-up prunes
1 cup mayonnaise or salad dressing
2 tablespoons lemon juice
2 cups sliced celery
1 cup coarsely chopped walnuts
1 can (16 ounces) sliced peaches, drained
1 can (16 ounces) sliced pears, drained
Lettuce leaves

Mix reserved pineapple juice, the prunes, mayonnaise and lemon juice. Mix pineapple and remaining ingredients except lettuce leaves; toss with mayonnaise mixture. Serve on lettuce. **8 servings; 430 calories per serving.**

WALDORF SALAD

2 medium apples, coarsely chopped (about 2 cups)
2 medium stalks celery, chopped (about 1 cup)
½ cup mayonnaise or salad dressing
⅓ cup coarsely chopped nuts

Toss all ingredients. Serve on salad greens if desired. **4 servings; 310 calories per serving.**

Pear Waldorf Salad: Substitute 4 pears, coarsely chopped, for the apples.

Waldorf Salad Supreme: Decrease celery to 1 medium stalk and nuts to ¼ cup. Stir in 1 can (8¼ ounces) pineapple chunks in syrup, drained, ½ cup miniature marshmallows and ⅓ cup cut-up dates.

APPLE-PEAR SALAD

- 2 medium apples, sliced
- 2 medium pears, sliced
- 1 medium stalk celery, diagonally sliced (about ½ cup)
- 2 tablespoons lemon juice
- 1 tablespoon honey
- ¼ teaspoon salt
- ¼ teaspoon pumpkin pie spice
    Lettuce leaves

Mix apples, pears and celery. Shake lemon juice, honey, salt and pumpkin pie spice in tightly covered container; toss with apple mixture. Cover and refrigerate at least 1 hour. Arrange on lettuce leaves. **8 servings** (about ⅔ cup each); 55 calories per serving.

AVOCADO-APPLE SALAD

    Poppy Seed Dressing (page 547)
- 2 avocados, cut into ¼-inch slices
- 1 large red apple, cut into ⅛-inch slices
    Lemon juice
    Endive
    Pomegranate seeds

Prepare Poppy Seed Dressing. Sprinkle avocado and apple slices with lemon juice. Arrange slices on endive. Sprinkle with pomegranate seeds; drizzle with dressing. **8 servings;** 280 calories per serving.

CANTALOUPE SALADS

    2   small cantaloupes
    1   cup sliced strawberries
    1   cup seedless green grapes
        Lettuce leaves
  ½   cup dairy sour cream
  ¼   cup mayonnaise or salad dressing
    2   tablespoons packed brown sugar
  ¼   cup chopped nuts

Pare each cantaloupe. Cut off about 1 inch from ends of each cantaloupe. Cut up end pieces; mix with strawberries and grapes. Remove seeds from cantaloupes. Cut each cantaloupe crosswise into 3 even rings. Place a ring on lettuce leaves on each of 6 salad plates; cut each ring into 1-inch pieces, retaining ring shape. Spoon fruit mixture onto each ring.

Mix sour cream, mayonnaise and brown sugar until sugar is dissolved and mixture is smooth; stir in nuts. Spoon onto each salad.   **6 servings; 245 calories per serving.**

CREAM CHEESE-GRAPE TOSS

        Ginger Dressing (below)
    6   cups bite-size pieces leaf lettuce
    1   cup seedless grapes
  ⅓   cup chopped toasted pecans
    1   green onion (with top), thinly sliced
    1   package (3 ounces) cream cheese, cut into small cubes

Toss all ingredients.   **5 servings; 215 calories per serving.**

Ginger Dressing
  ¼   cup bottled oil-and-vinegar dressing
    1   teaspoon lemon juice
  ¼   teaspoon ground ginger

Shake all ingredients in tightly covered container.

ORANGE-AVOCADO SALAD

    3 oranges, pared and sliced
    2 avocados, peeled and sliced
    6 thin slices red onion, separated into rings
       Salad greens
       Orange Dressing (below)

Arrange oranges, avocados and onion on salad greens on 6
salad plates. Serve with Orange Dressing. **6 servings; 250**
calories per serving.

Orange Dressing

    ⅓ cup vegetable oil
    1 teaspoon grated orange peel
    ¼ cup orange juice
    2 tablespoons sugar
    2 tablespoons lemon juice
    ½ teaspoon dry mustard
    ¼ teaspoon salt

Shake all ingredients in tightly covered container.

Orange-Jicama Salad: Cut 1 small jicama into halves; cut 1
half into julienne strips. Substitute jicama strips for the onion
rings.

ORANGE SALAD

    5 medium oranges, pared and each cut into 6 slices
    1 medium onion, thinly sliced and separated into rings
    1 medium green pepper, cut into thin rings
       Curly endive or other salad greens
       Lime-Honey Dressing (page 544)

Arrange oranges, onion and green pepper on endive. Drizzle
with Lime-Honey Dressing. **8 servings; 145** calories per
serving.

Lime-Honey Dressing

¼ cup vegetable oil
¼ teaspoon grated lime peel
3 tablespoons lime juice
3 tablespoons honey
½ teaspoon dry mustard
¼ teaspoon seasoned salt
¼ teaspoon paprika
Dash of white pepper

Shake all ingredients in tightly covered container.

PEAR SALAD

¼ cup lime juice
1 tablespoon snipped mint
3 tablespoons vegetable oil
2 tablespoons honey
1 teaspoon finely shredded lime peel
3 large pears
Bibb lettuce leaves

Mix lime juice and snipped mint. Let stand at room temperature at least 1 hour.

Remove mint and discard. Shake lime juice, oil, honey and lime peel in tightly covered container. Cut each pear lengthwise into halves; remove core and seeds. Place each pear half, cut side down, on cutting surface. Cut crosswise diagonally into thin slices.

Place each sliced pear half on lettuce leaves with spatula; separate and overlap slices slightly, retaining pear shape. Drizzle with lime juice mixture. Garnish with mint leaves if desired.   6 servings (½ pear each); 145 calories per serving.

PINEAPPLE RING SALADS

Poppy Seed Dressing (page 547)
1 small pineapple
Lettuce leaves
6 apricots, each cut into fourths
2 cups blueberries

Prepare Poppy Seed Dressing. Pare pineapple; cut crosswise into halves. Remove core with apple corer. Cut each half crosswise into 3 rings. Place a ring on lettuce leaves on each of 6 salad plates. Arrange 4 apricot pieces around each pineapple ring. Spoon blueberries into center of each pineapple ring and between apricot pieces. Serve with Poppy Seed Dressing.   **6 servings; 310 calories per serving.**

SALAD DRESSINGS

HERBED VINEGAR

Shake 1 cup white vinegar and one of the following in tightly covered jar. Refrigerate at least 4 days. Strain before serving. Use in salad dressings and marinades.　**1 cup herbed vinegar; 3 calories per tablespoon.**
- [ ] ¼ cup snipped chives
- [ ] ¼ cup snipped dill weed or ½ teaspoon dried dill weed
- [ ] 1 clove garlic, cut into fourths
- [ ] ⅓ cup snipped mint

RASPBERRY VINEGAR

Press 1 package (10 ounces) frozen raspberries, thawed, through strainer to measure ¾ cup juice. Heat raspberry juice, 3 cups vinegar and 1 cup sugar to boiling, stirring frequently. Boil and stir 1 minute; cool. Pour into bottles; cover tightly. Use in salad dressings and marinades.　**1 quart raspberry vinegar; 20 calories per tablespoon.**

　Strawberry Vinegar: Substitute 1 package (10 ounces) frozen strawberries, thawed, for the raspberries.

POPPY SEED DRESSING

⅓   cup sugar
2   tablespoons vinegar
1   tablespoon lemon juice
½   teaspoon salt
½   teaspoon dry mustard
½   cup vegetable oil
1   tablespoon poppy seed

Mix sugar, vinegar, lemon juice, salt and mustard in 1-quart bowl. Gradually add oil, beating with electric mixer or hand beater until thick and smooth; stir in poppy seed. Cover and refrigerate at least 2 hours.   **¾ cup dressing; 105 calories per tablespoon.**

ITALIAN DRESSING

1   cup vegetable oil
¼   cup vinegar
2   tablespoons finely chopped onion
1   teaspoon salt
1   teaspoon sugar
1   teaspoon dry mustard
1   teaspoon dried basil leaves
½   teaspoon dried oregano leaves
¼   teaspoon pepper
2   cloves garlic, crushed

Shake all ingredients in tightly covered container. Refrigerate at least 2 hours. Shake before serving.   **1¼ cups dressing; 100 calories per tablespoon.**

Creamy Italian Dressing: Beat ½ cup Italian Dressing and ½ cup mayonnaise or salad dressing with hand beater until smooth.   **About 1 cup dressing.**

FRENCH DRESSING

   1   **cup olive or vegetable oil or combination**
  ¼   **cup vinegar**
  ¼   **cup lemon juice**
   1   **teaspoon salt**
  ½   **teaspoon dry mustard**
  ½   **teaspoon paprika**

Shake all ingredients in tightly covered container; refrigerate. Shake before serving. **1½ cups dressing; 80 calories per tablespoon.**

   Lorenzo Dressing: Mix ½ cup French Dressing and 1 tablespoon chili sauce. **About ½ cup dressing.**

   Tomato Dressing: Mix ½ cup French Dressing and ½ cup catsup. **About 1 cup dressing.**

CLASSIC FRENCH DRESSING

  ½   **cup vegetable or olive oil**
  ¼   **cup tarragon or wine vinegar**
   1   **teaspoon salt**
   1   **medium clove garlic, crushed**
      Generous dash of freshly ground pepper

Shake all ingredients in tightly covered container; refrigerate. Shake dressing before serving. **About ¾ cup dressing; 90 calories per tablespoon.**

ORANGE-PECAN DRESSING

  ½   **cup vegetable oil**
  ½   **cup orange juice**
   2   **tablespoons chopped pecans**
   1   **tablespoon honey or sugar**
   1   **teaspoon celery salt**
   1   **teaspoon prepared mustard**

Shake all ingredients in tightly covered container; refrigerate. Shake dressing before serving. **About 1 cup dressing; 75 calories per tablespoon.**

Orange-Onion Dressing: Substitute 2 to 3 teaspoons grated onion for the pecans. Add ½ teaspoon salt and ¼ teaspoon pepper.

GINGER-HONEY DRESSING

2	tablespoons vegetable oil
2	tablespoons lime juice
2	tablespoons honey
¼	teaspoon salt
¼	teaspoon ground ginger

Shake all ingredients in tightly covered container. **About ⅓ cup dressing; 70 calories per tablespoon.**

COOKED SALAD DRESSING

¼	cup all-purpose flour
2	tablespoons sugar
1	teaspoon salt
1	teaspoon dry mustard
1½	cups milk
2	egg yolks, slightly beaten
⅓	cup vinegar
1	tablespoon margarine or butter

Mix flour, sugar, salt and mustard in 2-quart saucepan. Gradually stir in milk. Heat to boiling over medium heat, stirring constantly. Boil and stir 1 minute. Gradually stir at least half of the hot mixture into egg yolks. Stir into hot mixture in saucepan. Boil and stir 1 minute; remove from heat. Stir in vinegar and margarine. Cover and refrigerate. **About 2 cups dressing; 20 calories per tablespoon.**

MAYONNAISE

- 1   egg yolk
- 2   tablespoons lemon juice or vinegar
- 1   teaspoon dry mustard
- 1   teaspoon sugar
- ¼   teaspoon salt
-      Dash of ground red pepper
- 1   cup vegetable oil

Beat egg yolk, 1 tablespoon lemon juice, the mustard, sugar, salt and red pepper in 1½-quart bowl on medium speed until blended. Beat in oil, 1 drop at a time; increase rate of addition as mixture thickens. Beat in remaining lemon juice; refrigerate. (Any remaining dressing should be refrigerated immediately.) **About 1 cup dressing; 125 calories per tablespoon.**

Blender Mayonnaise: Substitute 1 egg for the egg yolk. Place egg, the 2 tablespoons lemon juice or vinegar, the mustard, sugar, salt, red pepper and ¼ cup of the oil in blender container. Cover and blend on high speed 5 seconds; stop blender. Blend on high speed, very gradually adding remaining ¾ cup oil and stopping blender occasionally to scrape sides; refrigerate. **About 1½ cups dressing.**

BUTTERMILK DRESSING

- ¾   cup mayonnaise or salad dressing
- ½   cup buttermilk
- 1   teaspoon parsley flakes
- ½   teaspoon instant minced onion
- ½   teaspoon salt
-      Dash of freshly ground pepper
- 1   clove garlic, crushed

Shake all ingredients in tightly covered container. Refrigerate at least 2 hours. Shake before serving. **1¼ cups dressing; 65 calories per tablespoon.**

Mayonnaise-Buttermilk Dressing: Increase mayonnaise to 1 cup and decrease buttermilk to ¼ cup.

GREEN GODDESS DRESSING

- 1 cup mayonnaise or salad dressing
- ½ cup dairy sour cream
- ⅓ cup finely snipped parsley
- 3 tablespoons finely snipped chives
- 3 tablespoons anchovy paste or
finely chopped anchovy fillets
- 3 tablespoons tarragon or wine vinegar
- 1 tablespoon lemon juice
- ¼ teaspoon salt
- ⅛ teaspoon freshly ground pepper

Mix all ingredients; cover dressing and refrigerate.   **About 2 cups dressing;** 60 calories per tablespoon.

BLUE CHEESE DRESSING

- ¾ cup crumbled blue cheese
- 1 package (3 ounces) cream cheese, softened
- ½ cup mayonnaise or salad dressing
- ⅓ cup half-and-half

Reserve ⅓ cup of the blue cheese. Beat remaining blue cheese and the cream cheese on low speed until blended. Add mayonnaise and half-and-half; beat on medium speed until creamy. Stir in reserved blue cheese. Cover and refrigerate at least 3 hours.   **About 1⅔ cups dressing;** 60 calories per tablespoon.

THOUSAND ISLAND DRESSING

- 1 cup mayonnaise or salad dressing
- 1 tablespoon snipped parsley
- 2 tablespoons chopped pimiento-stuffed olives or sweet pickle relish
- 2 tablespoons chili sauce or catsup
- 1 teaspoon finely chopped onion
- ½ teaspoon paprika
- 1 hard-cooked egg, chopped

Mix all ingredients; cover dressing and refrigerate. **About 1¼ cups dressing; 55 calories per tablespoon.**

Russian Dressing: Omit parsley, olives and egg. Increase chili sauce to ¼ cup; add 1 teaspoon prepared horseradish.

MOCK MAYONNAISE

    1   cup plain yogurt
    2   tablespoons mayonnaise or salad dressing
    ¼   teaspoon salt
        Dash of paprika
    1   drop yellow food color

Beat all ingredients with hand beater until smooth. Cover dressing; refrigerate at least 2 hours. **About 1 cup dressing; 20 calories per tablespoon.**

EASY YOGURT DRESSINGS

Blue Cheese Yogurt Dressing: Mix ⅔ cup plain yogurt, ¼ cup crumbled blue cheese, 1 green onion (with top), chopped, ½ teaspoon salt and ⅛ teaspoon garlic powder. **About 1 cup dressing; 15 calories per tablespoon.**

Cucumber Yogurt Dressing: Mix ⅔ cup plain yogurt, ½ cup chopped cucumber, 1½ teaspoons instant minced onion, 1½ teaspoons sugar, 1 teaspoon prepared horseradish and ½ teaspoon salt. Cover and refrigerate at least 2 hours. **About 1 cup dressing; 10 calories per tablespoon.**

Fruit Salad Yogurt Dressing: Mix ⅔ cup plain yogurt, 1 tablespoon honey and 1 tablespoon lemon juice. **About ¾ cup dressing; 15 calories per tablespoon.**

CREAMY LOW-CAL DRESSING

½   cup skim milk
2   tablespoons lemon juice
1   tablespoon vegetable oil
1½ cups low-fat cottage cheese (12 ounces)
1   small onion, chopped (about ¼ cup)
2   cloves garlic, crushed
½   teaspoon salt
¼   teaspoon pepper
¼   teaspoon paprika

Place all ingredients in blender container in order listed. Cover and blend on medium speed until smooth, about 1 minute; cover and refrigerate. **About 2 cups dressing; 15 calories per tablespoon.**

NO-OIL DRESSING

⅓   cup water
¼   cup lemon juice
2   tablespoons honey
1   tablespoon prepared mustard
½   teaspoon salt
¼   teaspoon paprika
1   clove garlic, crushed

Shake all ingredients in tightly covered container. Refrigerate at least 1 hour. Shake before serving. **About ¾ cup dressing; 15 calories per tablespoon.**

SOUPS
SANDWICHES
SAUCES

SOUPS

CHICKEN AND BROTH

3-	to 3½-pound broiler-fryer chicken, cut up*
4½	cups cold water
1½	teaspoons salt
½	teaspoon pepper
1	stalk celery with leaves, cut up
1	medium carrot, cut up
1	small onion, cut up
1	sprig parsley

Remove any excess fat from chicken. Place chicken, giblets (except liver) and neck in Dutch oven. Add remaining ingredients; heat to boiling. Skim foam; reduce heat. Cover and simmer until thickest pieces of chicken are done, about 45 minutes.

Remove chicken from broth; cool chicken just until cool enough to handle, about 10 minutes. Strain broth through cheesecloth-lined sieve. Remove chicken from bones and skin; cut up chicken. Discard bones, skin and vegetables. Skim fat from broth. Use immediately, or cover and refrigerate broth and chicken in separate containers up to 24 hours, or freeze for future use. **About 3 cups broth; 110 calories, and about 3 cups cooked chicken; 715 calories.**

*3 to 3½ pounds chicken necks, backs and giblets (except liver) can be used to make broth.

CHICKEN NOODLE SOUP

Chicken and Broth (page 557)
2 medium carrots, sliced (about 1 cup)
2 medium stalks celery, sliced (about 1 cup)
1 small onion, chopped (about ¼ cup)
1 tablespoon instant chicken bouillon
1 cup uncooked medium noodles (about 2 ounces)
Snipped parsley, if desired

Prepare Chicken and Broth; reserve cut-up chicken. Add enough water to broth to measure 5 cups. Heat broth, carrots, celery, onion and bouillon (dry) to boiling; reduce heat. Cover; simmer until carrots are tender, about 15 minutes. Stir in noodles and chicken. Heat to boiling; reduce heat. Simmer uncovered until noodles are done, 7 to 10 minutes. Sprinkle with parsley. **6 servings** (about 1 cup each); 185 calories per serving.

Chicken Rice Soup: Substitute ½ cup uncooked regular rice for the uncooked noodles. Stir in rice with the vegetables. Cover and simmer until rice is tender, about 15 minutes. Stir in chicken; heat until chicken is hot.

CHICKEN-VEGETABLE CHOWDER

1 package (10 ounces) frozen chopped broccoli
3 medium stalks celery, thinly sliced (about 2 cups)
1 medium onion, chopped (about ½ cup)
2 cups water
1 teaspoon salt
1 can (10¾ ounces) condensed chicken broth or
   1¼ cups chicken broth (page 557)
1 cup cold milk
½ cup all-purpose flour
1½ cups cut-up cooked chicken (page 557)
1 cup milk
6 ounces Swiss cheese, cut into cubes (about 1½ cups)

Rinse broccoli under running cold water to separate; drain. Heat broccoli, celery, onion, water, salt and broth to boiling in Dutch oven; reduce heat. Cover and simmer 10 minutes.

Shake 1 cup cold milk and the flour in tightly covered

container; gradually stir into hot mixture. Heat to boiling. Boil and stir 1 minute. Stir in chicken and 1 cup milk. Heat over low heat, stirring occasionally, just until hot, about 10 minutes. Stir in cheese; let stand just until cheese is melted, 3 to 5 minutes; stir.   **8 servings** (about 1 cup each); 225 calories per serving.

EGG DROP SOUP

3   cups chicken broth (page 557)
1   teaspoon salt
    Dash of white pepper
1   medium green onion (with top), chopped
2   eggs, slightly beaten

Heat chicken broth, salt and white pepper to boiling in 3-quart saucepan. Stir onion into eggs. Pour egg mixture slowly into broth, stirring constantly with fork until eggs form shreds.   **4 servings** (about ¾ cup each); 70 calories per serving.

MULLIGATAWNY SOUP

2½- to 3-pound broiler-fryer chicken, cut up
4   cups water
1½   teaspoons salt
1   teaspoon curry powder
1   teaspoon lemon juice
⅛   teaspoon ground cloves
⅛   teaspoon ground mace
1   medium onion, chopped (about ½ cup)
2   tablespoons margarine or butter
2   tablespoons all-purpose flour
2   medium tomatoes, chopped
1   large apple, coarsely chopped
1   medium carrot, thinly sliced
1   medium green pepper, cut into ½-inch pieces

Remove any excess fat from chicken. Heat chicken, giblets (except liver), neck, water, salt, curry powder, lemon juice, cloves and mace to boiling in Dutch oven; reduce heat. Cover and simmer until thickest pieces of chicken are done, about 45 minutes.

Remove chicken from broth; cool chicken just until cool enough to handle, about 10 minutes. Remove chicken from bones and skin; cut chicken into bite-size pieces. Skim fat from broth. Add enough water to broth, if necessary, to measure 4 cups.

Cook and stir onion in margarine in Dutch oven until tender; remove from heat. Stir in flour. Gradually stir in broth. Add chicken, tomatoes, apple, carrot and green pepper. Heat to boiling; reduce heat. Cover and simmer until carrot is tender, about 10 minutes. Garnish with parsley if desired. **6 servings** (about 1¼ cups each); 260 calories per serving.

CHICKEN AND LEEK SOUP

2½-	**to 3-pound broiler-fryer chicken, cut up**
1	**medium carrot, sliced (about ½ cup)**
1	**medium stalk celery, sliced (about ½ cup)**
1	**bay leaf**
½	**cup uncooked barley**
4	**cups water**
2	**teaspoons salt**
2	**teaspoons instant chicken bouillon (dry)**
¼	**teaspoon pepper**
1½	**cups sliced leeks (with tops)**

Heat all ingredients except leeks to boiling in Dutch oven reduce heat. Cover and simmer 30 minutes.

Add leeks. Heat to boiling; reduce heat. Cover and simmer until thickest pieces of chicken are done, about 15 minutes. Remove chicken from broth; cool chicken slightly. Remove chicken from bones and skin; cut chicken into 1-inch pieces. Skim fat from broth; remove bay leaf. Add chicken to broth; heat until hot, about 5 minutes. **7 servings** (about 1 cup each); 195 calories per serving.

BEEF AND BROTH

2	pounds beef shank cross cuts
6	cups cold water
1	teaspoon salt
¼	teaspoon dried thyme leaves
1	carrot, cut up
1	stalk celery with leaves, cut up
1	small onion, cut up
5	peppercorns
3	whole cloves
3	sprigs parsley
1	bay leaf

Remove marrow from center of bones. Heat marrow in Dutch oven over low heat until melted, or heat 2 tablespoons vegetable oil until hot. Cook beef shanks in marrow over medium heat until brown on both sides. Add water; heat to boiling. Skim foam. Stir in remaining ingredients; heat to boiling. Skim foam; reduce heat. Cover and simmer 3 hours.

Remove beef from broth; cool beef just until cool enough to handle, about 10 minutes. Strain broth through cheesecloth-lined sieve. Remove beef from bones; cut beef into ½-inch pieces. Discard bones, vegetables and seasonings. Skim fat from broth. Use immediately, or cover and refrigerate broth and beef in separate containers up to 24 hours, or freeze for future use. **About 4 cups broth;** 75 calories, and **about 3 cups cooked beef;** 840 calories.

VEGETABLE BEEF SOUP

Beef and Broth (page 561)
1 ear corn*
2 medium potatoes, cut into ¾-inch pieces
1 medium carrot, thinly sliced (about ½ cup)
1 medium stalk celery, sliced (about ½ cup)
1 medium onion, chopped (about ½ cup)
1 cup 1-inch pieces green beans*
1 cup shelled green peas*
1 tablespoon instant beef bouillon (dry)
¼ teaspoon pepper
1 can (16 ounces) whole tomatoes, undrained

Prepare Beef and Broth. Add enough water to broth to measure 5 cups; return beef and broth to Dutch oven. Cut kernels from corn.

Stir corn and remaining ingredients into broth; break up tomatoes with fork. Heat to boiling; reduce heat. Cover and simmer until vegetables are tender, about 30 minutes. **7 servings** (about 1½ cups each); 230 calories per serving.

Barley-Vegetable Beef Soup: Omit potatoes. Stir ⅔ cup uncooked barley and ½ teaspoon salt into Beef and Broth. Heat to boiling; reduce heat. Cover and simmer 30 minutes. Stir in remaining ingredients. Cover and simmer until barley and vegetables are tender, about 30 minutes longer.

*1 cup each frozen whole kernel corn, cut green beans and green peas can be substituted for the 1 ear corn, 1-inch pieces green beans and shelled green peas. Add potatoes, carrot, celery, onion, bouillon, pepper and tomatoes to beef broth. Simmer uncovered 15 minutes. Stir in frozen vegetables. Heat to boiling; reduce heat. Cover and simmer until vegetables are tender, about 15 minutes longer.

HAMBURGER MINESTRONE

1	pound ground beef
1	medium onion, chopped (about ½ cup)
1	clove garlic, crushed
1¼	cups water
1	stalk celery, thinly sliced (about 1 cup)
1	small zucchini, sliced (about 1 cup)
1	cup shredded cabbage
½	cup uncooked elbow macaroni or broken spaghetti
2	teaspoons instant beef bouillon (dry)
1	teaspoon Italian seasoning
½	teaspoon salt
1	can (28 ounces) whole tomatoes, undrained
1	can (8 ounces) kidney beans, undrained
1	can (8 ounces) whole kernel corn, undrained
	Grated Parmesan cheese

Cook and stir ground beef, onion and garlic in Dutch oven until beef is brown; drain. Stir in remaining ingredients except cheese; break up tomatoes with fork.

Heat to boiling; reduce heat. Cover and simmer, stirring occasionally, until macaroni is tender, about 15 minutes. Serve with cheese.   **6 servings** (about 1½ cups each); 320 calories per serving.

SCOTCH BROTH

1½	pounds lamb boneless shoulder
6	cups water
½	cup uncooked barley
2	teaspoons salt
½	teaspoon pepper
3	medium carrots, sliced (about 1½ cups)
2	stalks celery, sliced (about 1 cup)
1	large onion, chopped (about 1 cup)
1	cup diced rutabaga or turnips
	Snipped parsley

Trim fat from lamb; cut lamb into ¾-inch pieces. Heat lamb, water, barley, salt and pepper to boiling in Dutch oven; reduce heat. Cover and simmer 1 hour.

Add vegetables. Cover and simmer until lamb and vegetables are tender, about 30 minutes. Skim fat from broth if necessary. Sprinkle with parsley. **6 servings; 235 calories per serving.**

ITALIAN VEGETABLE SOUP

1	pound bulk Italian sausage
1	medium onion, sliced
1½	cups water
½	teaspoon dried basil leaves
2	medium zucchini or yellow summer squash, cut into ¼-inch slices
1	can (16 ounces) whole tomatoes, undrained
1	can (15 ounces) garbanzo beans, drained
1	can (10½ ounces) condensed beef broth
¼	cup grated Parmesan cheese

Cook and stir sausage and onion in 3-quart saucepan until sausage is light brown; drain. Stir in remaining ingredients except cheese; break up tomatoes with fork.

Heat to boiling; reduce heat. Cover and simmer until zucchini is tender, about 5 minutes. Serve with cheese. **8 servings** (about 1 cup each); **190 calories per serving.**

MANHATTAN CLAM CHOWDER

¼	cup finely cut-up lean salt pork or bacon
1	small onion, finely chopped
2	cans (8 ounces each) minced or whole clams*
2	cups finely chopped potatoes
⅓	cup chopped celery
1	cup water
2	teaspoons snipped parsley
1	teaspoon salt
¼	teaspoon dried thyme leaves
⅛	teaspoon pepper
1	can (16 ounces) whole tomatoes, undrained

*1 pint shucked fresh clams with liquid can be substituted for the canned clams. Chop clams and stir in with the potatoes.

Cook and stir salt pork and onion in Dutch oven until pork is crisp and onion is tender. Drain clams, reserving liquid. Stir clam liquid, potatoes, celery and water into onion and pork. Heat to boiling; reduce heat. Cover and boil until potatoes are tender, about 10 minutes. Stir in clams and remaining ingredients; break up tomatoes with fork. Heat to boiling, stirring occasionally.   **5 servings; 160 calories per serving.**

NEW ENGLAND CHOWDER

¼ cup cut-up bacon or lean salt pork
1 medium onion, chopped (about ½ cup)
2 cans (8 ounces each) minced clams, drained (reserve liquid)
1 cup finely chopped potato
½ teaspoon salt
   Dash of pepper
2 cups milk

Cook and stir bacon and onion in 2-quart saucepan until bacon is crisp and onion is tender. Add enough water, if necessary, to reserved clam liquid to measure 1 cup. Stir clams, liquid, potato, salt and pepper into onion mixture. Heat to boiling; reduce heat. Cover and boil until potato is tender, about 15 minutes. Stir in milk. Heat, stirring occasionally, just until hot (do not boil).   **4 servings; 240 calories per serving.**

SHRIMP GUMBO

2	medium onions, sliced
1	medium green pepper, cut into thin strips
2	cloves garlic, crushed
¼	cup margarine or butter
2	tablespoons all-purpose flour
3	cups water
1	tablespoon instant beef bouillon (dry)
1	teaspoon salt
¼	teaspoon pepper
½	teaspoon red pepper sauce
1	bay leaf
1	can (16 ounces) okra, drained, or 1 package (10 ounces) frozen cut okra, thawed
1	can (16 ounces) whole tomatoes, undrained
1	can (6 ounces) tomato paste
1½	pounds fresh or frozen raw shrimp (in shells),* thawed
3	cups hot cooked rice (page 85)
¼	cup snipped parsley

Cook and stir onions, green pepper and garlic in margarine in Dutch oven over low heat until onions are tender. Stir in flour. Cook over low heat, stirring constantly, until bubbly; remove from heat. Stir in remaining ingredients except shrimp, rice and parsley; break up tomatoes with fork. Heat to boiling; reduce heat. Simmer uncovered, stirring occasionally, 45 minutes.

Peel shrimp. Make a shallow cut lengthwise down back of each shrimp; wash out sand vein. Stir shrimp into tomato mixture. Cover and simmer until shrimp are pink, about 5 minutes. Remove bay leaf. Serve gumbo over rice; sprinkle with parsley. **6 servings** (about 1½ cups each); 345 calories per serving.

*1 pound frozen peeled and deveined shrimp, thawed, can be substituted for the 1½ pounds shrimp in shells.

ORIENTAL SEAFOOD SOUP

1	small cucumber
2	cans (10¾ ounces each) condensed chicken broth
2⅓	cups water
1	tablespoon soy sauce
⅛	teaspoon ground ginger
	Dash of pepper
2	ounces uncooked vermicelli
½	pound fish fillets, cut into ½-inch slices
1	can (4½ ounces) tiny shrimp, rinsed and drained
1	cup sliced mushrooms or 1 can (4 ounces) mushroom stems and pieces, drained
5	cups torn spinach (about 4 ounces)
¼	cup sliced green onions (with tops)

Cut cucumber lengthwise into halves; remove seeds. Cut each half crosswise into thin slices. Heat broth, water, soy sauce, ginger and pepper to boiling in 3-quart saucepan; stir in vermicelli. Heat to boiling; boil uncovered just until tender, about 4 minutes.

Stir in cucumber, fish, shrimp and mushrooms. Heat to boiling; reduce heat. Simmer uncovered until fish flakes easily with fork, about 1 minute. Stir in spinach until wilted. Sprinkle each serving with onions. **6 servings** (about 1 cup each); 160 calories per serving.

QUICK FISH SOUP

2	medium onions, chopped (about 1 cup)
2	cloves garlic, crushed
2	tablespoons vegetable oil
1½	pounds fish fillets, cut into 1-inch pieces
2	cans (10¾ ounces each) condensed chicken broth
2	soup cans water
3	medium tomatoes, coarsely chopped
2	medium green peppers, chopped
½	teaspoon salt
½	teaspoon dried oregano leaves
½	teaspoon ground red pepper

Cook and stir onions and garlic in oil in Dutch oven until onions are tender; add remaining ingredients. Heat to boiling; reduce heat. Cover and simmer until fish flakes easily with fork, about 5 minutes. **8 servings** (about 1¼ cups each); 210 calories per serving.

SALMON-WILD RICE SOUP

    3   slices bacon, cut into ½-inch pieces
    1   medium onion, sliced
    1   medium stalk celery, thinly sliced
    4   ounces mushrooms, sliced
    2   tablespoons all-purpose flour
    ½   teaspoon dry mustard
    ¼   teaspoon dried rosemary leaves
    1   cup cooked wild rice (page 85)
    2   cans (10¾ ounces each) condensed chicken broth
    1   cup half-and-half
    1   can (15½ ounces) salmon, drained and flaked

Cook bacon in 3-quart saucepan until crisp; drain, reserving fat in saucepan. Cook and stir onion, celery and mushrooms in bacon fat until celery is tender. Stir in flour, mustard and rosemary. Cook over low heat, stirring constantly, until bubbly; remove from heat. Stir in wild rice and broth.

Heat to boiling; reduce heat. Cover and simmer 10 minutes. Stir in bacon, half-and-half and salmon. Heat, stirring occasionally, until hot. **6 servings** (about 1 cup each); 280 calories per serving.

WILD RICE SOUP

2	medium stalks celery, sliced
1	medium carrot, coarsely shredded
1	medium onion, chopped (about ½ cup)
1	small green pepper, chopped
2	tablespoons margarine or butter
3	tablespoons all-purpose flour
1	teaspoon salt
¼	teaspoon pepper
1½	cups cooked wild rice (page 85)
1	cup water
1	can (10¾ ounces) condensed chicken broth
1	cup half-and-half
⅓	cup toasted slivered almonds
¼	cup snipped parsley

Cook and stir celery, carrot, onion and green pepper in margarine in 3-quart saucepan until celery is tender, about 5 minutes. Stir in flour, salt and pepper. Stir in wild rice, water and broth. Heat to boiling; reduce heat.

Cover and simmer, stirring occasionally, 15 minutes. Stir in half-and-half, almonds and parsley. Heat just until hot (do not boil). **5 servings** (about 1 cup each); 300 calories per serving.

CREAM OF VEGETABLE SOUP

2	cups water
1	cup cut fresh or frozen green beans
¾	cup fresh or frozen green peas
¼	small head cauliflower, separated into flowerets
2	small carrots, sliced
1	medium potato, cubed
2	ounces spinach, cut up (about 2 cups)
2	cups milk
2	tablespoons all-purpose flour
¼	cup whipping cream
1½	teaspoons salt
⅛	teaspoon pepper

Heat water, beans, peas, cauliflowerets, carrots and potato to boiling in 3-quart saucepan; reduce heat. Cover and simmer until vegetables are crisp-tender, 10 to 15 minutes.

Add spinach; cook uncovered about 1 minute. Mix ¼ cup of the milk and the flour; gradually stir into vegetable mixture. Heat to boiling. Boil and stir 1 minute. Stir in remaining milk, the whipping cream, salt and pepper. Heat just until hot (do not boil). Garnish each serving with snipped dill weed if desired.   **6 servings** (about 1¼ cups each); 150 calories per serving.

CREAM OF MUSHROOM SOUP

    8   **ounces mushrooms**
    4   **tablespoons margarine or butter**
    1   **medium onion, chopped**
    ¼   **cup all-purpose flour**
    1   **teaspoon salt**
    ¼   **teaspoon white pepper**
    1¼ **cups water**
    1   **can (10¾ ounces) condensed chicken broth**
    1   **cup half-and-half**
        Snipped parsley

Slice enough mushrooms to measure 1 cup; chop remaining mushrooms. Cook and stir sliced mushrooms in 2 tablespoons of the margarine in 3-quart saucepan over low heat until mushrooms are golden brown. Remove mushrooms with slotted spoon.

Cook and stir chopped mushrooms and onion in remaining 2 tablespoons margarine until onion is tender. Stir in flour, salt and white pepper. Cook over low heat, stirring constantly, until mixture is smooth and bubbly; remove from heat. Stir in water and broth. Heat to boiling, stirring constantly. Boil and stir 1 minute. Stir in half-and-half and sliced mushrooms. Heat just until hot (do not boil). Sprinkle with parsley.   **4 servings** (about 1 cup each); 260 calories per serving.

ZUCCHINI SOUP

1	small onion, chopped (about ¼ cup)
1	tablespoon margarine or butter
2	cups chicken broth (page 557)
2	tablespoons chopped canned green chilies
½	teaspoon salt
⅛	teaspoon pepper
2	small zucchini, chopped
1	can (8¾ ounces) whole kernel corn, drained
1	cup milk
2	ounces Monterey Jack cheese, cut into ¼-inch cubes (about ½ cup)
	Ground nutmeg
	Snipped parsley

Cook and stir onion in margarine until tender. Stir in broth, chilies, salt, pepper, zucchini and corn. Heat to boiling; reduce heat. Cover and cook 5 minutes. Stir in milk. Heat just until hot (do not boil). Add cheese; sprinkle with nutmeg and parsley.   5 servings (about 1 cup each); 150 calories per serving.

CREAMY BROCCOLI SOUP

1½	pounds broccoli
2	cups water
1	large stalk celery, chopped (about ¾ cup)
1	medium onion, chopped (about ½ cup)
2	tablespoons margarine or butter
2	tablespoons all-purpose flour
2½	cups water
1	tablespoon instant chicken bouillon
¾	teaspoon salt
⅛	teaspoon pepper
	Dash of ground nutmeg
½	cup whipping cream

Prepare broccoli as directed on page 625. Remove flowerets from broccoli; cut stalks into 1-inch pieces.

Heat 2 cups water to boiling in 3-quart saucepan. Add broccoli flowerets and pieces, celery and onion. Cover and heat to boiling. Boil until tender, about 10 minutes; do not drain. Place in blender container. Cover and blend until of uniform consistency.

Heat margarine in 3-quart saucepan over low heat until melted. Stir in flour. Cook, stirring constantly, until mixture is smooth and bubbly; remove from heat. Stir in 2½ cups water. Heat to boiling, stirring constantly. Boil and stir 1 minute. Stir in broccoli mixture, bouillon (dry), salt, pepper and nutmeg. Heat just to boiling. Stir in whipping cream. Heat just until hot (do not boil). Serve with shredded cheese if desired. **8 servings** (about 1 cup each); 115 calories per serving.

Creamy Cabbage Soup: Substitute 1 medium head green cabbage (about 1½ pounds), shredded, for the broccoli; decrease boiling time to 5 minutes.

Creamy Cauliflower Soup: Substitute 1 head cauliflower (about 2 pounds), separated into flowerets, for the broccoli; add 1 tablespoon lemon juice with the onion.

CORN CHOWDER

½	**pound bacon, cut up**
1	**medium onion, chopped (about ½ cup)**
2	**stalks celery, chopped (about 1 cup)**
2	**tablespoons all-purpose flour**
4	**cups milk**
½	**teaspoon salt**
⅛	**teaspoon pepper**
1	**can (17 ounces) cream-style corn**
1	**can (16 ounces) tiny whole potatoes, diced**
	Snipped parsley
	Paprika

Cook bacon in 3-quart saucepan until crisp; drain, reserving 3 tablespoons fat in saucepan. Cook and stir onion and celery in bacon fat until onion is tender; remove from heat. Stir in flour. Cook over low heat, stirring constantly, until mixture is bubbly; remove from heat. Stir in milk. Heat to boiling, stirring constantly. Boil and stir 1 minute. Stir in salt, pepper, corn and potatoes; heat through. Stir in bacon. Sprinkle each serving with parsley and paprika. **6 servings** (about 1 cup each); 320 calories per serving.

HEARTY TOMATO SOUP

---

1   medium onion, finely chopped (about ½ cup)
2   tablespoons margarine or butter
½   teaspoon paprika
½   teaspoon dried basil leaves
⅛   teaspoon garlic powder
2   packages (3 ounces each) cream cheese, softened
1¼   cups milk
2   cans (10¾ ounces each) condensed tomato soup
2   cans (16 ounces each) whole tomatoes, undrained

Cook and stir onion in margarine in 3-quart saucepan until onion is transparent, 2 to 3 minutes; remove from heat. Stir in paprika, basil, garlic powder and cream cheese. Gradually stir in milk and soup; beat with hand beater until smooth. Break up tomatoes with fork; stir into soup. Heat over medium heat, stirring frequently, until hot.   **8 servings** (about 1 cup each); 215 calories per serving.

EASY BORSCH

---

1   can (16 ounces) shoestring beets, undrained
1   can (10½ ounces) condensed beef broth
1   cup shredded cabbage
2   tablespoons finely chopped onion
1   teaspoon sugar
1   teaspoon lemon juice
     Dairy sour cream

Heat beets, broth, cabbage, onion and sugar to boiling; reduce heat. Simmer uncovered 5 minutes. Stir in lemon juice. Serve hot, or refrigerate until chilled. Top each serving with spoonful of sour cream.   **4 servings** (about 1 cup each); 85 calories per serving.

VEGETABLE-PASTA SOUP

1	cup chopped fully cooked smoked ham (about 4 ounces)
1	medium onion, sliced
2	cloves garlic, crushed
2	tablespoons olive or vegetable oil
3	cups water
1	teaspoon dried oregano leaves
½	teaspoon dried thyme leaves
¼	teaspoon pepper
1	can (16 ounces) whole tomatoes, undrained
1	cup uncooked spiral or elbow macaroni
2	medium potatoes, cut into ½-inch pieces
1	can (20 ounces) cannellini beans or 1 can (15 ounces) red kidney beans, drained
1	small zucchini, thinly sliced
⅓	cup grated Parmesan cheese

Cook and stir ham, onion and garlic in oil in Dutch oven over medium heat until onion is tender, about 5 minutes. Stir in water, oregano, thyme, pepper and tomatoes; break up the tomatoes. Heat to boiling. Stir in macaroni and potatoes; reduce heat. Cook uncovered until macaroni is tender, about 10 minutes.

Stir in beans and zucchini. Cook just until zucchini is crisp-tender, about 3 minutes. Sprinkle with cheese. **6 servings** (about 1⅓ cups each); 310 calories per serving.

FRENCH ONION SOUP

3	large onions, sliced
¼	cup margarine or butter
1	tablespoon all-purpose flour
2	cans (10½ ounces each) condensed beef broth
2	cups water
1	teaspoon Worcestershire sauce
6	slices French bread, toasted
3	cups shredded Monterey Jack or mozzarella cheese (12 ounces)

Cook onions in margarine in Dutch oven over medium heat, stirring occasionally, until onions are tender and just begin to brown; sprinkle with flour. Gradually stir in 1 can broth. Heat to boiling, stirring constantly. Stir in remaining broth, the water and Worcestershire sauce. Heat to boiling; reduce heat. Simmer uncovered 5 minutes.

Place 1 slice toast in each of 6 ovenproof soup bowls or casseroles. Pour soup over toast; sprinkle with cheese. Set oven control to broil and/or 550°. Broil soup with tops 3 to 4 inches from heat until cheese is melted and light brown, about 5 minutes. **6 servings** (about 1 cup each); 385 calories per serving.

CHEDDAR CHEESE SOUP

1	small onion, chopped (about ¼ cup)
1	medium stalk celery, thinly sliced (about ½ cup)
2	tablespoons margarine or butter
2	tablespoons all-purpose flour
¼	teaspoon pepper
¼	teaspoon dry mustard
1	cup milk
1	can (10¾ ounces) condensed chicken broth
2	cups shredded Cheddar cheese (8 ounces)

Cover and cook onion and celery in margarine in 2-quart saucepan until onion is tender, about 5 minutes. Stir in flour, pepper and mustard. Add milk and broth. Heat to boiling over medium heat, stirring constantly. Boil and stir 1 minute. Stir in cheese; heat over low heat, stirring occasionally, just until cheese is melted. Sprinkle with paprika if desired. **4 servings;** 355 calories per serving.

SPLIT PEA SOUP

8 cups water
1 pound dried split peas (about 2¼ cups)
2 - pound smoked ham
1 medium onion, chopped (about ½ cup)
1 teaspoon salt
¼ teaspoon pepper
2 medium carrots, cut into ½-inch pieces (about 1 cup)
2 medium stalks celery, cut into ½-inch pieces (about 1 cup)

Heat water and peas to boiling in Dutch oven. Boil 2 minutes; remove from heat. Cover and let stand 1 hour.

Stir ham, onion, salt and pepper into peas. Heat to boiling; reduce heat. Cover and simmer until peas are tender, about 1 hour. Skim fat if necessary.

Remove ham; trim fat and bone from ham. Cut ham into ½-inch pieces (about 4 cups). Stir ham, carrots and celery into soup. Heat to boiling; reduce heat. Cover and simmer until vegetables are tender, about 45 minutes. **8 servings** (about 1½ cups each); 365 calories per serving.

LENTIL-SPINACH SOUP

2 medium onions, sliced
1 clove garlic, finely chopped
2 tablespoons vegetable or olive oil
3 cups water
1 teaspoon salt
8 ounces dried lentils (about 1¼ cups)
1 teaspoon grated lemon peel
2 teaspoons lemon juice
10 ounces spinach, chopped (about 4 cups) or 1 package (10 ounces) frozen chopped spinach, thawed

Cook and stir onions and garlic in oil in 3-quart saucepan over medium heat until onions are tender. Stir in water, salt and lentils. Heat to boiling; reduce heat. Cover and simmer 1 hour.

Stir in lemon peel, lemon juice and spinach. Cover and simmer until spinach is tender, about 5 minutes. **4 servings** (about 1¼ cups each); 260 calories per serving.

BLACK BEAN SOUP

3	cups water
4	ounces dried black beans (½ cup)
1	ham bone or 1 pound ham shank or smoked pork hocks
½	teaspoon salt
1	clove garlic, finely chopped
1	small bay leaf
¼	teaspoon crushed dried chili pepper
1	medium carrot, sliced (about ½ cup)
1	medium stalk celery, chopped
1	medium onion, chopped (about ½ cup)
2	tablespoons chopped red onion
3	lemon slices, cut into halves
3	hard-cooked eggs, finely chopped

Heat water and beans to boiling in Dutch oven. Boil 2 minutes; remove from heat. Cover and let stand 1 hour.

Add ham bone to beans. Heat to boiling; reduce heat. Cover and simmer until beans are tender, about 2 hours (do not boil or beans will burst). Stir in salt, garlic, bay leaf, chili pepper, carrot, celery and ½ cup onion. Cover; simmer 1 hour.

Remove ham bone and bay leaf. (Place soup in blender container; cover and blend until uniform consistency if desired.) Trim ham from bone and stir into soup. Serve with red onion, lemon slices and eggs. **6 servings** (about 1 cup each); 160 calories per serving.

NAVY BEAN SOUP

7	cups water
1	pound dried navy or pea beans (2 cups)
2	cups cubed fully cooked smoked ham
1	ham bone
1	small onion, finely chopped
½	teaspoon salt
1	bay leaf
	Dash of pepper

Heat water and beans to boiling in Dutch oven. Boil 2 minutes; remove from heat. Cover and let stand 1 hour.

Stir remaining ingredients into beans. Heat to boiling; reduce heat. Cover and simmer, skimming off foam occasionally, until beans are tender, about 1¼ hours (do not boil or beans will burst). Add water during cooking if necessary. Remove ham bone and bay leaf; trim ham from bone and stir into soup.   **7 servings** (about 1 cup each); 130 calories per serving.

COLD CUCUMBER SOUP

    2 **cups buttermilk**
    2 **medium cucumbers, pared and cut into ¾-inch slices**
    1 **small onion, cut into eighths**
    1 **tablespoon prepared horseradish**
    1 **teaspoon salt**
    ¼ **teaspoon pepper**
    1 **small cucumber, seeded and coarsely shredded**

Pour ¼ cup of the buttermilk into blender container; add half of the cucumber slices. Cover and blend on high speed, stopping blender occasionally to scrape sides, until smooth. Add remaining cucumber slices, the onion, horseradish, salt and pepper. Cover and blend until smooth, about 1 minute.

Stir in remaining buttermilk and the shredded cucumber. Cover and refrigerate at least 2 hours. Garnish with additional coarsely shredded cucumber and fresh dill weed if desired.   **8 appetizer servings** (about ½ cup each); 40 calories per serving.

GAZPACHO

    1½ **cups tomato juice**
    ½ **cup chopped cucumber**
    ½ **cup chopped green pepper**
    ¼ **cup chopped onion**
    2 **tablespoons lemon juice**
    1 **tablespoon vegetable oil**
    ½ **teaspoon salt**
    ¼ **teaspoon red pepper sauce**
    2 **tomatoes, chopped**
       Accompaniments (about ½ cup each chopped cucumber, green pepper and onion and 1 cup seasoned croutons)

Place all ingredients except Accompaniments in blender container. Cover and blend on medium speed until smooth. Cover and refrigerate at least 4 hours. Serve with Accompaniments.   **8 appetizer servings** (about ½ cup each); 65 calories per serving.

GUACAMOLE SOUP

- 2   **medium avocados**
- 1½ **cups water**
- 1   **cup milk**
- 2   **tablespoons lemon juice**
- 2   **teaspoons seasoned salt**
-     **Dash of red pepper sauce**
- 1   **medium tomato, chopped**

Cut avocados lengthwise into fourths; remove pits and peel. Place avocados, water and milk in blender container. Cover and blend until smooth. Stir in remaining ingredients. Refrigerate until chilled. Garnish each serving with lemon slices if desired.   **8 appetizer servings** (about ½ cup each); 115 calories per serving.

FRESH FRUIT SOUP

- 3   **tablespoons sugar**
- 3   **tablespoons cornstarch**
- ⅛   **teaspoon salt**
- 1¼ **cups medium red wine**
- 1   **cup water**
- 1½ **cups cranberry juice cocktail**
- 1   **cup each strawberry halves, seedless green grapes and ½-inch cantaloupe pieces**

Mix sugar, cornstarch and salt in 3-quart saucepan; stir in wine and water. Heat to boiling, stirring constantly. Boil and stir 1 minute; remove from heat. Stir in cranberry juice. Cover loosely and refrigerate until chilled.

Stir in fruit. Garnish each serving with spoonful of dairy sour cream or whipped cream if desired.   **6 appetizer servings**; 150 calories per serving.

SANDWICHES

SEASONED SANDWICH SPREADS

Mix ½ cup margarine or butter, softened, and one of the
following seasonings. Serve on roast beef, pork, ham, lamb,
seafood or tongue sandwiches.   **Enough for 6 sandwiches.**

- [ ] 2 tablespoons snipped chives and
      2 tablespoons lemon juice
- [ ] 1 teaspoon dried dill weed
- [ ] 1 tablespoon prepared horseradish
- [ ] 1 tablespoon lemon juice, 1 tablespoon snipped parsley
      and ½ teaspoon dried basil leaves
- [ ] 1 tablespoon prepared mustard

REUBEN SANDWICHES

⅓	cup mayonnaise or salad dressing
1	tablespoon chili sauce
12	slices rye bread
6	slices Swiss cheese
¾	pound cooked corned beef, thinly sliced
1	can (16 ounces) sauerkraut, drained
	Margarine or butter, softened

Mix mayonnaise and chili sauce; spread over 6 slices bread.
Arrange cheese, corned beef and sauerkraut on mayonnaise
mixture; top with remaining bread slices. Spread top slices of
bread with margarine.

Place sandwiches, margarine sides down, in skillet. Spread
top of bread with margarine. Cook uncovered over low heat
until bottom is golden brown, about 10 minutes. Turn; cook
until golden brown and cheese is melted, about 8 minutes
longer.   **6 sandwiches; 650 calories per sandwich.**

Rachel Sandwiches: Substitute 1½ cups coleslaw for the sauerkraut and thinly sliced cooked turkey or chicken for half of the corned beef.

PHILLY BEEF SANDWICHES

2	medium onions, sliced
2	tablespoons margarine or butter
6	hoagie or frankfurter buns, split and toasted
1¼	pounds thinly sliced cooked roast beef
12	square process American cheese slices

Cook and stir onions in margarine until tender, about 10 minutes.

Set oven control to broil and/or 550°. Place bottom halves of buns on ungreased cookie sheet; top with onions and beef. Cut cheese slices into halves; place 4 halves on each sandwich.

Broil with tops 5 to 6 inches from heat just until cheese is melted, 2 to 3 minutes. Top each with remaining bun half.   **6 sandwiches;** 820 calories per sandwich.

BEEF-BAGUETTE SLICES

	Garlic Sauce (page 582)
1	baguette
1	cup shredded lettuce
1	pound thinly sliced cooked roast beef
12	thin red onion slices

Prepare Garlic Sauce. Cut baguette lengthwise into halves. Place lettuce on bottom half. Arrange beef on lettuce; arrange onion slices on beef. Spoon Garlic Sauce over onion and beef; top with remaining baguette half. Cut diagonally into 12 slices.   **6 servings** (2 slices each); 360 calories per serving.

Garlic Sauce

    1 hard-cooked egg
    2 cloves garlic, finely chopped
    1 tablespoon snipped parsley
    1 tablespoon Dijon-style mustard
    2 teaspoons lemon juice
    1 teaspoon water
    2 drops red pepper sauce
       Dash of salt
   ¼ cup olive or vegetable oil

Place all ingredients except oil in blender container. Cover and blend on low speed, stopping blender occasionally to scrape sides, until smooth, about 45 seconds. Add oil, 1 tablespoon at a time, blending after each addition until smooth.

Beef Sandwiches: Substitute 6 Kaiser rolls or hamburger buns for the baguette.

SLOPPY JOES

    1 pound ground beef
    1 medium onion, chopped (about ½ cup)
   ⅓ cup chopped celery
   ⅓ cup chopped green pepper
   ⅓ cup catsup
   ¼ cup water
    1 tablespoon Worcestershire sauce
    1 teaspoon salt
   ⅛ teaspoon red pepper sauce
    6 hamburger buns, split and toasted

Cook and stir ground beef and onion in 10-inch skillet until beef is brown; drain. Stir in remaining ingredients except buns. Cover and cook over low heat just until vegetables are tender, 10 to 15 minutes. Fill buns with beef mixture. **6 sandwiches; 325 calories per sandwich.**

HAMBURGERS

Prepare and cook Hamburger Patties as directed on page 376. Place in 4 split hamburger buns. Top each patty with catsup, prepared mustard, chopped onion, sliced pickles or relish if desired. **4 sandwiches; 390 calories per sandwich.**

California Hamburgers: Top each patty with lettuce, onion slice, tomato slice and about 1 teaspoon mayonnaise or salad dressing.

Cheeseburgers: About 1 minute before patties are done, top each with cheese slice (process American, Swiss, Monterey Jack, provolone, mozzarella). Continue cooking until cheese is melted. Top each with 2 slices crisply cooked bacon if desired.

OPEN-FACE HAMBURGERS

8	slices bread
1	egg, slightly beaten
1	pound ground beef
1	small onion, chopped (about ¼ cup)
¼	cup catsup
1	teaspoon salt
¼	teaspoon pepper

Set oven control to broil and/or 550°. Broil one side of bread about 4 inches from heat until toasted. Mix remaining ingredients; spread mixture to very edge of untoasted side of bread. Broil with tops about 4 inches from heat until done, 4 to 5 minutes. **8 open-face sandwiches; 225 calories per sandwich.**

CHILI BURGERS

1½   pounds ground beef
½   cup finely crushed corn chips
1   tablespoon chili powder
1   egg
1   small onion, chopped (about ¼ cup)
1   medium clove garlic, crushed
1   can (4 ounces) chopped green chilies, drained
2   medium tomatoes, each cut into 4 slices
1   cup shredded Monterey Jack cheese (4 ounces)
8   hamburger buns, split

Mix all ingredients except tomatoes, cheese and buns. Shape mixture into 8 patties, each about ½ inch thick.

Set oven control to broil and/or 550°. Broil patties with tops about 3 inches from heat until medium doneness, 5 to 7 minutes on each side. Place 1 tomato slice on each patty; sprinkle with 1 tablespoon cheese. Broil just until cheese is melted, about 2 minutes. Serve patties in buns.   **8 sandwiches;** 460 calories per sandwich.

BARBECUE HAMBURGERS

1½   pounds ground beef
1   medium onion, chopped (about ½ cup)
1   teaspoon salt
⅓   cup catsup
⅓   cup chili sauce
2   tablespoons packed brown sugar
1   tablespoon lemon juice
6   hamburger buns, split

Mix ground beef, onion and salt. Shape mixture into 6 patties, each about ¾ inch thick. Cook patties in 10-inch skillet over medium-high heat, turning once, until brown. Cover and cook over low heat 10 minutes; drain.

Mix catsup, chili sauce, brown sugar and lemon juice; pour over patties. Cover and simmer 15 minutes, spooning sauce onto patties occasionally. Place patties in buns; spoon sauce over patties.   **6 sandwiches;** 440 calories per sandwich.

GYROS

1	pound ground lamb or beef
2	tablespoons water
1	tablespoon lemon juice
1	teaspoon salt
½	teaspoon ground cumin
½	teaspoon dried oregano leaves
¼	teaspoon pepper
2	cloves garlic, crushed
1	small onion, chopped (about ¼ cup)
2	tablespoons vegetable oil
4	pita breads (6-inch diameter)
2	cups shredded lettuce
½	cup plain yogurt
1	tablespoon snipped mint or
	1 teaspoon dried mint leaves
1	teaspoon sugar
1	small cucumber, seeded and chopped (about ¾ cup)
1	medium tomato, chopped

Mix lamb, water, lemon juice, salt, cumin, oregano, pepper, garlic and onion. Shape into 4 thin patties. Cook patties in oil over medium heat, turning frequently, until done, 10 to 12 minutes.

Split each bread halfway around edge with knife; separate to form pocket. Place patty in each pocket; top with lettuce. Mix yogurt, snipped mint and sugar; stir in cucumber. Spoon onto lettuce; top with tomato. **4 sandwiches; 505 calories** per sandwich.

HOT DOG ROLL-UPS

8	frankfurters
8	slices white sandwich bread
¼	cup mayonnaise or salad dressing
2	tablespoons finely chopped onion
2	tablespoons pickle relish
1	tablespoon prepared mustard
¼	cup margarine or butter, melted

Place frankfurter in center of each slice bread. Mix mayonnaise, onion, relish and mustard. Spoon about 2 teaspoons mayonnaise mixture over each frankfurter. Bring sides of bread up over frankfurter; secure with wooden picks. Place roll-ups, seam sides down, in ungreased rectangular baking dish, 13 × 9 × 2 inches. Brush with margarine. Bake uncovered in 350° oven until hot and golden brown, about 20 minutes. **8 sandwiches; 335 calories per sandwich.**

CHILI DOGS

1	can (15 ounces) chili with beans
1	can (6 ounces) tomato paste
½	small green pepper, chopped (about ¼ cup)
1	small onion, chopped (about ¼ cup)
1	teaspoon prepared mustard
½	teaspoon salt
½	teaspoon chili powder
10	frankfurters
10	frankfurter buns, split and toasted

Heat all ingredients except frankfurters and buns to boiling; reduce heat. Simmer uncovered 10 minutes. Drop frankfurters into boiling water; reduce heat. Cover and simmer until hot, 5 to 8 minutes. Place frankfurters in buns; top with bean mixture. **10 sandwiches; 335 calories per sandwich.**

SLOPPY FRANKS

1	small green pepper, chopped (about ½ cup)
⅓	cup chopped onion
2	tablespoons margarine or butter
½	cup bottled barbecue sauce
1	can (8 ounces) tomato sauce
1	pound frankfurters, cut into ¼-inch slices
8	hamburger buns, split

Cook and stir green pepper and onion in margarine in 10-inch skillet until onion is tender. Stir in barbecue sauce, tomato sauce and sliced frankfurters. Heat to boiling; reduce heat. Simmer uncovered 10 minutes. Fill buns with mixture. **8 sandwiches; 330 calories per sandwich.**

FRANKS WITH SAUERKRAUT

10 frankfurters
1 can (16 ounces) sauerkraut
10 frankfurter buns
Prepared mustard
Chopped onion

Drop frankfurters into boiling water; reduce heat. Cover and simmer until hot, 5 to 8 minutes. Heat sauerkraut over low heat, stirring occasionally, until hot; drain. Place frankfurters in buns; top with mustard, sauerkraut and onion. **10 sandwiches; 295 calories per sandwich.**

PEPPERONI CALZONES

Pizza Dough (page 588)
1 can (8 ounces) tomato sauce
1 can (4 ounces) mushroom stems and pieces, drained
1 teaspoon dried basil leaves
1 teaspoon dried oregano leaves
1 clove garlic, crushed
8 ounces thinly sliced pepperoni
1 small green pepper, chopped
1 cup shredded mozzarella cheese (4 ounces)
1 egg, beaten

Prepare Pizza Dough. Punch down dough; divide into 6 equal parts. Roll each part into 7-inch circle on lightly floured surface. Mix tomato sauce, mushrooms, basil, oregano and garlic. Spread over half of each circle to within 1 inch of edge; top with pepperoni, green pepper and cheese. Carefully fold dough over filling; pinch edges to seal securely. Place sandwiches on greased cookie sheet; let rest 15 minutes.

Heat oven to 375°. Brush sandwiches with egg. Bake until golden brown, about 25 minutes. Garnish with ripe olives and green onions if desired. **6 sandwiches; 355 calories per sandwich.**

Pizza Dough

1 package regular or quick-acting active dry yeast
1 cup warm water (105 to 115°)
1 tablespoon sugar
2 tablespoons vegetable oil
1 teaspoon salt
2¾ to 3¼ cups all-purpose flour

Dissolve yeast in warm water in 3-quart bowl. Stir in sugar, oil, salt and 1 cup of the flour. Beat until smooth. Mix in enough remaining flour to make dough easy to handle.

Turn dough onto lightly floured surface; knead until smooth and elastic, about 5 minutes. Place in greased bowl; turn greased side up. Cover and let rise in warm place until almost double, about 30 minutes.

Ground Beef Calzones: Cook and stir 1 pound ground beef, 1 teaspoon salt and 1 medium onion, chopped (about ½ cup), until beef is done; drain. Substitute beef mixture for the pepperoni.

SAUSAGE BURRITOS

1 package (12 ounces) bulk seasoned pork sausage
1 medium onion, sliced
1 medium green pepper, cut into ¼-inch strips
6 flour tortillas (10 inches in diameter)
1 can (16 ounces) baked beans in molasses
½ head lettuce, shredded (about 3 cups)

Cook and stir pork, onion and green pepper over medium heat until pork is done, about 10 minutes; drain. Prepare tortillas as directed on package. Spoon about 3 tablespoons beans down center of each tortilla. Divide pork mixture among tortillas. Top with lettuce.

Fold 2 opposite sides of each tortilla over filling. Fold 1 end up and about ¼ over folded sides. Serve with taco sauce if desired.   **6 burritos; 385 calories per burrito.**

PEPPERONI PIZZA SLICES

- 2 cups buttermilk baking mix
- ½ cup cold water
- ⅓ cup tomato paste
- ¼ teaspoon Italian seasoning
- ¼ teaspoon garlic salt
- 1 package (3½ to 4 ounces) sliced pepperoni, cut up
- 1 cup shredded mozzarella cheese (4 ounces)

Heat oven to 425°. Mix baking mix and water until soft dough forms; beat vigorously 20 strokes. Turn dough onto lightly floured board. Knead 5 times. Roll into rectangle, 15 × 9 inches. Mix tomato paste, Italian seasoning and garlic salt; spread over dough to within ½ inch of edges. Sprinkle pepperoni and cheese over top. Roll up, beginning at 15-inch side. Pinch edge to seal. Place roll, seam side down, on ungreased cookie sheet. Bake until golden brown, 15 to 20 minutes. Cool 5 minutes; cut into about 3-inch slices.   **5 servings**; 370 calories per serving.

HEIDELBERG SANDWICHES

- 6 slices rye bread, toasted
    Margarine or butter, softened
    Lettuce leaves
- 3 medium tomatoes, sliced
- 1½ pounds Braunschweiger, sliced
- 1 small onion, thinly sliced
- ¾ cup Thousand Island Dressing (page 551) or
    bottled Thousand Island dressing

Spread toast with margarine. Arrange lettuce leaves on toast. Top with tomatoes, Braunschweiger and onion. Spoon about 2 tablespoons Thousand Island Dressing over top of each.   **6 open-face sandwiches**; 635 calories per sandwich.

SUBMARINE SANDWICH

1   loaf (1 pound) French bread
     Margarine or butter, softened
4   ounces Swiss cheese, sliced
½   pound salami, sliced
2   cups shredded lettuce
2   medium tomatoes, thinly sliced
1   medium onion, thinly sliced
½   pound fully cooked smoked ham, thinly sliced
1   medium green pepper, thinly sliced
¼   cup bottled creamy Italian dressing
6   long wooden picks or small skewers

Cut bread horizontally into halves. Spread bottom half with margarine. Layer cheese, salami, lettuce, tomatoes, onion, ham and green pepper on top. Drizzle with dressing; top with remaining bread half. Secure loaf with picks; cut into 6 pieces.   **6 servings; 545 calories per serving.**

HAM-PINEAPPLE SANDWICHES

8   slices whole wheat bread, toasted
     Mayonnaise or salad dressing
1   can (8¼ ounces) crushed pineapple, drained
1   can (6¾ ounces) chunk ham or
     8 slices fully cooked smoked ham
     Lettuce leaves

Spread toast with mayonnaise. Spread pineapple on 4 slices toast; top with ham and lettuce leaves. Top with remaining slices toast.   **4 sandwiches; 245 calories per sandwich.**

TURKEY PUFF SANDWICHES

6   slices bread
½   cup cranberry sauce or cranberry-orange relish
1   pound thinly sliced cooked turkey or chicken
2   egg whites
¼   teaspoon dry mustard
¼   cup mayonnaise or salad dressing

Heat oven to 400°. Spread bread with cranberry sauce. Place slices on ungreased cookie sheet; top each with turkey. Beat egg whites and mustard until stiff; fold in mayonnaise. Spread mixture evenly over turkey. Bake until topping is golden brown, about 10 minutes.   **6 open-face sandwiches; 295 calories per sandwich.**

CHICKEN SALAD FILLING

1½   cups chopped cooked chicken or turkey
½   cup mayonnaise or salad dressing
1   medium stalk celery, chopped (about ½ cup)
1   small onion, chopped (about ¼ cup)
½   teaspoon salt
¼   teaspoon pepper

Mix all ingredients.   **2 cups filling** (enough for 4 sandwiches); 305 calories per ½ cup filling.

Beef Salad Filling: Substitute 1½ cups chopped cooked beef for the chicken. Stir in 2 tablespoons sweet pickle relish, drained.

Egg Salad Filling: Substitute 6 hard-cooked eggs, chopped, for the chicken.

Ham Salad Filling: Substitute 1½ cups chopped fully cooked smoked ham for the chicken. Omit salt and pepper; stir in 1 teaspoon prepared mustard.

Tuna Salad Filling: Substitute 1 can (9¼ ounces) tuna, drained, for the chicken. Stir in 1 teaspoon lemon juice.

CHICKEN-AVOCADO SANDWICHES

2   cans (5 ounces each) chunk chicken
2   stalks celery, chopped (about 1 cup)
½   cup mayonnaise or salad dressing
¼   cup chopped toasted almonds
½   teaspoon onion salt
2   medium tomatoes, thinly sliced
3   whole wheat English muffins, split and toasted
1   container (6 ounces) frozen avocado dip, thawed

Mix chicken, celery, mayonnaise, almonds and onion salt. Arrange tomato slices on each muffin half. Spoon chicken mixture onto tomatoes. Spoon avocado dip onto chicken mixture. Sprinkle with sliced green onions or snipped parsley if desired. **6 open-face sandwiches; 410 calories per sandwich.**

TUNA PATTY SANDWICHES

     1   **egg, slightly beaten**
     1   **can (9¼ ounces) tuna, drained**
     4   **green onions (with tops), chopped**
     ¼   **cup cracker crumbs**
     1   **tablespoon lemon juice**
     ½   **teaspoon salt**
     ¼   **teaspoon pepper**
     2   **tablespoons margarine or butter**
     4   **hamburger buns, split and toasted**
     4   **slices process American cheese**
         Lettuce leaves
     1   **tomato, sliced**
     ¼   **cup Tartar Sauce (page 603)**

Mix egg, tuna, onions, cracker crumbs, lemon juice, salt and pepper. Shape into 4 patties, each about ½ inch thick. Heat margarine in 10-inch skillet over medium heat until melted. Cook patties in margarine until golden brown, about 5 minutes on each side.

Place a patty on each of 4 bun halves. Top each with cheese slice, lettuce, tomato, Tartar Sauce and remaining bun half.   **4 sandwiches; 505 calories per sandwich.**

Salmon Patty Sandwiches: Substitute 1 can (15½ ounces) salmon, drained and flaked, for the tuna.

SHRIMP CLUB SANDWICHES

12	slices white bread, toasted
	Mayonnaise or salad dressing
4	lettuce leaves
12	slices tomatoes (about 2 medium)
12	slices bacon, crisply cooked
2	cans (4½ ounces each) large shrimp, rinsed and drained
1	large avocado, thinly sliced

Spread toast with mayonnaise. Place lettuce leaf, 3 slices tomato and 3 slices bacon on each of 4 slices toast. Top with another slice toast. Arrange shrimp on toast; top with avocado slices. Top with third slice toast; secure with wooden picks. Cut sandwiches diagonally into 4 triangles. **4 sandwiches; 515 calories per sandwich.**

Club Sandwiches: Substitute 1 pound sliced cooked turkey or chicken for the shrimp and 4 additional lettuce leaves for the avocado.

DENVER SANDWICHES

8	slices bread or toast
	Margarine or butter, softened
1	small onion, chopped
½	small green pepper, chopped
1	tablespoon margarine or butter
1	tablespoon shortening
4	eggs
½	cup chopped fully cooked smoked ham
¼	teaspoon salt
⅛	teaspoon pepper

Spread 4 slices bread with margarine. Cook and stir onion and green pepper in 1 tablespoon margarine and the shortening in 10-inch skillet until onion is tender. Beat eggs slightly; stir in remaining ingredients. Pour egg mixture into skillet. Cook over low heat just until set. Cut into four wedges; turn. Cook until light brown. Serve between bread slices. **4 sandwiches; 350 calories per sandwich.**

EGGS IN BUNS

 6   unsliced hamburger buns
 ¼   cup margarine or butter, melted
 6   tablespoons shredded Cheddar cheese
 8   eggs
 ½   cup milk
 1   teaspoon salt
 ¼   teaspoon pepper
 2   tablespoons margarine or butter

Cut a hole about 2 inches in diameter in top of each bun; scoop out inside, leaving about a ¼-inch wall. Place buns on ungreased cookie sheet. Brush insides of buns with ¼ cup margarine; spoon 1 tablespoon cheese into each. Bake in 350° oven until buns are slightly crisp, 10 to 15 minutes.

Mix eggs, milk, salt and pepper with fork until uniform color. Heat 2 tablespoons margarine in 10-inch skillet over medium heat just until hot enough to sizzle a drop of water. Pour egg mixture into skillet. As mixture begins to set at bottom and side, gently lift cooked portions with spatula so that thin, uncooked portion can flow to bottom. Avoid constant stirring. Cook until eggs are thickened throughout but still moist. Spoon eggs into warm buns. Garnish with pimiento-stuffed olives if desired.   **6 servings;** 380 calories per serving.

EGGS WITH WINE SAUCE

 8   Poached Eggs (page 281)
 ¼   cup sliced green onions (with tops)
 3   tablespoons margarine or butter
 3   tablespoons all-purpose flour
 ½   teaspoon dry mustard
 ¼   teaspoon dried tarragon leaves
 ⅛   teaspoon white pepper
 ¾   cup dry white wine
 ¾   cup chicken broth (page 557)
 6   slices bacon, crisply cooked and crumbled
 4   croissants, split*

*Four English muffins, split and toasted, can be substituted for the croissants. Place 1 egg on each muffin half; spoon wine mixture over eggs.

Prepare Poached Eggs. Cook and stir onions in margarine in 1-quart saucepan over medium heat 3 minutes. Stir in flour, mustard, tarragon and white pepper. Cook over low heat, stirring constantly, until bubbly; remove from heat. Stir in wine and chicken broth. Heat to boiling, stirring constantly. Boil and stir 1 minute. Stir in bacon.

Place 2 eggs on bottom half of each croissant; spoon wine mixture over eggs. Top with remaining croissant halves. **4 servings; 430 calories per serving.**

MEXICAN EGG SANDWICHES

1	can (16 ounces) refried beans
3	English muffins, split and toasted
¾	cup shredded Cheddar cheese (3 ounces)
2	medium tomatoes, thinly sliced
6	Poached Eggs (page 281)
¼	cup chopped green onions (with tops)

Heat beans until hot. Spread muffin halves with beans; sprinkle with cheese. Top with tomatoes and eggs; sprinkle with onions. **6 open-face sandwiches; 230 calories per sandwich.**

CHILI-CHEESE SANDWICHES

8	ounces Monterey Jack cheese, cut into 16 slices
8	slices rye bread
4	tablespoons chili sauce
1	can (4 ounces) green chilies, drained
¼	cup milk
¼	teaspoon ground cumin
¼	teaspoon salt
1	egg
1	tablespoon margarine or butter

Place 4 slices cheese on each of 4 slices bread; spread each with 1 tablespoon chili sauce. Divide chilies equally among sandwiches. Top with remaining slices bread.

Beat milk, cumin, salt and egg with fork in pie plate until smooth. Dip both sides of sandwiches into egg mixture.

Heat margarine in 12-inch skillet until hot and bubbly;

reduce heat. Cover and cook sandwiches in margarine over low heat 5 minutes; turn. Cover and cook until cheese is melted and sandwiches are light brown, about 5 minutes longer. **4 sandwiches; 460 calories per sandwich.**

SUPER GRILLED CHEESE

8   ounces Monterey Jack, Muenster, provolone or
      mozzarella cheese, thinly sliced
8   slices white or whole wheat bread
1   small onion, chopped (about ¼ cup)
8   slices bacon, crisply cooked
1   medium tomato, thinly sliced
1   avocado, peeled and thinly sliced
      Margarine or butter, softened

Arrange half of the cheese on 4 slices bread; sprinkle with onion. Top each with bacon, tomato, avocado, remaining cheese and bread. Spread top slices of bread with margarine.

Place sandwiches, margarine sides down, in skillet. Spread top of bread with margarine. Cook uncovered over medium heat until golden brown, about 5 minutes; turn. Cook until golden brown and cheese is melted, 2 to 3 minutes longer. **4 sandwiches; 550 calories per sandwich.**

American Grilled Cheese: Substitute 12 slices process American cheese for the 8 ounces cheese. Omit onion, bacon, tomato and avocado.

BAKED VEGETABLE SLICES

1¼   cups buttermilk baking mix
¾   cup mayonnaise or salad dressing
1   egg
2   cups shredded Swiss cheese (8 ounces)
½   cup alfalfa sprouts
¼   teaspoon salt
1   medium tomato, chopped (about 1 cup)
½   medium cucumber, coarsely chopped
½ - pound loaf French bread, cut lengthwise into halves,
      or 6 slices bread

Heat oven to 450°. Mix baking mix, mayonnaise and egg. Stir in remaining ingredients except French bread. Spread about 1½ cups mixture evenly on cut sides of French bread, or spread about ½ cup mixture on each slice bread. Bake on ungreased cookie sheet until puffy and golden brown, 10 to 15 minutes. Cut each half French bread crosswise into thirds. Serve immediately.   **6 servings; 570 calories per serving.**

Baked Chicken Slices: Substitute Cheddar cheese for the Swiss cheese. Omit alfalfa sprouts, tomato and cucumber. Stir 1 cup cut-up cooked chicken, ¼ cup sliced green onions (with tops), dash of pepper and 1 can (4 ounces) mushroom stems and pieces, drained, into mayonnaise mixture.

Baked Chili Slices: Substitute Monterey Jack cheese for the Swiss cheese. Omit alfalfa sprouts, salt and cucumber. Stir ½ cup chopped onion, 1 tablespoon chili powder, 1 can (4 ounces) chopped green chilies, drained, and the tomato into mayonnaise mixture.

Baked Frankfurter Slices: Substitute process cheese spread loaf for the Swiss cheese. Omit alfalfa sprouts, salt, tomato and cucumber. Stir 4 frankfurters, cut into ¼-inch slices, ½ cup sweet pickle relish and 1 tablespoon prepared mustard into mayonnaise mixture.

Baked Tuna Slices: Substitute Cheddar cheese for the Swiss cheese. Omit alfalfa sprouts, salt, tomato and cucumber. Stir 1 can (6½ ounces) tuna, drained, ¼ cup chopped onion, ¼ cup sliced celery and 3 tablespoons lemon juice into mayonnaise mixture.

VEGGIE-FILLED CROISSANTS

  4   **croissants**
1½   **cups shredded Monterey Jack cheese (6 ounces)**
  1   **small zucchini, chopped (about ½ cup)**
  1   **small tomato, chopped (about ½ cup)**
  1   **small onion, chopped (about ¼ cup)**
  1   **can (4 ounces) chopped green chilies, drained**

Heat oven to 325°. Cut along outside curve of each croissant to within 1 inch of each end and ¼ inch of inside curve to form a pocket. Mix remaining ingredients; spoon into croissants. Heat on ungreased cookie sheet until cheese is melted, about 15 minutes.   **4 sandwiches; 360 calories per sandwich.**

HOT PROVOLONE SANDWICHES

4	English muffins, split and toasted
8	large mild sweet onion slices
2	cups shredded provolone or Monterey Jack cheese (8 ounces)
1	cup shredded zucchini (about 1 medium)
½	teaspoon dried basil leaves
½	teaspoon dry mustard
4	slices bacon, crisply cooked and crumbled

Heat oven to 350°. Place muffin halves on ungreased cookie sheet; top each with onion slice. Mix remaining ingredients. Place about ⅓ cup cheese mixture on each muffin half. Bake until cheese is melted, about 5 minutes. **8 open-face sandwiches;** 190 calories per sandwich.

SAUCES

WHITE SAUCE

2 tablespoons margarine or butter
2 tablespoons all-purpose flour
¼ teaspoon salt
⅛ teaspoon pepper
1 cup milk

Heat margarine in 1½-quart saucepan over low heat until melted. Stir in flour, salt and pepper. Cook over low heat, stirring constantly, until mixture is smooth and bubbly; remove from heat. Stir in milk. Heat to boiling, stirring constantly. Boil and stir 1 minute. **1 cup sauce; 25 calories per tablespoon.**

Thin White Sauce: Decrease margarine to 1 tablespoon and flour to 1 tablespoon.

Thick White Sauce: Increase margarine to ¼ cup and flour to ¼ cup.

Cheese Sauce: Prepare White Sauce as directed except— stir in ¼ teaspoon dry mustard with the flour. After boiling and stirring sauce 1 minute, stir in ½ cup shredded Cheddar cheese (2 ounces) until melted.

Curry Sauce: Prepare White Sauce as directed except— stir in ½ teaspoon curry powder with the flour. Serve with chicken, lamb or shrimp.

Dill Sauce: Prepare White Sauce as directed except—stir in 1 teaspoon snipped dill weed or ½ teaspoon dried dill weed and dash of ground nutmeg with the flour. Nice served with fish.

Mustard Sauce: Prepare White Sauce as directed except— decrease margarine to 1 tablespoon and flour to 1 tablespoon. After boiling and stirring sauce 1 minute, stir in 3 tablespoons prepared mustard and 1 tablespoon prepared horseradish. Serve with beef, veal, ham or vegetables.

HOLLANDAISE SAUCE

> 3 **egg yolks**
> 1 **tablespoon lemon juice**
> ½ **cup firm butter***

Stir egg yolks and lemon juice vigorously in 1½-quart saucepan. Add ¼ cup of the butter. Heat over *very low heat*, stirring constantly, until butter is melted. Add remaining butter. Continue stirring vigorously until butter is melted and sauce is thickened. (Be sure butter melts slowly as this gives eggs time to cook and thicken sauce without curdling.) Serve hot or at room temperature. Cover and refrigerate any remaining sauce; to serve, stir in small amount of hot water.   **About ¾ cup sauce; 85 calories per tablespoon.**

A lemon-flavored sauce to top vegetables, chicken, turkey, fish or poached or soft-cooked eggs.

Béarnaise Sauce: Prepare Hollandaise Sauce as directed except—stir in 1 tablespoon dry white wine with the lemon juice. After sauce thickens, stir in 1 tablespoon finely chopped onion, ½ teaspoon dried tarragon leaves and ¼ teaspoon dried chervil leaves. An herbed sauce to serve with fish or meat.

Maltaise Sauce: Prepare Hollandaise Sauce as directed except—after sauce thickens, stir in ½ teaspoon grated orange peel and 2 tablespoons orange juice. A nice flavor change for green vegetables.

Mousseline Sauce: Prepare Hollandaise Sauce; cool to room temperature. Just before serving, beat ¼ cup chilled whipping cream in chilled 1½-pint bowl until stiff; fold into sauce. Delicate-flavored sauce to serve with fish, eggs, artichokes, broccoli or cauliflower.

*We do not recommend margarine for this recipe.

BROWN SAUCE

2 tablespoons margarine or butter
1 thin slice onion
2 tablespoons all-purpose flour
1 cup beef broth (page 561)
¼ teaspoon salt
⅛ teaspoon pepper

Heat margarine in 8-inch skillet over low heat until melted. Cook and stir onion in margarine until onion is brown. Discard onion. Stir flour into margarine. Cook over low heat, stirring constantly, until flour is deep brown; remove from heat. Stir in broth. Heat to boiling, stirring constantly. Boil and stir 1 minute. Stir in salt and pepper. **1 cup sauce; 15 calories per tablespoon.**

Bordelaise Sauce: Prepare Brown Sauce as directed except— decrease broth to ½ cup and add ½ cup red wine. Stir in ½ teaspoon each snipped parsley, finely chopped onion and crushed bay leaves and ¼ teaspoon dried thyme leaves with the broth. Serve with steaks, pork chops or hamburgers.

Mushroom Sauce: Prepare Brown Sauce. Cook and stir 1 cup sliced mushrooms or 1 jar (4½ ounces) sliced mushrooms, drained, in margarine until brown. Stir mushrooms and a few drops of Worcestershire sauce into sauce. Serve with fish, meat or omelets.

Piquant Sauce: Prepare Brown Sauce as directed except— stir in ¼ cup dry white wine, 1 tablespoon snipped parsley, 1 tablespoon chopped gherkins, 1 tablespoon finely chopped onion and ½ teaspoon dried chervil leaves with the broth. Serve with tongue, beef, veal or fish.

Provençale Sauce: Prepare Brown Sauce. Gently stir 1 tomato, chopped, and 1 clove garlic, crushed, into sauce. Serve with meat, spaghetti, noodles or vegetables.

Spicy Brown Sauce: Prepare Brown Sauce as directed except—stir in 2 tablespoons chopped onion, 1 tablespoon snipped parsley, 1 tablespoon vinegar, ¼ teaspoon dried tarragon leaves, crushed, and ¼ teaspoon dried thyme leaves, crushed, with the broth. Serve with chicken or pork.

VELOUTE SAUCE

- 2   tablespoons margarine or butter
- 2   tablespoons all-purpose flour
- 1   cup chicken broth (page 557)
- ¼   teaspoon salt
- ⅛   teaspoon pepper
- ⅛   teaspoon ground nutmeg

Heat margarine in 1½-quart saucepan over low heat until melted. Stir in flour. Cook over low heat, stirring constantly, until mixture is smooth and bubbly; remove from heat. Stir in broth. Heat to boiling, stirring constantly. Boil and stir 1 minute. Stir in remaining ingredients. **About 1 cup sauce; 20 calories per tablespoon.**

Allemande Sauce: Heat margarine until melted as directed; reserve. Mix flour, salt, pepper and nutmeg in 1½-quart saucepan. Mix broth and 1 egg yolk until blended; stir into flour mixture. Heat to boiling, stirring constantly. Boil and stir 1 minute; remove from heat. Stir in margarine, 2 tablespoons half-and-half and 1 teaspoon lemon juice. Serve with eggs, fish or poultry.

Almond Velvet Sauce: Prepare Velouté Sauce. Just before serving, stir in ¼ cup toasted slivered almonds. Serve with poultry or fish.

Mornay Sauce: Prepare Velouté Sauce except—substitute ½ cup half-and-half for ½ cup of the chicken broth. After boiling and stirring 1 minute, stir in ⅛ teaspoon ground red pepper and ½ cup grated Parmesan or shredded Swiss cheese until melted. Serve with meat, fish, eggs or vegetables.

HORSERADISH SAUCE

- ½   cup chilled whipping cream
- 3   tablespoons well-drained prepared horseradish
- ½   teaspoon salt

Beat whipping cream in chilled 1½-pint bowl until stiff. Fold in horseradish and salt. **1 cup sauce; 25 calories per tablespoon.**

Delicious topping for beef, ham or pork.

CREAM MUSTARD SAUCE

½   cup chilled whipping cream
1   tablespoon prepared mustard
¼   teaspoon lemon juice
    Dash of salt
    Dash of pepper

Beat whipping cream in chilled 1½-pint bowl until stiff. Mix remaining ingredients; fold into whipped cream.   **About 1 cup sauce; 25 calories per tablespoon.**

A creamy mustard sauce to serve with corned beef, ham, pork, cauliflower or Brussels sprouts.

TARTAR SAUCE

1   cup mayonnaise or salad dressing
2   tablespoons finely chopped dill pickle
1   tablespoon snipped parsley
2   teaspoons chopped pimiento
1   teaspoon grated onion

Mix all ingredients; cover and refrigerate until chilled.   **About 1 cup sauce; 100 calories per tablespoon.**

COCKTAIL SAUCE

1   bottle (12 ounces) chili sauce
1   tablespoon prepared horseradish
1   tablespoon lemon juice
½   teaspoon Worcestershire sauce
¼   teaspoon salt
    Dash of pepper

Mix all ingredients. Cover and refrigerate until chilled.   **About 1¼ cups sauce; 20 calories per tablespoon.**

MEXICAN CASERA SAUCE

 2 medium tomatoes, finely chopped
 1 medium onion, chopped (about ½ cup)
 1 small clove garlic, finely chopped
 1 canned jalapeño pepper, seeded and finely chopped
 ½ teaspoon jalapeño pepper liquid
     (from jalapeño pepper can)
 1 tablespoon finely snipped cilantro, if desired
 1 tablespoon lemon juice
1½ teaspoons vegetable oil
 ½ teaspoon dried oregano leaves

Mix all ingredients. Cover and refrigerate in glass or plastic container up to 7 days. **About 2 cups sauce; 5 calories per tablespoon.**
  Serve with fish, beef or eggs.

BARBECUE SAUCE

 1 cup catsup
 ½ cup finely chopped onion
 ⅓ cup water
 ¼ cup margarine or butter
 1 tablespoon paprika
 1 teaspoon packed brown sugar
 ½ teaspoon salt
 ¼ teaspoon pepper
 ¼ cup lemon juice
 1 tablespoon Worcestershire sauce

Heat all ingredients except lemon juice and Worcestershire sauce to boiling in 1-quart saucepan over medium heat. Stir in lemon juice and Worcestershire sauce; heat until hot. **About 2 cups sauce; 25 calories per tablespoon.**

SPICY BARBECUE SAUCE

⅓   cup margarine or butter
2   tablespoons water
2   tablespoons vinegar
1   tablespoon Worcestershire sauce
1   teaspoon sugar
1   teaspoon onion salt
½   teaspoon garlic powder
½   teaspoon pepper
     Dash of ground red pepper

Heat all ingredients, stirring frequently, until margarine is melted.   **About ¾ cup sauce; 50 calories per tablespoon.**

ITALIAN TOMATO SAUCE

1   medium onion, chopped (about ½ cup)
1   small green pepper, chopped (about ½ cup)
1   large clove garlic, finely chopped
2   tablespoons olive or vegetable oil
1   can (16 ounces) whole tomatoes, undrained
1   can (8 ounces) tomato sauce
1   teaspoon dried basil leaves
½   teaspoon salt
½   teaspoon dried oregano leaves
¼   teaspoon fennel seed
⅛   teaspoon pepper

Cook and stir onion, green pepper and garlic in oil in 3-quart saucepan until onion is tender. Stir in remaining ingredients; break up tomatoes with fork. Heat to boiling; reduce heat. Cover and simmer 45 minutes.   **2 cups sauce; 15 calories per tablespoon.**

SWEET-AND-SOUR SAUCE

½ cup sugar
½ cup chicken broth or water
⅓ cup white vinegar
1 teaspoon vegetable oil
1 teaspoon soy sauce
¼ teaspoon salt
1 clove garlic, crushed
2 tablespoons cornstarch
2 tablespoons cold water
1 tomato, cut into 16 pieces
1 small green pepper, cut into 1-inch pieces
1 can (8¼ ounces) pineapple chunks in syrup, drained

Heat sugar, broth, vinegar, oil, soy sauce, salt and garlic to boiling in 2-quart saucepan over medium-high heat, stirring occasionally. Mix cornstarch and water; stir into sugar mixture. Cook and stir until thickened, about 10 seconds. Stir in tomato, green pepper and pineapple. Heat to boiling. **About 2½ cups sauce; 140 calories per ½ cup**

A colorful sauce to serve over meatballs, pork chops or shrimp.

RAISIN SAUCE

½ cup packed brown sugar
2 tablespoons cornstarch
1 teaspoon dry mustard
1½ cups water
¼ teaspoon grated lemon peel
2 tablespoons lemon juice
2 tablespoons vinegar
½ cup raisins

Mix brown sugar, cornstarch and mustard in 1½-quart saucepan. Mix water, lemon peel, lemon juice and vinegar; gradually stir into sugar mixture. Cook over low heat, stirring constantly, until mixture thickens. Stir in raisins. **About 2 cups sauce; 25 calories per tablespoon.**

Serve with ham or pork.

CHERRY SAUCE

½   cup sugar
2   tablespoons cornstarch
1   can (16 ounces) pitted red tart cherries, undrained

Mix sugar and cornstarch in 1-quart saucepan. Stir in cherries. Cook, stirring constantly, until mixture thickens and boils. Boil and stir 1 minute. Stir in several drops of red food color if desired. **About 2 cups sauce; 25 calories per tablespoon.**

Adds color and flavor to ham or pork.

ORANGE-MUSTARD SAUCE

Heat ½ cup orange marmalade and 2 tablespoons prepared mustard over low heat, stirring occasionally, until marmalade is melted. **About ½ cup sauce; 60 calories per tablespoon.**

Serve warm with pork, ham or beets.

Orange-Mint Sauce: Stir ¼ cup snipped mint into sauce before serving.

PESTO

2   cups firmly packed fresh basil leaves
¾   cup grated Parmesan cheese
¾   cup olive oil
2   tablespoons pine nuts
4   cloves garlic

Place all ingredients in blender container. Cover and blend on medium speed, stopping blender occasionally to scrape sides, until smooth, about 3 minutes. **About 1¼ cups sauce; 95 calories per tablespoon.**

Toss Pesto with hot cooked pasta.

Do-ahead Tip: Freeze Pesto up to 6 months. Let stand at room temperature until thawed, at least 4 hours.

VEGETABLES

VEGETABLES

CREAMED VEGETABLES

Stir 2 cups cooked vegetables into Thin White Sauce (page 599). **6 servings.**

Au Gratin Vegetables: Prepare Cheese Sauce (page 599). Stir in vegetables. Pour into ungreased 1-quart casserole. Mix ½ cup dry bread crumbs, 1 tablespoon margarine or butter, melted, and ⅛ teaspoon salt. Sprinkle over vegetables. Bake uncovered in 325° oven until heated through, about 15 minutes.

Scalloped Vegetables: Prepare Thin White Sauce (page 599). Stir in vegetables. Pour into ungreased 1-quart casserole. Bake uncovered in 325° oven until heated through, about 15 minutes.

Vegetables in Cheese Sauce: Prepare Cheese Sauce (page 599). Stir in vegetables; heat through.

CRUMB TOPPINGS

Mix ¼ cup dry bread crumbs, 1½ teaspoons margarine or butter, melted, and dash of salt. Sprinkle over hot cooked vegetables or creamed vegetables. **¼ cup topping.**

Garlic Crumb Topping: Mix in ½ small clove garlic, crushed.

Nutmeg Crumb Topping: Mix in ⅛ teaspoon ground nutmeg.

Oregano Crumb Topping: Mix in ¼ teaspoon dried oregano leaves and ⅛ teaspoon dried basil leaves.

BUTTER SAUCES

Drawn Butter: Heat margarine or butter over low heat until melted.

Browned Butter: Heat margarine or butter over low heat until light brown.

Black Butter: Heat ⅓ cup margarine or butter over low heat until golden brown, or microwave uncovered in 2-cup microwavable measure on high (100%) about 3½ minutes. Stir in 1 tablespoon vinegar or lemon juice; heat until bubbly or microwave uncovered 15 seconds. Add dash each of salt and pepper. Serve immediately.

SEASONED BUTTERS

Heat ¼ cup margarine or butter over low heat until melted, or microwave uncovered in 1-cup microwavable measure on high (100%) until hot and bubbly, about 45 seconds. Mix with one of the following:

☐ *Almond:* 1 tablespoon chopped toasted almonds

☐ *Basil:* 1 teaspoon snipped basil or ¼ teaspoon dried basil leaves

☐ *Cheese:* 2 tablespoons grated Parmesan cheese

☐ *Chive-Parsley:* 1 tablespoon snipped chives, 1 tablespoon snipped parsley and ½ teaspoon salt

☐ *Curry:* ¼ teaspoon curry powder

☐ *Garlic:* ¼ teaspoon garlic powder

☐ *Horseradish:* 1 tablespoon prepared horseradish

☐ *Lemon:* 1 tablespoon grated lemon peel, 2 tablespoons lemon juice and, if desired, 1 tablespoon snipped chives

☐ *Mustard-Dill:* ¼ teaspoon dry mustard and ¼ teaspoon dried dill weed

☐ *Sesame-Soy:* 1 tablespoon sesame seed and 2 tablespoons soy sauce

ARTICHOKES—FRENCH

Amount for 4 servings: 4 (1 per serving).

When shopping: Look for plump, heavy globes, compact scales (leaves).

TO PREPARE: Trim stem even with base of artichoke. Cutting straight across, slice 1 inch off top; discard top. Snip off points of the remaining leaves with scissors. Rinse artichoke under running cold water.

TO COOK: Heat 6 quarts water, ¼ cup vegetable oil, 2 tablespoons lemon juice, 1 clove garlic, cut into fourths, and 1 teaspoon salt to boiling in large kettle; add artichokes. Heat to boiling; reduce heat. Simmer uncovered, rotating occasionally, until leaves pull out easily and bottom is tender when pierced with knife, 30 to 40 minutes. Remove artichokes carefully from water (use tongs or two large spoons); place upside down to drain.

TO STEAM: Place steamer basket in ½ inch water (water should not touch bottom of basket). Place artichokes in basket. Cover tightly and heat to boiling; reduce heat. Steam until bottom is tender when pierced with knife, 20 to 25 minutes.

TO SERVE: Place hot artichoke upright on plate. Accompany with Hollandaise Sauce (page 600) or one of the Seasoned Butters (page 612). Or cool artichokes; cover and refrigerate at least 4 hours. Open each artichoke to reach the interior. Pull out tender center cone of leaves; scrape off exposed choke with spoon. Place each artichoke upright on plate. Accompany with Hollandaise Sauce (page 600).

TO EAT: Pluck leaves one at a time. Dip base of leaf into a sauce or butter. Turn leaf meaty side down and draw between teeth, scraping off meaty portion. Discard leaf on plate.

When all outer leaves have been removed, a center cone of small, light-colored leaves covering the fuzzy center choke will be exposed. Pull or cut off cone of leaves. Slice off fuzzy choke with knife and fork; discard. Eat the remaining "heart."

ARTICHOKE HEARTS SAUTE

2 slices bacon, cut into 1-inch pieces
1 can (14 ounces) artichoke hearts, drained and cut into halves
1 teaspoon lemon juice

Cook bacon in 10-inch skillet, stirring occasionally, until limp, about 1½ minutes. Stir in artichoke hearts; cook and stir until hot, about 3 minutes. Stir in lemon juice. **4 servings; 100** calories per serving.

ARTICHOKES—JERUSALEM

Amount for 4 servings: 1½ pounds.
When shopping: Look for firm, clean tubers.
TO PREPARE: Pare thinly. Leave whole, slice or dice; soak in water with a small amount of lemon juice to prevent discoloration.
TO COOK: Heat 1 inch salted water (½ teaspoon salt to 1 cup water) to boiling. Add artichokes. Cover and heat to boiling; reduce heat. Boil until crisp-tender, 15 to 35 minutes.
TO STEAM: Place steamer basket in ½ inch water (water should not touch bottom of basket). Place artichokes in basket. Cover tightly and heat to boiling; reduce heat. Steam until crisp-tender, 15 to 20 minutes.
TO MICROWAVE: Cover and microwave artichokes (¼-inch slices) and ¼ cup water in 1½-quart microwavable casserole on high (100%) 3 minutes; stir. Cover and microwave until crisp-tender, 3 to 4 minutes longer. Let stand covered 1 minute; drain.

BAKED HERBED ARTICHOKES

1½   pounds Jerusalem artichokes, unpared
¼   cup margarine or butter, melted
2   tablespoons snipped chives
1   tablespoon lemon juice
1   teaspoon dried dill weed
½   teaspoon salt
⅛   teaspoon pepper

Wash artichokes. Place in ungreased square baking dish, 8×8×2 inches. Mix remaining ingredients; pour over artichokes. Bake uncovered in 400° oven until crisp-tender, 35 to 40 minutes.   **4 servings; 130 calories per serving.**

ASPARAGUS

Amount for 4 servings: 1½ pounds.
   When shopping: Look for smooth, round, tender, medium-size green spears with closed tips.
   TO PREPARE: Break off tough ends as far down as stalks snap easily. Wash asparagus. Remove scales if sandy or tough. (If necessary, remove sand particles with a vegetable brush.) For spears, tie whole stalks in bundles with string, or hold together with band of aluminum foil. Or cut each stalk into 1-inch pieces.

TO COOK:
Spears—heat 1 inch salted water (½ teaspoon salt to 1 cup water) to boiling in deep, narrow pan or coffeepot. Place asparagus upright in pan. Heat to boiling; reduce heat. Boil uncovered 5 minutes. Cover and boil until stalk ends are crisp-tender, 7 to 10 minutes longer; drain. *Pieces*—cook lower stalk pieces uncovered in 1 inch boiling salted water (½ teaspoon salt to 1 cup water) 6 minutes. Add tips. Cover and cook until crisp-tender, 5 to 8 minutes longer; drain.
   TO STEAM: Place steamer basket in ½ inch water (water should not touch bottom of basket). Place asparagus (spears or 1-inch pieces) in basket. Cover tightly and heat to boiling; reduce heat. Steam until crisp-tender, 6 to 8 minutes.

TO MICROWAVE: Cover and microwave asparagus (spears or 1-inch pieces) and ¼ cup water in 2-quart microwavable casserole on high (100%) 4 minutes; turn asparagus over. Cover and microwave until crisp-tender, 4 to 6 minutes longer. Let stand covered 1 minute; drain.

BAKED ASPARAGUS

Prepare 1 to 1¼ pounds fresh asparagus as directed on page 615 except—do not tie the stalks in bundles.

Arrange asparagus in ungreased rectangular baking dish, 12 × 7½ × 2 inches. Cover and bake in 400° oven until tender, 20 to 30 minutes. Serve with Hollandaise Sauce (page 600). **4 servings; 250 calories per serving.**

ASPARAGUS IN PUFF PASTRY

¾	pound fresh asparagus
½	package (17¼-ounce size) frozen puff pastry, thawed (1 sheet)
¼	cup shredded Gruyère cheese
¼	cup dairy sour cream
1	tablespoon margarine or butter, melted
2	teaspoons all-purpose flour
¼	teaspoon salt
1	tablespoon margarine or butter, melted
½	teaspoon sesame seed

Prepare asparagus as directed on page 615. Cut stalks into 2-inch pieces. Heat oven to 425°. Roll pastry into rectangle, 12 × 10 inches, on lightly floured surface. Mix cheese, sour cream, 1 tablespoon margarine, the flour and salt; spread into rectangle, 8 × 3 inches, on center of pastry. Arrange asparagus on cheese mixture. Bring 10-inch sides of pastry up and over asparagus pieces; pinch edge and ends to seal. Place seam side down on ungreased cookie sheet. Brush with 1 tablespoon margarine; sprinkle with sesame seed. Bake 15 minutes.

Reduce oven temperature to 325°. Bake until pastry is puffed and deep golden brown, about 35 minutes longer. **6 servings; 270 calories per serving.**

STIR-FRIED ASPARAGUS

1	pound fresh asparagus
½	cup water
½	teaspoon instant chicken bouillon
1	tablespoon cornstarch
1	tablespoon cold water
2	tablespoons vegetable oil
4	ounces fresh mushrooms, sliced (about 1½ cups)
½	teaspoon salt
⅛	teaspoon freshly ground pepper

Prepare asparagus as directed on page 615 except—cut each stalk diagonally into ½-inch pieces. Mix ½ cup water and the bouillon (dry); reserve. Mix cornstarch and 1 tablespoon water; reserve.

Heat oil in 12-inch skillet over medium-high heat. Add asparagus, mushrooms, salt and pepper; stir-fry until asparagus is crisp-tender, about 3 minutes. Stir in bouillon mixture; heat to boiling. Stir in cornstarch mixture; cook and stir until thickened, about 10 seconds. **4 servings;** 90 calories per serving.

BEANS—GREEN AND WAX

Amount for 4 servings: 1 pound.

When shopping: Look for bright, crisp pods.

TO PREPARE: Wash beans; remove ends. Leave whole, or cut crosswise into 1-inch pieces.

TO COOK: Place beans in 1 inch salted water (½ teaspoon salt to 1 cup water). Heat to boiling; reduce heat. Boil uncovered 5 minutes. Cover and boil until tender, 5 to 10 minutes longer; drain.

TO STEAM: Place steamer basket in ½ inch water (water should not touch bottom of basket). Place beans in basket. Cover tightly and heat to boiling; reduce heat. Steam until tender, 10 to 12 minutes.

TO MICROWAVE: Cover and microwave beans (1-inch pieces) and ¼ cup water in 1½-quart microwavable casserole on high (100%) 6 minutes; stir. Cover and microwave until tender, 5 to 7 minutes longer. Let stand covered 1 minute; drain.

HERBED GREEN BEANS

1 **pound fresh green beans**
2 **tablespoons vegetable oil**
¼ **cup snipped parsley**
½ **teaspoon dried basil leaves**
½ **teaspoon dried oregano leaves**
⅛ **teaspoon crushed red pepper**
2 **medium tomatoes, cut into 1-inch pieces**
2 **cloves garlic, finely chopped**
1 **tablespoon grated Parmesan cheese**

Prepare and cook whole green beans as directed on page 617. Heat oil in 12-inch skillet until hot. Cook and stir remaining ingredients except cheese in oil until tomatoes are soft. Stir in beans. Cook, stirring occasionally, just until beans are hot, 1 to 2 minutes; sprinkle with cheese.   **6 servings; 75 calories** per serving.

■ **To Microwave:** Place 2 tablespoons water, ¼ teaspoon salt and the green beans in 2-quart microwavable casserole. Cover tightly and microwave on high (100%), stirring every 5 minutes, until tender, 16 to 18 minutes; drain. Stir in remaining ingredients except cheese. Cover tightly and microwave until tomatoes are hot, 3 to 5 minutes; sprinkle with cheese.

SAUCY GREEN BEANS

1 **pound fresh green beans***
¼ **cup chili sauce**
1 **tablespoon prepared horseradish**
⅛ **teaspoon pepper**
¼ **cup margarine or butter, softened**
4 **green onions (with tops), chopped**

*2 packages (9 ounces each) frozen cut green beans, cooked and drained, can be substituted for the 1 pound green beans. Or 2 cans (16 ounces each) cut green beans, drained, can be substituted for the 1 pound green beans; heat beans and remaining ingredients until hot.

Prepare and cook green beans, cut into 1-inch pieces, as directed on page 617. Mix chili sauce, horseradish and pepper. Stir margarine, onions and chili sauce mixture into beans. Cook, stirring occasionally, just until heated through, 2 to 3 minutes. **6 servings; 100 calories per serving.**

■ **To Microwave:** Place 2 tablespoons water, ¼ teaspoon salt and the fresh green beans in 2-quart microwavable casserole. Cover tightly and microwave on high (100%) 6 minutes; stir. Cover tightly and microwave until tender, 5 to 6 minutes longer. Stir in remaining ingredients. Cover tightly and microwave until hot, about 1 minute.

ITALIAN-STYLE BEANS

1½ **pounds fresh green beans***
1 **small red onion, thinly sliced**
1 **cup small pitted ripe olives**
½ **cup bottled Italian dressing**
1 **large tomato, chopped (about 1 cup)**

Prepare and cook green beans, cut into 1-inch pieces, as directed on page 617. Cook beans, onion, olives and dressing uncovered over medium heat just until onion is tender, about 3 minutes; sprinkle with tomato. **6 servings; 190 calories per serving.**

■ **To Microwave:** Cover and microwave green beans (1-inch pieces) in 3-quart microwavable casserole as directed on page 617. Stir in onion, olives and dressing. Microwave uncovered until onion is tender, 1 to 3 minutes; sprinkle with tomato.

BEANS—GREEN LIMAS

Amount for 4 servings: 3 pounds (unshelled).
  When shopping: Look for broad, thick, shiny pods that are plump with large seeds.

*2 packages (9 ounces each) frozen cut green beans, cooked and drained, can be substituted for the 1½ pounds green beans.

TO PREPARE: Wash lima beans; shell just before cooking. To shell beans, remove thin outer edge of pod with sharp knife or scissors. Beans will slip out.

TO COOK: Heat 1 inch salted water (½ teaspoon salt to 1 cup water) to boiling. Add beans. Heat to boiling; reduce heat. Boil uncovered 5 minutes. Cover and boil until tender, 15 to 20 minutes longer; drain.

TO MICROWAVE: Cover and microwave lima beans and ½ cup water in 1-quart microwavable casserole on high (100%), stirring every 6 minutes, until tender, 16 to 18 minutes. Let stand covered 1 minute; drain.

BEANS AND SOUR CREAM

2	packages (10 ounces each) frozen lima beans
1	cup dairy sour cream
2	tablespoons milk
¼	teaspoon salt
4	green onions (with tops), sliced
1	jar (2 ounces) diced pimientos, drained

Cook beans as directed on package; drain. Stir in remaining ingredients; heat until hot. **6 servings; 210 calories per serving.**

SUCCOTASH

3	pounds fresh lima beans
4	ears fresh corn
⅓	cup cut-up lean salt pork or bacon
¼	cup chopped onion
½	cup half-and-half
¼	teaspoon salt
⅛	teaspoon pepper

Prepare beans as directed above. Prepare corn as directed on page 637. Cut enough kernels from corn to measure 2 cups. Mix beans, pork and onion in 3-quart saucepan; add enough water to cover. Heat to boiling; reduce heat. Cover and simmer until beans are tender, 20 to 25 minutes. Stir in corn.

Heat to boiling; reduce heat. Cover and simmer until corn is tender, about 5 minutes; drain. Stir in half-and-half, salt and pepper. Heat, stirring occasionally, until half-and-half is hot. **6 servings;** 320 calories per serving.

CREOLE LIMA BEANS

1 **can (8 ounces) stewed tomatoes**
1 **package (10 ounces) frozen baby lima beans**
1 **large stalk celery, chopped (about ¾ cup)**
¾ **teaspoon salt**
⅛ **teaspoon pepper**

Heat tomatoes to boiling in 1-quart saucepan. Stir in remaining ingredients. Heat to boiling, separating beans with fork; reduce heat. Cover and simmer until beans are tender, about 5 minutes. **5 servings;** 75 calories per serving.

BEETS

Amount for 4 servings: 5 medium (about 1¼ pounds).

When shopping: Look for firm, round, smooth beets of a deep red color; fresh tops.

TO PREPARE: Cut off all but 2 inches of beet tops. Wash beets and leave whole with root ends attached.

TO COOK: Heat 6 cups water, 1 tablespoon vinegar (to preserve color) and 1 teaspoon salt to boiling. Add beets. Cover and heat to boiling; reduce heat. Boil until tender, 40 to 50 minutes; drain. Run cold water over beets; slip off skins and remove root ends. Slice, dice or cut into shoestring pieces.

TO STEAM: Place steamer basket in ½ inch water (water should not touch bottom of basket). Place medium whole beets in basket. Cover tightly and heat to boiling; reduce heat. Steam until tender, 45 to 50 minutes. Add boiling water during steaming if necessary. Run cold water over beets; slip off skins and remove root ends. Slice, dice or cut into shoestring pieces.

HARVARD BEETS

5   fresh medium beets (about 1¼ pounds)*
1   tablespoon cornstarch
1   tablespoon sugar
¾   teaspoon salt
    Dash of pepper
⅔   cup water
¼   cup vinegar

Prepare and cook beets as directed on page 621; cut into slices. Mix cornstarch, sugar, salt and pepper in saucepan. Gradually stir in water and vinegar. Cook, stirring constantly, until mixture thickens and boils. Boil and stir 1 minute. Stir in beets; heat through.   **4 servings; 50 calories per serving.**

Orange Beets: Substitute packed brown sugar for the sugar and ¾ cup orange juice for the ⅔ cup water. Mix in 1 teaspoon grated orange peel with the sugar. Decrease vinegar to 1 tablespoon.

HONEYED BEETS

5   fresh medium beets (about 1¼ pounds)**
1   medium onion, chopped (about ½ cup)
2   tablespoons margarine or butter
2   tablespoons honey
1   tablespoon lemon juice
½   teaspoon salt
⅛   teaspoon ground cinnamon
1   tablespoon snipped parsley

Prepare and cook beets as directed on page 621; cut into shoestring pieces. Cook and stir onion in margarine in 10-inch skillet over medium heat until onion is tender, about 5 minutes. Stir in beets, honey, lemon juice, salt and cinnamon.

*1 can (16 ounces) sliced beets, drained (reserve liquid), can be substituted for the 5 medium beets. Add enough water to reserved liquid to measure ⅔ cup. Substitute beet liquid mixture for the water.
**2 cans (16 ounces each) julienne beets, drained, can be substituted for the 5 medium beets; stir in with the onion.

Heat, stirring occasionally, until beets are hot, about 5 minutes; sprinkle with parsley. **7 servings** (about ½ cup each); 65 calories per serving.

BOK CHOY

Amount for 4 servings: 1½ pounds.

  When shopping: Look for firm, white stalks and shiny, dark leaves.

  TO PREPARE: Wash bok choy and cut off leaves. Cut stems into ¼-inch slices; cut leaves into ½-inch strips.

  TO COOK: Heat 1 inch salted water (½ teaspoon salt to 1 cup water) to boiling. Add bok choy stems. Cover and heat to boiling; reduce heat. Boil 5 minutes. Add bok choy leaves. Cover and boil until stems are crisp-tender, 2 to 3 minutes longer; drain.

  TO STEAM: Place steamer basket in ½ inch water (water should not touch bottom of basket). Place bok choy stems in basket. Cover tightly and heat to boiling; reduce heat. Steam 5 minutes. Add bok choy leaves; steam until stems are crisp-tender, 2 to 3 minutes longer.

  TO MICROWAVE: Place bok choy stems and 2 tablespoons water in 3-quart microwavable casserole. Cover tightly and microwave on high (100%) 4 minutes. Stir in bok choy leaves. Cover tightly and microwave until stems are crisp-tender, 3 to 4 minutes longer. Let stand covered 1 minute; drain.

BOK CHOY ORIENTAL STYLE

1½	pounds fresh bok choy
1	tablespoon cornstarch
2	tablespoons soy sauce
1	tablespoon vegetable oil
1	tablespoon margarine or butter
2	thin slices gingerroot, finely chopped
1	clove garlic, finely chopped
2	tablespoons water

Prepare bok choy as directed on page 623. Mix cornstarch and soy sauce. Heat oil and margarine in 12-inch skillet over medium-high heat until margarine is melted. Add gingerroot and garlic; stir-fry until garlic is light brown. Add bok choy stems; stir-fry 2 minutes. Add water; cover and cook until stems are crisp-tender, about 2 minutes. Stir in cornstarch mixture and bok choy leaves; cook and stir until leaves are wilted, 1 to 2 minutes. **6 servings; 60 calories per serving.**

BOK CHOY AU GRATIN

1½   **pounds fresh bok choy**
½   **cup shredded Swiss cheese (2 ounces)**
1   **tablespoon margarine or butter**
1   **tablespoon all-purpose flour**
¼   **teaspoon salt**
⅛   **teaspoon ground nutmeg**
1   **cup half-and-half**
2   **tablespoons fine dry bread crumbs**
1   **tablespoon margarine or butter, melted**

Prepare and cook bok choy as directed on page 623; drain thoroughly. Place bok choy in ungreased rectangular pan, 10 × 6 × 1½ inches, or square pan, 8 × 8 × 2 inches; sprinkle with cheese.

Heat 1 tablespoon margarine in 1-quart saucepan over low heat until melted. Stir in flour, salt and nutmeg. Cook over low heat, stirring constantly, until smooth and bubbly; remove from heat. Stir in half-and-half. Heat to boiling, stirring constantly. Boil and stir 1 minute. Pour over bok choy. Mix bread crumbs and 1 tablespoon melted margarine; sprinkle over bok choy.

Set oven control to broil and/or 550°. Broil with top about 4 inches from heat until golden brown and bubbly, 3 to 5 minutes. **6 servings; 130 calories per serving.**

BROCCOLI

Amount for 4 servings: 1½ pounds.
When shopping: Look for firm, compact dark green clusters. Avoid thick, tough stems.

   TO PREPARE: Trim off large leaves; remove tough ends of lower stems. Wash broccoli. If stems are thicker than 1 inch in diameter, make lengthwise gashes in each stem.

   TO COOK: Heat 1 inch salted water (½ teaspoon salt to 1 cup water) to boiling. Add broccoli. Cover and heat to boiling; reduce heat. Boil until stems are tender, 12 to 15 minutes; drain.

   TO STEAM: Place steamer basket in ½ inch water (water should not touch bottom of basket). Place broccoli in basket. Cover tightly and heat to boiling; reduce heat. Steam until stems are tender, 15 to 18 minutes.

   TO MICROWAVE: Cover and microwave broccoli (1-inch pieces or thin spears) and ¼ cup water in 3-quart microwavable casserole on high (100%) 5 minutes; stir. Cover and microwave until stems are tender, 4 to 6 minutes longer. Let stand covered 1 minute; drain.

BROCCOLI PIE

1½   **pounds fresh broccoli***
¼   **cup finely chopped onion**
1   **tablespoon margarine or butter**
3   **eggs, slightly beaten**
¼   **cup dry bread crumbs**
¼   **cup grated Parmesan cheese**
½   **cup milk**
¼   **teaspoon salt**
⅛   **teaspoon pepper**
   Mushroom Sauce (page 626)

Prepare and cook broccoli as directed above except—cook until crisp-tender, 10 to 12 minutes; drain and cool.

   Coarsely chop broccoli. Cook and stir onion in margarine until tender, about 3 minutes. Place broccoli in greased pie plate, 9 × 1¼ inches; sprinkle with onion. Mix remaining ingredients except Mushroom Sauce; pour over broccoli.

   Bake uncovered in 350° oven until knife inserted halfway between center and edge comes out clean, 30 to 35 minutes.

*2 packages (10 ounces each) frozen chopped broccoli can be substituted for the 1½ pounds broccoli. Rinse under running cold water to separate; drain. Increase salt to ½ teaspoon.

Serve pie with Mushroom Sauce.   **8 servings;** 160 calories per serving.

Mushroom Sauce

  2   tablespoons margarine or butter
  1   thin slice onion
  2   tablespoons all-purpose flour
  1   cup beef broth (page 561)
  1   jar (4½ ounces) sliced mushrooms, drained
 ¼   teaspoon salt
 ⅛   teaspoon pepper

Heat margarine in 8-inch skillet over low heat until melted. Cook and stir onion in margarine until onion is brown. Discard onion. Stir flour into margarine. Cook over low heat, stirring constantly, until flour is deep brown; remove from heat. Stir in broth and mushrooms. Heat to boiling, stirring constantly. Boil and stir 1 minute. Stir in salt and pepper and, if desired, a few drops of Worcestershire sauce.

BROCCOLI WITH CHEESE

1½ pounds fresh broccoli*
  6 ounces process American cheese, sliced
 ⅓ cup milk
 ¼ teaspoon onion salt
  1 drop red pepper sauce, if desired

Prepare and cook broccoli as directed on page 625. Heat remaining ingredients over medium heat, stirring frequently, until cheese is melted and mixture is smooth, 6 to 8 minutes; pour over broccoli.   **4 servings;** 190 calories per serving.

---

*1 package (10 ounces) frozen broccoli spears, cooked and drained, can be substituted for the 1½ pounds broccoli.

FRENCH-FRIED BROCCOLI

1½	pounds fresh broccoli
	Vegetable oil
1	cup all-purpose flour
¾	cup beer
¾	teaspoon salt
1½	teaspoons vegetable oil
2	eggs

Prepare broccoli as directed on page 625 except—cut lengthwise into ½-inch spears. Cook as directed until crisp-tender, about 8 minutes; drain and cool.

Heat oil (1½ inches) in deep fryer or Dutch oven to 375°. Beat remaining ingredients with hand beater until smooth. Dip each spear into batter, letting excess drip into bowl.

Fry 2 or 3 broccoli spears at a time in hot oil, turning once, until golden brown, about 2 minutes; drain.   6 servings; 260 calories per serving.

NOTE: To keep fried broccoli warm, place in 300° oven up to 5 minutes.

BRUSSELS SPROUTS

Amount for 4 servings: 1½ pounds.

When shopping: Look for unblemished, bright green sprouts; compact leaves.

TO PREPARE: Remove any discolored leaves. Cut off stem ends; wash sprouts.

TO COOK: Heat 1 inch salted water (½ teaspoon salt to 1 cup water) to boiling. Add Brussels sprouts. Cover and heat to boiling; reduce heat. Boil until stems are tender, 8 to 10 minutes; drain.

TO STEAM: Place steamer basket in ½ inch water (water should not touch bottom of basket). Place Brussels sprouts in basket. Cover tightly and heat to boiling; reduce heat. Steam until tender, 20 to 25 minutes.

TO MICROWAVE: Cover and microwave Brussels sprouts and ¼ cup water in 1½-quart microwavable casserole on high (100%) 4 minutes; stir. Cover and microwave until tender, 3 to 4 minutes longer. Let stand covered 1 minute; drain.

PARMESAN SPROUTS

1½ pounds fresh Brussels sprouts*
1 small onion, chopped (about ¼ cup)
¼ cup margarine or butter
¼ cup grated Parmesan cheese

Prepare and cook Brussels sprouts as directed on page 627. Cook and stir onion in margarine until tender. Pour over Brussels sprouts; sprinkle with cheese. **6 servings; 125 calories per serving.**

CABBAGE—GREEN, SAVOY AND RED

Amount for 4 servings: 1 medium head (about 1½ pounds).
   When shopping: Look for firm, heavy heads of good color.
   TO PREPARE: Remove outside leaves; wash cabbage. Cut into wedges; remove core after cooking. Or coarsely shred cabbage with knife and discard core.
   TO COOK: Heat 1 inch (½ inch for shredded) salted water (½ teaspoon salt to 1 cup water) to boiling. Add cabbage (and 2 tablespoons vinegar or lemon juice for red cabbage). Cover and heat to boiling; reduce heat. Boil, turning wedges once, until crisp-tender, wedges 10 to 17 minutes, shredded 5 to 8 minutes; drain.
   TO STEAM: Place steamer basket in ½ inch water (water should not touch bottom of basket). Place cabbage in basket. Cover tightly and heat to boiling; reduce heat. Steam until crisp-tender, wedges 18 to 24 minutes, shredded 5 to 7 minutes.

*2 packages (10 ounces each) frozen Brussels sprouts, cooked and drained, can be substituted for the 1½ pounds Brussels sprouts.

STIR-FRIED CABBAGE

1	medium head green cabbage (about 1½ pounds)
3	green onions (with tops)
1	tablespoon cornstarch
1	tablespoon cold water
3	tablespoons vegetable oil
2	large cloves garlic, finely chopped
¼	cup catsup
1	teaspoon salt
1	teaspoon red pepper sauce
½	cup chicken broth

Prepare cabbage as directed at left except—cut into 1½-inch pieces. Cut onions into 2-inch pieces. Mix cornstarch and water.

Heat oil in wok or 12-inch skillet over medium-high heat until hot. Add cabbage and garlic; stir-fry 1 minute. Add catsup, salt and pepper sauce; stir-fry 1 minute. Stir in chicken broth; heat to boiling. Stir in cornstarch mixture; cook and stir until thickened, about 10 seconds. Stir in onions. **3 servings;** 200 calories per serving.

SAVOY CABBAGE AND BACON

1	medium head savoy cabbage (about 1½ pounds), finely shredded (about 8 cups)
4	slices bacon, diced
¼	cup vinegar
1	teaspoon sugar
½	teaspoon dry mustard
¼	teaspoon salt
⅛	teaspoon pepper
5	green onions (with tops), sliced (about ½ cup)

Cover cabbage with boiling water in 4-quart bowl. Let stand 10 minutes; drain. Cook bacon in 12-inch skillet until crisp; remove from heat.

Add vinegar, sugar, mustard, salt and pepper; heat through over medium heat. Add cabbage and onions. Toss until cabbage is coated with bacon mixture. **6 servings;** 115 calories per serving.

SWEET-SOUR RED CABBAGE

1	medium head red cabbage (about 1½ pounds)
4	slices bacon, diced
¼	cup packed brown sugar
2	tablespoons all-purpose flour
½	cup water
¼	cup vinegar
1	teaspoon salt
⅛	teaspoon pepper
1	small onion, sliced

Prepare and cook 5 cups shredded cabbage as directed on page 628. (Be sure to add the 2 tablespoons vinegar or lemon juice to the salted water.)

Cook bacon, stirring occasionally, until crisp; drain. Drain fat from skillet, reserving 1 tablespoon. Stir brown sugar and flour into fat in skillet. Stir in water, vinegar, salt, pepper and onion. Cook, stirring frequently, until mixture thickens, about 5 minutes.

Stir bacon and sauce mixture into hot cabbage in saucepan; heat through. Garnish with additional crisply cooked diced bacon if desired.   **6 servings; 105 calories per serving.**

CABBAGE STRUDELS

1	medium head green cabbage (about 1½ pounds), finely shredded (about 8 cups)
1	cup dairy sour cream
2	teaspoons curry powder
½	teaspoon salt
8	frozen phyllo leaves, thawed
½	cup margarine or butter, melted

Cook cabbage as directed on page 628; drain thoroughly. Mix cabbage, sour cream, curry powder and salt.

Fold 1 phyllo leaf crosswise into halves; brush with margarine. (Cover remaining leaves with a damp towel to prevent them from drying out.) Fold leaf crosswise into halves again; brush with margarine.

Place about ½ cup cabbage mixture down center of leaf. Fold long sides up and over cabbage mixture; fold short sides up over cabbage mixture, overlapping ends. Place strudel, seam side down, on ungreased cookie sheet. (Cover with damp towel to prevent it from drying out.) Repeat with remaining phyllo leaves and cabbage mixture.

Bake strudels uncovered in 350° oven until golden brown, about 30 minutes. **8 servings; 225 calories per serving.**

Do-ahead Tip: Before baking, strudels can be covered with damp cloth and refrigerated up to 4 hours.

CABBAGE—CHINESE OR CELERY

Amount for 4 servings: 1 medium head.

When shopping: Look for crisp, green heads, either firm or leafy.

TO PREPARE: Remove root ends. Wash cabbage; shred.

TO COOK: Heat ½ inch salted water (½ teaspoon salt to 1 cup water) to boiling. Add cabbage. Cover and heat to boiling; reduce heat. Boil until crisp-tender, 4 to 5 minutes; drain.

TO STEAM: Place steamer basket in ½ inch water (water should not touch bottom of basket). Place coarsely shredded Chinese cabbage in basket. Cover tightly and heat to boiling; reduce heat. Steam until tender, 4 to 6 minutes.

TO MICROWAVE: Cover and microwave cabbage and 2 tablespoons water in 2-quart microwavable casserole on high (100%) 2 minutes; stir. Cover and microwave until crisp-tender, 2 to 3 minutes longer. Let stand covered 1 minute; drain.

CABBAGE AND SOUR CREAM

1	medium head Chinese cabbage, shredded (about 8 cups)
½	cup dairy sour cream
1	teaspoon all-purpose flour
1	tablespoon vegetable oil
1	tablespoon margarine or butter
½	teaspoon salt
½	teaspoon ground turmeric
½	teaspoon ground ginger
⅛	teaspoon pepper

Prepare cabbage as directed on page 631. Mix sour cream and flour. Heat remaining ingredients in 12-inch skillet over medium-high heat until margarine is melted. Add cabbage; cook and stir until crisp-tender, 2 to 3 minutes. Stir in sour cream mixture.   **6 servings; 95 calories per serving.**

■ **To Microwave:** Place 2 tablespoons water, ¼ teaspoon salt and the cabbage in 3-quart microwavable casserole. Cover tightly and microwave on high (100%) 3 minutes; stir. Cover tightly and microwave until crisp-tender, 3 to 5 minutes longer; drain. Mix sour cream and flour. Omit oil. Stir sour cream mixture and remaining ingredients into cabbage.

CARROTS

Amount for 4 servings: 1¼ pounds.

When shopping: Look for firm, nicely shaped carrots of good color.

TO PREPARE: Pare carrots thinly and remove ends. Leave carrots whole, shred or cut lengthwise into ⅜-inch strips or crosswise into ¼-inch slices.

TO COOK: Heat 1 inch salted water (½ teaspoon salt to 1 cup water) to boiling. Add carrots. Cover and heat to boiling; reduce heat. Boil until tender, whole 25 minutes, shredded 5 minutes, lengthwise strips 18 to 20 minutes, crosswise slices 12 to 15 minutes; drain.

TO STEAM: Place steamer basket in ½ inch water (water should not touch bottom of basket). Place carrots (slender whole or ¼-inch slices) in basket. Cover tightly and heat to boiling; reduce heat. Steam until tender, whole 12 to 15 minutes, slices 9 to 11 minutes.

TO MICROWAVE: Cover and microwave carrots (¼-inch slices) in 1½-quart microwavable casserole on high (100%) 5 minutes; stir. Cover and microwave until tender, 5 to 7 minutes longer. Let stand covered 1 minute; drain.

GLAZED CARROTS

1½ pounds fresh carrots
⅓ cup packed brown sugar
½ teaspoon salt
½ teaspoon grated orange peel
2 tablespoons margarine or butter

Prepare and cook carrots, cut into lengthwise strips, as directed on page 632. Cook and stir brown sugar, salt and orange peel in margarine in 12-inch skillet until bubbly. Add carrots; cook over low heat, stirring occasionally, until carrots are glazed and heated through, about 5 minutes. **6 servings;** 110 calories per serving.

CARROT CASSEROLE

About 6 medium fresh carrots
1 small onion, chopped (about ¼ cup)
½ teaspoon salt
½ teaspoon dried savory leaves
¼ teaspoon dry mustard
½ cup hot water
¼ cup coarsely chopped walnuts
1 tablespoon margarine or butter

Prepare 3 cups shredded carrots as directed on page 632. Mix carrots, onion, salt, savory and mustard in ungreased 1½-quart casserole. Pour water over top. Cover and bake in 350° oven until carrots are tender, about 45 minutes.

Cook and stir walnuts in margarine over medium heat until walnuts are toasted, about 2 minutes. Spoon over carrots.   **4 servings** (about ½ cup each); 115 calories per serving.

■ **To Microwave:** Mix shredded carrots, onion, salt, savory, mustard and 1 tablespoon water in ungreased 1½-quart microwavable casserole. Cover tightly and microwave on high (100%) 3 minutes; stir. Cover tightly and microwave until carrots are tender, 2 to 4 minutes longer. Place walnuts and margarine in 1-cup microwavable measure. Microwave uncovered, stirring every 30 seconds, until toasted, 3 to 4 minutes. Spoon over carrots.

CAULIFLOWER

Amount for 4 servings: 1 medium head (about 2 pounds).

When shopping: Look for clean, nonspreading flower clusters (the white portion); green "jacket" leaves.

TO PREPARE: Remove outer leaves and stalk. Cut off any discoloration; wash cauliflower. Leave whole, or separate into flowerets.

TO COOK: Heat 1 inch salted water (½ teaspoon salt to 1 cup water) to boiling. Add cauliflower. Cover and heat to boiling; reduce heat. Boil until tender, whole 20 to 25 minutes, cauliflowerets 10 to 12 minutes; drain.

TO STEAM: Place steamer basket in ½ inch water (water should not touch bottom of basket). Place cauliflower in basket. Cover tightly and heat to boiling; reduce heat. Steam until tender, whole 18 to 22 minutes, cauliflowerets 6 to 8 minutes.

TO MICROWAVE: Cover and microwave cauliflower and 2 tablespoons water in 2-quart microwavable casserole on high (100%) 6 minutes; rotate casserole ¼ turn (stir cauliflowerets). Cover and microwave until tender, 5 to 7 minutes longer. Let stand covered 1 minute; drain.

CHEESE CAULIFLOWER

Prepare and cook 1 medium head cauliflower (about 2 pounds) as directed above for whole cauliflower. Pour Cheese Sauce (page 599) over hot cauliflower; sprinkle with paprika if desired.   **4 servings; 250 calories per serving.**

BAKED CAULIFLOWER

1	medium head cauliflower (about 2 pounds)
½	cup dry bread crumbs
¼	cup margarine or butter, melted
2	tablespoons grated Parmesan cheese
⅛	teaspoon onion salt
⅛	teaspoon ground red pepper

Prepare and cook whole cauliflower as directed at left until crisp-tender, 12 to 15 minutes; drain. Place cauliflower in ungreased 1½-quart casserole. Mix remaining ingredients until crumbly; press evenly on cauliflower.

Bake uncovered in 375° oven until cauliflower is tender and bread crumb mixture is light brown, about 15 minutes.   **6 servings; 135 calories per serving.**

■ **To Microwave:** Cut cone-shaped center from core of cauliflower. Place 2 tablespoons water, ¼ teaspooon salt and the cauliflower in 1½-quart microwavable casserole. Cover tightly and microwave on high (100%) 5 minutes; rotate casserole ¼ turn. Microwave until tender, 4 to 5 minutes longer; drain. Mix remaining ingredients until crumbly; press evenly on cauliflower. Microwave uncovered until crumb mixture is hot, about 1 minute.

CELERY

Amount for 4 servings: 1 medium bunch.

When shopping: Look for crisp, unblemished stalks; fresh leaves.

TO PREPARE: Remove leaves and trim off root ends. Remove any coarse strings. Wash celery. Cut stalks into 1-inch pieces (about 4 cups).

TO COOK: Heat 1 inch salted water (½ teaspoon salt to 1 cup water) to boiling. Add celery pieces. Cover and heat to boiling; reduce heat. Boil until tender, 15 to 20 minutes; drain.

TO STEAM: Place steamer basket in ½ inch water (water should not touch bottom of basket). Place celery pieces in basket. Cover tightly and heat to boiling; reduce heat. Steam until crisp-tender, 18 to 20 minutes.

TO MICROWAVE: Cover and microwave celery pieces and 2 tablespoons water in 1½-quart microwavable casserole on high (100%) 4 minutes; stir. Cover and microwave until tender, 3 to 5 minutes longer. Let stand covered 1 minute; drain.

CELERY POLYNESIAN

10	medium stalks celery
1	can (8 ounces) water chestnuts, drained and sliced
1	tablespoon instant chicken bouillon
½	teaspoon salt
½	teaspoon celery salt
1	teaspoon vegetable oil
1	jar (2 ounces) sliced pimientos, drained

Prepare celery as directed on page 635 except—cut into ¼-inch diagonal slices. Cook and stir celery, water chestnuts, instant bouillon (dry), salt and celery salt in oil over medium heat, turning vegetables constantly with pancake turner, until celery is crisp-tender, about 10 minutes. Stir in pimientos; heat through. **5 servings** (1 cup each); 60 calories per serving.

CHINESE PEA PODS

Amount for 4 servings: 1 pound.
   When shopping: Look for flat, crisp, bright pods.
   TO PREPARE: Wash pea pods; remove tips and strings.
   TO COOK: Heat 1 inch salted water (½ teaspoon salt to 1 cup water) to boiling. Add pea pods. Boil uncovered, stirring occasionally, until crisp-tender, 2 to 3 minutes; drain.
   TO STEAM: Place steamer basket in ½ inch water (water should not touch bottom of basket). Place pea pods in basket. Cover tightly and heat to boiling; reduce heat. Steam until crisp-tender, 5 to 7 minutes.
   TO MICROWAVE: Cover and microwave pea pods and ¼ cup water in 2-quart microwavable casserole on high (100%) 3 minutes; stir. Cover and microwave until crisp-tender, 2 to 4 minutes longer. Let stand covered 1 minute; drain.

PEA PODS AND PEPPERS

1	pound fresh Chinese pea pods
2	red peppers, cut into ¼-inch strips
1	medium onion, cut into ¼-inch slices and separated into rings
2	tablespoons vegetable oil
2	tablespoons margarine or butter
½	teaspoon celery salt
⅛	teaspoon freshly ground pepper

Prepare pea pods as directed on page 636. Cook and stir red peppers and onion in oil and margarine in 12-inch skillet over medium-high heat until peppers are crisp-tender, about 3 minutes. Stir in pea pods, celery salt and pepper; cook and stir until pea pods are hot, about 1 minute.   **8 servings; 115 calories per serving.**

CORN

Amount for 4 servings: 4 to 8 ears.

When shopping: Look for bright green husks, fresh-looking silk and plump but not too large kernels.

TO PREPARE: Refrigerate unhusked corn until ready to use. Corn is best when eaten as soon after picking as possible. Husk ears and remove silk just before cooking.

TO COOK: Place corn in enough *unsalted* cold water to cover (salt toughens corn). Add 1 tablespoon sugar and 1 tablespoon lemon juice to each gallon of water. Heat to boiling. Boil uncovered 2 minutes; remove from heat. Let stand uncovered 10 minutes before serving.

TO STEAM: Place steamer basket in ½ inch water (water should not touch bottom of basket). Place 4 ears of corn in basket. Cover tightly and heat to boiling; reduce heat. Steam until tender, 6 to 9 minutes.

TO MICROWAVE: Wrap corn in waxed paper; twist ends. Microwave on high (100%) until tender, 7 to 9 minutes. Let stand 1 minute.

CORN WITH BASIL

6 ears fresh corn*
1 medium onion, chopped (about ½ cup)
½ cup thinly sliced celery
1 clove garlic, finely chopped
2 tablespoons margarine or butter
1 teaspoon snipped basil or ¼ teaspoon dried basil leaves
½ teaspoon salt
1 jar (2 ounces) diced pimientos, drained

Prepare corn as directed on page 637. Cut enough kernels from corn to measure 3 cups. Cook and stir corn, onion, celery and garlic in margarine in 3-quart saucepan over medium heat until onion is tender, about 10 minutes. Stir in remaining ingredients; reduce heat. Cover and cook until corn is tender, 3 to 5 minutes longer.   **8 servings;** 95 calories per serving.

SCALLOPED CORN

4 ears fresh corn**
1 small onion, chopped (about ¼ cup)
½ small green pepper, chopped
2 tablespoons margarine or butter
2 tablespoons all-purpose flour
1 teaspoon salt
½ teaspoon paprika
¼ teaspoon dry mustard
  Dash of pepper
¾ cup milk
1 egg, slightly beaten
⅓ cup cracker crumbs
1 tablespoon margarine or butter, melted

*2 packages (10 ounces each) frozen whole kernel corn can be substituted for the 6 ears corn.
**1 package (10 ounces) frozen whole kernel corn, cooked and drained, or 1 can (16 ounces) whole kernel corn, drained, can be substituted for the 4 ears corn.

Prepare and cook corn as directed on page 637. Cut enough kernels from corn to measure 2 cups.

Cook and stir onion and green pepper in 2 tablespoons margarine in 1-quart saucepan until onion is tender; remove from heat. Stir in flour, salt, paprika, mustard and pepper. Cook over low heat, stirring constantly, until mixture is bubbly; remove from heat. Gradually stir in milk. Heat to boiling, stirring constantly. Boil and stir 1 minute. Stir in corn and egg. Pour into ungreased 1-quart casserole.

Mix crumbs and 1 tablespoon melted margarine; sprinkle over corn. Bake uncovered in 350° oven until bubbly, 30 to 35 minutes.   **4 servings; 230 calories per serving.**

Cheese Scalloped Corn: Stir ½ cup shredded natural Cheddar cheese into sauce mixture.

SKILLET CORN

    4   **ears fresh corn***
    2   **tablespoons margarine or butter**
    2   **tablespoons milk**
    ¼   **teaspoon salt**
        Dash of pepper

Prepare corn as directed on page 637. Cut enough kernels from corn to measure 2 cups (scrape ears with back of knife to extract all pulp and milk).

Cook and stir all ingredients in 10-inch skillet over medium heat until margarine is melted. Cover and cook over low heat until corn is tender, 10 to 15 minutes.   **4 servings; 130 calories per serving.**

*1 package (10 ounces) frozen whole kernel corn can be substituted for the 4 ears corn.

CORN AND CHEESE

6 ears fresh corn*
1 small onion, chopped (about ¼ cup)
1 fresh hot green chili pepper, seeded
    and finely chopped (about 1 tablespoon)
2 tablespoons margarine or butter
½ teaspoon salt
½ cup shredded Cheddar cheese (2 ounces)

Prepare corn as directed on page 637. Cut enough kernels
from corn to measure 3 cups. Cook and stir onion and chili
pepper in margarine in 1½-quart saucepan until tender, about
3 minutes. Stir in corn and salt. Cover and cook over medium
heat, stirring occasionally, until corn is tender, 10 to 15
minutes. Just before serving, stir in cheese. **6 servings; 190**
calories per serving.

■ **To Microwave:** Mix 2 tablespoons water, the fresh corn
kernels, onion, chili pepper, margarine and salt in 2-quart
microwavable casserole. Cover tightly and microwave on high
(100%) 3 minutes; stir. Cover tightly and microwave until
corn is tender, 6 to 9 minutes longer. Stir in cheese.

CORN OYSTERS

1 cup bacon fat
1 cup vegetable oil
1 cup all-purpose flour
1 teaspoon baking powder
1 teaspoon salt
2 eggs, slightly beaten
1 can (16 ounces) whole kernel corn,
    drained (reserve ¼ cup liquid)

*2 packages (10 ounces each) frozen whole kernel corn can be substituted
for the 6 ears corn. Or 2 cans (12 ounces each) vacuum-packed whole
kernel corn, drained, can be substituted for the 6 ears corn; cook until
hot, about 5 minutes.

Heat fat and oil in deep fryer or Dutch oven to 375°. Mix flour, baking powder, salt, eggs and reserved corn liquid. Stir in corn. Drop by rounded tablespoonfuls into hot fat. Fry until golden brown, 4 to 5 minutes; drain. **6 servings; 230 calories per serving.**

Nutmeg Corn Oysters: Stir in 1 teaspoon ground nutmeg with the flour.

EGGPLANT

Amount for 4 servings: 1 medium (about 1½ pounds).

When shopping: Look for smooth, firm eggplants of an even dark purple.

TO PREPARE: Just before cooking, wash eggplant and, if desired, pare. Cut into ½-inch cubes, strips or ¼-inch slices.

TO BOIL: Heat small amount salted water (½ teaspoon salt to 1 cup water) to boiling. Add eggplant. Cover and heat to boiling; reduce heat. Boil until tender, 5 to 8 minutes; drain.

TO FRY: Cook and stir eggplant in margarine, butter or bacon fat until tender, 5 to 10 minutes.

TO STEAM: Place steamer basket in ½ inch water (water should not touch bottom of basket). Place eggplant (¼-inch slices) in basket. Cover tightly and heat to boiling; reduce heat. Steam until tender, 5 to 7 minutes.

TO MICROWAVE: Cover and microwave eggplant (¼-inch slices) in 2-quart microwavable casserole on high (100%) until tender, 5 to 7 minutes. Let stand covered 1 minute.

BROILED EGGPLANT

1	medium eggplant (about 1½ pounds)
1	teaspoon salt
¼	cup margarine or butter, melted
2	eggs
1	cup dry bread crumbs
¼	cup grated Parmesan cheese
½	teaspoon dried basil leaves
½	teaspoon parsley flakes

Prepare eggplant as directed on page 641, cutting into ¼-inch slices. Sprinkle cut sides with salt; let drain in colander 30 minutes.

Beat margarine and eggs. Mix remaining ingredients. Dip eggplant slices into egg mixture, then into bread crumb mixture. Place on greased broiler pan. Set oven control to broil and/or 550°. Broil with tops about 5 inches from heat, turning once, until light golden brown, about 4 minutes.   **6 servings; 195 calories per serving.**

RATATOUILLE

1	medium eggplant (about 1½ pounds)
2	small zucchini (about ½ pound)
1	medium green pepper, chopped (about 1 cup)
1	medium onion, finely chopped (about ½ cup)
4	medium tomatoes, each cut into fourths
¼	cup vegetable oil
2	teaspoons salt
¼	teaspoon pepper
1	clove garlic, crushed

Prepare 5 cups cubed eggplant as directed on page 641. Prepare 2 cups sliced zucchini as directed on page 663. Cook and stir all ingredients until heated through. Cover and cook over medium heat, stirring occasionally, until vegetables are crisp-tender, about 10 minutes.   **6 servings; 155 calories per serving.**

GREENS

Types: Mild-flavored—Beet Tops, Chicory (outer leaves), Collards, Escarole, Lettuce (outer leaves), Spinach; Strong-flavored—Kale, Swiss Chard, Mustard Greens, Turnip Greens.

Amount for 4 servings: 2 pounds.

When shopping: Look for tender, young, unblemished leaves of bright green color.

TO PREPARE: Remove root ends and imperfect leaves. Wash several times in water, lifting out each time; drain.

TO COOK: Cover and cook with just the water that clings to leaves until tender, beet tops 5 to 15 minutes, chicory, escarole, lettuce, mustard greens and Swiss chard 15 to 20 minutes, collards 10 to 15 minutes, spinach 3 to 10 minutes, kale and turnip greens 15 to 25 minutes; drain.

TO MICROWAVE: Place greens (beet tops, chicory, escarole, lettuce or spinach) with just the water that clings to leaves in 3-quart microwavable casserole. Cover and microwave on high (100%), stirring every 6 minutes, until tender, 15 to 18 minutes. Let stand covered 1 minute; drain.

WILTED SPINACH

1	pound fresh spinach
1	medium onion, chopped (about ½ cup)
1	slice bacon, cut up
1	clove garlic, finely chopped
2	tablespoons margarine or butter
2	tablespoons olive or vegetable oil
½	teaspoon salt
¼	teaspoon pepper
¼	teaspoon ground nutmeg
	Juice of ½ lime (about 2 tablespoons)

Prepare spinach as directed above. Cook and stir onion, bacon and garlic in margarine and oil in Dutch oven over medium heat until bacon is crisp; reduce heat. Stir in salt, pepper and nutmeg. Add spinach; toss just until spinach is wilted. Drizzle with lime juice.   **6 servings; 130 calories per serving.**

SPINACH SOUFFLE

1	pound fresh spinach
¼	cup margarine or butter
¼	cup all-purpose flour
¼	teaspoon salt
⅛	teaspoon pepper
1	cup milk
1	tablespoon finely chopped onion
1	teaspoon salt
⅛	teaspoon ground nutmeg
3	eggs, separated
¼	teaspoon cream of tartar

Prepare and cook spinach as directed on pages 642 and 643; chop and drain thoroughly. Heat oven to 350°. Butter 4-cup soufflé dish or 1-quart casserole. Heat margarine in saucepan over low heat until melted. Stir in flour, ¼ teaspoon salt and the pepper. Cook over low heat, stirring constantly, until mixture is smooth and bubbly; remove from heat. Stir in milk. Heat to boiling, stirring constantly. Boil and stir 1 minute; remove from heat. Stir in onion, 1 teaspoon salt and the nutmeg.

Beat egg whites and cream of tartar in 3-quart bowl until stiff. Beat egg yolks in 1½-quart bowl until very thick and lemon colored; stir into white sauce mixture. Stir in spinach.

Stir about ¼ of the egg whites into sauce mixture; fold into remaining egg whites.

Carefully pour into soufflé dish. Set soufflé dish in pan of water (1 inch deep). Bake until puffed and golden and knife inserted halfway between center and edge comes out clean, 50 to 60 minutes. Serve immediately. **4 servings; 265 calories per serving.**

Broccoli Soufflé: Substitute 1 pound fresh broccoli, prepared and cooked as directed on page 625, or 1 package (10 ounces) frozen chopped broccoli, cooked and drained, for the spinach.

LEEKS

Amount for 4 servings: 2 pounds.

When shopping: Look for bright green tops and white bulbs.

TO PREPARE: Remove green tops to within 2 inches of white part; peel outside layer of bulbs. Wash leeks several times in water; drain.

TO COOK: Heat 1 inch salted water (½ teaspoon salt to 1 cup water) to boiling. Add leeks. Cover and heat to boiling; reduce heat. Boil until tender, 12 to 15 minutes; drain.

TO STEAM: Place steamer basket in ½ inch water (water should not touch bottom of basket). Place leeks in basket. Cover tightly and heat to boiling; reduce heat. Steam until tender, 13 to 15 minutes.

TO MICROWAVE: Cover and microwave leeks and ¼ cup water in 3-quart microwavable casserole on high (100%) 3 minutes; turn leeks over. Cover and microwave until tender, 3 to 4 minutes longer. Let stand covered 1 minute; drain.

LEEKS IN TOMATO SAUCE

4	medium leeks (about 2 pounds)
1	cup sliced fresh mushrooms
1	tablespoon margarine or butter
1	can (8 ounces) tomato sauce
⅛	teaspoon freshly ground pepper

Prepare and cook leeks as directed above except—cut lengthwise into halves and cook until crisp-tender, 5 to 7 minutes; drain. Cook and stir mushrooms in margarine in 8-inch skillet 5 minutes. Stir in tomato sauce; cook until hot, about 5 minutes. Pour over leeks; sprinkle with pepper.   **4 servings;** 135 calories per serving.

MUSHROOMS

Amount for 4 servings: 1 pound.

When shopping: Look for creamy white to light brown caps, closed around the stems; if slightly open, gills should be light pink or tan.

TO PREPARE: Wash mushrooms and trim off stem ends. Do not peel. Slice parallel to stem if desired.

TO COOK: Heat ¼ cup margarine or butter in 10-inch skillet until bubbly. Cook mushrooms in margarine over medium heat, stirring occasionally, until tender, 6 to 8 minutes.

TO STEAM: Place steamer basket in ½ inch water (water should not touch bottom of basket). Place medium whole mushrooms in basket. Cover tightly and heat to boiling; reduce heat. Steam until tender, 6 to 8 minutes.

TO MICROWAVE: Cover and microwave mushrooms (¼-inch slices) in 2-quart microwavable casserole on high (100%) until tender, 4 to 5 minutes. Let stand covered 1 minute; drain. Stir in 3 tablespoons margarine or butter.

MUSHROOMS AND CUCUMBERS

 1   pound fresh mushrooms
 1   medium cucumber, cut into ¼-inch slices (about 2 cups)
 2   tablespoons margarine or butter
 1   tablespoon all-purpose flour
 ½   cup half-and-half
 ½   teaspoon salt
 ½   teaspoon Italian seasoning
 ⅛   teaspoon pepper

Prepare mushrooms as directed above except—cut into halves. Cook and stir cucumber in margarine in 12-inch skillet over medium-high heat until crisp-tender, 4 to 6 minutes; stir in mushrooms. Sprinkle with flour; stir until vegetables are coated. Stir in remaining ingredients. Cover and cook over medium heat, stirring occasionally, 3 minutes.   **6 servings; 95 calories per serving.**

SAUTEED MUSHROOMS

<table>
<tr><td>1</td><td>pound fresh mushrooms</td></tr>
<tr><td>2</td><td>slices buttered toast</td></tr>
<tr><td>1</td><td>small onion, chopped (about ¼ cup)</td></tr>
<tr><td>2</td><td>tablespoons margarine or butter</td></tr>
<tr><td>2</td><td>tablespoons olive or vegetable oil</td></tr>
<tr><td></td><td>Juice of 1 lemon (about ¼ cup)</td></tr>
<tr><td>1</td><td>teaspoon ground nutmeg</td></tr>
<tr><td>½</td><td>teaspoon salt</td></tr>
<tr><td></td><td>Dash of pepper</td></tr>
<tr><td>1</td><td>clove garlic, finely chopped</td></tr>
<tr><td>¼</td><td>cup snipped parsley</td></tr>
</table>

Prepare mushrooms as directed at left, slicing parallel to stem. Remove crusts from toast. Cut each slice into 4 triangles. Cook and stir onion in margarine and oil in 10-inch skillet over medium heat until tender. Stir in mushrooms, lemon juice, nutmeg, salt, pepper and garlic; reduce heat. Simmer uncovered 5 minutes; stir in parsley. Serve over toast triangles.   **4 servings; 200 calories per serving.**

OKRA

Amount for 4 servings: 1 pound.

When shopping: Look for tender, unblemished, bright green pods, less than 4 inches long.

TO PREPARE: Wash okra; remove ends and cut into ½-inch slices.

TO COOK: Heat 1 inch salted water (½ teaspoon salt to 1 cup water) to boiling. Add okra. Cover and heat to boiling; reduce heat. Boil until tender, about 10 minutes; drain.

TO STEAM: Place steamer basket in ½ inch water (water should not touch bottom of basket). Place whole okra in basket. Cover tightly and heat to boiling; reduce heat. Steam until tender, 6 to 8 minutes.

TO MICROWAVE: Cover and microwave okra and ¼ cup water in 1½-quart microwavable casserole on high (100%) 3 minutes; stir. Cover and microwave until tender, 2 to 3 minutes longer. Let stand covered 1 minute; drain.

OKRA SKILLET

¾ **pound fresh okra**
2 **to 3 ears fresh corn**
¼ **cup finely cut-up lean salt pork (about ¼ pound)**
1 **medium onion, chopped (about ½ cup)**
4 **medium tomatoes, each cut into eighths**
Dash of pepper

Prepare 2 cups sliced okra as directed on page 647. Prepare corn as directed on page 637. Cut enough kernels from corn to measure 1 cup. Cook and stir pork and onion in 10-inch skillet until pork is golden brown; stir in okra. Cook over medium-high heat, stirring constantly, 3 minutes. Stir in tomatoes and corn. Cover and simmer until corn is tender, 10 to 15 minutes; stir in pepper. **4 servings; 290 calories per serving.**

ONIONS

Types: Dry, small white (for whole-cooked); yellow or red (domestic, for seasoning); Spanish, Bermuda, Italian (sweet, for raw or French-fried slices).

Amount for 4 servings: 1½ pounds.

When shopping: Look for firm, well-shaped onions with unblemished, papery skins.

TO PREPARE: Peel onions under running cold water (to prevent eyes from watering).

TO BOIL: Heat several inches salted water (½ teaspoon salt to 1 cup water) to boiling. Add onions. Cover and heat to boiling; reduce heat. Boil until tender, small 15 to 20 minutes, large 30 to 35 minutes; drain.

TO BAKE: Place large onions in ungreased baking dish. Pour water into dish to ¼-inch depth. Cover and bake in 350° oven until tender, 40 to 50 minutes.

TO STEAM: Place steamer basket in ½ inch water (water should not touch bottom of basket). Place small white onions in basket. Cover tightly and heat to boiling; reduce heat. Steam until tender, 15 to 20 minutes.

TO MICROWAVE: Cover and microwave whole small onions of similar size and ¼ cup water in 2-quart microwavable casserole on high (100%) 3 minutes; stir. Cover and micro-wave until tender, 3 to 5 minutes longer. Let stand covered 1 minute; drain.

BAKED WHOLE ONIONS

6	medium white onions (with skins)
2	small cloves garlic, finely chopped
¼	cup margarine or butter
¼	cup dry white wine
¼	cup grated Parmesan cheese
2	tablespoons snipped parsley

Place onions directly on middle oven rack. Bake in 350° oven until tender, 30 to 40 minutes. Remove skins; place onions upright in serving dish. Cut each onion into fourths about halfway through; separate slightly. Cook garlic in margarine over medium heat until garlic is golden brown; remove from heat. Stir in wine; stir in cheese and parsley. Pour immediately over onions. **6 servings; 135 calories per serving.**

FRENCH-FRIED ONIONS

3	large Spanish or Bermuda onions
	Vegetable oil
¾	cup all-purpose flour
½	cup milk
½	teaspoon salt
1	egg

Prepare onions as directed on page 648; cut into ¼-inch slices and separate into rings. Heat oil (1 inch) in deep fryer or Dutch oven to 375°. Beat remaining ingredients with hand beater until smooth. Dip each onion ring into batter, letting excess drip into bowl.

Fry a few onion rings at a time in hot oil, turning once, until golden brown, about 2 minutes; drain. **4 servings; 290 calories per serving.**

NOTE: To keep fried onion rings warm, place in 300° oven until ready to serve.

ONIONS—GREEN

Amount for 4 servings: 3 bunches.

When shopping: Look for crisp green tops; 2 to 3 inches of white root.

TO PREPARE: Wash onions; remove any loose layers of skin. Leave about 3 inches of green tops.

TO COOK: Heat 1 inch salted water (½ teaspoon salt to 1 cup water) to boiling. Add green onions. Cover and heat to boiling; reduce heat. Boil just until tender, 8 to 10 minutes; drain.

TO STEAM: Place steamer basket in ½ inch water (water should not touch bottom of basket). Place green onions in basket. Cover tightly and heat to boiling; reduce heat. Steam until tender, 8 to 10 minutes.

TO MICROWAVE: Cover and microwave green onions and 2 tablespoons water in 1½-quart microwavable casserole on high (100%) just until tender, 1 to 2 minutes. Let stand covered 1 minute; drain.

ONIONS AND CARROTS

    3   bunches green onions (about 20)
    2   tablespoons vegetable oil
    2   thin slices gingerroot, finely chopped
    1   clove garlic, finely chopped
    1   medium carrot, shredded (about ⅔ cup)
   ¼   teaspoon salt
   ⅛   teaspoon freshly ground pepper

Prepare green onions as directed above. Cut diagonally into 1½-inch pieces.

Heat oil in 10-inch skillet over medium-high heat. Add onions, gingerroot and garlic; stir-fry until onions are crisp-tender, about 2 minutes. Stir in carrot and salt; sprinkle with pepper.   **4 servings; 95 calories per serving.**

PARSNIPS

Amount for 4 servings: 1½ pounds (about 6).

When shopping: Look for firm, nicely shaped, unblemished parsnips that are not too wide.

TO PREPARE: Scrape or pare. Leave whole or cut into halves, fourths, slices or ¼-inch lengthwise strips.

TO COOK: Heat 1 inch salted water (½ teaspoon salt to 1 cup water) to boiling. Add parsnips. Cover and heat to boiling; reduce heat. Boil until tender, about 30 minutes; drain.

TO STEAM: Place steamer basket in ½ inch water (water should not touch bottom of basket). Place parsnips (whole or ½-inch slices) in basket. Cover tightly and heat to boiling; reduce heat. Steam until tender, whole 20 to 25 minutes, slices 11 to 13 minutes.

TO MICROWAVE: Cover and microwave parsnips (¼-inch slices) and ¼ cup water in 1½-quart microwavable casserole on high (100%) 4 minutes; stir. Cover and microwave until tender, 4 to 6 minutes longer. Let stand covered 1 minute; drain.

GLAZED PARSNIPS

---

2   **pounds fresh parsnips**
2   **tablespoons margarine or butter**
1   **tablespoon packed brown sugar**
¼   **cup snipped parsley**

Prepare and cook parsnips cut into ¼-inch slices as directed above except—boil until tender, about 10 minutes. Heat margarine over medium heat until melted; stir in brown sugar. Mix parsnips and brown sugar mixture until parsnips are coated; stir in parsley. **6 servings** (about ½ cup each); 115 calories per serving.

■ **To Microwave:** Place parsnips, ¼ cup water and ⅛ teaspoon salt in 1½-quart microwavable casserole. Cover tightly and microwave on high (100%) 3 minutes; stir. Cover tightly and microwave until tender, 3 to 5 minutes longer. Let stand covered 1 minute; drain. Place margarine in 1-cup microwavable measure. Microwave uncovered on high (100%) until melted, about 15 seconds; stir in brown sugar. Continue as directed on page 651.

PARSNIP CAKES

1¼ pounds fresh parsnips (about 5 medium)
2 tablespoons all-purpose flour
½ teaspoon salt
   Dash of pepper
2 tablespoons margarine or butter, softened
1 tablespoon chopped onion
1 egg, beaten
   Dry bread crumbs or cracker crumbs
¼ cup shortening

Prepare and cook whole parsnips as directed on page 651; mash parsnips. Mix parsnips, flour, salt, pepper, margarine, onion and egg. Shape parsnip mixture into 8 patties; coat with bread crumbs. Heat shortening in 10-inch skillet over low heat until melted. Cook parsnip patties in shortening over medium heat, turning once, until golden brown, about 5 minutes.   **4 servings; 330 calories per serving.**

PEAS—GREEN

Amount for 4 servings: 3 pounds.

When shopping: Look for bright green pods, well filled and tender.

TO PREPARE: Wash and shell peas just before cooking.

TO COOK: Heat 1 inch salted water (½ teaspoon salt to 1 cup water) to boiling. Add peas. Heat to boiling; reduce heat. Boil uncovered 5 minutes. Cover and boil until tender, 3 to 7 minutes longer. If desired, add ½ teaspoon sugar and a few pea pods or lettuce leaf to boiling water for added flavor; drain.

TO STEAM: Place steamer basket in ½ inch water (water should not touch bottom of basket). Place peas in basket. Cover tightly and heat to boiling; reduce heat. Steam until tender, 10 to 12 minutes.

TO MICROWAVE: Cover and microwave peas and ¼ cup water in 1½-quart microwavable casserole on high (100%) 5 minutes; stir. Cover and microwave until tender, 5 to 6 minutes longer. Let stand covered 1 minute; drain.

PEAS AND ONIONS

1½	pounds fresh green peas*
1	slice (¼ inch thick) medium onion, separated into rings
½	teaspoon salt
½	teaspoon dried thyme leaves
2	tablespoons margarine or butter
1	tablespoon grated Parmesan cheese

Prepare peas as directed at left. Heat 1 inch water in 2-quart saucepan to boiling. Add peas, onion rings, salt and thyme. Heat to boiling; reduce heat. Boil uncovered 5 minutes. Cover and boil until tender, 3 to 7 minutes longer; drain. Stir in margarine; sprinkle with cheese. **6 servings; 130 calories per serving.**

■ **To Microwave:** Place 2 tablespoons water, ½ teaspoon salt, the peas, onion rings and thyme in 1-quart microwavable casserole. Cover tightly and microwave on high (100%) 2 minutes; stir. Cover tightly and microwave until peas are tender, 1 to 2 minutes longer; drain. Stir in margarine; sprinkle with cheese.

SESAME PEAS

1	package (10 ounces) frozen green peas
¼	cup margarine or butter
1	tablespoon sesame seed
1	teaspoon sugar
¼	teaspoon salt

Cook peas as directed on package; drain. Cook remaining ingredients over medium heat, stirring constantly, until golden brown; pour over peas. **4 servings; 170 calories per serving.**

*2 cups frozen green peas can be substituted for the 1½ pounds peas.

CURRIED PEAS

3	pounds fresh green peas*
2	tablespoons chopped onion
2	tablespoons margarine or butter
2	tablespoons all-purpose flour
½	teaspoon curry powder
¼	teaspoon salt
1½	cups milk

Prepare and cook peas as directed on page 652. Cook and stir onion in margarine in 1½-quart saucepan until tender; remove from heat. Stir in flour, curry powder and salt. Cook over low heat, stirring constantly, until mixture is bubbly; remove from heat. Stir in milk. Heat to boiling, stirring constantly. Boil and stir 1 minute. Gently stir in peas; heat through.   **4 servings; 175 calories per serving.**

PARMESAN PEAS

2	packages (10 ounces each) frozen green peas
1	tablespoon grated Parmesan cheese
⅛	teaspoon grated lemon peel
1	tablespoon lemon juice
½	teaspoon salt
⅛	teaspoon dried tarragon leaves

Cook peas as directed on package; drain. Toss with remaining ingredients. Serve with additional grated Parmesan cheese if desired.   **6 servings** (about ½ cup each); **70 calories per serving.**

PEPPERS—GREEN BELL

Amount for 4 servings: 4 green peppers.
   When shopping: Look for well-shaped, shiny, medium to dark green peppers with firm sides.

*1 package (10 ounces) frozen green peas, cooked and drained, or 1 can (17 ounces) green peas, drained, can be substituted for the 3 pounds peas.

TO PREPARE: Wash green peppers; remove stems, seeds and membranes. Leave whole to stuff and bake; cut into thin slices or rings to fry.

TO BAKE: Parboil green peppers until crisp-tender, 3 to 5 minutes; stuff and bake.

TO FRY: Fry green pepper slices or rings in small amount of margarine or butter until crisp-tender and light brown, 3 to 5 minutes.

TO STEAM: Place steam basket in ½ inch water (water should not touch bottom of basket). Place green peppers (½-inch strips) in basket. Cover tightly and heat to boiling; reduce heat. Steam until tender, 8 to 10 minutes.

SAUTEED PEPPERS

2   green peppers
2   red peppers
2   slices bacon, cut up
2   tablespoons margarine or butter
1   small onion, chopped (about ¼ cup)
2   tomatoes, chopped
1   teaspoon salt
1   teaspoon cumin seed
1   teaspoon dried oregano leaves
¼   teaspoon pepper
½   cup dairy sour cream
      Snipped parsley or cilantro

Prepare green and red peppers as directed above, cutting into ¼-inch strips. Cook and stir bacon in margarine in 10-inch skillet until crisp; remove bacon with slotted spoon. Cook and stir peppers and onion in bacon fat mixture over medium-high heat 2 minutes.

Add bacon and remaining ingredients except sour cream and parsley. Heat to boiling; reduce heat. Simmer uncovered 5 minutes; remove from heat. Stir in sour cream; sprinkle with parsley.   **6 servings; 165 calories per serving.**

PEPPERS AND CAULIFLOWER

4	medium green peppers
½	medium head cauliflower (about 1 pound)
2	tablespoons margarine or butter
2	tablespoons all-purpose flour
1	teaspoon dry mustard
¼	teaspoon salt
	Dash of pepper
1	cup milk
1	cup shredded mozzarella cheese (4 ounces)
¼	teaspoon red pepper sauce
	Paprika

Prepare green peppers as directed on pages 654 and 655 except—cut lengthwise into halves. Prepare cauliflower as directed on page 634, separating into flowerets. Heat 1 inch salted water (½ teaspoon salt to 1 cup water) to boiling. Add peppers and cauliflower. Cover and heat to boiling; reduce heat. Boil until crisp-tender, about 3 minutes; drain. Place peppers, cut sides up, in ungreased rectangular baking dish, 11 × 7 × 1½ inches. Place culiflowerets in pepper shells.

Heat margarine in 1½-quart saucepan over low heat until melted. Stir in flour, mustard, salt and pepper. Cook over low heat, stirring constantly, until mixture is smooth and bubbly; remove from heat. Stir in milk. Heat to boiling, stirring constantly. Boil and stir 1 minute. Stir in cheese and red pepper sauce. Cook over low heat, stirring constantly, until cheese is melted.

Spoon about 2 tablespoons sauce over each pepper; sprinkle with paprika. Bake uncovered in 375° oven until hot, 10 to 15 minutes.   **8 servings;** 80 calories per serving.

POTATOES—SMALL NEW

Amount for 4 servings: 1½ pounds (10 to 12).

When shopping: Look for nicely shaped, smooth, firm potatoes with unblemished skins, free from discoloration.

TO PREPARE: Wash potatoes lightly and leave whole. If desired, pare a narrow strip around centers.

TO COOK: Heat 1 inch salted water (1 teaspoon salt to 1 cup water) to boiling. Add potatoes. Cover and heat to boiling; reduce heat. Boil until tender, 20 to 25 minutes; drain.

TO STEAM: Place steamer basket in ½ inch water (water should not touch bottom of basket). Place potatoes in basket. Cover tightly and heat to boiling; reduce heat. Steam until tender, 18 to 22 minutes.

TO MICROWAVE: Prick potatoes of similar size with fork to allow steam to escape. Arrange potatoes about 1 inch apart in circle in microwave oven. Microwave uncovered on high (100%) until tender, 10 to 12 minutes. Let stand uncovered 1 minute.

LEMON-CHIVE POTATOES

1½	**pounds new potatoes (10 to 12 small)**
2	**tablespoons margarine or butter**
½	**teaspoon grated lemon peel**
1	**tablespoon lemon juice**
2	**teaspoons snipped chives**
½	**teaspoon salt**
⅛	**teaspoon pepper**
	Dash of ground nutmeg

Prepare and cook new potatoes as directed at left and above; keep warm. Heat remaining ingredients just to boiling. Turn hot potatoes into serving dish; pour lemon butter over potatoes.   **4 servings; 145 calories per serving.**

POTATOES—WHITE

Amount for 4 servings: 1½ pounds (about 4 medium).
   When shopping: Look for well-shaped, smooth, firm potatoes with unblemished skins, free from discoloration.

TO PREPARE:
For boiling—wash potatoes. Leave skins on whenever possible or pare thinly and remove eyes. Leave whole or cut into large pieces. *For baking*—scrub potatoes and, if desired, rub with shortening for softer skins. Prick with fork to allow steam to escape.

TO BOIL: Heat 1 inch salted water (½ teaspoon salt to 1 cup water) to boiling. Add potatoes. Cover and heat to boiling; reduce heat. Boil until tender, whole 30 to 35 minutes, pieces 20 to 25 minutes; drain.

TO BAKE: Bake until tender, in 375° oven 1 to 1¼ hours, in 350° oven 1¼ to 1½ hours, in 325° oven about 1½ hours.

TO STEAM: Place steamer basket in ½ inch water (water should not touch bottom of basket). Place whole potatoes in basket. Cover tightly and heat to boiling; reduce heat. Steam until tender, 30 to 35 minutes.

TO MICROWAVE: Prick potatoes of similar size with fork to allow steam to escape. Arrange potatoes about 1 inch apart in circle in microwave oven. Microwave uncovered on high (100%) until tender, 11 to 13 minutes. Let stand uncovered 1 minute.

MASHED POTATOES

2   **pounds potatoes (about 6 medium)**
⅓   **to ½ cup milk**
¼   **cup margarine or butter, softened**
½   **teaspoon salt**
     Dash of pepper

Prepare and boil pared potatoes as directed on page 657 and above. Shake pan gently over low heat to dry potatoes.

Mash potatoes until no lumps remain. Beat in milk in small amounts. (Amount of milk needed to make potatoes smooth and fluffy depends on kind of potatoes.) Add margarine, salt and pepper; beat vigorously until potatoes are light and fluffy. Dot with margarine or sprinkle with paprika, snipped parsley, watercress or chives if desired. **5 servings; 190 calories** per serving.

Duchess Potatoes: Beat 2 eggs; add to Mashed Potatoes and beat until blended. Drop mixture by spoonfuls in mounds onto ungreased cookie sheet, or form rosettes, using decorators' tube with tip. Brush mounds or rosettes with melted margarine or butter. Bake uncovered in 425° oven until potatoes are light brown, about 15 minutes. **About 10 mounds or rosettes.**

POTATO PLANKS

1   **pound potatoes (about 3 medium)**
     Vegetable oil
1   **teaspoon salt**
½   **teaspoon sugar**
½   **teaspoon paprika**
¼   **teaspoon dry mustard**
⅛   **teaspoon garlic powder**

Prepare potatoes as directed on page 657 for boiling (do not pare); cut lengthwise into eighths. Set oven control to broil and/or 550°. Place potatoes, cut sides down, in ungreased jelly roll pan, 15½ × 10½ × 1 inch; brush with oil. Mix remaining ingredients; sprinkle potatoes with half of the mixture. Broil potatoes with tops about 3 inches from heat until potatoes begin to bubble slightly, about 10 minutes. Turn; brush with oil and sprinkle with remaining salt mixture. Broil until golden brown and tender, about 5 minutes longer. Serve with dairy sour cream if desired.   **6 servings** (4 wedges each); 85 calories per serving.

FRENCH-FRIED POTATOES

Prepare 1½ pounds potatoes (about 4 medium) as directed on page 657 for boiling; cut into lengthwise strips, ¼ to ⅜ inch wide.

Fill deep fryer or Dutch oven ½ full with vegetable oil or shortening; heat to 375°. Fill basket ¼ full with potatoes. Slowly lower into hot oil. (If oil bubbles excessively, raise and lower basket several times.) Use long-handled fork to keep potatoes separated. Fry until potatoes are golden, 5 to 7 minutes; drain. Repeat; sprinkle with salt.   **4 servings; 215 calories per serving.

RAW FRIES

2   pounds potatoes (about 6 medium)
2   tablespoons shortening or vegetable oil
1   large onion, thinly sliced, if desired
1½   teaspoons salt
     Pepper
2   tablespoons margarine or butter

Prepare potatoes as directed on pages 657 and 658 for boiling; cut into enough thin slices to measure about 4 cups.

Heat shortening in 10-inch skillet until melted. Layer ⅓ each of the potato and onion slices in skillet; sprinkle with ½ teaspoon salt and dash of pepper. Repeat 2 times. Dot top layer with margarine. Cover and cook over medium heat 20 minutes. Uncover and cook, turning once, until potatoes are brown.   **4 servings; 305 calories per serving.**

POTATOES WITH TOPPERS

For each serving, prepare and bake 1 baking potato as directed on pages 657 and 658. To serve, cut crisscross gashes in top; squeeze gently until some potato pops up through opening. Top with 2 tablespoons dairy sour cream and ½ green onion (with top), finely chopped.   **1 serving; 255 calories per serving.**

Potatoes with Cheese Toppers: Substitute hot cooked chopped broccoli and shredded mozzarella cheese or crisply cooked and crumbled bacon and shredded process American cheese for the sour cream and green onion.

TWICE-BAKED POTATOES

Prepare and bake 4 baking potatoes as directed on pages 657 and 658. Cut thin lengthwise slice from each potato; scoop out inside, leaving a thin shell. Mash potatoes until no lumps remain. Beat in ⅓ to ½ cup milk in small amounts. (Amount of milk needed to make potatoes smooth and fluffy depends on kind of potatoes.) Add ¼ cup margarine or butter, softened, ½ teaspoon salt and dash of pepper; beat vigorously until fluffy.

Increase oven temperature to 400°. Place shells on ungreased cookie sheet; fill shells with potato mixture. Sprinkle with shredded cheese if desired. Bake uncovered until filling is golden brown, about 20 minutes.   **4 servings; 310 calories per serving.**

Pepper or Pimiento Potatoes: Stir ½ small green pepper, finely chopped, or ¼ cup drained chopped pimientos into mashed potato mixture.

AU GRATIN POTATOES

2	pounds potatoes (about 6 medium)
1	medium onion, chopped
¼	cup margarine or butter
1	tablespoon all-purpose flour
1	teaspoon salt
¼	teaspoon pepper
2	cups milk
2	cups shredded natural sharp Cheddar cheese (8 ounces)
¼	cup fine dry bread crumbs
	Paprika

Prepare potatoes as directed on pages 657 and 658 for boiling; cut into enough thin slices to measure about 4 cups. Cook and stir onion in margarine in 2-quart saucepan until tender. Stir in flour, salt and pepper. Cook over low heat, stirring constantly, until mixture is bubbly; remove from heat. Stir in milk and 1½ cups of the cheese. Heat to boiling, stirring constantly. Boil and stir 1 minute. Place potatoes in ungreased 1½-quart casserole. Pour cheese sauce on potatoes. Bake uncovered in 325° oven 1 hour 20 minutes or in 375° oven 1 hour.

Mix remaining cheese and the bread crumbs; sprinkle over potatoes. Sprinkle with paprika. Bake uncovered until top is brown and bubbly, 15 to 20 minutes longer.   **6 servings; 420 calories per serving.**

SCALLOPED POTATOES

2	pounds potatoes (about 6 medium)
3	tablespoons margarine or butter
3	tablespoons all-purpose flour
1	teaspoon salt
¼	teaspoon pepper
2½	cups milk
1	small onion, finely chopped (about ¼ cup)
1	tablespoon margarine or butter

Prepare potatoes as directed on pages 657 and 658 for boiling; cut into enough thin slices to measure about 4 cups. Heat 3 tablespoons margarine in saucepan over low heat until melted. Stir in flour, salt and pepper. Cook over low heat, stirring constantly, until mixture is smooth and bubbly; remove from heat. Stir in milk. Heat to boiling, stirring constantly. Boil and stir 1 minute.

Arrange potatoes in greased 2-quart casserole in 3 layers, topping each of the first 2 layers with ½ of the onion and ⅓ of the white sauce. Top with remaining potatoes and sauce. Dot with 1 tablespoon margarine. Cover and bake in 325° oven 40 minutes or in 350° oven 30 minutes. Uncover and bake until potatoes are tender, 60 to 70 minutes longer. Let stand 5 to 10 minutes before serving. **6 servings;** 265 calories per serving.

HASHED BROWNS

1½	pounds potatoes (about 4 medium)
2	tablespoons finely chopped onion
½	teaspoon salt
⅛	teaspoon pepper
2	tablespoons margarine or butter
2	tablespoons vegetable oil or bacon fat

Prepare and boil potatoes as directed on pages 657 and 658; cool slightly. Shred enough to measure 4 cups. Toss potatoes, onion, salt and pepper. Heat margarine and oil in 10-inch skillet until margarine is melted. Pack potato mixture firmly in skillet, leaving a ½-inch space around edge. Cook over low heat until bottom is brown, 10 to 15 minutes.

Cut potato mixture into fourths; turn. Add 1 tablespoon vegetable oil if necessary. Cook until bottom is brown, 12 to 15 minutes longer.   **4 servings; 240 calories per serving.**

NOTE: Potato mixture can be kept in one piece if desired. To turn, invert on plate and slide back into skillet.

SQUASH—SUMMER

Types: White—Cymling, Pattypan and Scalloped; Yellow—Straightneck and Crookneck; Light green—Chayote; Dark green—Zucchini.

Amount for 4 servings: 2 pounds.

When shopping: Look for firm, well-shaped squash and shiny, smooth skins. Should seem heavy for size.

TO PREPARE: Wash squash; remove stem and blossom ends but do not pare. Cut into ½-inch slices or cubes.

TO COOK: Heat 1 inch salted water (½ teaspoon salt to 1 cup water) to boiling. Add squash. Cover and heat to boiling; reduce heat. Boil until tender, slices 12 to 15 minutes, cubes 7 to 8 minutes; drain.

TO STEAM: Place steamer basket in ½ inch water (water should not touch bottom of basket). Place squash (slices or cubes) in basket. Cover tightly and heat to boiling; reduce heat. Steam until tender, 5 to 7 minutes.

TO MICROWAVE: Cover and microwave squash (½-inch slices) and ¼ cup water in 2-quart microwavable casserole on high (100%) 4 minutes; stir. Cover and microwave until tender, 3 to 5 minutes longer (pattypan 5 to 7 minutes). Let stand covered 1 minute; drain.

BROILED ZUCCHINI

Prepare 2 pounds zucchini (about 8 small) as directed above except—cut each zucchini lengthwise into halves. Brush each cut side with margarine or butter, melted; sprinkle with salt and pepper.

Set oven control to broil and/or 550°. Broil with tops 5 to 6 inches from heat until zucchini is tender, 10 to 12 minutes.   **4 servings; 100 calories per serving.**

DILLED ZUCCHINI

1½   pounds zucchini (about 6 small)
1   clove garlic, finely chopped
2   tablespoons olive or vegetable oil
1   small onion, sliced and separated into rings
½   teaspoon salt
     Dash of pepper
½   cup plain yogurt
3   tablespoons snipped fresh dill weed or
        1 teaspoon dried dill weed

Prepare 6 cups sliced zucchini as directed on page 663. Cook and stir zucchini and garlic in oil in 10-inch skillet over medium heat until zucchini is light brown, 5 to 8 minutes. Stir in onion rings; heat just until hot. Sprinkle with salt and pepper; remove from heat. Mix yogurt and dill; stir into zucchini mixture.   **6 servings; 75 calories per serving.**

ZUCCHINI-PEPPER SKILLET

1   pound zucchini (about 4 small)
1   onion, thinly sliced
1   small green pepper, chopped
1   clove garlic, crushed
2   tablespoons vegetable oil
1   teaspoon salt
⅛   teaspoon pepper
2   tomatoes, cut into wedges

Prepare zucchini as directed on page 663 except—cut into ¼-inch slices. Cook and stir zucchini and remaining ingredients except tomatoes in 10-inch skillet until heated through. Cover and cook over medium heat, stirring occasionally, until vegetables are crisp-tender, about 5 minutes.

Add tomatoes. Cover and cook over low heat just until tomatoes are heated through, about 3 minutes. Sprinkle with snipped parsley and grated Parmesan cheese if desired.   **4 servings; 110 calories per serving.**

Yellow Squash-Pepper Skillet: Substitute 1 pound yellow summer squash (about 2 medium) for the zucchini and 1 teaspoon ground ginger for the garlic; omit pepper.

SQUASH-WINTER

Types: Large—Banana, Buttercup, Hubbard; Medium—Acorn (Table Queen or Des Moines), Butternut, Spaghetti.

Amount for 4 servings: 3 pounds.

When shopping: Look for good yellow-orange color; hard, tough rinds; squash that is heavy.

TO PREPARE: Cut squash into serving pieces; remove seeds and fibers. For boiling, pare squash if desired; cut into slices or cubes.

TO BAKE: Place squash in ungreased rectangular baking dish, 13×9×2 inches. Sprinkle cut sides with salt and pepper; dot with margarine or butter. Pour water into dish to ¼-inch depth. Cover and bake until tender; in 400° oven 30 to 40 minutes, in 350° oven about 40 minutes, in 325° oven about 45 minutes.

TO BOIL (FOR LARGE SQUASH): Heat 1 inch salted water (½ teaspoon salt to 1 cup water) to boiling. Add squash. Cover and heat to boiling; reduce heat. Boil until tender, 15 to 20 minutes; drain.

TO STEAM: Place steamer basket in ½ inch water (water should not touch bottom of basket). Place squash (slices or cubes) in basket. Cover tightly and heat to boiling; reduce heat. Steam until tender, slices 12 to 15 minutes, cubes 7 to 10 minutes.

TO MICROWAVE: Acorn Squash—prick whole squash of similar size. Arrange at least 1 inch apart diagonally in microwave oven. Microwave uncovered on high (100%) 6 minutes; turn squash over. Microwave uncovered until tender, 7 to 9 minutes longer; cool slightly. Cut into halves; remove seeds. Hubbard Squash—prepare as directed above except—decrease second microwave time to 6 to 8 minutes.

MAPLE ACORN SQUASH

Cut 2 acorn squash (1 to 1½ pounds each) into halves; remove seeds and fibers. Place squash, cut sides up, in ungreased pan, 13×9×2 inches. Spoon 1 tablespoon maple-flavored syrup and 1 tablespoon cream into each half. Bake uncovered in 350° oven until tender, about 1 hour. **4 servings; 185 calories per serving.**

BAKED SQUASH CASSEROLE

3 pounds Hubbard squash*
1 cup dairy sour cream
2 tablespoons margarine or butter
1 teaspoon salt
¼ teaspoon pepper
1 medium onion, finely chopped

Prepare and boil cubed squash as directed on page 665. Mash squash; stir in remaining ingredients. Turn mixture into ungreased 1-quart casserole. Bake uncovered in 400° oven until hot, 20 to 30 minutes. **6 servings; 180 calories per serving.**

SQUASH WITH SALSA

Prick 1 spaghetti squash (about 3 pounds) with fork; place in ungreased square baking dish, 8 × 8 × 2 inches. Bake uncovered in 400° oven until soft, about 1½ hours.

Cut squash crosswise into halves; remove seeds and fibers. Cut each half crosswise into halves again to make four rings. Fluff squash with fork into strands. Serve with Avocado Salsa (below). **4 servings; 115 calories per serving.**

Avocado Salsa

1 avocado, cut up
2 sprigs parsley
1 small clove garlic, cut into fourths
¼ cup chopped onion
1 tablespoon lime juice
1 tablespoon water
2 teaspoons chopped canned jalapeño pepper
½ teaspoon salt

Place all ingredients in blender container. Cover and blend on high speed, stopping blender frequently to scrape sides, until smooth, about 3 minutes. Heat over low heat until warm.

*2 packages (12 ounces each) frozen cooked squash, thawed, can be substituted for the 3 pounds squash.

SWEET POTATOES—
JERSEY SWEETS, YAMS

Amount for 4 servings: 2 pounds (about 6 medium).

When shopping: Look for smooth, even-colored skins; potatoes that are firm and nicely shaped.

TO PREPARE: Wash sweet potatoes but do not pare.

TO COOK: Heat enough salted water to cover sweet potatoes (½ teaspoon salt to 1 cup water) to boiling. Add potatoes. Cover and heat to boiling; reduce heat. Boil until tender, 30 to 35 minutes; drain. Slip off skins. Leave potatoes whole, slice or mash.

TO STEAM: Place steamer basket in ½ inch water (water should not touch bottom of basket). Place sweet potatoes in basket. Cover tightly and heat to boiling; reduce heat. Steam until tender, 25 to 30 minutes. Slip off skins. Leave potatoes whole, slice or mash.

TO MICROWAVE: Prick 4 medium sweet potatoes of similar size (about 1½ pounds) to allow steam to escape. Arrange potatoes about 1 inch apart in circle in microwave oven. Microwave uncovered on high (100%) until tender, 8 to 9 minutes. Let stand uncovered 1 minute. Slip off skins. Leave potatoes whole, slice or mash.

CANDIED SWEET POTATOES

2	**pounds sweet potatoes or yams (about 6 medium)***
½	**cup packed brown sugar**
3	**tablespoons margarine or butter**
3	**tablespoons water**
½	**teaspoon salt**

Prepare and cook sweet potatoes as directed above; cut crosswise into ½-inch slices. Mix remaining ingredients in 10-inch skillet. Cook over medium heat, stirring constantly, until smooth and bubbly. Add sweet potato slices; stir gently until glazed and heated through.   **4 servings; 275 calories per serving.**

*1 can (18 ounces) vacuum-packed sweet potatoes, cut into ½-inch slices, can be substituted for the 2 pounds sweet potatoes.

Orange Sweet Potatoes: Substitute 3 tablespoons orange juice for the water. Mix in 1 tablespoon grated orange peel.

Pineapple Sweet Potatoes: Omit water and mix in 1 can (8¼ ounces) crushed pineapple (with syrup).

Sherry Sweet Potatoes: Substitute 3 tablespoons sherry or other white wine for the water.

Spicy Sweet Potatoes: Stir ½ teaspoon ground cinnamon or ¼ teaspoon ground allspice, cloves, mace or nutmeg into sugar mixture in skillet.

SWEET POTATO SLICES

4   medium sweet potatoes (about 1½ pounds), each cut
          lengthwise into ¼-inch slices
     Coating Mix (below)
¼   cup milk

Prepare sweet potatoes as directed on page 667. Prepare Coating Mix. Dip potatoes into milk, then shake in Coating Mix. Place in single layer on rack in shallow roasting pan. Bake uncovered in 425° oven until tender, 30 to 35 minutes. Serve with cranberry sauce if desired.   **4 servings; 260 calories per serving.**

Coating Mix

2   tablespoons yellow cornmeal
2   tablespoons whole wheat flour
1   teaspoon salt
1   teaspoon ground sage
½   teaspoon onion powder
½   teaspoon sugar
½   teaspoon paprika

Shake all ingredients in plastic bag.

SWEET POTATO MALLOW

1	pound sweet potatoes or yams (about 3 medium)*
½	cup dairy sour cream
½	teaspoon salt
¼	teaspoon ground mace
1	egg yolk
¾	cup miniature marshmallows

Prepare and cook sweet potatoes as directed on page 667. Beat sweet potatoes, sour cream, salt, mace and egg yolk on medium speed until smooth. Pour into buttered 1-quart casserole; top with marshmallows. Bake uncovered in 350° oven until marshmallows are puffed and golden brown, about 30 minutes. **4 servings; 245 calories per serving.**

TWICE-BAKED YAMS

2	pounds yams or sweet potatoes (about 6 medium)
	Vegetable oil
¼	cup dairy sour cream
¼	cup milk
2	tablespoons packed brown sugar
2	tablespoons margarine or butter
⅛	teaspoon salt
2	tablespoons coarsely chopped pecans

Prepare yams as directed on page 667. Rub with oil; prick with fork to allow steam to escape. Bake in 375° oven until tender, 35 to 45 minutes. Cut thin lengthwise slice from each yam; scoop out inside, leaving a thin shell. Mash yams until no lumps remain. Beat in sour cream and milk. Beat in brown sugar, margarine and salt until light and fluffy; stir in pecans.

Increase oven temperature to 400°. Place shells in ungreased rectangular baking dish, 13 × 9 × 2 inches; fill shells with yam mixture. Top each with pecan half if desired. Bake uncovered until filling is golden, about 20 minutes. **6 servings; 310 calories per serving.**

*1 can (18 ounces) vacuum-packed sweet potatoes can be substituted for the 1 pound sweet potatoes.

Do-ahead Tip: Before baking filled shells, cover and refrigerate up to 24 hours. About 30 minutes before serving, heat Twice-baked Yams uncovered in 400° oven until filling is golden, about 25 minutes.

TOMATOES

Amount for 4 servings: 2 pounds (about 6 medium).

When shopping: Look for ripe well-shaped tomatoes; fully ripe tomatoes should be slightly soft and have a rich red color.

TO PREPARE: Wash tomatoes; cut into fourths or ¾-inch slices. Peel tomatoes before cutting if desired. To remove skin easily, dip tomato into boiling water 30 seconds, then into cold water. Or scrape surface of tomato with blade of knife to loosen; peel.

TO COOK: Cover and cook tomatoes *without water* over low heat, stirring occasionally, until tender, 8 to 10 minutes.

TO MICROWAVE: Cover and microwave tomatoes (8 wedges or ½-inch slices) in 2-quart microwavable casserole on high (100%), wedges 4 minutes, slices 3 minutes. Stir and break up wedges with fork or rotate casserole ¼ turn for slices. Cover and microwave until tender, wedges 3 to 4 minutes longer, slices 2 to 3 minutes longer. Let stand covered 1 minute.

STEWED TOMATOES

　3　ripe large tomatoes (about 1½ pounds)*
　⅓　cup finely chopped onion
　2　tablespoons chopped green pepper
　1　tablespoon sugar
　½　teaspoon salt
　⅛　teaspoon pepper
　1　cup soft bread cubes

*1 can (16 ounces) peeled tomatoes can be substituted for the 3 large tomatoes.

Prepare and peel tomatoes as directed at left except—cut into small pieces. Mix tomatoes, onion, green pepper, sugar, salt and pepper. Cover and heat to boiling; reduce heat. Simmer until green pepper is tender, 8 to 10 minutes. Stir in the bread cubes.   **4 servings;** 75 calories per serving.

PANFRIED TOMATOES

4	firm ripe or green medium tomatoes (about 1½ pounds)
½	cup all-purpose flour
1	teaspoon salt
¼	teaspoon pepper
⅓	cup margarine or butter

Prepare tomato slices as directed at left. Mix flour, salt and pepper. Dip tomato slices into flour mixture. Heat margarine in 10-inch skillet until melted. Add tomato slices; cook, turning once, until golden brown.   **3 servings;** 290 calories per serving.

SKILLET CHERRY TOMATOES

2	pounds cherry tomatoes (about 48)
3	green onions (with tops), sliced (about ½ cup)
1	clove garlic, finely chopped
2	tablespoons margarine or butter
½	teaspoon salt
½	teaspoon dried dill weed

Cook and stir all ingredients in skillet until tomatoes are hot, about 5 minutes.   **6 servings;** 75 calories per serving.

■ **To Microwave:** Place all ingredients in 2-quart microwavable casserole. Cover tightly and microwave on high (100%) 2 minutes; stir. Cover tightly and microwave until tomatoes are hot, 1 to 2 minutes longer.

TOMATOES AND ARTICHOKES

½ cup coarsely chopped walnuts
2 tablespoons grated Parmesan cheese
½ teaspoon salt
⅛ teaspoon pepper
2 tablespoons olive oil
1 can (14 ounces) artichoke hearts,
    drained and cut into quarters
1 pint cherry tomatoes
¼ cup snipped parsley

Cook and stir walnuts, cheese, salt and pepper in oil in 10-inch skillet over medium heat until nuts are coated and golden brown, about 5 minutes. Add artichoke hearts and tomatoes. Cook, stirring constantly, just until vegetables are hot, about 3 minutes. Stir in parsley. **6 servings** (about ⅔ cup each); 175 calories per serving.

BAKED STUFFED TOMATOES

6 medium tomatoes (about 2 pounds)
½ small green pepper, finely chopped (about ¼ cup)
¼ cup grated Parmesan cheese
⅓ cup croutons
1 teaspoon salt

Remove stem ends from tomatoes; cut thin slice from bottom of each tomato to prevent tipping. Remove pulp from each tomato, leaving a ½-inch wall; chop enough pulp to measure ⅓ cup.

Mix tomato pulp, green pepper, cheese, croutons and salt. Fill the tomatoes with tomato-cheese mixture. Place filled tomatoes in ungreased rectangular baking dish, 12 × 7½ × 2 inches. Bake uncovered in 350° oven until tomatoes are heated through, about 20 minutes. Garnish tops with parsley sprigs or crisply cooked and crumbled bacon if desired. **6 servings;** 55 calories per serving.

BAKED PLUM TOMATOES

1½	pounds fresh Italian plum tomatoes (about 12)
1	medium onion
1	clove garlic, crushed
1	tablespoon vegetable or olive oil
1	tablespoon snipped fresh basil or
	1 teaspoon dried basil leaves
½	teaspoon salt
⅛	teaspoon freshly ground pepper
½	cup shredded provolone cheese (2 ounces)
¼	cup dry bread crumbs
1	tablespoon margarine or butter, melted
½	teaspoon paprika
¼	teaspoon garlic salt

Prepare tomatoes as directed on page 670 except—cut lengthwise into halves. Cut onion into ¼-inch slices; separate into rings. Cook and stir onion rings and garlic in oil until onion is tender, about 3 minutes. Stir in basil, salt and pepper. Place half of the tomatoes in ungreased 1½-quart casserole; top with onion. Sprinkle with cheese; top with remaining tomatoes. Mix remaining ingredients; sprinkle over top.

Bake uncovered in 375° oven until crumb mixture is golden brown and tomatoes are hot, 20 to 25 minutes. **6 servings; 125 calories per serving.**

TURNIPS, RUTABAGAS AND KOHLRABI

Amount for 4 servings: Turnips—2 pounds (about 6 medium); Rutabagas—1 large or 2 medium; Kohlrabi—4 to 6 medium.

When shopping: Look for turnips that are smooth, round and firm, with fresh tops; look for rutabagas that are heavy, well shaped (round or elongated) and smooth; look for kohlrabi that are young and small (not over 3 inches in diameter).

TO PREPARE:

Turnips—if necessary, cut off tops. Wash turnips and pare thinly; leave whole or cut into cubes. *Rutabagas*—wash ruta-

bagas and pare thinly. Cut into ½-inch cubes or 2-inch pieces.
Kohlrabi—trim off root ends and vinelike stems. Wash and
pare. Cube or cut into ¼-inch slices.

TO COOK: Heat 1 inch salted water (½ teaspoon salt to 1
cup water) to boiling. Add turnips, rutabagas or kohlrabi.
Cover and heat to boiling; reduce heat. Boil until tender—
turnips: whole 25 to 30 minutes, cubes 15 to 20 minutes;
rutabagas: cubes 20 to 25 minutes, pieces 30 to 40 minutes;
kohlrabi: 25 minutes. Drain.

TO STEAM: Place steamer basket in ½ inch water (water
should not touch bottom of basket). Place rutabaga cubes in
basket. Cover tightly and heat to boiling; reduce heat. Steam
until tender, 25 to 28 minutes.

TO MICROWAVE:
Turnips—cover and microwave turnips (½-inch pieces) and
¼ cup water in 3-quart microwavable casserole on high (100%),
stirring every 5 minutes, until tender, 12 to 14 minutes. Let
stand covered 1 minute; drain. *Rutabagas*—cover and microwave rutabagas (½-inch cubes) and ¼ cup water in 3-quart
microwavable casserole on high (100%), stirring every 6 minutes, until tender, 17 to 18 minutes. Let stand covered 1
minute; drain. *Kohlrabi*—cover and microwave kohlrabi (¼-
inch slices) and ¼ cup water in 1½-quart microwavable casserole on high (100%) 3 minutes; stir. Cover and microwave
until tender, 3 to 5 minutes longer. Let stand covered 1
minute; drain.

TURNIPS WITH CHEESE

1 **pound turnips (about 3 medium), cut into 2 × ½ × ½-
   inch strips**
2 **medium stalks celery, thinly sliced (about 1 cup)**
1 **medium onion, sliced**
   Dash of pepper
½ **cup shredded Cheddar cheese (2 ounces)**

Heat 1 inch salted water (½ teaspoon salt to 1 cup water) to
boiling. Add turnips, celery, onion and pepper. Cover and
heat to boiling; reduce heat. Simmer until turnips are tender,
about 20 minutes; drain. Toss vegetables with cheese. **6
servings** (about ½ cup each); 65 calories per serving.

GLAZED RUTABAGAS

2   medium rutabagas (about 2 pounds)
¼   cup margarine or butter
2   tablespoons packed brown sugar
1   tablespoon water
1   teaspoon salt

Prepare rutabagas, cut into ½-inch cubes, as directed on pages 673 and 674. Heat margarine in 10-inch skillet until melted. Add rutabagas. Cook uncovered over medium heat, stirring frequently, until light brown on all sides, about 10 minutes. Sprinkle with brown sugar, water and salt. Cover and simmer over low heat, stirring occasionally, until tender, about 20 minutes.   **6 servings; 130 calories per serving.**

RUTABAGA-POTATO WHIP

1   pound potatoes (about 3 medium)
1   large rutabaga (about 2 pounds)
1   teaspoon sugar
3   tablespoons margarine or butter
1   teaspoon salt
⅛   teaspoon pepper

Prepare and cook cut-up potatoes as directed on pages 657 and 658. Prepare and cook-cubed rutabaga as directed on pages 673 and 674 except—add 1 teaspoon sugar to water.

Mash potatoes and rutabaga together until no lumps remain. Beat in margarine, salt and pepper until mixture is smooth and fluffy. (Beat in enough hot milk to make mixture smooth and fluffy if necessary.)   **6 servings; 115 calories per serving.**

MUSTARD KOHLRABI

4   to 6 medium kohlrabi
2   tablespoons margarine or butter
1   tablespoon prepared mustard
½   teaspoon salt

Prepare and cook kohlrabi as directed on pages 673 and 674; cut into ¼-inch slices. Heat margarine in 8-inch skillet until melted. Stir in mustard and salt. Add kohlrabi and toss. Cook, turning slices, until golden brown. **4 servings; 80 calories per serving.**

SPECIAL HELPS

NUTRITION CHARTS

COOKING KNOW-HOW

TERMS YOU SHOULD KNOW

FOR PREPARING INGREDIENTS

Blanch: Plunge food into boiling water for a brief time to preserve color, texture and nutritional value or to remove skin from fruit or nuts.

Chop: Cut food into irregular-size pieces.

Cool: Allow hot food or liquid to come to room temperature.

Crush: Press with side of knife, mallet or rolling pin to break into small pieces.

Cube: Cut into ½-inch or wider strips; cut across into cubes.

Cut up: Cut into small pieces with kitchen scissors.

Dash: Less than ⅛ teaspoon of an ingredient.

Dice: Cut into ½-inch or narrower strips; cut across into cubes.

Grate: Cut into tiny particles by rubbing food across the small rough holes of a grater.

Julienne: Stack thin slices; then cut into matchlike sticks.

Lukewarm: A temperature of approximately 95°.

Marinate: Let food stand in a savory, usually acidic, liquid for several hours to add flavor or to tenderize.

Pare: Cut off outer covering with knife or vegetable parer.

Peel: Strip off outer covering with fingers.

Refrigerate: Place food in refrigerator to chill or store.

Shred: Cut into long thin pieces by rubbing food across the large holes of a shredder or using a knife.

Slice: Cut food into same-size flat pieces.

Snip: Cut into very small pieces with kitchen scissors.

Soften: Let cold margarine or butter stand at room temperature until soft.

Tear: Break into pieces, using fingers.

Toast: Brown food in oven or toaster.

FOR COMBINING INGREDIENTS

Beat: Make mixture smooth by a vigorous over-and-over motion with a spoon, hand beater, wire whisk or electric mixer.

Blend: Thoroughly combine all ingredients until very smooth and uniform.

Cut in: Distribute solid fat in dry ingredients by cutting with pastry blender with a rolling motion or cutting with two knives until particles are desired size.

Fold: Combine ingredients lightly using two motions: first, cut vertically through mixture with a rubber spatula; next, slide spatula across bottom of bowl and up the side, turning mixture over. Continue down-across-up-over motion while rotating bowl ¼ turn with each series of strokes.

Mix: Combine in any way that distributes all ingredients evenly.

Stir: Combine ingredients with a circular or figure eight motion until of uniform consistency.

Toss: Tumble ingredients lightly with a lifting motion.

FOR COOKING

Bake: Cook in oven.

Baste: Spoon a liquid over food during cooking to keep it moist.

Boil: Heat until bubbles rise continuously and break on the surface of liquid.

Broil: Cook by direct heat.

Brown: Cook until surface of food changes color, usually in a small amount of fat over medium heat.

Cook and stir: Cook rapidly in small amount of fat, stirring occasionally. We use this term rather than *sauté*.

Poach: Cook in hot liquid just below the boiling point.

Roast: Cook meat uncovered on rack in shallow pan in oven without adding liquid.

Rolling boil: Heat until bubbles form rapidly and break on the surface of liquid.

Scald: Heat liquid to just below the boiling point. Tiny bubbles form at the edge.

Simmer: Cook in liquid just below the boiling point. Bubbles form slowly and collapse below the surface.

Skim: Remove fat or foam from surface of liquid with a spoon.

Stir-fry: A Chinese method of cooking uniform pieces of food in small amount of hot oil over high heat, stirring constantly.

FOOD PREPARATION BASICS

Bread Crumbs (dry): Place bread in low oven until dry. Crush with rolling pin or mallet into very small pieces.

Bread Crumbs (soft): Tear soft bread into small pieces.

Chocolate Curls: Let a block or bar of chocolate stand in warm place for about 15 minutes before making curls. They will be easier to make if the chocolate is slightly warm. Slide a swivel-bladed vegetable parer or thin, sharp knife across the top of the chocolate in long, thin strokes. Sweet milk chocolate will make slightly larger curls than semisweet chocolate. To avoid breaking the curls, lift with a wooden pick in center of circle.

Chocolate—To Melt: Place in small heatproof bowl or in top of double boiler over hot (not boiling) water. Heat until chocolate is melted, stirring occasionally.

Coating Chicken: Place seasonings, crumbs or flour in plastic bag. Add a few pieces of chicken at a time; shake until each piece is evenly coated.

Croutons: Heat oven to 400°. Cut crusts from bread slices. Spread both sides generously with margarine or butter, softened; cut into ½-inch cubes. Bake in ungreased pan, stirring occasionally, until golden brown and crisp, 10 to 15 minutes.

Crumbled Blue Cheese: Freeze cheese until firm. Chop with knife into desired size pieces.

Tinted Coconut: Add a few drops food color to coconut in a jar; shake until evenly tinted.

Toasted Coconut: Heat oven to 350°. Bake in ungreased pan, stirring occasionally, until golden brown, 5 to 7 minutes.

Toasted Nuts: Heat oven to 350°. Bake in ungreased pan, stirring occasionally, until golden brown, about 10 minutes.

Toasted Sesame Seed: Heat oven to 350°. Bake in ungreased pan, stirring occasionally, until golden brown, 8 to 10 min-

MEASURING INGREDIENTS

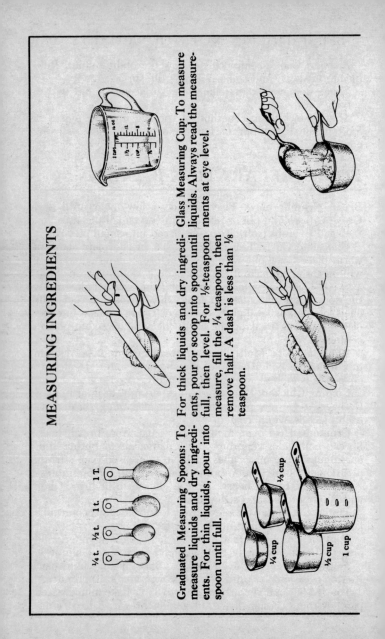

Graduated Measuring Spoons: To measure liquids and dry ingredients. For thin liquids, pour into spoon until full.

For thick liquids and dry ingredients, pour or scoop into spoon until full, then level. For ⅛-teaspoon measure, fill the ¼ teaspoon, then remove half. A dash is less than ⅛ teaspoon.

Glass Measuring Cup: To measure liquids. Always read the measurements at eye level.

Graduated Nested Measuring Cups: To measure dry ingredients and solid fats.

For all-purpose flour and granulated sugar, dip cup into ingredient to fill, then level with straight-edged spatula. Do not sift flour to measure or combine with other ingredients.

For cake flour, buttermilk baking mix and powdered sugar, spoon ingredient lightly into cup, then level. Sift powdered sugar only if lumpy.

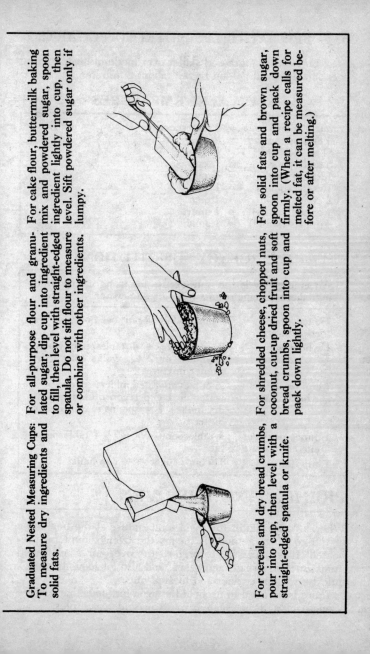

For cereals and dry bread crumbs, pour into cup, then level with a straight-edged spatula or knife.

For shredded cheese, chopped nuts, coconut, cut-up dried fruit and soft bread crumbs, spoon into cup and pack down lightly.

For solid fats and brown sugar, spoon into cup and pack down firmly. (When a recipe calls for melted fat, it can be measured before or after melting.)

utes. Or heat in ungreased skillet over medium heat, stirring occasionally, until golden brown, about 2 minutes.

EQUIVALENT MEASURES

3 teaspoons	=	1 tablespoon
4 tablespoons	=	¼ cup
5⅓ tablespoons	=	⅓ cup
8 tablespoons	=	½ cup
12 tablespoons	=	¾ cup
16 tablespoons	=	1 cup
2 cups	=	1 pint
4 cups (2 pints)	=	1 quart
4 quarts (liquid)	=	1 gallon

EMERGENCY SUBSTITUTIONS

An emergency is the only excuse for using a substitute ingredient—recipe results will vary somewhat.

1½ teaspoons cornstarch	1 tablespoon all-purpose flour
1 whole egg	2 egg yolks + 1 tablespoon water (cookies) or 2 egg yolks (custards, similar mixtures)
1 cup fresh whole milk	½ cup evaporated milk + ½ cup water or 1 cup reconstituted nonfat dry milk + 2 teaspoons margarine or butter
1 ounce unsweetened chocolate	3 tablespoons cocoa + 1 tablespoon fat
1 cup honey	1¼ cups sugar + ¼ cup liquid

PREHEATING THE OVEN

When a recipe states the oven temperature at the beginning of the cooking method, it means the oven should be preheated. It is necessary to preheat the oven for many baked items, such as breads and cakes, and also for foods that cook quickly, such as cookies and toasted nuts.

There is no need to preheat the oven for foods that require a long cooking time, such as roasts or some casseroles.

Remember, it takes only about 10 minutes to preheat the oven. Check your manufacturer's care and use information for preheating your oven and broiler.

HIGH-ALTITUDE COOKING

People who live in a high-altitude area—3500 feet or higher—face some unique cooking problems. Air pressure is lower, liquid evaporates faster and water has a lower boiling point. As certain foods and methods of preparation are affected by the pressure of high altitudes, recipes must be adjusted.

Because the boiling point of water is lower at high altitudes, foods that require boiling take longer to cook; the cooking time must be increased. Meats cooked in the oven need more time. Use a meat thermometer and record the time required as a guide for the future.

If you are new to a high-altitude area, call the Home Service Department of the local utility company or the State Extension Office for help in solving specific problems and for recipe booklets. Recipes are also available from Colorado State University, Fort Collins, Colorado 80521.

FOOD SAFETY

KEEP FOOD HOT OR COLD
The most perishable foods are those containing eggs, milk (creamed foods, cream pies), seafood (seafood salads), meat and poultry. When you shop, pick up your meat and poultry selections last. Take them straight home and refrigerate.

Don't allow hot or cold foods to remain at room temperature for more than 2 hours; bacteria thrive in lukewarm food. These germs seldom change the taste, odor or appearance of food. A standard rule, recommended by the U.S. Department of Agriculture, is to keep hot foods hot (above 140°) and cold foods cold (below 40°).

Once food has been cooked, keep it hot until serving time or refrigerate as soon as possible. If it will not raise the refrigerator temperature above 45°, hot food can be placed immediately in the refrigerator.

KEEP FOOD CLEAN
Germs are a natural part of the environment. Keep utensils, dishes, countertops and hands soap-and-hot-water clean. Don't handle food if you have infected cuts or sores on your hands.

Be careful not to transfer germs from raw meat to cooked meat. Do not, for example, carry raw hamburgers to the grill on a platter, then serve cooked meat on the same (unwashed) platter.

Another hazard to food is a wooden chopping board used for raw meat or poultry as well as other foods. A hard plastic cutting board is less porous and safer for meats. Wash boards with a mixture of 2 teaspoons chlorine bleach and 1 teaspoon vinegar to a gallon of water.

Use disposable paper towels when working with or cleaning up after raw foods.

Keep pets out of the kitchen. Teach children to wash their hands after playing with pets.

FOOD SAFETY TIPS

Eggs: Eggs with clean, uncracked, unbroken shells are safe to use raw in uncooked dishes that will be refrigerated immediately (cold soufflés, mousses, chiffon pies). Serve these foods cold and refrigerate any leftovers immediately. Storage for "do-ahead" recipes should not exceed 48 hours. Foods containing cooked eggs (such as cheesecakes, cream fillings, custards, quiches and potato salads) must be served hot or cold (depending on the recipe), with leftovers refrigerated immediately.

Ground meat: Cook thoroughly—it's handled often in preparation and germs can get mixed into it. Don't eat raw ground meat—it's not safe!

Ham: Know what kind of ham you're buying; some are fully cooked but others need cooking. Check the label. If you have any doubts, cook it.

Luncheon meat, frankfurters: Refrigerate; use within a week. Use a fork or tongs to handle.

Poultry: Cook all poultry products as long as directions require. Refrigerate cooked poultry, stuffing and giblets as soon as possible in separate containers; use within a few days or freeze.

Canned foods: Do not buy or use food from leaking, bulging or dented cans or jars with cracks or loose or bulging lids. If you are in doubt about a can of food, don't taste it! Return it to your grocer and report it to your local health authority.

Milk: Fresh milk products are highly perishable; refrigerate them as soon after purchase as possible. Unopened evaporated milk and nonfat dry milk may be stored in a cool area for several months. Unopened dry whole milk, which contains fat, should be refrigerated; use within a few weeks.

KEEP FOOD SAFE AT BUFFETS

Serve food in small dishes, refilling frequently from stove or refrigerator. Or keep food hot in electric skillet or chafing dish or on hot tray. Don't depend on warming units with candles. Refrigerate salads made with seafood, poultry or meat. Chill both food and dish before serving. Serve cold foods over crushed ice.

PACK SAFE LUNCHES

■ Wash fruits and vegetables before packing.

- Use fully cooked foods (bologna, frankfurters, canned meats and poultry). They keep well.

- Wash vacuum bottles and rinse with boiling water after each use. Be sure hot foods are boiling hot when poured into vacuum bottles.

- Lunch boxes insulate better than lunch bags.

NOTE: For a free copy of the Home and Garden Bulletin, *Safe Food Book*, write to Publications Room 1165–S, USDA, Washington, D.C. 20250.

FREEZER & REFRIGERATOR STORAGE

PREPARING FOODS FOR FREEZING

COOLING FOODS

The less time that food spends at temperatures between 45 and 140°, the better. If you allow foods to remain at these temperatures for more than 3 to 4 hours, they may not be safe to eat, so speed the cooling process. Hot foods can be placed right in the refrigerator provided they don't raise the refrigerator temperature above 45°.

A large quantity of hot food should be cooled in a big bowl (or a sink) filled with cold water and ice that almost reaches the top of the food container. Replace ice as it melts; freeze the food as soon as it is cool.

WRAPPING FOODS

To maintain the high quality of food in the freezer, it is necessary to use good packaging and wrapping materials. Freezer wraps and containers should be airtight, moistureproof and vaporproof. Best materials are heavy-duty aluminum foil, heavy-weight plastic wrap and freezer bags or containers.

When you wrap, press out the air and wrap tightly. Fragile foods are an exception—they may need to be protected in a box. Place the freezer-wrapped food in the box or overwrap the box.

LABELING FOODS

Label packages before you put them in the freezer. For labeling, you will need labels, a grease pencil or a felt-tipped pen (to avoid moisture smudges) and freezer tape. Include this information:

Name of recipe: If you have more than one package from the same recipe, note that on the label.

Last-stage ingredients: Write down and keep your own instructions for reheating or additional ingredients that are needed before serving.

Number of servings: Write down the number of servings the package contains. When you freeze meat, note its weight.

Storage time: Determine when the package should be used and put this "use before" date on the label. (If you leave the package in the freezer beyond the recommended storage time, the food won't spoil—but it may begin to lose some of its moisture, flavor or texture.)

FAST FREEZING

Thawing then refreezing is not recommended, so use meal-size containers and, at any one time, freeze only as much food as you can place against a freezing surface. The faster the food freezes, the better it retains flavor and texture. For fast freezing, food packages should be in direct contact with a freezing surface, at least 1 inch apart so the air can circulate.

DO-AHEAD MAIN DISHES

■ Slightly undercook meats, pasta and vegetables before freezing to prevent overcooking when reheating. When you prepare a double batch—one to eat and one to freeze—set the freezer batch aside a few minutes before it is fully cooked.

■ Season lightly and add more seasonings just before serving. Pepper and some other spices become strong and bitter when frozen.

■ Add crumb and cheese toppings to frozen foods just before reheating.

■ While thawing, sauces and gravies may appear curdled but you can stir them smooth.

■ Some good do-ahead main dishes are cooked poultry casseroles, many cooked meat stews, most vegetables used in casseroles (peas, carrots, celery, onions), meat loaves (baked) and dried beans (cooked just until tender).

DON'T FREEZE THESE
Some foods are not recommended for freezing. Cooked egg whites become tough. Mayonnaise or salad dressing may separate. Salad greens become soggy; raw tomatoes, limp and watery. Raw apples and grapes become mushy. Fried foods may taste warmed over when reheated.

FREEZER TEMPERATURE
The temperature for freezing and storing food is 0° or lower. At a low temperature (0°), foods freeze faster with less breakdown in cellular structure; they are more likely to retain true flavor and firm texture. We recommend that you buy a freezer thermometer. Check the thermometer often to make sure that your freezer actually maintains a temperature of 0° or lower.

GUIDELINES FOR FREEZER STORAGE

Keep freezer temperature at 0° or lower. To retain flavor, moisture and nutrients, wrap food in moisture/vaporproof materials (remove as much air from packages as possible). Foods purchased frozen should be kept frozen in original packages. Thaw frozen meats, poultry, fish and seafood in refrigerator.

Foods	Length of Time	Storage Precautions
Dairy		
Cheese, natural or process	3 to 4 months	Freezing is not recommended for creamed cottage cheese and cream cheese. Freeze other cheeses in small amounts; thaw in refrigerator to prevent crumbling.
Cream, whipping	2 to 3 months	Texture changes, but it can be whipped after thawing.
Ice cream, sherbet	1 month	Cover surface with aluminum foil to prevent ice crystals.
Milk	3 to 4 months	Freeze in original carton.
Eggs		
Fresh	Not recommended	
Whites	1 year	Use promptly after thawing.
Yolks	3 months	Add ⅛ teaspoon salt or ½ teaspoon sugar for each ¼ cup yolk.
Fats, Oils		
Butter, margarine	4 to 6 months	
Meats, Poultry, Fish, Seafood		
Meats, fresh		
Beef		
roasts or steaks	8 to 12 months	

ground or stew meat	2 to 3 months	
Lamb, roasts or steaks	8 to 12 months	
Veal, roasts or steaks	4 to 8 months	
Pork, fresh		
roasts, steaks, chops	4 to 6 months	May lose desirable color and flavor.
Pork, cured and/or smoked	1 to 2 months	Freeze in vacuum wrap. Overwrap for storage longer than 2 weeks.
bacon, frankfurters	1 month	
smoked ham	2 months	
luncheon meats	Not recommended	
Variety meats	1 to 2 months	
Meats, cooked	1 to 3 months	
Poultry		
cooked, no sauce	1 month	Wrap airtight; it dries out quickly.
uncooked		
whole	6 to 8 months	
cut up	4 to 6 months	
giblets	1 to 3 months	
ducks, geese	6 to 8 months	
Fish		
uncooked		
fatty	3 to 4 months	
lean	6 to 8 months	
breaded, cooked	2 to 3 months	
Seafood		
lobster or scallops	1 to 2 months	
shellfish	3 to 4 months	

GUIDELINES FOR REFRIGERATOR STORAGE

The temperature of your refrigerator should be at 40° or slightly lower for safe storage of perishable foods. It is best to store foods in containers with tight-fitting lids or in plastic bags to retain moisture and prevent transfer of odors to other foods. Remove foods from the refrigerator only when you are ready to cook or serve them.

Foods	Length of Time	Storage Precautions
Dairy		
Buttermilk, dairy sour cream, yogurt	2 weeks	Check the freshness date on container before purchase.
Cheese		
cottage	3 to 5 days	Refrigerate tightly covered.
cream	2 weeks	
hard	2 months	Wrap tightly; discard if moldy.
sliced	2 weeks	
spread	1 to 2 weeks	Refrigerate covered after opening.
Cream	3 to 5 days	Refrigerate tightly closed.
Milk (skim, whole and reconstituted dry)	5 days	Refrigerate evaporated and condensed tightly covered after opening.
Eggs		
Fresh	1 week	Can be refrigerated longer, but expect loss of some quality and flavor.
Yolks, white	2 to 4 days	Cover yolks with cold water. Refrigerate yolks and whites covered.

Fats, Oils

Butter	2 weeks	Refrigerate tightly covered.
Margarine	1 month	
Mayonnaise, salad dressings	3 months	Refrigerate after opening.

Meats, Poultry, Fish, Seafood

Meats, fresh		Cover tightly and refrigerate.
chops	2 to 3 days	
ground	1 day	
roasts	2 to 3 days	
steaks	2 to 3 days	
variety meats	1 day	
Meats		
processed		
luncheon meats (unopened)	2 weeks	
luncheon meats (opened)	3 to 5 days	
cured		
bacon	1 week	
frankfurters	1 week	
ham		
canned (unopened)	1 year	
half	5 days	
slices	3 days	
whole	1 week	
Poultry, Fish, Seafood	1 to 2 days	Refrigerate in plastic wrap or waxed paper.

MICROWAVE COOKING

This cool, convenient way of cooking simplifies life. It saves time, doesn't heat the kitchen, cuts dishwashing and oven scouring. It prevents waste (generally you are cooking just what you will eat), and uses 25 to 75% less energy than conventional cooking because only the food—not the oven cavity—is heated.

MICROWAVE COOKING PRINCIPLES

Temperature of food: The colder the food, the longer the cooking time. Testing for this book was done with foods taken from their normal storage areas, whether freezer, refrigerator or cupboard shelf.

Volume of food: As the bulk of food increases, so must the cooking time.

Size of pieces of food: Small pieces of food cook faster than large pieces, so keep pieces uniform in size.

Shape of food: Round or doughnut-shaped foods or foods in round or ring-shaped containers cook most evenly. Odd-shaped foods need more attention during cooking.

Density of food: Porous foods (breads, cakes) cook quickly; dense foods (roasts, potatoes) need longer cooking.

Moisture, sugar, fat in food: Microwaves are attracted to these ingredients. To heat cooked meat, add gravy or sauce for best results.

Standing time: This is indicated in recipes where it is important for completing cooking.

MICROWAVE TECHNIQUES
Commonly used techniques include:

- Covering tightly with a lid or plastic wrap (leaving a corner of plastic turned back) to speed heating.

- Covering foods loosely with waxed paper or microwavable paper towel (to prevent spatters).

- Stirring (from outside to inside).

- Rotating dish (for foods that cannot be stirred).

- Arranging foods in a circle.

- Turning foods over (for even heat).

- Elevating on an inverted dish (to cook bottom center of food).

- Covering uncooked food with a crumb or cracker coating, or adding a glaze (to add crispness and color appeal to food that browns or becomes crusty when cooked conventionally).

MICROWAVE UTENSILS
Use nonmetal utensils: glassware, plasticware, dishwasher-safe plastic containers, ceramic plates and casseroles containing no metal, and china with no metal trim. Avoid metal utensils; they are not suitable for microwaving because *arcing* (causing a flash, as in welding) can occur. Follow your microwave use and care guide in regard to using aluminum foil.

MICROWAVE SAFETY
The microwave is one of the safest appliances in the home. Strict limits on the level of energy emitted have been established by the government for the safety of microwave cooking.

TESTING FOR THIS BOOK
All the microwave recipes in this book were tested using countertop microwaves with 625 to 700 watts. If your microwave has a rating of 400 to 500 watts, cooking time must be lengthened.

NOT RECOMMENDED FOR MICROWAVING

Angel, foam-type cakes: Hot dry air needed.

Crisp, fried foods: Surface cooking needed.

Crusty breads: Reheat only.

Deep-fried foods: Fat may spatter; constant temperature needed.

Dried beans or peas: Reheat only.

Eggs in shells or whole cooked peeled: Eggs can burst during microwaving.

Hash-browned potatoes: Surface cooking only.

Home canning: Surface cooking only (to maintain safe temperature).

Pancakes: Surface cooking, reheating only.

Pasta: Only reheating saves time.

Popcorn: Use corn designed for microwaving or pop in a microwave popper.

Popovers: Reheat only.

Regular rice: Only reheating saves time.

Turkey (15 pounds or over): More attention needed than for conventional cooking.

FREEZING & CANNING

SELECTING PRODUCE

When selecting fruits and vegetables for freezing and canning, it is important to look for produce that appears fresh; avoid any that is wilted or has spots of decay. For successful freezing or canning, use produce at the peak of quality (never overripe) and gather or purchase only as much as you can handle within 2 or 3 hours. Thoroughly wash or peel any fruits or vegetables that have been sprayed with insecticides.

FRUIT AND VEGETABLE YIELDS

Produce	Amount (1 bushel) Pounds	Canned Yield Quarts	Frozen Yield Quarts
Apples	48	16 to 20	16 to 20
applesauce	48	15 to 18	15 to 18
Apricots	22 (1 lug)	7 to 11	12 to 14
Cherries	56	22 to 23*	18 to 22
	22 (1 lug)	9 to 11*	8 to 10
Peaches	48	18 to 24	16 to 24
	22 (1 lug)	8 to 12	8 to 10
Pears	50	20 to 25	18 to 24
	35 (1 box)	14 to 17	12 to 16
Plums	56	24 to 30	22 to 28
	24 (1 lug)	12	10 to 12
Beans			
green or wax	30	12 to 22	15 to 22
Beets			
without tops	52	14 to 22	17 to 22

*Unpitted

FRUIT AND VEGETABLE YIELDS

Produce	Amount (1 bushel) Pounds	Canned Yield Quarts	Frozen Yield Quarts
Carrots			
without tops	50	17 to 20	16 to 20
Corn			
in husks	35	6 to 10	7 to 9
Peas			
green, in pods	30	5 to 10	6 to 8
Squash			
summer	40	10 to 20	16 to 20
Squash			
winter	11	*	4
Tomatoes	53	14 to 22	*

*Not recommended

FOOD SAFETY GUIDE

Keep hot foods hot, cold foods cold! The following indicates temperature zones for control of bacteria.

240°F	Canning temperatures for low-acid vegetables, meat and poultry in steam-pressure canner.
212°F	Canning temperatures for fruits, tomatoes and pickles in water-bath canner. Boiling point of water.
165°F	Cooking temperatures destroy most bacteria. Time required to kill bacteria decreases as temperature is increased.
140°F	Warming temperatures prevent growth but allow survival of some bacteria.
125°F	Some bacterial growth may occur. Many bacteria survive.

DANGER ZONE

60°F	Foods held more than 2 hours in this zone are subject to rapid growth of bacteria and production of toxins by some bacteria.
40°F	Some growth of food poisoning bacteria may occur.
32°F	Cold temperatures permit slow growth of some bacteria that cause spoilage.
0°F	Freezing temperatures stop growth of bacteria, but may allow bacteria to survive. (Do not store food above 10° for more than a few weeks.)

INFORMATION SOURCES

Home Freezing of Fruits and Vegetables (about $2.00) and *Home Canning of Fruits and Vegetables* (about $1.50) are government Home and Garden bulletins with the latest information about home freezing and canning. For specific details about these and other bulletins, write to Superintendent of Documents, Consumer Information Center, Pueblo, Colorado 81009.

FREEZING

BLANCHING VEGETABLES

All vegetables must be blanched before freezing to preserve nutritional value, fresh color and flavor. Blanching is quick, partial cooking that stops the enzyme action that causes ripening and maturing in vegetables. It also stabilizes the vitamin content.

To blanch vegetables in boiling water: Use a blancher with a basket and cover. Or fit a wire basket into a large kettle. For each pound of prepared vegetables, use at least 1 gallon of boiling water in the blancher or kettle. Blanch only 1 pound at a time. Put vegetables in blanching basket and lower into the boiling water. Cover and start counting time immediately (see Timetable). Keep over high heat for the time given in directions for vegetable you are freezing.

To blanch vegetables in steam: Pour 1 inch water in kettle and bring to a rolling boil. Suspend a thin layer of vegetables in wire basket or loose cheesecloth over rapidly boiling water. Cover and start counting time immediately (see Timetable).

Immediately plunge vegetables into a large quantity of cold water (60° or below). Change water frequently or use running cold water or iced water. It will take about twice as long to cool the food as it does to heat it. Remove from water, drain and cool at room temperature. If desired, freeze on cookie sheet to keep vegetables from sticking together.

Pack the cold or frozen vegetables in bags or other containers. Leave ½-inch headspace and seal by twisting and folding back top of bag. Freeze at once. The packaging keeps the food moist and preserves food value, flavor, color and texture.

TIMETABLE FOR BLANCHING VEGETABLES

Asparagus, medium stalks	3 minutes
Beans, green or wax	3 minutes
Beans, lima, medium	3 minutes
Beets, medium	45 to 50 minutes
Broccoli, 1½-inch flowerets*	3 minutes
Brussels sprouts, medium heads	4 minutes
Carrots, whole, small	5 minutes
diced, sliced, strips	2 minutes
Cauliflower, 1-inch pieces*	3 minutes
Corn, sweet, on the cob, medium	9 minutes
whole kernel or cream style	4 minutes
Peas, green	1½ minutes
Peppers, halves or whole	2½ to 3 minutes
slices	2 minutes
Squash, summer, ¼-inch slices	3 minutes
Sweet potatoes	until tender

*Soak ½ hour in brine of ½ cup salt to 1 quart water.

FREEZING FRUIT

PREPARING AND PACKING THE FRUIT

Assemble all the equipment you will need. Make and refrigerate the syrup (page 710); if using an ascorbic acid mixture, do not add it to the syrup until just before using. Choose fully ripened (never overripe) fruits and keep them as cold as possible until you put them in the freezer.

Wash a small quantity of fruit at a time to prevent bruising. Lift fruit out of the water and drain thoroughly. Work quickly.

Fruit for freezing is usually prepared much as fruit for serving. Large pieces freeze better if cut into smaller pieces or crushed. Peel, pit and slice fruit as desired. It is best to prepare enough fruit for only a few containers at one time, especially those fruits that darken rapidly. Two or three quarts is a good amount to freeze at one time.

Most fruits have better texture and flavor if packed in sugar or syrup. Some can be packed without sweetening. See chart on page 704 for type of syrup and amount of sugar. Use Medium Syrup (page 710) for most fruits. Lighter syrups can be used for some mild-flavored fruits. Use ½ to ⅔ cup syrup for each pint of fruit. Fruits packed in syrup are usually best for desserts; those packed in sugar or unsweetened are best for most cooking (pies, fillings, jams).

Using one of the methods described below, pack fruit in freezerproof containers. (See pages 689 and 702 for information about freezer containers.) Place a small piece of crumbled parchment paper or freezer wrap on top and press fruit down into syrup. Leave ½-inch headspace; seal. Freeze at once.

Syrup Pack: Pack fruit in containers; add syrup. Be sure syrup covers fruit so that top pieces will not change in color or flavor. Seal and freeze.

Sugar Pack: Sprinkle cut fruit with sugar; mix gently with a large spoon until juice is drawn out and sugar is dissolved. Pack fruit and juice in containers. Seal and freeze.

Unsweetened Pack: Pack prepared fruit in containers without juice or sugar. Or pack crushed or sliced fruit in its own juice without sweetening. Seal and freeze.

SWEETENING FRUITS FOR FREEZING

Fruit	Syrup Pack: Type of Syrup*	Sugar Pack: Sugar for Each Pint	Unsweetened	Ascorbic Acid
Apples	Medium	¼ cup	omit sugar	yes
Apricots	Medium	¼ cup	**	yes
Berries	Medium/Heavy	⅓ cup	omit sugar	no
Cherries, sweet	Medium	⅓ cup	**	yes
Cranberries	Medium/Heavy	**	omit sugar	no
Peaches	Medium	⅓ cup	cover with cold water	yes
Pineapple	Light	**	omit sugar	no
Plums	Medium	**	omit sugar	yes
Raspberries	Medium	⅓ cup	omit sugar	no
Rhubarb	Medium	**	omit sugar	no
Strawberries	Heavy	⅓ cup	omit sugar	no

*See page 710 for Sugar Syrups. **Other methods preferred.

ABOUT ASCORBIC ACID

Most fruits will darken during freezing. Ascorbic acid (vitamin C) can be used to help preserve flavor as well as color, adding nutritive value at the same time. Buy ascorbic acid compounds intended for use in home food preservation (available at the supermarket) and follow the manufacturer's directions.

For syrup pack, the ascorbic acid mixture is dissolved in a small amount of cold water or in the syrup. For sugar pack, it is dissolved in water, then sprinkled over the fruit just before adding the sugar. For the unsweetened pack, the dissolved mixture is sprinkled over the fruit and mixed well just before packing.

CANNING

CANNING FOODS SAFELY

	Safe Method
Acid Foods: Fruits, red medium tomatoes, pickles	Boiling water bath (212°) or pressure canner at 5 pounds pressure
Low-Acid Foods: Meats, poultry, fish, vegetables (except red medium tomatoes)	Pressure canner only at 10 pounds pressure (240°)

A higher acidity level in foods such as fruits and red medium (not cherry) tomatoes helps stop the growth of dangerous bacteria. These foods are safe if processed in a boiling water bath (212°) or at 5 pounds pressure in a pressure canner. Failure to do this may allow growth of yeasts, molds or bacteria that can cause spoilage.

Foods in the low-acid group above must be processed at a heat of 240°, which can be reached only with steam under 10 pounds pressure in a pressure canner. This very high temperature will destroy dangerous heat-resistant, botulism-producing bacteria.

Processing times for foods vary because the rate of heat transfer is not the same in all vegetables and fruits. Recommended processing times are based on the length of time needed to reach the proper temperature in the slowest-heating part of the container.

TO CAN LOW-ACID FOODS WITHOUT SALT

The amount of salt called for in canning low-acid vegetables, meats, poultry and seafoods is too small to prevent spoilage and is added only for flavor. If you wish, follow the recipes for these foods; just omit the salt.

FOR CANNING SUCCESS

- To avoid spoilage, select only sound, unbruised foods at the peak of ripeness (do not can overripe fruits, especially tomatoes). Process immediately.

- Make small batches and never double a recipe.

- Use only standard jars and lids intended for home preserving and follow the manufacturer's instructions for sealing the jars.

- Do not reuse sealing lids or cracked, chipped jars, or jars not designed for canning.

- Jars used for jam and jelly preserving must be sterilized; jars used in boiling water processing do not need sterilization.

- Use open-kettle (hot-pack) canning only for jellies and jams. Use the boiling water method only for fruits and tomatoes and for pickles preserved in vinegar. Use a pressure canner for other vegetables and for meats, poultry and fish.

- Have the seal and pressure gauge on the pressure canner checked regularly for accuracy.

- Do not overpack jars; allow adequate headspace (see individual recipes).

TIMETABLE FOR PRESSURE CANNING

To acquire a complete list of vegetables, meats and fish that should be pressure canned, see Information Sources (page 701).

Low-Acid Produce	Minutes at 10 Pounds Pressure	
	Pints	Quarts
Beans, green	20	25
Beets	30	35
Carrots	25	30
Corn, whole kernel	55	*
Peas	40	40
Pumpkin	55	90
Squash, summer	25	30

*Corn should be canned in pints because the longer processing time for quarts causes the corn to darken.

PRESSURE CANNER PROCESSING

Prepare jars as directed below and on page 708. Follow the manufacturer's instructions for opening and closing the canner. Follow Timetable for Pressure Canning (above).

Have 2 to 3 inches of hot water in pressure canner. Stand the jars on a rack so they are not touching each other or sides of canner. Fasten lid to canner.

Turn heat on until steam flows from vent in a steady stream (10 minutes or more after steam first appears). At first a mixture of steam and air will be released as a white vapor or cloud. When all air is driven out, the steam from the vent will become nearly invisible. It is then time to put on or close the petcock or pressure regulator. All air must be exhausted from canner to make certain the internal temperature of pressure canner reaches 240°.

Raise pressure rapidly to 2 pounds less than required; reduce heat and bring up the last 2 pounds slowly to avoid over-pressure. Fluctuating pressure is one cause of liquid loss. from jars, so hold the pressure steady.

When processing time is up, remove the canner from heat and allow the pressure to return to zero. Do not attempt to cool the pressure canner with cold water.

When the pressure registers zero, wait 1 to 2 minutes,

then slowly remove or open petcock or pressure regulator. Unfasten cover; tilt the far side up so that any steam will escape away from you. Remove each jar with tongs or lift out in wire basket. Place jars upright on a dry, nonmetallic surface. Towels, boards or newspapers can be used. Space jars for free air circulation.

HOW TO CAN GREEN BEANS

Wash fresh, tender, crisp beans in several changes of water; drain. Trim ends; cut into 1-inch pieces.

Boil beans 5 minutes before packing or pack raw into hot jars. Add ½ teaspoon salt per pint. Add boiling water to within 1 inch of jar tops. Wipe tops, add lids, seal sides down; screw on bands.

Place in pressure canner in 2 to 3 inches hot water. See below for preparation of jars and page 707 for pressure canner processing. Process according to manufacturer's directions.

Remove from heat; let pressure fall to zero. Wait 2 minutes. Then open vent, open canner and remove jars. Do not tighten bands. Let stand 12 hours. Press center of lid; if down and stays down, jar is sealed.

BOILING WATER PROCESSING FOR FRUITS AND TOMATOES

This is also called water-bath processing. You need: a large covered kettle (deep enough for jars to be covered by 2 inches of water); a rack; a jar lifter; a ladle with a lip. You also need two measuring cups: one for dry ingredients, one for liquids. Work quickly; prepare no more food than you can process at one time.

To prepare jars and boiling water bath: Examine tops and edges of standard jars to see that there are no nicks, cracks or sharp edges on sealing surfaces. Wash jars in hot soapy water. Rinse; cover with hot water. Let jars remain in hot water until ready to use. Prepare lids as directed by manufacturer. About 10 minutes before ready to use, fill kettle half full with hot water; heat. (The water should be hot but not boiling when jars are placed in kettle.) Remove jars; invert jars on folded towel to drain.

To raw pack: Put cold raw fruits in jars and cover with boiling hot syrup, juice or water. For tomatoes, press down in the containers so they are covered with their own juice; add no liquid.

To hot pack: Heat fruits in syrup or water, or steam or juice them before packing. Juicy fruits and tomatoes can be preheated without added liquid and packed in the juice that cooks out.

To fill jars: Pack each hot jar to within ½ inch of top. Wipe top and screw threads of jar with damp cloth. Place hot metal lid on jar with sealing compound next to glass; screw metal band down firmly. Place sealed jar on rack in kettle, allowing enough space for water to circulate.

To process: When jars are in kettle, add hot (not boiling) water to cover them by 1 to 2 inches. Cover kettle. Heat water to boiling; reduce heat to steady but gentle boil. Start counting processing time (see Timetable); process as directed for each product. Remove jars. If center of lid is down and will not move, jar is sealed. Or tap center of lid with a spoon: a clear ringing sound means a good seal.

To cool jars: Place jars upright, not touching, on rack or folded cloth; keep out of drafts, but do not cover. Test for seal after 12 hours (caps or lids will be depressed in centers and will not move when pressed; lids with wire clamps and rubber seals will not leak when inverted). If seal is incomplete, empty jar; repack and reprocess food as if fresh, or refrigerate for immediate use. Remove screw bands from sealed jars. Label jars with product name and date. Store in a cool, dry place. Use within one year.

TIMETABLE FOR BOILING WATER BATH

High-Acid Produce	Minutes	
	Pints	Quarts
Apples, applesauce (hot)	20	20
Apricots, peaches, pears (raw)	25	30
Cherries, plums (raw)	20	25
Tomato juice (hot)	10	15
Tomatoes (raw)	35	45

SUGAR SYRUPS

These syrups are for canning or freezing fruits. For fruits to be canned, light corn syrup or mild-flavored honey can be substituted for as much as half of the sugar. For fruits to be frozen, corn syrup can replace up to one fourth of the sugar.

Syrup	Yield
Light	
2 cups sugar, 4 cups water	5 cups
Medium	
3 cups sugar, 4 cups water	5½ cups
Heavy	
4¾ cups sugar, 4 cups water	6½ cups

Cook sugar and water until sugar is dissolved. For canning, keep syrup hot until needed but do not boil down. For freezing, refrigerate until ice cold. The usual proportion of sugar to fruit for canned fruits is ½ to ¾ cup sugar for each quart of fruit. Types of syrup are shown below:

Fruit	Syrup
Apples	Light
Grapes, rhubarb	Light or Medium
Apricots, cherries, pears, prunes, grapefruit	Medium
Berries, figs, peaches, plums	Medium or Heavy

To help maintain quality of canned fruits, ¼ teaspoon ascorbic acid, dissolved in ¼ cup cold water, can be added for each quart of fruit.

HOW TO CAN PEACHES

After washing and draining peaches, fill canner half full with water; put canner on to heat. Prepare Medium Syrup above. See pages 708 and 709 for preparation of jars and boiling water processing. After dipping peaches into boiling water 30 to 60 seconds and then into cold water, drain and slip off skins. Cut into halves; remove pits.

Drop pitted, peeled peach halves into mixture of 1 gallon water and 2 tablespoons each salt and vinegar; rinse peaches before packing.

With layers overlapping, pack peaches cavity sides down in hot jars placed on board or cloth. Leave ½-inch headspace in jars.

Cover peaches with boiling syrup, leaving ½-inch headspace. Each pint takes ½ to ¾ cup syrup, each quart 1 to 1½ cups syrup. Run spatula or table knife gently between peaches and jar to release air bubbles. Add more hot syrup if necessary.

Wipe rims and threads of jars with clean, damp cloth. Put lids on; screw bands tightly and evenly to hold rubber sealing rings in place.

Stand filled jars on rack in hot water in canner. Add hot (not boiling) water to cover jars by 1 to 2 inches; heat to steady, gentle boil. Process pints 25 minutes, quarts 30 minutes. Remove jars; cool 12 hours. Test for seal; remove bands and store in cool, dry place.

HOW TO CAN TOMATOES

Wash and drain enough fresh, firm, red-ripe tomatoes* for one canner load. Place in wire basket.

After dipping into boiling water 30 seconds to loosen skins, dip into cold water; drain. Slip off skins. Cut out cores and trim any green spots. Pack small tomatoes whole, large ones in halves or wedges.

Pack tomatoes in hot jars, pressing tomatoes to fill spaces with juice to ½ inch of tops of jars. See pages 708 and 709 for preparation of jars and boiling water processing. Add ½ teaspoon salt per pint. Run spatula between tomatoes and jar to release air bubbles.

Wipe rims and threads of jars with damp cloth. Add lids, rubber sides down; screw bands tightly.

Stand filled jars on rack in hot water in canner. Add hot water to cover jars by 1 to 2 inches. Put cover on canner.

---

*In recent years, there has been a varying acidity level in tomatoes. Use only regular-size ripe tomatoes; avoid yellow and small tomatoes. The Extension Service of the USDA recommends any of the following additions: citric acid (available in drugstores) at a ratio of ¼ teaspoon per pint or ½ teaspoon per quart; or bottled or frozen lemon juice at a ratio of 1 teaspoon per pint, 2 teaspoons per quart; or 5% vinegar, same ratio as for lemon juice. Any of these additions will alter taste only slightly. Commercially prepared tablets containing salt and citric acid are available and can be added to jars before processing.

Heat water to steady, gentle boil. Process pints 35 minutes, quarts 45 minutes.

After removing jars and cooling 12 hours, test each seal (page 709). Remove bands; store in cool place.

PRESERVES, PICKLES AND RELISHES

ABOUT JELLIES AND JAMS
Containers: For jellies and jams firm enough to be sealed with paraffin, use glasses or straight-sided containers. For soft jams and preserves, use canning jars with lids that can be sealed tightly. In warm, humid climates, use canning jars with tight seals for all jams, conserves and marmalades.

To prepare jelly jars or glasses:

1. Examine tops and edges of standard jars; discard any with chips or cracks (which prevent an airtight seal).
2. Wash in hot, soapy water; rinse well.
3. Place in pan with rack or folded cloth on bottom.
4. Cover with hot (not boiling) water; heat to boiling.
5. After boiling gently 15 minutes, cover and let stand in hot water in pan.
6. About 5 minutes before filling, remove from hot water; invert on folded towel to drain away from draft. Prepare lids as directed by manufacturer.

To seal with lids: Use only standard home canning jars and lids. Fill one hot sterilized jar at a time, leaving the amount of headspace specified in recipe. Wipe tops and screw threads of jars with damp cloth. Place hot metal lid on jar with sealing compound next to glass. Screw band tightly; stand jar upright to cool. Work quickly when packing and sealing. Shake jars of jam occasionally as they cool to keep fruit from floating to top.

To seal with paraffin: Ladle fruit mixture into hot sterilized glasses, leaving the amount of headspace specified in recipe. Hold ladle close to tops to prevent air bubbles from forming in jelly or jam. Use only enough paraffin to make a ⅛-inch layer; it must touch side of glass and be even for a good seal. Prick any air bubbles—they prevent a proper seal. Check seal when paraffin has hardened.

Before storing: Let jellied fruit products stand at least 8 hours to avoid breaking the gel. Cover with metal or paper lids. Store in a cool, dry place. The shorter the storage time, the better the eating.

EQUIPMENT FOR JELLY MAKING

You will need a large kettle with a broad, flat bottom. This will allow the sugar and juice mixture to boil quickly and evenly. You will also need a long-handled spoon for skimming the jelly, a pair of tongs for removing the glasses from the hot water and a can and a small pan for heating the paraffin.

EASY JELLY

1   can (6 ounces) frozen orange, tangerine or grape juice
       concentrate, thawed
2   cups water
1   package (1¾ ounces) powdered fruit pectin
3¾ cups sugar

Stir juice, water and pectin in saucepan until pectin is dissolved. Heat to rolling boil over high heat, stirring constantly, about 2 minutes. Add sugar; heat to rolling boil, stirring constantly. Remove from heat. Immediately pour jelly into hot sterilized jars, leaving ½-inch headspace. Wipe rim of jars. Seal with paraffin as directed (left). Or cover with lids. Store in refrigerator no longer than 2 months.   **About 4 half-pints jelly.**

Herb Jelly: Wrap 2 tablespoons herbs tightly in cheesecloth (for orange juice, use dried marjoram leaves; for tangerine juice, use whole cloves; for grape juice, use dried tarragon leaves). Place in saucepan with 2 cups boiling water. Cover and let stand 10 minutes. To extract flavor, squeeze cheesecloth into water. Add enough water to herb water to measure 2 cups; substitute for the 2 cups water.

APPLE-PEPPER JELLY

1   jar (10 ounces) apple jelly
1   tablespoon crushed red peppers
6   drops red food color

Heat jelly and peppers to boiling, stirring constantly. Stir in food color. Immediately strain into hot sterilized jar; cover with lid. Refrigerate no longer than 1 month. **1 half-pint jelly.**

ROSY GRAPE JELLY

2	cups cranberry juice
¾	cup grape juice
1	package (1¾ ounces) powdered fruit pectin
3¼	cups sugar

Mix cranberry juice, grape juice and pectin until smooth in Dutch oven. Heat to boiling over high heat, stirring constantly. Stir in sugar, all at once. Heat to boiling, stirring constantly. Boil and stir 1 minute.

Remove from heat; quickly skim off foam. Immediately pour jelly into hot sterilized jars. Let jars stand 1 hour; cover with lids. Refrigerate no longer than 3 weeks. Or freeze no longer than 6 months. Thaw in refrigerator or at room temperature. **About 5 half-pints jelly.**

HOT WINE JELLY

1	tablespoon crushed dried hot peppers
2	cups sweet red wine
3	cups sugar
1	teaspoon yellow food color
¾	teaspoon red food color
½	bottle (6-ounce size) liquid fruit pectin

Stir peppers into wine. Cover and let stand at least 3 hours.

Strain wine into 3-quart saucepan; stir in sugar and food colors. Heat over low heat, stirring constantly, until sugar is dissolved, about 5 minutes. Remove from heat. Immediately stir in the pectin. Skim off foam. Immediately pour jelly into hot sterilized jars, leaving ½-inch headspace. Wipe rim of jars. Seal with paraffin as directed (page 712). **4 or 5 half-pints jelly.**

STRAWBERRY JAM

    8   cups strawberries (about 4 pints), crushed
    5   cups sugar
    2   tablespoons lemon juice

Mix all ingredients in Dutch oven. Heat to boiling over high heat, stirring frequently. Boil uncovered, stirring frequently, until translucent and jam is thick, about 25 minutes. Quickly skim off foam. Immediately pour jam into hot sterilized jars, leaving ¼-inch headspace. Wipe rim of jars. Seal as directed (page 712). **About 5 half-pints jam.**

Cherry Jam: Substitute 8 cups cut-up cherries (about 4 pounds) for the strawberries. Boil 30 minutes.

Peach Jam: Substitute 8 cups cut-up peeled peaches (about 12 medium) for the strawberries.

Raspberry Jam: Substitute 8 cups raspberries (about 4 pints), crushed, for the strawberries.

PEACH PRESERVES

    4   pounds ripe peaches, peeled and sliced (about 8 cups)
    6   cups sugar
    ¼   cup lemon juice

Toss peaches and sugar. Cover and refrigerate at least 12 hours but no longer than 24 hours.

Heat peach mixture to boiling, stirring constantly. Boil uncovered rapidly 20 minutes. Stir in lemon juice. Boil uncovered 10 minutes. Immediately pour mixture into hot jars, leaving ¼-inch headspace. Wipe rim of jars. Seal and process in boiling water bath 15 minutes (page 708). **About 6 half-pints preserves.**

Spiced Peach Preserves: Tie 8 whole cloves, 5 whole allspice, 2 sticks cinnamon, 2 blades mace and 1½ teaspoons ground coriander in cheesecloth bag; add to peach mixture before boiling. Remove bag before pouring mixture into jars.

PEAR CONSERVES

3   pounds winter pears, pared and sliced (about 8 cups)
4   cups sugar
¾   cup raisins
1   tablespoon grated orange peel
2   teaspoons grated lemon peel
¼   cup lemon juice
1   cup broken walnuts

Mix all ingredients except walnuts in Dutch oven. Heat to boiling, stirring frequently. Boil uncovered, stirring occasionally, until mixture thickens slightly, 25 to 30 minutes. Stir in walnuts. Immediately pour mixture into hot jars, leaving ¼-inch headspace. Wipe rim of jars. Seal and process in boiling water bath 15 minutes (page 708).   **4 or 5 half-pints conserves.**

APPLE BUTTER

4   quarts sweet apple cider
3   quarts pared and quartered cooking
     apples (about 4 pounds)
2   cups sugar
1   teaspoon ground cinnamon
1   teaspoon ground ginger
½   teaspoon ground cloves

Heat cider to boiling in 5-quart Dutch oven. Boil uncovered until cider measures 2 quarts, about 1¼ hours.

Add apples. Heat to boiling; reduce heat. Simmer uncovered, stirring frequently, until apples are soft and can be broken apart with spoon, about 1 hour. (Apples can be pressed through sieve or food mill at this point if smooth apple butter is desired.)

Stir in remaining ingredients. Heat to boiling; reduce heat. Simmer uncovered, stirring frequently, until no liquid separates from pulp, about 2 hours. Heat to boiling. Immediately pour mixture into hot jars, leaving ¼-inch headspace. Wipe rim of jars. Seal and process in boiling water bath 10 minutes (page 708).   **About 3 half-pints butter.**

LEMON CURD

1	cup sugar
2	teaspoons finely shredded lemon peel
1	cup lemon juice (about 5 large lemons)
3	tablespoons firm margarine or butter, cut up
3	eggs, slightly beaten

Mix sugar, lemon peel and lemon juice in heavy 1½-quart saucepan. Stir in margarine and eggs. Cook over medium heat, stirring constantly, until mixture thickens and coats back of spoon, about 8 minutes (do not boil). Immediately pour into 1-pint container or two 1-cup containers. Cover; refrigerate no longer than 2 months. **About 2 cups curd.**

ONION MARMALADE

1	jar (10 ounces) apple jelly
2	tablespoons finely chopped red onion
2	tablespoons thinly sliced green onion (with tops)

Heat all ingredients over low heat, stirring occasionally, until jelly is melted, about 10 minutes. Cook, stirring occasionally, 5 minutes. Pour into 1-cup container; cover and refrigerate no longer than 1 month. **About 1 cup marmalade.**

FRESH PINEAPPLE CHUTNEY

10	cups cut-up pared fresh ripe pineapples (about 2 large)
4	cups sugar
1½	cups raisins
1	cup cut-up crystallized ginger
½	cup finely chopped green pepper
3	cups vinegar
½	teaspoon salt
½	teaspoon whole cloves
½	teaspoon whole allspice
3	three-inch sticks cinnamon

Mix pineapple, sugar, raisins, ginger, green pepper, vinegar and salt in Dutch oven. Tie cloves, allspice and cinnamon sticks in double-thickness cheesecloth; place in pineapple mixture. Heat to boiling, stirring frequently; reduce heat. Simmer uncovered, stirring frequently, until mixture is dark and syrupy, 1½ to 2 hours.

Remove the spice bag from pineapple mixture. Immediately pour into sterilized jars, leaving ¼-inch headspace. Wipe rim of jars. Seal as directed (page 712). Test for seal when jars are completely cool. Store in cool, dark, dry place. **8 half-pints chutney.**

Fresh Peach Chutney: Substitute 10 cups sliced peeled peaches (about 5 pounds) for the pineapple.

Fresh Pear Chutney: Substitute 10 cups sliced pared pears (about 5 pounds) for the pineapple.

Fresh Plum Chutney: Substitute 12 cups sliced blue plums (about 5 pounds) for the pineapple.

GARLIC-DILL PICKLES

36	to 40 pickling cucumbers (3 to 3½ inches)
7½	cups water
5	cups vinegar (5 to 6% acidity)
½	cup plus 2 tablespoons pickling or noniodized salt
12	cloves garlic
6	heads fresh dill
6	slices onion, ½ inch thick

Wash and scrub cucumbers carefully. Cut ¼-inch slice from blossom end of each cucumber. Heat water, vinegar and salt to boiling in Dutch oven. Place 2 cloves garlic, 1 dill head and 1 onion slice in each of 6 hot jars. Pack cucumbers in jars, leaving ½-inch headspace. Cover with boiling brine, leaving ½-inch headspace. Wipe rim of jars. Seal and process in boiling water bath 10 minutes (page 708). **About 6 quarts pickles.**

Fresh-Pack Dill Pickles: Omit garlic.

BREAD AND BUTTER PICKLES

3	quarts thinly sliced unpared cucumbers (about 4 pounds)
7	cups thinly sliced onions (about 2 pounds)
1	red pepper, cut into strips
1	green pepper, cut into strips
½	cup pickling or noniodized salt
1	cup water
2½	cups sugar
2½	cups cider or white vinegar
2	tablespoons mustard seed
1	teaspoon celery seed
1	teaspoon ground turmeric

Mix cucumbers, onions and peppers. Dissolve salt in water; pour over vegetables. Place a solid layer of ice cubes or crushed ice over vegetables. Weight with a heavy object and let stand 3 hours.

Drain vegetables thoroughly. Mix remaining ingredients; heat to boiling. Add vegetables; heat to boiling. Immediately pack mixture in hot jars, leaving ¼-inch headspace. Wipe rim of jars. Seal and process in boiling water bath 10 minutes (page 708).   **About 6 pints pickles.**

RIPE CUCUMBER PICKLES

8	cups water
1	teaspoon salt
½	teaspoon lump alum
10	cups ¾-inch pieces cucumbers,* seeds removed
3	cups sugar
1½	cups white vinegar (5 to 6% acidity)
1	tablespoon plus 1 teaspoon whole mixed pickling spice
4	small onions, sliced (about 2 cups)

Mix water, salt and alum; add cucumbers and let stand at least 8 hours.

Drain cucumbers thoroughly. Heat sugar, vinegar and pickling spice to boiling in Dutch oven. Stir in cucumbers and onions. Heat to boiling; reduce heat. Simmer uncovered until

*This is a good recipe for overripe large cucumbers.

cucumbers are clear, about 5 minutes. Immediately pack in hot jars, leaving ¼-inch headspace. Wipe rim of jars. Seal and process in boiling water bath 10 minutes (page 708). About 3 pints pickles.

WATERMELON RIND PICKLES

¼	cup pickling or noniodized salt
8	cups cold water
4	quarts 1-inch cubes pared watermelon rind
1	piece gingerroot
3	sticks cinnamon, broken into pieces
2	tablespoons whole cloves
8	cups cider vinegar
9	cups sugar

Dissolve salt in cold water; pour over watermelon rind. Stir in additional water, if necessary, to cover rind. Let stand in cool place 8 hours.

Drain rind; cover with cold water. Heat to boiling. Cook uncovered just until tender, 10 to 15 minutes; drain. Tie spices in cheesecloth bag. Heat spice bag, vinegar and sugar to boiling; boil uncovered 5 minutes. Add rind; simmer uncovered 1 hour. Remove spice bag. Immediately pack mixture in hot jars, leaving ¼-inch headspace. Wipe rim of jars. Seal and process in boiling water bath 10 minutes (page 708). **7 or 8 pints pickles.**

SWEET PEPPER RELISH

12	large red or green peppers, finely chopped
1	tablespoon pickling or noniodized salt
3	cups sugar
2	cups white vinegar

Mix peppers and salt. Cover and let stand at least 12 hours.

Drain peppers, pressing out all liquid. Heat peppers, sugar and vinegar to boiling in 3-quart saucepan, stirring frequently; reduce heat. Simmer uncovered, stirring frequently, until mixture is thickened, about 45 minutes. Immediately pack in hot jars, leaving ¼-inch headspace. Wipe rim of jars. Seal and process in boiling water bath 10 minutes (page 708). **About 6 half-pints relish.**

NOTE: Peppers can be finely chopped in food processor following manufacturer's directions.

CORN RELISH

9	ears corn
1½	cups sugar
3	tablespoons all-purpose flour
2	tablespoons pickling or noniodized salt
2	teaspoons dry mustard
1	teaspoon ground turmeric
3	cups white vinegar
3	medium onions, chopped
2	red peppers, chopped
1	green pepper, chopped
1	small head green cabbage, chopped

Place corn in Dutch oven; add enough cold water to cover. Heat to boiling. Boil uncovered 3 minutes; cool. Cut enough kernels from corn to measure 5 cups.

Mix sugar, flour, salt, mustard and turmeric; stir in vinegar. Heat to boiling. Add vegetables. Simmer uncovered 25 minutes. Immediately pack mixture in hot jars, leaving ¼-inch headspace. Wipe rim of jars. Seal and process in boiling water bath 15 minutes (page 708). **5 or 6 pints relish.**

NOTE: Onions, peppers and cabbage can be chopped in blender or food processor following manufacturer's directions.

VEGETABLE RELISH

4	medium carrots, cut up
2	medium onions, cut up
2	medium stalks celery, cut up
1	medium cucumber, cut up
1	medium green pepper, cut up
1	cup chopped cabbage
1	cup cut-up green beans
1	cup cut-up wax beans
2	cloves garlic
2¼	cups sugar
2¼	cups vinegar (5 to 6% acidity)
2	tablespoons mustard seed
2	tablespoons celery seed

Place vegetables and garlic, about 2 cups at a time, in blender container; cover with water. Cover and blend until coarsely chopped; drain thoroughly. Pour into glass bowl or crock. Cover vegetables with salted water (¼ cup salt to 1 quart water); let stand at least 8 hours.

Drain vegetables thoroughly; press out excess liquid. Mix sugar, vinegar, mustard seed and celery seed. Heat to boiling, stirring until sugar is dissolved. Stir in vegetables; reduce heat. Simmer uncovered 10 minutes.

Immediately pack mixture in hot jars, leaving ¼-inch headspace. Wipe rim of jars. Seal and process in boiling water bath 10 minutes (page 708). **About 4 pints relish.**

NOTE: Vegetables and garlic can be chopped in food grinder using coarse blade.

NUTRITION

The newest trend in cooking means emphasis on vegetables and fruits; lighter meals with reduced servings of high-fat foods; moderate use of sugar and salt; and use of whole grains and cereals as inexpensive sources of protein, vitamins, minerals and dietary fiber. It means today's and yesterday's ingredients assembled in fresh ways to reflect the recent awakening to good nutrition and physical fitness. The key to good nutrition remains the same—eat a varied balanced diet.

NUTRIENTS IN FOOD

Protein: Occurs naturally in foods of animal and plant origin. Protein is necessary for growth and maintenance of body tissues.

Carbohydrates: Carbohydrates are the body's main source of energy. Carbohydrates are of two types: complex and simple. Increased amounts of complex carbohydrates are being encouraged in the diet—especially whole grain foods, fruits and vegetables.

Complex carbohydrates occur naturally in plants and include the starches in vegetables and grains as well as the fiber of many fruits, vegetables, legumes and whole grains. Fiber is the part of plant foods that cannot be completely digested by the body.

Simple carbohydrates include sugars found naturally in some foods and sweeteners. Regardless of whether a sugar is added to food or whether it occurs naturally in food, it is used in the same way by the body.

Fat: Fat is a nutrient found in many foods. The main functions of fat in the diet are to supply energy, provide essential fatty acids and aid in the transportation of the fat-soluble vitamins A, D, E and K. The body needs fat to insulate and cushion the organs. However, there is a concern

723

today about the fat and cholesterol in the diet and its relationship to heart disease.

Vitamins: Vitamins are compounds that are necessary for growth and development and maintenance of health. They are found in varying amounts in the food we eat. The vitamins most easily lost during cooking are the B vitamins (thiamin, riboflavin, niacin, B_6 and B_{12}) and vitamin C. Cooking foods, especially vegetables, in a small amount of water saves the greatest amount of these vitamins.

Minerals: Minerals are also important to the body because they are part of a rigid skeleton, are needed to help nerves and muscles function and are oxygen carriers.

The most prevalent minerals are calcium, phosphorus, sodium, potassium and magnesium. The trace minerals—those needed in smaller amounts—are iron, zinc, manganese, copper and iodine.

Calcium and iron are being consumed at less than adequate levels by many groups, especially teenage girls and adult women.

Sodium: Common table salt is a combination of sodium and chloride—both needed to help regulate the balance of water in the body. About one-fourth of the sodium in the average American diet occurs naturally in foods and the remaining amount comes from the use of salt in food preparation and at the table.

WATER—THE FORGOTTEN NUTRIENT

Water makes up about 70 percent of the human body and is second only to oxygen as being essential for life. We can survive only four days without water.

Because water is involved in so many body functions, maintenance of water balance is crucial. Balance is attained when we ingest at least as much water as we lose. Drinking six or more cups of liquids—including juices and broths—per day helps provide some of the water that is needed to maintain water balance. Sodium and potassium are the principal minerals responsible for the body's water balance along with adequate protein.

UNDERSTANDING THE BASIC FOOD GROUPS

If you use the Basic Food Groups below as a guide in planning meals, you will be meeting your nutritional needs.

Food Group	Recommended Daily Amounts	Equivalent of 1 Serving	Nutrient Contributions
Milk, Yogurt and Cheese	*Children under 9 years:* 2 to 3 servings *Children 9 to 12 years:* 3 servings *Teens:* 4 servings *Adults:* 2 to 3 servings	1 cup milk or yogurt or 1½ ounces cheese	Calcium Phosphorus Protein Riboflavin Vitamin A Vitamin D
Meat, Fish, Poultry and Legumes	2 servings	2 to 3 ounces cooked lean meat, fish or poultry or 1 to 1½ cups cooked dried beans or 2 eggs	Iron Niacin Phosphorus Protein Folic acid Vitamin B_6 Vitamin B_{12}*

*Animal products only

Food Group	Recommended Daily Amounts	Equivalent of 1 Serving	Nutrient Contributions
Breads and Cereals (whole grain, enriched and fortified)	4 servings	1 slice bread or 1 cup dry cereal or ½ cup cooked cereal, rice or pasta	Carbohydrate Iron Niacin Riboflavin Thiamin Magnesium
Vegetables and Fruits	4 servings Include one good source of vitamin C daily. Frequently include deep yellow or dark green vegetables.	1 cup raw vegetables or ½ cup fruit, fruit juice or cooked vegetables or 1 medium or 2 small fruits	Carbohydrate Vitamin A Vitamin C
Fats, Sweets and Alcohol	Number of servings depends on the individual's calorie needs		Fatty acids Vitamin E

NUTRITION CHARTS

GUIDELINES TO UNDERSTANDING NUTRITION INFORMATION ON RECIPES

The United States Recommended Daily Allowances (U.S. RDA) are based on Recommended Dietary Allowances established by the Food and Nutrition Board of the National Academy of Sciences and National Research Council. The dietary allowances were determined for adults and represent the average nutrient requirement plus an added margin to cover individual variations.

Calories per serving or unit are included with the recipes. Percent U.S. RDA in use in 1985 are included on the nutrition charts for protein, vitamin A, vitamin C, calcium and iron. Carbohydrates, fat and sodium are also listed. These nutrients are ones that receive considerable attention in American diets.

■ If ingredient choices are given, the first ingredient in the ingredient list is used to calculate the nutrition information. For example, when "catsup or chili sauce" is indicated, the nutrition was determined using catsup.

■ When a range is given for an ingredient or more than one serving is indicated, the lower weight or smaller serving size was used to calculate the nutrition content.

■ "If desired" ingredients are not included in the nutrition calculations. For example, for "top with strawberries and, if desired, whipped cream," the nutrition information was determined using strawberries only.

■ Nutrition information for variations of a recipe have not been calculated. For example, a salmon variation of a tuna recipe will have different calorie and nutrient values.

Per Serving or Unit Recipe, Page	Protein (grams)	Carbohydrates (grams)	Fat (grams)	Sodium (milligrams)	Percent U.S. Recommended Daily Allowance				
					Vitamin A	Vitamin C	Protein	Calcium	Iron
APPETIZERS/BEVERAGES									
FIRST COURSE									
Caviar Classic 5	10	14	5	755	0	0	15	10	20
Melon and Prosciutto 3	2	5	1	140	40	35	4	0	2
Oysters Rockefeller 4	13	18	26	770	55	80	20	15	40
Shrimp Cocktail 3	4	15	1	890	15	15	6	6	4
PICK-UP TIDBITS									
Barbecued Ribs 12	3	1	6	75	0	0	4	0	2
Broiled Potato Skins 9	1	4	1	45	0	6	2	2	0
Cheese Board 8	16	21	23	575	25	135	25	20	10
Cheese Sandwiches 14	1	3	1	35	0	0	0	0	0
Cheesy Bagel Bites 7	1	2	2	80	0	0	0	0	0
Chili-Cheese Balls 8	1	1	2	50	2	0	0	2	0
Cocktail Meatballs 10	2	6	2	125	2	2	2	0	2
Cucumber Sandwiches 14	2	9	2	110	2	0	2	0	2
Cucumber-Shrimp Sandwiches 14	1	3	0	30	0	0	0	0	0
Deviled Eggs 16	7	1	12	210	6	0	10	2	6
Dilled Vegetables 6	1	4	2	520	4	30	2	2	2
Ham Phyllo Rolls 15	4	9	3	160	15	10	6	0	6
Ham Sandwiches 14	2	6	3	165	0	0	2	0	2
Marinated Mushrooms 6	1	2	3	50	2	4	2	0	2
Olives and Onions 7	0	1	4	190	0	0	0	0	0
Oriental-style Nuts 17	7	10	21	100	2	0	10	6	10
Parmesan-Curry Popcorn 17	3	9	13	220	6	0	4	4	2
Pickled Eggs 16	7	15	6	315	6	2	10	4	8
Pizza Bites 12	3	5	4	175	4	2	4	4	2
Popcorn 17	2	9	5	0	0	0	2	0	2
Rumaki 13	4	4	2	115	40	2	4	0	6
Sauerkraut Balls 11	3	3	5	90	0	2	4	0	2

Per Serving or Unit	Protein (grams)	Carbohydrates (grams)	Fat (grams)	Sodium (milligrams)	Percent U.S. Recommended Daily Allowance				
					Vitamin A	Vitamin C	Protein	Calcium	Iron
Recipe, Page									
APPETIZERS/BEVERAGES *continued*									
Sausage-Cheese Chips 14	2	2	3	70	0	4	2	2	0
Shrimp-Bacon Bites 13	2	2	2	140	2	2	2	2	0
Stuffed Celery Sticks 7	3	1	6	135	2	2	4	4	0
Stuffed Mushrooms 5	1	4	2	80	0	2	0	0	0
DIPS & SPREADS									
Baked Cheese Spread 24	3	8	4	175	4	0	4	2	2
Buttermilk Dip 20	1	2	3	55	2	0	2	4	0
Cajun Crabmeat Mold 27	2	5	4	110	4	2	2	0	2
Cheese Ball 21	7	2	19	300	15	6	10	15	2
Chèvre Pâté 24	1	7	3	90	0	0	2	2	2
Fruit-Cheese Kabobs with Ginger Dip 20	2	5	4	55	2	6	2	6	0
Guacamole 19	0	2	2	70	2	4	0	0	0
Italian Sausage Terrine 23	6	1	8	170	45	4	10	0	8
Kielbasa in Fondue 21	23	5	33	860	10	0	35	50	6
Mexi-Dip 18	1	1	2	60	2	6	2	0	0
Mock Caviar 25	2	10	5	200	0	0	2	2	2
Mushroom Spread 22	2	5	6	160	4	2	2	2	2
Ricotta Cheese Spread 22	2	5	2	90	0	0	2	2	2
Salmon Mousse 27	1	0	1	45	0	0	2	2	0
Salsa Cheese Bake 25	11	23	18	760	15	15	15	25	6
Shrimp-Cheese Strata 26	1	0	2	30	2	0	0	0	0
Spinach Dip 19	0	1	1	35	6	2	0	0	0
Yogurt-Shrimp Spread 26	2	2	4	70	2	0	2	2	0
Zippy Chili Dip 18	4	5	3	90	8	10	8	0	6
BEVERAGES									
Apricot Aperitif 32	0	15	0	25	15	4	0	2	2
Brandy Cream 32	2	16	7	60	6	0	4	8	0
Café au Lait 35	3	5	3	45	2	0	4	10	0

Per Serving or Unit Recipe, Page	Protein (grams)	Carbohydrates (grams)	Fat (grams)	Sodium (milligrams)	Percent U.S. Recommended Daily Allowance				
					Vitamin A	Vitamin C	Protein	Calcium	Iron
APPETIZERS/BEVERAGES *continued*									
Chocolate Milk Shakes 32	7	44	11	130	8	2	10	20	4
Hot Chocolate 33	5	16	9	110	2	2	8	15	4
Hot Cocoa 33	5	14	5	120	2	0	8	15	2
Hot Cranberry Punch 29	0	25	0	15	0	30	0	0	2
Hot Orange Cider 30	1	33	0	10	2	95	0	2	4
Irish Coffee 35	1	28	11	15	8	0	0	2	0
Lemonade 31	0	23	0	5	0	35	0	0	0
Mexican Hot Chocolate 34	4	17	8	105	2	0	6	10	4
Pink Colada 31	0	30	0	15	0	6	0	0	0
Sangria Punch 30	0	12	0	10	0	10	0	0	2
Sparkling Cranberry Punch 30	0	16	0	15	0	60	0	0	0
Spiced Tea 37	0	8	0	5	2	20	0	0	0
Strawberry Spritzer 31	1	10	0	5	0	50	0	2	2
Tomato-Beer Cooler 30	1	8	0	135	8	15	0	0	2
Wassail 29	0	21	0	5	0	2	0	0	2
BREADS/GRAINS/PASTA									
QUICK BREADS									
Baking Powder Biscuits 42	3	16	9	290	0	0	4	8	4
Banana Bread 57	2	18	5	135	2	2	2	0	2
Blueberry Muffins 46	3	23	10	300	0	2	4	8	4
Bran-Raisin Muffins 47	4	31	6	250	0	10	6	4	8
Cake Doughnuts 50	3	21	7	105	0	0	4	4	4
Corn Bread 54	4	19	6	560	0	0	6	15	6
Cranberry-Orange Bread 56	2	16	4	140	2	8	2	2	2
Dumplings 43	2	14	5	255	0	0	4	8	4

Per Serving or Unit	Protein (grams)	Carbohydrates (grams)	Fat (grams)	Sodium (milligrams)	Percent U.S. Recommended Daily Allowance				
Recipe, Page					Vitamin A	Vitamin C	Protein	Calcium	Iron
BREADS/GRAINS/PASTA *continued*									
French Toast 44	6	22	5	250	2	0	10	6	6
Gruyère Puff Ring 53	9	13	13	195	10	0	15	15	6
Irish Soda Bread 52	3	21	3	270	2	0	4	4	4
Pancakes 45	3	12	4	275	0	0	4	10	4
Popovers 52	6	17	6	230	2	0	8	6	4
Raisin-Spice Coffee Cake 48	7	64	20	560	10	0	10	15	10
Scones 43	3	14	5	200	4	2	4	6	4
Sour Cream Coffee Cake 49	5	43	18	405	10	0	8	6	8
Spoon Bread 55	5	15	8	700	6	0	8	15	6
Waffles 44	18	71	40	1390	30	2	25	50	20
Zucchini Bread 55	2	19	4	125	0	0	2	0	2
YEAST BREADS									
Angel Biscuits 63	3	17	7	240	0	0	4	4	4
Bran-Oatmeal Bread 71	2	17	1	180	2	0	4	2	6
Brioche 67	3	14	9	185	6	0	4	0	4
Cheese Casserole Bread 72	4	12	7	175	6	0	6	6	2
Cinnamon Rolls 77	3	41	7	160	2	0	4	2	6
Danish Kringle 82	3	24	14	145	6	0	4	2	4
Danish Strip 80	2	23	6	110	20	0	2	0	2
Danish Twists 81	1	15	6	110	4	0	2	0	0
Dark Pumpernickel 69	2	12	1	155	0	0	2	2	6
Egg Bagels 65	4	24	3	215	0	0	6	0	6
English Muffins 62	3	25	4	185	0	0	4	0	6
French Bread 68	2	12	0	190	0	0	2	0	2
Garlic Bread 69	2	11	4	155	2	0	2	0	2
Hard Rolls 73	4	28	2	385	0	0	6	0	6
Honey Twist Coffee Cake 78	3	27	9	220	6	0	4	2	4

Per Serving or Unit Recipe, Page	Protein (grams)	Carbohydrates (grams)	Fat (grams)	Sodium (milligrams)	Percent U.S. Recommended Daily Allowance				
					Vitamin A	Vitamin C	Protein	Calcium	Iron
BREADS/GRAINS/PASTA *continued*									
Honey-Whole Wheat Bread 70	2	13	2	140	0	0	2	0	2
Jam Pastries 81	2	28	8	150	6	4	2	0	2
Orange Rolls 76	2	32	6	130	2	2	4	0	2
Raised Doughnuts 61	4	31	10	105	0	0	6	2	4
Soft Breadsticks 64	2	12	2	365	0	0	2	0	2
Traditional Roll Dough									
Cloverleaf Rolls 75	2	15	4	110	0	0	4	0	2
Crescent Rolls 75	2	11	3	90	0	0	2	0	2
Fan Tans 75	2	15	5	120	2	0	4	0	2
Pan Rolls 75	1	8	2	55	0	0	2	0	2
Parker House Rolls 75	2	15	6	130	2	0	4	0	2
Square Rolls 75	4	24	5	165	0	0	6	2	6
Traditional White Bread 66	2	13	1	140	0	0	2	0	2
GRAINS									
Barley with Mushrooms 88	5	30	5	430	2	8	8	2	6
Brown Rice 85	4	39	1	550	0	0	6	2	4
Bulgur Pilaf 90	5	20	5	425	2	2	8	2	6
Cheesy Grits 89	11	20	12	470	10	2	15	25	6
Cornmeal Mush 89	3	22	6	800	4	0	4	10	4
Curried Rice 87	5	39	12	990	6	0	8	4	10
Lemon Pilaf 86	2	23	7	760	8	6	4	2	4
Oven-steamed Rice 86	4	50	0	770	0	0	6	2	10
Regular Rice 85	4	50	0	770	0	0	6	2	10
Rice with Artichokes 86	4	31	1	365	20	30	6	2	10
Savory Mixed Rice 87	8	34	9	795	10	8	10	6	8
Wild Rice 85	9	46	1	730	0	0	10	2	15
Wild Rice and Mushrooms 88	8	21	8	440	8	2	10	15	8

Per Serving or Unit	Protein (grams)	Carbohydrates (grams)	Fat (grams)	Sodium (milligrams)	Percent U.S. Recommended Daily Allowance				
Recipe, Page					Vitamin A	Vitamin C	Protein	Calcium	Iron

BREADS/GRAINS/PASTA *continued*

PASTA									
Cooked Macaroni, Spaghetti and Noodles 91	6	37	9	100	8	0	10	2	8
Egg Noodles 92	5	17	3	450	0	0	8	2	6
Four-Cheese Fettuccine 94	20	45	31	1720	20	2	30	45	10
Green Fettuccine 93	4	16	2	210	30	15	6	2	8
Mexican-style Macaroni 98	10	45	11	350	10	30	15	15	10
Noodles Romanoff 95	8	25	22	490	15	0	10	15	4
Pepper Mostaccioli 97	4	20	8	175	10	85	6	4	6
Rigatoni and Tomatoes 98	8	45	9	250	10	10	10	8	10
Spaetzle 93	5	15	7	550	4	0	6	2	4
Spaghetti and Anchovies 97	7	36	8	920	10	40	10	4	10
Spaghetti with Mushrooms 96	8	33	13	340	10	8	10	10	8
Vermicelli and Spinach 95	5	25	5	150	50	30	8	6	10

CAKES/PIES

CAKES									
Angel Food Cake 124	3	29	0	80	0	0	4	0	0
Apple Cake 118	4	36	21	165	0	2	6	2	6
Applesauce Cake 117	4	52	10	350	0	0	6	2	6
Banana-Nut Cake 118	5	42	14	300	0	4	6	4	6
Chocolate Mousse Cake 106	5	31	37	310	20	0	8	4	8
Cocoa Fudge Cake 108	4	32	8	290	0	0	6	4	6
Cocoa Pecan Torte 106	5	22	28	165	10	0	8	4	8
Date-Chocolate Chip Cake 116	5	69	23	425	4	0	8	4	10
Double Chocolate Cake 110	3	47	11	250	0	0	4	2	10

Per Serving or Unit Recipe, Page	Protein (grams)	Carbohydrates (grams)	Fat (grams)	Sodium (milligrams)	Percent U.S. Recommended Daily Allowance				
					Vitamin A	Vitamin C	Protein	Calcium	Iron
CAKES/PIES *continued*									
Fruit-topped Cake 115	5	57	20	320	10	50	6	8	6
German Chocolate Cake 109	7	60	31	480	15	0	10	10	4
Jelly Roll 125	3	44	2	125	0	0	4	4	4
Jeweled Fruitcake 123	3	23	6	50	10	6	4	2	6
Lemon Chiffon Cake 126	4	29	9	250	0	0	6	6	6
Pineapple-Apricot Cake 119	4	49	13	280	8	2	6	2	8
Pineapple Upside-down Cake 114	3	38	10	320	2	2	4	6	4
Pound Cake 113	6	51	18	270	15	0	8	6	6
Silver White Cake 111	4	35	10	270	0	0	4	8	4
Sour Cream Chocolate Cake 107	4	40	11	270	2	0	4	2	6
Sour Cream Spice Cake 121	4	44	13	260	6	0	6	8	10
Williamsburg Orange Cake 120	5	44	14	340	6	0	8	4	6
Yellow Cake 112	4	32	9	260	0	0	4	8	4
Zucchini Spice Cake 122	5	31	14	260	4	2	6	2	6
FROSTINGS									
Almond Topping 133	1	2	11	15	8	0	0	2	0
Caramel Frosting 130	0	32	6	80	4	0	0	2	2
Chocolate Chip Glaze 132	0	5	3	20	0	0	0	0	0
Chocolate Frosting 131	1	18	6	50	2	0	0	0	0
Chocolate Sour Cream Frosting 131	1	28	9	50	4	0	0	0	2
Cocoa Fluff 133	1	10	11	10	8	0	2	2	2
Cream Cheese Frosting 130	1	34	5	45	4	0	2	0	0
Creamy Vanilla Frosting 129	0	26	4	50	2	0	0	0	0
Fudge Frosting 131	1	23	3	55	2	0	0	0	2

| Per Serving or Unit | Protein (grams) | Carbohydrates (grams) | Fat (grams) | Sodium (milligrams) | Percent U.S. Recommended Daily Allowance | | | | |
Recipe, Page					Vitamin A	Vitamin C	Protein	Calcium	Iron
CAKES/PIES *continued*									
Vanilla Glaze 132	0	16	4	45	2	0	0	0	0
White Mountain Frosting 128	0	10	0	15	0	0	0	0	0
PIES									
Apple-Cinnamon Tart 140	2	42	11	155	2	6	2	0	4
Apple Deep-Dish Pie 139	2	55	9	160	2	8	2	0	2
Apple Dumplings 142	5	133	29	390	2	15	6	8	20
Apple Pie 138	5	77	30	455	4	8	6	2	8
Apple-Sour Cream Pie 140	4	50	20	230	8	2	6	6	6
Apple Squares 141	3	51	21	190	2	4	6	0	6
Blueberry Grenadine Pie 143	3	55	21	360	6	10	4	4	4
Blueberry Pie 143	5	64	30	415	4	20	8	2	8
Cherry Cream Pie 146	3	58	13	290	2	0	4	8	6
Cherry Phyllo Pie 145	3	50	12	140	20	2	4	0	10
Cherry Pie 144	5	101	30	420	15	2	8	2	15
Chocolate Angel Pie 160	2	22	16	30	10	0	2	2	2
Chocolate-Banana Pie 154	4	47	18	350	10	6	6	8	4
Chocolate Brownie Pie 158	6	50	28	220	4	0	10	4	15
Classic French Silk Pie 153	6	41	46	355	25	0	10	4	10
Coconut Cream Pie 152	7	41	33	390	15	0	10	15	6
Coffee Cordial Pie 161	3	34	25	235	15	0	4	4	6
Custard Pie 159	8	31	16	350	4	0	10	10	6
French Strawberry Tart 151	2	30	14	290	10	50	2	4	2
Frozen Lemon Pie 162	5	35	24	260	15	6	6	4	6
Frozen Pumpkin Pie 162	3	33	17	280	50	2	4	6	4
Fruit Salad Pie 146	4	62	29	390	6	20	6	4	6
Glazed Cherry Tarts 145	5	59	21	210	10	10	8	4	10
Lemon Chiffon Pie 160	5	36	13	180	0	4	8	0	4
Lemon Coconut Pie 159	8	71	38	450	20	10	10	6	8

Per Serving or Unit	Protein (grams)	Carbohydrates (grams)	Fat (grams)	Sodium (milligrams)	Percent U.S. Recommended Daily Allowance				
Recipe, Page					Vitamin A	Vitamin C	Protein	Calcium	Iron

CAKES/PIES continued

Lemon Meringue Pie 156	4	63	16	210	4	10	6	2	4
Peach Melba Tarts 148	3	49	15	180	6	8	4	6	4
Peach-Pecan Tart 148	5	65	28	310	30	30	8	4	8
Peach Pie 147	5	77	30	410	15	10	8	0	8
Pear Tart 149	3	49	17	200	2	6	4	4	6
Pecan Pie 157	5	59	29	420	8	0	8	4	15
Pumpkin Pie 156	7	38	15	340	80	6	10	15	6
Raisin-Sour Cream Pie 150	6	76	21	260	8	0	10	8	10
Rhubarb Pie 150	5	80	30	410	4	10	8	8	8
Strawberry Glacé Pie 152	3	46	14	170	4	100	4	2	6

COOKIES/CANDY

COOKIES									
Acorn Cookies 188	1	7	4	30	0	0	2	0	2
Almond Brownies 176	3	22	11	85	0	0	4	4	4
Butterscotch Brownies 177	2	18	6	105	0	0	2	4	4
Candy Cookies 168	1	14	5	75	2	0	2	0	2
Caramel-Apple Bars 182	1	23	4	110	2	0	2	0	2
Caramel-Oat Bars 181	1	11	4	65	2	0	2	0	2
Cashew Triangles 179	2	10	7	70	4	0	2	0	2
Chocolate Chip Cookies 167	1	10	5	65	2	0	2	0	2
Chocolate Crinkles 185	1	10	3	30	0	0	0	0	2
Chocolate Drop Cookies 171	1	12	5	60	2	0	2	0	2
Chocolate-Mint Cookies 170	1	21	8	95	4	0	2	0	2
Chocolate-Nut Slices 190	1	11	5	75	2	0	2	0	2
Cocoa Brownies 175	3	18	9	160	6	0	4	2	4
Coconut-Macadamia Cookies 174	1	10	5	65	2	0	0	0	2

Per Serving or Unit Recipe, Page	Protein (grams)	Carbohydrates (grams)	Fat (grams)	Sodium (milligrams)	Percent U.S. Recommended Daily Allowance				
					Vitamin A	Vitamin C	Protein	Calcium	Iron

COOKIES/CANDY *continued*

Coconut Macaroons 173	1	7	2	25	0	0	0	0	0
Colorful Cookies 187	1	12	3	55	2	0	0	0	0
Cream Cheese Cookies 173	1	8	4	65	2	0	0	0	2
Deluxe Brownies 175	4	31	18	105	8	0	6	2	8
Easy Praline Bars 177	0	5	3	45	0	0	0	0	0
Fudgy Oatmeal Bars 183	2	18	6	95	2	0	2	2	4
Gingerbread People 198	3	37	3	165	0	0	4	10	20
Gingersnaps 185	1	13	3	60	0	0	0	0	2
Grasshopper Bars 176	1	19	6	90	2	0	2	0	2
Hazelnut Bars 179	1	8	3	20	0	0	0	0	0
Hidden Mint Cookies 187	1	29	4	90	0	0	0	0	2
Honey-Spice Cookies 195	1	16	1	15	0	0	0	0	2
Italian Sweets 196	1	15	3	55	2	0	2	2	2
Jumbo Molasses Cookies 198	1	21	3	130	0	0	2	6	10
Lemon Cookie Sandwiches 192	1	8	3	55	2	0	0	0	0
Lemon Squares 181	1	13	4	80	4	0	2	0	0
Nut Roll-ups 197	1	3	4	25	2	0	0	0	0
Oatmeal Cookies 169	2	16	5	80	2	0	2	0	2
Peanut Butter Cookies 184	2	9	5	85	0	0	2	0	2
Peanut Butter Squares 180	2	12	4	65	0	0	2	0	2
Pretzel Cookies 186	1	12	4	70	2	0	2	0	2
Rosettes 200	1	3	7	65	0	0	0	0	0
Russian Teacakes 189	1	8	5	55	2	0	0	0	0
Scotch Shortbread 196	1	9	6	70	4	0	2	0	0
Sour Cream Cookies 193	1	9	3	60	0	0	0	0	0
Spritz 199	1	5	3	55	2	0	0	0	0
Spumoni Cookies 191	1	4	3	45	2	0	0	0	0
Sugar Cookies 193	1	8	3	55	2	0	0	0	0

Per Serving or Unit Recipe, Page	Protein (grams)	Carbohydrates (grams)	Fat (grams)	Sodium (milligrams)	Percent U.S. Recommended Daily Allowance				
					Vitamin A	Vitamin C	Protein	Calcium	Iron
COOKIES/CANDY *continued*									
Thumbprint Cookies 190	1	7	4	35	0	0	0	0	0
Toffee Bars 178	2	15	8	90	4	0	2	2	2
Zucchini Cookies 172	1	14	3	55	2	0	0	0	2
CANDY									
Almond Bark Fudge 204	1	6	3	10	0	0	2	2	0
Almond Butter Crunch 206	0	4	4	25	2	0	0	0	0
Bourbon Balls 211	1	11	2	15	0	0	0	0	0
Caramels 207	0	9	3	25	2	0	0	0	0
Cashew Clusters 209	2	6	7	25	0	0	2	0	2
Chocolate Fudge 202	1	14	3	30	0	0	0	0	0
Cocoa Fudge 203	1	15	2	20	0	0	0	0	0
Divinity 205	0	14	1	5	0	0	0	0	0
Easy Fudge 203	1	7	2	10	0	0	0	2	0
Easy Turtle Candies 209	1	12	6	5	0	0	0	0	0
Mint Wafers 211	0	6	0	5	0	0	0	0	0
Peanut Brittle 206	2	9	4	35	0	0	2	0	2
Peanut Butter Candy Bars 210	4	21	12	190	8	4	6	2	6
Pralines 207	1	40	8	35	0	0	2	4	6
Sponge Candy 208	0	12	0	100	0	0	0	0	2
Taffy 208	0	8	0	55	0	0	0	0	0
Truffles 204	1	14	10	20	2	0	2	0	4
SWEET SNACKS									
Candied Citrus Peel 212	0	30	0	5	0	60	0	4	0
Caramel-Nut Corn 212	4	29	19	190	4	0	6	4	8
Chocolate-Caramel Apples 213	2	80	9	5	0	10	2	2	4
Granola Bark 215	1	6	2	15	0	0	0	0	0

Per Serving or Unit Recipe, Page	Protein (grams)	Carbohydrates (grams)	Fat (grams)	Sodium (milligrams)	Percent U.S. Recommended Daily Allowance				
					Vitamin A	Vitamin C	Protein	Calcium	Iron

COOKIES/CANDY *continued*

Marshmallow Bars 214	0	5	1	45	4	2	0	0	4
Popcorn Balls 213	2	36	6	220	4	0	2	0	6
S'more Bars 215	1	14	2	75	4	4	0	0	6

DESSERTS

FRUIT DESSERTS									
Apple Crisp 220	2	47	11	125	10	6	2	4	10
Applesauce 220	0	46	1	10	0	0	0	2	6
Apricot-Banana Cream 221	2	43	22	210	40	4	2	4	0
Apricot-glazed Pears 231	1	42	1	5	0	25	0	2	2
Baked Apples 219	1	37	4	45	4	15	0	2	2
Caribbean Bananas 222	1	45	12	140	10	15	2	2	6
Cherries and Kiwifruit 224	1	35	1	15	2	110	2	2	2
Cherries Jubilee 223	3	51	10	85	8	4	4	10	4
Cinnamon Oranges 228	2	19	3	25	6	110	2	6	2
Creamy Filled Mango 226	1	26	3	10	100	60	2	4	2
Fresh Blueberry Cobbler 222	3	48	8	300	2	20	4	10	6
Fresh Fruit Cups 225	1	21	0	5	20	60	0	2	2
Fruit Ambrosia 224	1	22	4	30	4	65	2	4	4
Fruit in Orange Cream 224	2	29	15	20	15	110	2	4	2
Fruit-Wine Compote 225	1	36	10	130	15	10	0	2	6
Gingered Pineapple 229	1	27	4	25	0	45	2	0	4
Glazed Apple Rings 219	0	46	12	135	10	10	0	0	2
Melon Balls in Wine 226	1	17	0	10	50	55	0	0	0
Minted Melon 228	1	20	0	30	30	15	0	0	0
Orange Dessert Omelets 228	3	18	2	25	4	70	4	2	4

Per Serving or Unit Recipe, Page	Protein (grams)	Carbohydrates (grams)	Fat (grams)	Sodium (milligrams)	Percent U.S. Recommended Daily Allowance				
					Vitamin A	Vitamin C	Protein	Calcium	Iron
DESSERTS *continued*									
Papaya Dessert 229	2	30	11	20	90	210	2	6	4
Peach Melba 230	3	91	7	75	10	20	6	10	8
Peaches Flambé 230	5	57	17	85	20	15	8	15	4
Pears Helene 231	3	37	9	75	6	2	4	10	0
Poached Plums 232	1	33	1	35	8	15	0	0	0
Raspberries Romanoff 232	1	18	4	25	4	20	2	4	2
Rhubarb Sauce 233	0	32	0	2	0	4	0	10	0
Rhubarb with Macaroons 232	3	45	12	30	8	15	4	10	2
Strawberry Shortcakes 233	6	75	28	640	10	95	10	20	10
Watermelon Supreme 227	1	18	1	10	20	50	0	0	2
Whipped Avocado Dessert 221	3	24	27	20	20	15	4	2	6
Winter-Fruit Compote 225	1	62	0	10	20	15	2	4	4
BAKED & COOKED DESSERTS									
Apple Pudding 252	4	34	8	165	0	0	6	8	6
Baked Chocolate Soufflé 240	6	34	31	340	25	0	10	8	4
Baked Custard 248	7	16	7	140	6	0	10	15	4
Bread Pudding 252	9	49	14	435	10	2	15	15	10
Cherry Blintzes 247	14	60	29	480	20	2	20	20	10
Chocolate Cheesecake 243	7	34	29	300	20	0	10	8	10
Chocolate Pots de Crème 249	6	28	20	130	8	0	10	8	8
Cream Puffs 245	10	34	28	360	20	0	15	15	10
Crème Brûlée 249	3	22	25	30	25	8	4	6	4
Crepes 246	4	14	5	165	4	0	6	6	4
English Trifle 251	7	56	23	200	20	35	10	15	8
Fudgy Meringue Mallow 256	6	66	25	185	20	0	10	6	6

| Per Serving or Unit | | | | | | | | |
Recipe, Page	Protein (grams)	Carbohydrates (grams)	Fat (grams)	Sodium (milligrams)	Vitamin A	Vitamin C	Protein	Calcium	Iron

| | Protein (grams) | Carbohydrates (grams) | Fat (grams) | Sodium (milligrams) | Percent U.S. Recommended Daily Allowance | | | | |
Recipe, Page					Vitamin A	Vitamin C	Protein	Calcium	Iron
DESSERTS *continued*									
Gingerbread 239	4	51	12	330	0	0	6	10	15
Hot Fudge Sundae Cake 235	7	69	19	230	6	0	10	20	10
Lemon Pudding Cake 236	4	38	3	130	2	8	6	4	2
Lemon Schaum Torte 257	3	40	15	125	10	8	4	2	2
Lindy's Cheesecake 241	7	27	31	270	25	2	15	6	6
Meringue Shell 258	1	18	0	25	0	0	2	0	0
Noodle-Raisin Pudding 254	12	53	13	375	10	0	20	10	10
Pavlova 258	2	27	11	35	10	60	2	2	0
Peanut Cheesecake 242	8	43	23	305	10	0	15	4	8
Plantation Cake 238	4	59	24	255	8	2	6	10	15
Plum Pudding Cake 237	3	83	8	250	2	2	4	15	10
Pumpkin Cheesecake 244	8	31	34	300	75	2	10	8	10
Raspberry Crepes 247	12	75	21	480	15	25	20	25	10
Rice Pudding 253	7	45	5	390	4	2	10	10	6
Rice Pudding Mold 253	5	49	8	320	6	8	8	10	6
Rum-Cracker Torte 237	7	35	29	160	15	0	10	8	10
Steamed Chocolate Pudding 254	6	71	22	505	15	0	10	8	8
Steamed Molasses Pudding 255	4	61	21	480	15	0	6	10	15
Vanilla Pudding 250	5	26	13	200	10	2	8	15	2
REFRIGERATED & FROZEN DESSERTS									
Angel Toffee Dessert 267	4	44	14	100	10	0	6	4	0
Cherry Freeze 265	6	39	5	60	15	2	10	15	2
Cherry Layer Dessert 264	3	42	7	260	4	0	6	8	6
Chocolate Baked Alaska 267	4	38	10	130	4	0	6	8	4
Chocolate Frango 266	2	16	22	35	15	0	2	4	2
Chocolate Mousse 262	4	22	18	40	10	0	6	4	6

Per Serving or Unit Recipe, Page	Protein (grams)	Carbohydrates (grams)	Fat (grams)	Sodium (milligrams)	Percent U.S. Recommended Daily Allowance				
					Vitamin A	Vitamin C	Protein	Calcium	Iron

DESSERTS *continued*

Coconut Snowballs 270	4	26	14	110	8	0	6	10	2
Cranberry Ice 264	0	55	0	5	0	15	0	0	0
Frozen Chocolate Cream 266	4	32	24	50	15	0	8	8	4
Frozen Lemon Cream 264	1	33	22	25	15	10	2	4	0
Graham Cracker Torte 263	5	45	22	345	15	0	8	6	6
Ice-cream Bombe 269	5	32	14	115	10	0	8	15	0
Lemon Soufflé 260	4	27	17	90	15	10	6	4	2
Orange Bavarian 261	2	34	15	60	15	35	4	2	0
Orange Mousse 263	3	21	18	50	10	0	4	6	0
Sherbet-Berry Parfaits 265	2	55	3	60	2	15	2	8	4
Vanilla Ice Cream 268	3	16	25	110	20	0	4	8	2
Watermelon Mousse 261	2	18	8	70	10	10	4	2	0
DESSERT SAUCES									
Butterscotch Sauce 271	0	12	5	90	4	0	0	0	0
Caramel Sauce 271	0	10	3	30	2	0	0	0	0
Crunchy Chocolate Sauce 272	1	6	9	30	2	0	0	0	2
Fudge Sauce 272	1	9	2	15	0	0	0	2	0
Lemon Sauce 273	0	7	1	20	0	0	0	0	0
Marshmallow Sauce 272	0	10	0	15	0	0	0	0	0
Nutmeg Sauce 273	0	12	7	70	6	0	0	0	0
Orange Sauce 274	0	8	0	20	0	8	0	0	0
Raspberry-Currant Sauce 274	0	9	0	5	0	2	0	0	0
Sweetened Whipped Cream 274	0	1	6	10	4	0	0	0	0

Per Serving or Unit	Protein (grams)	Carbohydrates (grams)	Fat (grams)	Sodium (milligrams)	Percent U.S. Recommended Daily Allowance				
Recipe, Page					Vitamin A	Vitamin C	Protein	Calcium	Iron
EGGS/CHEESE/LEGUMES									
EGGS									
Broccoli Oven Omelet 288	15	6	12	435	30	65	35	15	10
Cheese Soufflé 292	20	12	37	895	30	0	30	40	10
Creamed Eggs with Ham 291	17	9	18	560	10	0	25	15	10
Egg-Bacon Bake 291	16	9	29	590	25	2	35	20	10
Egg Foo Yong 290	22	10	34	2235	10	6	35	8	20
Eggs Benedict 284	16	15	32	860	20	0	25	10	15
Eggs Benedict Casserole 283	25	11	28	755	25	4	55	35	20
Eggs in Rolls 289	19	31	29	1025	15	0	30	15	15
Eggs on English Muffins 282	13	20	17	680	20	10	20	15	15
Eggs on Tortillas 284	16	16	25	505	25	45	25	30	15
French Omelet 285	21	2	31	370	25	0	45	10	20
Oven Omelet 287	19	7	22	640	20	30	25	45	8
Puffy Omelet 286	14	2	18	500	15	0	30	6	15
Vegetable Frittata 288	14	6	24	365	15	55	20	15	10
CHEESE									
Cheese Enchiladas 302	18	29	34	785	45	40	40	50	15
Cheese Fondue 303	44	71	37	1270	25	0	65	115	15
Cheese Pie 296	15	6	16	410	15	15	30	35	6
Cheese Pizza 297	9	22	9	490	8	15	15	15	6
Cheese Strata 300	21	26	32	1025	25	6	45	45	10
Cheesy French Bread Bake 301	18	20	16	580	15	2	30	30	10
Impossible Broccoli Pie 295	23	19	26	885	40	90	35	55	10
Macaroni and Cheese 298	17	32	27	1015	20	4	25	40	6
Manicotti 299	24	38	12	1025	100	55	35	30	20

Per Serving or Unit	Protein (grams)	Carbohydrates (grams)	Fat (grams)	Sodium (milligrams)	Percent U.S. Recommended Daily Allowance				
Recipe, Page					Vitamin A	Vitamin C	Protein	Calcium	Iron
EGGS/CHEESE/LEGUMES *continued*									
Quiche Lorraine 296	15	19	54	640	30	2	25	25	8
Welsh Rabbit 301	19	23	33	925	20	0	40	50	8
LEGUMES									
Baked Black Beans 305	13	54	8	975	2	8	20	8	25
Baked Pinto Beans 307	13	51	3	430	0	2	20	10	20
Boston Baked Beans 304	16	68	6	335	0	2	25	20	35
Chalupas 309	12	26	26	570	25	10	15	30	10
Cheesy Lentils 310	10	22	3	445	6	55	15	8	10
Chili Beans with Dumplings 311	20	62	18	575	4	6	30	25	25
Italian Lima Beans 309	17	45	4	1190	30	150	25	15	35
Red Beans and Rice 312	7	41	8	1165	2	65	10	4	15
Refried Bean Bake 313	11	10	12	450	20	55	15	20	10
Savory Baked Beans 308	15	47	8	1310	30	65	25	10	35
Skillet Beans 314	15	49	17	1290	10	15	25	15	25
Three-Bean Casserole 311	27	55	22	1970	10	40	40	15	35
Western-style Beans 312	30	74	12	720	20	40	45	8	15
FISH/SHELLFISH									
FISH									
Baked Fish 319	35	1	14	590	10	2	75	4	6
Baked Stuffed Fish 323	26	11	20	925	45	15	40	6	8
Broiled Fish Steaks 324	34	0	14	585	10	0	75	4	6
Cod and Vegetable Bake 322	39	16	23	1200	70	10	60	8	10
Cold Poached Salmon 328	73	4	21	1020	35	40	160	35	20
Creamy Tuna Casserole 333	23	31	24	940	20	15	35	15	15

Per Serving or Unit Recipe, Page	Protein (grams)	Carbohydrates (grams)	Fat (grams)	Sodium (milligrams)	Percent U.S. Recommended Daily Allowance				
					Vitamin A	Vitamin C	Protein	Calcium	Iron
FISH/SHELLFISH *continued*									
Creole Catfish 319	30	33	2	830	25	60	45	4	15
Crustless Salmon Quiche 334	26	6	17	765	10	2	40	45	10
Curried Tuna 332	17	26	13	1060	10	4	25	2	10
Deep-fried Fish 331	41	27	19	650	6	0	65	8	15
Fish a la Meunière 329	26	12	33	540	15	6	40	6	8
Fish in Foil 324	43	0	23	1070	15	0	95	6	8
Fish with Garlic Salsa 326	32	5	11	350	15	20	50	4	8
Halibut with Grapefruit Sauce 320	35	7	14	630	15	40	75	6	8
Mustard-topped Fish 327	51	1	16	740	10	0	110	10	10
Orange Roughy with Tarragon 327	31	0	10	350	8	0	45	4	6
Oven-fried Fish 330	36	9	19	560	15	0	80	10	8
Panfried Fish 329	38	15	16	510	4	0	85	4	10
Salmon Loaf 335	28	24	16	1110	6	2	40	35	15
Salmon Puff 334	17	10	13	840	10	2	25	20	8
Salmon Shortcakes 335	20	42	28	1660	10	6	30	30	10
Tuna Spaghetti 331	19	28	20	880	15	0	30	10	10
Vegetable-stuffed Sole 321	21	8	7	920	55	60	30	15	8
SHELLFISH									
Boiled Lobster 346	33	1	2	2840	0	0	70	15	8
Broiled Ginger Scallops 342	19	8	6	915	0	4	30	10	15
Broiled Lobster Tails 346	24	2	52	1950	45	6	55	10	6
Chinese-fried Shrimp 339	16	55	28	720	0	4	25	20	15
Company Crab Casserole 345	13	9	13	1030	45	60	20	15	15
Lobster Newburg with Popovers 347	18	24	17	640	10	0	25	20	8

Per Serving or Unit Recipe, Page	Protein (grams)	Carbohydrates (grams)	Fat (grams)	Sodium (milligrams)	Percent U.S. Recommended Daily Allowance				
					Vitamin A	Vitamin C	Protein	Calcium	Iron

FISH/SHELLFISH *continued*

Scalloped Oysters 347	20	61	30	1460	25	60	30	25	55
Scallops in Cream Sauce 343	16	28	20	315	15	0	25	15	15
Seafood Lasagne 348	17	22	16	680	15	2	25	25	8
Shrimp Jambalaya 341	20	30	12	1150	15	50	30	15	20
Skewered Shrimp 338	9	9	15	285	6	100	15	15	8
Stir-fried Shrimp with Vegetables 340	12	8	18	940	30	30	20	20	10

BEEF/VEAL

BEEF									
Beef Brisket Barbecue 361	34	4	12	450	4	6	75	2	25
Beef Burgundy Popovers 373	37	25	16	800	2	6	55	8	30
Beef Steak Provençale 367	25	13	8	320	150	15	55	6	20
Beef Stew 372	19	17	8	1115	60	95	30	4	15
Beef Stroganoff 370	26	9	20	735	10	6	40	6	20
Beef Teriyaki 364	33	4	11	1110	0	0	70	2	25
Beef with Mustard Sauce 365	18	7	10	360	4	2	25	4	10
Corned Beef and Cabbage 361	15	5	19	590	2	35	25	4	10
Fajitas 369	47	49	44	800	120	200	70	35	45
French-style Beef Roast 359	26	9	18	380	90	30	60	6	20
London Broil 364	27	6	16	490	2	10	60	2	20
Mushroom Minute Steaks 365	27	3	14	795	2	20	40	2	20
Mushroom Steak 366	24	4	7	610	0	4	55	2	15

Per Serving or Unit Recipe, Page	Protein (grams)	Carbohydrates (grams)	Fat (grams)	Sodium (milligrams)	Percent U.S. Recommended Daily Allowance				
					Vitamin A	Vitamin C	Protein	Calcium	Iron
BEEF/VEAL *continued*									
Mustard Short Ribs 376	39	12	77	330	2	20	85	4	30
New England Pot Roast 359	38	26	11	790	150	35	60	8	100
Savory Beef Short Ribs 375	31	8	65	450	4	6	45	4	20
Sesame Beef 374	24	32	10	615	0	0	35	2	20
Skillet Hash 374	23	14	21	325	0	25	35	2	15
Stir-fried Beef 371	26	12	22	830	8	20	40	2	20
Swiss Steak 368	33	10	11	360	15	75	50	2	25
GROUND BEEF									
Beef in Potato Shells 382	22	27	21	410	20	50	35	10	15
Chèvre Burgers 377	35	2	32	665	4	2	55	15	20
Chili con Carne 387	32	28	21	780	35	40	50	8	35
Giant Burger 377	24	1	24	680	4	0	55	2	15
Hamburger Patties 376	23	1	19	330	0	0	35	0	15
Hidden Beef Ring 388	18	35	21	1015	6	6	25	10	15
Impossible Cheeseburger Pie 384	28	18	26	580	15	10	60	25	15
Lasagne Roll-ups 388	26	32	24	825	85	30	40	20	25
Meat-and-Potato Pie 378	31	20	29	835	4	10	70	15	20
Meat Loaf 379	27	15	22	750	8	10	60	8	20
Meatballs 380	27	12	22	590	2	4	60	6	20
Mexican Hash 385	30	54	25	1670	15	90	45	8	30
Salisbury Steaks 378	30	12	21	800	2	6	45	4	20
Saucy Meatballs 380	31	20	31	1210	10	6	45	10	20
Spaghetti and Meatballs 381	23	38	15	930	25	60	35	8	25
Stuffed Cabbage Rolls 383	26	16	20	1110	25	125	40	8	30
Stuffed Peppers 389	20	16	16	920	20	140	30	10	20
Taco Dinner 385	26	44	39	950	20	15	40	25	20

Per Serving or Unit Recipe, Page	Protein (grams)	Carbohydrates (grams)	Fat (grams)	Sodium (milligrams)	Percent U.S. Recommended Daily Allowance				
					Vitamin A	Vitamin C	Protein	Calcium	Iron
BEEF/VEAL *continued*									
Tortilla Casserole 386	29	20	33	720	90	30	45	35	20
VEAL									
Braised Veal Shanks 394	56	33	36	1150	2	6	85	4	40
Veal Oscar 393	20	14	34	700	25	20	30	6	20
Veal Sauté 394	23	12	14	750	80	8	35	4	15
Veal with Tuna Sauce 392	22	2	17	405	0	4	45	2	15
VARIETY MEATS									
Glazed Beef Tongue 398	44	15	34	130	0	4	95	2	25
Liver and Onions 396	24	13	21	570	900	40	55	2	45
PORK/LAMB									
PORK									
Bacon-Cheese Pastries 427	12	13	24	725	8	15	20	15	6
Breaded Pork Chops 408	17	8	21	720	4	0	25	4	15
Choucroute 422	29	34	53	1630	2	50	45	6	25
Corn Dogs 426	17	26	46	1420	2	4	25	15	15
Country-style Ribs 412	19	26	35	400	6	8	30	2	15
Fresh Ham with Stuffing 407	38	11	51	580	2	10	60	4	25
Gingered Ham Slice 421	20	4	21	710	0	0	30	0	15
Ham and Scalloped Potatoes 421	15	26	14	820	8	30	25	15	10
Ham Loaf 422	18	6	18	600	2	10	25	4	15
Ham with Spiced Fruits 420	27	81	9	915	100	20	40	6	25
Italian Sausage Lasagne 424	25	37	23	960	35	60	35	35	20

Per Serving or Unit Recipe, Page	Protein (grams)	Carbohydrates (grams)	Fat (grams)	Sodium (milligrams)	Percent U.S. Recommended Daily Allowance				
					Vitamin A	Vitamin C	Protein	Calcium	Iron
PORK/LAMB *continued*									
Lemon Pork Chops 409	41	19	21	530	4	10	90	4	30
Mustard Spareribs 411	38	18	71	250	0	0	60	10	35
Polish Sausage in Beer 425	15	2	31	1220	0	0	25	4	10
Pork Chow Mein 416	25	28	19	1510	15	15	35	4	15
Pork Fried Rice 415	17	42	21	1410	6	6	25	4	20
Pork Hocks with Sauerkraut 416	66	16	10	3210	2	50	100	10	25
Pork Piccata 412	15	11	16	330	4	2	20	2	10
Pork Pies 413	20	39	30	1160	10	60	40	8	15
Pork Roast with Rosemary 404	31	2	18	255	0	0	45	0	20
Pork with Parsnips 409	20	18	23	425	4	20	45	6	15
Sweet-and-Sour Pork 414	30	60	27	1050	40	50	45	6	30
Sweet and Zesty Spareribs 411	29	20	52	570	2	6	60	4	25
Tenderloin with Peppers 406	24	7	30	340	6	170	35	2	20
LAMB									
Irish Stew 434	34	23	12	805	2	45	50	2	15
Italian Lamb Shanks 434	51	8	47	1070	4	2	110	15	20
Lamb and Couscous 435	24	30	14	660	85	100	35	4	15
Lamb Ragout 436	34	34	16	1000	85	70	50	8	25
Lamb with Kasha 437	23	11	11	530	4	8	50	4	15
Mustard Lamb Chops 433	28	7	40	575	70	70	60	6	15
Shish Kabobs 432	22	7	28	330	2	90	30	2	10
Stuffed Lamb Shoulder 430	23	2	32	325	20	2	35	2	8

Per Serving or Unit	Protein (grams)	Carbohydrates (grams)	Fat (grams)	Sodium (milligrams)	Percent U.S. Recommended Daily Allowance				
Recipe, Page					Vitamin A	Vitamin C	Protein	Calcium	Iron

POULTRY

CHICKEN									
Autumn Roast Chicken 444	29	39	28	255	130	50	45	8	15
Batter-fried Chicken 446	20	24	37	870	4	0	30	10	10
Brunswick Stew 455	23	28	19	1180	30	50	35	6	20
Chicken a la King 462	22	31	27	1340	20	40	35	25	10
Chicken and Peppers 461	26	7	10	615	.8	190	40	2	8
Chicken Curry 459	22	43	15	935	10	4	30	4	15
Chicken Fricassee 452	28	32	24	935	15	2	40	15	15
Chicken in Red Wine 453	23	16	16	780	65	8	35	4	10
Chicken Jambalaya 454	28	30	22	1270	25	20	45	4	20
Chicken Livers with Bacon 449	10	6	10	200	110	15	15	0	15
Chicken Paprika 456	27	9	15	490	40	70	40	8	10
Chicken-Pasta Primavera 464	20	26	12	500	45	60	30	10	10
Chicken-Rice Supper 465	19	23	16	1150	10	30	30	10	10
Chicken Tostadas 463	19	25	16	620	30	45	30	20	15
Chicken with Vegetables 454	21	14	10	485	25	30	45	4	10
Chicken with Yogurt 458	32	6	23	470	10	4	70	8	10
Country Broiled Chicken 450	22	3	30	970	15	4	35	2	6
Dinner Casserole 465	17	12	8	490	90	5	25	4	8
Fried Chicken 445	27	8	19	440	6	0	40	2	8
Golden Nuggets 446	17	25	16	450	4	4	25	2	6
Macaroni Casserole 463	26	38	16	900	15	15	40	25	15
Oven-barbecued Chicken 447	20	12	5	695	8	6	45	0	8
Oven Chicken Kiev 460	28	13	11	320	25	15	60	2	10
Oven-fried Chicken 445	27	8	14	530	10	0	40	2	8

Per Serving or Unit Recipe, Page	Protein (grams)	Carbohydrates (grams)	Fat (grams)	Sodium (milligrams)	Percent U.S. Recommended Daily Allowance				
					Vitamin A	Vitamin C	Protein	Calcium	Iron
POULTRY *continued*									
Stir-fried Chicken 448	21	9	14	665	2	10	30	2	8
Tandoori-style Chicken 461	25	1	3	165	2	0	35	2	4
Wheat-stuffed Drumsticks 457	34	36	25	565	15	4	75	2	15
TURKEY									
Bread Stuffing 472	6	31	29	1090	20	6	8	6	8
Impossible Turkey Pie 467	22	12	12	430	10	4	35	25	10
Rice Stuffing 471	6	38	17	750	6	4	10	4	10
Turkey Divan 468	28	8	16	840	20	60	40	15	10
Turkey Meatballs 474	20	22	11	1160	20	15	30	10	10
Turkey Pot Pie 466	28	41	41	980	95	8	40	8	15
Turkey with Pineapple 473	25	9	6	185	0	10	55	2	8
GAME									
Cornish Hens with Glazed Oranges 475	29	25	12	360	10	65	60	2	15
Pheasant and Gravy 475	75	25	38	2210	25	50	115	10	30
Stewed Rabbit 476	39	14	16	505	60	4	85	4	15
Venison Sauerbraten 477	28	10	9	545	0	4	45	4	35
SALADS									
MAIN DISH SALADS									
Beef-Bulgur Salad 498	18	19	21	325	30	30	25	4	20
Beef-Eggplant Salad 499	15	5	24	350	4	10	30	2	15
Chef's Salad 498	19	10	33	350	40	35	30	30	15
Chicken Salad 483	23	4	33	540	2	4	35	6	8
Chicken Salad Cups 484	23	19	44	860	20	15	35	8	15

Per Serving or Unit Recipe, Page	Protein (grams)	Carbohydrates (grams)	Fat (grams)	Sodium (milligrams)	Percent U.S. Recommended Daily Allowance				
					Vitamin A	Vitamin C	Protein	Calcium	Iron
SALADS *continued*									
Club Salads 483	27	32	24	600	40	35	40	8	15
Curried Chicken Salad 485	18	38	34	780	10	40	25	4	15
Curried Shrimp Salad 489	8	10	14	275	25	50	10	15	15
Fish and Pepper Salad 491	30	8	18	935	20	160	65	6	10
Fruited Turkey Salad 486	23	19	5	440	10	20	35	6	10
Glazed Ham Salad 497	4	19	17	275	15	30	10	6	10
Ham-Pasta Salad 495	24	40	28	72	20	90	50	10	20
Ham-Swiss Cheese Salad 496	3	8	11	410	20	45	6	4	6
Macaroni-Shrimp Salad 488	15	32	30	660	15	25	20	20	15
Marinated Chicken Salad 482	23	11	30	820	20	25	35	4	12
Mediterranean Salad 494	16	15	42	1000	25	50	25	35	10
Oriental Chicken Salad 481	22	6	23	370	25	8	35	2	8
Seafood-stuffed Shells 490	30	31	6	1400	10	15	45	15	15
Seafood-Wild Rice Salad 489	14	22	22	595	25	20	20	8	15
Smoked Fish Salad 491	18	30	14	475	50	55	40	10	8
Taco Salads 500	23	28	40	750	25	25	50	20	20
Tuna-Bean Salad 493	20	45	12	1070	15	100	30	15	25
Tuna-Cantaloupe Salads 494	24	52	18	1050	190	160	35	6	20
Tuna-Macaroni Salad 493	21	25	38	970	8	15	30	4	15
Tuna-Pasta Toss 492	16	38	11	325	10	25	25	4	15
Turkey-Fruit Salad 486	23	23	16	335	6	50	50	4	10
Turkey-Pasta Salad 487	30	37	16	290	75	65	65	20	25
Turkey-Vegetable Salads 485	26	7	21	240	6	50	60	6	10
Vegetable-Beef Salad 499	13	10	43	495	15	30	30	4	15

Per Serving or Unit Recipe, Page	Protein (grams)	Carbohydrates (grams)	Fat (grams)	Sodium (milligrams)	Percent U.S. Recommended Daily Allowance				
					Vitamin A	Vitamin C	Protein	Calcium	Iron
SALADS *continued*									
PASTA & GRAIN SALADS									
Bulgur-Tomato Salad 503	3	20	7	280	10	30	4	2	8
Dilled Pasta Salad 501	4	27	9	315	22	2	6	4	6
Rice-Spinach Salad 502	5	21	18	560	40	8	8	4	10
Tomato-Pasta Salad 502	4	27	5	185	10	15	6	2	8
TOSSED SALADS									
Caesar Salad 509	5	8	16	400	20	25	8	10	8
Easy Caesar Salad 509	4	11	8	390	25	20	6	10	8
Elegant Tossed Salad 510	2	7	4	50	35	25	2	2	4
Greek Salad 510	3	7	11	270	70	50	6	10	15
Lettuce-Mushroom Salad 508	1	3	17	60	4	6	2	0	2
Mandarin Salad 512	2	10	12	220	10	10	2	4	4
Spinach-Mushroom Salad 506	4	4	10	130	90	50	6	6	10
Spinach Tossed Salad 506	6	17	14	425	120	70	10	12	16
Walnut Tossed Salad 511	3	5	15	185	2	6	4	0	4
Wilted Lettuce Salad 508	2	6	15	170	20	15	2	4	10
Winter Vegetable Toss 511	1	5	8	25	25	25	2	2	4
VEGETABLE SALADS									
Asparagus Salad 513	9	13	17	690	10	25	10	6	10
Broiled Tomato Salads 525	4	6	13	200	20	15	6	8	4
Cabbage Salad 517	1	5	2	105	4	65	0	2	2
Carrot-Raisin Salad 519	1	18	18	170	120	10	2	2	4
Cauliflower Salad 520	4	12	11	430	18	100	6	4	10
Coleslaw 515	1	4	9	160	4	35	2	4	0
Confetti Slaw 516	2	5	11	520	0	35	2	6	4
Creamy Cucumber Salad 521	1	4	1	170	4	15	2	4	4

Per Serving or Unit	Protein (grams)	Carbohydrates (grams)	Fat (grams)	Sodium (milligrams)	Percent U.S. Recommended Daily Allowance				
Recipe, Page					Vitamin A	Vitamin C	Protein	Calcium	Iron
SALADS *continued*									
Cucumber Salad 521	0	2	0	45	0	4	0	0	0
Cucumbers and Shrimp 522	7	6	1	275	6	15	10	4	10
Cucumbers and Tomatoes 520	3	7	1	385	15	35	4	8	8
Garbanzo Bean Salad 514	10	29	16	250	15	55	15	10	20
Garlic Tomato Slices 524	1	3	7	35	10	10	0	0	2
Hot German Potato Salad 523	3	26	9	800	0	35	6	2	4
Kidney Bean Salad 514	9	27	4	55	10	30	15	6	15
Marinated Carrot Salad 519	2	15	19	455	270	14	4	4	4
Marinated Peppers 522	2	7	7	155	10	270	2	2	6
Marinated Whole Tomatoes 524	2	8	5	5	20	50	2	2	4
Mixed Vegetable Salad 518	5	12	8	600	40	85	8	6	8
Pickled Beets 519	0	27	0	85	0	2	0	0	2
Potato Salad 523	6	26	15	520	4	35	8	2	6
Ratatouille Salad 517	2	6	9	275	10	50	2	2	6
Sweet-sour Cabbage Slaw 516	2	12	5	440	6	75	4	4	2
Three-Bean Salad 515	4	15	8	290	10	15	6	6	15
Tomato-Cheese Salads 525	4	4	8	195	15	10	6	10	2
MOLDED SALADS									
Ambrosia Salad Mold 533	2	22	5	45	4	35	2	4	2
Apple-Cherry Salad 530	2	27	0	65	2	35	2	0	0
Artichoke Salad 529	3	23	4	280	6	20	4	2	2
Berry-Wine Salad 531	3	29	1	65	2	35	4	6	2
Carrot-Pineapple Salad 528	2	22	0	100	40	6	2	0	0

Per Serving or Unit	Protein (grams)	Carbohydrates (grams)	Fat (grams)	Sodium (milligrams)	Percent U.S. Recommended Daily Allowance				
Recipe, Page					Vitamin A	Vitamin C	Protein	Calcium	Iron
SALADS *continued*									
Cherry Layered Salad 531	1	13	0	45	0	10	0	0	2
Citrus Salad 532	1	14	0	10	4	60	0	2	0
Confetti Cabbage Mold 527	2	15	15	260	2	35	2	2	2
Corn-Relish Mold 528	2	19	0	220	8	40	4	0	2
Cran-Raspberry Mold 532	3	42	6	100	4	2	4	4	0
Cucumber-Relish Mold 529	2	21	0	390	2	10	4	2	0
Frozen Fruit Salad 535	5	34	21	225	30	8	8	8	4
Frozen Raspberry Salad 535	4	42	13	155	10	10	6	8	4
Molded Apricot Salad 530	2	10	1	10	25	4	2	0	2
Sangria Mold 534	3	42	0	95	2	50	4	2	2
Spiced Peach Mold 533	1	21	0	40	4	2	2	0	0
Strawberry-Cheese Salad 534	4	23	9	90	4	60	6	2	4
Triple-Orange Salad 532	3	37	1	90	2	25	4	4	0
FRUIT SALADS									
Apple-Pear Salad 541	1	13	0	75	4	10	0	0	2
Avocado-Apple Salad 541	2	20	22	145	10	15	2	2	4
Cantaloupe Salads 542	3	27	14	90	130	125	4	6	10
Chow Mein Fruit Salad 539	4	37	9	190	8	15	6	4	2
Cream Cheese-Grape Toss 542	3	11	18	60	10	15	4	4	6
Easy Fruit Salad 537	2	34	2	25	4	30	4	6	4
Fruit and Cheese Salad 538	8	16	13	185	15	10	10	20	2
Fruit Platter 538	2	31	0	5	15	130	2	6	2
Fruit-Prune Salad 540	3	38	30	210	15	15	4	4	8

Per Serving or Unit Recipe, Page	Protein (grams)	Carbohydrates (grams)	Fat (grams)	Sodium (milligrams)	Percent U.S. Recommended Daily Allowance				
					Vitamin A	Vitamin C	Protein	Calcium	Iron
SALADS *continued*									
Fruit-Walnut Salad 536	5	32	6	60	40	80	8	10	4
Mixed Fruit Salad 537	1	29	5	10	45	170	2	4	2
Orange-Avocado Salad 543	2	17	20	100	10	70	2	4	4
Orange Salad 543	2	19	7	55	15	120	2	4	2
Pear Salad 544	1	20	7	5	6	15	0	2	4
Pineapple Ring Salads 544	2	33	20	190	20	40	2	4	4
Summer Fruit Salad 536	3	28	10	30	15	35	4	6	2
Twenty-four-hour Salad 539	3	35	11	85	10	50	4	6	4
Waldorf Salad 540	2	12	28	210	2	8	4	2	2
Winter Fruit Salad 538	1	36	9	5	4	60	0	2	2
SALAD DRESSINGS									
Blue Cheese Dressing 551	1	1	6	90	2	0	2	2	0
Blue Cheese Yogurt Dressing 552	1	1	1	100	0	0	0	2	0
Buttermilk Dressing 550	0	1	7	110	0	0	0	0	0
Classic French Dressing 548	0	1	10	205	0	0	0	0	0
Cooked Salad Dressing 549	1	2	1	80	0	0	0	0	0
Creamy Low-Cal Dressing 553	2	1	1	80	0	0	2	0	0
Cucumber Yogurt Dressing 552	0	1	0	75	0	0	0	0	0
French Dressing 548	0	1	9	90	0	0	0	0	0
Fruit Salad Yogurt Dressing 552	0	2	1	5	0	0	0	0	0
Ginger-Honey Dressing 549	0	7	5	100	0	0	0	0	0

Per Serving or Unit	Protein (grams)	Carbohydrates (grams)	Fat (grams)	Sodium (milligrams)	Percent U.S. Recommended Daily Allowance				
Recipe, Page					Vitamin A	Vitamin C	Protein	Calcium	Iron
SALADS *continued*									
Green Goddess Dressing 551	1	1	6	250	2	2	0	0	0
Herbed Vinegar 546	0	1	0	0	0	0	0	0	0
Italian Dressing 547	0	1	11	110	0	0	0	0	0
Mayonnaise 550	0	0	14	35	0	0	0	0	0
Mock Mayonnaise 552	1	1	2	50	0	0	0	2	0
No-Oil Dressing 553	0	4	0	110	0	2	0	0	0
Orange-Pecan Dressing 548	0	2	8	75	0	4	0	0	0
Poppy Seed Dressing 547	0	6	9	90	0	0	0	0	0
Raspberry Vinegar 546	0	5	0	0	0	0	0	0	0
Thousand Island Dressing 551	1	3	4	110	2	0	0	0	0
SOUPS/SANDWICHES/SAUCES									
SOUPS									
Beef and Broth 561									
Beef	122	0	39	300	2	0	190	4	85
Broth	5	8	3	5430	0	0	8	2	0
Black Bean Soup 577	13	14	6	460	30	10	20	6	15
Cheddar Cheese Soup 575	20	8	27	950	20	4	30	50	4
Chicken and Broth 557									
Chicken	115	0	28	300	4	0	180	6	25
Broth	15	3	4	2330	0	0	20	2	8
Chicken and Leek Soup 560	23	14	5	870	30	10	35	2	8
Chicken Noodle Soup 558	23	10	6	775	55	4	35	2	10
Chicken-Vegetable Chowder 558	19	13	11	660	20	45	30	30	6

Per Serving or Unit				Percent U.S. Recommended Daily Allowance				
Recipe, Page	Protein (grams)	Carbohydrates (grams)	Fat (grams)	Sodium (milligrams)	Vitamin A	Vitamin C	Protein	Calcium	Iron

SOUPS/SANDWICHES/SAUCES continued

	Protein (grams)	Carbohydrates (grams)	Fat (grams)	Sodium (milligrams)	Vitamin A	Vitamin C	Protein	Calcium	Iron
Cold Cucumber Soup 578	3	6	1	345	0	15	4	8	2
Corn Chowder 572	10	35	16	540	10	20	15	20	6
Cream of Mushroom Soup 570	8	14	20	1190	15	10	10	8	6
Cream of Vegetable Soup 569	6	16	7	640	90	50	10	15	10
Creamy Broccoli Soup 571	3	6	9	510	35	80	4	6	2
Easy Borsch 573	5	10	3	550	2	20	6	4	4
Egg Drop Soup 559	7	1	4	1170	4	0	10	2	6
French Onion Soup 574	21	18	25	1000	15	15	30	45	8
Fresh Fruit Soup 579	0	31	0	55	2	70	0	0	2
Gazpacho 578	2	10	2	270	15	65	2	2	6
Guacamole Soup 579	2	6	9	430	10	10	2	4	4
Hamburger Minestrone 563	23	23	15	740	30	50	35	10	20
Hearty Tomato Soup 573	6	19	13	790	40	100	8	8	10
Italian Vegetable Soup 564	13	14	9	590	15	25	20	8	10
Lentil-Spinach Soup 576	15	37	7	600	110	40	20	10	25
Manhattan Clam Chowder 564	6	17	8	770	15	45	8	2	8
Mulligatawny Soup 559	29	11	11	630	40	80	45	4	12
Navy Bean Soup 577	11	15	3	360	0	0	15	4	8
New England Chowder 565	9	17	15	610	2	15	15	15	6
Oriental Seafood Soup 567	23	12	2	890	35	20	50	8	15
Quick Fish Soup 567	26	7	8	700	15	90	40	4	8
Salmon-Wild Rice Soup 568	24	14	14	1110	8	8	35	25	10
Scotch Broth 563	26	20	6	830	80	20	40	6	15
Shrimp Gumbo 566	18	44	11	1360	50	120	25	25	25
Split Pea Soup 576	35	38	8	1080	40	4	55	4	30
Vegetable Beef Soup 562	22	20	7	1210	35	40	35	4	20

Per Serving or Unit Recipe, Page	Protein (grams)	Carbohydrates (grams)	Fat (grams)	Sodium (milligrams)	Percent U.S. Recommended Daily Allowance				
					Vitamin A	Vitamin C	Protein	Calcium	Iron
SOUPS/SANDWICHES/SAUCES *continued*									
Vegetable-Pasta Soup 574	17	42	8	365	15	35	25	10	20
Wild Rice Soup 569	9	26	18	1190	65	50	15	10	10
Zucchini Soup 571	8	12	8	720	15	10	10	15	4
SANDWICHES									
Baked Vegetable Slices 596	18	40	38	870	10	6	25	40	10
Barbecue Hamburgers 584	27	34	22	940	8	10	40	6	20
Beef-Baguette Slices 581	27	23	18	350	2	4	60	4	20
Chicken-Avocado Sandwiches 591	20	20	28	475	15	10	30	8	10
Chicken Salad Filling 591	16	2	26	500	2	2	25	2	4
Chili Burgers 584	26	30	26	415	15	20	40	15	20
Chili-Cheese Sandwiches 595	23	40	23	1070	20	30	35	50	15
Chili Dogs 586	12	30	19	995	15	60	20	4	15
Denver Sandwiches 593	16	27	19	705	10	20	35	8	15
Eggs in Buns 594	15	23	25	865	20	0	30	15	15
Eggs with Wine Sauce 594	19	25	25	825	15	2	45	4	10
Franks with Sauerkraut 587	10	25	17	1125	0	30	15	6	10
Gyros 585	30	46	23	920	2	10	45	6	10
Ham-Pineapple Sandwiches 590	14	31	7	940	0	25	20	6	10
Hamburgers 583	26	22	22	530	0	0	40	4	20
Heidelberg Sandwiches 589	20	28	49	1705	340	30	30	4	65
Hot Dog Roll-ups 585	8	16	27	850	4	20	10	2	6
Hot Provolone Sandwiches 598	11	17	9	470	6	4	15	25	6

Per Serving or Unit	Protein (grams)	Carbohydrates (grams)	Fat (grams)	Sodium (milligrams)	Percent U.S. Recommended Daily Allowance				
Recipe, Page					Vitamin A	Vitamin C	Protein	Calcium	Iron

SOUPS/SANDWICHES/SAUCES *continued*

Mexican Egg Sandwiches 595	14	14	13	380	10	4	30	15	10
Open-face Hamburgers 583	15	16	11	515	2	2	20	2	10
Pepperoni Calzones 587	13	51	11	665	15	60	20	15	15
Pepperoni Pizza Slices 589	12	35	20	1110	15	10	20	20	10
Philly Beef Sandwiches 581	51	79	33	1505	15	6	80	35	35
Reuben Sandwiches 580	28	39	43	1660	15	15	40	35	20
Sausage Burritos 588	12	31	24	635	6	65	15	10	15
Shrimp Club Sandwiches 593	23	47	26	625	20	20	35	15	25
Sloppy Franks 586	11	26	21	1010	10	45	15	4	10
Sloppy Joes 582	19	27	15	780	4	30	30	4	15
Submarine Sandwich 590	26	50	27	1720	15	95	40	25	20
Super Grilled Cheese 596	21	33	37	710	25	15	30	50	15
Tuna Patty Sandwiches 592	26	28	32	1445	20	10	40	20	15
Turkey Puff Sandwiches 590	26	22	12	260	0	0	40	4	12
Veggie-filled Croissants 597	15	23	23	480	25	30	20	35	8
SAUCES									
Barbecue Sauce 604	0	3	2	135	6	4	0	0	0
Brown Sauce 601	0	1	2	100	0	0	0	0	0
Cherry Sauce 607	0	7	0	5	2	0	0	0	0
Cocktail Sauce 603	1	4	0	260	4	4	0	0	0
Cream Mustard Sauce 603	0	0	3	35	2	0	0	0	0
Hollandaise Sauce 600	1	0	9	80	6	0	0	0	0
Horseradish Sauce 602	0	1	3	75	2	0	0	0	0

Per Serving or Unit Recipe, Page	Protein (grams)	Carbohydrates (grams)	Fat (grams)	Sodium (milligrams)	Percent U.S. Recommended Daily Allowance				
					Vitamin A	Vitamin C	Protein	Calcium	Iron
SOUPS/SANDWICHES/SAUCES *continued*									
Italian Tomato Sauce 605	0	2	1	85	4	15	0	0	0
Mexican Casera Sauce 604	0	1	0	5	0	2	0	0	0
Orange-Mustard Sauce 607	0	14	0	50	0	2	0	0	0
Pesto 607	2	2	9	60	4	2	2	8	6
Raisin Sauce 606	0	6	0	5	0	0	0	0	0
Spicy Barbecue Sauce 605	0	1	5	165	4	2	0	0	0
Sweet-and-Sour Sauce 606	1	32	1	330	6	70	0	0	2
Tartar Sauce 603	0	1	11	105	0	2	0	0	0
Velouté Sauce 602	0	1	2	100	0	0	0	0	0
White Sauce 599	1	1	2	60	0	0	0	2	0
VEGETABLES									
Artichoke Hearts Sauté 614	2	5	8	45	2	8	2	0	2
Asparagus in Puff Pastry 616	5	14	22	390	10	10	6	6	6
Au Gratin Potatoes 661	17	37	23	760	15	50	25	40	8
Baked Asparagus 616	3	3	26	280	30	25	4	2	4
Baked Cauliflower 634	4	11	9	240	8	100	6	6	6
Baked Herbed Artichokes 615	2	4	12	420	10	10	4	4	4
Baked Plum Tomatoes 673	5	11	7	410	25	40	8	10	6
Baked Squash Casserole 666	3	15	12	430	95	20	4	8	4
Baked Stuffed Tomatoes 672	3	8	1	460	20	30	4	6	4
Baked Whole Onions 649	3	11	9	170	10	22	4	8	4
Beans and Sour Cream 620	9	25	9	250	15	35	15	10	15
Bok Choy au Gratin 624	4	9	9	210	65	40	6	20	6

Per Serving or Unit Recipe, Page	Protein (grams)	Carbohydrates (grams)	Fat (grams)	Sodium (milligrams)	Percent U.S. Recommended Daily Allowance				
					Vitamin A	Vitamin C	Protein	Calcium	Iron
VEGETABLES *continued*									
Bok Choy Oriental Style 623	2	5	4	390	60	40	4	15	5
Broccoli Pie 625	9	11	9	520	50	130	15	20	8
Broccoli with Cheese 626	12	4	14	830	40	80	25	35	4
Broiled Eggplant 641	7	16	12	665	10	4	10	10	8
Broiled Zucchini 663	2	6	8	365	20	30	2	6	4
Cabbage and Sour Cream 631	2	4	8	240	8	40	2	6	4
Cabbage Strudels 630	3	13	18	420	15	25	4	8	4
Candied Sweet Potatoes 667	2	48	9	400	140	20	2	4	8
Carrot Casserole 633	2	11	7	345	235	15	4	6	6
Celery Polynesian 636	2	11	1	840	10	30	2	6	4
Cheese Cauliflower 634	12	13	17	655	15	150	15	25	8
Corn and Cheese 640	7	29	8	290	15	20	10	8	8
Corn Oysters 640	6	25	12	580	6	2	8	6	8
Corn with Basil 638	2	15	3	180	10	20	4	0	4
Creole Lima Beans 621	4	15	0	475	10	25	6	2	6
Curried Peas 654	7	16	9	250	15	25	10	15	8
Dilled Zucchini 664	2	6	5	195	10	8	2	4	4
French-fried Broccoli 627	8	21	16	580	60	170	10	12	10
French-fried Onions 649	7	28	17	310	2	20	10	6	6
French-fried Potatoes 659	3	26	11	180	0	20	4	0	4
Glazed Carrots 633	1	18	4	260	180	8	0	4	4
Glazed Parsnips 651	2	18	4	330	8	20	2	6	4
Glazed Rutabagas 675	1	14	8	750	20	50	2	8	2
Harvard Beets 622	1	12	0	450	0	10	0	0	2
Hashed Browns 662	4	27	13	340	4	50	6	0	6
Herbed Green Beans 618	2	7	5	20	20	35	4	6	6
Honeyed Beets 622	1	9	3	520	4	8	0	0	0
Italian-style Beans 619	2	10	16	845	10	25	4	8	6

Per Serving or Unit Recipe, Page	Protein (grams)	Carbohydrates (grams)	Fat (grams)	Sodium (milligrams)	Percent U.S. Recommended Daily Allowance				
					Vitamin A	Vitamin C	Protein	Calcium	Iron
VEGETABLES *continued*									
Leeks in Tomato Sauce 645	4	23	3	295	100	170	6	15	15
Lemon-Chive Potatoes 657	3	20	6	340	6	35	4	0	4
Maple Acorn Squash 665	3	34	4	10	115	25	4	6	6
Mashed Potatoes 658	3	22	10	340	8	35	6	4	4
Mushrooms and Cucumbers 646	3	7	6	250	6	10	4	4	6
Mustard Kohlrabi 675	2	5	6	390	4	60	2	4	2
Okra Skillet 648	7	20	21	200	30	50	10	10	10
Onions and Carrots 650	1	7	7	180	70	35	2	4	4
Panfried Tomatoes 671	4	22	21	970	45	25	6	4	8
Parmesan Peas 654	5	11	1	305	10	20	8	2	10
Parmesan Sprouts 628	5	7	9	160	15	130	8	8	6
Parsnip Cakes 652	6	30	21	900	6	20	8	8	8
Pea Pods and Peppers 637	4	10	7	170	10	70	6	2	6
Peas and Onions 653	6	16	5	345	15	35	10	4	10
Peppers and Cauliflower 656	3	8	4	565	10	180	4	6	4
Potato Planks 659	2	15	2	365	2	25	2	0	2
Potatoes with Toppers 660	6	44	6	25	6	60	10	6	8
Ratatouille 642	3	14	10	940	25	100	6	4	10
Raw Fries 660	6	44	12	890	4	80	10	2	8
Rutabaga-Potato Whip 675	2	15	6	1010	10	40	2	4	2
Saucy Green Beans 618	1	8	8	230	20	20	2	4	4
Sautéed Mushrooms 647	4	13	15	430	10	25	6	2	6
Sautéed Peppers 655	3	10	13	440	25	250	4	6	8
Savoy Cabbage and Bacon 629	2	7	9	140	6	70	2	6	2
Scalloped Corn 638	6	25	12	740	20	50	10	4	8
Scalloped Potatoes 662	7	35	11	500	8	50	12	15	6
Sesame Peas 653	5	10	13	270	15	20	6	2	8

Per Serving or Unit Recipe, Page	Protein (grams)	Carbohydrates (grams)	Fat (grams)	Sodium (milligrams)	Percent U.S. Recommended Daily Allowance				
					Vitamin A	Vitamin C	Protein	Calcium	Iron
VEGETABLES *continued*									
Skillet Cherry Tomatoes 671	2	8	4	230	30	60	2	2	6
Skillet Corn 639	3	16	7	210	10	10	4	0	2
Spinach Soufflé 644	11	13	19	960	190	50	18	20	20
Squash with Salsa 666	3	13	6	280	25	50	6	8	8
Stewed Tomatoes 670	3	15	1	320	25	60	4	2	6
Stir-fried Asparagus 617	2	5	7	375	15	25	2	2	2
Stir-fried Cabbage 629	3	16	14	1100	15	105	4	8	4
Succotash 620	11	31	18	360	10	30	15	8	15
Sweet Potato Mallow 669	4	40	8	320	200	30	6	6	6
Sweet Potato Slices 668	5	55	2	630	240	50	8	10	10
Sweet-sour Red Cabbage 630	2	18	3	690	2	60	4	6	4
Tomatoes and Artichokes 672	4	15	11	215	15	30	6	6	15
Turnips with Cheese 674	4	5	3	100	95	80	6	20	6
Twice-baked Potatoes 660	6	44	12	430	10	65	10	4	8
Twice-baked Yams 669	5	49	11	105	110	25	8	4	8
Wilted Spinach 643	3	5	11	270	120	40	4	8	10
Zucchini-Pepper Skillet 664	2	10	7	555	20	110	4	4	6

INDEX

A

Acorn cookies, 188
Acorn squash, 665
Alexander pie, 161
Allemande sauce, 602
Almond
  bark fudge, 204
  brickle cookies, 168
  brownies, 176–77
  butter crunch, 206
  pound cake, 113–14
  taffy, 208–9
  topping, 133
  truffles, 204–5
  velvet sauce, 602
  white cake, 111–12
Ambrosia, fruit, 224
Ambrosia salad mold, 533
Angel biscuits, 63
Angel food cake(s), 123–25
Angel toffee dessert, 267
Appetizers, 3–28. *See also*
      Beverages; Dip(s);
      Spread(s).
  barbecued ribs, 12
  caviar classic, 5
  celery sticks, stuffed, 7
  cheese board, 8–9
  cheesy bagel bites, 7–8
  chili-cheese balls, 8
  cucumbers and shrimp, 522
  eggs
    deviled, 16
    pickled, 16–17
  ham phyllo rolls, 15–16

meatballs, cocktail, 10
melon and prosciutto, 3
mushrooms
  marinated, 6
  stuffed, 5
nuts, Oriental-style, 17
olives and onions, 7
oysters
  Parmesan, 4
  Rockefeller, 4
pizza bites, 12–13
popcorn, 14
  Parmesan-curry, 17–18
potato skins, broiled, 9
rumaki, 13
sandwiches, party, 14–15
sauerkraut balls, 11
sausage(s)
  -cheese chips, 14
  cocktail, 10
shrimp
  -bacon bites, 13–14
  cocktail, 3
soups, 557–79
vegetables, dilled, 6
Apple(s). *See also* applesauce.
  avocado-, salad, 541
  baked, 219–20
  butter, 716
  cake, 118
    spiced, upside-down, 115
  caramel, 214
    bars, 182
  -cheese coleslaw, 516
  -cherry salad, 530
  chocolate-caramel, 213–14

Apple(s) *(continued)*
crisp, 220
dumplings, 142
muffins, 46
-pear salad, 540
-pepper jelly, 713–14
pie(s), 138–39
pudding, 252
-raisin stuffing, 472
rings, glazed, 219
squares, 141
tart, -cinnamon, 140–41
Waldorf salads, 540–41
Applesauce, 220
cake(s), 117
cookies, 173
Apricot
aperitif, 32
-banana cream, 221
crisp, 221
-glazed peaches, 231
-glazed pears, 231
pie(s), 148
-prune upside-down cake, 115
rum cake, 116
salad, molded, 530–31
spiced, mold, 534
truffles, 205
Artichoke(s), French, 613. *See
also* Jerusalem artichokes.
hearts sauté, 614
rice with, 86
salad, 529–30
tomatoes and, 672
Asparagus, 615–16
baked, 616
in puff pastry, 616
salad, 513
stir-fried, 617
Au gratin potatoes, 661
Au gratin vegetables 611
Autumn roast chicken, 444
Avocado(s)
-apple salad, 541
chicken-, sandwiches, 591–92
dessert, whipped, 221
guacamole, 19

soup, 579
orange-, salad, 543

B
Bacon, 426–27. *See also*
Canadian-style bacon.
curls, 426
guacamole, 19
omelet, 285
rumaki, 13
shrimp-, bites, 13–14
Bagel(s)
bites, cheesy, 7–8
egg, 65
Baked Alaska, chocolate, 267–68
Baking powder biscuits, 42
Banana(s)
apricot-, cream, 221
bread, 57
Caribbean, 222
cream pie, 153
-nut cake, 118–19
Banana squash, 665
Barbecue hamburgers, 584
Barbecue sauce(s), 604–5
Barbecued ribs, 12
Barley, 84
-vegetable beef soup, 562
with mushrooms, 88
Bavarian, orange, 261
Bean(s). *See also specific kind.*
baked, 304–8
chalupas, 309
chili, with dumplings, 311–12
red, and rice, 312–13
refried, bake, 313
skillet, 314
three-, casserole, 311
three-, salad, 515
Western-style, 312
Béarnaise sauce, 600
Beef, 354–90
about, 354–56
and broth, 561
-baguette slices, 581
brisket barbecue, 361
Burgundy popovers, 373

Beef *(continued)*
  corned, *See* Corned beef.
  cuts, 352–53
  ground. *See* Ground beef.
  hash, 374
  pot roast. *See* Pot roast(s).
  ragout, 436
  roast, 356
    carving, 355–56
  salad filling, 591
  salads, 498–500
  sandwiches, 580–84
  sesame, 374–75
  shanks, braised, 395
  short ribs, 375
  soups, 561–63
  steak(s)
    beef with mustard sauce, 365–66
    broiled, 362–63
    fajitas, 369–70
    London broil, 364
    minute, mushroom, 365
    mushroom, 366
    Provençale, 367
    Swiss, 368
  stew, 372–73
    oxtail, 373
    Provençale, 367
  stir-fried, 371–72
  stroganoff, 370
  teriyaki, 364–65
  tongue, glazed, 398
Beer, tomato-, cooler, 30
Beet(s), 621–23
  borsch, easy, 573
  Harvard, 622
  honeyed, 622–23
  orange, 622
  pickled, 519
  tops, 642
Berry-wine salad, 531
Beverages, 29–38
  apricot aperitif, 32
  brandy cream, 32
  chocolate, 33–34
  cocoa, hot, 33
  coffee, 34–36
  fruit brandy cream, 32
  lemonades, 31
  limeade, 31
  milk shakes, 32–33
  pink colada, 31
  punches, 29–30
  strawberry spritzer, 31–32
  tea, 36–38
  tomato-beer cooler, 30
Biscuit(s)
  angel, 63
  baking powder, 42
  basics, 41
  blue cheese, 42
  buttermilk, 42
  cornmeal, 42
  drop, 42
  herb, 42
Black bean(s)
  baked, 305
  soup, 577
Blackberry pie, 143
Black-eyed peas
  hoppin' John, 313
Blanching vegetables, 701–2
Blintzes, cherry, 247
Blue cheese
  biscuits, 42
  dressing, 551
  to crumble, 681
  yogurt dressing, 552
Blueberry
  cobbler, fresh, 222–23
  muffins, 46
  pancakes, 45
  pies, 143, 151
  waffles, 44–45
Boiling water processing, 708–9
Bok choy, 623–24
  au gratin, 624
  Oriental style, 623–24
Bologna, macaroni-, salad, 488
Bonbons, easy, 211
Bordelaise sauce, 601
Borsch, easy, 573
Boston baked beans, 304–6

Bourbon balls, 211
Boysenberry pie, 143
Brains, 398–99
Bran
  -oatmeal bread, 71–72
  -raisin muffins, 47
Brandy
  Alexander bars, 176
  balls, 211
  chocolate mousse, 262
  cream, 32
  fruit, cream, 32
  -pecan pie, 157–58
Bratwurst in beer, 425
Brazil nut bars, 177
Bread(s). *See also* Coffee cake(s);
      Roll(s); Sweet roll(s).
  quick, 41–57
    about, 41
    banana, 57
    biscuits, 42
    corn, 54
    cranberry-orange, 56
    dumplings, 43–44
    Gruyère puff ring, 53
    Irish soda bread, 52
    muffins, 46–47
    popovers, 52–53
    pumpkin, 56
    scones, 43
    spoon, 55
    zucchini, 55–56
  yeast, 58–83
    about, 58, 59, 60
    bagels, egg, 65
    biscuits, angel, 63
    bran-oatmeal, 71–72
    breadsticks, 64
    brioches, 67–68
    casserole, 72–73
    cinnamon-raisin, 66
    English muffins, 62–63
    French, 68–69
    garlic, 69
    herb-cheese, 69
    honey-whole wheat, 70–71
    onion, 69

      pumpernickel, dark, 69–70
      white, traditional, 66
Bread and butter pickles,
      719
Bread crumbs, 681
Bread pudding, 252
Bread stuffing, 472
Breadsticks, soft, 64
  whole wheat, 64
Brioche(s), 67–68
  individual, 67–68
Broccoli, 624–25
  French-fried, 627
  omelet, oven, 287
  pie(s), 295, 625–26
  soufflé, 644
  soup, creamy, 571–72
  with cheese, 626
Broth
  beef, 561
  chicken, 557
Brown rice, 85
  savory mixed rice, 87
Brown sauce, 601
  spicy, 601
Brown sugar
  glaze, 417
  measuring, 683
  meringue, 155
Brownies
  almond, 176–77
  brandy Alexander bars, 176
  Brazil nut bars, 177
  butterscotch, 177
    coconut-, 177
    date-, 177
  cocoa, 175–76
  deluxe, 175
  grasshopper bars, 176
  mint bars, 176
Brunswick stew, 455
Brussels sprouts, 627
  Parmesan sprouts, 628
Buckwheat pancakes, 45
Bulgur, 84
  beef-, salad, 498
  pilaf, 90

Bulgur *(continued)*
-tomato salad, 503
wheat-stuffed drumsticks, 457
Burritos, sausage, 588
Butter(s)
black, 612
browned, 612
drawn, 612
frosting, browned, 129
-rum glaze, 132
seasoned, 612
storage, 692, 695
Buttercup squash, 665
Buttermilk
biscuits, 42
dip, 20
doughnuts, 51
dressing, 550
fried chicken, 445
mayonnaise-, dressing, 550
pancakes, 45
Butternut squash, 665
Butterscotch
brownies, 177
-pecan rolls, 77
pudding, 250
sauce, 271
slices, 191
sundae cake, 235

C
Cabbage, 628. *See also*
Coleslaw.
and sour cream, 631–32
Chinese or celery, 631
green, 628
mold confetti, 527–28
red, 630
sweet-sour, 630
rolls, stuffed, 383–84
salad, 517
savoy, 629
and bacon, 629
soup, creamy, 572
stir-fried, 629
strudels, 630–31
Caesar salad(s) 509–10

Café au lait, 35
Cajun crabmeat mold, 27–28
Cake(s), 103–27. *See also* Cake
desserts; Cupcakes;
Torte.
almond
pound, 114
white, 111
angel food, 124–25
apple, 118
spiced, upside-down, 115
applesauce, 117
apricot
-prune upside-down, 115
rum, 116
baking, about, 103–5, 123–24
banana-nut, 118–19
carrot, 118
cherry-nut, 111
chiffon, 126–27
chocolate
angel food, 125
-cherry, 110
cocoa fudge, 108
cocoa spice, 108
devils food, red, 108
double, 110
German, 109–10
ice-cream roll, 126
mousse, 106–7
sour cream, 107
-spice, 110
triple fudge, 108
-walnut, 110
chocolate chip white, 111–12
coconut angel food, 125
date-chocolate chip, 116–17
devils food, red, 108
eggnog, 112
frostings. *See* Frosting(s).
fruit-topped, 115–16
fruitcake, jeweled, 123
German chocolate 109–10
glazes. *See* Glaze(s), cake.
hazelnut, 112
jelly roll, 125–26
layer, basics, 103–4

Cake(s) *(continued)*
 lemon
  chiffon, 126–27
  -filled white, 112
  -filled yellow, 112
  pound, 113–14
  roll, 126
 maple-nut, 111
 maraschino cherry, 113
 marble, 113
 oatmeal-molasses, 111
 orange
  chiffon, 127
  -coconut pound, 114
  Williamsburg, 120
 peanut, 113
 pineapple
  -apricot, 119–20
  upside-down, 114–15
 pound, 113–14
 prune-walnut, 120
 pumpkin, 111
 rhubarb, 122
 sheet, silver white, 112
 silver white, 111
 sour cream spice, 121
 spice, 121, 122
  chocolate-, 110
  cocoa, 108
 sponge, 123–24
 toppings, 133
 upside-down, 114–15
 white, 111
 Williamsburg orange, 120
 yellow, 112–13
 zucchini spice, 122
Cake desserts
 gingerbread, 239
 plantation cake, 238–39
 pudding cake
  lemon, 236
  lime, 236
  plum, 237
 rum-cracker torte, 237–38
 sundae cake
  butterscotch, 235
  hot fudge, 235

  mallow, 235
  peanutty, 236
  raisin, 236
California hamburgers, 583
California-style potato salad, 524
Calzones
 ground beef, 588
 pepperoni, 587–88
Canadian-style bacon, 427
 bacon-cheese pastries, 427
Candied citrus peel, 212
Candied sweet potatoes, 667
Candy(-ies), 201–11. *See also*
  Sweet snacks.
 about, making, 201–2
 almond
  bark fudge, 204
  butter crunch, 206
  taffy, 208–9
  truffles, 204–5
 apricot truffles, 205
 bars, 168
 bonbons, easy, 211
 bourbon balls, 211
 brandy balls, 211
 caramels, 207
 cashew
  clusters, 209–10
  truffles, 205
 cherry truffles, 205
 chocolate caramels, 207
 cocoa fudge, 203
 coconut clusters, 210
 cookies, 168
 divinity, 205
 fudge, 202–4
 mint wafers, 211
 orange truffles, 205
 peanut brittle, 206–7
 peanut butter
  bars, 210
  cups, 210
  fudge, 203
 penuche, 203
 peppermint taffy, 209
 pralines, 207–8
 raisin clusters, 210

Candy(-ies) *(continued)*
  raisin-nut clusters, 210
  rum balls, 211
  sponge, 208
  taffy, 208–9
  tests for, 202
  truffles, 204–5
  turtle, easy, 209
Canning, 699–701, 704–12
  boiling water processing,
    708–9
  green beans, 708
  information sources, 701
  peaches, 710–11
  pressure canner processing,
    707–8
  safety, 700–1, 705–6
  sugar syrups, 710
  tomatoes, 711–12
  yields, 699–700
Cantaloupe. *See also* Melon.
  dessert, 230
  salads, 542
  tuna-, salads, 492–94
Caramel
  apple(s), 214
    bars, 182
  corn, 213
  custard, 248–49
  fluff, 133
  frosting, 130
  -nut corn, 212–13
  -oat bars, 181–82
  popcorn balls, 213
  sauce, 271
Caramels, 207
Caraway salt, 406
Caribbean bananas, 222
Carrot(s), 632
  cake, 118
  casserole, 633
  cookies, 172
  glazed, 633
  onions and, 650
  -pineapple salad, 528
  -raisin salad, 519–20
  salad, marinated, 519

Cashew
  clusters, 209–10
  triangles, 179
  truffles, 204–5
Casserole breads, 72–73
Catfish, creole, 319–20
Cauliflower, 634
  baked, 634–35
  cheese, 634
  peppers and, 656
  salad, 520
  soup, creamy, 572
Caviar classic, 5
Celery, 635
  Polynesian, 636
  sticks, stuffed, 7
Celery cabbage, 631
Chalupas, 309
Chayote, 663
Cheddar cheese soup, 575
Cheese, 293–303. *See also*
    Egg(s); *specific kind.*
  about, 293–95
  and bacon waffles, 45
  bacon-, pastries, 427
  ball, 21
  board, 8–9
  casserole bread, 72–73
  cheesecake. *See* Cheesecake.
  chili-, balls, 8
  dumplings, 43–44
  enchiladas, 302–3
  fondue, 303
    kielbasa in, 21
  four-, fettuccine, 94–95
  French bread bake, cheesy,
    301
  fruit-, kabobs with ginger dip,
    20
  grits, cheesy, 89
  macaroni and, 298–99
  macaroni-, salad, 488
  manicotti, 299–300
  omelet, 285
  pie, 296
  pizza, 297–98
  quiches, 296–97

Cheese (*continued*)
  salsa, bake, 25
  sandwiches, 14–15, 595–98
  sauce, 599
  sausage-, chips, 14
  shrimp-, strata, 26
  soufflé, 292
  spread, baked, 24
  strata, 300
  turnips with, 674
  varieties, 293–95
  Welsh rabbit, 301–2
Cheeseburger(s), 583
  pie, impossible, 384
Cheesecake
  chocolate, 243–44
  lemon, 244
  Lindy's, 241
    squares, 241–42
  peanut, 242
  pumpkin, 244
Chef's salad, 498
Cherry(-ies)
  and kiwifruit, 224
  blintzes, 247
  cobbler, fresh, 223
  cordial pie, 161
  -cream cheese cookies, 173
  crisp, 221
  freeze, 265–66
  frostings, 128–31
  jam, 715
  jubilee, 223
  layer dessert, 264
  layered salad, 531–32
  milk shakes, 33
  -nut cake, 111
  pie(s), 144–46
  sauce, 607
  tarts, glazed, 145–46
  truffles, 204–5
Chèvre
  burgers, 377–78
  pâté, 24
Chicken, 441–66. *See also*
    Turkey.
  a la king, 462
  about, 441
  and broth, 557
  and brown gravy, 475
  and leek soup, 560
  and peppers, 461
  -avocado sandwiches, 591–92
  batter-fried, 446
  broiled, 450–51
  Brunswick stew, 455
  carving, 472
  cilantro, 461
  coating, 681
  cordon bleu, oven, 460
  curry, 459
  cutting up, 443
  dinner casserole, 465
  drumsticks, wheat-stuffed, 457
  fricassee, 452
  fried, 445–46
  fried rice, 416
  giblets, 442
  golden nuggets, 446–47
  in potato shells, 382
  in red wine, 453
  jambalaya, 454–55
  Kiev, oven, 460
  livers
    rumaki, 13
    with bacon, 449
    with sour cream, 450
  macaroni casserole, 463–64
  noodle soup, 558
  oven-barbecued, 447–48
  oven-fried, 445–46
    crunchy, 446
  paprika, 456
  -pasta primavera, 464
  piccata, 413
  poached, 451
  quiche, 297
  rice soup, 558
  -rice supper, 465–66
  roast, 441–42, 444
  salad(s), 481–85
    -bacon, 483
    club, 483
    cups, 484

Chicken (*continued*)
  curried, 485
  filling, 591
  fruited, 483
  macaroni, 488, 493
  marinated, 482
  Oriental, 481–82
  -wild rice, 489
  sandwiches, 591–92
  slices, baked, 597
  soups, 557–60
  spaghetti and, sauce, 381
  stewed, 451–52
  stir-fried, 448–49
  tandoori-style, 461–62
  tostadas, 463
  -vegetable chowder, 558–59
  with vegetables, 454
  with yogurt, 458
Chicory, 642
Chiffon cakes, 126–27
Chiffon pies, 160
Chili
  beans with dumplings,
    311–12
  burgers, 584
  -cheese balls, 8
  -cheese sandwiches, 595–96
  -chicken, broiled, 450–51
  Cincinnati-style, 387
  con carne, 387
    easy, 387
  corn bread, 54
  dip, zippy, 18
  dogs, 586
  slices, baked, 597
Chinese cabbage, 631
Chinese-fried shrimp, 339–40
Chinese pea pods, 636
  and peppers, 637
Chive omelet, 285
Chocolate. *See also* Chocolate
    chip; Cocoa.
  baked Alaska, 267–68
  cakes. *See* Cake(s).
  -caramel apples, 213–14
  caramels, 207

cashew clusters, 209–10
cheesecake, 243–44
coconut clusters, 210
cookies. *See* Cookies.
cream, frozen, 266
cream puffs, 245
curls, 681
frango, 266–67
frostings. *See* Frosting(s).
fudge, 202–3
granola bark, 215
hot, 33
  Mexican, 34
ice cream, 268
  sandwich cookie, 268
malts, 33
-marshmallow bars, 214
melting, 681
milk shakes, 32
mousse, 262
  brandy, 262
-nut logs, 189
pies. *See* Pie(s).
popcorn balls, 213
pots de crème, 249–50
pudding, 250
  steamed, 254–55
raisin clusters, 210
raisin-nut clusters, 210
sauces, 272
s'more bars, 215
soufflé, baked, 240
truffles, 204–5
Chocolate chip
  cookies. *See* Cookies, choco-
    late chip.
  glaze, 132–33
  white cake, 111–12
Choucroute, 422–23
Chow mein
  fruit salad, 539
  pork, 416
Chowder
  chicken-vegetable, 558–59
  clam
    Manhattan, 564–65
    New England, 565

Chowder *(continued)*
  corn, 572
Chutney
  peach, fresh, 718
  pear, fresh, 718
  pineapple, fresh, 717–18
  plum, fresh, 718
Cider
  hot orange, 30
  wassail, 29
Cincinnati-style chili, 387
Cinnamon
  meringue, 259
  oranges, 228
  -raisin bread, 66
  rolls, 77
Citrus. *See also specific kind.*
  peel, candied, 212
  salad, 532
Clam(s)
  chowder
    Manhattan, 564–65
    New England, 565
  deep-fried, 349
  panfried, 349
  steamed, 343
Cloverleaf rolls, 75
Club sandwiches, 593
  shrimp, 593
Cobblers, 222–23
Cocktail meatballs, 10
Cocktail sauce, 603
Cocktail sausages, 10
Cocoa
  brownies, 175–76
  drop cookies, 171
  fluff, 133
  frosting, 129
    creamy, 132
  fudge, 203
    cake, 108
    cupcakes, 108
  hot, 33
  pecan torte, 106
  spice cake, 108
  triple fudge cake, 108
Coconut

angel food cake, 125
  -butterscotch brownies, 177
  clusters, 210
  -macadamia bars, 174
  -macadamia cookies, 174
  macaroons, 173–74
  measuring, 683
  orange-, pound cake, 114
  pies, 152–53, 159
  slices, toasted, 191
  snowballs, 270
  tinted, 681
  toasted, 681
Coconutty-marshmallow bars,
  214
Cod and vegetable bake, 322–23
Coffee
  about, 34–35
  café au lait, 35
  cordial pie, 161
  frosting, 129
  Irish, 35–36
  large-quantity, 36
  -peach meringue, 259
Coffee cake(s). *See also* Sweet
  roll(s).
  Danish kringle, 82
  Danish strip, 80
  honey twist, 78
  raisin-spice, 48
  sour cream, 49
  streusel, 48
Coleslaw, 515
  apple-cheese, 516
  cabbage salad, 517
  confetti slaw, 516–17
  pineapple-marshmallow, 516
  sweet-sour cabbage slaw,
    516
Collards, 642
Colorful cookies, 187–88
Compotes, fruit, 225–26
Confetti cabbage mold, 527–28
Confetti slaw, 516–17
Conserves, pear, 716
Cooked salad dressings, 549
Cookie crumb pie crust, 138

Cookies, 165–200
  about, making, 165–67
  acorn, 188
  almond brickle, 168
  applesauce, 173
  bar, 166, 175–83
  brownies. *See* Brownies.
  butterscotch slices, 191
  candy, 168
    bars, 168
    teacakes, surprise, 189
  caramel
    -apple bars, 182
    -oat bars, 181–82
  carrot, 172
  cashew triangles, 179
  cherry-cream cheese, 173
  chocolate
    -cherry drop, 171
    cocoa drop, 171
    crinkles, 185
    drop, 171
    grasshopper bars, 176
    -mint, 170
    mint bars, 176
    -nut logs, 189
    -nut slices, 190–91
    spritz, 199
  chocolate chip, 167
    bars, 168
    crisp, 168
    jumbo, 168
  coconut
    -macadamia, 174
    -macadamia bars, 174
    macaroons, 173–74
    slices, toasted, 191
  colorful, 187–88
  cream cheese, 173
  date bars, 182
  drop, 165–66, 167–74
  gingerbread people, 198–99
  gingersnaps, 185–86
  hazelnut bars, 179–80
  holiday decorated spritz, 199
  honey-spice, 195
  Italian sweets, 196
  lemon
    -coconut squares, 181
    cookie sandwiches, 192–93
    squares, 181
  macaroons, 173–74
    mint, 174
  mincemeat bars, 182
  mint, hidden, 187
  molasses, jumbo, 198
  molded, 166, 185–90
  Neapolitan, 192
  nut roll-ups, 197
  oatmeal, 169
    -coconut slices, 191
    crispies, 169
    fudgy, bars, 183
    squares, 169
  paintbrush, 194
  peanut butter, 184
    and jelly, 184
    fingers, 184
    squares, 180–81
  peppermint candy canes, 189
  praline bars, easy, 177–78
  pressed (shaped), 167, 198
  pretzel, 186
  refrigerator, 166, 190–93
  rolled, 166–67, 192–99
  rosettes, 200
  Russian teacakes, 189
  Scotch shortbread, 196–97
  sour cream, 193
  spritz, 199
  spumoni, 191–92
  sugar, 193–94
    decorated, 194
    filled, 194
  thumbprint, 190
  toffee bars, 178
  zucchini, 172
Cooking terms, 679–81
Corn, 637–41. *See also* Corn
    bread(s); Cornmeal.
  and cheese, 640
  chowder, 572
  oysters, 640–41
    nutmeg, 641

Corn *(continued)*
 relish, 721
 -relish mold, 528–29
 scalloped, 638–39
  cheese, 639
 skillet, 639
 succotash, 620–21
 with basil, 638
Corn bread(s), 54
 chili, 54
 corn muffins, 54
 corn sticks, 54
 cornmeal biscuits, 42
 onion-cheese, 54
 skillet, 54
 spoon bread, 55
 stuffing, 473
Corn dogs, 426
Corned beef
 and cabbage, 361–62
 hash
  oven, 374
  red flannel skillet, 374
  skillet, 374
 New England boiled dinner,
  362
 Reuben sandwiches, 580
Cornish hens
 about, 441
 with glazed oranges, 475–76
cornmeal, 84
 biscuits, 42
 mush, 89
 noodles, 92
Country broiled chicken,
 450
Country-style ribs, 412
Couscous, lamb and, 435–36
Crab(meat)
 casserole, company, 345
 Dungeness, boiled, 344
 hard-shell, boiled, 344
 mold, Cajun, 27–28
 Newburg with popovers, 347
 quiche, 297
 seafood salad, 483
Cracked wheat, 84

Cranberry
 cran-raspberry mold, 532
 ice, 264
 -orange
  bread, 56
  muffins, 46
 punch
  hot, 29
  sparkling, 30
Cream, whipped. *See* Whipped
 Cream.
Cream cheese
 cookies, 173
 frosting, 130
 -grape toss, 542
Cream pies, 152–53
Cream puffs, 245
 chocolate, 245–46
Creamed eggs, 291
 with ham, 291
 with seafood, 291
Creamed vegetables, 611
Crème brûlée, 249
Crème de cacao topping, 133
Crème de menthe
 meringue, 259
 topping, 133
Creole catfish, 319–20
Creole lima beans, 621
Crepes, 246–47
 raspberry, 247–48
Crescent rolls, 75
Crisps, 220–21
Crookneck squash, 663
Croutons, 681
Crumb crusts for pies, 138
Crumb toppings, 611
Crusts, pie, 134–38
Cucumber(s)
 and shrimp, 522
 and tomatoes, 520–21
 mushrooms and, 646
 pickles, 719–20
 -relish mold, 529
 salad, 521
  creamy, 521
 sandwiches, 14

Cucumber(s) *(continued)*
-shrimp, 14
soup, cold, 578
yogurt dressing, 552
Cupcakes
cocoa fudge, 108
silver white, 112
yellow, 113
Curd, lemon, 717
Curry(ied)
chicken, 459
salad, 485
peas, 654
rice, 87
sauce, 599
shrimp, 459
salad, 489
tuna, 332
Custard
baked, 248–49
caramel, 248
crème brûlée, 249
pie(s), 159
raspberry, 248–49
Cymling squash, 663

D
Danish kringle, 82–83
Danish pastry dough, 79–80
Danish strip, 80
Danish twists, 81
Dark pumpernickel, 69–70
Date
bars, 182
-butterscotch brownies, 177
-chocolate chip cake, 116–17
-nut muffins, 46
Deep-fried foods, 51–52
Denver sandwiches, 593
Dessert(s), 219–70. *See also*
Dessert sauces.
angel toffee, 267
avocado, whipped, 221
Bavarian, orange, 261
blintzes, cherry, 247
cake desserts, 235–39
cakes, 103–27

cantaloupe, 230
cheesecakes, 241–44
cherry freeze, 265–66
cherry layer, 264
chocolate cream, frozen, 266
chocolate frango, 266–67
cobblers, 222–23
cookies, 164–215
cranberry ice, 264
cream puffs, 245–46
crepes, 246–48
crisps, 220–21
custards, 248–49
eclairs, 246
fruit, 219–34. *See also specific
kind.*
ice creams, 268–70
lemon cream, frozen, 264–65
meringues, 258–59
mousse. *See* Mousse.
omelets, orange, 228–29
papaya, 229–30
Pavlova, 258
pies, 134–62
pots de crème, chocolate,
249–50
puddings, 250–55
sherbet-berry parfaits, 265
shortcakes, strawberry, 233–34
soufflé
chocolate, baked, 240
lemon, 260–61
tortes. *See* Torte.
trifle, English, 251
Dessert sauces. *See also*
Whipped cream.
butterscotch, 271
caramel, 271
chocolate, crunchy, 272
fudge, 272
orange, 272
lemon, 273
marshmallow, 272–73
nutmeg, 273
orange, 274
raspberry-currant, 274
rhubarb, 233

Dessert sauces *(continued)*
  strawberry-rhubarb, 233
Deviled eggs, 16
Devils food cake, red, 108
Dill(ed)
  pasta salad, 501
  pickles, 718
  pot roast, 359–60
  sauce, 599
  vegetables, 6
  zucchini, 664
Dinner casserole, 465
Dip(s)
  buttermilk, 20
  fondue, kielbasa in, 21
  ginger, fruit-cheese kabobs
    with, 20
  guacamole, 19
  Mexi-, 18
  spinach, 19
  zippy chili, 18
Divinity, 205
Doughnuts
  buttermilk, 51
  cake, 50
  raised, 61
Drop biscuits, 42
Duchess potatoes, 658
Duck, roast, 441–42
Dumplings, 43
  apple, 142
  cheese, 44
  herb, 44
  parsley, 44
Dungeness crabs, 344
Dutch apple pie, 139

E
Easy main dishes
  beef, 361, 364, 374–75, 378,
    380, 384–85
  cheese, 296, 300
  eggs, 287
  fish and shellfish, 319, 324,
    327, 329–30, 342–43,
    347–48
  pork, 408, 409, 422, 425

  poultry, 461, 463–65, 467–68,
    473–74
Eclairs, 246
Egg(s), 279–92. *See also*
    Custard; Soufflé.
  about, 279–80
  -bacon bake, 291–92
  bagels, 65
  baked, 282
  Benedict, 284–85
    casserole, 283–84
  creamed, 291
    with ham, 291
    with seafood, 291
  deviled, 16
  drop soup, 559
  foo yong, 290
  fried, 281
  frittata, vegetable, 288–89
  hard-cooked, 280–81
  in buns, 594
  in rolls, 289
  noodles, 92
  omelets, 285–88
  on English muffins, 282–83
  on tortillas, 284
  pickled, 16–17
  poached, 281
  poached-fried, 281
  salad filling, 591
  sandwiches, 595
  scrambled, 281–82
    fancy, 282
  shirred, 282
  soft-cooked, 280
  storage, 691, 692, 694
  with wine sauce, 594–95
Eggnog cake, 112
Eggplant, 641–42
  beef-, salad, 499
  broiled, 641–42
  ratatouille, 642
  salad, 517–18
Enchiladas, cheese, 302–3
English muffins, 62–63
English trifle, 251
Equivalent measures, 684

Escarole, 642

F
Fajitas, 369–70
Fan tans, 75
Fettuccine
four-cheese, 94–95
green, 93–94. *See also* Salmon;
Fish, 317–36. *See also* Salmon;
    Seafood; Shellfish;
    Tuna.
a la meunière, 329–30
about, 317–19
and pepper salad, 491–92
baked, 319
    stuffed, 323
batter-fried, 331
carving, 325
catfish, creole, 319–20
cod and vegetable bake,
    322–23
deep-fried, 331
fillets, broiled, 325–26
halibut with grapefruit sauce,
    320–21
in foil, 324
mustard-topped, 327
orange roughy with tarragon,
    327
oven-fried, 330
panfried, 329
smoked, salad, 491
sole, vegetable-stuffed, 321–22
soup, quick, 567–68
steaks, broiled, 324–25
with garlic salsa, 326
Flour
about, 58
measuring, 683
Fondue
cheese, 303
kielbasa in, 21
Swiss cheese, 303
Food groups, basic, 725–26
Food preparation
basics, 681, 684
terms, 679–81, 684

Food safety, 686–88
Four-cheese fettuccine, 94–95
Frankfurters, 425
chili dogs, 586
corn dogs, 426
franks with sauerkraut,
    587
hot dog roll-ups, 585–86
macaroni-frank salad, 488
slices, baked, 596–97
sloppy franks, 586
storage, 687, 692–95
Freezer storage, 691–93
Freezing, 699–705
fruit, 699–700, 703–5
main dishes, 690–91
vegetables, 699–700, 701–2
French apple pie, 139
French bread, 68–69
bake, cheesy, 301
French dressing(s), 548
French-fried broccoli, 627
French-fried onions, 649
French-fried potatoes, 659
French omelet, 285
French onion soup, 574–75
French puffs, 46
French silk pies, 153–54
French strawberry tart, 151–52
French-style beef roast, 359
French toast, 44
Fried rice
chicken, 416
pork, 415–16
Frittata, vegetable, 288–89
Fritters, 51
Frosting(s), 128–32. *See also*
    Glaze(s), cake.
browned butter, 129
caramel, 130
cherry
    creamy, 129
    -nut, 129
chocolate, 131–32
    fudge, 131
    revel, 129
    sour cream, 131

Frosting(s) *(continued)*
  cocoa, 129
    creamy, 132
  coffee, 129
  cream cheese, 130
  fudge, 131
  how-to tips, 128
  lemon, creamy, 129
  maple-nut, 130
  mocha, 132
  orange, creamy, 129
  peanut butter, 130
  peppermint, 129
  pineapple, 130
  satiny beige, 129
  vanilla, creamy, 129
  white mountain, 128–29
Frozen desserts, 264–67. *See
    also* Ice cream.
Fruit(s). *See also specific kind.*
  ambrosia, 224
  brandy cream, 32
  canning, 700–701
  -cheese kabobs with ginger
    dip, 20
  cups, fresh, 225
  desserts, 219–34
  freezing, 699, 703–5
  in orange cream, 224
  pie(s), 138–52
  salad pie, 146–47
  salad(s). *See* Salad(s), fruit.
    frozen, 535
    yogurt dressing, 552
  soup, fresh, 579
  spiced, ham with, 420
  -topped cake, 115–16
  turkey-, salad, 486
  -wine compote, 225–26
  winter-, compote, 225
Fruitcake, jeweled, 123
Fruited chicken salad, 483
Fruited pot roast, 360
Fruited rice stuffing, 471
Fruited turkey salad, 486
Fudge
  almond bark, 204

cake
  cocoa, 108
  triple, 108
  chocolate, 202
  cocoa, 203
  cupcakes, cocoa, 108
  easy, 203
  frosting, 131
  hot, sundae cake, 235
  peanut butter, 203
  sauce, 272
    orange, 272
Fudgy meringue mallow,
    256–57
Fudgy oatmeal bars, 183

G
Game, 475–78
Garbanzo bean salad, 514–15
Garden potato salad, 524
Garlic
  bread, 69
  crumb topping, 611
  -dill pickles, 718
  salsa, fish with, 326
  tomato slices, 524
Gazpacho, 578–79
Gelatin, about, 526
Giant burger, 377
Giblet(s), 442
  stuffing, 473
Ginger(ed)
  dip, fruit-cheese kabobs with,
    20
  ham slice, 421
  -honey dressing, 549
  pineapple, 229
  scallops, broiled, 342
Gingerbread, 239
  people, 198–99
Gingersnaps, 185–86
Glaze(s)
  cake
    butter-rum, 132
    chocolate chip, 132–33
    how-to tips, 128
    lemon, 132

Glaze(s) *(continued)*
  orange, 132
  vanilla, 132
 ham
  brown sugar, 417
  pineapple, 417
Golden nuggets, 446–47
Goose, roast, 441–42
Graham cracker
 pie crust, 138
 torte, 263
Grains, 84–90. *See also specific kind.*
 about, 84–85
Granola
 bark, 215
 pie crust, 138
Grape jelly, rosy, 714
Grasshopper bars, 176
Grasshopper pie, 161
Gravy
 creamy, 358
 pan, 358
 thin, 358
Great northern beans
 savory baked beans, 308
Greek salad, 510
Green beans, 617–18
 canning, 708
 herbed, 618
 Italian-style, 619
 saucy, 618–19
Green chili omelet, 285
Green fettuccine, 93–94
Green goddess dressing, 551
Green lima beans, 619–20. *See also* Lima beans.
Green onions, 650
 onions and carrots, 650
Green peppers, 654–55
 chicken and peppers, 461
 fish and pepper salad, 491–92
 pepper macaroni and cheese, 299
 pepper mostaccioli, 97–98
 pepper potatoes, 661
 peppers and cauliflower, 656

 sautéed peppers, 655
 stuffed peppers, 389–90
 sweet pepper relish, 720–21
 tenderloin with peppers, 406
Greens, 504–7, 642–43
Grenadine apples, baked, 220
Grits, 84
 cheesy, 89
Ground beef, 376–90. *See also* Hamburger(s); Meat loaf(-ves); Meatballs.
 beef in potato shells, 382
 burger, giant, 377
 cabbage rolls, stuffed, 383–84
 calzones, 587
 cheeseburger pie, impossible, 384
 chili con carne, 387
 chili dip, zippy, 18
 gyros, 585
 hash, Mexican, 385–86
 hidden beef ring, 388–89
 lasagne, beef, 425
 lasagne roll-ups, 388
 meat-and-potato pie, 378
 Mexi-dip, 18
 minestrone, hamburger, 563
 peppers, stuffed, 389–90
 pizza, hamburger, 298
 Salisbury steaks, 378
 sloppy Joes, 582
 spaghetti and beef sauce, 381
 taco dinner, 385
 taco salads, 500
 tortilla casserole, 386
Gruyère puff ring, 53
Guacamole, 19
 bacon, 19
 creamy, 19
 soup, 579
Gumbo, shrimp, 566
Gumdrop-marshmallow bars, 214
Gyros, 585

H
Halibut
 mustard-topped fish, 327

Halibut *(continued)*
with grapefruit sauce, 320–21
Ham
and scalloped potatoes,
421–22
baked, 417
glazes for, 417
carving, 418–19
creamed eggs with, 291
fresh, with stuffing, 407
loaf, 422
macaroni and cheese, 298–99
pancakes, 45
phyllo rolls, 15–16
pie, impossible, 467
salad
filling, 591
glazed, 497
-pasta, 495
-Swiss cheese, 496
sandwich(es), 14–15
-pineapple, 590
submarine, 590
slice, smoked, 420
gingered, 421
storage, 693, 695
Western omelet, 286
with spiced fruits, 420–21
Hamburger(s), 583–84. *See also*
Ground beef.
barbecue, 584
California, 583
cheeseburgers, 583
chèvre burgers, 377–78
chili burgers, 584
giant burger, 377
open-face, 583
patties, 376–77
Hard rolls, 73–74
Harvard beets, 622
Hash
Mexican, 385–86
oven, 374
red flannel skillet, 374
skillet, 374
Hashed browns, 662–63
Hazelnut

bars, 179–80
cake, 112
Heart, 397
Heart meringue, 259
Heidelberg sandwiches, 589
Herb(ed)
biscuits, 42
-cheese bread, 69
dumplings, 44
green beans, 618
jelly, 713
omelet, 285
pot roast, 359–60
salt, 406
seasonings for roast lamb, 428
vinegar, 546
Herbs for roast pork, 406
Hidden beef ring, 388–89
Hidden mint cookies, 187
High-altitude cooking, 685
Hollandaise sauce, 600
Honey
apples, baked, 220
ginger-, dressing, 549
-spice cookies, 195
twist coffee cake, 78
-whole wheat bread, 70
Honeyed beets, 622–23
Hoppin' John, 313
Horseradish sauce, 602
Hot chocolate, 33
Mexican, 34
Hot dog. *See also* Frankfurters.
roll-ups, 585–86
Hot German potato salad, 523
Hubbard squash, 665

I
Ice, cranberry, 264
Ice cream
chocolate, 268
chocolate sandwich cookie,
268
desserts
baked Alaska, chocolate,
267–68
bombe, 269

Ice cream *(continued)*
    cherries jubilee, 223
    chocolate ice-cream roll, 126
    meringue(s), 258–59
    peach Melba, 230
    pears Helene, 231
    raspberries Romanoff, 232
    snowballs, 270
    sundae cakes, 235
  nut brittle, 269
  peach, fresh, 268
  peppermint, 269
  storage, 694
  strawberry, 269
  vanilla, 268–69
  vanilla bean, 269
Iced tea, 38
  do-ahead, 38
Impossible broccoli pie, 295
Impossible cheeseburger pie, 384
Impossible ham pie, 467
Impossible turkey pie, 467
Ingredients
  emergency substitutions, 684
  measuring, 682–83
  terms, 679–81
Irish coffee, 35–36
Irish soda bread, 52
Irish stew, 434–35
Italian dressings, 547
Italian lamb shanks, 434
Italian lima beans, 309–10
Italian sausage
  vegetable soup, 564
  lasagne, 424
  pizza, 297–98
  terrine, 23
Italian-style beans, 619
Italian sweets, 196
Italian tomato sauce, 605
Italian vegetable soup, 564

J
Jam(s)
  about, 712–13

  cherry, 715
  pastries, 81
  peach, 715
  raspberry, 715
  strawberry, 715
Jambalaya
  chicken, 454–55
  shrimp, 341–42
Jelly(-ies)
  about, 712–13
  apple-pepper, 713–14
  easy, 713
  grape, rosy, 714
  herb, 713
  omelet, 286
  roll, 125–26
  wine, hot, 714
Jersey sweets, 667
Jerusalem artichokes, 614
  baked herbed, 615
Jeweled fruitcake, 123
Jicama, orange-, salad, 543

K
Kabobs
  fruit-cheese, with ginger dip, 20
  shish kabobs, 432
Kale, 642
Kasha, 84
  lamb with, 437
Kidney bean(s)
  red beans and rice, 312–13
  salad, 514
Kidneys, 397
Kielbasa in fondue, 21
Kiwifruit, cherries and, 224
Kohlrabi, 673–74
  mustard, 675–76

L
Lamb, 428–37
  about, 428
  and couscous, 435
  broiled, 431–32
  chops, mustard, 433
  cuts, 352–53

Lamb *(continued)*
gyros, 585
Irish stew, 434–35
ragout, 436
roast, 428–29
carving, 430
seasonings for, 428
Scotch broth, 563–64
shanks, Italian, 434
shish kabobs, 432
shoulder, stuffed, 430–31
with kasha, 437
Lasagne
beef, 425
Italian sausage, 424
roll-ups, 388
seafood, 348
Leek(s), 645
chicken and, soup, 560
in tomato sauce, 645
Legumes, 304–14
about, 304, 306
Lemon
cakes. *See* Cake(s).
cheesecake, 244
chicken, broiled, 450–51
-chive potatoes, 657
cookie sandwiches, 192–93
cream, frozen, 264–65
curd, 717
filling, 113
frosting, creamy, 129
glaze, 132
pies. *See* Pie(s).
pilaf, 86
pork chops, 409
pudding cake, 236
rice, 85
sauce, 273
schaum torte, 257
soufflé, 260–61
squares, 181
-coconut, 181
Lemonades, 31
Lentil(s)
cheesy, 310
-spinach soup, 576

Lettuce, 642
dill wilted, salad, 508
-mushroom salad, 508
wilted, salad, 508
Lima beans
and sour cream, 620
creole, 621
green, 619–20
Italian, 309–10
savory baked beans, 308
succotash, 620–21
Lime
chiffon pie, 160
pudding cake, 236
schaum torte, 258
Limeade, 31
Lindy's cheesecake, 241
squares, 241–42
Liver, 396. *See also* Chicken
livers.
and onions, 396
Lobster
boiled, 346
Newburg with popovers, 347
seafood salad, 483
tails, broiled, 346–47
Loganberry pie, 143
London broil, 364
Lorenzo dressing, 548
Low-cal dressing, creamy, 553

M
Macaroni
and cheese, 298–99
casserole, 463–64
cooking methods, 91
Mexican-style, 98–99
salads, 488, 493
Macaroons, 173–74
rhubarb with, 232–33
Main dish pies. *See also*
Quiche.
broccoli, 295
cheese, 296
cheeseburger, 384
ham, 467
meat-and-potato, 378

Main dish pies(*continued*)
  pork, 413–14
  turkey, 467
Main dish salads, 481–500
  beef
    -bulgur, 498
    -eggplant, 499
    vegetable-, 499
  chef's, 498
  chicken, 483
    -bacon, 483
    cups, 484
    curried, 485
    fruited, 483
    -macaroni, 493
    marinated, 482
    Oriental, 481–82
    -wild rice, 489
  club, 483
  fish
    and pepper, 491–92
    smoked, 491
  ham
    glazed, 497
    -pasta, 495
    -Swiss cheese, 496
  macaroni
    -bologna, 488
    -cheese, 488
    -chicken, 488
    -frank, 488
    -shrimp, 488
  Mediterranean, 494–95
  salmon-macaroni, 493
  seafood, 483
    -stuffed shells, 490
    -wild rice, 489
  shrimp, curried, 489
  taco, 500
  tomatoes, stuffed, 484
  tuna, 483
    -bean, 493–94
    -cantaloupe, 494
    -macaroni, 493
    -pasta toss, 492
  turkey
    -fruit, 486–87

    fruited, 486
    -pasta, 487
    smoked, glazed, 497
    -vegetable, 485
Maltaise sauce, 600
Mango, creamy filled, 226
Manhattan clam chowder,
    564–65
Manicotti, 299–300
Maple acorn squash, 665
Maple-nut
  cake, 111
  frosting, 130
Marble cake, 113
Marinated carrot salad, 519
Marinated chicken salad, 482
Marinated mushrooms, 6
Marinated peppers, 522
Marinated whole tomatoes,
    524
Marmalade, onion, 717
Marshmallow(s)
  bars, 214
  fudgy meringue mallow,
    256–57
  mallow sundae cake, 235
  sauce, 272–73
  sweet potato mallow, 669
Maryland fried chicken, 445
Mashed potatoes, 658
Mayonnaise, 550
  blender, 550
  -buttermilk dressing, 550
  mock, 552
Measuring ingredients, 682–83
Meat(s), 352–437. *See also
    specific kind.*
  cuts, 352–53
  freezing, 690–91, 692–93
  pies. *See* Main dish pies.
  storage, 686, 687, 695
Meat loaf(-ves), 379–80
  ham loaf, 422
  individual, 379
  Spanish, 379
  stuffed, 379
  vegetable, 379–80

Meatballs
  cocktail, 10
  saucy, 380–81
  spaghetti and, 381
  turkey, 474
Mediterranean salad, 494–95
Melon. *See also* Cantaloupe;
      Watermelon.
  and prosciutto, 3
  balls in wine, 226
  minted, 228
Meringue(s), 256–59
  brown sugar, 155
  cinnamon, 259
  coffee-peach, 259
  crème de menthe, 259
  for 9-inch pie, 155
  heart, 259
  ice cream, 259
  individual, 259
  mallow, fudgy, 256–57
  pies, 154–55
  shells, 155, 258–59
Mexican casera sauce, 604
Mexican egg sandwiches, 595
Mexican hash, 385–86
Mexican hot chocolate, 34
Mexican-style macaroni, 98–99
Mexi-dip, 18
Microwave cooking, 696–98
Microwave recipes
  artichokes, Jerusalem, 614
  asparagus, 616
  bok choy, 623
  broccoli, 625
  Brussels sprouts, 627
  cabbage
    and sour cream, 632
    Chinese or celery, 631
    rolls, stuffed, 383
  carrot(s), 632
    casserole, 633
  catfish, creole, 319–20
  cauliflower, 634
    baked, 634
  celery, 635
  chicken

  dinner casserole, 465
  Kiev, oven, 460
  microwaved stuffed, 444
  oven-barbecued, 447–48
  -rice supper, 465–66
Chinese pea pods, 636
corn, 637
  and cheese, 640
eggplant, 641
green beans, 617–18
  herbed, 618
  Italian-style beans, 619
  saucy, 619
green onions, 650
greens, 643
hamburger patties, 376–77
kohlrabi, 674
leeks, 645
lima beans, green, 620
macaroni casserole, 463–64
meatballs, 380
  saucy, 380–81
mushrooms, 646
okra, 647
onions, 648–49
parsnips, 651
  glazed, 651–52
peas, green, 653
  and onions, 653
peppers, stuffed, 389–90
potatoes, 657, 658
rutabagas, 674
salmon
  cold poached, 328–29
  puff, 334
sole, vegetable-stuffed, 321–22
squash
  acorn, 665
  Hubbard, 665
  summer, 663
sweet potatoes, 667
tomatoes, 670
  cherry, skillet, 671
tortilla casserole, 386
tuna
  curried, 332
  casserole, creamy, 333

Microwave recipes *(continued)*
  turnips, 674
  wax beans, 617–18
Milk shakes, 32–33
Mincemeat
  apples, baked, 220
  bars, 182
Minestrone, hamburger, 563
Mint(ed)
  bars, 176
  hidden, cookies, 187
  lemonade, 31
  macaroons, 173–74
  melon, 228
  orange-, sauce, 607
  wafers, 211
Minute steaks, mushroom, 365
Mocha
  fluff, 133
  French silk pie, 153–54
  frosting, 132
Mock caviar, 25–26
Mock mayonnaise, 552
Molasses
  cookies, jumbo, 198
  oatmeal-, cake, 111
  pudding, steamed, 255
Molded salads, 526–35
  about, making, 526–27
  ambrosia salad mold, 533
  apple-cherry salad, 530
  apricot
    mold, spiced, 534
    salad, molded, 530–31
  artichoke salad, 529–30
  berry-wine salad, 531
  cabbage mold, confetti,
    527–28
  carrot-pineapple, 528
  cherry layered salad, 531–32
  citrus salad, 532
  corn-relish mold, 528–29
  cran-raspberry mold, 532
  cucumber-relish mold, 529
  fruit salad, frozen, 535
  nectarine salad, molded, 531
  peach mold, spiced, 533–34

  raspberry salad, frozen, 535
  sangria mold, 534
  strawberry-cheese salad, 534
  triple-orange salad, 532–33
  zucchini-pineapple salad, 528
Mornay sauce, 602
Mostaccioli, pepper, 97–98
Mousse
  brandy chocolate, 262
  chocolate, 262
  orange, 263
  salmon, 27
  watermelon, 261–62
Mousseline sauce, 600
Muffins
  apple, 46
  blueberry, 46
  bran-raisin, 47
  corn, 54
  cranberry-orange, 46
  date-nut, 46
  English, 62–63
  French puffs, 46
  oatmeal-raisin, 47
Mulligatawny soup, 559–60
Mush, cornmeal, 89
Mushroom(s), 645–47
  and cucumbers, 646
  barley with, 88
  lettuce-, salad, 508
  marinated, 6
  minute steaks, 365
  quiche, 297
  rice, 85
  sauce, 601
  sautéed, 647
  soup, cream of, 570
  spaghetti with, 96
  spinach-, salad, 506, 508
  spread, 22
  steak, 366
  stuffed, 5
  stuffing, 473
  wild rice and, 88
Mustard
  kohlrabi, 675–76
  lamb chops, 433

Mustard *(continued)*
    sauce, 599–600
        cream, 603
        orange-, 607
    short ribs, 376
    spareribs, 411–12
    -topped fish, 327
Mustard greens, 642, 643

N
Navy bean(s)
    Boston baked beans, 304, 306
    soup, 577–78
Neapolitan cookies, 192
Nectarine salad, molded, 531
New England boiled dinner,
        362
New England chowder, 565
No-oil dressing, 553
Noodle(s)
    cooking methods, 91
    cornmeal, 92
    egg, 92
    -raisin pudding, 254
    Romanoff, 95
Nut(s). *See also specific kind.*
    breads, 55–57
    brittle ice cream, 269
    measuring, 683
    Oriental-style, 17
    pie crust, 138
    roll-ups, 197
    toasted, 681
Nutmeg
    corn oysters, 640–41
    crumb topping, 611
    sauce, 273
Nutrition, 723–64
    basic food groups, 725–26
    charts, 727–64
    nutrients in food, 723–24
    water, 724

O
Oatmeal
    bars, fudgy, 183
    bran-, bread, 71–72

caramel-oat bars, 181–82
    -coconut slices, 191
    cookies, 169
    crispies, 169
    -molasses cake, 111
    -raisin muffins, 47
    squares, 169
Okra, 647
    skillet, 648
Olive(s)
    and onions, 7
    macaroni and cheese, 298–99
    mock caviar, 25–26
Omelet(s)
    bacon, 285
    cheese, 285
    chive, 285
    dessert, orange, 228–29
    French, 285
    green chili, 285
    herbed, 285
    jelly, 286
    oven, 287
        broccoli, 288
    puffy, 286–87
    Western, 286
Onion(s), 648–49
    and carrots, 650
    baked whole, 649
    bread, 69
    -cheese corn bread, 54
    -dill casserole bread, 73
    French-fried, 649
    green. *See* Green onions.
    marmalade, 717
    olives and, 7
    peas and, 653
    rice, 85
    soup, French, 574–75
Orange(s)
    -avocado salad, 543
    Bavarian, 261
    beets, 622
    cakes. *See* Cake(s).
    candied citrus peel, 212
    chiffon pie, 160
    cider, hot, 30

Orange(s) *(continued)*
  cinnamon, 228
  citrus salad, 532
  cream, fruit in, 224
  dessert omelets, 228–29
  frosting, creamy, 129
  glaze, 132
  -jicama salad, 543
  mandarin salad, 512
  mousse, 263
  muffins, cranberry, 46
  -onion dressing, 549
  -pecan dressing, 548
  rolls, 76–77
  salad, 543–44
  sauce, 274
    fudge, 272
    -mint, 607
    -mustard, 607
  sweet potatoes, 668
  topping, 133
  triple-, salad, 532–33
  truffles, 205
Orange roughy with tarragon,
    327
Oregano crumb topping, 611
Oriental chicken salad, 481–82
Oriental seafood soup, 567
Oriental-style nuts, 17
Oven, preheating, 684–85
Oxtail stew, 373
Oyster(s)
  deep-fried, 349
  panfried, 349
  Parmesan, 4
  Rockefeller, 4
  scalloped, 347–48
  stuffing, 473

P
Paintbrush cookies, 194
Pan gravy, 358
Pan rolls, 75
Pancakes, 45
  blueberry, 45
  buckwheat, 45
  buttermilk, 45–46

  ham, 46
  whole wheat, 46
Papaya dessert, 229–30
Parfaits, sherbet-berry, 265
Parker House rolls, 75
Parmesan
  -curry popcorn, 17–18
  peas, 654
  sprouts, 628
Parsley
  dumplings, 44
  rice, 85
Parsnip(s), 651
  cakes, 652
  glazed, 651–52
  pork with, 409
Party deviled eggs, 16
Party sandwiches, 14–15
Pasta, 91–99. *See also* Lasagne;
    Macaroni; Noodle(s);
    Spaghetti.
  chicken-, primavera, 464
  fettuccine
    four-cheese, 94–95
    green, 93–94
  manicotti, 299–300
  mostaccioli, pepper, 97–98
  rigatoni and tomatoes, 98
  salad(s)
    dilled, 501
    ham-, 495–96
    tomato-, 502
    tuna-, toss, 492
    turkey-, 487–88
  shells, seafood-stuffed, 490
  spaetzle, 93
  vegetable-, soup, 574
  vermicelli and spinach, 95–96
  yields, 92
Pastry(-ies)
  bacon-cheese, 427
  baked tart shells, 137
  basics, 136
  Danish, dough, 79–80
  edges, 136, 137
  for pies, about, 134
  jam, 81

Pastry(-ies) *(continued)*
  lattice top, 137
  standard, 135–36
Pat-in-the-pan shortcake, 234
Pâté, chèvre, 24
Pattypan squash, 663
Pavlova, 258
Peach(es)
  apricot-glazed, 231
  -banana cream, 221
  canning, 710–11
  chutney, fresh, 718
  cobbler, fresh, 223
  coffee-, meringue, 259
  crisp, 221
  flambé, 230–31
  ice cream, fresh, 268
  in wine, 226
  jam, 715
  Melba, 230
  pie(s), 147–48, 152
  preserves, 715
  spiced, mold, 533–54
  tarts, 148–49
Peanut
  brittle, 206–7
  cake, 113
  cheesecake, 242
  -chocolate chip pie, 158
Peanut butter
  and jelly cookies, 184
  candy bars, 210
  cookies, 184
  cups, 210
  fingers, 184
  frosting, 130
  fudge, 203
  -marshmallow bars, 214
  squares, 180–81
Peanutty sundae cake, 236
Pear(s)
  apple-, salad, 541
  apricot-glazed, 231
  chutney, fresh, 718
  conserves, 716
  Helene, 231
  salad, 544

  tart, 149–50
  Waldorf salad, 540
Peas, green, 652–53
  curried peas, 654
  Parmesan peas, 654
  peas and onions, 653
  sesame peas, 653
Pecan pie, 157–58
  brandy-, 158
  chocolate-, 158
Penuche, 203
Peppermint
  candy canes, 189
  fluff, 133
  frosting, 129
  ice cream, 269
  taffy, 209
Pepperoni
  calzones, 587–88
  pizza, 298
  slices, 589
Peppers. *See* Green peppers;
    Red peppers.
Pesto, 607
Pheasant and gravy, 475
Philly beef sandwiches, 581
Phyllo
  pie, cherry, 145
  rolls, ham, 15–16
Pickled beets, 519
Pickled eggs, 16–17
Pickles
  about, 712
  bread and butter, 719
  cucumber, ripe, 719–20
  dill, fresh-pack, 718
  garlic-dill, 718
  watermelon rind, 720
Pie(s), 134–62. *See also* Main
    dish pies; Tart(s).
  Alexander, 161
  apple, 138–39
    deep-dish, 139
    Dutch, 139
    easy, 139
    French, 139
    -sour cream, 140

Pie(s) *(continued)*
  apricot, 148
  banana cream, 153
  blackberry, 143
  blueberry, 143
    easy, 143
    grenadine, 143–44
  boysenberry, 143
  brandy-pecan, 158
  cherry, 144–45
    cordial, 161
    cream, 146
    fresh, 144–45
    frozen, 144–45
    phyllo, 145
  chiffon, 160
  chocolate
    angel, 160–61
    -banana, 154
    brownie, 158
    classic French silk, 153–54
    cream, 153
    -pecan, 157–58
  coconut cream, 152–53
  coffee cordial, 161
  cream, 152–53
  crusts, crumb, 138. *See also*
      Pastry(-ies).
  custard, 156–59
  French silk, classic, 153–54
  frozen, 162
  fruit, 138–52
    salad, 146–47
  grasshopper, 161
  lemon
    chiffon, 160
    coconut, 159
    frozen, 162
    meringue, 154–56
  lime chiffon, 160
  loganberry, 143
  meringue, 154–56
  mocha French silk, 154
  orange chiffon, 160
  peach, 147–48
    -apricot, 148
    easy, 148

  glacé, 152
  peanut-chocolate chip, 158
  pecan, 157–58
  plum, 143
  pumpkin, 156–57
    frozen, 162
    praline, 157
  raisin-sour cream, 150
  raspberry, 143
    glacé, 152
  refrigerated, 159–62
  rhubarb, 150–51
    blueberry, 151
    frozen, 151
    -strawberry, 151
  shell(s)
    baked, 136
    crumb crusts, 138
    meringue, 155
  strawberry
    glacé, 152
    rhubarb-, 151
  sweet potato, 157
Pilaf
  bulgur, 90
  lemon, 86
Pimiento potatoes, 661
Pineapple
  -apricot cake, 119–20
  carrot-, salad, 520
  chutney, fresh, 717–18
  crisp, 221
  frosting, 130
  gingered, 229
  glaze, 417
  -marshmallow coleslaw, 516
  milk shakes, 33
  ring salads, 544–45
  sweet potatoes, 668
  turkey with, 473–74
  upside-down cake, 114–15
  zucchini-, salad, 528
Pink colada, 31
Pink lemonade, 31
Pinto beans
  baked, 307
  Western-style beans, 312

Piquant sauce, 601
Pizza
  bites, 12–13
  cheese, 297–98
  hamburger, 298
  Italian sausage, 298
  pepperoni, 298
  slices, 589
Plantation cake, 238–39
Plum(s)
  chutney, fresh, 718
  cobbler, fresh, 223
  pie, 143
  poached, 232
  pudding cake, 237
Polish sausage in beer, 425
Popcorn, 17
  balls, 213
    caramel, 213
    chocolate, 213
  caramel corn, 213
  -nut, 212–13
  Parmesan-curry, 17–18
Popovers, 52–53
  beef burgundy, 373
  crab Newburg with, 347
  lobster Newburg with, 347
Poppy seed dressing, 547
Pork, 403–27. *See also* Ham;
    Sausage(s).
  about, 403–4
  braised fresh, 410
  broiled fresh, 407
  chops
    breaded, 408
    lemon, 409
    pork with parsnips, 409
  choucroute, 422–23
  chow mein, 416
  cooked in liquid, 410
  cuts, 352–53
  fried rice, 415
  hocks with sauerkraut, 416–17
  piccata, 412–13
  pies, 413–14
  ribs
    barbecued, 12

    country-style, 412
    mustard spareribs, 411–12
    sweet and zesty spareribs, 411
  roast, 403–404
    carving, 405
    herbs for, 406
    with rosemary, 404–5
  sauerkraut balls, 11
  spareribs, 411–12
  sweet-and-sour, 414–15
  tenderloin with peppers, 406
Pot roast(s)
  barbecue, 360
  beef brisket barbecue, 361
  carving, 356, 362
  dilled, 360
  French-style beef roast, 359
  fruited, 360
  herbed, 360
  New England, 359–60
Potato(es), 656–63
  au gratin, 661
  duchess, 658
  French-fried, 659
  hashed browns, 662–63
  lemon-chive, 657
  mashed, 658
  meat-and-, pie, 378
  oven-browned, 357
  pepper or pimiento, 661
  planks, 659
  raw fries, 660
  rutabaga-, whip, 675
  salad, 523–24
    California-style, 524
    garden, 524
    hot German, 523
    Scandinavian-style, 524
  scalloped, 662
    ham and, 421–22
  shells
    beef in, 382
    chicken in, 382
  skins, broiled, 9
  twice-baked, 660–61
  varieties, 657
  with toppers, 660

Pots de crème, chocolate, 249–50
Poultry, 441–76. *See also*
    Chicken; Cornish hens;
    Duck; Goose; Turkey.
  safety tips, 686–88
  storage, 690, 693, 695
Pound cakes, 113–14
Praline(s), 207–8
  bars, easy, 177–78
  pumpkin pie, 157
Preserves. *See also* Chutney;
    Jam(s); Jelly(-ies).
  apple butter, 716
  lemon curd, 717
  onion marmalade, 717
  peach, 715
    spiced, 715
  pear conserves, 716
Pressure canner processing,
    707–8
Pretzel cookies, 186
Prosciutto, melon and, 3
Provençale sauce, 601
Provolone sandwiches, hot, 598
Prune-walnut cake, 120
Pudding(s), 250–56. *See also*
    Custard.
  apple, 252
  bread, 252
  butterscotch, 250
  cakes, 236, 237
  chocolate, 250
    steamed, 254–55
  molasses, steamed, 255–56
  noodle-raisin, 254
  rice, 253
    mold, 253–54
    -nut, 253
  vanilla, 250
  Yorkshire, 358
Pumpernickel, dark, 69–70
Pumpkin
  bread, 56
  cake, 111
  cheesecake, 244
  pie, 156–57

    frozen, 162
    praline, 157
Punch(es)
  cranberry
    hot, 29
    sparkling, 30
  orange cider, hot, 30
  sangria, 30
  wassail, 29

Q
Quiche
  chicken, 297
  crab, 297
  Lorraine, 296–97
  mushroom, 297
  salmon, crustless, 334–35
  tuna, crustless, 335
Quick breads. *See* Bread(s), quick.

R
Rabbit, stewed, 476–77
Rachel sandwiches, 581
Ragout. *See also* Stew(s).
  beef, 436
  lamb, 436
Raisin
  bran-, muffins, 47
  bread, cinnamon-, 66
  clusters, 210
  oatmeal-, muffins, 47
  -nut clusters, 210
  sauce, 606
  -sour cream pie, 150
  -spice coffee cake, 48
  sundae cake, 236
Raspberry(-ies)
  cran-, mold, 532
  crepes, 247–48
  -currant sauce, 274
  custard, 248–49
  glacé pie, 152
  jam, 715
  pie, 143
  Romanoff, 232
  salad, frozen, 535
  vinegar, 546

Ratatouille, 642
 salad, 517–18
Raw fries, 660
Red cabbage, 628
 sweet-sour, 630
Red devils food cake, 108
Red flannel skillet hash, 374
Red peppers. *See also* Green
  peppers.
 Chinese pea pods and
  peppers, 637
 marinated peppers, 522
 sweet pepper relish, 720–21
Refried bean bake, 313
Refrigerator storage, 686, 689,
  694–95
Relish
 corn, 721
 sweet pepper, 720–21
 vegetable, 722
Reuben sandwiches, 580
Rhubarb
 cake, 122
 pie, 150–51
  -blueberry, 151
  frozen, 151
  -strawberry, 151
 sauce, 233
  strawberry-, 233
 with macaroons, 232–33
Rice, 84, 85. *See also* Wild rice.
 brown, 85
 chicken-, supper, 465–66
 curried, 87
 curried chicken salad, 485
 fried
  chicken, 416
  pork, 415–16
 lemon, 85
 mushroom, 85
 -nut pudding, 253
 onion, 85
 oven-steamed, 86
 parsley, 85
 pilaf, lemon, 86
 pudding(s), 253
 red beans and, 312–13

 regular, 85
 savory mixed, 87
 -spinach salad, 502
 stuffing, 471
  fruited, 471
 with artichokes, 86
Ricotta cheese spread, 22
Rigatoni and tomatoes, 98
Rock Cornish hens. *See* Cornish
  hens.
Roll(s). *See also* Sweet roll(s).
 cloverleaf, 75
 crescent, 75
 dough, traditional, 74–75
 fan tans, 75
 hard, 73–74
 pan, 75
 Parker House, 75
 square, 75
Rosettes, 200
Rum
 apricot, cake, 116
 balls, 211
 -cracker torte, 237–38
Rumaki, 13
Russian dressing, 552
Russian teacakes, 189
Rutabaga(s), 673–674
 glazed, 675
 -potato whip, 675

S
Salad(s), 481–545. *See also* Main
    dish salads; Molded
    salads.
 asparagus, 513
 beets, pickled, 519
 bulgur-tomato, 503
 cabbage, 517
 Caesar, 509–10
  easy, 509
 carrot
  marinated, 519
  -pineapple, 520
  -raisin, 519–20
 cauliflower, 520
 coleslaw. *See* Coleslaw.

Salad(s) *(continued)*
  cream cheese-grape toss, 542
  cucumber(s), 521
    and shrimp, 522
    and tomatoes, 520–21
    creamy, 521
  dressings. *See* Salad dressings.
  elegant tossed, 510–11
  fruit, 536–45. *See also specific kind.*
    and cheese, 538
    chow mein, 539
    easy, 537
    mixed, 537
    platter, 538
    -prune, 540
    summer, 536
    twenty-four-hour, 539–40
    Waldorf, 540–41
    Waldorf, pear, 540
    Waldorf, supreme, 541
    -walnut, 436–37
    winter, 538
  garbanzo bean, 514–15
  Greek, 510
  greens, 504–5, 507
  kidney bean, 514
  lettuce-mushroom, 508
  mandarin, 512
  pasta, dilled, 501
  peppers, marinated, 522
  potato, 523–24
    California-style, 524
    garden, 524
    hot German, 523
    Scandinavian-style, 524
  ratatouille, 517–18
  rice-spinach, 502
  spinach
    -mushroom, 506–8
    tossed, 506
  three-bean, 515
  tomato(es)
    broiled, 525
    -cheese, 525
    marinated whole, 524
    -pasta, 502

    slices, garlic, 524
    tossed, 504–12
      chart, 507
    vegetable, 513–25. *See also specific kind.*
      mixed, 518
      winter, toss, 511
    walnut tossed, 511–12
    wilted lettuce, 508
      dill, 508
Salad dressings, 546–53
  blue cheese, 551
    yogurt, 552
  buttermilk, 550
  cooked, 549
  cucumber yogurt, 552
  French, 548
    classic, 548
  fruit salad yogurt, 552
  ginger-honey, 549
  green goddess, 551
  Italian, 547
    creamy, 547
  Lorenzo, 548
  low-cal, creamy, 553
  mayonnaise, 550
    blender, 550
    -buttermilk, 550
    mock, 552
  no-oil, 553
  orange-onion, 549
  orange-pecan, 548
  poppy seed, 547
  Russian, 552
  Thousand Island, 551–52
  tomato, 548
  yogurt, easy, 552
Salami
  Mediterranean salad, 494–95
  submarine sandwich, 590
Salisbury steaks, 378
Salmon
  cold poached, 328–29
  loaf, 335
  -macaroni salad, 493
  mousse, 27
  patty sandwiches, 592

Salmon *(continued)*
  puff, 334
  quiche, crustless, 334–35
  shortcakes, 335–56
  -wild rice soup, 568
Salsa cheese bake, 25
Salt
  caraway, 406
  herb, 406
Sandwich(es), 580–98
  beef, 580–82
    -baguette slices, 581–82
    salad filling, 591
  calzones
    ground beef, 588
    pepperoni, 589
  cheese
    American, grilled, 596
    chili, 595–96
    hot provolone, 598
    super grilled, 596
  chicken
    -avocado, 591–92
    club, 593
    salad filling, 591
    slices, baked, 597
  chili slices, baked, 597
  club, 593
  Denver, 593
  egg(s)
    in buns, 594
    Mexican, 595
    salad filling, 591
    with wine sauce, 594–95
  frankfurters. *See* Frankfurters.
  gyros, 585
  ham
    -pineapple, 590
    salad filling, 591
  hamburgers. *See*
    Hamburger(s).
  Heidelberg, 589
  party, 14–15
  pepperoni pizza slices, 589
  Philly beef, 581
  Rachel, 581
  Reuben, 580
  salmon patty, 592
  sausage burritos, 588
  shrimp club, 593
  sloppy Joes, 582
  spreads, seasoned, 580
  submarine, 590
  tuna
    patty, 592
    salad filling, 591
    slices, baked, 597
  turkey
    club, 593
    puff, 590–91
  vegetable slices, baked,
    596–97
  veggie-filled croissants, 597
Sangria
  mold, 534
  punch, 30
Sauce(s), 599–607. *See also*
    Dessert sauces.
  allemande, 602
  almond velvet, 602
  barbecue, 604
    spicy, 605
  béarnaise, 600
  bordelaise, 601
  brown, 601
    spicy, 601
  butter, 612
  cheese, 599
  cherry, 607
  cocktail, 603
  curry, 599
  dill, 599
  hollandaise, 600
  horseradish, 602
  maltaise, 600
  Mexican casera, 604
  Mornay, 602
  mousseline, 600
  mushroom, 601
  mustard, 599–600
    cream, 603
  orange-mint, 607
  orange-mustard, 607
  pesto, 607

Sauce(s) *(continued)*
  piquant, 601
  Provençale, 601
  raisin, 606
  sweet-and-sour, 606
  tartar, 603
  tomato, Italian, 605
  velouté, 602
  white, 599
Sauerbraten, venison, 477–78
Sauerkraut
  balls, 11
  choucroute, 422–23
  franks with, 587
  pork hocks with, 416–17
Sausage(s). *See also specific*
      kind.
  burritos, 588
  -cheese chips, 14
  cocktail, 10
  fresh, 423
  pork pies, 413–14
  smoked, 425
  stuffing, 473
  submarine sandwich, 590
  three-bean casserole, 311
  Western-style beans, 312
Savoy cabbage, 629
  and bacon, 629
Scalloped corn, 638–39
  cheese, 639
Scalloped oysters, 347–48
Scalloped potatoes, 662
  ham and, 421–22
Scalloped squash, 663
Scalloped vegetables, 611
Scallops
  batter-fried, 349
  broiled ginger, 342
  deep-fried, 349
  in cream sauce, 343
  seafood salad, 483
Scandinavian-style potato salad,
      524
Scones, 43
Scotch broth, 563–64
Scotch shortbread, 196–97

Seafood. *See also* Fish;
      Shellfish; *specific kind.*
  creamed eggs with, 291
  lasagne, 348
  salad, 483
  soup(s), 564–68
    Oriental, 567
  storage, 693, 695
  -stuffed shells, 490
  -wild rice salad, 489
Seasonings for roast lamb, 428
Sesame
  beef, 374–75
  peas, 653
  seed, toasted, 681, 684
Shellfish, 337–49. *See also*
      specific kind.
  about, 337–38
  batter-fried, 349
  deep-fried, 349
  storage, 693, 695
Sherbet-berry parfaits, 265
Sherry sweet potatoes, 668
Shish kabobs, 432
Short ribs
  mustard, 376
  savory beef, 375
Shortbread, Scotch, 196–97
Shortcake(s)
  pat-in-the-pan, 234
  salmon, 335–36
  strawberry, 233–34
  tuna, 336
Shortening, measuring, 683
Shrimp, 337
  -bacon bites, 13–14
  batter-fried, 349
  -cheese strata, 26
  Chinese-fried, 339–40
  club sandwiches, 593
  cocktail, 3
  cucumber-, sandwiches, 14
  cucumbers and, 522
  curry, 459
  deep-fried, 349
  gumbo, 566
  jambalaya, 341–42

Shrimp (continued)
  salad
    curried, 489
    macaroni-, 488
  seafood salad, 483
  skewered, 338–39
  stir-fried, with vegetables,
    340–41
  yogurt-, spread, 26
Silver white cakes, 111–12
Silver white cupcakes, 112
Skewered shrimp, 338–39
Sloppy franks, 586
Sloppy Joes, 582
Smoked fish salad, 491
Smoked turkey salad, 497
S'more bars, 215
Soft breadsticks, 64
Sole, vegetable-stuffed, 321–22
Soufflé
  broccoli, 644
  cheese, 292
  chocolate, baked, 240
  lemon, 260–61
  spinach, 644
Soup(s), 557–79. see also
    Chowder.
  barley-vegetable beef, 562
  beef, 561
    and broth, 561
  black bean, 577
  borsch, easy, 573
  broccoli, creamy, 571–72
  cabbage, creamy, 572
  cauliflower, creamy, 572
  Cheddar cheese, 575
  chicken, 557–60
    and broth, 557
    and leek, 560
    noodle, 558
    rice, 558
  cold, 578–79
  cucumber, cold, 578
  egg drop, 559
  fish, quick, 567–68
  fruit, fresh, 579
  gazpacho, 578–79

  guacamole, 579
  hamburger minestrone, 563
  lentil-spinach, 576
  mulligatawny, 559–60
  mushroom, cream of, 570
  navy bean, 577–78
  onion, French, 574–75
  salmon-wild rice, 568
  Scotch broth, 563–64
  seafood, 564–68
    Oriental, 567
  shrimp gumbo, 566
  split pea, 576
  tomato, hearty, 573
  vegetable, 569–74
    beef, 562
    cream of, 569–70
    Italian, 564
    -pasta, 574
  wild rice, 569
  zucchini, 571
Sour cream
  apple-, pie, 140
  chicken livers with, 450
  chocolate cake, 107
  coffee cake, 49
  cookies, 193
  frosting, chocolate 131
  raisin-, pie, 150
  spice cake, 121
  storage, 692, 694
Spaetzle, 93
Spaghetti
  and anchovies, 97
  and beef sauce, 381
  and chicken sauce, 381
  and meatballs, 381
  Cincinnati-style chili, 387
  cooking methods, 91–92
  tuna, 331
  with mushrooms, 96
Spaghetti squash, 665
Spareribs. See Pork ribs.
Spice cakes. See Cake(s), spice.
Spiced tea, 37–38
Spinach, 642
  dip, 19

Spinach *(continued)*
  lentil-, soup, 576
  -mushroom salad, 506
  rice-, salad, 502
  soufflé, 644
  tossed salad, 506
  vermicelli and, 95–96
  wilted, 643
Split pea soup,. 576
Sponge cakes, 123–27
Sponge candy, 208
Spoon bread, 55
Spread(s). *See also* Butter(s);
      Preserves.
  baked cheese, 24
  cheese ball, 21
  chèvre pâté, 24
  crabmeat mold, Cajun,
    27–28
  Italian sausage terrine, 23
  mock caviar, 25–26
  mushroom, 22
  ricotta cheese, 22
  salmon mousse, 27
  salsa cheese bake, 25
  shrimp-cheese strata, 26
  yogurt-shrimp, 26
Spritz, 199
  chocolate, 199
  holiday decorated, 199
Spumoni cookies, 191–92
Squash. *See also specific kind.*
  acorn, maple, 665
  casserole, baked, 666
  summer, 663
  winter, 665
  with salsa, 666
  yellow, -pepper skillet,
    664
Steaming equipment, 256
Stew(s)
  beef, 372–73
    Provençale, 367
    ragout, 436
  chicken
    Brunswick, 455–56
    fricassee, 452

    in red wine, 453
  lamb
    Irish, 434–35
    ragout, 436
  oxtail, 373
Storage charts, 692–95
Straightneck squash, 663
Strawberry(-ies)
  -cheese salad, 534
  ice creams, 268–69
  in wine, 226
  jam, 715
  pies, 151–52
  -rhubarb sauce, 233
  shortcakes, 233–34
  spritzer, 31–32
  tart, French, 151–52
  vinegar, 546
Stroganoff, beer, 370
  economy, 370
Strudels, cabbage, 630–31
Stuffing
  apple-raisin, 472
  bread, 472
  casserole, 473
  corn bread, 473
  giblet, 473
  mushroom, 473
  oyster, 473
  rice, 471
    fruited, 471
  sausage, 473
  vegetable, 473
Submarine sandwich, 590
Substitutions, emergency, 684
Succotash, 620–21
Sugar, measuring, 683
Sugar cookies, 193–94
Summer fruit salad, 536
Surprise candy teacakes, 189
Sweet-and-sour pork, 414–15
Sweet-and-sour sauce, 606
Sweet and zesty spareribs, 411
Sweet pepper relish, 720–21
Sweet potato(es), 667
  candied, 667
  mallow, 669

Sweet potato(es) *(continued)*
    orange, 668
    pie, 157
    pineapple, 668
    sherry, 668
    slices, 668
    spicy, 668
    twice-baked yams, 669–70
Sweet roll(s). *See also* Coffee
        cake(s).
    butterscotch-pecan rolls, 77
    cinnamon rolls, 77
    Danish twists, 81
    dough, 76
    jam pastries, 81
    orange rolls; 76–77
Sweet snacks, 212–15. *See also*
        Candy(-ies).
    candied citrus peel, 212
    caramel apples, 214
    caramel corn, 213
    caramel-nut corn, 212–13
    chocolate-caramel apples,
        213–14
    granola bark, 215
    marshmallow bars, 214
        chocolate-, 214
        coconutty-, 214
        gumdrop-, 214
        peanut butter-, 214
    popcorn balls, 213
        caramel, 213
        chocolate, 213
    s'more bars, 215
Sweet-sour cabbage slaw, 516
Sweet-sour red cabbage, 630
Sweetbreads, 398–99
Swiss chard, 642
Swiss cheese fondue, 303
Swiss steak, 368

T
Taco dinner, 385
Taco salads, 500
Taffy, 208–9
    almond, 209
    peppermint, 209

Tandoori-style chicken, 461–62
Tart(s)
    apple-cinnamon, 140–41
    glazed cherry, 145–46
    peach Melba, 148
    peach-pecan, 148–49
    pear, 149–50
    shells, baked, 137
    strawberry, French, 151–52
Tartar sauce, 603
Tea
    about, 36–37
    iced, 38
        do-ahead, 38
        spiced, 37–38
Tenderloin with peppers, 406
Teriyaki, beef, 364–65
Terrine, Italian sausage, 23
Thousand Island dressing,
        551–52
Three-bean casserole, 311
Three-bean salad, 515
Thumbprint cookies, 190
Toffee
    bars, 178
    dessert, angel, 267
Tomato(es), 670
    and artichokes, 672
    baked stuffed, 672
    -beer cooler, 30
    bulgur-, salad, 503
    canning, 711–12
    -cheese salads, 525
    cherry, skillet, 671
    cucumbers and, 520–21
    dressing, 548
    macaroni and cheese, 299
    marinated whole, 524
    panfried, 671
    -pasta salad, 502
    plum, baked, 673
    rigatoni and, 98
    salads, broiled, 525
    sauce, Italian, 605
    slices, garlic, 524
    soup, hearty, 573
    stewed, 670–71

Tomato(es) (*continued*)
  stuffed, 484
Tongue, 398
  beef, glazed, 398
Toppings
  for desserts. *See* Whipped
      cream.
  for potatoes, 660
  for vegetables, 611
Torte
  cocoa pecan, 106
  graham cracker, 263
  lemon schaum, 257
  lime schaum, 258
  rum-cracker, 237–38
Tortilla(s)
  casserole, 386
  chalupas, 309
  cheese enchiladas, 302–3
  eggs on, 284
  fajitas, 369–70
  sausage burritos, 588
Tostadas, chicken, 463
Traditional roll dough, 74–75
  whole wheat, 75
Traditional white bread, 66
Trifle, English, 251
Triple-orange salad, 532–33
Truffles, 204–5
  almond, 205
  apricot, 205
  cashew, 205
  cherry, 205
  orange, 205
Tuna
  casserole, creamy, 333
  curried, 332
  macaroni and cheese, 298–99
  patty sandwiches, 592
  quiche, crustless, 334–35
  salad(s), 483
    -bean, 493–94
    -cantaloupe, 494
    filling, 591
    -macaroni, 493
    -pasta toss, 492
  sauce, veal with, 392

shortcakes, 336
slices, baked, 597
spaghetti, 331
Turkey, 466–74. *See also*
      Chicken.
  about, 468–70
  carving, 472
  dinner casserole, 465
  divan, 468
  macaroni casserole, 463
  meatballs, 474
  pie, impossible, 467
  pot pie, 466–67
  roast, 469–70
  salad(s)
    -fruit, 486–87
    fruited, 486
    glazed smoked, 497
    -pasta, 487–88
    -vegetable, 485
  sandwiches
    club, 593
    puff, 590–91
    Rachel, 581
  with pineapple, 473–74
Turnip(s), 673–74
  greens, 642
  with cheese, 674
Turtle candies, easy, 209
Twenty-four-hour salad, 539–40
Twice-baked potatoes, 660–61
Twice-baked yams, 669–70

U
Upside-down cake
  apricot-prune, 115
  pineapple, 114–15
  spiced apple, 115

V
Vanilla
  frosting, creamy, 129
  glaze, 132
  ice cream(s), 268
  pudding, 250
Variety meats, 396–99
  brains, 398–99

Variety meats (continued)
heart, 397
kidneys, 397
liver, 396
and onions, 396
storage, 693, 695
sweetbreads, 398–99
tongue, 398
beef, glazed, 398
Veal, 391–95
about, 354–55
cuts, 352–53
Oscar, 393
piccata, 413
roast, 391–92
sauté, 394
shanks, braised, 394–95
with tuna sauce, 392
Vegetable(s), 611–76. See also
specific kind.
au gratin, 611
blanching, 701–2
canning, 699–701
creamed, 611
dilled, 6
freezing, 701–2
frittata, 288–89
in cheese sauce, 611
meat loaf, 379–80
relish, 722
salad(s), 513–25
beef, 499
mixed, 518
winter, toss, 511
scalloped, 611
slices, baked, 596–97
soup(s), 569–75
barley-, beef, 562
beef, 562
cream of, 569–70
Italian, 564
-pasta, 574
-stuffed sole, 321–22
stuffing, 473
veggie-filled croissants, 597
Velouté sauce, 602
Venison sauerbraten, 477–78

Vermicelli and spinach, 95–96
Vinegar
herbed, 546
raspberry, 546
strawberry, 546

W
Waffles, 44
blueberry, 45
cheese and bacon, 45
whole wheat, 45
Waldorf salad, 540
pear, 540
supreme, 541
Walnut tossed salad, 511–12
Wassail, 29
Water-bath processing, 708–9
Watermelon
mousse, 261–62
rind pickles, 720
supreme, 227
Wax beans, 617–18
Welsh rabbit, 301–2
Western omelet, 286
Western-style beans, 312
Wheat-stuffed drumsticks, 457
Whipped cream
almond topping, 133
caramel fluff, 133
cocoa fluff, 133
crème de cacao topping, 133
crème de menthe topping,
133
flavored, 275
mocha fluff, 133
orange topping, 133
peppermint fluff, 133
sweetened, 274
White bread, traditional, 66
White cakes, 111–12
White mountain frosting,
128–29
White sauce, 599
Whole wheat
breadsticks, soft, 64
honey-, bread, 70–71
pancakes, 46

Whole wheat *(continued)*
  roll dough, traditional, 75
  waffles, 45
Wieners. *See* Frankfurters.
Wild rice, 85
  and mushrooms, 88
  chicken-, salad, 489
  salmon-, soup, 568
  savory mixed rice, 87
  seafood-, salad, 489
  soup, 569
Williamsburg orange cake, 120
Wilted lettuce salad, 508
Wilted spinach, 643
Wine jelly, hot, 714
Winter-fruit compote, 225
Winter-fruit salad, 538
Winter vegetable toss, 511

Y
Yams, 667. *see also* Sweet
       potato(es).
  twice-baked, 669–70

Yeast, about, 58–60
Yellow çake(s), 112–13
Yellow cupcakes, 113
Yellow squash-pepper skillet,
       664
Yogurt
  chicken with, 458
  dressings, easy, 552
  mock mayonnaise, 552
  -shrimp spread, 26
  storage, 694
Yorkshire pudding, 358

Z
Zucchini, 663
  bread, 55–56
  broiled, 663
  cookies, 172
  dilled, 664
  -pepper skillet, 664
  -pineapple salad, 528
  soup, 571
  spice cake, 122

Special Offer
Buy a Bantam Book
for only 50¢.

Now you can have Bantam's catalog filled with hundreds of titles plus take advantage of our unique and exciting bonus book offer. A special offer which gives you the opportunity to purchase a Bantam book for only 50¢. Here's how!

By ordering any five books at the regular price per order, you can also choose any other single book listed (up to a $5.95 value) for just 50¢. Some restrictions do apply, but for further details why not send for Bantam's catalog of titles today!

Just send us your name and address and we will send you a catalog!

HANDSOME, SPACE-SAVER
BOOKRACK

ONLY
$9.95

- hand-rubbed walnut finish
- patented sturdy construction
- assembles in seconds
- assembled size 16" x 8"

Perfect as a desk or table top library— Holds both hardcovers and paperbacks.

Nevco US Pat. 3,464,565
